The Oxford Handbook of Social Exclusion

OXFORD LIBRARY OF PSYCHOLOGY

Editor in Chief PETER E. NATHAN

The Oxford Handbook of Social Exclusion

Edited by

C. Nathan DeWall

OXFORD

UNIVERSITY PRESS

OXFORD
UNIVERSITY PRESS

Oxford University Press is a department of the University of Oxford.
It furthers the University's objective of excellence in research, scholarship,
and education by publishing worldwide.

Oxford   New York
Auckland   Cape Town   Dar es Salaam   Hong Kong   Karachi
Kuala Lumpur   Madrid   Melbourne   Mexico City   Nairobi
New Delhi   Shanghai   Taipei   Toronto

With offices in
Argentina   Austria   Brazil   Chile   Czech Republic   France   Greece
Guatemala   Hungary   Italy   Japan   Poland   Portugal   Singapore
South Korea   Switzerland   Thailand   Turkey   Ukraine   Vietnam

Published in the United States of America by
Oxford University Press
198 Madison Avenue, New York, NY 10016

Library of Congress Cataloging-in-Publication Data
The Oxford handbook of social exclusion / edited by C. Nathan DeWall.
    p. cm. — (Oxford library of psychology)
    ISBN 978-0-19-539870-0
    1. Marginality, Social—Handbooks, manuals, etc.   I. DeWall, C. Nathan, 1954-   II. Title: Handbook of social exclusion.
HM1136.O94 2013
306—dc23
2012025641

9 8 7 6 5 4 3 2 1
Printed in the United States of America
on acid-free paper

SHORT CONTENTS

OXFORD LIBRARY OF PSYCHOLOGY

The *Oxford Library of Psychology*, a landmark series of handbooks, is published by Oxford University Press, one of the world's oldest and most highly respected publishers, with a tradition of publishing significant books in psychology. The ambitious goal of the *Oxford Library of Psychology* is nothing less than to span a vibrant, wide-ranging field and, in so doing, to fill a clear market need.

Encompassing a comprehensive set of handbooks, organized hierarchically, the *Library* incorporates volumes at different levels, each designed to meet a distinct need. At one level are a set of handbooks designed broadly to survey the major subfields of psychology; at another are numerous handbooks that cover important current focal research and scholarly areas of psychology in depth and detail. Planned as a reflection of the dynamism of psychology, the *Library* will grow and expand as psychology itself develops, thereby highlighting significant new research that will impact on the field. Adding to its accessibility and ease of use, the *Library* will be published in print and, later on, electronically.

The *Library* surveys psychology's principal subfields with a set of handbooks that capture the current status and future prospects of those major subdisciplines. This initial set includes handbooks of social and personality psychology, clinical psychology, counseling psychology, school psychology, educational psychology, industrial and organizational psychology, cognitive psychology, cognitive neuroscience, methods and measurements, history, neuropsychology, personality assessment, developmental psychology, and more. Each handbook undertakes to review one of psychology's major subdisciplines with breadth, comprehensiveness, and exemplary scholarship. In addition to these broadly conceived volumes, the *Library* also includes a large number of handbooks designed to explore in depth more specialized areas of scholarship and research, such as stress, health and coping, anxiety and related disorders, cognitive development, or child and adolescent assessment. In contrast with the broad coverage of the subfield handbooks, each of these latter volumes focuses on an especially productive, more highly focused line of scholarship and research. Whether at the broadest or most specific level, however, all of the *Library* handbooks offer synthetic coverage that reviews and evaluates the relevant past and present research and anticipates research in the future. Each handbook in the *Library* includes introductory and concluding chapters written by its editor to provide a roadmap to the handbook's table of contents and offer informed anticipations of significant future developments in that field.

An undertaking of this scope calls for handbook editors and chapter authors who are established scholars in the areas about which they write. Many of the nation's and world's most productive and best-respected psychologists have agreed to edit *Library* handbooks or write authoritative chapters in their areas of expertise.

For whom has the *Oxford Library of Psychology* been written? Because of its breadth, depth, and accessibility, the *Library* serves a diverse audience, including graduate students in psychology and their faculty mentors, scholars, researchers, and practitioners in psychology and related fields. Each will find in the *Library* the information they seek on the subfield or focal area of psychology in which they work or are interested.

Befitting its commitment to accessibility, each handbook includes a comprehensive index, as well as extensive references to help guide research. And because the *Library* was designed from its inception as an online as well as a print resource, its structure and contents will be readily and rationally searchable online. Further, once the *Library* is released online, the handbooks will be regularly and thoroughly updated.

In summary, the *Oxford Library of Psychology* will grow organically to provide a thoroughly informed perspective on the field of psychology, one that reflects both psychology's dynamism and its increasing interdisciplinarity. Once published electronically, the *Library* is also destined to become a uniquely valuable interactive tool, with extended search and browsing capabilities. As you begin to consult this handbook, we sincerely hope you will share our enthusiasm for the more than 500-year tradition of Oxford University Press for excellence, innovation, and quality, as exemplified by the *Oxford Library of Psychology*.

Peter E. Nathan
Editor-in-Chief
Oxford Library of Psychology

ABOUT THE EDITOR

C. Nathan DeWall

C. Nathan DeWall is an Associate Professor of Psychology at the University of Kentucky. He has published over 100 peer-reviewed articles, chapters, and books. The Association for Psychological Science identified him as a "Rising Star," and the Foundation for Personality and Social Psychology awarded him a SAGE Young Scholars award. He is a sought-after speaker (this year he will be giving talks in China, Hong Kong, the Netherlands, Luxembourg, Australia, and many locations in the United States). His research on social connections is currently supported by grants from the National Institutes of Health, National Science Foundation, and the Templeton Foundation. He is frequently featured in the national media, including the *New York Times*, *LA Times*, *Harvard Business Review*, *Time*, and National Public Radio.

CONTRIBUTORS

Ashley Batts Allen
Department of Psychology and
Neuroscience
Duke University
Durham, NC

Roy F. Baumeister
Department of Psychology
Florida State University
Tallahassee, FL

Terry K. Borsook
Department of Psychology
University of Toronto
Toronto, Ontario, Canada

John T. Cacioppo
Department of Psychology
University of Chicago
Chicago, IL

W. Keith Campbell
Department of Psychology
University of Georgia
Athens, GA

Justin V. Cavallo
Department of Psychology
Wilfrid Laurier University
Waterloo, Ontario, Canada

Tanya L. Chartrand
Fuqua School of Business
Duke University
Durham, NC

Joshua Correll
Department of Psychology
University of Chicago
Chicago, IL

Catherine A. Cottrell
Department of Psychology
New College of Florida
Sarasota, FL

C. Nathan DeWall
Department of Psychology
University of Kentucky
Lexington, KY

Sally S. Dickerson
Department of Psychology and Social
Behavior
University of California, Irvine
Irvine, CA

Naomi I. Eisenberger
Department of Psychology
University of California, Los Angeles
Los Angeles, CA

Susan T. Fiske
Psychology and Public Affairs
Princeton University
Princeton, NJ

Jeff Greenberg
Department of Psychology
University of Arizona
Tucson, AZ

Louise C. Hawkley
Department of Psychology
University of Chicago
Chicago, IL

Michelle Hebl
Department of Psychology
Rice University
Houston, TX

John G. Holmes
Department of Psychology
University of Waterloo
Waterloo, Ontario, Canada

Thomas E. Joiner, Jr.
Department of Psychology
Florida State University
Tallahassee, FL

Jaana Juvonen
Department of Psychology
University of California
Los Angeles, CA

Megan L. Knowles
Department of Psychology
Franklin & Marshall College
Lancaster, PA

Jessica L. Lakin
Psychology Department
Drew University
Madison, NJ

Mark R. Leary
Department of Psychology and
Neuroscience
Duke University
Durham, NC

Bonita London
Department of Psychology
Stony Brook University
Stony Brook, NY

Geoff MacDonald
Department of Psychology
University of Toronto
Toronto, Ontario, Canada

Juan M. Madera
Conrad N. Hilton College of Hotel and
Restaurant Management
University of Houston
Houston, TX

Jon K. Maner
Department of Psychology
Florida State University
Tallahassee, FL

Ashley E. Mason
Department of Psychology
University of Arizona
Tucson, AZ

Amori Yee Mikami
Department of Psychology
University of British Columbia
Vancouver, British Columbia, Canada

Mario Mikulincer
New School of Psychology
Interdisciplinary Center (IDC) Herzliya
Herzliya, Israel

Daniel C. Molden
Department of Psychology
Northwestern University
Evanston, IL

Michael S. North
Department of Psychology
Princeton University
Princeton, NJ

Laura Smart Richman
Department of Psychology and
Neuroscience
Duke University
Durham, NC

Lisa Rosenthal
Department of Psychology
Stony Brook University
Stony Brook, NY

David A. Sbarra
Department of Psychology
University of Arizona
Tucson, AZ

Jeff Schimel
Department of Psychology
University of Alberta
Edmonton, Alberta, Canada

Norman B. Schmidt
Department of Psychology
Florida State University
Tallahassee, FL

Kristin L. Scott
College of Business and Behavioral
Science
Clemson University
Clemson, SC

Phillip R. Shaver
Department of Psychology
University of California, Davis
Davis, CA

Tyler F. Stillman
Department of Marketing and
Management
Southern Utah University
Cedar City, UT

Stefan Thau
London Business School
London, UK

Jean M. Twenge
Department of Psychology
San Diego State University
San Diego, CA

Kimberly A. Van Orden
University of Rochester Medical
Center
Rochester, NY

Michelle R. vanDellen
Department of Psychology
University of Georgia
Athens, GA

Adam Waytz
Department of Psychology
Northwestern University
Kellogg School of Management
Evanston, IL

Eric D. Wesselmann
Department of Psychology
Illinois State University
Normal, IL

Kipling D. Williams
Department of Psychological Sciences
Purdue University
Lafayette, IN

Peggy M. Zoccola
Department of Psychology
Ohio University
Athens, OH

CONTENTS

PART 1

Introduction and Overview

1

Emerging Perspectives on the Study of Social Exclusion

C. Nathan DeWall

Abstract

From its beginning, the field of psychology emphasized the importance of social connections. Whether it was monkeys who preferred terrycloth mothers to wired ones, therapists who gave their clients unconditional positive regard, or establishing social relationships as a means of enabling self-actualizing, dominant psychological theories highlighted the need to have few positive and lasting relationships. Yet systematic research on the need to belong remained sparse over several decades. The past 15 years have seen the most active period of research on the need to belong in the history of psychology. This chapter outlines emerging perspectives from this pioneering period.

Key Words: social exclusion, social rejection, ostracism, need to belong, interpersonal relationships

Introduction

Scientists have a knack for disagreement. Many questions—Does personality change after age 30? Does conscious thought matter? Does altruism exist?—show no signs of reaching a resolution anytime soon. Scientists battle each other in journals and occasionally at conferences hoping to reach resolutions, only to be left with more questions than when they started. But among psychologists, there is a rare sense of agreement on at least one observable fact: social exclusion thwarts a fundamental human motivation to have a few positive and lasting relationships. *The Oxford Handbook of Social Exclusion* offers the most comprehensive body of social exclusion research ever assembled.

Despite the current acceptance of social exclusion as a topic worthy of study, it went understudied for many years. To be sure, the importance of social connections had been stressed by early thinkers including William James (1890), Sigmund

Freud (1930), and Abraham Maslow (1968). Yet, this work was almost entirely theoretical, which left a systematic field of empirical research fallow for decades. The past 15 years has seen a surge in social exclusion research, which was aided in large part from narrative reviews of the literature (Baumeister & Leary, 1995; Williams, 2009) and the advent of novel paradigms to manipulate social exclusion (e.g., ball-tossing paradigms, autobiographical narratives, group rejection, priming concepts related to social exclusion). *The Oxford Handbook of Social Exclusion* brings together innovative theory and findings from this golden age of social exclusion research.

The "Basic and Historical Perspectives" section provides a foundation on why people have a need to belong, why people exclude others, and how people respond to various forms of social exclusion. Mark Leary and Catherine Cottrell review theoretical and empirical research that argues that people evolved psychological adaptations to selectively exclude people from groups and to cope with social exclusion. Far from being a random event, Leary and Cottrell suggest that social exclusion is used systematically to enhance survival and reproductive goals. Michael North and Susan Fiske examine how social exclusion relates to five core social motives: belonging, understanding, controlling, enhancing self, and trusting others. They assert that people feel driven to fulfill these motives within the in-group, which fosters exclusion of people outside of the group. Eric Wesselmann and Kipling Williams present a temporal model of responses to social exclusion, in which people have immediate reflexive reactions, which are followed by reflection and finally resignation. Laura Smart Richman describes how social exclusion prompts three sets of competing motives: the need to aggress toward the source of exclusion, to repair the relationship, or to withdraw.

The next two sections, "Exclusion at the Group Level" and "Exclusion within the Family and Romantic Relations" showcase research on how social exclusion affects people according to their stage of development, their involvement in romantic relationships, and within their work relationships. Juan Madera and Michelle Hebl conclude the section by discussing how people of various groups experience social exclusion through formal (overt, illegal) and interpersonal behaviors (more subtle, legal). Kristin Scott and Stefan Thau put forth a theoretical model on when social exclusion within the workplace will bring about prosocial or antisocial responses. David Sbarra and Ashley Mason review research on how martial separation and divorce relate to lower mental well-being, lower physical well-being, and greater relational violence. Justin Cavallo and John Holmes review research on how people cope with social exclusion at the hands of their romantic partners. They emphasize the importance of how much people feel valued by their partner as a key moderator in driving behaviors aimed at pursuing intimacy or protecting oneself from the threat of social exclusion. Finally, Jaana Juvonen discusses research on subtypes of socially excluded youth and how this approach can inform laboratory social exclusion research.

The section "Individual Exclusion: Behavior and Cognition" is filled with chapters that display the power of social exclusion in shaping a variety of behavioral and cognitive processes. Jean Twenge and I discuss research linking social exclusion to aggression. We explain why such paradoxical

behavior occurs, who is at risk for exclusion-related aggression, and how to prevent such aggression. Daniel Molden and Jon Maner discuss how social exclusion motivates people to reconnect with potential new friends and why such reconnection occurs. Tyler Stillman and Roy Baumeister review research on how and why social exclusion impairs intelligent thought and self-regulation.

The next section, "Individual Exclusion: Physiological, Neural, and Emotional Responses," extends the previous section by showing how social exclusion influences hormonal, neurological, and emotional responses. Sally Dickerson and Peggy Zoccola show how social evaluative threat, of which social exclusion is a part, influences cortisol and inflammatory responses. Naomi Eisenberger catalogues a program of research testing pain overlap theory, which argues that responses to social pain share common neurological overlap with physical pain. Terry Borsook and Geoff MacDonald discuss when social exclusion reduces and enhances physical and emotional sensitivity.

The following section, "Exclusion Across Individuals," shifts the focus to personal characteristics that pertain to social exclusion. John Cacioppo, Louise Hawkley, and Joshua Correll discuss the evolution of loneliness, with an emphasis on its adaptive nature within an evolutionary timescale. Bonita London and Lisa Rosenthal discuss how individual differences in rejection sensitivity modulate responses to various forms of social exclusion. Kimberly Van Orden and Thomas Joiner discuss the interplay between depression and social exclusion, which can inform understanding of suicidal thoughts and behavior. Michelle van-Dellen, Ashley Allen, and Keith Campbell review research examining how individual differences in self-esteem, narcissism, and self-compassion play distinct roles in shaping responses to social exclusion. Amori Mikami goes on to describe how and why individuals with attention deficit hyperactivity disorder (ADHD) often experience social exclusion—and what interventions may reduce such social exclusion. Mario Mikulincer and Phillip Shaver round out the section by providing an overview of attachment theory, along with new empirical evidence regarding the role of attachment style in moderating the effect of social exclusion on reduced meaning.

The final section, "Combating Social Exclusion," is devoted to research on how to reduce the often negative consequences of social exclusion. Adam Waytz discusses how people attribute human qualities to nonhuman objects as a means of warding off the effects of social exclusion. Norman Schmidt reviews research on how training attention away from threatening images can provide an effective way to reduce affective responses to stress, with a focus on interventions for people suffering from anxiety psychopathology. Jessica Lakin and Tanya Chartrand describe how people can use mimicry to make friends and to cope with social exclusion. In the following chapter, Megan Knowles describes how people use parasocial attachments, such as television characters, as reservoirs of belonging. Finally, Jeff Schimel and Jeff Greenberg describe how people form social connections in order to reduce existential fear.

The volume ends with a chapter that ties together these perspectives and findings, with an eye toward possible future directions in the social exclusion literature. Although the research reviewed and presented will likely spark as many questions as it answers, it shows how much knowledge has been gained regarding the causes and consequences of social exclusion. What was once fallow ground now represents a fertile area of study from which future insights can be gained.

References

Baumeister, R. F., & Leary, M. R. (1995). The need to belong: Desire for interpersonal attachments as a fundamental human motivation. *Psychological Bulletin, 117,* 497–529.

Freud, S. (1930). *Civilization and Its Discontents* (J. Riviere, Trans.). London: Hogarth Press.

James, W . (1890). *The Principles of Psychology.* New York: Dover Publications.

Maslow, A. H. (1968). *Toward a Psychology of Being.* New York: Van Nostrand.

Williams, K. D. (2009). Ostracism: A temporal need-threat model. In M. Zanna (Ed.), *Advances in Experimental Social Psychology* (Vol. 41, pp. 279–314). NY: Academic Press.

PART 2

Basic and Historical Perspectives

Evolutionary Perspectives on Interpersonal Acceptance and Rejection

Mark R. Leary *and* Catherine A. Cottrell

Abstract

Establishing and maintaining relationships with other people was among the most crucial tasks faced by our evolutionary ancestors. As a result, human beings possess adaptations not only to seek acceptance by other people and to respond adaptively to threats of social rejection but, ironically, to avoid and reject individuals who are judged to be poor relational partners and group members. This chapter examines the interplay of these opposing inclinations, the evolved adaptations that may underlie them, and implications of an evolutionary perspective for understanding emotional and behavioral reactions to interpersonal rejection.

Key Words: evolutionary psychology, hurt feelings, interpersonal rejection, need to belong, self-presentation

Introduction

At least since Darwin's theory of natural selection began to filter into psychology late in the 19th century, the idea that human beings evolved to live in social groups has been widely endorsed by social and behavioral scientists. Most evolutionary theorists believe not only that the strong human tendency toward sociality evolved because group-living had adaptive value but also that many other aspects of human nature arose because they were beneficial in the context of social groups and relationships (for examples, see Schaller, Simpson, & Kenrick, 2006). Put simply, most social and behavioral scientists take it as a given that human beings evolved psychological adaptations designed to form relationships and live in social groups. This chapter looks at the other side of the coin, focusing on the strong possibility that people also evolved psychological adaptations designed to selectively exclude other people and to deal with instances in which they were, or might be, excluded themselves.

We begin by examining why natural selection might have prepared people to reject certain categories of other individuals, along with the counter-adaptations that might have evolved to help people avoid being rejected for those kinds of reasons. We then examine aspects of human psychology that appear designed to detect and respond to cues that connote interpersonal rejection.

The Necessity of Social Exclusion and Rejection

According to an evolutionary perspective, hominids evolved their strong tendency toward sociality and group-living because solitary individuals were unlikely to survive, reproduce, and have offspring who survived to reproduce. Lacking the typical defenses of most other large mammals—such as ferocity, fangs and claws, speed, or brute strength—the hominids survived harsh natural and social environments only by living in cooperative groups. Not only could groups of prehumans defend themselves against predators and out-groups in ways that individuals could not, but cooperative hunting and sharing of resources allowed groups of early humans to flourish under conditions where solitaires would perish. And, because human infants depend on adults for care and protection much longer than most other mammals (Montagu, 1961), group living provided a context for the cooperative care of children.

Although many theorists have recognized that people are motivated to live in groups and form close relationships, early analyses did not fully appreciate the fact that people are also motivated to behave in ways that lead others to accept them as group members and relational partners. That is, the inclination for people to join groups and form relationships does not ensure that others will, in fact, accept them as group members and relational partners. In fact, as we will discuss, other people have many reasons to be selective in choosing the individuals with whom they form relationships and may occasionally desire to avoid, exclude, or reject others altogether. Thus, people not only have an evolved inclination to form groups and relationships but also to behave in ways that will lead others to accept and include them. This need for acceptance and belonging seems to underlie a great deal of human behavior (Baumeister & Leary, 1995).

Although people are inherently motivated to seek acceptance from others, there are also strong evolutionary reasons why people cannot form social connections with everyone they meet or allow all-comers into their groups. As Alexander (1974) observed, "There is no automatic or universal benefit from group living. Indeed the opposite is true: there are automatic and universal detriments, namely increased intensity of competition for resources, including mates, and increased likelihood of disease and parasite transmission" (p. 328). As a result, people need to be selective about their relational partners and fellow group members in order to minimize these detriments of group living.

In fact, other species also are selective about their social partners (Gruter & Masters, 1986; Lancaster, 1986), and it is instructive to consider why other animals sometimes exclude conspecifics. In her work with the chimpanzees of Gombe, Goodall (1986b) identified three basic reasons why chimpanzees exclude one another. First, like many social species, chimps are hostile toward out-group strangers, whom they typically drive away by force because out-groups compete for resources such as food, territory, or mates. Second, chimps occasionally try to exclude members of their own groups who vie with them for status, mates, or membership in cliques and coalitions (see also de Waal, 2000). Third, like

many species, chimps exclude those who look or behave oddly, presumably because such cues may signal that another animal is diseased, erratic, or dangerous. Human beings regularly exclude other people for these same three reasons, along with others that we discuss, suggesting that these tendencies are part of our evolved primate nature.

From an evolutionary perspective, then, animals presumably avoid, ignore, and exclude others selectively. Each potential relationship with another individual carries the possibility of both fitness opportunities and fitness costs. Members of social species, including hominids, face an ongoing adaptive problem of affiliating and forming relationships with individuals who are likely to provide fitness benefits and avoiding those who generate fitness costs (Kurzban & Leary, 2001; Kurzban & Neuberg, 2005). Thus, psychological adaptations may have evolved for helping people decide which relationships would be particularly disadvantageous.

The list of ways in which other people can harm and disadvantage one another is nearly endless. Even so, certain types of harm with implications for reproductive fitness would have recurred throughout human evolution, setting the stage for possible adaptations to avoid particularly harmful social associations. Here we identify seven broad categories of individuals who are, from the standpoint of maximizing individual fitness, fruitfully avoided, excluded, or rejected.

Avoidance of Out-Group Members

As noted, chimpanzees drive away members of other groups, and human beings also exclude those who are not members of their groups. The reasons are clear. First, members of other groups are unlikely to be close kin, making them less desirable coalition partners (Hamilton, 1964). Moreover, in the ancestral environment, other early humans would have been in direct competition for vital resources, particularly food. Because a certain geographical area can sustain only a limited number of individuals of a given species, forming relationships with outsiders likely undermined one's reproductive fitness by increasing competition for limited resources. Furthermore, members of groups with whom one did not have ongoing, cooperative ties could not be trusted to share resources in the same way as members of one's own group; different norms about cooperative exchange would have hindered intergroup interactions and created fitness costs (Gil-White, 2001).

Thus, once people formed groups (often along kinship lines), they would have resisted the intrusion of members of other groups and used whatever cues were available to distinguish "us" from "them." Many theorists have suggested that this adaptation underlies the human penchant for distinguishing so strongly between in-group and out-group members on the basis of seemingly arbitrary criteria and then treating the groups quite differently (Campbell, 1965; Sherif et al., 1961).

Avoidance of Intragroup Competitors

Even in the most cooperative groups, members compete with one another for limited resources, mates, status, alliances (including friendships), and influence. People who are in explicit and implicit competition within a group understandably view one another with a certain degree of distance and suspicion even as they often cooperate on group tasks. In many cases, each competitor would be quite pleased if the other was no longer a member of the group, and in some instances, they may even work covertly to undermine the other's position in the group. People are particularly likely to avoid in-group members with whom they are socially or instrumentally redundant (i.e., they possess similar characteristics and abilities).

In some cases, this intragroup competition may lead to physical violence (Daly & Wilson, 1988). This potential danger represents another reason underlying the rejection of competitors within one's own group (Kurzban & Neuberg, 2005).

Avoidance of Exploitative Relationship Partners

People obviously prefer to enter into relationships and alliances with people who behave in cooperative, reciprocating, and mutually beneficial ways and to avoid relationships with those who exploit or disadvantage them. Thus, people are highly sensitive to the degree to which others violate basic norms regarding social exchange and exclude those who do so (Cosmides, 1989; Kerr & Levine, 2008; Kurzban & Leary, 2001). For example, we tend to avoid, if not reject, people who violate norms of reciprocity (Gouldner, 1960), fairness (Miller, 2001), in-group loyalty (Tajfel, 1970), sharing (Kameda, Takezawa, & Hastie, 2003), and trustworthiness (Cottrell, Neuberg, & Li, 2007). Such actions on the part of other people harm one's fitness greatly and would have presumably done so throughout evolutionary history. As a result, people may possess adaptations that help them to monitor and respond to others' unfair, selfish, dishonest, and otherwise disadvantageous actions. The fact that no otherwise normal adult is indifferent to being taken advantage of, betrayed, or treated unfairly or selfishly suggests that such concerns are a part of human nature.

Avoidance of Those Who Violate Interaction Norms and Group Values

Some social norms involve arbitrary conventions that simplify and facilitate interpersonal interactions. Unlike norms involving fair and cooperative social exchange described earlier, violations of interaction norms typically do not harm or disadvantage others. For example, norms involving politeness, appropriate attire, forms of address, nonverbal behaviors, privacy, and decorum standardize interpersonal encounters within a group or culture, but violations of such norms do not directly harm anyone.

Even so, people who consistently violate interaction norms and folkways are often avoided or ostracized (Boyd & Richerson, 1985; Schachter, 1951), although the reasons are less clear than in the case of violations of mores and social exchange norms. In part, violations of certain interaction norms create awkward and stilted encounters that simply make others uncomfortable. In addition, adherence to these arbitrary norms may be a way for people to assess another person's similarity and in-groupness (Park & Schaller, 2005). Precisely because they are arbitrary, interaction norms and folkways reveal the degree to which another person is familiar with the rules of the group and willing to abide by them in the service of being a member-in-good-standing.

Of course, some deviations from common group values do harm others. Interestingly, people seem responsive to norm violations that do not disadvantage them directly but still suggest that the violator cannot be counted on to be a good group member, friend, or other relational partner. Thus, people are rejected for behaving in ways that are so outside the pale that their reputation as a reasonable and trustworthy member of society is called into question. For example, parents who abandon or have sex with their children are generally ostracized (Fitness, 2005), even though those behaviors may not be directly relevant to their interactions with other people. People who violate the mores of a group or society are rejected because they cannot be trusted to abide by basic group standards.

Avoidance of Vectors of Disease

Schaller (2006) proposed that people possess a suite of evolved mechanisms—the behavioral immune system—that allows people to detect and avoid potential sources of disease in their immediate environment. One feature of this system leads people to avoid and even exclude individuals who might be a source of disease. We tend to steer clear of people who look ill and avoid people who are known to have serious illnesses whether or not they appear sick (Park, Faulkner, & Schaller, 2003; Rozin, Markwith, & Nemeroff, 1992). Indeed, in modern Westernized cultures, the avoidance and ostracism of the ill has become institutionalized as many workplaces now insist that employees experiencing specific symptoms stay home from work until the symptoms abate.

In many instances, avoiding people who might be contagious reflects a conscious and deliberate effort to stay healthy. However, nonhuman species lacking the cognitive ability to understand the process of disease transmission can also detect when other members of their species are sick and preferentially avoid associating and mating with them (Clayton, 1990; Fedorka & Mousseau, 2007; Hamilton & Zuk, 1982; Møller, 1990; Pomiankowski, 1989; see however, Cramer & Cameron, 2007). Likewise, evidence suggests that human beings also possess automatic inclinations to avoid or ostracize those who are ill (Grammer & Thornhill, 1994; Low, 1990; Shackelford & Larsen, 1997, 1999; Schaller, 2006). For example, people naturally withdraw from and avoid stimuli that evoke a disgust reaction, including other people who show evidence of being ill or infected, such as skin lesions, oozing sores, and discharges from the eyes or nose (Oaten, Stevenson, & Case, 2009).

Avoidance of Disengaged Others

Kerr and Levine (2008) suggested that "disengagement" is an additional cue that might lead people to reject others. Indications that another person is disengaged from social interaction may lead to rejection via two routes. First, disengagement renders a person a poor group member and relational partner because it signals a lack of interest and involvement in group endeavors and a failure to pay sufficient attention to what occurs within the group. Disinterested group members are arguably less effective than members who are attentive and engaged.

Second, disengagement often indicates that the person does not regard his or her relationship with others as sufficiently important or valuable. Because rewarding interdependent relationships require involvement by both parties, perceiving that another person is disengaged raises red flags regarding the other's commitment. People who are not attentive and engaged may not be trusted to devote time and

effort to group goals or other people's well-being. All other things being equal, people should want to form connections with those who consider them valuable as relational partners because people for whom we have high relational value have a greater stake in our well-being than people who do not (Tooby & Cosmides, 1996). Engagement is one indicator of our value to other people. Furthermore, according to the principle of least interest, the person with the least emotional attachment and interest in continuing a relationship has more power and control in the relationship (Waller & Hill, 1951). Thus, disengagement may indicate that one's relative power in a relationship is low or declining.

The use of engagement as a social glue can be seen in the grooming behavior of nonhuman primates. Baboons and apes groom one another far more than is needed to remove insects and irritants and to maintain healthy skin. Rather, grooming signals engagement and investment and is perhaps all the more useful as a social cue because it is largely unnecessary (Byrne, 1995). Like interpersonal engagement in human beings, grooming not only signals the strength of social bonds but also increases them (Dunbar, 1991).

Avoidance Due to Limited Time, Energy, and Other Resources

Finally, people may sometimes avoid or reject others for no reason other than the fact that they have a limited amount of time, energy, and other resources to devote to various relationships. Developing a new relationship with another person, or even having an interaction with him or her, may draw one's time and energy away from established relationships and memberships and from other important activities.

Along these lines, Tooby and Cosmides (1996) proposed that people have a limited number of friendship or association niches. They suggested that people face an ongoing problem of how to fill these niches with individuals from whom they will receive the best outcomes over the long haul. As with economic investments, people must decide which relationships they will invest in and how much they will invest. And, just as with economic investments, investing one's resources in one relationship can preclude investing in another. Tooby and Cosmides proposed that evolution has provided mechanisms to facilitate these calculations, and we would add only that the results of those calculations may lead people to exclude those individuals who are judged to be bad relational investments.

The Pursuit of Acceptance

As we have seen, people are excluded and rejected by other people for seven primary sets of reasons—because they are viewed as out-group members, in-group competitors, poor social exchange partners by virtue of being exploitative, unabashed norm violators, potentially infectious, inexplicably disengaged, or a drain on time and energy that could be devoted to more beneficial relationships. Furthermore, it is not unreasonable to assume that each of these bases of rejection may have an evolutionary basis and that psychological adaptations exist to facilitate people's judgments of them.

Viewed from the standpoint of the person who desires acceptance, these seven bases of rejection also shine light on the basic ways in which people try to minimize the chances of rejection. In fact, we surmise that at least some of the ways in which people avoid rejection are linked evolutionarily to the reasons that people are rejected. That is, if people are predisposed to avoid, exclude, and reject others for a finite set of recurrent reasons, counter-adaptations may have emerged that help people to act in ways that minimize those particular rejection criteria. For example, out-group members who wish admission to a group may mimic the appearance or behaviors of in-group members, and psychologically disengaged partners and group members often feign a minimal level of interest and involvement.

For the person who seeks to avoid rejection, the most important consideration is to appear as the kind of person who makes a good friend, group member, or other relational partner. Thus, we would expect evolution to have prepared people to be attuned to how they are perceived by others and motivated to convey the kinds of impressions that would increase their relational value in other people's eyes (Cottrell, 2009). Of course, all well-adjusted people are concerned with others' impressions and evaluations of them, try to convey impressions of themselves that help them to obtain desired outcomes and achieve desired goals, and are particularly responsive to situations in which they believe that they have made an undesired impression that might lead others to devalue or reject them (Leary, 1995). People may use self-presentation in the service of many goals other than social acceptance, so we should not expect that people will always try to convey impressions that increase their relational value. Even so, many, if not most, of people's concerns with their social images appear to involve concerns with promoting acceptance and avoiding rejection (Leary, 2010). Taking our list of seven bases of rejection as a starting point, we hypothesize that, all other things being equal, people prefer for others to see them as a member of the in-group (and especially as sharing kin ties; Webster, 2008), cooperative rather than competitive, fair, norm abiding, physically healthy, socially engaged, and worth the investment of time and effort needed to sustain a relationship.

Reactions to Real and Potential Rejection

Given the vital importance of social acceptance to reproductive fitness, we should not be surprised that many features of the human psyche appear designed to monitor and respond to events that have implications for people's value and acceptance to other people, and particularly to events that connote the possibility of devaluation and rejection.

Monitoring and Detecting Rejection

The specific mechanisms that monitor the social environment for cues regarding interpersonal acceptance and rejection are not well understood, but we know a few things about their properties. Notably, the psychological systems that detect interpersonal rejection are exceptionally sensitive, to the point that Williams and Zadro (2005) characterized this early-warning system as "indiscriminant" (p. 19). This system activates quickly to warn people of potential threats that are often minor, remote, or even imagined. Most systems that monitor the environment for potential threats and opportunities are designed with a bias toward false positives under nature's assumption that it's better to be safe than sorry (Haselton, Nettle, & Andrews, 2005). Just as animals are more likely to respond fearfully to innocuous stimuli than they are to remain calm when surrounded by threats, people are similarly more likely to interpret neutral or ambivalent cues as rejecting than they are to overestimate their social acceptance (Leary, Haupt, Strausser, & Chokel, 1998).

As a result, people often respond automatically to neutral reactions, minor snubs, and trivial exclusions as if they had exceptionally important consequences, even when coming from people whose acceptance does not matter (Gonsalkorale & Williams, 2007; Wirth & Williams, 2009). A meta-analysis of research on reactions to rejection concluded that rejection does not cause immediate distress (Blackhart, Nelson, Knowles, & Baumeister, 2009), but many studies have found effects of rejection on people's immediate emotional reactions. We suspect that being told "I never want to see you again," "You're fired," or "You've been voted out of the group" would elicit a strong, immediate reaction in virtually everyone.

Once the alarm is sounded, people's conscious assessment of the situation may show that they need not be as concerned as they first thought, but their first reaction is, in fact, nearly indiscriminant. Of course, people can cognitively override their initial reactions when they realize that a particular rejection does not actually present a meaningful threat. But the ability to override one's initial response would have developed relatively late in evolutionary history, after the emergence of self-awareness and the capacity to regulate one's own thoughts and emotions deliberately and consciously (Leary & Buttermore, 2003).

Emotional Reactions

To the extent that emotions evolved to manage animals' reaction to threats and opportunities (Cosmides & Tooby, 2000), emotional reactions can reveal a great deal about the processes that underlie reactions to particular stimuli and events. Here we examine the emotions that are most closely associated with social rejection.

HURT FEELINGS

Hurt feelings results from the appraisal that one is being insufficiently relationally valued or outright rejected and, thus, can be regarded as the "rejection emotion" (Leary & Leder, 2009). The major categories of events that cause hurt feelings involve indications that other people do not value their relationship with the person as much as he or she would like (Feeney, 2004, 2005; Leary, Springer, Negel, Ansell, & Evans, 1998; Mills, Nazar, & Farrell, 2002). Furthermore, experimental studies that lead participants to believe that others do not wish to interact with or get to know them—that is, manipulations that induce a sense of low relational value or rejection—reliably elicit hurt feelings (Bourgeois, & Leary, 2001; Buckley, Winkel, & Leary; 2003; Eisenberger, Lieberman, & Williams, 2003; Snapp & Leary, 2001).

MacDonald and Leary (2005) reviewed a wide range of evidence suggesting that the physiological mechanisms that mediate hurt feelings evolved on top of existing mechanisms that are associated with physical pain (see also MacDonald, Kingsbury, & Shaw, 2005; Panksepp, 1998). They suggested that social animals, including human beings, require a system that punishes individuals who do not avoid social exclusion and motivates quick responses to signs of rejection. In support of this hypothesis,

they reviewed physiological evidence that social and physical pain operate via shared mechanisms (specifically, the anterior cingulate cortex and periaqueductal gray brain structures and the opioid and oxytocin neuroendocrine systems) and that the cognitive, emotional, and behavioral features of social and physical pain overlap considerably. The fact that people possess a system that evokes strong, painful feelings in response to interpersonal rejection provides additional evidence that the regulation of social acceptance was critical to survival throughout human evolution.

Although situations in which people feel devalued reliably elicit hurt feelings, rejections tend to evoke other emotions as well, particularly anger and sadness (Leary, Twenge, & Quinlivan, 2006). However, Leary and Leder (2009) presented evidence that only hurt feelings result directly from appraisals of low relational evaluation and that other emotions that often accompany rejection arise from other features of the situation. For example, rejections that are perceived as unfair may elicit anger, and those that are experienced as losses of relationships may cause sadness.

EMBARRASSMENT, GUILT, AND SHAME

Embarrassment is typically defined as an emotional response to self-presentational predicaments—situations in which people believe that they have conveyed undesired impressions of themselves to others (Miller, 1996). However, in a broader sense, embarrassment may be thought of as a reaction to situations in which one has conveyed images that may lower one's relational value and likelihood of acceptance by other people. The events that evoke embarrassment tend to be those in which a person violates generic social norms involving how one should interact with other people, and as we have noted, violations of interaction norms and folkways reliably lead to devaluation and rejection. It is therefore likely that embarrassment functions to signal possible interpersonal rejection to an individual.

Historically, guilt and shame have been conceptualized as emotions that arise from unfavorable comparisons between people's personal ideals or moral standards and their actual behavior (Lewis, 2000). However, when one considers the evolutionary bases of guilt and shame, they must involve systems that are designed to regulate one's behavior with respect to other people's standards rather than merely one's own. Of course, social standards can become internalized so that the immediate comparison is with one's internal standards (or, perhaps, the standards of some generalized other). Yet, the systems that underlie guilt and shame presumably evolved to prevent people from violating social standards that might cause others to reject them and to motivate remedial behavior in the aftermath of such violations (Fessler, 2007). Thus, in our view, guilt and shame are also involved in systems that mediate reactions to real, anticipated, and imagined rejection.

An interesting question is why people have different emotional responses to different kinds of situations that undermine relational value and social acceptance. Specifically, embarrassment arises in response to violations of social norms (such as burping in front of others, falling down in public, or forgetting an appointment), whereas guilt and shame generally occur when people violate moral or ethical standards (such as infidelity, damaging another's property, or malfeasance) (Tangney, Miller, Flicker, & Barlow, 1996). Granted, embarrassing events are usually less serious than those that cause guilt and shame, but one might expect that such differences in severity of the antecedent would be reflected in differences in the intensity of the reaction rather than in qualitative differences in the reaction.

Self-Esteem

People's feelings about themselves are intimately involved in their reactions to interpersonal rejection. Indications that one has been, or is about to be, rejected from groups and relationships reliably lowers state self-esteem compared to indications that one is relationally valued and socially accepted (for reviews, see Leary, 2006, Leary & Baumeister, 2000). According to sociometer theory, rejection and state self-esteem are so closely related because self-esteem is part of the system that monitors and responds to threats to social acceptance.

When people perceive that their relational value has declined, they naturally assess the role that they might have played in the rejection and entertain the possibility that they were rejected on the basis of their own behavior, personality, ability, appearance, or other attributes. Whatever the circumstances of a particular rejection episode, at minimum it is always the case that the rejector did not see sufficient value in relating to the rejectee, which influences how people feel about themselves. The pangs of lowered self-esteem not only alert people to potential problems but also focus them on the question of whether their personal attributes played some role in the rejection. Furthermore, research suggests that changes in state self-esteem cause changes in people's interpersonal

aspirations following rejection (Kavanagh, Robins, & Ellis, in press). That is, when people feel less positively about themselves, they gravitate toward safer and less demanding people as interaction and relational partners, thereby increasing the chances that they will be accepted.

Appeasement Displays

Many species, including nonhuman primates, possess a repertoire of appeasement behaviors that they display under conditions of social threat. As the label implies, appeasement behaviors have typically been conceptualized as actions that appease a conspecific and lower the likelihood of conflict and aggression. Although this characterization is true, appeasement behaviors also deter social exclusion. That is, a lower-status primate that fails to engage in appropriate appeasement behavior not only risks the possibility of aggression from a higher-status conspecific but may also be marginalized or excluded by that individual or other members of the group.

Chimpanzees who feel threatened by another chimp, particularly one who is more dominant, display a stereotypic pattern of behaviors that involves avoiding eye contact, a slightly bowed head, and sometimes a submissive open mouth grin (Estes, 1991). Human beings display a similar response to certain social threats that must certainly share some evolutionary roots with nonhuman primates (Leary, Britt, Cutlip, & Templeton, 1992). First, when people become concerned about how they are being evaluated by others, they often display gaze aversion and downcast eyes. People who feel socially anxious have difficulty maintaining eye contact with other people, and experiences of embarrassment, guilt, and shame are likewise accompanied by averted gaze (Keltner, 1995). Furthermore, people who are embarrassed, ashamed, or guilty typically desire to withdraw from social contact with the sources of the threat. This urge to withdraw is particularly pronounced in the case of shame but is also seen when people feel socially anxious, embarrassed, or guilty (Leary & Kowalski, 1995; Tangney et al., 1996). And, when the episode involves a minor infraction of social norms, people sometimes display a mirthless grin that closely resembles the open mouth grin seen in appeasing chimpanzees (Estes, 1991; Leary et al., 1992).

At times, people also respond to possible rejection with facial blushing, a reaction that appears to have no nonhuman counterpart. People who feel embarrassed or ashamed sometimes blush, and many theorists have interpreted blushing as an involuntary appeasement behavior that conveys to others that the person recognizes his or her misbehavior and feels sorry for it (Castelfranchi & Poggi, 1990; Keltner, 1995). Conveying embarrassment or shame may mitigate the negative social impression that was caused by the infraction (de Jong, 1999; de Jong, Peters, & De Cremer, 2003; Dijk, Jong, & Peters, 2009; Keltner, Young, & Buswell, 1997).

Although most theorists link blushing to situations in which people behave inappropriately or convey undesired images of themselves, people sometimes blush in response to positive events that would seem to connote that they are regarded positively and socially accepted (Leary et al., 1992). For example, people may blush when being complimented, receiving an award, or being serenaded by friends with "Happy Birthday to You." Leary et al. (1992) suggested that, rather than being a reaction only to self-presentational predicaments, blushing is a response to undesired social attention. Attention from other people in the wake of embarrassing, humiliating, or shameful events is obviously undesired, but sometimes positive attention from other people is discomfiting as well. By signaling that the person feels uncomfortable with accolades and other positive attention, blushing moderates appearances of deservedness, self-satisfaction, grandiosity, and other attributes that may not be desired in group members and relational partners.

Motives

Evolved mechanisms for dealing with threats generally do three things. They monitor the environment for cues indicating the presence of the threat, evoke aversive emotions when such cues are detected, and instigate a motivation or action tendency to behave in ways that minimize or eliminate the threat. As we have seen, human beings possess systems that detect and respond to real and potential rejection. However, the subsequent motivations are a bit complicated because evidence suggests that people may respond to rejection in at least three quite disparate ways—by trying to enhance their relational value and acceptance, lashing out aggressively, or withdrawing socially by avoiding the person who rejected them (Buckley et al., 2003; Leary et al., 2006; Maner, DeWall, Baumeister, & Schaller, 2007).

Each of these reactions could be functional under certain circumstances. Enhancing one's relational value could restore social connections with the rejector or others, aggression could punish people for unfair rejections and possibly deter future exclusion, and withdrawal reduces the likelihood of further rejection and hurt feelings. Although we can imagine natural selection designing systems to facilitate each of these responses, their operation must be sensitive to nuances in each particular rejection episode.

Richman and Leary (2009; Richman, this volume) have offered a multi-motive model of responses to rejection that specifies the circumstances under which people who are rejected will tend to respond prosocially, antisocially, or asocially. Specifically, they identified six sets of factors that should moderate people's reactions to rejection—the fairness of the rejection, expectations of relationships repair, pervasiveness or chronicity of the rejection, value of the damaged relationship, perceived costs of the rejection, and the possibility of relational alternatives. The model predicts that these six construals explain which of the three motives (seeking acceptance, harming others, or withdrawal) dominates people's responses after being rejected.

Whether there are dedicated evolved mechanisms that mediate these three reactions is not clear. On one hand, natural selection might have fostered systems that led people to make judicious choices regarding how to respond to particular rejections. Given the importance of acceptance to reproductive fitness, cues indicating rejection might naturally induce behavioral responses to deal with it, and the optimal response may involve motives to be accepted, to harm others, or to withdraw, depending on the circumstances. People may possess mechanisms that take into account the specific contingencies in a particular situation. On the other hand, natural selection might have created systems that detect rejection but that do not specify a particular kind of response.

Conclusions

Much of human life is played out on a field on which people selectively avoid and reject other people even as they try to minimize their own chances of rejection by others. Moreover, people are evolutionarily prepared both to distance themselves from those who may be poor relational partners and group members and to monitor and respond to events in which their own relational value and social acceptance is in jeopardy. Given the importance of strong interpersonal relationships to human survival and reproduction throughout evolutionary history and the disastrous effects of social exclusion and rejection, natural selection fashioned systems that help human beings to manage their social lives in ways that increase the quality of their social connections.

References

Alexander, R. D. (1974). The evolution of social behavior. *Annual Review of Ecology and Systematics, 5*, 325–383.

Baumeister, R. F., & Leary, M. R . (1995). The need to belong: Desire for interpersonal attachments as a fundamental human motivation. *Psychological Bulletin, 117*, 497–529.

Blackhart, G. C., Nelson, B. C., Knowles, M. L., & Baumeister, R. F. (2009). Rejection elicits emotional reactions but neither causes immediate distress nor lowers self-esteem: a meta-analytic review of 192 studies on social exclusion. *Personality and Social Psychology Review, 13*, 269–309.

Bourgeois, K. S., & Leary, M. R. (2001). Coping with rejection: Derogating those who choose us last. *Motivation and Emotion, 25*, 101–111.

Boyd, R., & Richerson, P. J. (1985). *Culture and the Evolutionary Process.* Chicago: University of Chicago Press.

Buckley, K. E., Winkel, R. E., & Leary, M. R. (2003). Reactions to acceptance and rejection: Effects of level and sequence of relational evaluation. *Journal of Experimental Social Psychology, 40*, 14–28.

Byrne, R. (1995). *The Thinking Ape: Evolutionary Origins of Intelligence.* Oxford: Oxford University Press.

Campbell, D. T. (1965). Ethnocentric and other altruistic motives. In D. Levine (Ed.), *Nebraska Symposium on Motivation* (Vol. 13, pp. 283–311). Lincoln, NE: University of Nebraska Press.

Castelfranchi, C., & Poggi, I. (1990). Blushing as a discourse: Was Darwin wrong? In W. R. Crozier (Ed.), *Shyness and Embarrassment: Perspectives from Social Psychology* (pp. 230–251). Cambridge, UK: Cambridge University Press.

Clayton, D. (1990). Mate choice in experimentally parasitized rock doves: Lousy males lose. *American Zoology, 30*, 251–262.

Cosmides, L. (1989). The logic of social exchange: Has natural selection shaped how humans reason? Studies with the Wason selection task. *Cognition, 31*, 187–276.

Cosmides, L., & Tooby, J. (2000). Evolutionary psychology and the emotions. In M. Lewis & J. M. Haviland-Jones (Eds.), *Handbook of Emotions* (pp. 91–115). New York: Guilford Press.

Cottrell, C. A. (2009, February). *From playing dead to playing dumb: An evolutionary analysis of self-presentation.* Paper presented at the annual meeting of the Society for Personality and Social Psychology, Tampa, FL.

Cottrell, C. A., Neuberg, S. L., & Li, N. P. (2007). What do people desire in others? A sociofunctional perspective on the importance of different valued characteristics. *Journal of Personality and Social Psychology, 92*, 208–231.

Cramer, M. J., & Cameron, G. N. (2007). Effects of bot fly, Cuterebra fontinella, parasitism on male aggression and female choice in Peromyscus leucopus. *Animal Behaviour, 74*(5), 1419–1427.

Daly, M., & Wilson, M. (1988). *Homicide.* Hawthorne, NY: Aldine de Gruyter.

de Jong, P. J. (1999). Communicative and remedial effects of social blushing. *Journal of Nonverbal Behavior, 23*, 197–218.

de Jong, P. J., Peters, M. L., & De Cremer, D. (2003). Blushing may signify guilt: Revealing effects of blushing in ambiguous social situations. *Motivation and Emotion, 27*, 225–249.

De Waal, F. B. M. (2000). *Chimpanzee Politics: Power and Sex among Apes.* Baltimore: Johns Hopkins University Press.

Dijk, C., de Jong, P. J., & Peters, M. L. (2009). The signaling value of blushing in the context of transgressions and mishaps. *Emotion, 9*, 287–291

Dunbar, R. I. M. (1991). Functional significance of social grooming in primates. *Folia Primatologia, 57*, 121–131.

Eisenberger, N. I., Lieberman, M. D., & Williams, K. D. (2003). Does rejection hurt? An fMRI study of social exclusion. *Science, 302*, 290–292.

Estes, R. D. 1991. *The Behavior Guide to African Mammals.* Berkeley, CA: University of California Press.

Fedorka, K. M., & Mousseau, T. A. (2007). Immune system activation affects male sexual signal and reproductive potential in crickets. *Behavioral Ecology, 18*, 231–235.

Feeney, J. A. (2004). Hurt feelings in couple relationships: Toward integrative models of the negative effects of hurtful events. *Journal of Social and Personal Relationships, 21*, 487–508.

Feeney, J. A. (2005). Hurt feelings in couple relationships: Exploring the role of attachent and percpetions of personal injury. *Personal Relationships, 12*, 253–271.

Fessler, D. M. T. (2007) From appeasement to conformity: Evolutionary and cultural perspectives on shame, competition, and cooperation. In J. L. Tracy, R. W. Robins, & J. P. Tangney (Eds.), *The Self-Conscious Emotions: Theory and Research* (pp. 174–193). New York: Guilford Press.

Fitness, J. (2005). Bye bye, black sheep: The causes and consequences of rejection in family relationships. In K. D. Williams, J. P. Forgas, & W. von Hippel (Eds.), *The Social Outcast: Ostracism, Social Exclusion, Rejection, and Bullying (pp. 263–276).* New York: Psychology Press.

Gil-White, F. J. (2001) Are ethnic groups biological "species" to the human brain?: Essentialism in our cognition of some social categories. *Current Anthropology, 42*, 515–554.

Gonsalkorale, K., & Williams, K. D. (2007). The KKK won't let me play: Ostracism even by a despised outgroup hurts. *European Journal of Social Psychology, 37*, 1176–1186.

Goodall, J. (1986b). *The Chimpanzees of Gombe: Patterns of Behavior.* Cambridge, MA: Belknap Press.

Gouldner, A. W. (1960.) The norm of reciprocity: A preliminary statement. *American Sociological Review, 25*, 161–178.

Grammer, K., & Thornhill, R. (1994). Human (Homo sapiens) facial attractiveness and sexual selection: The role of symmetry and averageness. *Journal of Comparative Psychology, 108*, 223–242.

Gruter, M., & Masters, R. D. (1986). Ostracism as a social and biological phenomenon. *Ethology and Sociobiology, 7*, 149–158.

Hamilton, W. D. (1964). The genetical evolution of social behaviour. *Journal of Theoretical Biology, 7*, 1–16.

Hamilton, W. D., & Zuk, M. (1982). Heritable true fitness and bright birds: A role for parasites? *Science, 218*, 383–387.

Haselton, M. G., Nettle, D., & Andrews, P. W. (2005). The evolution of cognitive bias. In D. M. Buss (Ed.), *Handbook of Evolutionary Psychology* (pp. 724–746). Hoboken, NJ: Wiley.

Kameda, T., Takezawa, M., & Hastie, R. (2003). The logic of social sharing: An evolutionary game analysis of adaptive norm development. *Personality and Social Psychology Review, 7*, 2–19.

Kavanagh, P. S., Robins, S., & Ellis, B. J. (2010). The mating sociometer: A regulatory mechanism for mating aspirations. *Journal of Personality and Social Psychology, 99*(1), 1120–132.

Keltner, D. (1995). Signs of appeasement: Evidence for the distinct displays of embarrassment, amusement, and shame. *Journal of Personality and Social Psychology, 68*, 441–454.

Keltner, D., Young, R. C., & Buswell, B. N. (1997). Appeasement in human emotion, social practice, and personality. *Aggressive Behavior, 23*, 359–374.

Kerr, N. L., & Levine, J. M. (2008) The detection of social exclusion: Evolution and beyond. *Group Dynamics: Theory, Research, and Practice, 12*, 39–52.

Kurzban, R., & Leary, M. R. (2001). Evolutionary origins of stigmatization: The functions of social exclusion. *Psychological Bulletin, 127*, 187–208.

Kurzban, R., & Neuberg, S. (2005). Managing ingroup and outgroup relationships. In D. Buss (Ed.), *The Handbook of Evolutionary Psychology* (pp. 653–675). Hoboken, NJ: Wiley.

Lancaster, J. B. (1986). Primate social behavior and ostracism. *Ethology and Sociobiology, 7*, 215–225.

Leary, M. R. (1995). *Self-presentation: Impression management and interpersonal behavior.* Boulder: Westview Press.

Leary, M. R. (2006). Sociometer theory and the pursuit of relational value: Getting to the root of self-esteem. *European Review of Social Psychology, 16*, 75–111.

Leary, M. R. (2010). Social anxiety as an early warning system: A refinement and extension of the self- presentational theory of social anxiety. In S. G. Hofman & P. M. DiBartolo (Eds.), *Social Anxiety: Clinical, Developmental, and Social Perspectives* (2nd ed.). New York: Allyn & Bacon.

Leary, M. R., & Baumeister, R. F. (2000). The nature and function of self-esteem: Sociometer theory. In M.P. Zanna (Ed.), *Advances in Experimental Social Psychology* (Vol. 32, pp. 1–62). San Diego: Academic Press.

Leary, M. R., Britt, T. W., Cutlip, W. D., & Templeton, J. L. (1992). Social blushing. *Psychological Bulletin, 112*, 446–460.

Leary, M. R., & Buttermore, N. E. (2003). Evolution of the human self: Tracing the natural history of self-awareness. *Journal for the Theory of Social Behaviour, 33*, 365–404.

Leary, M. R., Haupt, A. L., Strausser, K. S., & Chokel, J. T. (1998). Calibrating the sociometer: The relationship between interpersonal appraisals and state self-esteem. *Journal of Personality and Social Psychology, 74*, 1290–1299.

Leary, M. R., & Kowalski, R. M. (1995). *Social Anxiety.* New York: Guilford Press.

Leary, M. R., & Leder, S. (2009). The nature of hurt feelings: Emotional experience and cognitive appraisals. In A. Vangelisti (Ed.), *Feeling Hurt in Close Relationships.* New York: Cambridge University Press.

Leary, M. R., Springer, C., Negel, L., Ansell, E., & Evans, K. (1998). The causes, phenomenology, and consequences of hurt feelings. *Journal of Personality and Social Psychology, 74*, 1225–1237.

Leary, M. R., Twenge, J. M., & Quinlivan, E. (2006). Interpersonal rejection as a determinant of anger and aggression. *Personality and Social Psychology Review, 10*, 111–132.

Lewis, M. (2000). Self-conscious emotions: Embarrassment, pride, shame, and guilt. In M. Lewis & J. M. Haviland-Jones (Eds.), *Handbook of Emotions* (2nd ed., pp. 623–636). New York: Guilford Press.

Low, B. (1990). Marriage systems and pathogen stress in human societies. *American Zoology, 30*, 325–339.

MacDonald, G., Kingsbury, R., & Shaw, S. (2005). Adding insult to injury: Social pain theory and response to social exclusion. In K. Williams, J. Forgas, & W. von Hippel (Eds.), *The Social Outcast: Ostracism, Social Exclusion, Rejection, & Bullying* (pp. 77–90). New York: Psychology Press.

MacDonald, G., & Leary, M. R. (2005). Why does social exclusion hurt? The relationship between social and physical pain. *Psychological Bulletin, 131*, 202–223.

Maner, J. K., DeWall, C. N., Baumeister, R. F., & Schaller, M. (2007). Does social exclusion motivate interpersonal reconnection? Resolving the "porcupine problem." *Journal of Personality and Social Psychology, 92*, 42–55.

Miller, D. T. (2001). Disrespect and the psychology of injustice. *Annual Review of Psychology, 52*, 527–553.

Miller, R. S. (1996). *Embarrassment: Poise and Peril in Everyday Life.* New York: Guilford.

Mills, R. S. L., Nazar, J., & Farrell, H. M. (2002). Child and parent perceptions of hurtful messages. *Journal of Social and Personal Relationships, 19*, 731–754.

Møller, A. P. Parasites and sexual selection: Current studies of the Hamilton and Zuk hypothesis. *Journal of Evolutionary Biology, 3*, 319–328.

Montagu, M. F. A. (1961). Neonatal and infant maturity in man. *The Journal of the American Medical Association, 178*, 56–57.

Oaten, M. Stevenson, R. J., & Case, T. I. (2009). Disgust as a disease-avoidance mechanism. *Psychological Bulletin, 135*, 303–321.

Panksepp, J. (1998). *Affective Neuroscience: The Foundations of Human and Animal Emotions.* London: Oxford University Press.

Park, J. H., Faulkner, J., & Schaller, M. (2003). Evolved disease-avoidance processes and contemporary anti-social behavior: Prejudicial attitudes and avoidance of people with disabilities. *Journal of Nonverbal Behavior, 27*, 65–87.

Park, J. H., & Schaller, M. (2005). Does attitude similarity serve as a heuristic cue for kinship? Evidence of an implicit cognitive association. *Evolution and Human Behavior, 26*, 158–170.

Pomiankowski, A. (1989). Choosing parasite-free mates. *Nature, 338*, 115–116.

Richman, L. S., & Leary, M. R. (2009). Reactions to discrimination, stigmatization, ostracism, and other forms of interpersonal rejection: A dynamic, multi-motive model. *Psychological Review, 116*, 365–383.

Rozin, P., Markwith, M., & Nemeroff, C. (1992). Magical contagion beliefs and fear of AIDS. *Journal of Applied Social Psychology, 22*, 1081–1092.

Schachter, S. (1951). Deviance, rejection, and communication. *Journal of Abnormal and Social Psychology, 46*, 190–207.

Schaller, M. (2006). Parasites, behavioral defenses, and the social psychological mechanisms through which cultures are evoked. *Psychological Inquiry, 17*, 96–101.

Schaller, M., Simpson, J. A., & Kenrick, D. T. (Eds.) (2006). *Evolution and Social Psychology.* New York: Psychology Press.

Shackelford, T. K., & Larsen, R. J. (1999). Facial attractiveness and physical health. *Evolution and Human Behavior, 20*, 71–76.

Sherif, M., Harvey, O. J., White, B. J., Hood, W. R., & Sherif, C. W. (1961): *Intergroup Conflict and Cooperation: The Robbers Cave Experiment.* Norman, OK: University of Oklahoma Book Exchange.

Snapp, C. M., & Leary, M. R. (2001). Hurt feelings among new acquaintances: Moderating effects of interpersonal familiarity. *Journal of Personal and Social Relationships, 18*, 315–326.

Tajfel, H. (1970) Experiments in intergroup discrimination. *Scientific American, 223*, 96–102.

Tangney, J. P. Miller, R. S., Flicker, L., & Barlow, D. H. (1996). Are shame, guilt, and embarrassment distinct emotions? *Journal of Personality and Social Psychology, 70*, 1256–1269.

Tooby, J., & Cosmides, L. (1996). Friendship and the banker's paradox: Other pathways in the evolution of altruism. *Proceedings of the British Academy, 88*, 119–143.

Waller, W. W., & Hill, R. (1951). *The Family: A Dynamic Interpretation*. New York: Dryden.

Webster, G. D. (2008). The kinship, acceptance, and rejection model of altruism and aggression (KARMAA): Implications for interpersonal and intergroup aggression. *Group Dynamics: Theory, Research, and Practice, 12*, 27–38.

Williams, K. D., & Zadro, L. (2005). Ostracism: The indiscriminate early detection system. In K. D. Williams, J. P. Forgas, & W. von Hippel (Eds.), *The Social Outcast* (pp. 19–34). New York: Psychology Press.

Wirth, J., & Williams, K. D. (2009). "They don't like our kind": Consequences of being ostracized while possessing a group membership. *Group Processes and Intergroup Relations, 12*, 111–127.

Ostracism and Stages of Coping

Eric D. Wesselmann *and* Kipling D. Williams

Abstract

Ostracism—being ignored and excluded—is a painful event that many individuals experience. Williams (2009) proposed a temporal model of ostracism, arguing that reactions to ostracism change over time. Individuals have *reflexive* reactions to ostracism, characterized by immediate distress and threat to various basic needs. Next, ostracized individuals enter the *reflective* stage, in which they strive to recover basic needs satisfaction. Individuals only enter the *resignation* stage if they experience chronic ostracism. Research has focused on the first two stages, but the resignation stage remains largely unexplored. The goal of this chapter is to generate future directions for research on each of the stages of ostracism, particularly the resignation stage. We propose that individuals in the resignation stage may be more likely to engage in maladaptive behaviors (e.g., extreme violence), than individuals who are not in the resignation stage. We close this chapter by speculating on potential intervention techniques to help individuals in the resignation stage cope with chronic ostracism.

Key Words: coping and recovery, need to belong, ostracism, social exclusion

Introduction

Ostracism—being ignored and excluded—is a situation that occurs in myriad cultures and contexts (Williams, 2001; Williams & Nida, 2011). Researchers from various disciplines have argued ostracism served useful functions in humans' evolutionary past (Gruter & Masters, 1986; Kerr & Levine, 2008; Kurzban & Leary, 2001; Williams, 2009). Groups of humans and other social animals use ostracism as a form of social control to deal with deviant or burdensome group members, thus strengthening the group by motivating individual members to obey certain social norms and to contribute to the collective (Dijker & Koomen, 2007; Gruter & Masters, 1986; Juvonen & Gross, 2004; Kurzban & Leary, 2001; Ouwerkerk, Kerr, Gallucci, & Van Lange, 2005; Williams, 2001; Zippelius, 1986). There are two approaches to research on ostracism—researchers can focus on the

functions of ostracism (e.g., Wesselmann, Wirth, Pryor, Reeder, & Williams, 2012), or they can focus on the experiences of the individuals who experience ostracism (Williams, 2009). In this chapter, we discuss research that has examined the effects of ostracism on individuals who experience it.

Ostracism is a painful situation that the majority of individuals have experienced at least once in their lives, and sometimes on a daily basis (Nezlek, Wesselmann, Wheeler, & Williams, 2012; Williams, 2009). Social psychologists have studied ostracism systematically for the past 20 years, focusing on the effects of ostracism in social interactions (Williams, 2009). Ostracism occurs in three main modes of interaction—physical, face-to-face, and cyberostracism (Williams, Cheung, & Choi, 2000). *Physical* ostracism involves being separated physically from the group (e.g., incarceration, exile). *Face-to-face* ostracism involves being ignored and excluded while in the physical presence of others (e.g., the "silent treatment"). *Cyberostracism* occurs via electronic media wherein recognition and communication is anticipated but does not occur within an acceptable time frame (e.g., ignored email, texts). Experimental research in psychology has focused considerable attention on face-to-face and cyberostracism, but it is important to note little research thus far has investigated physical ostracism.

Ostracism can be psychologically harmful to the target, leading to impaired self-regulation (Baumeister, DeWall, Ciarocco, & Twenge, 2005; Oaten, Williams, Jones, & Zadro, 2008). It also increases self-perceptions of dehumanization (Bastian & Haslam, 2010). Furthermore, fMRI data demonstrate that ostracism activates the dorsal anterior cingulate cortex (dACC), the same region of the brain that is associated with physical pain (Eisenberger, Lieberman, & Williams, 2003).

Ostracism threatens individuals' satisfaction of four basic human needs: belonging, control, meaningful existence, and self-esteem (Williams, 2001; 2009; Williams et al., 2000; Zadro, Williams, & Richardson, 2004). Humans are social animals who desire *belonging* to groups and other interpersonal relationships (Baumeister & Leary, 1995). Additionally, humans desire some perceived *control* over their environment, even if it is only illusory (Rothbaum, Weisz, & Snyder, 1982). Humans are also motivated to have *self-esteem* that is reasonably positive (Leary, Tambor, Terdal, & Downs, 1995). Finally, humans have a need to know that their *existence* matters to others (Solomon, Greenberg, & Pyszczynski, 1991).

Williams's Temporal Model of Ostracism

Williams (2009) posits that individuals' experiences of ostracism are not uniform over time, and that ostracism's impact can be influenced by different personality and situational factors. Williams's (2009) temporal model has three stages: reflexive (Stage 1), reflective (Stage 2), and resignation (Stage 3).

Reflexive Stage

Humans evolved to detect the slightest cues of ostracism, which helped them forestall or avoid permanent expulsion. Once individuals detect these cues, their reflexive responses are characterized by immediate pain, distress and thwarted need satisfaction. Typical research in this area uses self-report scales to measure need threat and negative affect, but other researchers have also used physiological measures to assess pain and distress. This research

finds ostracism immediately increases blood pressure along with activating the dACC region of the brain (Eisenberger et al. 2003; Williams & Zadro, 2004). Other studies have found that ostracism can have other physiological effects (e.g., increased cortisol) that can become harmful if experienced chronically (Dickerson & Kemeny, 2004; Josephs et al., 2012; Moor, Crone, & van der Molen, 2010).

These negative effects of ostracism occur regardless of whether it occurs in a face-to-face situation (Williams & Sommer, 1997) or in electronic social interactions (Smith & Williams, 2004; Williams et al, 2000; Williams, Govan, Crocker, Tynan, Cruickshank, & Lam, 2002). Even simple nonverbal cues, such as lack of eye contact, are sufficient to threaten need satisfaction and increase negative mood (Wirth, Sacco, Hugenberg, & Williams, 2010; see also Williams, Shore, & Grahe, 1998). The power of eye contact recently was demonstrated in a field study. Pedestrians who were given an "air-gaze" (i.e., having someone look in their direction, but looking just past them as if they didn't exist) by a passerby felt decreased social connection (Wesselmann, Cardoso, Slater, & Williams, 2012). Other research suggests that individuals do not have to be the direct recipients of ostracism to feel its reflexive effects; simply observing the ostracism of another individual can threaten the observer's need satisfaction and worsen mood (Wesselmann, Bagg, & Williams, 2009).

Reflexive reactions to ostracism have been resistant to moderation by several individual or situational factors (Williams, 2009; c.f., Boyes & French, 2009). Ostracism still threatens need satisfaction when participants are told the ostracism was unintentional, or planned by a computer program (Eisenberger et al. 2003; Zadro et al. 2004). Ostracism also hurts under conditions when it could be considered desirable to targets, such as when the sources of ostracism are members of a despised out-group (i.e., the Klu Klux Klan; Gonsalkorale & Williams, 2007), when inclusion would cost participants money (van Beest & Williams, 2006), or when inclusion increased participants' chances to lose a game akin to cyber "Russian Roulette" (van Beest, Williams, & van Dijk, 2011). Finally, Schefske, Wirth, and Williams (2008) found that sharing ostracism with another coplayer does not reduce ostracism's immediate mood effects or thwarted need satisfaction.

Recent studies have demonstrated moderation for some of the reflexive effects of ostracism. Zhou, Vohs, and Baumeister (2009) found that participants who counted money before being ostracized received a boost in self-esteem, and experienced less threat to their self-esteem when ostracized compared with participants who did not count money. Capezza, Reed, Arriaga and Williams (2009) found that romantic couples experienced less need threat and immediate distress when they believed they were being ostracized by their partner and a stranger compared with being ostracized by two strangers. Wirth, Lynam, and Williams (2010) found that participants who had higher levels of personality traits symptomatic of Cluster A personality disorders (e.g., severe interpersonal distrust, detachment, and/or discomfort with social interaction) experienced less adverse effects of ostracism compared with participants with lower levels of these traits. Finally, individual differences in age can moderate ostracism's immediate effects: elderly participants who were ostracized self-reported experiencing less aversive effects than younger ostracized participants (Hawkley, Williams, & Cacioppo, 2011).

Reflective Stage

Williams's (2009) reflective stage of ostracism focuses on an individual's recovery from ostracism's negative effects. This stage can begin within minutes after the initial effects of ostracism are experienced (Wirth & Williams, 2009). Research on the reflective stage has approached recovery from two main directions: the situational and personality factors that influence recovery and the behavioral responses that individuals use to facilitate recovery.

FACTORS THAT INFLUENCE RECOVERY

Recent research has investigated how the group membership of the ostracized individual (and of the sources of ostracism) can influence recovery of need satisfaction. Wirth and Williams (2009) found that ostracized participants who made attributions to their temporary group membership (i.e., minimal group assignment) recovered their need satisfaction more quickly than did ostracized participants who made attributions to their permanent group membership (i.e., gender). Goodwin, Williams, and Carter-Sowell (2010) extended research on permanent group members, examining how race influences reactions to ostracism in a sample that was nationally representative. These researchers found that participants who attributed their ostracism to racism had a more difficult time recovering need satisfaction compared with participants who did not make these attributions. The effect of racist attributions was not moderated by

the participants' race or the race of the sources of ostracism.

Zadro, Boland, and Richardson (2006) focused on how individual differences in social anxiety influenced recovery from ostracism. The researchers found that the ostracized participants had significant recovery for levels of need satisfaction after 45 minutes, but participants who had higher levels of social anxiety recovered more slowly than did participants who had less social anxiety, presumably due to rumination during the distraction period. Swim and Williams (2008) investigated the role of rumination on recovery from ostracism in an experimental study. Ostracized participants were either asked to focus on a cognitive task meant to distract participants from ruminating on their Cyberball game, or encouraged to write down their thoughts about why things occurred as they did during the game. Participants who were distracted were then asked to write about their current thoughts to confirm that they were thinking about the cognitive task. The researchers found a significant interaction between the ostracism and distraction manipulations: distracting participants increased their recovery from ostracism, but participants who were encouraged to ruminate did not fully recover.

Finally, recent research suggests that individual differences in depression and rumination can influence speed of recovery from ostracism. Poznanski (2010) indexed participants' scores on the Beck Depression Inventory and individual differences in rumination prior to assigning them randomly to an inclusion or ostracism manipulation. Participants reported their levels of need satisfaction immediately after the manipulation, and then again after a 7-minute period. She found a significant four-way interaction, with ostracism × depression × rumination as between-subjects factors and reflexive versus reflective need satisfaction as a within-subjects factor. Participants who were ostracized and also had high levels of depressive symptoms and ruminative tendencies had a more difficult time recovering need satisfaction over time; this relation was not found for ostracized participants who were low in both of these individual difference measures.

BEHAVIORAL RESPONSES

Williams (2009) argues that individuals' behavioral responses in the reflective stage serve to fortify need satisfaction threatened by ostracism (see also Leary, Twenge, & Quinlivan, 2006). Research has found two main types of behavioral responses to ostracism: pro- and antisocial responses. Several studies demonstrate that ostracized individuals may respond to their treatment with prosocial behavior as a way to become reincluded. Ostracized individuals have been more likely to work harder on a collective group task (Williams & Sommer, 1997), conform (Williams et al., 2000), focus on strategies for reinclusion (Molden, Lucas, Gardner, Dean, & Knowles, 2009), comply with social influence tactics (Carter-Sowell, Chen, & Williams, 2008), and show interest in new groups (Maner, DeWall, Baumeister, & Schaller, 2007; Predmore & Williams, 1983) than those individuals who are included. Ostracized individuals are also more likely to emulate a cooperative group member (Ouwerkerk et al., 2005), engage in nonconscious mimicry (Lakin & Chartrand, 2005; Lakin, Chartrand, & Arkin, 2008), and be more attentive to social information (Bernstein, Young, Brown, Sacco, & Claypool, 2008; Gardner, Pickett, & Brewer, 2000; Pickett, Gardner, & Knowles, 2004; Sacco, Wirth, Hugenberg, Chen, & Williams, 2011) than included individuals.

Individuals are also more likely to behave aggressively towards another person after being ostracized, and it does not matter whether that person was involved or uninvolved in the ostracism (Buckley, Winkel, & Leary, 2004; Carter-Sowell, Van Beest, van Dijk, & Williams, in preparation; Chow, Tiedens, & Govan, 2008; Twenge, Baumeister, Tice, & Stucke, 2001; Twenge & Campbell, 2003; Warburton, Williams, & Cairns, 2006; Williams, 2001). Ostracism's link with aggressive behavior is not limited to current ostracism episodes—simply recalling a previous experience of ostracism can increase a person's temptations for aggression (Riva, Wirth, & Williams, 2011).

At first blush, these patterns of behavior appear contradictory. Williams (2009) argues that the specific type of behavioral response to ostracism corresponds to the main type of need individuals are motivated to fortify. Prosocial responses are focused on fortifying *inclusionary* needs (i.e., belonging and self-esteem), and aggressive responses are focused on fortifying *power/provocation* needs (i.e., meaningful existence and control). Williams's argument has yet to be tested directly in an experimental setting, but several studies provide indirect evidence. Warburton, Williams, and Cairns (2006) demonstrated that control restoration attenuates ostracized participants' aggressive responses; ostracized participants who did not have their control restored replicated the typical ostracism→aggression relation (see Twenge et al, 2001). This relation between control needs and aggression can be bidirectional.

Subsequent research has found that participants who were treated negatively during a group discussion had some warning of their subsequent exclusion, and these participants were less likely to aggress than participants who were treated positively and did not expect the exclusion (Wesselmann, Butler, Williams, & Pickett, 2010).

Other research focuses Williams's (2009) argument for inclusionary needs. Twenge and colleagues (Twenge, Zhang, Catanese, Dolan-Pascoe, Lyche, & Baumeister, 2007) found that ostracized participants who either had a pleasant interaction with an experimenter or were reminded of positive social relationships were less likely to behave aggressively. Other research suggests that even small amounts of inclusion in a group context can help individuals recover from ostracism, reducing the need for subsequent aggression (DeWall, Twenge, Bushman, Im, & Williams, 2010). Bernstein and colleagues (Bernstein, Sacco, Brown, Young, & Claypool, 2010) demonstrated that participants' needs for belonging and self-esteem influenced prosocial responses to ostracism (i.e., desire to interact with potential sources of affiliation). Participants were asked to recall a time where they were excluded, included, or experiencing a mundane event (control condition). Participants were then shown a series of faces displaying both genuine (Duchenne) and deceptive (non-Duchenne) smiles, and asked to indicate their desire to interact with each stimulus person. As hypothesized, participants who recalled past exclusion showed more preference for faces displaying genuine smiles than deceptive smiles, compared to the other two conditions. These researchers also found that participants' feelings of threatened inclusionary needs mediated the relation between exclusion and the desire to interact with faces showing genuine smiles.

Wesselmann and Williams (2010) proposed that the basic needs thwarted by ostracism could be fortified by religious/spiritual beliefs or affiliation. Aydin, Fischer, and Frey (2010) presented compelling empirical evidence supporting the coping mechanism argument (see also Epley, Akalis, Waytz, & Cacioppo, 2008). These researchers found that members of groups that felt consistently excluded (e.g., Turkish immigrants in Germany) reported higher levels of religious affiliation than members of groups that did not perceive constant exclusion (e.g., Turkish natives). They replicated and extended these results with experimental manipulations of exclusion and found that excluded individual had stronger intentions to perform religious behaviors than included individuals. Finally, they found that excluded individuals who were then presented with a religious prime were less aggressive than excluded individuals who did not receive the prime. This last finding is most germane to Williams's (2009) need fortification hypothesis: individuals who were primed to think of how important religion was in their lives likely had their needs fortified and thus found aggression less necessary.

It is important to note that research on using religion/spirituality as a balm for ostracism is still in its infancy, and there are areas that we should remain agnostic about until more empirical work is conducted. Religion/spirituality may not always be the best solution to coping with exclusion or ostracism, particularly for individuals who do not adhere to a particular set of beliefs or affiliation (Aydin et al., 2010; Wesselmann & Williams, 2010). Not only may religion/spirituality be ineffective as a coping tool for these individuals, but it may intensify need threat for individuals who may feel disenfranchised or excluded from a previous affiliation, or even have a conception of God as exclusionary (e.g., van Beest & Williams, 2011). It is also important to note that any benefits religion/spirituality offer ostracized individuals may be exploited. We have argued elsewhere that ostracized individuals may be likely candidates for recruitment by extremists groups (e.g., cults or fundamentalist groups, terrorist organizations) because these groups offer an opportunity for need satisfaction that these individuals have been denied elsewhere (Wesselmann & Williams, 2010; Williams & Wesselmann, 2010). Not only do these groups offer a source for fortifying inclusionary needs, but many of these groups can also fortify power/provocation because they promise retribution, worldwide attention, and personal significance (Kruglanski, Chen, Dechesne, Fishman, & Orehek, 2009). Schaafsma and Williams (2012) recently demonstrated that individuals from three ethnic groups (Dutch, Moroccans, and Turks) responded to ostracism differently depending on the group membership of the ostracizers. Individuals who were ostracized by ethnic out-group members responded with increased hostility toward the ostracizers and their respective ethnic groups. Further, Christians and Muslims who were ostracized by members of their ethnic in-group increased endorsement of fundamentalist religious beliefs. These researchers argued that individuals who find themselves ostracized by members of their ethnic ingroup may be particularly at risk for recruitment to religious extremist groups. A potential implication of this research is that if these extremist groups also feel ostracized by outgroup members, intergroup conflict may also increase. Regardless of these caveats, the role of religion/spirituality in coping with ostracism remains a promising new direction for empirical research.

Resignation Stage

Finally, Williams (2009) argues that if ostracism persists for an extended period of time, individuals will enter the third stage—*resignation*. Individuals who find that their behavioral responses to ostracism fail either to restore their need satisfaction consistently or end the ostracism may learn that any attempt to recover from ostracism will be futile. Individuals in the resignation stage should then experience an acceptance of the lost needs: alienation (need to belong), depression (self-esteem), learned helplessness (control), and unworthiness (meaningful existence).

This third stage of Williams's temporal model (2009) has received little empirical study, but preliminary evidence suggests that consistent exposure to ostracism can lead to extreme consequences. Zadro (2004; see also Williams, 2001) conducted qualitative interviews with over 50 individuals who reported experiencing chronic ostracism from friends, coworkers, or family members. The themes that emerged from the interviews suggest that interviewees exhibited exacerbated need threat (i.e., feelings of alienation and isolation, learned helplessness, meaninglessness, and feelings of low self-worth and depression). These themes are similar to the experiences of individuals who report chronic loneliness (Cacioppo & Patrick, 2008). These various studies present a solid foundation to generate future research hypotheses in a systematic study of the cognitive and emotional implications of chronic ostracism.

Chronically ostracized individuals likely resign themselves to lack of opportunities for reinclusion. Williams and Wesselmann (2010) argue that these expectations for reinclusion should be a predictor of whether ostracized individuals respond in a pro- or antisocial manner (see also Twenge, 2005). Chronically ostracized individuals find themselves in a situation where any attempts to fortify their inclusionary needs (commonly via prosocial behavior) have been consistently thwarted and they do not expect to be reincluded. Thus, chronically ostracized individuals are left with behaviors focused on fortifying power/provocation (commonly via antisocial behavior) as their best chance for need satisfaction. In some cases, these individuals may resort to extreme violence to fortify power/provocation needs. Since 1994, in US schools alone, there have been over 220 separate shooting incidents in which at least 1 person was killed (Anderson et al., 2001). Research suggests long-term ostracism was a potential impetus for many of these school shooters (Leary, Kowalski, Smith, & Phillips, 2003; Twenge, 2000). The potential link between long-term ostracism and extreme violence is not limited to the United States. Studies of perpetrators in countries such as Tasmania and Germany suggest they experienced ostracism in myriad social situations (Bingham, 2000; Crook, 1997; Lemonick, 2002). These acts of extreme violence may also be directed at oneself. Williams (2001) notes that it is common for chronically ostracized individuals to contemplate or attempt suicide. Zadro (2004) interviewed one woman who said that after experiencing 159 days of ostracism from her classmates she elected to take 29 Valium pills as a way to escape from her experience. This woman had been consistently thwarted from any attempts to fortify her inclusionary needs, but she could at least exercise control by attempting suicide.

These conclusions about the link between chronic ostracism/exclusion and extreme violence are based on correlational data and case studies, but are consistent with experimental data on short-term exclusion. DeWall, Twenge, Gitter, and Baumeister (2009) found that exclusion manipulations increase participants' hostile cognitions, and these cognitions mediate the relation between exclusion and aggressive responses. DeWall and colleagues interpret these findings within the general aggression model (Anderson & Bushman, 2002), which argues that hostile cognitions promote aggression by causing individuals to perceive ambiguous acts as hostile, to perceive aggression as common, and ultimately to expect aggression from most other social interactions. By this logic, individuals who are chronically ostracized should be most likely to develop a set of hostile cognitive biases facilitating aggressive behavior.

The extant research is consistent with Williams's (2009) proposed resignation stage, but direct empirical tests of this stage are needed. We propose that future research should approach the resignation stage from multiple methods. One potential method is to measure individual differences in chronic ostracism and assess its correlation with its theorized negative outcomes (i.e., alienation, depression, helplessness, and meaninglessness). These studies could be conducted using various measures. Nezlek and colleagues (2012) utilized event-contingent daily diaries to assess how frequently ostracism occurs in participants' daily lives. This study did not assess any outcomes at the end of the study that were related to chronic ostracism, but future researchers could utilize this type of diary method to answer those questions.

Other researchers have been developing individual difference measures of chronic ostracism that could also be used as a predictor of theorized negative outcomes (Carter-Sowell, 2010; Saylor, et al., in press). These measures have thus far been utilized in both children and college student samples, but may be used to study members of various social groups that typically are ostracized from mainstream society, such as persons with mental illness (Farina, 2000; Feldman & Crandall, 2007), elderly or infirm individuals in institutionalized care (Goffman, 1961), and homeless individuals (Hulme, 2000). Future research should measure the degree to which members of these groups report experiencing chronic ostracism and its negative outcomes.

The methods thus far have been correlational in nature. Experimental research on chronic ostracism may prove to be difficult, because one ethically cannot ostracize participants for an extended period of time. We have suggestions on how research on chronic ostracism may address this limitation. Research on understanding the effects of chronic stress has begun using animal models to answer research questions that cannot be ethically or practically studied in humans. One animal model—the prairie vole—has been particularly useful for comparisons with humans because this is a social animal that forms socially monogamous pair-bonds, engages in biparental care of offspring, and has stress reactions similar to humans (Grippo, 2009). Research using this animal model has found that prairie voles who are isolated for 4 weeks are more likely than socially included voles to show increased aggression (Grippo, Wu, Hassan, & Carter, 2008), depression-like symptoms (Grippo, Cushing, & Carter, 2007), and learned helplessness (Grippo, et al., 2008); each of these are theorized outcomes for chronic ostracism in humans (Williams, 2009). Future research programs should combine studies using social animal models (e.g., prairie voles) with studies using human participants to elucidate the complicated experience and implications of chronic ostracism.

POTENTIAL INTERVENTIONS
Because the resignation stage of ostracism has received little empirical attention, potential

interventions for individuals who find themselves in this stage are far from forthcoming. However, there are two promising areas of research that may inform researchers who are interested in developing interventions for individuals who experience chronic ostracism. Recent research demonstrates that regular doses of acetaminophen can dampen the negative effects of ostracism in a laboratory setting (DeWall et al., 2010). It is possible that individuals who are in the resignation stage may be able to cope with the negative effects of chronic ostracism with regular doses of acetaminophen.

Another potential treatment may be regular doses of the social-affiliative hormone oxytocin. Gaertner (2009) has begun to examine the influence oxytocin has on group bonding and interactions. Preliminary evidence suggests that individuals who are assigned randomly to high interdependence groups have higher levels of oxytocin than individuals in groups with low interdependence. Further, oxytocin was related to perceptions of entititivity, attraction, and cooperation in these high interdependence groups. More germane to ostracism research, research demonstrates that doses of oxytocin can reduce the harmful effects of isolation in social animals such as prairie voles (Grippo, Trahanas, Zimmerman, Porges, & Carter, 2009). Both research on the effects of acetaminophen and oxytocin suggest that biochemical interventions may be developed to help individuals cope with the consequences of chronic ostracism (but see Campbell, 2010, for caveats about extending oxytocin research in animal models to understanding human behavior).

Research on social networking sites also provides potential for developing interventions for chronic ostracism. The advent of social networking sites, email, and other modes of electronic-based communication has afforded individuals the ability to form meaningful social relationships regardless of geographic or time constraints (Bargh & McKenna, 2004; McKenna & Bargh, 1999). These forms of electronic-based communication also afford individuals opportunities to overcome obstacles that normally inhibit them in face-to-face interactions, such as stigma, social anxiety, loneliness, or lack of social skills (McKenna & Bargh, 1998; 1999; McKenna, Green, & Gleason, 2002; Peter & Valkenburg, 2006; Peter, Valkenburg & Schouten, 2005; Reid & Reid, 2007; Sheeks & Birchmeier, 2007; Stritzke, Nguyen, & Durkin, 2004). It is possible that individuals who experience chronic ostracism in face-to-face interactions could seek out online relationships to fortify their threatened needs.

Conclusions

Ostracism—being ignored and excluded—is a situation that occurs in groups of humans and other social animals, and has been investigated by researchers from various disciplines (Gruter & Masters, 1986; Williams, 2009). The majority of research from social psychology has focused on individuals' experiences of ostracism, and ultimately how they respond to this aversive experience. Williams (2009) argues individuals' experiences of ostracism change over time. Individuals first have *reflexive* reactions to ostracism, characterized by immediate distress and threat to various basic needs (i.e., belonging, control, self-esteem, and meaningful existence). Ostracized individuals then progress to the *reflective* stage, where they strive to recover satisfaction of their basic needs. Individuals only enter the *resignation* stage if they experience chronic ostracism and are thwarted consistently in their attempts to fortify their need satisfaction. Social psychological research has focused on the first two stages predominately, but there is a dearth of systematic research on the resignation stage (Williams, 2009). Qualitative interviews and anecdotes have provided preliminary evidence that the need threat exhibited consistently in laboratory studies of ostracism can become exacerbated in chronic ostracism. We build upon this framework by proposing that individuals in the resignation stage may be more likely to engage in maladaptive behaviors, such as acts of extreme violence. Finally, we close this chapter by speculating on potential intervention techniques that clinicians and therapists could use to help individuals in this stage cope with chronic ostracism. The ultimate goal of this chapter was to generate future directions for research in unexplored areas, particularly the resignation stage of ostracism and potential methods for individuals to cope with this stage.

References

Anderson, C. A., & Bushman, B. J. (2002). Human aggression. *Annual Review of Psychology, 53,* 27–51.

Anderson, M. A., Kaufman, J., Simon, T. R., Barrios, L., Paulozzi, L., Ryan, G., Hammond, R., Modzeleski, W., Feucht, T., Potter, L., & the School-Associated Violent Deaths Study Group. (2001). School-associated violent deaths in the United States. *Journal of the American Medical Association, 286,* 2695–2700.

Aydin, N., Fischer, P., & Frey, D. (2010). Turing to God in the face of ostracism: Effects of social exclusion on religiousness. *Personality and Social Psychology Bulletin, 36*, 742–753.

Bargh, J. A., & McKenna, K. Y. A. (2004). The Internet and social life. *Annual Review of Psychology, 55*, 573–590.

Bastian, B., & Haslam, N. (2010). Excluded from humanity: The dehumanizing effects of social ostracism. *Journal of Experimental Social Psychology, 46*, 107–113.

Baumeister, R. F., DeWall, C. N., Ciarocco, N. J., & Twenge, J. M. (2005). Social exclusion impairs self-regulation. *Journal of Personality and Social Psychology, 88*, 589–604.

Baumeister, R. F., & Leary, M. R. (1995). The need to belong: Desire for inter-personal attachments as a fundamental human motivation. *Psychological Bulletin, 117*, 497–529.

Bernstein, M. J., Sacco, D. F., Brown, C. M., Young, S. G., & Claypool, H. M. (2010). A preference for genuine smiles following social exclusion. *Journal of Experimental Social Psychology, 46*, 196–199.

Bernstein, M. J., Young, S. G., Brown, C. M., Sacco, D. F., & Claypool, H. (2008). Adaptive responses to social exclusion: Social rejection improves detection of real and fake smiles. *Psychological Science, 19*, 981–983.

Bingham, M. (2000). *Suddenly One Sunday* (2nd Ed.). Pymble, NSW: Harper Collins.

Boyes, M. E., & French, D. J. (2009). Having a Cyberball: Using a ball-throwing game as an experimental social stressor to examine the relationship between neuroticism and coping. *Personality and Individual Differences, 47*, 396–401.

Buckley, K. E., Winkel, R. E., & Leary, M. R. (2004). Reactions to acceptance and rejection: Effects of level and sequence of relational evaluation. *Journal of Experimental Social Psychology, 40*, 14–28.

Cacioppo, J. T., & Patrick, B. (2008). *Loneliness: Human Nature and the Need for Social Connection.* New York: W. W. Norton & Company.

Campbell, A. (2010). Oxytocin and human social behavior. *Personality and Social Psychology Review, 14*, 281–295.

Capezza, N.M., Reed, J.T., Arriaga, X.B., & Williams, K.D. (2009, February). Does being ostracized by a romantic partner hurt as much as being ostracized by a stranger? Poster presented at the annual meeting of the Society for Personality and Social Psychology, Tampa, FL.

Carter-Sowell, A. R. (2010). Salting a wound, building a callous, or throwing in the towel? The measurement and effects of chronic ostracism experiences. Unpublished doctoral dissertation. Purdue University.

Carter-Sowell, A. R., Chen, Z., & Williams, K. D. (2008). Ostracism increases social susceptibility. *Social Influence, 3*, 143–153.

Carter-Sowell, A. R., Van Beest I., van Dijk, E., & Williams, K. D. Groups being ostracized by groups: Is the pain shared, is recovery quicker, and are groups more likely to be aggressive? Manuscript in preparation.

Chow, R. M., Tiedens, L. Z., & Govan, C. L. (2008). Excluded emotions: The role of anger in antisocial responses to ostracism. *Journal of Experimental Social Psychology, 44*, 896–903.

Crook, J. B. (1997). *Port Arthur: Gun Tragedy, Gun Law Miracle.* Melbourne: Gun Control Australia.

DeWall, C. N., MacDonald, G., Webster, G. D., Masten, C., Baumeister, R. F., Powell, C., Combs, D., Schurtz, D. R., Stillman, T. F., Tice, D. M., & Eisenberger, N. I. (2010). Acetaminophen reduces social pain: Behavioral and neural evidence. *Psychological Science, 21*, 931–937.

DeWall, C. N., Twenge, J. M., Bushman, B., Im, C., & Williams, K. D. (2010). A little acceptance goes a long way: Applying Social Impact Theory to the rejection-aggression link. *Social Psychological and Personality Science, 1*, 168–174.

DeWall, C. N., Twenge, J. M., Gitter, S. A., & Baumeister, R. F. (2009). It's the thought that counts: The role of hostile cognition in shaping aggressive responses to social exclusion. *Journal of Personality and Social Psychology, 96*, 45–59.

Dickerson, S. S., & Kemeny, M. E. (2004). Acute stressors and cortisol responses: A theoretical integration and syntehsis of laboratory research. *Psychological Bulletin, 130*, 355–391.

Dijker, A. J. M., & Koomen, W. (2007). *Stigmatization, Tolerance And Repair: An Integrative Psychological Analysis of Responses to Deviance.* New York: Cambridge University Press.

Eisenberger, N. I., Lieberman, M. D., & Williams, K. D. (2003). Does rejection hurt? An fMRI study of social exclusion. *Science, 302*, 290–292.

Epley, N., Akalis, S., Waytz, A., & Cacioppo, J. T. (2008). Creating social connection through inferential reproduction: Loneliness and perceived agency in gadgets, gods, and greyhounds. *Psychological Science, 19*, 114–120.

Farina, A. (2000). The few gains and many losses for those stigmatized by psychiatric disorders. In J. H. Harvey & E. D. Miller (Eds.), *Loss and Trauma: General and Close Relationship Perspectives* (pp. 183–207). Philadelphia: Brunner-Routledge.

Feldman, D. B., & Crandall, C. S. (2007). Dimensions of mental illness stigma: What about mental illness causes social rejection? *Journal of Social and Clinical Psychology, 26*, 137–154.

Gaertner, L. A. (2009, October). A bio-social model of positive in-group regard: Oxytocin as an evolved hormonal mediator of intragroup social-regulation. Presented at the Society for Experimental Social Psychology, Portland, ME.

Gardner, W., Pickett, C. L., & Brewer, M. B. (2000). Social exclusion and selective memory: How the need to belong influences memory for social events. *Personality and Social Psychology Bulletin, 26*, 486–496.

Goffman, E. (1961). *Asylums: Essays on the Social Situation of Mental Patients and Other Inmates.* Garden City, NY: Anchor Books.

Gonsalkorale, K., & Williams, K. D. (2007). The KKK won't let me play: Ostracism even by a despised outgroup hurts. *European Journal of Social Psychology, 37*, 1176–1186.

Goodwin, S. A., Williams, K. D., & Carter-Sowell, A. R. (2010). The psychological sting of stigma: The costs of attributing ostracism to racism. *Journal of Experimental Social Psychology, 46*, 612–618.

Grippo, A. J. (2009). Mechanisms underlying altered mood and cardiovascular dysfunction: The value of neurobiological and behavioral research with animal models. *Neuroscience and Biobehavioral Reviews, 33*, 171–180.

Grippo, A. J., Cushing, B. S., & Carter, C. S. (2007). Depression-like behavior and stressor-induced neuroendocrine activation in female prairie voles exposed to chronic social isolation. *Psychosomatic Medicine, 69*, 149–157.

Grippo, A. J., Trahanas, D. M., Zimmerman II, R. R., Porges, S. W., & Carter, C. S. (2009). Oxytocin protects against negative behavioral and autonomic consequences of long-term social isolation. *Psychoneuroendocrinology, 34*, 1542–1553.

Grippo, A. J., Wu, K. D., Hassan, I., & Carter, C. S. (2008). Social isolation in prairie voles induces behaviors relevant to negative affect: Toward the development of a rodent model focused on co-occurring depression and anxiety. *Depression and Anxiety, 25,* E17–E26.

Gruter, M., & Masters, R. D. (Eds.). (1986). Ostracism: A social and biological phenomenon. *Ethology and Sociobiology, 7,* 149–395.

Hawkley, L. C., Williams, K. D., & Cacioppo, J. T. (2011). Responses to ostracism across adulthood. *SCAN, 6,* 234–243.

Hulme, T. (2000). Societies ostracized: The homeless. Unpublished honors thesis. Macquarie University.

Josephs, R. A., Telch, M. J., Hixon, J. G., Evans, J. J., Lee, H., Knopik, V. S., McGeary, J. E., Hariri, A. R., & Beevers, C. G. (2012). Genetic and hormonal sensitivity to threat: Testing a serotonin transporter genotype × testosterone interaction. *Psychoneuroendocrinology, 37*(6), 752–761.

Juvonen, J., & Gross, E. F. (2004). The rejected and the bullied: Lessons about social misfits from developmental psychology. In K. D. Williams, J. P. Forgas, & W. von Hippel (Eds.), *The Social Outcast: Ostracism, Social Exclusion, Rejection, and Bullying* (pp. 155–170). New York: Psychology Press.

Kerr, N. L., & Levine, J. M. (2008). The detection of social exclusion: Evolution and beyond. *Group Dynamics: Theory, Research, and Practice, 12,* 39–52.

Kruglanski, A. W., Chen, X., Dechesne, M., Fishman, S., & Orehek, E. (2009). Fully committed: Suicide bombers' motivation and the quest for personal significance. *Political Psychology, 30,* 331–357.

Kurzban, R., & Leary, M. R. (2001). Evolutionary origins of stigmatization: The functions of social exclusion. *Psychological Bulletin, 127,* 187–208.

Lakin, J. L., & Chartrand, T. L. (2005). Exclusion and nonconscious behavioral mimicry. In K. D. Williams, J. P. Forgas, & W. von Hippel (Eds.), *The Social Outcast: Ostracism, Social Exclusion, Rejection, and Bullying* (pp. 279–295). New York: Psychology Press.

Lakin, J. L., Chartrand, T. L., & Arkin, R. M. (2008). I am too just like you: Nonconscious mimicry as an automatic behavioral response to social exclusion. *Psychological Science, 19,* 816–822.

Leary, M. R., Kowalski, R. M., Smith, L., & Phillips, S. (2003). Teasing, rejection, and violence: Case studies of the school shootings. *Aggressive Behavior, 29,* 202–214.

Leary, M. R., Tambor, E. S., Terdal, S. K., & Downs, D. L. (1995). Self-esteem as an interpersonal monitor: The sociometer hypothesis. *Journal of Personality and Social Psychology, 68,* 518–530.

Leary, M. R., Twegne, J. M., & Quinlivan, E. (2006). Interpersonal rejection as a determinant of anger and aggression. *Personality and Social Psychology Review, 10,* 111–132.

Lemonick, M. D. (2002, May 6). Germany's Columbine. *Time Magazine* (New York), *159* (18), 36–39.

Maner, J. K., DeWall, C. N., Baumeister, R. F., & Schaller, M. (2007). Does social exclusion motivate interpersonal reconnection? Resolving the "porcupine problem." *Journal of Personality and Social Psychology, 92,* 42–55.

McKenna, K. Y. A., & Bargh, J. A. (1998). Coming out in the age of the Internet: Identity "demarginalization" through virtual group participation. *Journal of Personality and Social Psychology, 75,* 681–694.

McKenna, K. Y. A., & Bargh, J. A. (1999). Causes and consequences of social interaction on the Internet: A conceptual framework. *Media Psychology, 1,* 249–269.

McKenna, K. Y. A., Green, A. S., & Gleason, M. E. J. (2002). Relationship formation on the Internet: What's the big attraction? *Journal of Social Issues, 58,* 9–31.

Molden, D. C., Lucas, G. M., Gardner, W. L., Dean, K., & Knowles, M. L. (2009). Motivations for prevention or promotion following social exclusion: Being rejected versus being ignored. *Journal of Personality and Social Psychology, 96,* 415–431.

Moor, B. G., Crone, E. A., & van der Molen, M. W. (2010). The heartbreak of social rejection: Heart rate deceleration in response to unexpected peer rejection. *Psychological Science, 21,* 1326–1333.

Nezlek, J. B., Wesselmann, E. D., Wheeler, L., & Williams, K. D. (2012). Ostracism in everyday life. *Group Dynamics: Theory, Research, and Practice, 16,* 91–104.

Oaten, M., Williams, K. D., Jones, A., & Zadro, L. (2008). The effects of ostracism on self-regulation in the socially anxious. *Journal of Social and Clinical Psychology, 27,* 471–504.

Ouwerkerk, J. W., Kerr, N. L., Gallucci, M., & Van Lange, P. A. M. (2005). Avoiding the social death penalty: Ostracism and cooperation in social dilemmas. In K. D. Williams, J. P. Forgas, & W. von Hippel (Eds.), *The Social Outcast: Ostracism, Social Exclusion, Rejection, and Bullying* (pp. 321–332). New York: Psychology Press.

Peter, J., & Valkenburg, P. M. (2006). Research note: Individual differences in perceptions of Internet communication. *European Journal of Communication, 21,* 213–226.

Peter, J., Valkenburg, P. M., & Schouten, A. P. (2005). Developing a model of adolescent friendship formation on the Internet. *CyberPsychology & Behavior, 8,* 423–430.

Pickett, C. L., Gardner, W. L., & Knowles, M. (2004). Getting a cue: The need to belong and enhanced sensitivity to social cues. *Personality and Social Psychology Bulletin, 30,* 1095–1107.

Poznanski, K. J. (2010). *I can't stop thinking about it: Increased rumination and depression reduces recovery from a brief episode of ostracism.* Unpublished honors thesis. Purdue University.

Predmore, S. J., & Williams, K. D. (1983, May). *The Effects of Social Ostracism on Affiliation.* Paper presented at the meeting of the Midwestern Psychological Association, Chicago.

Reid, D. J., & Reid, F. J. M. (2007). Text or talk? Social anxiety, loneliness, and divergent preferences for cell phone use. *CyberPsychology & Behavior, 10,* 424–435.

Rothbaum R., Weisz, J.R., & Snyder, S.S. (1982). Changing the world and changing the self: a two-process model of perceived control. *Journal of Personality & Social Psychology, 42,* 5–37.

Riva, P., Wirth, J. H., & Williams, K. D. (2011). The consequences of pain: the social and physical pain overlap on psychological responses. *European Journal of Social Psychology, 41,* 681–687.

Sacco, D., Wirth, J. H., Hugenberg, K., Chen, Z., & Williams, K. D. (2011). The world in black and white: Ostracism enhances the categorical perception of social information. *Journal of Experimental Psychology, 47,* 836–842.

Saylor, C. F., Nida, S. A., Williams, K. D., Taylor, L. A., Smyth, W., Twyman, K. A., Macias, M. M., & Spratt, E. G. Bullying and Ostracism Screening Scales (BOSS): Development and applications. *Children's Health Care.* In press.

Schaafsma, J., & Williams, K. D. (2012). Exclusion, intergroup hostility and religious fundamentalism. *Journal of Experimental Social Psychology, 48,* 829–837. doi:10.1016/j.jesp.2012.02.015.

Schefske, E., Wirth, J. H., & Williams, K. D. (2008, May). *Number of sources and targets in the ostracism experience.* Presented at the Midwestern Psychological Association, Chicago.

Sheeks, M. S., & Birchmeier, Z. P. (2007). Shyness, sociability, and the use of computer mediated communication in relationship development. *CyberPsychology & Behavior, 10,* 64–70.

Smith, A., & Williams, K. D. (2004). R U There? Effects of ostracism by cell phone messages. *Group Dynamics: Theory, Research, and Practice, 8,* 291–301.

Solomon, S., Greenberg, J., & Pyszczynski, T. (1991). A terror management theory of self-esteem and its role in social behavior. In M. Zanna (Ed.), *Advances in Experimental Social Psychology* (pp. 93–159). New York: Academic Press.

Stritzke, W. G. K., Nguyen, A., & Durkin, K. (2004). Shyness and computer-mediated communication: A self-presentational theory perspective. *Media Psychology, 6,* 1–22.

Swim, E., & Williams, K. D. (2008, May). Does distraction following ostracism decrease aggression? The effects of rumination. Presented at the Midwestern Psychological Association, Chicago.

Twenge, J. M. (2000). The age of anxiety? The birth cohort change in anxiety and neuroticism. *Journal of Personality and Social Psychology, 79,* 1007–1021.

Twenge, J. M. (2005). When does social rejection lead to aggression? The influences of situations, narcissism, emotion, and replenishing connections. In K. D. Williams, J. P., Forgas, & W. von Hippel (Eds.), *The Social Outcast: Ostracism, Social Exclusion, Rejection, and Bullying* (pp. 201–212). New York: Psychology Press.

Twenge, J. M., Baumeister, R. F., Tice, D. M., & Stucke, T. S. (2001). If you can't join them, beat them: Effects of social exclusion on aggressive behavior. *Journal of Personality and Social Psychology, 81,* 1058–1069.

Twenge, J. M., & Campbell, W. K. (2003). "Isn't it fun to get the respect that we're going to deserve?" Narcissism, social rejection, and aggression. *Personality and Social Psychology Bulletin, 29,* 261–272.

Twenge, J. M., Zhang, L., Catanese, K. R., Dolan-Pascoe, B., Lyche, L. R., & Baumeister, R. F. (2007). Replenishing connectedness: Reminders of social activity reduce aggression after social exclusion. *British Journal of Social Psychology, 46,* 205–224.

van Beest, I., & Williams, K. D. (2006). When inclusion costs and ostracism pays, ostracism still hurts. *Journal of Personality and Social Psychology, 91,* 918–928.

van Beest, I., & Williams, K. D. (2011). "Why hast thou forsaken me?": The effects of thinking about being ostracized by God on well-being and prosocial behavior. *Social Psychology and Personality Science, 2,* 379–386.

van Beest, I., Williams, K. D., & van Dijk, E. (2011). Cyberbomb: Effects of being ostracized from a death game. *Group Processes and Intergroup Relations, 14,* 581–596.

Warburton, W. A., Williams, K. D., & Cairns, D. R. (2006). When ostracism leads to aggression: The moderating effects of control deprivation. *Journal of Experimental Social Psychology, 42,* 213–220.

Wesselmann, E. D., Bagg, D., & Williams, K. D. (2009). "I feel your pain": The effects of observing ostracism on the ostracism detection system. *Journal of Experimental Social Psychology, 45,* 1308–1311.

Wesselmann, E. D., Butler, F. A., Williams, K. D., & Pickett, C. L. (2010). Adding injury to insult: Unexpected rejection leads to more aggressive responses. *Aggressive Behavior, 36,* 232–237.

Wesselmann, E. D., Cardoso, F. D., Slater, S., & Williams, K. D. (2012). "To be looked at as though air": Civil attention matters. *Psychological Science, 23,* 166–168

Wesselmann, E. D., & Williams, K. D. (2010). The potential balm of religion and spirituality for recovering from ostracism. *Journal of Management, Spirituality, and Religion, 7,* 29–45.

Wesselmann, E. D., Wirth, J. H., Pryor, J. B., Reeder, G. D., & Williams, K. D. (2012). When do we ostracize? *Social Psychological and Personality Science.* doi: 10.1177/1948550612443386.

Williams, K. D. (2001). *Ostracism: The Power of Silence.* New York: Guilford Press.

Williams, K. D. (2009). Ostracism: Effects of being excluded and ignored. In M. P. Zanna (Ed.), *Advances in Experimental Social Psychology* (Vol. 41, pp. 275–314). New York: Academic Press.

Williams, K. D., Cheung, C. K. T., & Choi, W. (2000). Cyberostracism: Effects of being ignored over the Internet. *Journal of Personality and Social Psychology, 79,* 748–762.

Williams, K. D., Govan, C. L., Croker, V., Tynan, D., Cruickshank, M., & Lam, A. (2002). Investigations into differences between social and cyberostracism. *Group Dynamics: Theory, Research, and Practice, 6,* 65–77.

Williams, K. D., & Nida, S. A. (2011). Ostracism: Consequences and coping. *Current Directions in Psychological Science, 20,* 71–75.

Williams, K. D., Shore, W. J., & Grahe, J. E. (1998). The silent treatment: Perceptions of its behaviors and associated feelings. *Group Processes & Intergroup Relations, 1,* 117–141.

Williams, K. D., & Sommer, K. L. (1997). Social ostracism by coworkers: Does rejection lead to social loafing or compensation. *Personality and Social Psychology Bulletin, 23,* 693–706.

Williams, K. D., & Wesselmann, E. D. (2010). The link between ostracism and aggression. In J. P. Forgas, A. W. Kruglanski, & K. D. Williams, (Eds.), *The Psychology of Social Conflict and Aggression* (pp. 37–51). New York: Psychology Press.

Williams, K. D., & Zadro, L. (January, 2004). *Ostracism: Empirical Studies Inspired by Real-World Experiences of Silence and Exclusion.* Paper presented at the meeting of the Society for Personality and Social Psychology.

Wirth, J. H., Lynam, D. R., & Williams, K. D. (2010). When social pain is not automatic: Personality disorder traits buffer ostracism's immediate negative impact. *Journal of Research in Personality, 44,* 397–401.

Wirth, J. H., Sacco, D. F., Hugenberg, K., & Williams, K. D. (2010). Eye gaze as relational evaluation: Averted eye gaze leads to feelings of ostracism and relational devaluation. *Personality and Social Psychology Bulletin, 36,* 869–882.

Wirth, J.H. and Williams, K.D. (2009). "They don't like our kind": consequences of being ostracized while possessing a group membership. *Group Processes and Intergroup Relations, 12,* 111–127.

Zadro, L. (2004). *Ostracism: Empirical studies inspired by real-world experiences of silence and exclusion.* Unpublished doctoral dissertation. University of New South Wales, Sydney, NSW.

Zadro, L., Boland, C., & Richardson, R. (2006). How long does it last? The persistence of the effects of ostracism in the socially anxious. *Journal of Experimental Social Psychology, 42*, 692–697.

Zadro, L., Williams, K. D., & Richardson, R. (2004). How low can you go? Ostracism by a computer is sufficient to lower self-reported levels of belonging, control, self-esteem, and meaningful existence. *Journal of Experimental Social Psychology, 40*, 560–567.

Zhou, X., Vohs, K. D., & Baumeister, R. F. (2009). The symbolic power of money: reminders of money alter social distress and physical pain. *Psychological Science, 20,* 700–706.

Zippelius, R. (1986). Exclusion and shunning as legal and social sanctions. *Ethology and Sociobiology, 7*, 159–166.

Driven to Exclude: How Core Social Motives Explain Social Exclusion

Michael S. North *and* Susan T. Fiske

Abstract

This chapter explores how social exclusion operates via core social motives: Belonging, Understanding, Controlling, Enhancing Self, and Trusting Others (BUC[K]ET; Fiske, 2010a). Within this framework, we explore how people's desire to fulfill each motive with the in-group fosters exclusion of people outside the group. Moreover, we delineate the consequences for people who face social exclusion: Because exclusion severely hinders their ability to achieve the core social motives, excluded people may develop *shattered assumptions* (Janoff-Bulman, 1992) about their social world. This not only undermines excluded people's physical and mental well-being, but also their ability to survive and thrive in the social world.

Key Words: belonging, controlling, core social motives, exclusion, self-enhancing, trusting, understanding

Introduction

Virtually everyone can picture the typical high-school cafeteria. Aside from the cuisine—which often pushes the envelope on novel food textures—the cafeteria's more striking image concretely represents the students' social divisions. Sure, the popular jocks, cheerleaders, cool guys, and popular girls each have their own table, but so do the artists, band geeks, and drama nerds. Oftentimes the minority students cluster with one another, much in the way that all of the black-clad, metal-wearing goth kids do. And, for better or for worse, there are always the loners, who sit solo, excluded from everyone. Every day the pattern repeats; although rarely stated, these divisions are rigid, with a virtually unanimous understanding of which students belong where and which do not belong anywhere.

Social sorting outlasts the high school bubble. Long after graduation, people find themselves continually attempting to join other types of groups. Sometimes they are successful, and sometimes they are not, but their attempts teach them a familiar lesson: Whereas exclusion may not always be intentional, it is inevitable, because in each group certain people belong whereas others do not. At college, some students gain admittance to selective fraternities, sororities, clubs, and secret societies, whereas the rest do not. Postbaccalaureates breaking into the workforce quickly learn that employers hire only some potential job candidates, while rejecting many others who do not fit a certain standard. Even the gainfully employed soon come to realize that they are figuratively barred from certain upscale neighborhoods, sorted by affordability. Thus, in many ways, the further beyond the high school dining area one looks, the higher the stakes of group membership become.

The lifelong ubiquity of differentiating the Included from the Excluded shows that exclusion is, for better or for worse, a fundamental social process. One might argue that the process is necessary, too, given that by definition not everyone can join any subset of the population. Regardless, people who make it into a given group usually feel good about belonging, not only because people feel more comfortable with others who share their attitudes, career interests, class background, and so on, but also because they avoid the sting of rejection. Unfortunately, others must face the reality that not everyone can belong; at least some must remain on the outside looking in.

This chapter utilizes a core social motives perspective (Fiske, 2010a) to explain the tenacity with which people seek and maintain group membership. This lens makes clear that people who adequately bond with the group greatly increase their chances of social survival, because effective, adaptive in-groups fulfill fundamental social needs. As we will also discuss, these motives create consequences for others: people who are not allowed into the group. In having their core social motives frustrated, targets of exclusion face different types of *shattered assumptions*—a phrase coined by Janoff-Bulman (1992) to explain trauma's impact on people's fundamental beliefs about survival in the world. In the case of exclusion, failing to be included in the group undermines many core beliefs and needs concerning the *social* world—the impact of which also has grave consequences for adaptive survival.

Five Core Social Motives (Plus or Minus Five)

Philosophers from Aristotle to John Locke have referred to humans as social animals. Similarly, one of us has asserted that human beings are social beings, social to the core (Fiske, 2010a). The basic idea is that people have evolved to fit in with adaptive, functional groups, in a process sometimes referred to as *social selection* (making oneself a desirable group member or interaction partner; Caporael, 1997; Nesse, 2010). Though a select few choose to make do on their own, this situation generally presents numerously more physical and mental health risks. Thus, across the board, people are highly motivated to fit in with adaptive groups.

Most social and personality psychologists agree about the broad motive to get along with others, but not always on its implications for other kinds of social motives. That is, while most theorists agree that motives are general motors for behavior, and that they systematically drive behavior in social situations, a cohesive integration has been elusive (Fiske, 2010a). Coming up with a framework to understand fundamental motives has been

treacherous—or at least unresolved—territory in social psychology.

One synthesis proposes a set of *core social motives,* or fundamental, underlying psychological processes that drive people's thinking, feeling, and behaving in social situations. These motives comprise five: Belonging, Understanding, Controlling, Enhancing Self, and Trusting Others (BUC[K]ET; Fiske, 2010a). Because humans have evolved over time to survive in groups, these driving forces are adaptive, and interact with particular social situations. Although we do not claim that these are the only fundamental motives that guide social behavior, they are clearly important ones, providing benefits for those who are able to fulfill them, and consequences for those who cannot.

Belonging

The *belonging* motive, which underlies the other four core social motives, represents people's inherent desire to form strong social relationships with others—essentially, to be part of a group and get along with the group. In many ways, this motive downplays individualistic motivations in favor of group harmony and well-being. Thus, belonging underlies the other four core social motives, and represents a pillar of social psychology—the study of how people's thoughts, behaviors and beliefs are driven largely by their social situations. The social situation comprises other people, and often groups. The fundamental place of the belonging motive in social and personality psychology manifests itself across various theories throughout the 20th century (e.g., chronologically, Freud, 1915; Rank, 1929; Horney, 1945; Maslow, 1962; Staub, 1989; Baumeister & Leary, 1995).

The social-adaptational desire to belong appears in people's readiness to form attachments (Baumeister & Leary, 1995). Some of the classic experiments in social psychology demonstrate how rapidly attachment formation occurs. The experiment conducted at the Robbers Cave Summer Camp (Sherif, Harvey, White, Hood, & Sherif, 1961) randomly assigned unacquainted boys into one of two groups. Despite the clearly arbitrary nature of these divisions, on each side the boys nevertheless formed quick, strong loyalties toward the in-group and intense hostility toward the other group. A second classic experiment randomly assigned World War II veterans' families to different housing locations (Festinger, Schachter, & Back, 1950). Despite the relatively haphazard creation of their social situation, people nonetheless formed more friendships with those who lived closest. Many subsequent studies have demonstrated that group loyalties not only form quickly but also resist termination. For instance, people usually choose to maintain their ties even when better outcomes are available by leaving the group (Van Vugt & Hart, 2004).

The desire to belong also produces conformity to in-group roles and norms. Classic social psychological theories are largely founded on people's willingness to go along with group, from Cooley's early (1902) notion of the human "looking glass self" (in which others' perceptions notify people of their social place), Mead's (1934) theory of the "mind, self, and society" (in which other people construct the realities that shape individuals' minds), to Goffman's (1959) "presentation of self" (in which actors adjust to different social settings, "performing" for other actors). Newcomb's classic (1943) Bennington experiment, demonstrating political attitude change from enrollment to graduation, shows how people's desire to establish and maintain relationships spurs them to comply with group norms. This is a recurring theme in more recent studies (e.g., Cialdini & Goldstein, 2004). Ensuring that people know "how we do things around here" serves to define the individual's rightful place within the group (Fiske, 2010a).

How In-Group Belonging Yields Out-Group Exclusion

Intense, unyielding group loyalties and shared group norms inevitably preclude people who do not share these rules. Thus, conformity to in-group standards shapes beliefs about who is worth including and excluding. As demonstrated by the Robbers Cave study, people's fierce loyalties to the group can produce hostilities toward those perceived to threaten it.

Research on stereotyping and prejudice has also demonstrated the excluding power of in-group belonging. For example, in-group favoritism typically leads people to reward and value the in-group, as exemplified by Social Identity Theory and Self-Categorization Theory (SIT/SCT; Tajfel & Turner, 1979). Indeed, societal in-groups, a country's "we," are typically deemed high in warmth and competence, whereas most other groups are regarded as inferior, lacking in either warmth, competence, or both (Fiske, Cuddy, Glick, & Xu, 2002). These attitudes can transform mere in-group fans into outright endorsers of out-group harm, as evidenced by the prevalence of *Schadenfreude,* or malicious pleasure at out-group

misfortune (e.g., Cikara, Botvinick, & Fiske, 2011; Combs, Powell, Schurtz, & Smith, 2009).

The motive to belong makes people within the group perceive it as a coherent whole, because it facilitates identification and attachment. People generally favor *in-group entitativity*, or clear definitions and boundaries for the group (Yzerbyt, Castano, Leyens, & Paladino, 2000). When the in-group is threatened, the belonging motivation intensifies. People fiercely stick behind their group, barring others who "are not like us," as was the case with post-9/11 American responses to Muslims and people perceived to be (e.g., Sikhs and south Asians; Chandrasekhar, 2003). Perceiving high entitativity within an in-group helps maximize its psychological utility because it fulfills a series of individual needs for group members (such as self-verification and power; Correll & Park, 2005) and also because it reduces uncertainty (Hogg, 2000).

The Excluded: Shattered Assumptions of Belonging

Whereas people inside the selective group reap various benefits, people outside find their need to belong deeply threatened. Numerous studies have shown a lack of belonging relates to negative outcomes. People with poor social networks are more likely to commit suicide (Berkman, Glass, Brissette, & Seeman, 2000; Durkheim, 1951) and in general ostracized people are more at risk for physical health problems and mortality (House, Landis, & Umberson, 1988) and mental ailments, such as anxiety and depression (Baumeister & Tice, 1990). The costs of not belonging also manifest at the macro level. For example, more firearm-based violent crimes occur in states where fewer people join voluntary groups (Kennedy, Kawachi, Prothrow-Stith, Lochner, & Gupta, 1998), consistent with the idea that a societal tendency to belong correlates with less aggression.

Various experimental manipulations of social exclusion demonstrate how people's need to belong is directly threatened. Participants who receive the silent treatment report broken feelings of belonging (Williams, Shore, & Grahe, 1998), as do participants who are deliberately left out of a game of catch between two confederates (Williams & Sommer, 1997). Demonstrating the robustness of this latter effect, the same finding replicates in a completely internet-based, electronic version of a ball-tossing game (Williams, Cheung, & Choi, 2000). In all these instances, belonging has important salutary effects, and exclusion has damaging effects.

Understanding

Related to Belonging is the motive to *understand* what others in the group believe, or to reach shared agreement with others. Achieving collective understanding with others allows people to predict what will happen in the face of uncertainty, as well as to make sense of what does happen. At the individual level, people share their theories about the social world with others in an effort to foster similar *social representations* (Moscovici, 1988) or create *group meaning* (Zajonc & Adelmann, 1987). Naturally, becoming part of the group entails perceiving the world in the same way that other group members do, but doing so also allows people to develop greater confidence in their conceptualization of the social world than they are generally able to do as individuals alone (Hardin & Higgins, 1996; Hogg, 2000).

Like belonging, the drive to understand the social world underlies multiple classic experiments in social psychology. Solomon Asch's famous (1956) study demonstrated that people who ordinarily have no trouble making the correct judgment of a line length when alone tend to go along with unanimous, incorrect judgments expressed by a group of several confederates. Sherif's autokinetic study showed how group judgment norms formed in a task estimating the (illusory) movement of a still point of light in a dark room (Sherif, 1935). In both cases, the motivation to conform to the beliefs of the group shaped people's development of norms for appropriate judgments. Outside of perceptual judgment, Schachter (1959) demonstrated that, when frightened, people cope by affiliating with one another in an effort to reach shared understanding. Indeed, recent research shows that people affiliate with informed others over similar others, to facilitate socially shared understanding (Kulik & Mahler, 2000).

More recent trends in social psychology have expanded on people's core need to understand. Understanding buffers against threat, when in-group members carefully guard their own group's boundaries; this is reflected in the *in-group overexclusion effect* (Leyens & Yzerbyt, 1992) and endorsement of *in-group homogeneity* (Castano, Yzerbyt, Paladino, & Sacchi, 2002). More broadly, the field of social cognition—the study of how people think about other people—has shown that people are determined to understand their social worlds in order to navigate them. In other words, "thinking is for doing" (Fiske's 1992 paraphrase of William James, 1890/1983).

Another important line of research in social psychology lies within the realm of cultural psychology,

which has compared different norms for understanding the world. Generally, collectivist cultures tend to emphasize harmonious, unanimous agreement, whereas individualistic ones tend to tolerate individual interpretations that may go against social consensus (Heine, 2010). Underscoring the fundamental nature of the understanding motive, social cognition and cultural psychology both continue to shape voluminous psychological research.

How Understanding Fosters Social Exclusion

Whereas people are motivated to understand their social worlds, they seek a level of comprehension satisfactory for staying within the group. Therefore, perhaps more than any of the other core social motives, the drive to understand along with other people in the group fosters shared stereotypes about people outside of it. Whereas these stereotypes naturally foster shared social understanding, they also foster exclusion, as evidenced by various forms of prejudice. For instance, tightly-knit, male-dominated "good old boy" networks engage in *dominance bonding* with one another, which excludes women and people of lower classes (Farr, 1988). Moreover, spurring age-based prejudice, younger people more often mimic and favor in-group members who express stereotypic beliefs about older people than those who do not (Castelli, Pavan, Ferrari, & Kashima, 2009).

At the societal level, the drive to create coherent social representations impels societies to create shared understandings about historical events, as well as new ideas and technologies (Moscovici, 1988). Unfortunately, not everyone partakes in the decision-making process. For instance, social progress and industrialization historically have had the deleterious effect of reducing the usefulness of the elderly and consequently excluding them from mainstream society (Nelson, 2005). The young may also be excluded on account of lacking experience and understanding; that is, of not knowing the ways of the world. As a result, age-based stereotyping and prejudice disproportionately target both the younger and older people, sparing the middle-aged (Garstka, Schmitt, Branscombe, & Hummert, 2004; North & Fiske, 2012).

A lack of mainstream understanding is implicated across other types of social exclusion. Education is often cited as a mechanism that perpetuates social marginalization in "knowledge-rich societies" that base cultural opportunities on the assumption of being educated (Baatjes, 2003). Indeed, in the

United States, a major barrier to poor people's ability to increase their social standing is not only a lack of formal education, but is also lack of general knowledge of the ins and outs of society, or *cultural capital* (Bourdieu, 1986). For many ethnic minorities and immigrants, too, lack of shared social understanding predicts disadvantage, such as in income inequality (Ooka & Wellman, 2003).

The Excluded: Shattered Assumptions of Understanding

The phrase "knowledge is power" may be centuries old (Bacon, 1597), but the idea that understanding is integral to one's social status still applies in most industries, perhaps especially politics and Hollywood. As such, the excluded endure a lack of understanding, which undermines their power. People desire informational control in the social world, and its lack reduces physical and mental health (Thompson, 1981). People who lack sufficient understanding are also more susceptible to persuasion, in that they are more likely to evaluate an argument based on peripheral factors that may have little regard for the central message (Petty & Cacioppo, 1981).

Small group dynamics shed light on the effects of failing to achieve a shared social understanding. In the early stages of group membership, people seek information, when they try to ascertain the roles and norms of the group. Any behavioral irregularities from these shared group understandings cast actors in a deviant light (Levine & Moreland, 1998), which puts them at heightened risk for devaluation, which is a core component of social exclusion (Eidelman, Silvia, & Biernat, 2006; Leary & Downs, 1995).

People who are denied understanding from the group are more at risk for antisocial behaviors. Aggression is a typical response among extreme outcasts, whose idiosyncratic understanding of being victims then justifies their actions as retaliation against the oppressors (Fiske, 2010a). Insufficient understanding between ethnic groups also fosters pluralistic ignorance about each other's intentions, which undermines interracial interactions (Shelton & Richeson, 2005). Overall, a socially shared sense of understanding has many benefits.

Controlling

The third core social motive encompasses people's need to have *control* over their social environment. People want to feel competent and effective, generally seeking a contingency between their actions and their social outcomes. Control is a motive that starts early, from young infants' crying or snuggling to get what they want, and continues through adolescent bullying or bonding. These early motives often predict control-based behaviors in adulthood, such as individual differences in the need for power (McClelland & Pilon, 1983). The need for control is so strong that extreme deprivation of perceived control is linked to frightening consequences, such as the first step on the path to becoming a terrorist (Moghaddam, 2005).

The idea that people want their actions to have a direct impact on their social outcomes is a long-standing theme in social and personality psychology. At least half of Erik Erikson's stages of psychosocial development emphasize the goal of attaining control or competence: *autonomy* versus shame and doubt, *initiative* versus guilt, *industry* versus inferiority, and *generativity* versus stagnation (Erikson, 1959). White's (1959) effectance motivation theory also posits that people and animals are driven by "a feeling of efficacy" to interact competently with their environment. Moreover, the drive for effectance is a key component explaining why people anthropomorphize nonhuman objects (Epley, Waytz, & Cacioppo, 2007; Waytz, this volume).

Later studies have shown that feeling in control produces a variety of individual benefits. Indeed, people are happier and healthier in general when they feel they are in control than when they are not (Taylor & Brown, 1988; Thompson, Armstrong, & Thomas, 1998). Further corroborating the control motive, people fixate significantly more on people who have control over them, that is, those on whom their social outcomes depend (Erber & Fiske, 1984), and engage in more sophisticated mind-perception for those people (Ames & Fiske, under review). Even in situations governed by chance, such as choosing a lottery ticket, people often create *illusions of control* to feel more efficacious (Langer, 1975).

How Controlling Fosters Out-Group Social Exclusion

The motive to control fosters exclusion in two primary ways. The first, more active of the two spurs people to control out-groups who may threaten in-group autonomy (Fiske & Ruscher, 1993). For example, social dominance theory (Sidanius & Pratto, 1999) asserts that members of dominant groups seek to maintain power hierarchies. In this sense, the motivation to have social control hoards resources from lower-status social groups.

Maintaining traditional values is a more symbolic form of social control that excludes minority and new groups (Altemeyer, 1988). Various theories of stereotyping and prejudice also theorize about power as a controlling component toward a specific out-group (Fiske, 1993), which may be involved in racism (Operario & Fiske, 1998), sexism (Rudman & Glick, 2001), and ageism (North & Fiske, 2012). People's desire to limit the autonomy of out-groups stems from common stereotypes about them as both concretely and symbolically dangerous (Stangor & Crandall, 2000). As a result, people tend to scapegoat out-group members when events go wrong (Glick, 2005).

More passively, the second form of control-relevant exclusion occurs when people ignore people on whom their outcomes do not depend. People are seldom motivated to individuate outcome-irrelevant people (Fiske, 2003), that is, people whom they do not need for anything. Recent neural and behavioral evidence indicates that people harbor an extreme form of this exclusion toward the homeless poor. Specifically, they come to *dehumanize* them, excluding them from full humanity (Harris & Fiske, 2006, 2009).

The Excluded: Shattered Assumptions of Control

According to Janoff-Bulman (1992), trauma shatters the core assumption is that the world is a meaningful place, which includes the idea that one's outcomes are contingent on one's actions. Likewise, in the social realm, exclusion demolishes feelings of social control. Having one's goal-directed behaviors persistently blocked increases frustration, which can cause people to behave aggressively (Dollard, Doob, Miller, Mowrer, & Sears, 1939). Theorists have extended this pattern to social behavior, demonstrating that socially excluded people may aggress toward their excluders (Twenge, Baumeister, Tice, & Stuck, 2001)—though others have argued that exclusion at least at first spurs appeasing behaviors from its targets (Williams, 1997). Either way, most agree that when social exclusion combines with a perceived loss of control, the excluded tend to respond antisocially, which further undermines their place within the group (Williams, 2007).

Over time, perpetual exclusion that causes a perceived lack of social control may result in long-term feelings of helplessness. Seligman and Maier (1967) famously demonstrated the phenomenon of *learned helplessness* using restrained, electrically-shocked dogs, but people may also develop this pattern of thinking if they have grown accustomed to having no control over their social outcomes. Therefore, socially excluded people are at particular risk for anxiety, depression, and loneliness, all arising in part from a perceived lack of competence and control (Baumeister & Tice, 1990; Leary, 1990). A sense of control serves many useful functions beyond the actually ability to predict and control events.

Enhancing Self

In their dealings with others, people continually strive to feel good about themselves, maintain a degree of self-worth, and raise their self-esteem. These strivings relate to the fourth social motive of *self-enhancement*. People who feel moderately good about themselves tend to be healthier (Taylor & Brown, 1988). The motivation to maintain and raise self-esteem in the social world underlies the work of various psychological theorists since the early 20th century, including Alfred Adler (1930), Gordon Allport (1955), and Carl Rogers (1959). More emphatically, some theorists have suggested that humans as a species have evolved to monitor their self-esteem as a sociometer, an indicator of their group standing (Leary & Baumeister, 2000).

The benefits of self-esteem generally fall into two categories: pleasant personal feelings and increased assertiveness. Evidence for other suggested benefits is less clear because the direction of causality is often uncertain (Baumeister, Campbell, Krueger, & Vohs, 2003). However, other work indicates that self-esteem does provide certain short-term, personal, emotional benefits. For instance, people high in self-esteem optimistically view their present selves as better off than their past selves, even in the face of contradictory evidence (Wilson & Ross, 2001). Moreover, high self-esteem people tend to hold positive outlooks about their futures (Taylor & Brown, 1988). Conversely, low self-esteem correlates with various antisocial behaviors, such as substance abuse, aggression, eating disorders, and sexual promiscuity (Leary, 2005).

Like other social motives, the pursuit of self-esteem varies across cultures. Individualistic cultures such as the United States tend to emphasize self-esteem to the point of obsession, as evidenced by the wealth of self-help books, childrearing manuals, and school programs on the subject (Crocker & Park, 2004). Because collectivist cultures emphasize interdependence and group harmony, an emphasis on blatant self-enhancement is not apparent. However, in an interdependent spirit, people may enhance their selves indirectly by viewing themselves more sympathetically, compared with others (Kitayama & Markus, 1999).

How Enhancing Self Fosters Social Exclusion (for Self and for Others)

Contrary to common sense, the pursuit of self-esteem is often costly, even for individuals within the group. When people experience threats in those domains on which their self-esteem is contingent, this tends to undermine interpersonal relationships with other members of the group, as measured by supportiveness and likeability (Park & Crocker, 2005). Failures in contingent domains of self-worth lead to a host of negative emotions (e.g., sadness, anger, and shame) and an increased focus on the self, thereby detracting attention from group goals (Crocker & Park, 2004).

When people's self-esteem is particularly tied to their group membership, exclusion of out-group members often ensues. The motive to self-enhance drives in-group favoritism, rather than outright disapproval or putting down of the out-group. For instance, as per SIT, people favor the in-group, but they are reluctant to punish out-groups (e.g., Brewer, 1999). This pattern also occurs at the implicit level when people hold positive, self-enhancing attitudes toward the in-group, but they do not have directly negative attitudes toward the out-group (Gaertner & McLaughlin, 1983).

As in threats to belonging, threats to self-enhancement increase the exclusion of out-group members. In such cases, people's allegiance to the in-group often intensifies, causing them to become especially prejudiced toward those outside of it. This is particularly so for people with high self-esteem (Crocker, Major, & Steele, 1998). Moreover, terror management theory (e.g., Solomon, Greenberg, & Pyszczynski, 2000) posits that when people are reminded of their eventual mortality, their self-image is threatened, causing them to identify more strongly with others who share their cultural worldview (and push away those who do not). Thus, moderate self-enhancement may help maintain the group and one's position within it, but it does so at the cost of excluding people not allowed into the group, especially for extreme forms of self-enhancement.

The Excluded: Shattered Assumptions of Enhancing Self

Another of Janoff-Bulman (1992)'s fundamental assumptions is that the self is worthy. When people are faced with trauma, they doubt their self-worth.

From a social psychological perspective, people use group membership to enhance their self-esteem. Group rejection may predict similar consequences. Being excluded from the group threatens people's self-esteem, as well as increasing anxiety, depression, and loneliness (Leary, 1990). The reverse is also true. People with low self-esteem are more sensitive to social exclusion than those with high self-esteem. Low self-esteem exacerbates the sting of social rejection, producing even more self-devaluation than exclusion per se (Neziek, Kowalski, Leary, Blevins, & Holgate, 1997). In its worst form, self-esteem threat deriving from social exclusion results in violence toward the self and others. An analysis of 15 school shootings from 1995 to 2001 found that all but two of them involved some sort of esteem-related social rejection: ostracism, bullying, or romantic rejection (Leary, Kowalski, Smith, & Phillips, 2003).

The sting of social exclusion is less clear at the group level. Although group-based self-esteem theories historically assume that members of stigmatized groups have lower global self-esteem, empirical evidence suggests otherwise. Members of excluded groups often cope with negative group-level feedback by attributing it to irrational prejudice, comparing their own outcomes to other in-group members rather than comparatively advantaged out-group members, or by disproportionately focusing on characteristics on which their group fares well (Crocker & Major, 1989). Nevertheless members of stigmatized groups occasionally experience lowered self-esteem. For instance, overweight people who endorse individualistic ideologies (such as Protestantism) may experience lowered self-esteem, due to their ideology blaming and therefore devaluing themselves (Crocker & Quinn, 2000). Altogether, people's sense of being worthy determines important life outcomes.

Trusting Others

The fifth and final core social motive involves the need to perceive the social world as a benevolent place. In forming close bonds with others, people develop faith in the group and learn to *trust others* within it. Like the other core social motives, trusting others reflects various social and personality theories, including some influential clinical (e.g. Rogers, 1959) and developmental ones (Bowlby, 1969). Trusting is so basic a need that it extends to nonhuman creatures (Harlow, 1958). The earliest explanations for intergroup prejudice centered on lack of trust between competing out-groups (Allport, 1954).

For most people, at least Westerners, trust is built-in. People perceive other people as basically trustworthy and benign until proven otherwise, a concept reflected in the *person-positivity bias* (Sears, 1983). Similarly, people are at baseline slightly optimistic, expecting positive social outcomes (Matlin & Stang, 1978). This is even the case in two-person games where people know that the other person has the option to act in his or her own self-interest (Orbell & Dawes, 1993). Highlighting our sensitivity to trust, trustworthiness is one of the two primary traits we infer from facial features, even from exposures of less than 100 milliseconds (Todorov, Said, Engell, & Oosterhof, 2008). In non-Western cultures, people's circle of trust may be narrower and deeper, the in-group limited to the closest family members and time-tested associates, such as well-established personal and professional relationships (Yamagishi, Cook, & Watabe, 1998).

Having high levels of trust in others generally yields a number of personal benefits. Trusting people tend to be more at ease with things; they are content to let outside influences—such as other people, luck, or a higher power—govern their life (Morling & Fiske, 1999). They're also less resentful, more socially successful, and less lonely than distrusting people (Gurtman, 1992; Rotenberg, 1994). Because trusting people see the social world as largely benevolent, they are more empathic and helpful compared to non-trusting people (Fiske, 2010a).

How Trusting Some Excludes Others

In the process of ensuring in-group success, people explicitly contrast in-group members against people who allegedly cannot be trusted. Real-world examples include civil rights symbols of the 1960s that epitomized stark in-group–out-group differentiation, such as the youth rallying cry, "Never Trust Anyone Over 30," the raised fist of the Black Power separatist movement, or the feminist claim of self-sufficiency, "A woman without a man is like a fish without a bicycle." People are extremely sensitive to trust-versus-mistrust differentiations in the social world; of the two fundamental dimensions that guide social perceptions, warmth/trustworthiness is more immediate (Ohman, 1997) and more resistant to change (Fiske, Cuddy, & Glick, 2007).

Like the other social motives, strengthening in-group bonds excludes out-group members. For example, people who are particularly high group-identifiers tend to be hesitant toward cooperative

contact with out-group members (Hewstone & Brown, 1986). People may distrust out-groups because they perceive them as threats to in-group goals (Cottrell & Neuberg, 2005). As such, a pillar of the "contact hypothesis" about reducing intergroup prejudice is fostering trustful interdependence to achieve common aims (Dovidio & Gaertner, 1999).

The Excluded: Shattered Assumptions of Trust

To call upon Janoff-Bulman (1992) once again, a final fundamental assumption undermined by trauma is that the world is a benevolent and trustworthy place. Excluding people compromises their ability to form trusting bonds with others. An inability to trust others has dire consequences for social functioning, because people conceive trust as a "social reality" (Lewis & Weigert, 1985).

Paralleling the other core social motives, shattered assumptions of trust have long-term social consequences. Lack of trust damages people's ability to form constructive relationships with others. For instance, people who are betrayed or exploited may become hyper-sensitive to the negative behaviors of others (Fiske, 2010a). Compared with people who have not been betrayed, the betrayed are more likely to lie, cheat, and steal, and less likely to give people a second chance or respect others' rights (Rotter, 1980). Betrayed people are also typically higher in monitoring, and consequently less cooperative with others (Ferrin, Bligh, & Kohles, 2007). Moreover, long-term violations of trust between groups can undercut potentially beneficial interactions between individuals of those groups (Shelton & Richeson, 2005).

Lacking trust predicts deleterious outcomes in more intimate relationships as well. As measured by infant attachment styles, early trust predicts relationship success in adult life. Anxious and avoidant infants tend to feel less frequent positive and more frequent negative emotions in their adult romantic relationships (Mikulincer & Shaver, this volume; Simpson, 1990). People whose trust has been violated may also develop high *rejection sensitivity*, which undermines supportiveness and fosters jealousy and hostility between romantic partners (Downey & Feldman, 1996; London & Rosenthal, this volume).

Conclusions

New opportunities for research on social inclusion and exclusion appear at levels from culture to the brain. We still do not know enough about how different cultures manage social belonging and rejecting, a pivotal set of processes that ramify to other social motives. As examples from our own lab, we are learning that expectations differ about friendship initiation and dissolution, about roles in courtship and marriage (Chen, Fiske, & Lee, 2009; Lee, Fiske, & Glick, 2010). We need to know more about how societies divide groups from each other, considering some select and some not; although status hierarchies and interdependence are universal features of intergroup relations, they operate in culturally specific ways (Fiske, 2010b). For example, in the United States, we know more about race and gender divides than about age and class as bases for acceptance and rejection (North & Fiske, 2012; Russell & Fiske, 2008, under review). We need to know more about how core adaptive social motives operate through neural, hormonal, and even genetic contributions to inclusion and exclusion (Fiske, 2010b). As this volume indicates, the opportunities are many.

However, we do know some fundamental principles. Across each of the five core social motives, the drive to thrive in the group benefits people. The most fundamental goal is to feel that one's place in the group is secure, having formed strong social bonds with other group members (Belonging). Moreover, people within the group also reap the luxury of having their view of the social world constantly reinforced by others (Understanding) and believing that they can sufficiently affect their outcomes with their actions (Control). By belonging to the group, in-group members also feel good about themselves, with opportunities to feel even better (Self-Enhancing), and can rely on others as they navigate their social worlds (Trusting Others). For those who are not let into the group, things are less rosy. Excluded people face shattered assumptions across each of these domains, primarily demoralizing people's sense that they belong, but also their supposedly shared understanding of the social world, their sense of control, their feelings of being basically good and worthy, and their ability to have confidence in the intentions of others. In this sense, the excluded find many of their assumptions about the social world to be damaged, sometimes beyond repair.

Thankfully, given that everyone faces some sort of social exclusion, only in rare cases are people unable to overcome all ostracism and eventually join some groups they desire. Moreover, given that the modern world offers more opportunities than ever to join groups and connect with others, even if only virtually, the consequences of being barred from certain groups may not be as dire as they once might have been. Therefore, for the vast majority of the students in the high school cafeteria, no matter which groups they belong to (or don't), they can hope that things will turn out okay—even if they may never know exactly what's in the sloppy joes.

References

Adler, A. (1930). Individual psychology. In C. Murchison (Ed.), *Psychologies of 1930* (pp. 395–405). Worcester, MA: Clark University Press.

Allport, G. (1955). *Becoming: Basic Considerations for a Psychology of Personality*. New Haven, CT: Yale University Press.

Allport, G. W. (1954). *The Nature of Prejudice*. Reading, MA: Addison-Wesley.

Altemeyer, B. (1988). *Enemies of Freedom: Understanding Right-Wing Authoritarianism*. San Francisco: Jossey-Bass.

Ames, D. L., & Fiske, S. T. (under review). Outcome dependency makes you smarter.

Asch, S. E. (1956). Studies of independence and conformity: A minority of one against a unanimous majority. *Psychological Monographs: General and Applied, 70*, 1–70.

Baatjes, X. (2003). The new knowledge-rich society: Perpetuating marginalization and exclusion. *Journal of Education, 29*, 179–210.

Bacon, F. (1597). *Meditationes Sacrae*. London: De Hæresibus.

Baumeister, R. F., Campbell, J. D., Krueger, J. I., & Vohs, K. D. (2003). Does high self-esteem cause better performance, interpersonal success, happiness, or healthier lifestyles? *Psychological Science in the Public Interest, 4*(1), 1–4.

Baumeister, R. F., & Leary, M. R. (1995). The need to belong: Desire for interpersonal attachments as a fundmanetal human motivation. *Psychological Bulletin, 117*, 497–529.

Baumeister, R. F., & Tice, D. M. (1990). Anxiety and social exclusion. *Journal of Social and Clinical Psychology, 9*(2), 165–195.

Berkman, L. F., Glass, T., Brissette, I., & Seeman, T. E. (2000). From social integration to health: Durkheim in the new millennium. *Social Science and Medicine, 51*, 843–857.

Bourdieu, P. (1986). The forms of capital. In J. Richardson (Ed.), *Handbook of Theory and Research for the Sociology of Education* (pp. 241–258). New York: Greenwood.

Bowlby, J. (1969). *Attachment and Loss. Vol. 1: Attachment*. New York: Basic Books.

Brewer, M. B. (1999). The psychology of prejudice: Ingroup love or outgroup hate? *Journal of Social Issues, 55*(3), 429–444.

Caporael, L. R. (1997). The evolution of truly social cognition: The core configurations model. *Personality and Social Psychology Review, 1*, 276–298.

Castano, E., Yzerbyt, V., Paladino, M. P., & Sacchi, S. (2002). I belong, therefore, I exist: Ingroup identification, ingroup entitativity, and ingroup bias. *Personality and Social Psychology Bulletin, 28*, 135–143.

Castelli, L., Pavan, G., Ferrari, E., & Kashima, Y. (2009) The stereotyper and the chameleon: The effects of stereotype use on perceivers' mimicry. *Journal of Experimental Social Psychology, 45*, 835–839.

Chandrasekhar, C. A. (2003). Flying while brown: Federal civil rights remedies to post-9/11 airline racial profiling of south Asians. *Asian Law Journal, 10*, 215–252.

Chen, Z., Fiske, S. T., & Lee, T. L. (2009). Ambivalent sexism and power-related gender-role ideology in marriage. *Sex Roles, 60*, 765–778.

Cialdini, R. B., & Trost, M. R. (1998). Social influence, social norms, conformity, and compliance. In D. T. Gilbert, S. T. Fiske, & G. Lindzey (Eds.), *The Handbook of Social Psychology* (Vol. 2, 4th ed., pp. 151–192). New York: McGraw-Hill.

Cialdini, R. B., & Goldstein, N. J. (2004). Social influence: Compliance and conformity. *Annual Review of Psychology, 55*, 591–621.

Cikara, M., Botvinick, M. M., & Fiske, S. T. (2011). Us versus them: Social identity shapes neural responses to intergroup competition and harm. *Psychological Science, 22*, 306–313.

Combs, D.J.Y., Powell, C.A.J., Schurtz, D.R., & Smith, R.H. (2009). Politics, schadenfreude, and ingroup identification: The sometimes happy thing about a poor economy and death. *Journal of Experimental Social Psychology, 45*, 635–646.

Cooley, C. H. (1902). *Human Nature and the Social Order*. New York: Charles Scribner's Sons.

Correll, J., & Park, B. (2005). A model of the ingroup as a social resource. *Personality and Social Psychology Review, 9*(4), 341–359.

Cottrell, C. A., & Neuberg, S. L. (2005). Different emotional reactions to different groups: A sociofunctional threat-based approach to "prejudice." *Journal of Personality and Social Psychology, 88*(5), 770–789.

Crocker, J., & Major, B. (1989). Social stigma and self-esteem: The self-protective properties of stigma. *Psychological Review, 96*(4), 608–630.

Crocker, J., Major, B. & Steele, C. (1998). Social stigma. In D. T. Gilbert, S. T. Fiske & G. Lindzey (Eds.), *The Handbook of Social Psychology* (Vol. 2, 4th ed., pp. 504–553). New York: McGraw-Hill.

Crocker, J. & Park, L. E. (2004). The costly pursuit of self-esteem. *Psychological Bulletin, 130*(3), 392–414.

Crocker, J., & Quinn, D. M. (2000). Social stigma and the self: Meanings, situations, and self-esteem. In T. F. Heatherton, R. E. Kleck, M. R. Hebl, & J. G. Hull (Eds.), *The Social Psychology of Stigma* (pp. 153–183). New York: Guilford Press.

Dollard, J., Doob, L. W., Miller, N. E., Mowrer, O. H., & Sears, R. R. (1939). *Frustration and Aggression*. New Haven, CT: Yale University Press.

Dovidio, J. F., & Gaertner, S. L. (1999). Reducing prejudice: Combating intergroup biases. *Current Directions in Psychological Science, 8*(4), 101–104.

Downey, G., & Feldman, S. I. (1996). Implications of rejection sensitivity for intimate relationships. *Journal of Personality and Social Psychology, 70*(6), 1327–1343.

Durkheim, E. (1951). *Suicide*. New York: Free Press.

Eidelman, S., Silvia, P. J., & Biernat, M. (2006). Responding to deviance: Target exclusion and differential devaluation. *Personality and Social Psychology Bulletin, 32*(9), 1153–1164.

Epley, N., Waytz, A., & Cacioppo, J. T. (2007). On seeing human: A three-factor theory of anthropomorphism. *Psychological Review, 114*(4), 864–886.

Erber, R., & Fiske, S. T. (1984). Outcome dependency and attention to inconsistent information. *Journal of Personality and Social Psychology, 47*, 709–726.

Erikson, E. (1959). *Identity and the Life Cycle: Selected Papers*. New York: International Universities Press, Inc.

Farr, K. A. (1988). Dominance bonding through the good old boys sociability group. *Sex Roles, 18*(5–6), 259–277.

Ferrin, D. L., Bligh, M. C., & Kohles, J. C. (2007). Can I trust you to trust me?: A theory of trust, monitoring, and cooperation in interpersonal and intergroup relationships. *Group and Organization Management, 32*, 465–499.

Festinger, L., Schachter, S., & Back, K. (1950). *Social Pressures in Informal Groups: A Study of a Housing Community*. Palo Alto, CA: Stanford University Press.

Fiske, S. T. (1992). Thinking is for doing: Portraits of social cognition from daguerreotype to laserphoto. *Journal of Personality and Social Psychology, 63*, 877–889.

Fiske, S. T. (1993). Controlling other people: The impact of power on stereotyping. *American Psychologist, 48*(6), 621–628.

Fiske, S. T. (2003). Five core motives, plus or minus five. In S. J. Spencer, S. Fein, M. P. Zanna, & J. M. Olson (Eds.), *Motivated Social Perception: The Ontario Symposium* (pp. 233–246). Mahwah, NJ: Erlbaum.

Fiske, S. T. (2010a). *Social Beings: A Core Motives Approach to Social Psychology* (2nd ed.). New York: Wiley.

Fiske, S. T. (2010b). Envy up, scorn down: How comparison divides us. *American Psychologist, 65*(8), 698–706.

Fiske, S. T., Cuddy, A. J. C., & Glick, P. (2007). Universal dimensions of cognition: Warmth and competence. *Trends in Cognitive Science, 11*(2), 77–83.

Fiske, S. T., Cuddy, A. J., Glick, P., & Xu, J. (2002). A model of (often mixed) stereotype content: Competence and warmth respectively follow from perceived status and competition. *Journal of Personality and Social Psychology, 82*, 878–902.

Fiske, S. T., & Ruscher, J. B. (1993). Negative interdependence and prejudice: Whence the affect? In D. M. Mackie & D. L. Hamilton (Eds.), *Affect, Cognition, and Stereotyping: Interactive Processes in Group Perception* (pp. 239–268). San Diego, CA: Academic Press.

Freud, S. (1915/1963). Instincts and their vicissitudes. In P. Rieff (Ed.), *Sigmund Freud: General Psychological Principles: Papers on Metapsychology* (pp. 83–103). New York: Collier.

Gaertner, S. L., & McLaughlin, J. P. (1983). Racial stereotypes: Associations and ascriptions of positive and negative characteristics. *Social Psychology Quarterly, 46*(1), 23–30.

Garstka, T.A., Schmitt, M.T., Branscombe, N.R., & Hummert, M.L . (2004). How young and older adults differ in their responses to perceived age discrimination. *Psychology and Aging, 19*(2), 326–335.

Glick, P. (2005). Choice of scapegoats. In J. F. Dovidio, P. Glick, & L. A. Rudman (Eds.), *On the Nature of Prejudice: Fifty Years after Allport* (pp. 244–261). Malden, MA: Blackwell.

Goffman, E. (1959). *The Presentation of Self in Everyday Life*. New York: Academic.

Gurtman, M. B. (1992). Trust, distrust, and interpersonal problems: A circumplex analysis. *Journal of Personality and Social Psychology, 62*, 989–1002.

Hardin, C. D., & Higgins, E. T. (1996). Shared reality: How social verification makes the subjective objective. In R. M. Sorrentino & E. T. Higgins (Eds.), *Handbook of Motivation and Cognition* (Vol. 3, pp. 28–34). New York: Guilford.

Harlow, H. (1958). The nature of love. *American Psychologist, 13*(12), 673–685.

Harris, L. T., & Fiske, S. T. (2006). Dehumanizing the lowest of the low: Neuro-imaging responses to extreme outgroups. *Psychological Science, 17*, 847–853.

Harris, L. T., & Fiske, S. T. (2009). Dehumanized perception: The social neuroscience of thinking (or not thinking) about disgusting people. In M. Hewstone & W. Stroebe (Eds.), *European Review of Social Psychology* (Vol. 20, pp. 192–231). London: Wiley.

Heine, S. J. (2010). Cultural psychology. In S. T. Fiske, D. T. Gilbert, & G. Lindzey (eds.), *Handbook of Social Psychology* (5th ed., pp. 1423–1464). New York: Wiley

Hewstone, M., & Brown, R. J. (1986). Contact is not enough: An intergroup perspective on the "contact hypothesis." In M. Hewstone & R. Brown (Eds.), *Contact and Conflict in Intergroup Encounters* (pp. l-44). Oxford: Blackwell .

Hogg, M. A. (2000). Subjective uncertainty reduction through self-categorization: A motivational theory of social identity processes. *European Review of Social Psychology, 11*, 223–255.

Horney, K. (1945). *Our Inner Conflicts: A Constructive Theory of Neurosis*. New York: Free Press.

House, J. S., Landis, K. R., & Umberson, D. (1988). Social relationships and health. *Science, 241*(4865), 540–545.

James, W. (1983). *The Principles of Psychology*. Cambridge, MA: Harvard University Press. (Original work published 1890)

Janoff-Bulman, R. (1992). *Shattered Assumptions: Towards a New Psychology of Trauma*. New York: The Free Press.

Kennedy, B. P., Kawachi, I., Prothrow-Stith, D., Lochner, K., & Gupta, V. (1998). Social capital, income inequality, and firearm violent crime. *Social Science and Medicine, 47*, 7–17.

Kitayama, S., & Markus, H. R. (1999). Yin and yang of the Japanese self: The cultural psychology of personality. In D. Cervone & Y. Shoda (Eds.), *The Coherence of Personality: Social-Cognitive Bases of Consistency, Variability, and Organization* (pp. 242–302). New York: Guilford.

Kulik, J. A., & Mahler, H. I. M. (2000). Social comparison, affiliation, and emotional contagion under threat. In J. Suls & L. Wheeler (Eds), *Handbook of Social Comparison: Theory and Research* (pp. 295–320). Dordrecht, NL: Kluwer Academic Publishers.

Langer, E. J. (1975). The illusion of control. *Journal of Personality and Social Psychology, 32*(2), 311–328.

Leary, M. R. (1990). Responses to social exclusion: Social anxiety, jealousy, loneliness, depression, and self-esteem. *Journal of Social & Clinical Psychology, 9*(2), 221–229.

Leary, M. R. (2005). Sociometer theory and the pursuit of relational value: Getting to the root of self-esteem. *European review of Social Psychology, 16*, 75–111.

Leary, M. R., & Baumeister, R. F. (2000). The nature and function of self-esteem: Sociometer theory. In M. P. Zanna (Ed.), *Advances in Experimental Social Psychology* (Vol. 32, pp. 1–62). San Diego, CA: Academic Press.

Leary, M.R., & Downs, D.L. (1995). Interpersonal functions of the self-esteem motive: The self-esteem system as a sociometer. In M. H. Kernis (Ed.), *Efficacy, Agency, and Self-Esteem* (pp. 123–144). New York: Plenum Press.

Leary, M. R., Kowalski, R. M., Smith, L., & Phillips, S. (2003). Teasing, rejection, and violence: Case studies of the school shootings. *Aggressive Behavior, 29*(3), 202–214.

Lee, T. L., Fiske, S. T., & Glick, P. (2010). Ambivalent sexism in close relationships: (Hostile) power and (benevolent) romance shape relationship ideals. *Sex Roles, 62*(7–8), 583–601.

Levine, J. M., & Moreland, R. L. (1998). Small groups. In D. T. Gilbert, S. T. Fiske, & G. Lindzey (Eds.), *The Handbook of Social Psychology* (Vol. 2, 4th ed., pp. 415–469). New York: Oxford University Press.

Lewis, J. D., & Weigert, A. (1985). Trust as a social reality. *Social Forces, 63*(4), 967–985.

Leyens, J. -Ph., & Yzerbyt, V. Y. (1992). The ingroup overexclusion effect: Impact of valence and confirmation on stereotypical information search. *European Journal of Social Psychology, 22*, 549–569.

Maslow, A. H. (1962). Some basic propositions of a growth and self-actualization psychology. In A. W. Combs (Yearbook Committee Chairman), *Perceiving, Behaving, Becoming: A New Focus for Education* (pp. 34–49). Washington, DC: Yearbook of the Assocation for Supervision and Curriculum Development.

Matlin, M., & Stang, D. (1978). *The Pollyana Principle*. Cambridge, MA: Schenkman.

McClelland, D. C., & Pilon, D. A. (1983). Sources of adult motives in patterns of parent behavior in early childhood. *Journal of Personality and Social Psychology, 44*(3), 564–574.

Mead, G. H. (1934). *Mind, Self, and Society*. Chicago: The University of Chicago Press.

Moghaddam, F. M. (2005). The staircase to terrorism: A psychological exploration. *American Psychologist, 60*, 161–169.

Morling, B., & Fiske, S. T. (1999). Defining and measuring harmony control. *Journal of Research in Personality, 33*, 379–414.

Moscovici, S. (1988). The history and actuality of social representations. In U. Flick (Ed.), *The Psychology of the Social* (pp. 209–247). Cambridge: Cambridge University Press.

Nelson, T. D. (2005). Ageism: Prejudice against our feared future self. *Journal of Social Issues, 61*(2), 207–221.

Nesse, R. M. (2010). Social selection and the origins of culture. In M. Schaller, A. Norenzayan, S. J. Heine, T. Yamagishi, & T. Kameda (Eds), *Evolution, Culture, and the Human Mind*. (pp. 137–150). New York: Psychology Press.

Newcomb, T. M. (1943). Personality and social change: Attitude formation in a student community. Fort Worth, TX: Dryden Press.

Neziek, J. B., Kowalski, R. M., Leary, M. R., Blevins, T., & Holgate, S. (1997). Personality moderators of reactions to interpersonal rejection: Depression and trait self-esteem. *Personality and Social Psychology Bulletin, 23*(12), 1235–1244.

North, M. S., & Fiske, S. T. (2012). An inconvenienced youth? Ageism and its potential intergenerational roots. *Psychological Bulletin*. doi: 10.1037/a0027843.

Ohman, A. (1997). As fast as the blink of an eye: Evolutionary preparedness for preattentive processing of threat. In P.J. Lang, R.F. Simons, & M. Balaban (Eds.), *Attention and Orienting: Sensory and Motivational Processes* (pp. 165–184). Hillsdale, NJ: Erlbaum.

Ooka, E., & Wellman, B. (2003). Does social capital pay off more within or between ethnic groups? Analyzing job searchers in five Toronto ethnic groups. In E. Fong (Ed.), *Inside the mosaic* (pp. 199–226). Toronto: University of Toronto Press.

Operario, D., & Fiske, S. T. (1998). Racism equals power plus prejudice: A social psychological equation for racial oppression. In J. L. Eberhardt & S. T. Fiske (Eds.), *Confronting Racism: The Problem and the Response* (pp. 33–53). Thousand Oaks, CA: Sage.

Orbell, J. M., & Dawes, R. M. (1993). Social welfare, cooperators' advantage, and the option of not playing the game. *American Sociological Review, 58*, 787–800.

Park, L. E., & Crocker, J. (2005). The interpersonal costs of seeking self-esteem. *Personality and Social Psychological Bulletin, 31*, 1587–1598.

Petty, R. E., & Cacioppo, J. T., (1981). *Attitudes and Persuasion: Classic and Contemporary Approaches*. Dubuque, IA: Brown.

Rank, O. (1929). *The Trauma of Birth*. New York: Harcourt Brace.

Rogers, C. R. (1959). A theory of therapy, personality, and interpersonal relationships, as developed in the client-centered framework. In S. Kock (Ed.), *Psychology: A Study of a Science* (Vol. 3, pp. 184–256). New York: McGraw-Hill.

Rotenberg, K. J. (1994). Loneliness and interpersonal trust. *Journal of Social and Clinical Psychology, 13*, 152–173.

Rotter, J. B. (1980). Interpersonal trust, trustworthiness, and gullibility. *American Psychologist, 35*(1), 1–7.

Rudman, L. A., & Glick, P. (2001). Prescriptive gender stereotypes and backlash toward agentic women. *Journal of Social Issues, 57*(4), 743–762.

Russell, A. M., & Fiske, S. T. (2008). It's all relative: Social position and interpersonal perception. *European Journal of Social Psychology, 38*, 1193–1201.

Russell, A. M., & Fiske, S. T. (under review). Social class ambivalence: Polarized reactions to the poor.

Schachter, S. (1959). *The Psychology of Affiliation: Experimental Studies of the Sources of Gregariousness*. Oxford, UK: Stanford University Press.

Sears, D. O. (1983). The person-positivity bias. *Journal of Personality and Social Psychology, 44*, 233–250.

Seligman, M. E. P., & Maier, S. F. (1967). Failure to escape traumatic shock. *Journal of Experimental Psychology, 74*, 1–9.

Shelton, J. N., & Richeson, J. A. (2005). Intergroup contact and pluralistic ignorance. *Journal of Personality and Social Psychology, 88*(1), 91–107.

Sherif, M. (1935). A study of some social factors in perception. *Archives in Psychology, 27*, 1–60.

Sherif, M., Harvey, O. J., White, B. J., Hood, W. R., & Sherif, C. W. (1961/1988). *The Robbers Cave Experiment: Intergroup Conflict and Cooperation*. Middletown, CT: Wesleyan University Press.

Sidanius, J., & Pratto, F. (1999). *Social Dominance*. New York: Cambridge University Press.

Simpson, J. A. (1990). Influence of attachment styles on romantic relationships. *Journal of Personality and Social Psychology, 59*(5), 971–980.

Solomon, S., Greenberg, J., & Pyszczynski, T. (2000). Pride and prejudice: Fear of death and social behavior. *Current Directions in Psychological Science, 9*, 200–204.

Stangor, C., & Crandall, C. S. (2000). Threat and the social construction of stigma. In T.F. Heatherton, R. E. Kleck, M. R. Hebl, & J. G. Hull (Eds.), *The Social Psychology of Stigma* (pp. 62–87). New York: Guilford.

Staub, E. (1989). *The Roots of Evil: The Origins of Genocide and Other Group Violence*. New York: Cambridge University Press.

Tajfel, H., & Turner, J. (1979). An integrative theory of intergroup conflict. In W. G. Austin, & S. Worchel, *The Social Psychology of Intergroup Relations* (pp. 94–109). Monterey, CA: Brooks-Cole.

Taylor, S. E., & Brown, J. D. (1988). Illusion and well-being: A social-psychological perspective on mental health. *Psychological Bulletin, 103*, 193–210.

Thompson, S. C. (1981). Will it hurt less if I can control it? A complex answer to a simple question. *Psychological Bulletin, 90*, 89–101.

Thompson, S. C., Armstrong, W., & Thomas, C. (1998). Illusions of control, underestimations, and accuracy: A control heuristic explanation. *Psychological Bulletin, 123*, 143–161.

Todorov, A., Said, C. P., Engell, A. D., & Oosterhof, N. N. (2008). Understanding evaluation of faces on social dimensions. *Trends in Cognitive Sciences, 12*(12), 455–460.

Twenge, J. M., Baumeister, R. F., Tice, D. M., & Stucke, T. S. (2001). If you can't join them, beat them: Effects of social exclusion on aggressive behavior. *Journal of Personality and Social Psychology. 81*(6), 1058–1069.

Van Vugt, M. & Hart, C. M. (2004). Social identity as social glue: The origins of group loyalty. *Journal of Personality and Social Psychology, 86*(4), 585–598.

White, R. W. (1959). Motivation reconsidered: The concept of competence. *Psychological Review, 66*, 297–333.

Williams, K. D. (1997). Social ostracism. In R. M. Kowalski (Ed.), *Aversive Interpersonal Behaviors* (pp. 133–170). New York: Plenum.

Williams, K. D. (2007). Ostracism. *Annual Review of Psychology, 58*, 425–452.

Williams, K. D., Cheung, C. K. T., & Choi, W. (2000). Cyberostracism: Effects of being ignored over the internet. *Journal of Personality and Social Psychology, 79*, 748–762.

Williams, K. D., Shore, W. J., & Grahe, J. E. (1998). The silent treatment: Perceptions of its behaviors and associated feelings. *Group Processes and Intergroup Relations, 1*, 117–141.

Williams, K. D., & Sommer, K. L. (1997). Social ostracism by coworkers: Does rejection lead to loafing or compensation? *Personality and Social Psychology Bulletin, 23*, 693–706.

Wilson, A. E., & Ross, M. (2001). From chump to champ: People's appraisals of their earlier and present selves. *Journal of Personality and Social Psychology, 80*, 572–584.

Yamagishi, T., Cook, K. S., & Watabe, M. (1998). Uncertainty, trust, and commitment formation in the United States and Japan. *American Journal of Sociology, 104*, 165–194.

Yzerbyt, V., Castano, E., Leyens, J.-Ph., & Paladino, M. P. (2000). The primacy of the ingroup: The interplay of entitativity and identification. *European Journal of Social Psychology, 11*, 257–295.

Zajonc, R. B., & Adelmann, P. K. (1987). Cognition and communication: A story of missed opportunities. *Social Science Information, 26*(1), 3–30.

The Multi-Motive Model of Responses to Rejection-Related Experiences

Laura Smart Richman

Abstract

This chapter describes a multimotive model of responses to rejection-related experiences. Social exclusion, like other forms of rejection, represents a threat to our need to be valued and accepted by others. In response to social exclusion, people often experience three sets of motives that promote competing behaviors: to aggress against the source of rejection, repair the relationship, and withdraw. According to the multimotive model, the ways in which the exclusion is construed determines when each of these behaviors are most likely to occur. The various construals are described in the context of different rejection-related experiences, and the model is applied to understand some of the long-term mental and physical health consequences of unrestored belonging.

Key Words: antisocial, avoidance, construal, exclusion, motive, prosocial

How people respond to experiences of social exclusion is dynamic, contextually driven, and often counterintuitive. In his book, *The Nature of Prejudice,* Gordon Allport (1954) recognized that in response to prejudice, a form of social exclusion, a person may feel "like a dwarf in a world of menacing giants," and may do a great many things that, in Allport's view, could serve his [or her] "ego-defenses." The person may (1) try to cheat the giants when possible and thus have a taste of sweet revenge … or in desperation occasionally push some giants off the sidewalk or throw a rock at them when it is safe to do so; (2) band together with other dwarfs, sticking close to them for comfort and self-respect; or (3) withdraw into himself or herself, speaking little to the giants. Interestingly, the range of responses to prejudice that Allport described more than 50 years ago correspond remarkably well to the current empirical findings on a range of different forms of social exclusion. A large body of literature now establishes that people who experience or even anticipate exclusion have competing motives to verbally or physically aggress against the rejector, regain a sense of social acceptance, and/or withdraw from further social interaction.

The range of responses to social exclusion can be somewhat perplexing in light of what we know about the strong, fundamental human drive to avoid rejection and be accepted by others. This motive, termed the *need to belong* (Baumeister & Leary, 1995) is thought to have its origins in evolutionary needs to function within social groups and depend on the group for survival. Given this need, how can one make sense of another instinctual impulse to aggress against or withdraw from a source of pain—social pain, as exclusion invariably is—leading to further distancing from an individual or social group and thus greater threat to survival?

The goal of this chapter is to describe a model developed by Richman and Leary (2009) that predicts the multiple motives that are activated in response to various forms of social exclusion. The Multi-Motive model describes that these disparate motives, and the behaviors they promote, can be predicted by how people construe the rejection they experienced. The model suggests that even the motives that are counterproductive to restoring belonging needs can be understood in the context of these construals and the complex interplay between the multiple motives that are activated. Based on the Multi-Motive model, the meaning of the construals as they relate to the different forms of social exclusion and the predictions for which motives will be activated based on a particular construal are described, and the literature is reviewed in these areas. The model is also applied to understand some of the long-term implications of social exclusion for mental and physical health.

Motive-Activating Construals

The Multi-Motive model proposes that in response to rejection, the ability to predict whether motives to harm others, seek support and acceptance, or withdraw will predominate at a given time lies in the understanding of the construals people have about the rejection experience. According to this model, people make one or more of six possible construals, involving the fairness of the rejection, expectations of relationship repair, pervasiveness or chronicity of the rejection, value of the damaged relationship, perceived costs of the rejection, and the possibility of relational alternatives. These six construals can be applied to explain which of the three motives dominates people's responses after being rejected.

The Perception of Unfairness or Injustice

The nature of exclusion is such that it is frequently viewed as being unfair. Being excluded, and thus not valued and appreciated by an individual or group, runs contrary to the generous views we often have of ourselves. Such a construal also reflects the seeming capriciousness of rejection. Most often, not only is the rejection inconsistent with self-views, but it is also coupled with unknowns (Why me? Why not me? How could she?). A failure to conjure up or comprehend reasons for the rejection contributes to a feeling of injustice.

We find evidence for this response across many different forms of laboratory-induced experiences of rejection, in which the reasons for exclusion are rarely provided to the individual. In one frequently used paradigm, participants take part in a getting-acquainted session in which they converse about topics of interest. They are then led to separate rooms and are told that working groups will be formed in which members like and respect each other. The participants are asked to name two people from the group with whom they would like to work and are told that the others will be making these same ratings. After a supposed exchange of information, those in the rejection condition are told, "I hate to tell you this, but no one chose you as someone they wanted to work with, so I'll have you do the next task alone" (Baumeister, DeWall, Ciarocco, & Twenge, 2005; adapted from Leary, Tambor, Terdal, & Downs, 1995). Another popular exclusion manipulation, the alone-later-in life paradigm, provides people with feedback that, based on a bogus personality measure they complete, they are "the type who will end up alone later in life … relationships don't last, and when you're past the age where people are constantly forming new relationships, the odds are you'll end up being alone more and more" (Twenge, Baumeister, DeWall, Ciarocco, & Bartels, 2007). The numerous studies on ostracism also use a paradigm in which the participant tosses a ball—or virtual ball in the Cyberball paradigms—to the other participants who then, suddenly and without explanation, stop tossing the ball to him or her. Rejection based on seemingly arbitrary, confusing criteria is apt to induce a sense of unfairness and has been found to predict aggressive behavior in numerous studies (e.g., Twenge et al., 2007; Warburton, Williams, & Cairns, 2006). In a direct test of this construal, when people were asked to reflect on a past experience of rejection, they were most likely to report having responded with aggression or by withdrawing from further contact with the rejector, rather than engaging in efforts to repair the relationship, when they construed the rejection as being unfair (Richman, Leary, & Robinson, 2010). On a societal level, mass protest on the part of oppressed groups is often grounded in the belief that their exclusion and marginalization in society are perceived as being unjust and unfair.

Expectations of Relational Repair

The perception of whether an exclusion episode reflects a relationship that is irreparable, or whether there is still hope that repair efforts could be successful, also determine how people are motivated to respond. The assessment that a relationship holds the potential for restoration following rejection motivates efforts to cooperate on a group task (Ouwerkerk et al., 2005) and work harder on a subsequent group task following ostracism on a ball-toss game (Williams & Sommer, 1997).

In contrast, when the possibility of repair is perceived as unlikely, prosocial motives are not activated and instead, antisocial responses predominate.

Evidence for how people engage in this calculation is provided in a set of studies manipulating social exclusion (Maner et al., 2007). Excluded participants were motivated to act in ways that would increase their acceptance, such as working with others rather than alone on a task, allocating cash rewards to other participants, and rating a potential interaction partner positively. However, these behaviors only occurred in conditions in which the participants expected that they would be interacting with the other person later on in the course of the experiment, reflecting an assessment that these behaviors may serve the function of regaining acceptance. When the possibility for future interaction was not available, participants treated the rejectors with contempt and did not allocate rewards when the opportunity was made available to them.

The Value of the Relationship

The degree to which people value the relationship in which exclusion occurred is another construal that determines motivational responses. Put simply, if people are excluded from a relationship they care about—whether it be with a friend, romantic partner, boss, or group—they will be motivated to do what they can to repair the relationship. Such prosocial responses may consist of increased cooperation, conformity to group opinions, or expressing regret for a misdeed. Alternatively, people can experience exclusion from a relationship that they do not care about and have little desire to continue, as in the context of a struggling friendship or romantic relationship. In these cases, people may express hostility because they care little about whether their actions lead to further exclusion or may withdraw from the current relationship and seek out alternative sources by turning to other relationships in which they feel a sense of belonging.

The Possibility of Alternatives

When people are able to imagine or pursue relationship alternatives, withdrawal motivations dominate. Rather than engage in efforts to repair the relationship or express hostility toward the rejector, attention may be withdrawn and instead be directed to new sources of acceptance. In the service of searching for acceptance beyond the relationship in which exclusion occurred, people may also turn to established support networks. Such sources of support may provide reminders that one has important relationships and may help restore a sense of belonging. Increases in group identification following prejudice may serve a similar function. Schmitt

and Branscombe (2002) describe a process of how increases in group-based identification may enhance well-being for chronically rejected groups. They propose that by becoming more engaged with their in-group, socially devalued groups can benefit from the social support they receive. In addition, a strong sense of group identity may provide a buffer to the rejection from the dominant group and reduce its negative impact. In this way, when members of disadvantaged groups believe that acceptance by the dominant group is unlikely, investing in alternative sources of support such as one's in-group is a way to feel accepted and enhance well-being.

Chronicity and Pervasiveness

Rejection episodes also differ on the dimension of typicality. A rebuff by a romantic interest, not being invited to a friend's party, or receiving a snide remark from a sales clerk may be perceived as anomalies, exceptions to how one is normally treated by others, and thus can be easily dismissed. When such experiences are perceived as being chronic and pervasive, however, people may be motivated to withdraw and avoid the possibility of further rejection. This response of withdrawal is most apparent with low-status groups that are chronically the target of social exclusion. In these situations, people may be motivated to withdraw from the source of rejection and sometimes from others whose acceptance they may doubt. Mendoza-Denton, Purdie, Downey, and Davis (2002) developed a measure of race-based sensitivity for blacks that measures the extent to which they anxiously expect to be rejected because of their race resulting from previous experiences with discrimination and awareness of stereotypes associated with their group. Consistent with the Multi-Motive model, blacks high in race-based rejection sensitivity showed evidence of withdrawal behavior. They were found to have fewer white friends and interacted less with professors and teaching assistants (who were primarily white) compared with black students low in race-based rejection sensitivity.

The Perceived Costs of Rejection

Some experiences of rejection are particularly weighty because of the costs associated with loss of the relationship. When there are high costs to being rejected, people are motivated to try to repair the relationship and act in prosocial ways to win favor with the rejector. These costs are often in terms of a loss of resources. Being left out of an important business decision may have meaning for future work productivity, the potential dissolution of a marriage may have strong negative financial consequences, and the loss of a friendship may have meaning for access to certain social groups or other resources. A high perceived cost may also be calculated in terms of the potential social costs. When the loss of relationship may lead to future embarrassment, ridicule, or shame, people are motivated to act in ways to repair the damaged relationship or prevent these events from occurring. These cost construals are evident in close relationships in which a high perceived investment (e.g., time, effort, money, shared experiences, and social identity) predict more costs associated with a rejection and a stronger motivation to repair the relationship(Rusbult, 1980).

Multiple Construals and Motives

A major challenge in the study of motivational responses to exclusion is that people often have multiple construals of their experience. The perception that an unwanted romantic breakup was unfair can also be coupled with highly valuing the relationship and a perception that losing the relationship would be devastating. Furthermore, a combination of such construals would predict competing motives to express anger and hostility toward the rejector, but also to try to win the person back. One construal and one motive may predominate to predict an initial response, but construals may quickly change, which may then lead to alternative motives and behaviors. Much of the work in this area has focused on a single behavioral response, and these responses are usually limited to how the rejected person reacts to the rejector (e.g., doling out hot sauce for him or her to consume, blasting the person with white noise, or engaging in altruistic behaviors to win favor with the person or group).

A different story may emerge if multiple responses are measured over time. Williams (2007) delineates a temporal model of responses to ostracism that takes into account these fluctuations in responses over time. It may be that people lash back as an immediate or "reflexive" response, but then moments later, or upon longer reflection, realize that they value the relationship or understand the reason for the rejection and may instead be motivated to respond with repair efforts. Our understanding of these motivation processes would be increased by incorporating measurements of these temporal processes into experimental studies of social exclusion.

The Case of Interracial InteractionsInterracial interactions provide an ideal context for illustrating the complexity of motivational processes that stem from the experience, or even the anticipation, of rejection. Although people are often strongly motivateds for an interracial interaction go smoothly, the discomfort and miscommunications that often plague these interactions contribute to the urge to avoid them if possible (e.g., Plant, 2004). Interracial interactions have been likened to a stress process in which individuals appraise the interaction as a threat, experience stress, and then are motivated to cope in a variety of ways (Trawalter, Richeson, & Shelton, 2009). Some coping responses — antagonizing, avoiding, or freezing — can be counterproductive to effective interactions. According to this framework, when people instead determine that they have the resources to have a positive interaction, they feel challenged and can engage in more prosocial behaviors.

The experimental work on interracial interactions provides evidence for these varied responses. Active engagement is a common characteristic of interracial interactions. People do and say things to accommodate their partner, such as asking questions and affirming the partner's comments during the interaction. They may do positive, intimacy-building behaviors such as smiling, head nodding, and leaning forward (e.g., Shelton, Richeson, & Salvatore, 2004). However, other behaviors that are distancing or even antagonizing such as reduced eye contact (Dovidio et al., 1997) and avoiding interracial contact are also common. Consistent with this experimental work, data from the National Longitudinal Survey of Freshmen on interracial friendships on college campuses suggests that interracial relationships are rare (Fischer, 2008).

An examination of the likely construals made about interracial interactions allows for some insight into when people may be motivated to respond in a certain way and why the behaviors often work at cross-purposes to gaining acceptance from a member of the out-group. Historically, interracial interactions have been fraught with difficulties, which increases the likelihood that members of different racial groups approach such an interaction with the expectation of rejection, or at a minimum, limited acceptance. Based on the Multi-Motive model, this construal—that the relationship represents a context in which rejection is chronic and pervasive—should motivate both whites and racial and ethnic minorities to avoid interracial interactions to avoid such rejection. The perceived likelihood for rejection, coupled with a combination of construals such as a high value placed on being accepted and low expectations of being able to act in a way that will yield acceptance (low expectations of repair), can have powerful influences on how people are motivated to behave in interracial interactions. Ironically, when people are highly concerned with the interaction going smoothly, their behaviors may be interpreted as antagonistic or patronizing, and create an awkward and uncomfortable interaction. In contrast, whites and racial minorities who have positive racial attitudes and previous experiences with interracial contact may feel efficacious in their capacity to enable a smooth interaction and are more likely to engage effectively.

Long-Term Consequences of Unrestored Belonging

The underlying assumption of the Multi-Motive model is that people are motivated to increase their sense of belonging and acceptance when they perceive that there is utility in doing so. People have an extensive repertoire of strategies that they can employ following rejection experiences that provide the capacity to restore threatened belonging needs. Despite their best efforts, people are sometimes not able to restore acceptance after social bonds have been weakened or severed. The Multi-Motive model suggests that when efforts to repair a damaged relationship or find alternative sources of belonging are not successful, chances are increased for the experience of long-term psychological or physical consequences. The long-term effects of rejection experiences are most evident in cases in which the rejection is based on group membership, personality traits, stigmatizing characteristics, or other permanent factors that contribute to construals that the rejection is chronic and unavoidable.

Psychological Consequences

Rejection research primarily employs one-shot experimental paradigms, so potential long-term consequences remain largely unexamined. However, researchers have investigated the cumulative impact of two varieties of rejection over time—discrimination and peer rejection. First, targets of discrimination based on group memberships such as race, gender, or ethnicity often experience repeated episodes of rejection and few opportunities to achieve acceptance, at least with respect to those who discriminate against them. Indeed, one of the reasons that discrimination may be highly stressful and detrimental to well-being involves repeated exposure paired with a lack of recourse and control over time. Numerous lab-based and community studies find strong support for an association between

self-reports of discrimination and lower psychological well-being (D. R. Williams et al., 2003). Perceived discrimination is a potent stressor that leads to a variety of negative mental health outcomes (e.g., poor mental health).

Similarly, peer rejection in childhood has been associated with loneliness, low self-esteem, and internalizing problems including anxiety and depression. In a meta-analytic review of the personality correlates of peer rejection, Newcomb, Bukowski, and Pattee (1993) found that children who are chronically rejected tend to be more aggressive, more withdrawn, less cognitively skilled, and less socially adept, characteristics that make it difficult for children to maintain successful peer relationships. Research into the long-term effects of ostracism also suggests that persistent exposure to these experiences leads eventually to "resignation, alienation, helplessness, and depression" (Williams, 2010, p. 52).

Of course, some of the psychological correlates of discrimination and peer rejection may precede rejection rather than result from it, but evidence suggests that both directions of influence occur. Longitudinal studies of children have found significant links between early social rejection and psychopathology later in life (see Parker & Asher, 1987 for a review). In one study, peer rejection predicted psychological maladjustment later in life, even after controlling for individual differences in behaviors that may precipitate rejection, such as aggressiveness and social withdrawal (Ladd, 2006). Furthermore, evidence suggests that peer rejection is a distinct experience from being unpopular for other reasons. Using a peer nomination technique, Asher and Wheeler (1985) had children indicate who they liked and disliked the most. Children who were rejected—lacking friends because others did not like them—were lonelier than neglected children who lacked friends but were not disliked.

Physiological Consequences

Long-term patterns of rejection—such as ongoing discrimination, peer rejection, or ostracism— also influence physical health. Physiologically, rejection induces autonomic arousal, triggers the release of certain hormones, and elicits certain neurological responses that resemble those associated with physical pain.

Rejection and ostracism, such as being excluded from a group task, elicit a stress response involving increased systolic and diastolic blood pressure (Stroud, Tanofsky-Kraff, Wilfley, & Salovey,

2000). Similarly, other events that make people feel excluded—such as perceptions of unfair treatment that appear to be caused by one's appearance—are related to elevated ambulatory blood pressure readings over the course of 2 days (Matthews, Salomon, Kenyon, & Zhou, 2005; see also Richman, Pek, Pascoe, & Bauer, 2010).

Physiological responses have been examined most extensively in the context of racial discrimination. Laboratory analogs of ethnic discrimination and mistreatment are associated with immediate physiological arousal (Harrell, Hall, & Taliaferro, 2003). Chronic experiences of mistreatment and discrimination may also be related to increased physiological reactivity to subsequent stressors. In a study of African-American and European-American women, Guyll et al. (2001) found that past experiences of subtle mistreatment (e.g., being ignored or being treated with less courtesy and respect than other people) were related to higher diastolic blood pressure reactivity among African Americans during a speech task in which participants gave a speech in their own defense after imagining being wrongfully accused of shoplifting. This effect was not observed among European Americans. Such findings and other related studies (e.g., Richman et al., 2007) suggest that pervasive and chronic exclusion experiences may have long-term effects on physiological responses to socially stressful events, possibly paving the way for pathogenic processes associated with heightened physiological reactivity.

Negative interpersonal experiences are also associated with the release of cortisol, a hormone that is associated with reactions to stressful events. For example, situations that involve the mere potential for negative evaluations and exclusion by other people (such as giving a speech or performing a difficult task in front of an evaluative audience) elicit cortisol release (Dickerson, Mycek, & Zaldivar, 2008). Similarly, feelings of loneliness, which arise from perceived deficits in people's social relationships, are associated with higher levels of cortisol on the following day (Adam, Hawkley, Kudielka, & Cacioppo, 2006).

Although the release of cortisol is beneficial in helping people deal with threats, ongoing threats to acceptance may lead to excessive cortisol activity that puts the person at risk for cardiovascular damage, comprised immune function, and other health problems over the long run (Miller, Chen, & Zhou, 2007). Along similar lines, studies of nonhuman primates have documented an association between the chronic stress of social subordination (in which a subordinate animal is subjected to repeated acts of exclusion, bullying, and rejection by more dominant animals) and coronary artery atherosclerosis, a link that is primarily mediated by neuroendocrine factors such as hypersecretion of cortisol (e.g., Sapolsky, 2005).

Another pathway by which exclusion experiences may affect health involves the negative emotions that are associated with rejection, including hurt, anger, sadness, and anxiety. As noted earlier, anger is particularly pronounced in the case of discrimination because anger arises from harm and threats that are perceived as unjustified (Solomon, 1990). When highly arousing emotions are triggered in response to threat, blood pressure increases, lipids and glucose are mobilized to increase energy and sensory vigilance, and in many cases cortisol is released. Unfortunately, repeated activation of these physiological pathways can have detrimental effects on cardiovascular outcomes such as an increased risk for hypertension (Krieger, 2000). Furthermore, the persistence or chronicity of stressors over time contributes to cardiovascular outcomes more strongly than the experience of an acute event or series of discrete events in a given year (Williams et al., 1999). Thus, people who perceive themselves to be regularly devalued or excluded because of ongoing discrimination, rejection, or ostracism are presumably at greatest risk for cardiovascular disease. In support of this hypothesis, research on loneliness and chronic states of low belonging finds increased morbidity and premature mortality (Cacioppo & Hawkley, 2003).

Social exclusion can also lead to failures of self-regulation (Twenge et al., 2003), and these self-regulatory failures provide another pathway by which exclusion contributes to long-term health outcomes. To the extent that exclusion depletes people's self-regulatory strength and interferes with self-control in other ways, it may lead to unhealthy behaviors of both commission (such as splurging on unhealthy foods, overusing alcohol, or smoking) and omission (such as not being able to make oneself exercise or follow medical regimens). In support of this notion, studies have found a relationship between experiences with discrimination and the use of cigarettes, alcohol, and other substances, as well an unhealthy eating (see Pascoe & Richman, 2009 for a meta-analysis of these effects). In a panel study of perceived discrimination and substance use, Gibbons et al. (2004) found evidence that discrimination produces alienation and dismissal of conventional values among black adolescents, as well as increased acceptance of deviance and rebellion and increased affiliation with friends who use drugs. The role of exclusion experiences on patterns of unhealthy and risky behaviors is an important avenue for future research.

The Zero-Miss Strategy in Rejection Detection

People's long-term challenges in dealing with social exclusion may be compounded by changes in how they perceive and interpret signs of potential rejection. People who have been excluded are understandably vigilant for future instances of devaluation and may attempt to minimize the possibility of missing future indications of potential rejection. This strategy is adaptive in protecting people from future occurrences of rejection, but it may have the unfortunate consequence of producing a high "false alarm" rate in which benign actions are interpreted as rejecting (Barrett & Swim, 1998).

This effect may be particularly likely when people possess a visible stigmatizing attribute that might lead others to devalue them, such as being overweight or being the member of a socially devalued racial or ethnic group. Such individuals may interpret others' reactions as more devaluing or rejecting than they actually are. When this happens, people are unable to repair damaged relationships fully because they detect signs of rejection that do not exist. A number of studies have shown that people who believe that they are stigmatized perceive negative reactions from others, even when they are not actually stigmatized or others are not aware of their stigma (Kleck & Strenta, 1980; Miller, Rothbaum, Felicio, & Brand, 1995).

Undetected Rejection

The Multi-Motive model focuses on the motivational underpinnings of people's responses once rejection is detected, yet for some forms of rejection—most notably, stigmatization and discrimination—people may develop conscious or nonconscious strategies to minimize or deny these experiences. The tendency to ignore, downplay, or fail to acknowledge that rejection has occurred can be attributable to a host of dispositional, situational, and societal factors (see Major, Quinton, & McCoy, 2002) that go beyond the scope of this chapter, but an important question to consider is which aspects of the Multi-Motive model of responses to rejection are applicable when people are rejected but fail to recognize it.

Consider, for example, the case of a female engineering student who does not acknowledge that she is being called on less frequently or is being treated less respectfully than her male classmates. By dismissing the experiences as harmless, she may minimize her distress and the perceived need to take action, but she also misses opportunities to change how she is treated. The concept of false consciousness suggests that social systems of inequality persist because low status groups do not recognize the illegitimacy of the status system and their own disadvantaged position within it (e.g., Jost & Banaji, 1994). Most pertinent to the Multi-Motive model, the student may miss the opportunity to reclaim a sense of acceptance, and the subtle, yet pervasive sense of not belonging could eventually lead her to experience negative emotions and lower self-esteem and decide not to pursue a career in engineering (e.g., Murphy, Steele, & Gross, 2007; Richman, vanDellen, & Wood, 2010). Most relevant to understanding the negative mental and physical health outcomes predicted by the Multi-Motive model is the fact that denying discrimination and rejection experiences may lead members of chronically oppressed groups to fail to respond in ways that, over time, may increase their sense of acceptance. Krieger and Sidney (1996) described this experience in terms of an "internalized racism," finding that among working-class black men and women, resting blood pressure was highest among those reporting having experienced no racial discrimination and lowest among those reporting discrimination in one or two situations.

Summary

People's construals of a rejection event determine the particular motive(s) that guide behavioral responses. Although a given construal does not definitively determine a particular motive, the Multi-Motive model suggests that particular patterns of construals make certain responses more likely. For example, when the rejection is perceived as unfair, then antisocial responses are more likely. When expectations of repairing the relationship are high, the relationship is highly valued, and the costs of losing the relationship are high, then people will likely be motivated to behave in prosocial ways that promote acceptance with the rejector and use tactics that restore a sense of belonging. In contrast, withdrawal motivations are generated from the beliefs that viable alternative relationships are available and that the rejection is chronic and pervasive. Over time, each of these responses will either restore the person's sense of belonging and acceptance or fail to do so.

Whether or not belonging is restored has important consequences for whether the person experiences positive or negative outcomes with respect to psychological and physical well-being. People have an extensive repertoire of strategies for restoring real or perceived acceptance following rejection, and such strategies reduce the chances of incurring long-term psychological or physical consequences. However, cases arise in which opportunities for belongingness restoration are not possible. Researchers have investigated the long-term effects of discrimination and peer rejection, but many other cases of chronic rejection have yet to be examined, such as people who possess stigmatizing physical conditions, socially undesirable identities (such as as an ex-con, child molester, or drug addict), or blemished reputations. (A single public display of incompetent or inappropriate behavior may turn a previously acceptable person into a social or political pariah.) Although limited research has been conducted on the longitudinal effects of these experiences, evidence suggests that chronic deprivation of belonging leads to prolonged negative affect (particularly depression, loneliness, and anger) and negative physical health outcomes either directly through chronic activation of stress responses or through behaviors that increase the risk for health problems.

Future Directions

1. How can the presence of three competing motives be considered in the context of a given exclusion experience?

2. What are the temporal features of how an experience of exclusion unfolds?

3. How are immediate responses different from more long-term responses?

4. How are the multiple strategies that people employ to cope with an experience of exclusion related to one another?

References

Adam, E. K., Hawkley, L., Kudielka, M. M., & Cacioppo, J. T. (2006). Day-to-day dynamics of experience-cortisol associations in a population-based sample of older adults. *Proceedings of the National Academy of Sciences, 103*, 17058–17063.

Allport, G. (1954). *The Nature of Prejudice*. Cambridge, MA: Addison-Wesley.

Asher, S. R., & Wheeler, V. A. (1985). Children's loneliness: A comparison of rejected and neglected peer status. *Journal of Consulting and Clinical Psychology, 53*, 500–505.

Barrett, L. F., & Swim, J. (1998). Appraisals of prejudice: A signal detection framework. In J. Swim & C. Stangor (Eds.), *Prejudice: The target's perspective* (pp. 11–36). Academic Press.

Baumeister, R. F., Dewall, C. N., Ciarocco, N. J., & Twenge, J. M. (2005). Social exclusion impairs self-regulation. *Journal of Personality and Social Psychology, 88*, 589–604.

Baumeister, R. F., & Leary, M. R. (1995). The need to belong: Desire for interpersonal attachments as a fundamental human motivation. *Psychological Bulletin, 117*, 497–529.

Caciopppo, J. T., & Hawkley, L. C. (2003). Social isolation and health, with an emphasis on underlying mechanisms. *Perspectives in Biology and Medicine, 46*, 839–852.

Dickerson, S. S., Mycek, P. J., & Zaldivar, F. (2008). Negative social evaluation—but not mere social presence—elicits cortisol responses to a laboratory stressor task. *Health Psychology, 27*(1), 116–121.

Dovidio, J. F., Kawakami, K., Johnson, C., Johnson, B., & Howard, A. (1997). On the nature of prejudice: Automatic and controlled processes. *Journal of Experimental Social Psychology, 33*, 510–540.

Fischer, M. J. (2008). Does campus diversity promote friendship diversity? A look at interracial friendships in college. *Social Science Quarterly, 89*, 631–655.

Gibbons, F. X., Gerrard, M., Cleveland, M. J., Wills, T. A., & Brody, G. H. (2004). Perceived discrimination and substance use in African-American parents and their children: A panel study. *Journal of Personality and Social Psychology, 86*, 517–529.

Guyll, M., Matthews, K. A., & Bromberger, J. T. (2001). Discrimination and unfair treatment: relationship to cardiovascular reactivity among African American and European American women. *Health Psychology, 20*, 315–325.

Harrell, J. P. Hall, S., & Taliaferro J. (2003). Physiological responses to racism and discrimination: An assessment of the evidence. *American Journal of Public Health, 93*, 243–248.

Jost, J. T., & Banaji, M. R. (1994). The role of stereotyping in system-justification and the production of false consciousness. *British Journal of Social Psychology, 33*, 1–27.

Kleck, R. E., & Strenta, A. (1980). Perceptions of the impact of negatively valued physical characteristics on social interaction. *Journal of Personality and Social Psychology, 39*, 861–873.

Krieger, N. (2000). Discrimination and health. In L. F. Berkman, & I. Kawachi (Eds). *Social Epidemiology* (pp. 36–75) New York: Oxford University Press.

Krieger, N., & Sidney S. (1996). Racial discrimination and blood pressure: The CARDIA study of young black and white adults. *Am J Public Health, 86*, 1370–1378.

Ladd, G. W. (2006). Peer rejection, aggressive or withdrawn behavior, and psychological maladjustment from ages 5 to 12: An examination of four predictive models. *Child Development, 77*, 822–846.

Leary, M. R., Tambor, E. S., Terdal, S. K., & Downs, D. L. (1995). Self-esteem as an interpersonal monitor: The sociometer hypothesis. *Journal of Personality and Social Psychology, 68*, 518–530.

Major, B., Quinton, W. J., & McCoy, S. K. (2002). Antecedents and consequences of attributions to discrimination: Theoretical and empirical advances. In M. P. Zanna (Ed.), *Advances in Experimental Social Psychology* (Vol. 34, pp. 251–300). San Diego: Academic Press.

Maner, J. K., DeWall, C. N., Baumeister, R. F., & Schaller, M. (2007). Does social exclusion motivate interpersonal reconnection? Resolving the "porcupine problem." *Journal of Personality and Social Psychology, 92*, 42–55.

Matthews, K. A., Salomon, K., Kenyon, K., & Zhou, F. (2005). Unfair treatment, discrimination, and ambulatory blood pressure in Black and White adolescents. *Health Psychology, 24,* 258–265.

Mendoza- Denton, R., Purdie, V., Downey, G., & Davis, A. (2002). Sensitivity to status-based rejection: Implications for African-American students' college experience. *Journal of Personality and Social Psychology, 83,* 896–918.

Miller, C., Rothbaum, E. D., Felicio, D., & Brand, P. (1995). Do obese women have poorer social relationships than non-obese women? *Personality and Social Psychology Bulletin, 21,* 1093–1106.

Miller, G. E., Chen, E., & Zhou, E. S. (2007). If it goes up, must it come down? Chronic stress and the hypothalamic-pituitary-adrenocorticol axis in humans. *Psychological Bulletin, 133,* 25–45.

Murphy, M. C., Steele, C. M., & Gross, J. J. (2007). Signaling threat: How situational cues affect women in math, science, and engineering settings. *Psychological Science, 18,* 879–885.

Newcomb, A. F., Bukowski, W. M., & Pattee, L. (1993). Children's peer relations: A meta-analytic review of popular, rejected, neglected, controversial, and average sociometric status. *Psychological Bulletin, 113*(1), 99–128.

Ouwerkerk, J. W., Kerr, N. L., Gallucci, M., & Van Lange, P. (2005). Avoiding the social death penalty: Ostracism and cooperation in social dilemmas. In K. D. Williams, & W. von Hippel (Eds.). *The Social Outcast: Ostracism, Social Exclusion, Rejection, and Bullying* (pp. 321–332). New York: Psychology Press.

Parker, J. G., & Asher, S. R. (1987). Peer relations and later personal adjustment: are low-accepted children at risk? *Psychological Bulletin, 102,* 357–389.

Pascoe, E., & Smart Richman, L. (2009). Perceived discrimination and health: A meta-analytic review. *Psychological Bulletin, 135,* 531–554.

Plant, E. A. (2004). Responses to interracial contact over time. *Personality and Social Psychology Bulletin, 30,* 1458–1471.

Richman, L., Bennett, G., Pek, J., Siegler, I. C., & Williams, R. B. (2007). Discrimination, dispositions, and cardiovascular responses to stress. *Health Psychology, 26,* 675–683.

Richman, L., & Leary, M. (2009). Reactions to discrimination, stigmatization, ostracism, and other forms of interpersonal rejection: A Multimotive model. *Psychological Review, 116,* 365–383.

Richman, L., Leary, M., & Robinson, K. (2010). An empirical test of the multi-motive model. *Unpublished data.*

Richman, L., vanDellen, M., & Wood, W. (2010). Mechanisms for coping with stereotype threat cues: Women in engineering. *Journal of Social Issues.*

Richman, L. S., Pek, J., Pascoe, E., & Bauer, D. (2010). The Effects of Perceived Discrimination on Ambulatory Blood Pressure and Affective Responses to Interpersonal Stress Modeled Over 24 Hours. *Health Psychology, 29,* 403–411.

Rusbult, C. E. (1980). Commitment and satisfaction in romantic associations: A test of the investment model. *Journal of Experimental Social Psychology, 16,* 172–186.

Sapolsky, R. M. (2005). The influence of social hierarchy on primate health. *Science, 308*(5722), 648–652.

Schmitt, M. T., & Branscombe, N. L. (2002). The meaning and consequences of perceived discrimination in disadvantaged and privileged social groups. *European Review of Social Psychology, 12,* 167–199.

Shelton, J. N., Richeson, J. A., & Salvatore, J. (2004). Expecting to be the target of prejudice: Implications for interethnic interactions. *Personality and Social Psychology Bulletin, 31,* 1189–1202.

Solomon, R. S. (1990). *A Passion for Justice: Emotions and the Origins of the Social Contract.* Reading, MA: Addison-Wesley.

Stroud, L. R., Tanofsky-Kraff, M., Wilfley, D. E., & Salovey, P. (2000). The Yale Interpersonal Stressor (YIPS): Affective, physiological, and behavioral responses to a novel interpersonal rejection paradigm. *Annals of Behavioral Medicine, 22,* 204–213.

Trawalter, S., Richeson, J. A., & Shelton, J. N. (2009). Predicting behavior during interracial interactions: A stress and coping approach. *Personality and Social Psychology Review, 13,* 243–268.

Twenge, J. M., Baumeister, R. F., DeWall, C. N., Ciarocco, N. J., & Bartels, J. M. (2007). Social exclusion decreases prosocial behavior. *Journal of Personality and Social Psychology, 92,* 56–66.

Twenge, J. M., Catanese, K. R., & Baumeister, R. F. (2003). Social exclusion and the deconstructed state: Time perception, meaninglessness, lethargy, lack of emotion, and self-awareness. *Journal of Personality and Social Psychology, 85,* 409–423.

Warburton, W. A., Williams, K. D., & Cairns, D. R. (2006). When ostracism leads to aggression: The moderating effects of control deprivation. *Journal of Experimental Social Psychology, 42,* 213–220.

Williams, D. R., Neighbors, H. W., & Jackson, J. S. (2003). Racial/ethnic discrimination and health: Findings from community studies. *American Journal of Public Health, 93,* 200–208.

Williams, D. R., Spencer, M. S., & Jackson, J. S. (1999). Race, stress, and physical health: The role of group identity. In R. J. Contrada, & R. D. Ashmore (Eds.), *Self, Social Identity, and Physical Health: Interdisciplinary Explorations* (pp. 71–100). New York: Oxford University Press.

Williams, K. D. (2007). Ostracism. *Annual Review of Psychology, 58,* 425–452.

Williams, K. D., & Sommer, K. L. (1997). Social ostracism by one's coworkers: Does rejection lead to loafing or compensation? *Personality and Social Psychology Bulletin, 23,* 693–706.

PART 3

Exclusion at the Group Level

Social Exclusion of Individuals through Interpersonal Discrimination

Juan M. Madera *and* Michelle Hebl

Abstract

In this chapter, we discuss the social exclusion that many individuals from stigmatized groups experience. Social exclusion may happen through the expression of formal (overt, illegal) behaviors and/or through the expression of interpersonal (more subtle, legal) behaviors. In this chapter, we begin by describing these different types of discrimination and describe why we focus our discussion and research on interpersonal discrimination. Then, we review the interpersonal discrimination that members of a wide variety of stigmatized groups (e.g., obese, ethnic minorities, physically disabled) experience. We consider the consequences of such interpersonal discrimination, and argue that such behavior is paramount to excluding individuals from many domains of life, although the majority of research thus far has been conducted in workplace settings. Finally, we end by considering strategies that individuals might use to reduce such interpersonal discrimination, and ultimately social exclusion.

Key Words: social exclusion, social rejection, belonging, stigma, interpersonal discrimination

Introduction

Discrimination continues to be a modern day reality for many individuals in our society. Such discrimination may range from overt, explicit expressions for which there are legal and societal repercussions to more subtle, interpersonal expressions that are not prohibited by law. The purpose of this chapter is to focus on the latter, more interpersonal types of behaviors that often result in individuals being excluded from full acceptance into social interactions and sometimes society as a whole. The majority of research on interpersonal types of discrimination has been conducted in workplace contexts (e.g., Hebl, Foster, Mannix, & Dovidio, 2002; Hebl, King, Glick, Singletary, & Kazama, 2007; King, Shapiro, Hebl, Singletary, & Turner, 2006; Shapiro, King, & Quinones, 2007; Singletary & Hebl, 2009); however, such findings provide important implications for the everyday dyadic and group interactions that often lead to the social exclusion of stigmatized individuals. We begin by briefly distinguishing the differences between overt

(or *formal discrimination*) and subtle (or *interpersonal discrimination*) and then review the relevant research on interpersonal discrimination. Then, we consider how interpersonal discrimination leads to social exclusion of a variety of individuals who have appearance-based stigmas (e.g., ethnic minorities, obese). Finally, we describe strategies that individuals might use to reduce interpersonal discrimination and ultimately social exclusion.

Formal and Interpersonal Discrimination

To distinguish the way in which people express discrimination, Hebl et al. (2002) conducted a study and differentiated between two forms of discrimination, *formal discrimination* and *interpersonal discrimination*.

Formal Discrimination

Formal discrimination involves behaviors that are often obvious, overt, and illegal, and include examples such as excluding ethnic minorities from housing or rental opportunities (Turner & Ross, 2005;

Turner & Ross, 2003), spending less time in the hospital with obese- than average-weight patients (Allon, 1982; Hebl & Xu, 2001), and calling back African-American applicants significantly less than Euro-American applicants despite the exact same credentials (Bertrand & Mullainathan, 2004). Such forms of exclusion often involve conscious or overt intentions to discriminate against stigmatized individuals (see Dovidio, Kawakami, & Gaertner, 2002). In addition to being illegal, formal discrimination also involves behaviors that are required of a job. That is, if an organization defines a job by specifying a given set of behaviors that *must* be performed, failure to do them (because one harbors prejudice against an individual) would also constitute formal discrimination. For instance, sales personnel are supposed to greet and offer customers assistance with questions that they have. Ignoring them and/or failing to respond to their requests for help, then, would also constitute formal discrimination.

Interpersonal Discrimination

Interpersonal discrimination involves the display of behaviors that tend to be subtle and are often nonverbal. Additionally, interpersonal discrimination may be the result of unconscious intentions to discriminate and/or may result when individuals' are trying to consciously control their verbal reactions and hence, their nonverbal reactions "leak out" prejudicial reactions. For example, individuals might stand farther distances away from, spend less time with, or smile less often at stigmatized (versus nonstigmatized) targets (Hebl et al., 2002, 2007; King et al., 2006; Singletary & Hebl, 2009). Although interpersonal discrimination often involves nonverbal behavior, it may include nonverbal, verbal, and paraverbal expressions, such as being ruder, asking fewer questions of, giving shortened responses to, or using an unfriendly tone of voice with stigmatized (versus nonstigmatized) targets (Hebl et al., 2002). In contrast to formal discrimination, interpersonal discrimination has been largely ignored until recently (Dovidio et al., 2002; Hebl et al., 2002). However, we argue that it may be a particularly important type of discrimination to investigate for several reasons.

First, and as mentioned previously, the display of formal discrimination is prohibited by laws such as Title VII of the Civil Rights Act, the Americans with Disabilities Act (ADA), the Age Discrimination in Employment Act of 1967, the Equal Pay Act of 1963, the Fair Housing act of Title VIII of the Civil Rights Act, and Title IX of the Education Amendments of 1972. These laws mandate equal access to resources and provide protection from educational and employment discrimination. Such laws, however, do not restrict the displays of interpersonal discrimination. That is, interpersonal discrimination remains outside the parameters of law, and so targets of interpersonal discrimination have no legally recognized course of action to pursue. There are simply not laws in place to sanction behaviors such as the amount of smiling, eye contact, and friendliness in which one must engage. Thus, it is important to examine interpersonal discrimination because it is often overlooked and not prohibited in any way.

Second, many organizational policies, city ordinances, and state laws have been adopted to protect stigmatized individuals from formal discrimination, particularly when there is not already protection at the federal level. For example, obese individuals, openly gay and lesbian individuals, and physically unattractive people are not protected by federal laws, but some states and municipalities and many organizations are extending protected group status to include members of these and other groups as well. For example, 470 of the Fortune 500 companies provide nondiscrimination protection for their gay and lesbian employees (Lazin, 2007). The state of Michigan and the cities of San Francisco, Santa Clara, and the District of Columbia have ordinances that protect people from weight discrimination. Not surprisingly, however, such policies do not extend to restricting interpersonal forms of discrimination, because such behaviors simply have not yet been considered.

Third, research shows that peoples' overt behaviors are influenced by politically correct or socially desirable expectations, which may lead individuals to consciously monitor, restrict, or reduce formal discriminatory behaviors that they display toward targets (Dovidio, Glick, & Rudman, 2005). However, people are more likely to express discrimination (even formally) in ways and situations in which their prejudicial motives are ambiguous or cannot clearly be discerned. For instance, Snyder, Kleck, Strenta, and Mentzer (1979) found that individuals indicated preferring to watch a movie in the presence (versus watching this same movie in the absence) of a physically disabled individual. However, if two different movies were offered, individuals indicated that they always preferred to watch the movie that was being shown in the absence (versus presence) of the disabled individual, even though the movies were counterbalanced. Thus, when their motives could not go undetected, nonstigmatized individuals indicated wanting to be in the company of a disabled individual, but if they could avoid and attribute avoiding the disabled individual because of movie selection, they opted to do so. By smiling less, shortening a conversion, or keeping a larger social distance toward a stigmatized target, individuals may be able to express discrimination in ways that are not uniformly interpreted as necessarily being racist, sexist, or homophobic. However, very little research has examined how these more ambiguous behaviors may also (like more overt behaviors) create mountains of disparate experiences for stigmatized individuals.

Fourth, research has shown that explicit, conscious attitudes (i.e., explicit statements of individuals' attitudes) are correlated with formal types of discrimination, whereas implicit attitudes are correlated with nonverbal and more interpersonal discriminatory behaviors (Dovidio et al., 2002; Dovidio, Kawakami, Johnson, Johnson, & Howard, 1997). It seems that people can readily monitor their obvious behaviors (i.e., what they say) more than they can monitor and alter their interpersonal, nonverbal behaviors (e.g., how they say it) (Dovidio, Kawakami, & Gaertner, 2002). As such, it is more difficult for people to regulate negativity that manifests itself in interpersonal discrimination. Add to this the fact that people do not always have ready access to their true attitudes (Greenwald & Banaji, 1995) and it becomes clear that nonstigmatized individuals do not even realize sometimes that they are engaging in interpersonal discrimination. Given that individuals do not report engaging in and even being aware of this type of discrimination, it seems very important to particularly focus research attention on it, because the targets of interpersonal discrimination report being aware and negatively affected by such behaviors (Richeson, Trawalter, & Shelton, 2005; Singletary & Hebl, 2010).

In sum, formal discrimination seems to be more clearly understood, consciously chosen, and mutable via laws and organizational policies than does interpersonal discrimination. Interpersonal discrimination, we argue, is more ambiguous but unequivocal way in which social exclusion of stigmatized groups continues to be achieved and maintained. We next review empirical studies that have been conducted on interpersonal discrimination.

A Review of Interpersonal Discrimination Research

In this section, we provide a brief review of research on interpersonal discrimination. We demarcate research that has been done on different groups of stigmatized individuals, although all of them share the commonality of having appearance-based stigmas. The visibility of such stigmas may accentuate the extent to which nonstigmatized individuals interpersonally discriminate against and exclude them (see Jones et al., 1984). In reviewing this research, three points become apparent. First, interpersonal discrimination is consistently present, despite the fact that formal discrimination sometimes is not. Second, there are consequences of interpersonal discrimination. Although stigmatized individuals' experiences may seem like they are simply targets of benign microinequities, we argue that interpersonal discrimination may be just as harmful and socially excluding; and in fact, sometimes interpersonal discrimination has even graver consequences for stigmatized individuals than does formal discrimination (see Singletary & Hebl, 2010). Third and finally, a wide range of differentially stigmatized individuals experience interpersonal discrimination in almost identical ways. Although they share the experience of having an appearance-based stigma, the particular stigmas and features of them differ dramatically. Yet, nonstigmatized individuals often treat them similarly and consistently react by social excluding them.

Discernibly Gay Individuals

In one of the first studies to examine different types of discrimination, Hebl et al. (2002) examined measures of both formal (i.e., hiring decisions) and interpersonal (i.e., nonverbal behaviors, amount of conversation) discrimination that both job applicants (either homosexual or assumed heterosexual) perceived from store employers and store employers actually displayed toward the applicants. Wearing hats labeled with "Gay and Proud" or "Texan and Proud," 18 trained confederates entered and formally applied for positions at retail stores that were hiring. The results of the study showed that store employers did not formally discrimination against the ostensibly gay applicants. Regardless of the hat they were wearing, applicants were equally likely to be told jobs were available, provided with job applications, and called back for job interviews. However, the results did reveal significant differences on the interpersonal discrimination measures. Employers interacting with applicants wearing the "Gay and Proud" hats (compared with those wearing "Texan and Proud" hats) spoke fewer words, had shorter interactions, and displayed more negativity (as reported from the perspectives of both the applicants and independent observers). Displays of negativity involved the store employers expressing more nervousness and hostility, ending the conversation prematurely, and being unfriendly toward the stigmatized than nonstigmatized individuals. The results from this study show that social exclusion is not happening through formal channels but through microinequities that emerge in interpersonal exchanges.

Discernible Religious Minorities

As with sexual orientation, individuals can choose to conceal their religious affiliation. At other times, individuals specifically choose to disclose such affiliations and, as with sexual orientation (i.e., when people wear pink triangles, hats or t-shirts that identify themselves as "out"), there are visible symbols and cues that identify people's religion, too. For instance, they may wear a cross, a Star of David, a Kippah, or a Hijab. In a study examining religious discrimination in employment settings, King and Ahmad (2010) examined applicant–manager interactions and coded formal and interpersonal discrimination against individuals either wearing (or not wearing) Muslim attire, using the procedures already described by Hebl et al. (2002). Additionally, King and Ahmad (2010) also examined how applicants who provided stereotype-consistent or -inconsistent information were treated by managers. The results revealed that applicants wearing a Hijab (versus those who did not) had more negative interactions involving interpersonal discrimination, particularly when they did not provide any stereotypic-inconsistent information to the managers. That is, applicants in the stereotypic inconsistent condition expressed warmth by describing their volunteer experience and were able to overcome the negativity associated with their stigmatized status. As we will discuss later, then, there are certainly ways in which stigmatized individuals may be able to compensate for the interpersonal discrimination they experience.

Obese Individuals

In a study examining the experiences of customer service that obese (versus nonobese) individuals received, King et al., (2006) also measured both formal discrimination (e.g., were customers greeted, offered assistance when requested) and interpersonal discrimination (e.g., interaction length, friendliness, eye contact). King et al. (2007) had women wearing obesity prostheses (or not) enter stores seeking help in finding items ostensibly for their sister's upcoming birthday. King et al. (2007) found, similar to Hebl et al. (2002), the presence of interpersonal discrimination and absence of formal discrimination. Specifically, store personnel displayed microinequities—they smiled less, they spoke fewer words, and they were more rude and less friendly with heavy (versus nonheavy) individuals. It is important to note that this behavior was identified by the confederates, corroborated by observers who witnessed the entire interaction, and further corroborated by independent coders who listened to audiotapes of the conversation and remained blind to the fact that there were different conditions.

This study was recently repeated to assess the experiences that heavy (and nonheavy) men have. Obesity researchers often overlook the experiences of men because the stigma of obesity seems to impact women so much more; however, Ruggs, Williams, and Hebl (2010) wanted to identify the experiences that heavy (and nonheavy) men have. The results showed a similar pattern to the earlier findings of King et al. (2007). Essentially, heavy men (relative to their thinner counterparts) experienced customer service marred by significant amounts of interpersonal (but not formal) discrimination as well.

In an additional study, Shapiro, King, and Quinones (2007) examined the quality of training that was given to obese versus nonobese individuals. Using a laboratory experiment, trainers were led to believe that they were training an obese or an average-weight (manipulated through a picture) trainee in a computer task. The trainers noted their expectations of the training interaction and the trainee before they conducted the training. In reality, those that were being trained were naïve participants who simply believed they were being trained at a task and had no knowledge of the weight manipulation. The results demonstrated that trainers in the obese condition had lower expectations from the trainee and evaluated the trainee more negatively than trainers in the average-weight condition. Additional results suggested that the obese individuals actually were trained more poorly and performed worse. Although the particular microbehaviors were not measured, it is very likely that the self-fulfilling prophecy lead trainers to actually train heavy (versus nonheavy) individuals differently via interpersonal behaviors. That is, the insidious effects of low expectations were likely born out in the verbal and nonverbal exchanges that trainer and trainees had, thereby resulting in lower performances on the part of heavy trainees.

Pregnant (and Nonpregnant) Women

The manifestation of interpersonal discrimination may depend on situation variables. For example, the discriminatory interpersonal behavior toward pregnant women seems to depend on whether they are depicted in nontraditional (job applicant) or traditional (store customer) roles (Hebl et al., 2007). Using experimental methods, female confederates wore either a pregnancy prosthesis or did not, and entered retail stores posing as job applicants or customers. Consistent with the findings from Hebl et al. (2002), the results did not show evidence of formal discrimination for applicants (i.e., permission to complete applications, number of job callbacks) or customers (i.e., being greeted, having merchandise recommended when requested). The results did show interpersonal discrimination, which depended on the role of the "pregnant" woman. When the confederate was in the role of a pregnant job applicant, employees exhibited more hostile interpersonal behavior, which was measured by less smiling, less eye contact, and higher rates of unfriendliness, hostility, and rudeness. When the confederate was in the role of a pregnant store customer, however, store employees exhibited more benevolent behavior (e.g., touching, overfriendliness, diminutive name calling) toward the "pregnant" than toward the nonpregnant confederates. Such research suggests that individuals may be using interpersonal discrimination to both socially exclude individuals from societal roles that are deemed to be incongruent with stereotypes (i.e., "pregnant women should not be working"), and also reinforce individuals into paths that are congruent with social stereotypes (i.e., "pregnant women can shop"). Such a pattern of interpersonal behaviors is further in line with ambivalent sexism research (Glick & Fiske, 1996).

Feeling excluded may also result when verbal, overt behaviors are at odds with more nonverbal, behavioral expressions. For example, in a study of gender and leadership, Butler and Geis (1990) trained male and female confederates to become leaders in leaderless mixed-sex groups. The confederates used the same scripts and were trained to make the same suggestions, wording, and tactics in trying to get their respective groups to follow them. When asked, members of the groups verbally expressed that they had nothing against female leadership. Their nonverbal behaviors, however, did not match their verbal expressions. The results showed that female leaders received more nonverbal disapproval (i.e., negative facial expressions) from both male and female group members than did their male counterparts. Similarly, male leaders received more positive nonverbal expressions (i.e., smiles, nods) than did the female (versus male) leaders. Such results show that individuals may explicitly claim to be accepting of female leaders, but their nonverbal behaviors tell a different story.

Physically Disabled and Facially Scarred Individuals

The same disparities witnessed in verbal and nonverbal displays toward female leaders have also been documented in a series of class studies conducted on physically disabled individuals. Specifically, Kleck and colleagues (Kleck, 1968; Kleck, Ono, & Hastorf, 1966) had nonstigmatized individuals act the part of interviewers engaging in an interaction with disabled (or not disabled) applicants. The interviewers were explicitly positive toward the disabled applicants—they distorted their own personal opinions in a direction consistent with those thought to be held by the disabled applicants and they also reported enhanced positive impressions of the physically disabled applicants relative to the able-bodied applicants. Yet, the nonverbal behaviors of the interviewers revealed interpersonal discrimination—interviewers were more physiologically aroused during the interaction, took a longer time deciding what interview questions to ask, terminated the interview sooner, showed more behavioral inhibitions, and maintained greater interaction distance with the disabled than the nondisabled applicants.

To examine the effect of interpersonal discrimination on other workplace-related outcomes, Madera and Hebl (2012) examined how interviewers' memories and ratings of applicants were influenced by the presence (or absence) of a facial disfigurement (e.g., a port-wine stain birthmark or severe scar on the face). The more interviewers stared at an applicants' facial stigma, the more they tended to be distracted and recall less information pertaining to what the interviewee said during the interview. The participants' impaired memory was also negatively correlated with their ratings of the interviewee.

Blacks

As with other stigmatized individuals, research suggests a mismatch in the verbal and nonverbal displays that white individuals show toward black individuals. That is, Dovidio et al. (2002) found that whites who reported less explicit prejudice were more positive in their conscious and controllable interpersonal behavior (i.e., verbal friendliness) during their interactions with black (compared with white) partners. However, whites' implicit racial attitudes (not their self-reported prejudice) predicted bias in their less controllable and monitored nonverbal behaviors. Thus, whites' verbal and nonverbal responses were typically mismatched in their interactions with black partners.

Interpersonal discrimination directed toward black individuals also has been shown to negatively impact their performance. In a seminal study, Word, Zanna, and Cooper (1974) illustrated the impact that subtle differences in nonverbal behavior had on applicants by examining a context in which white interviewers interviewed black or white applicants. Their first experiment revealed that white interviewers displayed more interpersonal discrimination toward black than white applicants (i.e., spaced themselves farther apart, made more speech errors, and terminated interviews more quickly). In a second experiment, participants were subjected to the same behaviors that were directed toward black applicants from the first experiment. The results showed that the subjects playing the role of an applicant were more nervous during the interview and ultimately performed worse than those who were not subjected to the negative interpersonal behaviors.

It is important to note that nonstigmatized versus stigmatized individuals pay very different amounts of attention to interpersonal behaviors (Vorauer & Kumhyr, 2001). That is, when asked to assess social interaction outcomes, nonstigmatized interactants focus on the verbal behaviors that they display to their stigmatized interactants. As such, nonstigmatized individuals may perceive that their interaction was positive and no social exclusion occurred because they verbally articulated (and were consciously aware of expressing) positivity. However, the stigmatized interactants tend to focus on the nonverbal (as compared with the verbal) behaviors displayed by their interactants. They many not trust what is said and hence, focus more attention on nonverbal behaviors for signs about how the interactant authentically feels. Because nonverbal behaviors may be much less likely to be volitionally controlled, stigmatized individuals may rely on these cues to assess how truly included (or socially excluded) they are in social interaction with others (Vorauer & Kumhyr, 2001).

Social Exclusion and Workplace-Related Consequences of Interpersonal Discrimination

Although some of the consequences of interpersonal discrimination are already inherent in the descriptions of the previous studies, we articulate these consequences again briefly in this section to highlight the negative impact that such microinequities can have in so many different and important spheres of peoples' lives.

Social Exclusion

Interpersonal discrimination is inextricably linked to social exclusion. By nature of the fact that interpersonal discrimination involves social exclusion itself, the two constructs may not be entirely orthogonal. Yet, a few studies have specifically shown how interpersonal discrimination can directly result in greater amounts of social exclusion. For instance, in a very well-known study on the self-fulfilling prophecy, Snyder, Tanke, and Berscheid (1977) gave male participants a packet of information about a woman and a photograph in which she was depicted as either attractive or unattractive. Men then interviewed the woman over the phone and the results showed that men who thought they were talking to an attractive woman responded to her in a warmer, more sociable manner than did the men who thought they were talking to an unattractive woman. Furthermore, the women who were believed to be attractive actually were rated as being warmer and more sociable too. Thus, the men who discriminated interpersonally against the ostensibly unattractive women behaved in such a way as to make them actually perform worse socially.

A number of the studies that we reviewed in the previous section also revealed that nonstigmatized individuals prematurely terminated interactions, spent less time with, and spoke fewer words to stigmatized (than nonstigmatized) individuals (e.g., Hebl et al., 2002; King et al., 2007). Add to this the fact that Hebl et al. (2007) found evidence that individuals may use interpersonal discrimination to directly reinforce societal behaviors that are acceptable and punish those that are unacceptable; it seems very likely that individuals also use interpersonal discrimination to specifically exclude others from all sorts of interaction outcomes.

Decreased Workplace-Related Performance

Interpersonal discrimination also has been directly and empirically linked to decreased performance in a workplace setting. In fact, research by Singletary and Hebl (2010) found that interpersonal discrimination (and not formal discrimination) significantly reduced individuals performance on job-related tasks. This was particularly noted with women who participated in a study on "job-related tasks," in which an experimenter induced interpersonal and/or formal discrimination (or no discrimination) and then had the women perform in-basket and attentional resource tasks. The women who experienced interpersonal discrimination (i.e., less eye contact, less friendliness, less smiling) performed significantly worse on the two tasks than the women who did not receive discrimination *and* when only formal discrimination occurred (i.e., hearing a man say, "I don't like the thought of having a female boss" and "We aren't going to hire a woman"). This evidence suggests that interpersonal discrimination actually has a significantly more negative impact on job-related performance than does formal discrimination.

Also showing performance decrements associated with interpersonal discrimination, Word, Zanna, and Cooper (1974) found that applicants who experienced interpersonal discrimination (versus those who did not) performed worse in job interviews. Similarly, Shapiro et al. (2007) found that in one-on-one training sessions, trainers interacted with their trainees substantially differently and less effectively if they were heavy versus thinner. Although the specific interpersonal behaviors that led to different outcomes were not measured, the effects were clearly due to such behavioral differences. Such behaviors may have included differences in negative affect, paraverbal behaviors, and word choices that either encouraged or discouraged the trainees, as demonstrated by Singletary and Hebl (2010).

Workplace Advancement

Another consequence of interpersonal discrimination is the exclusion of stigmatized individuals from advancement in the workplace. For example, in a study of developmental experiences that lead to workplace advancement in a 5-year period, men and women received the same amount of experiences, but they were qualitatively different (King et al., in press). Men received more challenging experiences than did women across this and two other samples, despite the fact that men and women were equally likely to express interest in challenging experiences. Moreover, women were less likely to receive negative feedback than were men, which may restrict growth and be attributable to benevolent sexism (see Glick & Fiske, 1996).

Patronage

In a study examining the interpersonal discrimination that authentically heavy (versus not-heavy)

shoppers received in retail stores, King et al. (2006) found that heavy individuals experienced more interpersonal discrimination. Additionally, the experience of interpersonal discrimination was negatively related to customer loyalty, purchasing behavior, and intentions to return to the store in the future. Such results suggest that interpersonal discrimination can have a substantial impact on excluding people from consumer patronage, a finding that has important implications not only for stigmatized individuals but also for organizations as a whole that should be servicing all clientele.

Strategies to Reduce Interpersonal Discrimination

Given that interpersonal discrimination is a common and consistent experience for stigmatized individuals, and that it is clearly associated with social exclusion and other negative outcomes, remediation becomes an important goal. A number of studies have examined remediation strategies particularly associated with reducing interpersonal discrimination and we describe some of these. We do not review an exhaustive list of such strategies; rather we describe the potential utility of several strategies that have been the focus of recent empirical attention. Before discussing these, we also note that the utility and success of each strategy likely depends on a number of factors, such as the individual engaging in them and the situation in which the individual finds her- or himself. Thus, one particular strategy might not work for everyone and should be enacted only after careful consideration of the potential personal and professional consequences—both positive and negative—that might result from each.

Reducing Justifications for Expression

Crandall and Eshleman (2003) proposed the Justification-Suppression Model of Prejudice (JSM) in which they suggested that people seek information that justifies the expression of their prejudices. However, people may be *less* likely to express prejudices when the justifications for expressing prejudices have been reduced, and this may happen when individuals are presented with information that runs contrary to their stereotypes. For instance, in a study that we mentioned earlier, King and Ahmad (2010) found that Muslim job applicants were less likely to have received interpersonal discrimination if they made statements that were counterstereotypical (i.e., they presented themselves as warm by stating that they volunteered). Thus, managers may have wanted to express prejudice (and display interpersonal discrimination) but when they discovered that the applicants were warm people, their justifications were reduced.

This strategy was also shown to be effective in work by King et al. (2007). In the study examining the customer service that obese female shoppers experienced, two additional studies (other than the one already discussed earlier) were conducted to try to remediate the interpersonal discrimination that heavy (but not less heavy) individuals experience. Specifically, in one study, King et al. (2007) tried to reduce expressions of prejudice by targeting the stereotype that individuals have of heavy people being sloppy, unkempt, and unprofessional (e.g., Hebl & Heatherton, 1997). In this study, confederates wore the obesity prosthesis (or not) and wore very professional clothes (i.e., a suit) or very casual clothes (i.e., a sweatshirt/pants). The results revealed that wearing professional clothes negated the interpersonal discrimination displayed toward heavy individuals, consistent with the JSM (Crandall & Eshleman, 2003). In one additional follow-up experiment, King et al. (2007) also tried to remediate the interpersonal discrimination by focusing on the stereotype that individuals have of heavy people overeating, being lazy, and not exercising (e.g., Hebl & Xu, 2001). In particular, confederates wore the obesity prosthesis (or not) and either (a) carried a Diet Coke into the store and mentioned that they were training to walk a half-marathon, or (b) carried a Dairy Queen Blizzard into the store and mentioned that their friend was training a half-marathon but that they could personally never imagine doing this. Again, the results showed that making the earlier statement negated the display of interpersonal discrimination, consistent with the notion that reducing justifications for displaying prejudice (Crandall & Eshleman, 2003) can be an effective strategy to combat interpersonal discrimination.

Compensation Strategies: Acknowledgment, Increased Positivity, and Individuation.

In a study specifically intended to examine several strategies designed to potentially reduce interpersonal discrimination, Singletary and Hebl (2009) examined three specific strategies that outwardly gay and lesbian job applicants might engage in during social interactions. The first strategy involved acknowledgment, or directly referring to one's stigma during an interaction in an attempt to move beyond otherwise distracting stigmatizing characteristics that impede social interactions (Hebl & Kleck, 2002; Hebl & Skorinko, 2005). The second strategy involved an

increase in the display of positivity, which included increases in smiling and being very friendly (Miller, Rothblum, Felicio, & Brand, 1995). The third strategy involved providing individuating information that distinguishes oneself apart from a stereotype or stigmatized group (Fiske & Neuberg, 1990).

Using the methodology previously outlined in Hebl et al. (2002), the results showed that adopting any of the three strategies at least partially resulted in a reduction of interpersonal discrimination relative to adopting no strategy. That is, those wearing "Gay and Proud" hats who also enacted any of the three strategies showed at least some reduction in the interpersonal discrimination they received relative to the individual wearing the "Gay and Proud" hat who did not enact any strategies (the control condition). In additional research conducted by Shelton, Richeson, and Salvatore (2005), they similarly found that the behaviors of stigmatized individuals (in this case, blacks) may strategically change into compensatory strategies when they anticipate bias. In particular, blacks who were primed with whites' prejudice, compared with those who were not, compensated for anticipated stigmatization by behaving in a more verbally and nonverbally engaged manner during these interactions. White interactants' liking for the black partner and enjoyment of the interaction were directly related to the level of black engagement overall. As consequence, blacks expectations of bias from whites in this study led to more negative experiences for blacks but, ironically, more positive experiences for whites.

There may be important issues to consider when choosing to enact compensation strategies (i.e., what exactly to say, how to say it, when to say it, how it impacts self versus others), but it is clear from the Singletary and Hebl (2009) study that these strategies certainly have the potential to be successful in reducing interpersonal discrimination in at least some conditions.

Group Identification

Group identification can also influence the displays of interpersonal discrimination in social interactions (Barron, King, & Hebl, 2010). In a field experiment, authentically black, Hispanic, and Irish individuals applied for retail jobs with or without visible display of their ethnic identification on hats as used in Hebl et al. (2002). That is, in some cases applicants simply wore a blank hat. In other cases, however, applicants wore a hat that said "[Their Race] Student Association" or "[Their Race] and Proud." The results showed that store personnel interacting with other-race applicants exhibited less interpersonal discrimination (e.g., interaction length, nonverbal negativity) when applicants displayed ethnic identification (either set of words written on the hat) than when they simply wore a plain hat. Thus, group identity serves as a boundary condition, at least in some cases, for the display of interpersonal discrimination toward stigmatized individuals. We believe that group identification may have primed people to act favorably and in an egalitarian manner.

Scripted Roles

Another social context that can influence the amount of interpersonal discrimination displayed is the presence of scripted social roles (Avery, Richeson, Hebl, & Ambady, 2009). In two studies, Avery et al. (2009) examined white participants' anxiety during dyadic interactions with black partners and found that white participants exhibited greater discomfort in black–white interactions than in same-race interactions unless their interaction role offered an accessible script to guide behavior. That is, providing a script for black-white interactions (i.e., assigning participants as interviewers or applicants) reduced the anxiety displayed by white partners. Interracial interactions can be threatening for white individuals because of fears of saying inappropriate comments or the uncertainty of the situation, and therefore, providing a script, at least in some cases, may ease this preoccupation.

Conclusions

In sum, interpersonal discrimination is alive and well, and leads to social exclusion of and other negative outcomes for stigmatized individuals. On the face of it, interpersonal discrimination may seem benign and inconsequential but to the contrary, research shows that these microinequities can lead to large amounts of disparate treatment for stigmatized individuals (Valian, 1998). Furthermore, interpersonal discrimination has been shown, in some situations (e.g., Singletary & Hebl, 2010), to be even more pernicious than the more overt, formal types of discrimination. What makes interpersonal discrimination more complex than formal discrimination is that the motivation for and causes of interpersonal discrimination are often not due to conscious, malicious intentions, but rather due to unconscious mechanisms (Dovidio et al., 1997; Dovidio et al., 2002; Greenwald & Banaji, 1995; Hebl & Dovidio, 2005). Additionally, there is no legal protection for those who face interpersonal discrimination. As such, the importance of identifying and understanding the strategies that individuals can use to reduce interpersonal discrimination becomes critically important. We hope future research will continue to focus on better understanding the display, consequences, and remediation of interpersonal discrimination.

Note

Correspondence concerning this chapter should be addressed to Michelle Hebl at Rice University, Department of Psychology, 6100 Main Street—MS 205, Houston, TX, 77005, or hebl@rice.edu.

References

Allon, N. (1982). The stigma of overweight in everyday life. In B. B. Wolfman, & S. DeBerry (Eds.), *Psychological Aspects of Obesity: A Handbook* (pp. 130–174). New York: Van Nostrand Reinhold.

Avery, D. R., Richeson, J. A., Hebl, M. R., & Ambady, N. (2009). It does not have to be uncomfortable: The role of behavioral scripts in black-white interracial interactions. *Journal of Applied Psychology, 94*, 1382–1393.

Barron, L. G., King, E. B., & Hebl, M. (2010). Manifesting one's ethnic identification: Liability in the lab but strategy in the field? Paper presented at the annual conference of the Society of Personality and Social Psychology in Las Vegas, NV.

Butler, D., & Geis, F. L. (1990). Nonverbal affect responses to male and female leaders: Implications for leadership evaluations. *Journal of Personality and Social Psychology, 58*, 48–59.

Bertrand, M., & Mullainathan, S. (2004). Are Emily and Greg more employable than Lakisha and Jamal? A field experiment on labor market discrimination. *American Economic Review, 94*, 991–1013.

Crandall, C. S., & Eshleman, A. (2003). A justification-suppression of expression and the appearance of prejudice. *Psychological Bulletin, 129*, 414–446.

Dovidio, J. F., Glick, P. G., & Rudman, L. (Eds.). (2005). *On the Nature of Prejudice: Fifty Years after Allport*. Malden, MA: Blackwell.

Dovidio, J. F., Kawakami, K., & Gaertner, S. L. (2002). Implicit and explicit prejudice and interracial interaction. *Journal of Personality and Social Psychology, 82*, 62–68.

Dovidio, J. F., Kawakami, K., Johnson, C., Johnson, B., & Howard, A. (1997). On the nature of prejudice: Automatic and controlled processes. *Journal of Experimental Social Psychology, 33*, 510–540.

Fiske, S. T., & Neuberg, S. L. (1990). A continuum of impression formation, from category–based to individuating processes: Influences of information and motivation on attention and interpretation. In M. P. Zanna (Ed.), *Advances in experimental social psychology* (Vol. 23, pp. 1–74). San Diego, CA: Academic Press.

Glick, P., & Fiske, S. T, (1996). The Ambivalent Sexism Inventory: Differentiating hostile and benevolent sexism. *Journal of Personality and Social Psychology, 70*, 491–512.

Greenwald, A. G., & Banaji, M. R. (1995). Implicit social cognition: Attitudes, self-esteem, and stereotypes. *Psychological Review, 102*, 4–27.

Hebl, M., & Heatherton, T. F. (1997). The stigma of obesity in women: The difference is Black and White. *Personality and Social Psychology Bulletin, 24*, 417–426.

Hebl, M., & Kleck, R. (2002). Acknowledging one's stigma in the interview setting: Strategy or liability? *Journal of Applied Social Psychology, 32*, 223–249.

Hebl, M., Madera, J., & King, E. B. (2007). Exclusion, avoidance, and social distancing. In K. M. Thomas (Ed.), *Diversity Resistance: Manifestation and Solutions* (pp. 127–150). NJ: Lawrence Erlbaum Associates.

Hebl, M., & Skorinko, J. L. (2005). Acknowledging one's physical disability in the interview: Does when make a difference. *Journal of Applied Social Psychology, 35*, 1–17.

Hebl, M., & Xu, J. (2001). Weighing the care: Physicians' reactions to the size of a patient. *International Journal of Obesity, 25*, 1246–1252.

Hebl, M. R., & Dovidio, J. F. (2005). Promoting the "social" in the examination of social stigmas. *Personality and Social Psychology Review, 9*, 156–182.

Hebl, M. R., Foster, J. B., Mannix, L. M., & Dovidio, J. F. (2002). Formal and interpersonal discrimination: A field study of bias toward homosexual applicants. *Personality and Social Psychology Bulletin, 28*, 815–825.

Hebl, M. R., King, E. B., Glick, P., Singletary, S., & Kazama, S. (2007). Hostile and benevolent behaviors toward pregnant women: Complementary interpersonal punishments and rewards that maintain traditional roles. *Journal of Applied Psychology, 92*, 1499–1511.

Jones, E. E., Farina, A., Hastrof, A. H., Marcus, H., Miller, D. T., & Scott, R. A. (1984). *Social Stigma: The Psychology of Marked Relationships*. NY: Freeman and Compaany.

King, E. B., & Ahmad, A. (2010). An experimental field study of interpersonal discrimination toward Muslim job applicants. *Personnel Psychology, 63*, 881–906.

King, E. B., Botsford, W., Kazama, S., Hebl, M., Dawson, J., & Perkins, A. (in press). Benevolent sexism at work: Gender differences in the distribution of challenging workplace experiences. *Journal of Management.*

King, E. B., Shapiro, J. L., Hebl, M., Singletary, S., & Turner, S. (2006). The stigma of obesity in customer service: A mechanism for remediation and bottom-line consequences of interpersonal discrimination. *Journal of Applied Psychology, 91*, 579–593.

Kleck, R. E. (1968). Physical stigma and nonverbal cues emitted in face-to-face interaction. *Human Relations, 21*, 19–28.

Kleck, R. E., Ono, H., & Hastorf, A. H. (1966). The effects of physical deviance upon face-to-face interaction. *Human Relations, 4*, 425–436.

Lazin, M. (2007). Record 94% of Fortune 500 companies provide sexual orientation discrimination protection. Equalityforum.com

Madera, J. M., & Hebl, M. R. (2012). Discrimination against facially stigmatized applicants in interviews: An eye tracking and face-to-face investigation. *Journal of Applied Psychology, 97*(2), 317–330.

Miller, C. T., Rothblum, E. D., Felicio, D., & Brand, P. (1995). Compensating for stigma: Obese and nonobese women's reactions to being visible. *Personality and Social Psychology Bulletin, 21*, 1093–1106.

Richeson, J. A., Trawalter, S., & Shelton, J. N. (2005). African Americans' implicit racial attitudes and the depletion of executive function after interracial interactions. *Social Cognition, 23*, 336–352.

Ruggs, E., Williams, A., & Hebl, M. (2010). The customer service experiences of obese men. Unpublished manuscript. Rice University, Houston TX.

Shapiro, J., King, E. B., & Quinones, M. (2007). Expectations of obese trainees: How stigmatized trainee characteristics influence training effectiveness. *Journal of Applied Psychology, 92*, 239–249.

Shelton, J. N., & Richeson, J. A. (2005). Intergroup contact and pluralistic ignorance. *Journal of Personality and Social Psychology, 88*, 91–107.

Singletary, S. L., & Hebl, M. R. (2009). Compensatory strategies for reducing interpersonal discrimination: The effectiveness of acknowledgments, increased positivity, and individuating information. *Journal of Applied Psychology, 94*, 797–805

Singletary, S. L., & Hebl, M. R. (2010). The impact of formal and interpersonal discrimination on performance. (Unpublished doctoral dissertation).. Rice University, Houston, TX.

Snyder, M., Tanke, E. D., & Berscheid, E. (1977). Social perception and interpersonal behavior: On the self-fulfilling nature of social stereotypes. *Journal of Personality and Social Psychology, 35*, 656–666.

Snyder, M. L., Kleck, R. E., Strenta, A., & Mentzer, S. J. (1979). Avoidance of the handicapped: An attributional ambiguity analysis. *Journal of Personality and Social Psychology, 12*, 2297–2306.

Turner, M. A., & Ross, S. L. (2003). *Discrimination in Metropolitan Housing Markets: National Results from Phase 2—Asians and Pacific Islanders.* Washington, DC: Department of Housing Urban Development.

Turner, M. A., & Ross, S. L. (2005). How racial discrimination affects the search for housing. In: Briggs X Souzade., editor. *The Geography of Opportunity: Race and Housing Choice in Metropolitan America* (pp. 81–100). Washington, DC: Brookings Inst. Press.

Valian, V. (1998). *Why So Slow? The Advancement of Women.* Cambridge, MA: MIT Press.

Vorauer, J. D., & Kumhyr, S. M. (2001). Is this about you or me? Self- versus other-directed judgments and feelings in response to intergroup interaction. *Personality and Social Psychology Bulletin, 27*, 706–719.

Word, C. O., Zanna, M. P., & Cooper, J. (1974). The nonverbal mediation of self-fulfilling prophecies in interracial interaction. *Journal of Experimental Social Psychology, 10*, 109–120.

Theory and Research on Social Exclusion in Work Groups

Kristin L. Scott *and* Stefan Thau

Abstract

We offer a theoretical model outlining the antecedents and consequences of work group exclusion. We theorize that individuals who threaten the work group's stability or existence are most likely to become the target of exclusion. We assume that, once excluded, employees will respond in a socially functional manner, such as by increasing helping or conforming behaviors, but only if they perceive there is an opportunity to reconnect with their group. If exclusion is more final, we believe this arouses an innate tendency to aggress against those who threaten the work group's stability or existence and excluded members will become socially dysfunctional, such as undermining or refusing to help others. We also suggest that once the group has mobilized efforts to exclude, reconnection efforts by members will be discounted and acceptance less attainable, because most group members are risk averse in their inclusion decisions.

Key Words: dysfunctional organizational behavior, social exclusion, work groups

Introduction

Employed adults spend a substantial amount of their waking hours at work interacting with group members to achieve organizational goals. Many employees derive a number of positive outcomes from *belonging* to a work group, including opportunities to enhance their self-worth (Crocker & Wolfe, 2001), receive social support (Beehr, Jex, Stacy, & Murray, 2000), and establish a shared worldview (Seashore, 1977). Because of the importance employees place on the outcomes they can extract from work groups, most workers are averse to the possibility of being excluded from them socially. There are many disjointed examples in the organizational behavior literature describing what we refer to as social exclusion in this chapter. Work group members risk being ignored (Salin, 2001), ostracized (Ferris, Brown, Berry, & Lian, 2008), avoided (Aquino, Tripp, & Bies, 2001), rejected (LePine & Van Dyne, 2001), and sometimes voted out from group membership (Sherer & Lee, 2002). These examples vary in how *final* the exclusion is (Derfler-Rozin, Pillutla, & Thau, 2010; Scott, Brass, Duffy, & Labianca, 2008), but they have in common that they diminish the target's sense of belongingness. Surprisingly, we currently know little about how work group members react to social exclusion, and even less about what motivates work groups to exclude their members. In this chapter, we present a theoretical model of the antecedents and consequences of social exclusion in work groups. We use this framework to review existing theory and research on exclusion and offer directions for future research on social exclusion in organization behavior.

A Model and Review of Social Exclusion in Work Groups

Our model is premised on the assumption that human beings possess a biologically driven desire to form lasting social bonds with other individuals (Baumeister & Leary, 1995). From an evolutionary perspective, the need to belong motivates individuals to seek stable, high-quality relationships within groups. Humans could not successfully survive and reproduce without group membership that provided many benefits such as access to resources and information, social support, and safety (Buss & Kenrick, 1998; Stevens & Fiske, 1995). Being excluded from group relationships was, in essence, a death sentence as it diminished the excluded individual's ability to adapt to and survive the many challenges posed by the environment (Brewer, 1997; Caporael, 1997).

Whereas the outcomes associated with present-day group affiliation are not quite as consequential, individuals still maintain a strong need to belong within groups to fulfill a variety of their social needs. Compared with other social groups, employed adults are likely to invest more effort in forming and maintaining stable, high-quality relationships with their work groups. One reason for this is that the amount of time employed adults spend at work limits their possible investments into alternative social groups. This may explain why many people stake their self-worth on the approval of their coworkers (Brockner, 1988; Pierce & Gardner, 2004). Work group members also rely on each other to accomplish joint tasks (Bowles, 1985; Lindenberg, 1997), which is why their members have an incentive to establish positive group relationships to be successful. Many people believe that success at work, in turn, is a central driver for their happiness (Buss, 2000) and they depend on work-related income to fulfill other social needs (e.g., status; Thierry, 2001).

The arguments we presented above suggest that a number of socially valued outcomes depend on the acceptance and inclusion by other group members. Consequently, our model of work group exclusion assumes that group members seek social acceptance and inclusion from coworkers because they need the group to secure these desired outcomes. This justifies why we assume that most people are averse to being excluded by work group members. However, we posit that it is the *finality* of exclusion that will influence their perceived ability to restore or gain inclusion and determine whether reactions to exclusion will be socially functional (i.e., prepare them to reconnect socially) or socially dysfunctional (i.e., prompt negative reactions that make social acceptance less likely) (Derfler-Rozin et al., 2010; Scott et. al., 2008).

The vast majority of studies investigating responses to social exclusion reveal behaviors that are dysfunctional to social reconnection. Most of this research has been conducted in experimental settings and not in interdependent groups with a history of interaction (like work groups). During these experiments, subjects experienced high levels of exclusion finality (e.g., were deliberately not selected to participate in a task or told they were going to end up alone) and exhibited high levels of aggression (e.g., Bourgeois & Leary, 2001; DeWall, Twenge, Gitter & Baumeister, 2009; Kirkpatrick, Waugh, Valencia, & Webster, 2002; Twenge, Baumeister, Tice, & Stucke, 2001), self-defeating behaviors (Twenge, Catanese & Baumeister, 2002), lowered performance on complex tasks (Baumeister, Twenge & Nuss, 2002) and impaired self-regulatory control (Baumeister, DeWall, Ciarocco, & Twenge, 2005).

One potential reason why much of past research on exclusion in social psychology found dysfunctional reactions to exclusion may be that these studies focused on individuals' reactions to exclusion with high levels of finality (Derfler-Rozin et al., 2010). In the few experimental studies where exclusion was less final (e.g., previously rejected individuals could be selected again for participation), the subjects displayed behaviors that were more likely to help them reconnect with the group, such as increasing their levels of conformity, effort, or behavioral mimicry (Lakin & Chartrand, 2005; Williams, Cheung & Choi, 2000; Williams & Sommer (women only), 1997). One study directly manipulated exclusion finality and showed that participants who risked being excluded (i.e., told that the group would probably not choose them as a member) trusted and reciprocated more compared to participants who were actually excluded (i.e., told that no one chose them as a group member) (Derfler-Rozin et al., 2010).

Based on these findings, our model proposes that whether exclusion is more, rather than less, final will predict the target's perceived ability to regain inclusion and influence their efforts to reconnect socially. Below, we further explicate our definition of finality and expound on our theoretical model that accounts for both socially functional and dysfunctional employee reactions to work group exclusion as well as the various antecedent conditions that may prompt workers to exclude other group members.

Exclusion Finality

Our model defines exclusion finality through variables reflecting duration and/or severity of exclusionary efforts by the work group. For example, when a work group member is avoided the first time after previously being included, then the exclusion is less final as compared to when the work group member is repeatedly avoided for a longer duration. Likewise, being avoided is less final than being voted out of group membership because the latter implies fewer, if any, chances to regain inclusion. We also posit that exclusion is perceived as more final when the group exerts exclusionary efforts through many, rather than few, of their members (but see Chernyak & Zayas, 2010, for an exception). That is, individuals may believe that an aspect of their self is less changeable when the social consensus on that aspect is high rather than low (Backman, Secord, & Pierce, 1963). Lastly, exclusionary efforts that are supported or even initiated by an organizational authority are also more final than those of fellow colleagues. We make this assumption because people typically see the behaviors of others who are in authority as more consequential and therefore less changeable compared with workers with no authority (e.g., Aquino, Tripp & Bies, 2001; Duffy, Ganster & Pagon, 2002).

Reactions to Work Group Exclusion
SOCIALLY FUNCTIONAL REACTIONS

As noted earlier, individuals are presumed to possess a biologically driven need to belong (Baumeister & Leary, 1995) and, we argue, that this need underlies a range of cognitive, emotional, and behavioral responses to varying degrees of exclusion. Whereas little research attention has been devoted to understanding reactions to less final exclusion, a handful of studies indicate that when individuals believe that opportunities for reinclusion exist, they are more likely to think and behave in ways that will prepare them to reconnect socially with others and, ultimately, satisfy belonging needs. For example, less final exclusion may be associated with a temporary, or moderate, loss of self-esteem (Leary, Tambor, Terdal, & Downs, 1995), possibly prompting individuals to think carefully about the reasons for their exclusion in the work group (Watson & Andrews, 2002) and subsequently motivate them to demonstrate their value to and willingness to reconnect with the group. Consistent with this idea, in experimental studies when subjects were offered the chance to gain acceptance by their peers they were more likely to display increased helping or conforming behaviors (e.g., Lakin & Chartrand, 2005; Williams et al., 2000; Williams & Sommer, 1997) as well as high levels of affective commitment to the group (Hogg, 2005). We thus contend that subjects experiencing less final exclusion are more likely to think and behave in a socially functional way to demonstrate their value to the group so as to gain belonging and acceptance.

SOCIALLY DYSFUNCTIONAL REACTIONS

Cognitive, emotional, and behavioral reactions to exclusion that either motivate or directly signal the target's unwillingness to benefit the group are defined here as socially dysfunctional, because these responses impose social burdens on the group (Allen & Badcock, 2003) and hinder one's ability to gain acceptance and inclusion. Whereas these outcomes may be dysfunctional in terms of establishing social reconnection within modern work groups, the evolutionary perspective in which belongingness theory is grounded offers some explanation for why these reactions are likely to be associated with final exclusion. One argument consistent with the evolutionary framework is that when belongingness needs are not being met and individuals realize they are being decisively shut out of social relationships, they may become aggressive in their thoughts and actions in hopes of eliminating the barrier to inclusion (Vaughn & Santos, 2007). Final exclusion arouses our innate tendency to behave aggressively towards those who threaten our social survival. Historically, if the "excluder(s)" could be eliminated or their behavior changed so that exclusion is no longer a problem then, possibly, inclusion or social acceptance (and therefore the ability to survive and prosper more successfully) was more likely to be restored.

Thus, the survival threat of exclusion suggests that final exclusion is likely to prompt aggressive, yet by today's standards, socially dysfunctional (e.g., distressed, hostile, unfriendly) reactions. Compared with less final exclusion, final exclusion may also be accompanied with drastic loss in self-esteem and/or an increase in sadness, which may lead the target to endlessly ruminate about the causes and consequences of exclusion without any constructive attempts to fix their inclusionary status in the work group (c.f. Nettle, 2004). Related research corroborates this argument by demonstrating that more severely excluded individuals exhibit less intelligent thought (Baumeister, Twenge, & Nuss, 2002) and have difficulty concentrating and self-regulating thoughts and behaviors (Baumeister et al., 2005).

EXCLUSION IN WORK GROUPS

Replicating the laboratory findings in organizational field studies is not a trivial task because—compared with the laboratory—organizations constrain their members in ways that provide incentives for excluded individuals to regulate their emotional, cognitive, and behavioral reactions to exclusion. For example, most work group members have some common expectations about future interaction. Work group members may also be concerned about their organizational reputation because they are embedded into a larger organizational network in which information travels and is consequential. Typically, these constraints provide employees with incentives to cooperate (Buskens, Raub & Snijders, 2003, for a review), and so we may not observe the same kind (or less) of dysfunctional exclusion reactions in the organizational field as in the laboratory.

Yet, a handful of studies suggest that workplace exclusion is an aversive experience with similarly dysfunctional consequences as shown in laboratory studies. For example, excluded workers report low levels of organizational commitment (Hitlan, Kelly, Schepman, Schneider & Zárate, 2006), coworker satisfaction and well-being (Hitlan, Cliffton & DeSoto, 2006), and self-esteem (Penhaligon, Louis, & Restubog, 2009). Moreover, work group members who experienced a deficit in coworker belongingness were more likely to engage in interpersonally harmful behaviors (e.g., slander, verbal abuse) and less likely to help others than their colleagues who did not feel any deficit in belongingness (Thau, Aquino, & Poortvliet, 2007). A recent study by O'Reilly and Robinson (2009) is also consistent with these findings and showed that being excluded by others at work diminished the target employee's sense of belonging, which was associated with lowered performance and work withdrawal.

Although the studies we review above suggest reactions that we would refer to as dysfunctional to reestablishing social relationships (lowered commitment, lowered performance, lowered helping, increased harming), these studies do not explicitly distinguish between exclusion that is more rather than less final. Further, some of the findings (increased withdrawal, lowered self-esteem, lowered well-being) cannot be readily interpreted as dysfunctional reactions. For example, withdrawal can signal the victim's willingness not to further burden the work group through negative contributions (Allen & Badcock, 2003) and lowered self-esteem could, in moderate levels, function to prompt the victim to find a solution to the problem of exclusion risk. Indeed, some research suggests that exclusion and other forms of rejection or loss are literally painful and trigger the same parts of the brain that respond to physical injury or danger (e.g., MacDonald &

Leary, 2005). Thus, being excluded by others is likely to be perceived as a threat to one's social safety that is not only detrimental to one's feelings of self-worth but also can subsume the target's cognitive attention and invoke responses that, under the right circumstances, may help the individual overcome his or her pain to being excluded.

That being said, the ambiguities associated with past findings of workplace exclusion have recently prompted researchers to theorize and investigate more complex models of reactions to exclusion in the workplace. For example, Scott and her colleagues (2008) argued that excluded employees' prosocial (preparing for social reconnection) and antisocial (dysfunctional to social reconnection) responses are curvilinear and will vary across different levels of coworker and supervisor exclusion severity (i.e., finality). Specifically, being moderately excluded by coworkers was positively related to prosocial responses (i.e., extra role or helping) and negatively related to social undermining behaviors. However, these relationships were reversed when employees reported being severely excluded by their coworkers. These findings provide support for the model we present in this paper such that when employees believe that exclusion is not final, they are likely to attempt to reconnect. However, reconnection behavior wanes at severe levels of exclusion where exclusion is final. Instead, severely excluded employees are likely to adopt more aggressive behavior (i.e., undermining).

Another study also supports the exclusion finality prediction of our model. Grosser, Sterling, Scott, and Labianca (2010) used social network analyses to evaluate employee prosocial and antisocial behavioral responses to both perceived and what they refer to as "actual workplace exclusion." Actual workplace exclusion means that coworkers identify the focal worker as being excluded from informal networks. In their study, Grosser et al., (2010) predicted and confirmed that employees who perceive themselves as excluded, and who are socially identified as actually being excluded from informal networks were rated by their supervisor as being more deviant (e.g., sabotaging others' work) and less helpful than those for whom exclusion consensus was low. These results are consistent with our model because they further demonstrate that socially dysfunctional behaviors are a likely response to exclusion by consensus, which is more severe and less changeable, and therefore, more final.

We further suggest that exclusion by one's supervisor may be perceived as more final by excluded work group members given that they have the ability to enact disciplinary measures or terminate employment. Indeed, Scott et al.'s (2008) study found that employees exhibited fewer helping behaviors and displayed higher levels of undermining in response to supervisor exclusion as compared to coworker exclusion. Building on this work, Scott, Lee, and Duffy (2010) found that supervisor exclusion triggered increased levels of moral disengagement mechanisms (Bandura, 1991) and decreased levels of affective-cognitive self-regulatory mechanisms, which in turn affected a range of employee behavioral and health outcomes. Specifically, these investigators found that employees excluded by their supervisor morally disengaged, which in turn increased antisocial (i.e., undermining) behavior and reduced helping behavior. This indirect effect of exclusion on undermining through moral disengagement was strengthened when employees endorsed punishment norms (i.e., believed bad deeds should be punished). In addition, supervisor exclusion inhibited the excluded employees' ability to sustain their mental concentration and focus, which was associated with higher levels of depression and diminished well-being. Consistent with prior research (e.g., Costanza, Derlega, & Winstead, 1988), these authors also found that social support actually exacerbated this mediated relationship. Researchers speculate that discussing stressful situations with peers can intensify negative feelings and cause the focal employee to further ruminate about the stressor, which can worsen health-related outcomes (e.g., O'Reilly & Robinson, 2009). Although this study offers additional insight into the "black-box" that explains why individuals respond negatively to being excluded by a more powerful other, more work is needed to further understand when these mediated relationships hold and when they do not. For instance, individual difference variables such as highly anxious employees or those who are especially sensitive to rejection may perceive being excluded when in reality they are not.

In sum, studies of exclusion at work have begun to explore and subsequently reveal that worker reactions to exclusion can be socially functional or dysfunctional in terms of pursuing reconnection with others and are highly dependent on the degree of finality associated with the exclusion experience. Socially functional reactions that facilitate inclusion tend to occur when exclusion is less final and, therefore, excluded targets likely believe they have the ability to restore or gain inclusion. In contrast, socially dysfunctional reactions that are inherently more aggressive are likely to follow more final exclusion experiences where the target's ability to restore or regain inclusion is absent.

Antecedents of Social Exclusion

Whereas being excluded from a group impedes an employee's ability to thrive and prosper, we argue that for work groups to function successfully and attain important group outcomes depends on the members' ability to work *interdependently* via joint production. Consequently, groups also depend on their members in order to survive (Hirshleifer & Rasmusen, 1998; Levine, Moreland & Hausmann, 2005). This makes the decision to exclude a member a consequential one for work groups. What motivates groups to mobilize exclusion efforts? To our knowledge, there is virtually no research on the antecedents of social exclusion in work groups (see Scott, Restubog, & Zagenczyk, forthcoming for an exception).

We assume that group members make both negative and positive contributions to groups. Most groups are accountable for the solutions to the problems they face in joint production which, in turn, evolve into group norms (Bettenhausen & Murnighan, 1991; Coleman, 1990). Norms are shared expectations of what is and is not acceptable in terms of displayed emotions, attitudes, and behaviors within the group. Compliance with these norms can be thought of as collectively beneficial for joint production (Ullman-Margalit, 1977) because this helps the group to adapt to the environment and compete efficiently with other groups. Consequently, we define negative contributions as the group-specific emotions, attitudes, and behaviors that impede joint production. What exactly groups will define as negative contributions to joint production will vary somewhat from group to group, but a cursory review of the literature suggests that group members who display negative affect, free-ride, do not reciprocate help, choose to harm others, or are poor task performers put themselves at risk of exclusion because these are examples of emotions, attitudes, and behaviors that most groups consider as undesirable (c.f., Kurzban & Leary, 2001). Positive contributions, however, are defined as group-specific emotion displays, attitudes, and behaviors that comply or exceed expectations for what is supportive of joint production. Again, there will be variation from group to group in what they define as acceptable standards, but we assume that group members who display positive affect, offer valuable information or insight, reciprocate help, and are good task performers—among other things—are those who minimize their risk of exclusion.

When a member's negative contributions exceed their positive contributions, they hinder rather than help the work group's ability to adapt to the demands of their environment, and to compete efficiently with other groups (Allen & Badcock, 2003; Pillutla & Thau, 2009). Consequently, according to our model, we predict that group members will mobilize exclusionary efforts towards an individual when they believe that the target's net contributions to the group are negative and unsatisfactory. A study with two samples of coworker dyads found that workers who were rated as rude and discourteous (i.e., a social burden) by the focal employee were more likely to become targets of exclusion (as rated by the target employee) (Scott et al., 2011a). These researchers also found that the social burden-exclusion relationship was mediated by perceptions of distrust but this mediated effect was weakened when the excluders thought that the target was a positive social exchange partner (i.e., had much to offer in terms of social knowledge or capital in the workplace), These results are consistent with the idea that employees who pose a burden to the group elicit exclusionary efforts, but only if they fail to generate social value in other ways, like being a high quality exchange partner.

A secondary prediction we make is that the greater the net negative contribution of a member, the more final the exclusionary efforts from the group will be. For example, if a group member is perceived to constantly display negative affect and to underperform, the group's exclusionary efforts will be more final (e.g., by telling the member to leave) compared with when a member is perceived to sometimes display negative affect and to perform well (e.g., by avoiding the group member when in a bad mood).

However, there is a chance that work groups could falsely exclude members who are needed for joint production or continue to include members who are actually hurtful to the group. This makes both exclusion (and nonexclusion) a potentially costly and survival-impeding decision. A corollary, therefore, is that work groups take a risk-averse approach when making exclusion decisions in an attempt to manage costly errors. The risk-averse approach itself leads to a number of group biases in the context of exclusion. We assume that, like in other tasks in which individuals need to manage potentially costly errors (Haselton & Buss, 2000), groups will use criteria for their exclusion decision that are *overgeneralized*

and not necessarily externally valid (cf. Zebrowitz & Montepare, 2008). In doing so, group members are likely to err on the side of excluding a group member even if there is only a small chance that the target may be detrimental to group functioning. In a similar vein, we argue that once a group member has become the target of exclusion, it will be much harder for that person to gain acceptance because the group has identified them as a potential liability. Thus, one prediction we can derive from this assumption is that when workers exhibit certain qualities that hinder joint production (e.g., the display of negative affect) this will lead to exclusionary efforts even if only a few members recognize these qualities or when there are only minimal levels of that quality present.

Another prediction based on the assumption that groups are risk-averse in exclusion is that once the group enacts exclusionary efforts towards a member, even moderately negative contributions from the target will be perceived by group members as more negative once exclusionary efforts are enacted. Likewise, we predict that the group will discount positive contributions of group members who try to reconnect, or perceive them altogether as negative. This supposition leads to a number of predictions about the likelihood that groups will reciprocate reconnection efforts from group members. One is that the group member at risk of being excluded will need to make excessively generous contributions to be deemed worthy of reinclusion (Pillutla & Thau, 2009). In addition, the target should avoid minor mishaps because risk-averse group members are likely to interpret these as more serious negative contributions. These final two predictions bring our model full circle and illustrate how workers both respond to and decide to engage in exclusionary behaviors. We close this chapter with some concluding remarks about our work and discuss future research directions that follow from our model and review.

Conclusions

Despite the potential pervasiveness and range of serious consequences associated with organization-based social exclusion, very little research attention has been devoted to understanding this far-reaching phenomenon. Taking steps to address this gap, we offer a theoretical model that outlines predictions concerning the antecedents and consequences of social exclusion within a work group context. Specifically, we argue that the motives for excluding others as well as the reactions to being excluded are fundamentally driven by a biological need to be part of a socially successful group because such membership, historically, has enabled human beings to better adapt to and survive within their environment.

Therefore, we argue that individuals who threaten the work group's stability or existence are most likely to become the target of exclusion. Once excluded, we posit that employees will respond in a socially functional way—such as by increasing helping or conforming behaviors—if exclusion is perceived as less final and the opportunity to reconnect with group members exists. However, if exclusion is more severe we believe that this will arouse the worker's innate tendency to aggress against those who threaten their social status (i.e., belongingness) and they are likely to display behaviors that are considered, by today's standards, socially dysfunctional such as undermining or refusing to help others—all of which are likely to lead to further exclusion. Because negative contributors threaten groups' long term viability, team members' exclusion efforts will typically be risk-averse. Consequently, the criteria that groups use to exclude members will be overgeneralized such that negative contributions from members facing final exclusion will have more impact—and positive contributions will have less impact—compared with those who have not been excluded. The risk averse approach to group functioning also has implications for the extremity of reconnection efforts that members need to exhibit for the group to reciprocate.

Future Research Directions

Opportunities for future research in the area of workplace exclusion are fruitful. We already mentioned that there is clearly a need to undertake research that examines the antecedents of exclusion. Currently, we have little understanding of who is likely to become the target of exclusion as well as the reasons why groups choose to exclude others, particularly in an organizational setting. Our model offers a number of parsimonious starting points for these investigations that remain largely untested.

We suggest one particular stream of future research based on our observation that the major focus of prior exclusion research has been on a range of antisocial or retaliatory responses. Future research should move beyond these outcomes and investigate the effect of workplace exclusion on a more diverse range of attitudinal (e.g., commitment, satisfaction, intent to quit), health (e.g., job-related tension, burnout), and behavioral (e.g., absence, job seeking-behavior, turnover, harassment) outcomes.

While doing so, researchers should also take exclusion finality into account, as well as other mediating or moderating variables that may be related to the exclusion event and their influence on these various outcomes.

Also absent from workplace exclusion research is how group members can regulate their socially dysfunctional responses when exclusion is more rather than less final. Baumeister et. al.'s (2005) studies revealed that individuals were able to overcome their negative reaction to being excluded and put greater effort into behaving in socially acceptable ways when a performance-based reward was provided. In addition, DeWall, Twenge, Bushman, Im, & Williams (2010) showed that offering rejected participants a small amount of acceptance reduced aggressive reactions. Other work has shown that linking performance to possible future acceptance also eliminates deficits in self-regulation (DeWall, Baumeister & Vohs, 2008). These findings raise the possibility that organizational incentive or recognition programs that reward inclusiveness may deter employees from engaging in exclusionary behavior as well as minimize the antisocial or self-defeating reactions often displayed by individuals who are excluded. This is a promising area for future research that needs to be explored.

Finally, although there is little research on exclusion in work organizations, the phenomenon of exclusion poses a number of methodological challenges to the traditional cross-sectional survey methods of organizational behavior research. This research suffers from a number of issues, including self-report biases, limited conclusions regarding causality, one-study papers without sufficient replication, and many more. We encourage researchers to combine multiple methods of investigation (including laboratory studies to garner evidence on causal relationships), combinations of cross-sectional and longitudinal designs, and the collection of multisource data so that we may gain a more substantive understanding of the antecedents and consequences of social exclusion in the workplace.

References

Allen, N. B., & Badcock, P. B. T. (2003). The social risk hypothesis of depressed mood: evolutionary, psychosocial and neurobiological perspectives. *Psychological Bulletin, 129,* 887–913.

Aquino, K., Tripp, T. M., Bies, R. J. (2001). How employees respond to personal offense: The effects of blame attribution, victim status, and offender status on revenge and reconciliation in the workplace. *Journal of Applied Psychology, 86,* 52–59.

Backman, C. W., Secard, P. F., & Pierce, J. R. (1963). Resistance to change in the self-concept as a function of consensus among significant others. *Sociometry, 26*, 102–111.

Bandura, A. (1991). Social cognitive theory of moral thought and action. In W. M. Kurtines & J. L. Gerwitz, (Eds.), *Handbook of Moral Behavior and Development* (Vol. 1, pp. 45–103). Hillsdale, NJ: Erlbaum.

Baumeister, R. F., & Leary, M. R. (1995). The need to belong: Desire for interpersonal attachments as a fundamental human motivation. *Psychological Bulletin, 117*, 497–497.

Baumeister, R. F., Twenge, J., & Nuss, C. (2002). Effects of social exclusion on cognitive processes: Anticipated aloneness reduces intelligent thought. *Journal of Personality and Social Psychology, 83*, 817–827.

Baumeister, R. F, DeWall, C. N, Ciarocco, N., & Twenge, J. (2005). Social exclusion impairs self-regulation. *Journal of Personality and Social Psychology, 88*, 589–604.

Beehr, T. A., Jex, S. M., Stacy, B. A., & Murray, M. A. (2000). Work stressors and coworker support as predictors of individual strain and job performance. *Journal of Organizational Behavior, 21*, 391–405.

Bettenhausen, K. L., & Murnighan, J. K. (1991). The development of an intragroup norm and the effects of interpersonal and structural challenges. *Administrative Science Quarterly, 36*, 20–35.

Bourgeois, K. S., & Leary, M. R. (2001). Coping with rejection. Derogating those who choose us last. *Motivation and Emotion, 25*, 101–111.

Bowles, S. (1985). The production process in a competitive economy: Walrasian, Neo-Hobbesian, and Marxian models. *American Economic Review, 75*, 16–36.

Brewer, M. B. (1997). On the social origins of human nature. In McGarty, C., & Haslam, S. A. (Eds.), *The Message of Social Psychology: Perspectives on Mind in Society* (pp. 54–62). Cambridge, MA: Blackwell Publishers.

Brockner, J. (1988). *Self-Esteem at Work.* Lexington, MA: Lexington.

Buskens, V., Raub, W., & Snijders, C. (2003). Theoretical and empirical perspectives on the governance of relations in markets and organizations. In V. Buskens, W. Raub, & C. Snijders (Eds), *Research in the Sociology of Organizations* (Vol. 20, pp. 1–18). Oxford: Elsevier Science.

Buss, D. M. (2000). The evolution of happiness. *American Psychologist, 55*, 15–23.

Buss, D.M & Kenrick, D.T . (1998). Evoluationary social psychology. In Gilbert, D.T., Fiske, S.T. & Lindzey, G. (Eds.), *The Handbook of Social Psychology* (4th ed., pp. 982–1026). New York: Oxford University Press.

Caporael, L. R. (1997). The evolution of truly social cognition: The core configurations model. *Personality and Social Psychology Bulletin, 23*, 276–298.

Chernyak, N., & Zayas, V. (2010). Being excluded by one means being excluded by all: Perceiving exclusion from inclusive others during one-person social exclusion. *Journal of Experimental Social Psychology, 46*, 582–585.

Coleman, J. S. (1990). *Foundations of Social Theory.* Cambridge, MA: Harvard University Press.

Costanza, R. S., Derlega, V. J., & Winstead, B. A. (1988). Positive and negative forms of social support: Effects of conversational topics on coping with stress among same-sex friends. *Journal of Experimental Social Psychology, 24*, 182–193.

Crocker, J., & Wolfe, C. T. (2001). Contingencies of self-worth. *Psychological Review, 108*(3), 593–623.

Derfler-Rozin, R. Pillutla, M., & Thau, S. (2010). Social reconnection revisited: The effects of social exclusion risk on reciprocity, trust, and general risk-taking. *Organizational Behavior and Human Decision Processes, 112* (2), 140–150.

DeWall, C. N., Baumeister, R. F., & Vohs, K. D. (2008). Satiated with belongingness?: Effects of acceptance, rejection, and task framing on self-regulatory performance. *Journal of Personality and Social Psychology, 95*, 1367–1382.

DeWall, C. N., Twenge, J. M., Bushman, B. J., Im, C., & Williams, K. D. (2010). Acceptance by one differs from acceptance by none: Applying social impact theory to the rejection-aggression link. *Social Psychological and Personality Science, 1*, 168–174.

DeWall, C. N., Twenge, J. M., Gitter, S. A., & Baumeister, R. F. (2009). It's the thought that counts: The role of hostile cognition in shaping aggressive responses to social exclusion. *Journal of Personality and Social Psychology, 96*(1), 45–59.

Duffy, M., Ganster, D., & Pagon, M. (2002). Social undermining in the workplace. *The Academy of Management Journal, 45*, 331–351.

Ferris, D. L, Brown, D. J., Berry, J. W., & Lian, H. (2008). The development and validation of the Workplace Ostracism Scale. *Journal of Applied Psychology, 93*(6), 1348–1366.

Grosser, T., Sterling, C., Scott, K. L., & Labianca, G., (2010). A social network perspective on social exclusion. In Neider, L. L., & Chester A. Schriesheim, (Eds.), *Research in Management: The Dark Side Series* (Vol. 8, pp. 143–191). Charlotte, NC: Information Age Publishing.

Haselton M. G., & Buss, D. M. (2000). Error management theory: A new perspective on biases in cross-sex mind reading. *Journal of Personality and Social Psychology, 78*, 81–91.

Hirshleifer, D., & Rasmusen, E. (1989). Cooperation in a repeated prisoner's dilemma with ostracism. *Journal of Economic Behavior and Organization, 12*, 87–106.

Hitlan, R., Cliffton, R., & Desoto, C. (2006). Perceived exclusion in the workplace: The moderating effects of gender on work-related attitudes and psychological health. *North American Journal of Psychology, 8*, 217–236.

Hitlan, R., Kelly, K., Schepman, S., Schneider, K., & Zá rate, M. (2006). Language exclusion and the consequences of perceived ostracism in the workplace. *Group Dynamics: Theory, Research, and Practice, 10*, 56–70.

Hogg, M. A. (2005a). All animals are equal but some animals are more equal than others: Social identity and marginal membership. In K. D. Williams, J. P. Forgas, & W. von Hippel (Eds.), *The Social Outcast: Ostracism, Social Exclusion, Rejection and Bullying* (pp. 243–261). New York: Psychology Press.

Kirkpatrick, L., Waugh, C., & Valenica, A., & Webster, G. (2002). The functional domain specificity of self-esteem and the differential prediction of aggression. *Journal of Personality and Social Psychology, 82*, 756–767.

Kurzban R., & Leary, M. R. (2001). Evolutionary origins of stigmatization: The function of social exclusion. *Psychological Bulletin, 127*(2), 187–208.

Lakin, J. L., & Chartrand, T. L. (2005). Exclusion and nonconscious behavioral mimicry. In K. D. Williams, J. P. Forgas, & W. von Hippel (Eds.), *The Social Outcast: Ostracism, Social Exclusion, Rejection, and Bullying* (pp. 279–296). New York: Psychology Press.

Leary, M. R., Tambor, E. S., Terdal, S. K., & Downs, D. L. (1995). Self-esteem as an interpersonal monitor: The sociometer hypothesis. *Journal of Personality and Social Psychology, 68*, 519–530

LePine, J. A., & Van Dyne, L. (2001). Peer responses to low performers: An attributional model of helping in the context of work groups. *Academy of Management Review, 26*, 67–84.

Levine, J. M., Moreland, R. L., & Hasuman L. R. M. (2005). Managing group composition: Inclusive and exclusive role transitions. In D. Abrams, M. A. Hogg, & J. M. Margues (Eds.), *The social psycology of inclusion and exclusion* (pp. 137–160). New York: Psychology Press.

Lindenberg, S. (1997). Grounding groups in theory: Functional, cognitive, and structural interdependencies. *Advances in Group Processes, 14*, 281–331.

MacDonald, G., & Leary, M. R. (2005). Why does social exclusion hurt? The relationship between social pain and physical pain. *Psychological Bulletin, 131*, 202–223.

Nettle, D. (2004). Evolutionary origins of depression: A review and reformulation. *Journal of Affective Disorders, 81*, 91–102.

O' Reilly, J., Robinson, S. L. (2009). Ostracism at Work: The Impact of Ostracism on Belonging and Work Contributions. Proceedings of the *Best Paper Proceedings, Academy of Management Meeting*, Chicago, IL.

Penhaligon, N., Louis, W., & Restubog, S. (2009). Emotional anguish at work: The mediating role of perceived rejection on workgroup mistreatment and affective outcomes. *Journal of Occupational Health Psychology, 14*, 34–45.

Pierce, J. L., & Gardner, D. G. (2004). Self-esteem within the work and organizational context: A review of the organization-based self-esteem literature. *Journal of Management, 30*, 591–622.

Pillutla, M. M., & Thau, S. (2009). Actual and potential exclusion as determinants of individual's unethical behavior in groups. In D. De Cremer (Ed.), *Psychological Perspectives on Ethical Behavior and Decision-Making in Groups* (pp. 121–134). Charlotte, NC: IAP.

Salin, D. (2001). Prevalence and forms of bullying among business professionals: A comparison of two different strategies for measuring bullying. *European Journal of Work and Organizational Psychology, 10*(4), 425–441.

Scott, K. D., Brass, D. J., Duffy, M. K., & Labianca, G. (2008). *Interpersonal workplace exclusion: A social exchange-based model*. Presented at the Annual Meeting of the Academy of Management, Anaheim, CA.

Scott, K. L., Lee, K. Y., & Duffy, M. K. (2010). *An examination of the mediating roles of moral disengagement and self-regulation between supervisor exclusion and employee behavioral and health outcomes*. Presented at the Annual Meetings of the Academy of Management: Montreal, Canada.

Scott, K. L., Restubog, S. L. D., & Zagenczyk, T. J. (forthcoming). *exchange A social exchange model of the antecedents of workplace exclusion. Journal of Applied Psychology*.

Scott, K. L., Tams, S., Schippers, M., & Lee, K. Y. (2011). *Opening the blackbox: Exploring the link between workplace exclusion, perceptions of envy and worker helping behavior, health and turnover*. Presented at the Annual Meetings of the Academy of Management, San Antonio, TX.

Seashore, S. E. (1977). *Group Cohesiveness in the Industrial Work Group*. New York: Arno.

Sherer, P. D., & Lee, K. (2002). Institutional change in large law firms: A resource dependency and institutional perspective. *Academy of Management Journal, 45*, 102–121.

Stevens, L., & Fiske, S. (1995). Motivation and cognition in social life: A social survival perspective. *Social Cognition, 13*, 189–214.

Thau, S., Aquino, K., & Poortvliet, P. M. (2007). Self-defeating behaviors in organizations: The relationship between thwarted belonging and interpersonal work behaviors. *Journal of Applied Psychology, 92*, 840–847.

Thierry, H. (2001). The reflection theory on compensation. In M. Erez, U. Kleinbeck, & H. Thierry, H. (Eds.), *Work motivation in the context of a globalizing economy* (pp. 149–166). Hove, UK: Psychology Press.

Twenge, J. M., Baumeister, R. F., Tice, D., & Stucke, T. (2001). If you can't join them, beat them: Effects of social exclusion on aggressive behavior. *Journal of Personality and Social Psychology, 81*, 1058–1069.

Twenge, J. M., Catanese, K., & Baumeister, R. F. (2002). Social exclusion causes self-defeating behavior. *Journal of Personality and Social Psychology, 83*, 606–615.

Ullman-Margalit, E. (1977). *The Emergence of Norms*. Oxford: Clarendon Press.

Vaughn, B. E., & Santos, A. J. (2007). An evolutionary/ecological account of aggressive behavior and trait aggression in human children and adolescents. In P. H. Hawley, T. D. Little, & P. C. Rodkin (Eds.), *Aggression and Adaptation* (pp. 31–63). Mahwah, NJ: Lawrence Erlbaum Associates.

Watson, P. J., & Andrews, P. W. (2002). Toward a revised evolutionary adaptationist analysis of depression: The social navigation hypothesis. *Journal of Affective Disorders, 72*, 1–14.

Williams, K. D., Cheung, C. K. T., & Choi, W. (2000). Cyberostracism: Effects of being ignored over the Internet. *Journal of Personality and Social Psychology, 79*, 748–762.

Williams, K. D., & Sommer, K. (1997). Social ostracism by coworkers: Does rejection lead to loafing or compensation? *Personality and Social Psychology Bulletin, 23*, 693–706.

Zebrowitz, L. A., & Montepare, J. M. (2008). Social psychological face perception: Why appearances matters. *Social and Personality Psychology Compass, 2/3*, 1497–1517.

PART 4

Exclusion within the Family and Romantic Relations

The Dark Side of Divorce

David A. Sbarra *and* Ashley E. Mason

Abstract

This chapter reviews research linking marital separation and divorce to three important outcomes in adults: mental health problems, physical health outcomes, and relational violence, including risk for homicide at the hands of an ex-partner. Following marital separation and divorce, most adults experience transient distress that abates relatively quickly over time; however, for a small percentage of people, the end of marriage represents a life-altering negative experience. This chapter catalogs a range of adverse outcomes with a focus on the potential mechanisms linking marital status and mental and physical health. The outcomes in question are discussed in terms of an overarching model for why social separations have the potential to be a particularly distressing class of negative life events, as well as methodological research highlighting the need to distinguish between social selection and social causation when considering the putative effects of marital separation and divorce.

Key Words: biology, divorce, health, homicide, loss, marriage, mechanisms, mental health, physical health, separation, suicide, violence

The Dark Side of Divorce

From *The Washington Post*, Wednesday, May 5, 2010: "This is how police say the story ended: George Huguely kicked through Yeardley Love's bedroom door early Monday. They fought. He grabbed her and shook her, slamming her head repeatedly into the wall. He seized her computer, the one on which she'd read his angry e-mails. Then he left her lying face down on a pillow that would soon be soaked with her blood" (Yanda, de Vise, and Johnson, 2010).

The recent alleged murder of a University of Virginia student by her ex-boyfriend calls attention to some of the most extreme and pathological end-points that can follow a romantic breakup. Although homicide and suicide occur rarely, nonmarital break-ups, marital separations, and divorce are unquestionably painful events. It is arguable that periods of loneliness, estrangement, frustration, guilt, and

identity disruption characterize *almost all* separation experiences. At the same time, these experiences are not fixtures of postrelationship life. In the divorce outcome literature, systematic reviews and empirical studies generally yield two broad conclusions. First, when marriages dissolve, the majority of children and adults are resilient (showing minimal changes in functioning or psychological well-being during the transition) and recover well in time (showing a period of disrupted functioning followed by gradual and steady movement toward predivorce levels of well-being) (Amato, 2000; Amato, 2010; Emery, 1999; Hetherington, Bridges, & Insabella, 1998; Hetherington & Kelly, 2002). Second, a small percentage of people experience considerable suffering following the end of marriage (Lucas, 2005; Mancini, Bonanno, & Clark, 2011). Unfortunately, because divorce is relatively common, this small percentage translates to a large number of people for whom the end of a marriage constitutes a major stressor. The negative outcomes in question span a number of different domains, including changes in financial security, increases in conflict and, potentially, relational violence, elevated risks for mental health problems, and increased likelihood of early death from all causes. In this chapter, we review the empirical evidence on these topics and attempt to quantify how many adults and children experience truly adverse outcomes. Our focus on the so-called "dark side" of divorce should not be misconstrued as a statement of the modal response to the end of marriage. Most people cope well with divorce and move forward to live fulfilling lives with opportunities for personal growth that follow directly from the end of their marriage. In cataloging some of the worst possible outcomes in this chapter, our primary goal is to underscore psychological mechanisms of action and, when the mechanisms are unclear or understudied, to pinpoint areas for future research.

The chapter is organized into six sections. The first three are brief and provide critical orienting remarks on the demographics associated with divorce, a theory about why social separations may be an especially painful class of negative life events, and a framework for considering different explanations linking marital status and health outcomes. We then review literature in three specific outcome domains: adults' mental health, adults' physical health, and relational violence/homicide. When considering these outcomes, our intention is to provide a broad overview of the research in this area that includes specific citations for readers interested in focusing on any one of the topics in greater detail. Finally, given space constraints, we omit consideration of co-parenting custody conflict, parental alienation, and child outcomes. To be sure, these are important topics, and they are reviewed in detail elsewhere (Cummings, Davies, & Cummings, 2010; Emery, 2004; Kelly & Johnston, 2005).

The Demographics of Divorce: Who and How Many?

In a recent panel study of over 16,000 German adults and over 600 divorces, Mancini et al. (2011) found that about 71% of divorcing adults report little change in subjective well-being from 4 years prior to and up to 4 years following divorce. Among the adults sampled, about 9% move from low levels of well-being predivorce to high levels of well-being postdivorce and about 19% move from moderate levels of well-being predivorce to low levels of well-being postdivorce. This latter group constitutes

those people who are most adversely impacted by the end of marriage—they experience decrements in well-being and do not recover to predivorce functioning in the subsequent 4 years. The unfortunate and sometimes unrecognized side of studying divorce resilience is that because divorce is such a common event, 10% to 20% of people experiencing precipitous drops in their well-being represents many people for whom this life event has lasting negative effects. Although the incidence of divorce in the United States has decreased over the last 35 years, from 5.0/1,000 marriages in 1970 to 3.5/1,000 in 2008 (Amato & James, 2010; Bramlett & Mosher, 2002; Tejada-Vera & Sutton, 2009), it remains a relatively common life event.

Using data from the National Survey of Family Growth, which involved face-to-face interviews with 10,847 women ages 15 to 44 years, Bramlett and Mosher (2002) estimated the divorce rate for first marriages in the United States to be 43%. Among adults who do divorce, 15% remarry within 1 year, 39% within 3 years, and 75% with 10 years (Bramlett & Mosher, 2002). Second marriages comprise approximately half of marriages in the United States (Bumpass, Sweet, & Martin, 1990), and they both dissolve more quickly than first marriages and are more likely than first marriages to end in divorce (~ 60%). Close to 40% of second marriages end within 5 years (Coleman, Ganong, & Fine, 2000). Men remarry more often than women, and African- and Hispanic-Americans remarry less often than Caucasian-Americans (South, 1991). Adults who remarry in middle and later-life (~ 40 years old) are less likely to divorce, especially if both partners were previously married (Wu & Penning, 1997). Given these estimates, it is crucial to better understand the variables and processes that help explain why marital separation is an acute, transient stressor for some adults but can evolve into a chronic stressor for others (cf. Amato, 2000, 2010).

The Pain of Social Separations: Coregulation and Dysregulation

Are relationship disruptions uniquely stressful? At the end of the first decade of the 21st century, in a time of nearly unprecedented financial calamity, it is reasonable to argue that divorce is just a single event amongst a long list of difficult life experiences, such as sustained unemployment or losing a home to foreclosure. Although the literature contains no direct comparisons of the differential stress associated with divorce and, for example, unemployment, it is long recognized that social disruptions are among life's most stressful events (Bowlby, 1980; Cacioppo & Patrick, 2008; Holmes & Rahe, 1967; Weiss, 1975). Mounting evidence suggests it is not a coincidence that the unwanted endings of social relationships are so distressing. Sbarra and Hazan (2008) reviewed literature on the psychobiology of attachment to propose an integrative coregulation-dysregulation model (CDM) of human loss experiences (also see Coan, 2008). A primary hypothesis of this model is that mammalian loss experiences disrupt the biological systems that subserve the psychological experience of felt security. From this perspective, the well-documented biological and psychological dysregulation people experience during unwanted social separations is a consequence of removing the functional components of the attachment system (Shear & Shair, 2005). When this occurs, the biological systems that regulate and that are regulated by a relationship go unchecked, which can lead to a number of undesirable endpoints.

One of the main implications of the CDM is that psychological reactions to a separation experience can prolong biological dysregulation. Of course, this is the case for any stressful event, and the manner in which people appraise difficult events has distinct biological correlates that are believed to be harmful to health (Dickerson & Kemeny, 2004; Kiecolt-Glaser, McGuire, Robles, & Glaser, 2002; Tomaka, Blascovich, Kibler, & Ernst, 1997). With respect to separation and loss experiences, the CDM holds that the disruption of coregulation, defined as the reciprocal maintenance of psychophysiological homeostasis within a relationship, engenders a biological response akin to a withdrawal reaction. How adults regulate this state has important implications for their long-term health and well-being. One way of suppressing physiological dysregulation in the aftermath of a separation is with alcohol and other substances (Agrawal & Lynskey, 2009; Dawson, Grant, Stinson, & Chou, 2006). Alternatively, people can succeed or fail in creating meaning from the event, and this process has clear health correlates. For example, in a study of 40 HIV-positive men following the loss of their partner from AIDS, cognitive processing that resulted in finding meaning from the loss experience proved protective to immune system declines that index the emergence of full-blown AIDS (Bower, Kemeny, Taylor, & Fahey, 1998). Most interestingly, this study demonstrated that cognitive processing in the *absence* of finding meaning was associated with a significant drop in immune functioning over time; repetitively processing loss-related thoughts without coming to some type of larger realization or insight is correlated with distinct biological risk.

These simple examples suggest that the manner in which adults regulate their sense of felt security in the aftermath of a loss experience is associated with long-term health outcomes. Because disruptions in felt security are a core feature of relationship disruptions like divorce, there is reason to believe that these events—relative to other potentially negative life events—have relatively unique potential to activate biological profiles that are consistent with threat appraisals. The experience of felt security is maintained in the context of personal relationships, and the loss of an attachment relationship is doubly stressful because it charges many adults to deal with both the loss of one's primary form of social support and the general stress of loss. In concluding his trilogy on attachment, Bowlby (1980), aptly described this process in the following way:

> Not infrequently after a person has been bereaved the situation with which he has to deal is unique, for the death entails the loss of the very person in whom he has been accustomed to confide. Thus, not only is the death itself an appalling blow but the very person towards who it is natural to turn in calamity is no longer there. For that reason, if mourning is to follow a favorable course, it is essential that the bereaved be able to turn for comfort elsewhere (p. 232).

This quote refers to bereavement; add to this description the emotional difficulties and conflict that typically accompany separation and divorce, and the resulting context has the potential to promote considerable emotional distress.

Divorce Outcomes: Social Selection or Social Causation?

When considering the putative consequences of marital separation/divorce for adults and children, it is critical to distinguish between two competing explanations, both of which have empirical support. The *social selection* perspective holds that some people possess characteristics that increase risks for both separation/divorce and poor health outcomes, and that poor mental or physical health itself can operate to select people out of marriage (Amato, 2000; Goldman, 1993; Osler, McGue, Lund, & Christensen, 2008b; Overbeek et al., 2006; Wade & Pevalin, 2004). From this point of view, the outcomes thought to be associated with marital dissolution are merely third variable correlates. For example, in a large, three-wave epidemiological study, Overbeek et al. (2006) found that the incidence of diagnosable mental disorders following divorce was attributable to the marital discord that predated the separation. Similarly, prospective epidemiological evidence indicates that the poor mental health outcome(s) observed after marital separations in fact often preceded the separation experience itself (Wade & Pevalin, 2004).

The social selection perspective, holding that separation/divorce outcomes are nonrandom, is further supported by the well-known existence of gene by environment correlations (i.e., the observation that environments are shaped by genotypes; Scarr & McCartney, 1983) and by evidence from the behavioral genetic study of marital dissolution. McGue and Lykken (1992) found greater concordance of divorce in monozygotic than dyzygotic twins, indicating that a substantial portion of the risk for marital dissolution can be explained by genetic factors. A follow-up study demonstrated that between 30% (in women) and 42% (in men) of heritable divorce risk was attributable to personality differences (Jocklin, McGue, & Lykken, 1996), and other work has shown the genetic association with controllable life events, of which divorce is one, is entirely explained by differences in personality (Saudino, Pedersen, Lichtenstein, McClearn, & Plomin, 1997).

In contrast to the social selection perspective, the *social causation* perspective holds that the structural and psychological changes following divorce play a causal role in poor mental and physical health outcomes. Some of the best evidence in support of this perspective comes from research on monozygotic twins who are discordant for a diagnosis of major depressive disorder (MDD) (Kendler & Gardner, 2001). This design is particularly strong because any differences between twins that are not due to measurement error must be caused by environmental influences. Indeed, evidence indicates that a history of divorce is among a group of variables that reliably discriminates affected and unaffected twins (Kendler & Gardner, 2001). One additional approach for separating selection and causation effects is the children of twins (CoT) model (D'Onofrio et al., 2003), which allows for a quantification of the environmental and genetic processes underlying the association between marital disruption and outcomes of interest. Results using the CoT model indicate that, on average, the association between parents' marital separation and adolescent/young adult children's behavioral and emotional problems is causal (although

evidence exists for selection effects as well). These behavioral and emotional problems include substance abuse, educational problems, and the earlier initiation of sexual intercourse (D'Onofrio et al., 2007a, 2007b; D'Onofrio et al., 2006).

In summary, when taking stock of the associations between marital status and child or adult mental or physical health outcomes, researchers must attend to issues of both social selection and social causation. Although evidence exists for selection processes, these findings cannot account for the entirety of the observed divorce-health associations. Credible evidence exists for the social causation perspective across a range of different outcomes and for both children and adults.

Adults' Mental Health Following Marital Separation/Divorce

Numerous reviews now catalog the adult mental health outcomes associated with separation and divorce. Research accounting for selection effects (i.e., affective distress selecting individuals out of marriage) consistently demonstrates that separation and divorce are associated with increased risks for a range of negative outcomes including mood, anxiety, sleep, and substance use disorders (Aseltine & Kessler, 1993; Doi, Minowa, Okawa, & Uchiyama, 2000; Hajak, 2001; Lorenz, Simons, & Conger, 1997; Menaghan & Lieberman, 1986). In a 3-year follow-up study of over 30,000 adults, separating/divorcing was significantly associated with the initial use of cannabis in previous abstainers (Agrawal & Lynskey, 2009). Among adults diagnosed with prior to past-year alcohol dependence, the end of a first marriage is associated with an increased risk for nonabstinent recovery (Dawson et al., 2006). Among women not diagnosed with substance dependent, alcohol intake also increases immediately prior to a marital separation (Mastekaasa, 1997). Perhaps the best studied mental health outcome following divorce is MDD. Marital dissolution has proven a robust predictor of the onset of MDD in genetically-controlled studies, which is strong (although not conclusive) evidence for the *causal* role of this environmental stressor in the development of an affective disorder (Kendler et al., 1995; Kendler, Karkowski, & Prescott, 1999). In a sample of 7,322 adults, Kendler et al. (2003) found that marital separation experiences (rated as significant losses) yielded a raw risk of 21.6% for MDD onset in the first month after the separation. According to these estimates, roughly one in five individuals experiencing a difficult, other-initiated separation that involves feelings of public humiliation (e.g., being left following a marital infidelity) will evidence a diagnosable MDD.

One of the primary weaknesses of the literature on divorce and adult mental health outcomes is that few studies have focused on the mechanisms, or psychological processes, that connect the end of marriage and subsequent emotional distress. High-quality, processes-focused research in this area is almost absent. This lack of empirical research on mechanisms is surprising, given observations that divorce can induce shame, longing, loneliness, humiliation, rumination, identity disruptions, and prolonged anger or grief (Emery, 1994; Hetherington & Kelly, 2002; Weiss, 1975). Presumably, it is these emotional experiences that give rise to, or at least covary with, more severe forms of psychopathology. Using a dyadic model, Sbarra and Emery (2005) recently showed that fathers' rates of coparenting conflict following child custody dispute settlements depended on mothers' rates of acceptance of the relationship termination. Specifically, fathers who reported the greatest levels of conflict were previously married to mothers who reported the greatest acceptance of the separation, and the authors interpreted this finding to suggest that prolonged coparenting conflict following divorce can operate as an attempt to promote a reunion with an ex-partner who is no longer invested in the relationship. In a prospective analysis over 12-years, Sbarra and Emery (2005) also reported that mothers who continued to show regrets about the separation experience (i.e., low levels of acceptance) also reported the highest rates of depression. In the context of a divorce mediation study, these effects were interpreted to suggest that a potentially adverse effect of helping parents cooperatively renegotiate their separation relationship may be to prolong feelings of grief. Although these studies provide some insight into the correlates of better and worse adjustment to divorce, we still have a great deal to learn about both the mechanisms of recovery (i.e., variables associated with changes in psychological adjustment) and the variables that explain the association between marital status and mental health outcomes.

One of the most complete descriptive accounts of the emotional processes that unfold following a separation experience is Emery's (1994) cyclical model of divorce-related grief. Central to this model is the simultaneous existence of three competing emotions: love, anger, and sadness. From this perspective, "Love" includes the intense longing that follows separation from a loved one, as well as vague hopes for reconciliation, guilt-ridden concern, and related emotions that cause a person to want to move closer to another. "Anger" refers to a variety of affective states ranging from feelings of frustration and resentment to the far more intense fury and/or rage that is commonly experienced in divorce; and, in this model. "Sadness" refers to a constellation of associated feelings including loneliness, depression, and despair. Unlike anger, these sad feelings are directed inward toward the self, rather than outward toward the other. Rather than a linear progression from distress to resolution, the grief process is characterized by constant cycling back and forth between the conflicted feelings of longing for a partner, feeling frustrated with and resentful toward this person, and being saddened by the end of the relationship. The model also allows for specific hypotheses regarding atypical patterns of emotional grief reactions. An individual who maintains, for example, elevated levels of anger and frustration with a former partner without experiencing associated feelings of longing or sadness would be described as "stuck" in anger. Hence, the predominance or maintained elevation of any one emotional state is hypothesized to portend an atypical grief reaction. Although the model provides a useful heuristic for understanding divorce-related grief and for deriving testable hypotheses, no research has used the model for empirically evaluating questions surrounding divorce and mental health outcomes. Research in this area will benefit from a much clearer focus on the mechanisms of action, and the Emery (1994) model provides a useful starting point for making predictions about adults' emotional responses to the end of marriage.

SUMMARY OF MENTAL HEALTH CORRELATES OF MARITAL SEPARATION/DIVORCE

A considerable literature links the experience of marital separation with a range of poor mental health outcomes, including diagnosable mood and substance abuse disorders. Noticeably absent from this literature is a focus on the proximal emotional experiences that increase or decrease risk for prolonged emotion distress. Emery's (1994) model of divorce-related grief presents a framework for considering the relevant affective processes. We suggest further research focus on mechanisms, in addition to quintessentially social emotions, including shame, guilt, and humiliation, as well as other topics that are germane to grief but rarely draw the attention of empirical research, including frustration, emptiness, and identity disruptions (cf. Lewandowski, Aron, Bassis, & Kunak, 2006).

Adults' Physical Health Outcomes
BROAD-BASED EFFECT SIZES

One of the most consistently replicated effects in the social relationships and health literature is the epidemiological finding that marital status is associated with risk for early death. Two very large meta-analyses document that divorce is associated with a significant increased risk for all-cause mortality. Integrating research in psychology, sociology, and epidemiology, Sbarra and colleagues (Sbarra, Law, & Portley, 2011) synthesized data from 32 prospective studies (involving more than 6.5 million people, 160,000 deaths, and over 755,000 divorces in 11 different countries). The overall risk hazard (RH) linking divorce and risk for early death was 1.23, which indicates that relative to married adults divorced adults evidenced, on average and across all the studies in the review, a 23% greater risk of being dead each successive follow-up period. (The RH is a relative risk statistic; thus, this index does not translate into some type of calibrated metric that suggests divorced adults lose some definable number of years life relative to married adults. Instead, the RH quantifies the difference in event occurrence between two ground at each successive measurement period in standard prospective research designs.) Although both men and women are at increased risk for early death following divorce, the meta-analysis revealed that divorced men evidenced greater risk for early death (RH = 1.31) than divorced women (RH = 1.13).

Based on the idea that the potential health effects following from divorce—if casual—take time to accrue, the Sbarra et al. (2011) meta-analysis focused exclusively on prospective studies, with average study length being 14 years. More recently, Shor, Roelfs, Bugyi, and Schwartz (2012) have taken a broader look at the potential association between divorce and death by studying every published report on this topic, including cross-sectional studies from very large census samples. Their final included *600 million people* from more than 24 countries. Consistent with the results of the more narrowly focused meta-analysis, Shor et al. (2012) observed a significant average RH of 1.30, as well as significant differences between men (RH = 1.37) and women (RH = 1.22).

Given these findings, we can conclude with certainty that divorced or separated adults evidence increased rates of early, all-cause mortality even in the fully adjusted models (that control not only for age, but also a variety of sociodemographic, health, and health behavior covariates). The effect sizes observed in these meta-analyses are consistent with the magnitude of association observed in other large-scale (nonprospective) studies, and it is notable that divorced men appear to have the highest death rates among unmarried adults (for a review of evidence from 16 developed countries, see Hu & Goldman, 1990).

The research reviewed above focuses on all-cause mortality, but a more specific literature also focuses on suicide. (We review evidence about homicide in the next section.) For example, in a 10-year, prospective epidemiological study of mortality risk in 471,922 noninstitutionalized adults living in the United States, Kposowa (2000) found that men who were separated or divorced at the start of the study were 2.28 times more likely to kill themselves during the follow-up period than their married counterparts, whereas no significant association was found between marital status and suicide for women. In a follow-up analysis, Kposowa (2003) reported that divorced men were more than 9 times more likely to kill themselves than were divorced women.

What do we know about the mechanisms linking the end of marriage and risk for poor health outcomes? First, consistent with the discussion above, social selection explains some of the physical health outcomes observed following divorce. For example, Osler and colleagues (2008a) recently used a cotwin control design to investigate rates of health outcomes between twins who were discordant for widowhood or divorce. The results indicated that depression and rates of smoking may follow from the ending of a marriage, but that differences in many other health outcomes (e.g., self-rated health, alcohol use, body mass index [BMI]) may be due to underlying genetic explanations, and not the stress of a relationship transition. In addition, the association between divorce and physical health may be explained by third variables that both increase the risk for divorce and increase the risk for poor health, such as hostility and neuroticism. The evidence for this hypothesis is relatively scant. Using data from the Terman Life Cycle study, Tucker and colleagues (Tucker, Friedman, Wingard, & Schwartz, 1996) reported that the risk associated with having ever experienced a divorce and early mortality could be reduced (by 21% for men and 15% for women) after accounting for childhood conscientiousness and a history of parental divorce. This paper aside, documenting the existence of third-variable selection processes is often one of piecing together established associations. If divorce risk can be explained by personality (Jocklin et al., 1996; Whisman, Tolejko, & Chatav, 2007), and there is a voluminous literature linking personality and health outcomes (Miller, Cohen, Rabin, Skoner, & Doyle, 1999; Roberts, Kuncel, Shiner, Caspi, & Goldberg, 2007), working hypotheses must include personality attributes as predictors of both the ending of romantic relationships and the associated health outcomes.

HEALTH BEHAVIORS

Beyond social selection processes, separation and divorce can instantiate changes in health behaviors that have long-term implications for physical health. Cross-national epidemiological data indicate that, as a demographic variable, being separated/ divorced is associated with substantially elevated risk for severe insomnia and problems of sleep maintenance (Doi et al., 2000; Hajak, 2001). Joung and colleagues (1995) found that a set of health behavior variables (including tobacco use, alcohol consumption, eating a regular breakfast, rates of exercise, and body mass index) significantly reduced differences between married and divorced adults' perceived general health and subjective complaints, as well as the difference in the number of women's chronic medical conditions. Accounting for this set of health behaviors led to an 11% reduction in the difference between married and divorced men's ratings of subjective health and a 14% reduction in the difference between married and divorced women's ratings of subjective health. Ikeda and colleagues (2007) conducted a similar study on objective risk for early mortality and found that a set of health behavior predictors reduced, but did not eliminate, the association between divorce and risk for early mortality in men. Additionally, divorced Japanese women were not at elevated risk for early mortality relative to their married counterparts. In a sample of over 80,000 US women from the Nurse's Health Study, Lee and colleagues (2005) reported that women who became divorced over a 4-year period evidenced significant decreases in their BMI (relative to women who remained married), evidenced a significant likelihood of smoking relapse (among prior smokers who were abstaining at the start of the study), and evidenced a significant decrease in fruit and vegetable consumption (also see Eng, Kawachi, Fitzmaurice, & Rimm, 2005). Finally, evidence from the ATTICA study (an epidemiological sample in the Attica region of Greece) demonstrates that differences in BMI and total serum cholesterol between married and divorced participants could be statistically eliminated by accounting for dietary differences between the groups, including the consumption of cereals and soft drinks. This suggests that divorced adults' health behaviors play a key role in altering biomarkers that have distinct negative associations with endpoint outcomes such as cardiovascular disease (Yannakoulia, Panagiotakos, Pitsavos, Skoumas, & Stafanadis, 2008).

PSYCHOLOGICAL STRESS AND DIVORCE-HEALTH OUTCOMES

Only a handful of studies have examined how the psychological responses to marital separation/ divorce may be associated with biomarkers that have health implications. The work in this area began in the 1980s with a series of now seminal studies by Kiecolt-Glaser and colleagues (1987, 1988). In the first report of this series, women who recently separated from their spouse (within the past year) evidenced poorer immune functioning than socio-demographically matched married women. Specifically, recently separated women demonstrated poorer immune proliferation in response to two mitogens in that they exhibited significantly lower percentages of natural killer cells, and significantly higher antibody titers to the Epstein-Barr virus (EBV), which serves as an indirect measure of cellular immune responses. Within the separated/ divorced sample, the degree of attachment to an ex-partner also was associated with greater impairments in immune responding (Kiecolt-Glaser et al., 1987). In a separate study, similar results were observed for men, although immunological differences between married and separated/divorced men were not as pronounced as those observed in women. Separated/divorced men evidenced significantly higher functional immune parameters, including elevated antibodies to EBV and herpes simplex virus. Among the separated/divorced men, those who initiated the separation reported better health and evidenced better antibody titer responses to EBV (Kiecolt-Glaser et al., 1988).

After Kielcolt-Glaser and colleagues published their findings on immune responses following separation/divorce, research investigating how the stress of marital dissolution may be correlated with health-relevant biomarkers came to a virtual standstill.[1] Since the late 1980s, only two studies have been conducted in this area. Powell and colleagues (2002) used divorce as a model of chronic stress in middle-aged women and examined neuroendocrine and catecholamine responses compared to a matched sample of nonstressed women. Divorced women evidenced significantly elevated cortisol responses in the evening relative to nondivorced women; surprisingly, divorced women also evidenced elevated rates of testosterone, which the authors interpreted as a possible effect of experiencing an emotional release from a poor marriage (cf. Mazur & Michalek, 1998). The findings from this study thus revealed a mixed picture for the health of divorced women.

More recently, Sbarra and colleagues (2009) designed a laboratory-based study of autonomic nervous system responses to test the idea that physiological reactivity following marital separation is correlated with the degree of emotion regulatory effort adults need to invoke when thinking about their separation experience. The overarching theory behind this research is that emotion regulatory responses (e.g., catastrophizing an event in your mind, or reappraising an event as benign and personally significant) serve as the mediators connecting specific individual difference variables with poor divorce-related outcomes; for example, one hypothesis consistent with this idea is that people with a high degree of attachment anxiety show greater physiological responses to thinking about their separation experience because they view (i.e., appraise) the separation as a chronically threatening event for their well-being. Using these ideas as a basis for their study, Sbarra et al. (2009) found that participants who reported greater divorce-related emotional intrusion (e.g., dreaming about the separation, experiencing waves of sudden emotion about the separation) entered the study with significantly higher levels of resting systolic and diastolic blood pressure. In addition, during a task in which participants mentally reflected on their separation experience, men who reported that the task required a great deal of emotion regulatory effort (i.e., feeling upset combined with a need to exert control of one's emotions in order to prevent a worsening of distress) evidenced the largest increases in BP, and these effects were in addition to those observed for baseline functioning.

One important aspect of the Sbarra et al. (2009) study was that the observed changes in blood pressure among highly distressed men placed them in a hypertensive range (systolic BP > 150 mg/mm) that would typically warrant medical intervention if observed as resting BP. Although many activities elevate BP into this range on a temporary basis, it is plausible that one way in which divorce may exert health compromising effects is through emotion regulatory demands: Highly distressed men may repeatedly push their BP responses into the range of hypertensive functioning, and this is of clinical significance. This idea is consistent with current models of allostatic load (McEwen, 1998), in which psychological stress can exert its effects on health by taxing regulatory systems (e.g., the vascular system) through repeated "hits" of high activity or a failure to shut-down normative responses to stress.

SUMMARY OF DIVORCE-PHYSICAL HEALTH LITERATURE

Marital separation and divorce are associated with a statistically reliable increase in the probability of early death, yet we know little about the mechanisms that explain this association. This section of the chapter reviewed evidence on two potential pathways, health behaviors and emotional responding. We reviewed evidence that marital separation increases the likelihood of poor health behaviors and that the broad-based mortality effect can be explained, in part, by health behaviors, although this conclusion depends on the ability to show that *changes* in health behaviors systematically follow changes in marital status. Only a few studies have examined emotional responding to divorce and associations with biomarkers that have distinct implications for endpoint health outcomes. Despite the nascent nature of this work, studies demonstrate that divorce-related subjective emotional experiences are consistently associated with heightened biological stress responses. Future research is needed to see if these emotional responses predict clinically meaningful health outcomes over the long term.

Marital Separation, Divorce, and Relational Violence

One of the most controversial and debated questions in all of the social sciences is the degree to which men and women perpetrate relational violence (Hamby, 2005; Johnson, 2006; Kimmel, 2002). While the so-called "gender symmetry" in rates of relational violence appear highly dependent on the definitions used to define the violence in question, evidence from representative population-based studies indicates that woman are much more likely to be the victims of behaviorally-defined acts of physical aggression within relationships. For example, in a sample of 16,000 men and women in the United States, Tjaden and Thoennes (2000) reported that more than 20% of women reported being the victim of forcible rape, physical assault (e.g., being slapped, kicked, or beat up), or stalking, whereas just 7.3% of married men reported being a victim of the same behaviors. With these rates as a backdrop, there is fairly clear evidence that when relationships come to an end, women are much more likely to be the victims of violence resulting in death than their male counterparts. In the remainder of the chapter, we address some of the literature on this topic.

According to the Federal Bureau Investigation (FBI) published homicide statistics for the year 2008, men committed some 90% of homicides. In the context of general homicide, women kill 6 non-romantic partners for every 100 nonromantic partners killed by men, yet killing ratios in the context of relationships tell a different story. In their investigation of gender differences in spousal homicides from 1988 to 1992 across 190 US cities, Gauthier and Bankston (1997) found that for every 100 spousal murders completed by men, there are some 62 spousal murders completed by women. More specifically, according to FBI 2008 homicide statistics, of the 1,176 reported homicides committed by women, 119 were committed against husbands (~10%), whereas of the 10,568 reported homicides committed by men, 577 were committed against wives (~5%). Other census data indicate that as many as half of all homicides committed by women involve murdering a spouse or ex-spouse (Gauthier & Bankston, 1997; Gauthier & Bankston, 2004) and that divorced men and women often have similar histories of domestic violence within their relationships (Johnson & Hotton, 2003). It is important to recognize that although the rate of homicide against men and women may not differ, estranged or divorced women comprise more than 90% of intimate partner homicide victims (for a review of the evidence, see Adams, 2007).

WHAT EXPLAINS THE DISCREPANCY IN SPOUSAL MURDER AMONG MEN AND WOMEN?

Some data suggest that being divorced doubles or even quadruples a woman's likelihood of experiencing domestic violence (Brownridge et al., 2008a; Brownridge et al., 2008b). Historically, the introduction of unilateral divorce laws, in which one member of a couple does not need the consent of the other member in order to procure a divorce, did not lead to a reduction in lethal spousal violence against women (as intended), but rather led to a 21% to 23% increase in the number of husbands killed by their wives (Dee, 2007). Gender differences in sexual jealousy and the desire to maintain control over a former partner are widely cited as motives for men killing their ex-partners, and self-defense is cited as a major reason that women kill

their partners (Campbell, 1992; Johnson & Hotton, 2003; Serran & Firestone, 2004; Wilson, Johnson, & Daly, 1995).

WHEN IS RISK GREATEST?

Data indicate that the periods of time during, and directly following, a wife leaving a husband, are the most likely occasions for violence against wives. Wilson and Daly (1993) found that among spousal homicides committed by separated men, the 2-month period following a separation was the time during which 50% of husbands murdered their ex-wives, and 85% had murdered their ex-wives within 1 year of the separation. Attempts to desert, or actually deserting, a relationship are also related to increased violence against women (Johnson & Hotton, 2003), and are especially risky for women who are currently in abusive relationships and attempting to leave them (Block, 2000). Women's threats and initiations of marital separation are events that can trigger violence acts or sexual abuse from their spouses (DeKeseredy, Rogness, & Schwartz, 2004; Wilson & Daly, 1993). Similarly, Wallace (1986) found that of 217 women killed by their ex-husbands, 98 had either left their husbands or were in the process of doing so. In contrast, of the 79 men killed by their ex-wives, only three had left their wives or were in the process of leaving.

WHO IS AT RISK?

Wilson and Daly (1993) reported that a combination of physical and legal separation poses a significant risk for murder by an ex-spouse. Similarly, more separated wives (as opposed to cohabiting wives) have reported experiencing violence from husbands (Ellis & DeKeseredy, 1989) and are more likely to be victims of homicide (Wilson & Daly, 1993). These findings lend credence to the fear that many women in abusive relationships have of leaving their partners. Women who choose not to leave their husbands may correctly infer that they are more likely to be physically attacked if they attempt to leave than if they stay in their marriages. Brownridge and colleagues (2008b) found that being young, dependent (unemployed), and less educated, in addition to having children and a sexually jealous ex-partner, were also strong (positive) predictors for domestic violence against divorced women in comparison with married women. In comparison with married women, divorced women's ex-husbands scored higher on measures of patriarchal dominance, which was in turn a significant predictor of violence toward ex-wives.

Data regarding the relationship between female education and risk for domestic violence and homicide have been mixed (Brownridge et al., 2008a, 2008b; Dawson & Gardner, 1998). Whereas Brownridge and colleagues (2008a) did not find education to be a significant predictor of violence for separated, married, or divorced women, they subsequently (2008b) found that each additional year of education was associated with an increase in odds of violence for separated women (29%) and married women (13%) but a 42% *decrease* in odds of violence for divorced women. One potential explanation for this difference is that the legal interventions and/or mediation that are often involved in formal divorce proceedings buffer divorced women from a certain degree of violence. Similarly, although employment status and having children with an ex-husband did not impact odds of violence for married or separated women, employment was associated with an 88% decrease in odds of violence for divorced women (compared with unemployed divorced women), and having children with an ex-husband was associated with 787% increase in odds for divorced women (compared with childless divorced women). One explanation for these findings may be that women who are employed and educated are less dependent on their ex-spouses for child support, which may decrease retaliation motives of the ex-husbands who may want little to do with their ex-wives.

WHAT MOTIVATES VIOLENCE AGAINST EX-SPOUSES?

Brownridge (2006) suggested that three potential motivations (restoration of control, reconciliation, and retaliation) might explain domestic violence against ex-partners. In other words, men may be attempting to restore their relationships via forced reconciliation, or may be retaliating against their ex-wives due to feeling abandoned, cheated, robbed, or betrayed. Along these lines, Campbell and colleagues (2007) note that male partners may be threatened by a loss of control over their relationship when women declare their intentions to desert the relationship, and this may explain why women's threats to end a relationship and their actual initiation of a marital separation may potentially trigger violence from their spouses.

One hypothesis from an evolutionary perspective is that men's sexual proprietariness motivates ex-partner violence (Wilson & Daly, 1992, 1993). Data show that while men and women kill their spouses at similar rates (keeping base rates in mind, see above), men often "hunt down and kill spouses who have left them; women hardly ever behave similarly" (Wilson & Daly, 1992, p. 206). Police reports of documented homicides committed against ex-husbands/wives show that women were more likely to be killed by ex-partners motivated by jealousy than were men, and that men were also more likely to take their own lives after taking those of their ex-spouses than were women (Johnston & Hotton, 2003). This evolutionary perspective builds on the cross-cultural body of literature examining when, how, and why men employ violent measures to obtain and maintain control over their romantic partners (cf. Wilson, Johnson, & Daly, 1995). That not all men who were violent toward their ex-wives are highly sexually proprietary or domineering suggests that their violent behavior may be out-of-character and not intended toward controlling their ex-wives. In other words, for some men, retaliation might be a stronger motive for violence against divorced women than attempts to restore control as consequences of women's independence.

SUMMARY OF RELATIONAL VIOLENCE LITERATURE.

Relational violence is a major public health concern. In the time immediately surrounding a marital separation, women are at a significantly increased risk for death at their ex-partner's hands than at any other time. Although the explanations for this increased risk are multifaceted, it is clear that a history of violence within the relationship, prior to its ending, is among the most systematic predictors of the future likelihood of a homicidal outcome. Studying the mechanisms surrounding these tragic outcomes is difficult; perhaps the best methods for doing so are qualitative summaries from in-depth interviews with the perpetrators (see Adams, 2007). This perspective suggests that psychological science will benefit by looking to other fields (such as anthropology) for the most appropriate tools to better understand research questions in this important area of study.

Conclusions

The most well-replicated finding in the divorce literature is that, on average, when marriages come to an end, most adults can be described as resilient. For most adults, periods of intense emotional distress are transient. For some adults, however, marital separation and divorce are associated with considerable risk for poor mental and physical health outcomes, as well as relational violence that can end in homicide. Prior to reviewing these areas of study, we described a theory for understanding why social separations, relative to other negative life events, can be particularly challenging. In addition, we underscored the importance of considering both social selection and social causation processes when considering the putative health outcomes of separation of divorce. Although a large and growing literature indicates that many of the outcomes believed to be caused by divorce predate the separation or can be better explained by genetic mechanisms (as opposed to the stress of separation), it is clear that selection processes cannot account for all of the variance in the mental and physical health outcomes that covary with separation and divorce. In terms of potentially causal mechanisms that connect the end of marriage with poor mental health, future research should focus on emotional responses such as shame, humiliation, and loneliness. Relative to the frequency with which divorcing adults report experiencing these emotional states, the field still knows relatively little about how these emotional states might serve to increase risk for significant psychopathology. Future research also should address changes in physical health as they pertain to changes in marital status. Do changes in marital status lead to changes in health behaviors and emotional responses that are associated with important health outcomes? Thus, in terms of the three major outcome areas addressed in this chapter, it is reasonable to conclude the field knows much more about broad-based associations than about mechanisms of action. Process-focused research targeting mechanisms has potential to reveal precisely why and how some adults experience truly adverse outcomes when their marriages end.

Note

1. One possible explanation for why research in this area slowed quite dramatically is that (in the 1990s) researchers in psychoneuroimmunology (PNI) focused a great deal of effort creating research paradigms that could interrogate clearly defined biological endpoints. In the study of relationships, Kiecolt-Glaser and colleagues (1995) introduced a wound healing paradigm that had clear relevance clinical health outcomes. These models dominated the study of close relationships for a long period of time, and it is only recently, as the PNI and health psychology fields have become more refined, that investigators have once again cast the study of relationships more broadly.

References

Adams, D. (2007). *Why Do They Kill: Men Who Murder Their Intimate Partners*. Nashville, TN: Vanderbilt Univ Press.

Agrawal, A., & Lynskey, M. T. (2009). Correlates of later-onset cannabis use in the national epidemiological survey on alcohol and related conditions (NESARC). *Drug and Alcohol Dependence, 105,* 71–75.

Amato, P. R. (2000). The consequences of divorce for adults and children. *Journal of Marriage & Family, 62,* 1269–1287.

Amato, P. R. (2010). Research on divorce: Continuing trends and new developments. *Journal of Marriage & Family, 72,* 650–666.

Amato, P. R., & James, S. (2010). Divorce in europe and the united states: Commonalities and differences across nations. *Family Science, 1,* 2–13.

Aseltine, R. H., & Kessler, R. C. (1993). Marital disruption and depression in a community sample. *Journal of Health and Social Behavior, 34,* 237–251.

Ben-Shlomo, Y., Smith, G. D., & Shipley, M. (1993). Magnitude and causes of mortality differences between married and unmarried men. *J Epidemiology Community Health, 47,* 200–205.

Block, C. R. (2000). *Chicago Women's Health Risk Study: Risk of Serious Injury or Death in Intimate Violence: A Collaborative Research Project*. Washington, DC: U.S. Department of Justice, National Institute of Justice.

Bower, J. E., Kemeny, M. E., Taylor, S. E., & Fahey, J. L. (1998). Cognitive processing, discovery of meaning, cd4 decline, and aids-related mortality among bereaved HIV-seropositive men. *Journal of Consulting & Clinical Psychology, 66,* 979–986.

Bowlby, J. (1980). *Attachment and Loss: Vol. 3. Loss: Sadness and Depression*. New York: Basic Books.

Bramlett, M. D., & Mosher, W. D. (2002). *Cohabitation, Marriage, Divorce, and Remarriage in the United States*. Hyattsville, MD: National Center for Health Statistics.

Brownridge, D. A. (2006). Violence against women post-separation. *Aggression and Violent Behavior, 11,* 514–530.

Brownridge, D. A., Chan, K. L., Hiebert-Murphy, D., Ristock, J., Tiwari, A., Leung, W. C., et al. (2008a). The elevated risk for non-lethal post-separation violence in Canada: A comparison of separated, divorced, and married women. *Journal of Interpersonal Violence, 23,* 117.

Brownridge, D. A., Hiebert-Murphy, D., Ristock, J., Chan, K. L., Tiwari, A., Tyler, K. A., et al. (2008b). Violence against separated, divorced, and married women in Canada, 2004. *Journal of Divorce & Remarriage, 49,* 308–329.

Bumpass, L., Sweet, J., & Martin, T. C. (1990). Changing patterns of remarriage. *Journal of Marriage and the Family, 52,* 747–756.

Cacioppo, J. T., & Patrick, W. (2008). *Loneliness: Human Nature and the Need for Social Connection*: New York: W. W. Norton & Company.

Campbell, J. C. (1992). "If I can't have you, no one can": Power and control in homicide of female partners. In J Radford & D.E.H. Russell (Eds.), *Femicide: The Politics of Woman Killing* (pp. 99–113). New York: Twayne Publishers.

Campbell, J. C., Glass, N., Sharps, P. W., Laughon, K., & Bloom, T. (2007). Intimate partner homicide: Review and implications of research and policy. *Trauma, Violence, & Abuse, 8,* 246.

Cheung, Y. B. (2000). Marital status and mortality in British women: A longitudinal study. *Int J Epidemiol, 29,* 93–99.

Coan, J. A. (2008). Toward a neuroscience of attachment. In J. Cassidy & P. R. Shaver (Eds.), *Handbook of Attachment: Theory, Research, and Clinical Applications* (2nd ed., pp. 241–265). New York: Guildford Publications.

Coleman, M., Ganong, L., & Fine, M. (2000). Reinvestigating remarriage: Another decade of progress. *Journal of Marriage and the Family, 62*, 1288–1307.

Cummings, E. M., Davies, P. T., & Cummings, M. E. (2010). *Marital Conflict and Children: An Emotional Security Perspective*: New York: The Guilford Press.

Dawson, D. A., Grant, B. F., Stinson, F. S., & Chou, P. S. (2006). Maturing out of alcohol dependence: The impact of transitional life events. *Journal of Studies on Alcohol, 67*, 195–203.

Dee, T. S. (2007). Until death do you part: The effects of unilateral divorce on spousal homicides. *Economic Inquiry, 41*, 163–182.

DeKeseredy, W. S., Rogness, M. K., & Schwartz, M. D. (2004). Separation/divorce sexual assault: The current state of social scientific knowledge. *Aggression and Violent Behavior, 9*, 675–691.

Dickerson, S. S., & Kemeny, M. E. (2004). Acute stressors and cortisol responses: A theoretical integration and synthesis of laboratory research. *Psychological Bulletin, 130*, 355–391.

Doi, Y., Minowa, M., Okawa, M., & Uchiyama, M. (2000). Prevalence of sleep disturbance and hypnotic medication use in relation to sociodemographic factors in the general japanese adult population. *J Epidemiol, 10*, 79–86.

D' Onofrio, B. M., Slutske, W. S., Turkheimer, E., Emery, R. E., Harden, K. P., Heath, A. C., et al. (2007b). Intergenerational transmission of childhood conduct problems: A children of twins study. *Arch Gen Psychiatry, 64*, 820–829.

D' Onofrio, B. M., Turkheimer, E., Emery, R., Maes, H., Silberg, J., & Eaves, L. (2007a). A children of twins study of parental divorce and offspring psychopathology. *Journal of Child Psychology and Psychiatry, 48*, 667–675.

D' Onofrio, B. M., Turkheimer, E., Emery, R. E., Slutske, W. S., Heath, A. C., Madden, P. A., et al. (2006). A genetically informed study of the processes underlying the association between parental marital instability and offspring adjustment. *Developmental Psychology, 42*, 486–499.

D' Onofrio, B. M., Turkheimer, E. N., Eaves, L. J., Corey, L. A., Berg, K., Solaas, M. H., et al. (2003). The role of the children of twins design in elucidating causal relations between parent characteristics and child outcomes. *J Child Psychol Psychiatry, 44*, 1130–1144.

Dupre, M. E., Beck, A. N., & Meadows, S. O. (2009). Marital trajectories and mortality among us adults. *American Journal of Epidemiology, 170*, 546–555.

Ebrahim, S., Wannamethee, G., McCallum, A., Walker, M., & Shaper, A. G. (1995). Marital status, change in marital status, and mortality in middle-aged British men. *Am J Epidemiology, 142*, 834–842.

Ellis, D., & DeKeseredy, W. S. (1989). Marital status and woman abuse: The dad model. *International Journal of Sociology of the Family, 19*, 67–87.

Emery, R. E. (1994). *Renegotiating Family Relationships: Divorce, Child Custody, and Mediation*. New York: The Guilford Press.

Emery, R. E. (1999). *Marriage, Divorce, and Children's Adjustment* (2nd ed.). Thousand Oaks, CA: Sage Publications, Inc.

Emery, R. E. (2004). *The Truth About Children and Divorce: Dealing with the Emotions So You and Your Children Can Thrive*. New York: Viking/Penguin.

Eng, P. M., Kawachi, I., Fitzmaurice, G., & Rimm, E. B. (2005). Effects of marital transitions on changes in dietary and other health behaviours in US male health professionals. *J Epidemiology Community Health, 59*, 56–62.

Gauthier, D. A. K., & Bankston, W. B. (1997). Gender equality and the sex ratio of intimate killing. *Criminology, 35*, 577.

Gauthier, D. K., & Bankston, W. B. (2004). "Who kills whom" Revisited: A sociological study of variation in the sex ratio of spouse killings. *Homicide Studies, 8*, 96.

Goldman, N. (1993). Marriage selection and mortality patterns: Inferences and fallacies. *Demography, 30*, 189–208.

Hajak, G. (2001). Epidemiology of severe insomnia and its consequences in germany. *European Archives of Psychiatry and Clinical Neuroscience, 251*, 49–56.

Hamby, S. L. (2005). Measuring gender differences in partner violence: Implications from research on other forms of violent and socially undesirable behavior. *Sex Roles, 52*, 725–742.

Hetherington, E. M., Bridges, M., & Insabella, G. M. (1998). Five perspectives on the association between marital transitions and children's adjustment. *American Psychologist, 53*, 167–184.

Hetherington, E. M., & Kelly, J. (2002). *For better or for worse: Divorce reconsidered*. New York: Norton & Company.

Holmes, T. H., & Rahe, R. H. (1967). The social readjustment rating scale. *Journal of Psychosomatic Research, 11*, 213–218.

Hu, Y. R., & Goldman, N. (1990). Mortality differentials by marital-status- an international comparison. *Demography, 27*, 233–250.

Ikeda, A., Iso, H., Toyoshima, H., Fujino, Y., Mizoue, T., Yoshimura, T., et al. (2007). Marital status and mortality among Japanese men and women: The Japan collaborative cohort study. *BMC Public Health, 7*, 73.

Iwasaki, M., Otani, T., Sunaga, R., Miyazaki, H., Xiao, L., Wang, N., et al. (2002). Social networks and mortality based on the Komoise cohort study in Japan. *International Journal of Epidemiology, 31*, 1208.

Jocklin, V., McGue, M., & Lykken, D. T. (1996). Personality and divorce: A genetic analysis. *Journal of Personality and Social Psychology, 71*, 288–299.

Johnson, H., & Hotton, T. (2003). Losing control: Homicide risk in estranged and intact intimate relationships. *Homicide Studies, 7*, 58.

Johnson, M. P. (2006). Conflict and control: Gender symmetry and asymmetry in domestic violence. *Violence Against Women, 12*, 1003.

Johnson, N. J., Backlund, E., Sorlie, P. D., & Loveless, C. A. (2000). Marital status and mortality: The national longitudinal mortality study. *Ann Epidemiology, 10*, 224–238.

Joung, I. M., Stronks, K., Van de Mheen, H., & Mackenbach, J. P. (1995). Health behaviours explain part of the differences in self reported health associated with partner/marital status in the netherlands. *Journal of Epidemiology and Community Health, 49*, 482–488.

Kelly, J. B., & Johnston, J. R. (2005). The alienated child: A reformulation of parental alienation syndrome. *Family Court Review, 39*, 249–266.

Kendler, K., Kessler, R., Walters, E., MacLean, C., Neale, M., Heath, A., et al. (1995). Stressful life events, genetic liability, and onset of an episode of major depression in women. *American Journal of Psychiatry, 152*, 833–842.

Kendler, K. S., & Gardner, C. O. (2001). Monozygotic twins discordant for major depression: A preliminary exploration of the role of environmental experiences in the aetiology and course of illness. *Psychological Medicine, 31*, 411–423.

Kendler, K. S., Hettema, J. M., Butera, F., Gardner, C. O., & Prescott, C. A. (2003). Life event dimensions of loss, humiliation, entrapment, and danger in the prediction of onsets of major depression and generalized anxiety. *Arch Gen Psychiatry, 60*, 789–796.

Kendler, K. S., Karkowski, L. M., & Prescott, C. A. (1999). Causal relationship between stressful life events and the onset of major depression. *American Journal of Psychiatry, 156*, 837–841.

Kiecolt-Glaser, J. K., Fisher, L. D., Ogrocki, P., Stout, J. C., & et al. (1987). Marital quality, marital disruption, and immune function. *Psychosomatic Medicine, 49*, 13–34.

Kiecolt-Glaser, J. K., Kennedy, S., Malkoff, S., Fisher, L., & et al. (1988). Marital discord and immunity in males. *Psychosomatic Medicine, 50*, 213–229.

Kiecolt- Glaser, J. K., Marucha, P. T., Malarkey, W., Mercado, A. M., & Glaser, R. (1995). Slowing of wound healing by psychological stress. *Lancet, 346*, 1194–1196.

Kiecolt- Glaser, J. K., McGuire, L., Robles, T. F., & Glaser, R. (2002). Emotions, morbidity, and mortality: New perspectives from psychoneuroimmunology. *Annual Review of Psychology, 53*, 83–107.

Kimmel, M. S. (2002). " Gender symmetry" In domestic violence: A substantive and methodological research review. *Violence Against Women, 8*, 1332.

Kposowa, A. J. (2000). Marital status and suicide in the national longitudinal mortality study. *J Epidemiol Community Health, 54*, 254–261.

Kposowa, A. J. (2003). Divorce and suicide risk. *Journal of Epidemiology and Community Health, 57*, 993.

Lee, S., Cho, E., Grodstein, F., Kawachi, I., Hu, F. B., & Colditz, G. A. (2005). Effects of marital transitions on changes in dietary and other health behaviours in us women. *Int J Epidemiology, 34*, 69–78.

Lewandowski, G. W., Jr., Aron, A., Bassis, S., & Kunak, J. (2006). Losing a self-expanding relationship: Implications for the self-concept. *Personal Relationships, 13*, 317–331.

Lorenz, F. O., Simons, R. L., & Conger, R. D. (1997). Married and recently divorced mothers' stressful events and distress: Tracing change across time. *Journal of Marriage & the Family, 59*, 219–232.

Lucas, R. E. (2005). Time does not heal all wounds: A longitudinal study of reaction and adaptation to divorce. *Psychological Science, 16*, 945–950.

Lund, R., Christensen, U., Holstein, B. E., Due, P., Osler, M., Ebrahim, S., et al. (2006). Influence of marital history over two and three generations on early death. A longitudinal study of danish men born in 1953. *J Epidemiology Community Health, 60*, 496–501.

Malyutina, S., Bobak, M., Simonova, G., Gafarov, V., Nikitin, Y., & Marmot, M. (2004). Education, marital status, and total and cardiovascular mortality in novosibirsk, russia: A prospective cohort study. *Annals of Epidemiology, 14*, 244–249.

Mancini, A. D., Bonanno, G. A., & Clark, A. E. (2011). Stepping off the hedonic treadmill. *Journal of Individual Differences, 32*, 144–152.

Mastekaasa, A. (1997). Marital dissolution as a stressor: Some evidence on psychological, physical, and behavioral changes in the pre-separation period. *Journal of Divorce & Remarriage, 26*, 155–183.

Mazur, A., & Michalek, J. (1998). Marriage, divorce, and male testosterone. *Social Forces, 77*, 315–330.

McEwen, B. S. (1998). Protective and damaging effects of stress mediators. *New England Journal of Medicine, 338*, 171–179.

McGue, M., & Lykken, D. T. (1992). Genetic influence on risk of divorce. *Psychological Science, 3*, 368–373.

Menaghan, E. G., & Lieberman, M. A. (1986). Changes in depression following divorce: A panel study. *Journal of Marriage and the Family, 48*, 319–328.

Miller, G. E., Cohen, S., Rabin, B. S., Skoner, D. P., & Doyle, W. J. (1999). Personality and tonic cardiovascular, neuroendocrine, and immune parameters. *Brain Behavior and Immunity, 13*, 109–123.

Molloy, G. J., Stamatakis, E., Randall, G., & Hamer, M. (2009). Marital status, gender and cardiovascular mortality: Behavioural, psychological distress and metabolic explanations. *Social Science & Medicine, 69*, 223–228.

Nilsson, P. M., Nilsson, J. A., Ostergren, P. O., & Berglund, G. (2005). Social mobility, marital status, and mortality risk in an adult life course perspective: The malmo preventive project. *Scandinavian Journal of Public Health, 33*, 412.

Osler, M., McGue, M., Lund, R., & Christensen, K. (2008a). Marital status and twins' health and behavior: An analysis of middle-aged Danish twins. *Psychosomatic Medicine, 70*, 482–487.

Overbeek, G., Vollebergh, W., de Graaf, R., Scholte, R., de Kemp, R., & Engels, R. (2006). Longitudinal associations of marital quality and marital dissolution with the incidence of DSM-III-R disorders. *Journal of Family Psychology, 20*, 284–291.

Powell, L. H., Lovallo, W. R., Matthews, K. A., Meyer, P., Midgley, A. R., Baum, A., et al. (2002). Physiologic markers of chronic stress in premenopausal, middle-aged women. *Psychosomatic Medicine, 64*, 502–509.

Roberts, B. W., Kuncel, N. R., Shiner, R., Caspi, A., & Goldberg, L. R. (2007). The power of personality: The comparative validity of personality traits, socioeconomic status, and cognitive ability for predicting important life outcomes. *Perspectives on Psychological Science, 2*, 313.

Saudino, K. J., Pedersen, N. L., Lichtenstein, P., McClearn, G. E., & Plomin, R. (1997). Can personality explain genetic influences on life events? *Journal of Personality and Social Psychology, 72*, 196–206.

Sbarra, D. A., Law, R. W., & Portley, R. M. (2011). Divorce and death: A meta-analysis and research agenda for clinical, social, and health psychology. *Perspectives on Psychological Science, 6*, 454–474.

Sbarra, D. A., & Emery, R. E. (2005). Co-parenting conflict, nonacceptance, and depression among divorced adults: Results from a 12-year follow-up study of child custody mediation using multiple imputation. *American Journal of Orthopsychiatry, 75*, 73–75.

Sbarra, D. A., & Hazan, C. (2008). Co-regulation, dysregulation, and self-regulation: An integrative analysis and empirical agenda for understanding attachment, separation, loss, and recovery. *Personality & Social Psychology Review, 12*, 141–167.

Sbarra, D. A., Law, R. W., Lee, L. A., & Mason, A. E. (2009). Marital dissolution and blood pressure reactivity: Evidence for the specificity of emotional intrusion-hyperarousal and task-rated emotional difficulty. *Psychosomatic Medicine, 71*, 532–540.

Scarr, S., & McCartney, K. (1983). How people make their own environments: A theory of genotype environment effects. *Child Development, 54*, 424–435.

Serran, G., & Firestone, P. (2004). Intimate partner homicide: A review of the male proprietariness and the self-defense theories. *Aggression and Violent Behavior, 9*, 1–15.

Shear, K., & Shair, H. (2005). Attachment, loss, and compli-cated grief. *Developmental Psychobiology, 47*, 253–267.

Shor, E., Roelfs, D. J., Bugyi, P., & Schwartz, J. E. (2012). Meta-analysis of marital dissolution and mortality: Reevaluating the intersection of gender and age. *Social Science & Medicine.* Published ahead online April 5, 2012: http://dx.doi.org/10.1016/j.socscimed.2012.03.010

South, S. J. (1991). Sociodemographic differentials in mate selection preferences. *Journal of Marriage and the Family, 53*, 928–940.

Tejada- Vera, B., & Sutton, P. (2009). *Births, Marriages, Divorces, and Deaths: Provisional Data for July 2008. National Vital Statistics Reports* (Vol. 57, no 13). Hyattsville, MD: National Center for Health Statistics.

Tjaden, P., & Thoennes, N. (2000). Prevalence and consequences of male-to-female and female-to-male intimate partner vio-lence as measured by the national violence against women survey. *Violence against women, 6*, 142.

Tomaka, J., Blascovich, J., Kibler, J., & Ernst, J. M. (1997). Cognitive and physiological antecedents of threat and chal-lenge appraisal. *Journal of Personality & Social Psychology, 73*, 63–72.

Tucker, J. S., Friedman, H. S., Wingard, D. L., & Schwartz, J. E. (1996). Marital history at midlife as a predictor of longevity: Alternative explanations to the protective effect of marriage. *Health Psychology, 15*, 94–101.

Wade, T. J., & Pevalin, D. J. (2004). Marital transitions and mental health. *Journal of Health & Social Behavior, 45*, 155–170.

Wallace, A. (1986). *Homicide: The Social Reality.* Sydney, Australia: New South Wales Bureau of Crime Statistics and Research.

Weiss, R. S. (1975). *Marital separation.* New York: Basic Books.

Whisman, M. A., Tolejko, N., & Chatav, Y. (2007). Social con-sequences of personality disorders: Probability and timing of marriage and probability of marital disruption. *Journal of Personality Disorders, 21*, 690–695.

Wilson, M. I., & Daly, M. (1992). Who kills whom in spouse killings-on the exceptional sex ratio of spousal homicides in the united states. *Criminology, 30*, 189–215.

Wilson, M., & Daly, M. (1993). Spousal homicide risk and estrangement. *Violence and Victims, 8*, 3–16.

Wilson, M., Johnson, H., & Daly, M. (1995). Lethal and nonle-thal violence against wives. *Canadian Journal of Criminology, 37*, 331–362.

Wu, Z., & Penning, M. J. (1997). Marital instability after midlife. *Journal of Family Issues, 18*, 459.

Yanda, S., de Vise, D., and Johnson, J. (2010, May 5). George Huguely, suspect in U-Va. Murder case, accused of slamming Yeardley Love's head into wall during fight. *The Washington Post.* Retrieved from http://www.washingtonpost.com/wp-dyn/content/article/2010/05/04/AR2010050402215.html

Yannakoulia, M., Panagiotakos, D., Pitsavos, C., Skoumas, Y., & Stafanadis, C. (2008). Eating patterns may mediate the association between marital status, body mass index, and blood cholesterol levels in apparently healthy men and women from the ATTICA study. *Social Science & Medicine, 66*, 2230–2239.

The Importance of Feeling Valued: Perceived Regard in Romantic Relationships

Justin V. Cavallo *and* John G. Holmes

Abstract

Romantic relationships present people with unparalleled opportunity to fulfill fundamental intimacy goals. However, they also present the risk of experiencing social pain. Recent research has identified perceived regard—how much one feels valued by one's romantic partner—as a critical moderator that determines when people set aside interpersonal risk in pursuit of connectedness or instead, forego intimacy to protect oneself from the threat of rejection. In the present chapter, we detail how chronic beliefs about perceived regard shape romantic outcomes by influencing relational cognition and self-regulation, particularly when interpersonal risk is salient. We also explore emerging research highlighting the mechanisms underlying these processes. Feeling valued is important to relationship well-being across all interpersonal contexts, but it is particularly critical in determining the longevity and quality of romantic bonds.

Key Words: interpersonal social cognition; perceived regard, romantic relationships, self-esteem

Introduction

Interpersonal life is fraught with both opportunity and peril. Establishing meaningful psychological connections with close others allows people to satisfy deep-seated and fundamental belongingness needs. However, as evidenced by the diversity and depth of chapters in this volume, the possibility of social exclusion and the pain that accompanies it is ubiquitous. Across social contexts, perceived or anticipated rejection experiences not only exert an immediate influence on affect, cognition, and behavior, but they also guide future interactions. The power of rejection is particularly evident in romantic relationships.

For many people, romantic relationships offer opportunities for intimacy that cannot be derived from other social bonds. However, obtaining these strong social connections often requires partners to be dependent and to give one another great control over their individual outcomes. Such interdependence often puts people in a precarious situation

should their partner reject them or not be responsive to their needs. Thus, romantic relationships present people with an inherent dilemma—to maximize intimacy and satisfy the essential motivation to belong, one must think and act in ways that leave one vulnerable to rejection and thereby run counter to the motivation to avoid social pain (Murray, Holmes, & Collins, 2006).

Relationship science has devoted itself to understanding how people respond to actual or perceived rejection from romantic partners, and most recently, the conditions under which people are willing to set aside rejection concerns in pursuit of intimacy goals. Though these attempts to understand interpersonal self-regulation have identified several important situational and personality variables that moderate reactions to rejection experiences, perceived regard has emerged as a central construct that governs much of romantic experience. A person's perceptions of how much their partner values them and cares for them exert considerable influence on interpersonal self-regulation and in turn, have a profound effect on both proximal and distal relationship outcomes.

In this chapter, we outline recent research that has highlighted the importance of perceived regard as a key factor in interpersonal cognition. We begin by exploring the origin and nature of perceived regard. We then examine how chronic perceptions of a partner's regard guide relational goal pursuit and subsequently, we detail recent findings elucidating the precise operation of these self-regulatory processes. Finally, we suggest avenues for future research that may generate a more comprehensive understanding of perceived regard and its influence on relationship functioning. We restrict our focus primarily to romantic relationships in the present chapter as it is these contexts that have received the most research attention thus far. However, perceived regard likely guides relationship processes in other types of interdependent relationships as well.

What is Perceived Regard?

The belief that one is regarded positively by others is important to all social relationships (Leary & Baumeister, 2000), but it is of even greater importance in romantic contexts. Romantic partners are central members of one's social network and acceptance by these important figures serve to bolster self-esteem and feelings of self-worth (Cooley, 1902; Leary, Tambor, Terdal, & Downs, 1995) in ways that less meaningful relationships cannot. In addition to the numerous intrapersonal benefits that stem from believing a romantic partner views oneself in a positive light, there are substantial interpersonal benefits as well. Conviction in romantic partners' valuation engenders positive expectations about a partner's responsiveness in times of need (Holmes & Cameron, 2005; Reis, Clark & Holmes, 2004) and thereby serves as the gateway to intimacy. That is, trusting that a partner will accommodate one's own needs in situations of dependence affords people confidence to pursue connectedness with their partners without concern of being rebuffed and thereby heightens mutual intimacy (Reis & Shaver, 1988). Thus, greater perceived regard emboldens people to set aside concerns about rejection and act in ways that further intimacy with romantic partners, for example by disclosing privileged information to them (Laurenceau, Feldman-Barrett, & Pietromonaco, 1998) or forgiving minor transgressions (Rusbult, Verette, Whitney, Slovik, & Lipkus, 1991).

Beliefs about a partner's regard are clearly important to both person and interpersonal functioning,

but how are such beliefs formed? The development of perceived regard with specific romantic partners has been somewhat understudied in the close relationships literature. However, notions about a partner's caring likely emerge as the result of both situational experiences and more stable personality characteristics. Clearly, a romantic partner's regard (or lack thereof) may be communicated directly through praise or criticism. More commonly however, it is inferred from partners' actions in diagnostic situations that commonly arise in romantic relationships. When one's outcomes are tied directly to his/her romantic partner's actions or cognitions, that person's behavior may connote perceived regard indirectly. Such situations may be relatively mundane, for example, when partners disagree on what restaurant to eat at, or may be relatively impactful, for example, when partners discuss having another child or relocating for a potential new job opportunity.

In these contexts, a partner may demonstrate responsiveness that engenders or sustains positive perceptions of regard by taking into consideration one's needs in addition to their own (Impett, Gable, & Peplau, 2005; Van Lange et al., 1997). Alternatively, a partner may respond negatively in such situations, declining to sacrifice for the sake of their partners or relationships. This may indicate to people a lack of responsiveness or caring that may undermine perceptions of regard (Rusbult & Van Lange, 2003). Though these diagnostic situations are highly informative, perceived regard may also shift as a function of more subtle relationship processes. For example, partners' efforts to change aspects of one's own personality or behavior often undermine perceived regard, particularly when partner regulations strategies are negative or hostile (Overall, Fletcher, & Simpson, 2006). A recent longitudinal study of romantic couples demonstrated that attempts at partner regulation predicted declines in perceived regard over a six-month period, suggesting that perceptions of regard can shift in accordance with relationship events (Overall & Fletcher, 2010).

Although beliefs about a partner's caring are subject to situational influence, people also maintain stable and chronic beliefs about partners' regard that affect relationship cognitions, motivation, and behavior. These chronic beliefs provide the basis for relational self-regulation because they shape the interpretation of relationship events and inform responses to these events. In most research, self-esteem serves as a proxy for these chronic beliefs about one's relational value (Leary et al., 1995). For low self-esteem people (LSEs), negative self-views elicit doubts about their partners' positive regard and lessen their willingness to forgo their own needs in situations of dependency (Murray et al., 2006). In contrast, high self-esteem people (HSEs) hold positive views about themselves and are eminently confident that their partners value them and will be responsive to their needs (Murray, Holmes, & Griffin, 2000; Murray, Holmes, MacDonald, & Ellsworth, 1998). It is these relatively fixed beliefs about the self that serve as the basis for the present chapter. Chronic perceived regard (used interchangeably with self-esteem from here forward) guides interpersonal self-regulatory processes through its impact on relational goal pursuit.

Before we proceed to examine how perceived regard influences relationship functioning, it is useful to highlight the self-perpetuating nature of chronic perceived regard. Preexisting beliefs about perceived regard often bias subsequent evaluations of a partner's regard that are consistent with (and thereby reinforce) chronic beliefs. This is particularly evident among LSEs, who utilize their own negative self-beliefs as a template for assessing their partner's regard (Murray et al., 1998). As a result, their judgments about a partner's caring are highly erroneous and widely discrepant from partner's reports of positive regard (Murray et al., 2000). In contrast, HSEs' perceptions of regard are not only more positive than those of LSEs, but also more accurate (Murray et al., 2000). They see themselves as positively as their partners see them, and they do not place the same contingencies on continued acceptance that LSEs do. This allows them to seek support from their partners in times of trouble and also enter other diagnostic situations that confirm their beliefs.

Regardless of the accuracy of one's perceived regard, such beliefs are critical to relationship functioning. A large body of research has been devoted to examining how chronic perceived regard governs important and diverse aspects of interpersonal dynamics and how this influence extends to relationship outcomes.

The Role of Perceived Regard in Romantic Risk Regulation

As discussed earlier, situations in which one must sacrifice control over personal outcomes to one's partner in service of relationship goals are ubiquitous in romantic relationships. Such situations offer unmatched opportunity to pursue closeness and thereby satisfy the fundamental motivation to belong (Baumeister & Leary, 1995). However, many of the behaviors and cognitions that facilitate pursuit of connectedness goals simultaneously leave one vulnerable to rejection and thereby oppose the strong motivation to avoid social pain (MacDonald & Leary, 2005). These interpersonally "risky" situations allow one to set aside rejection concerns and pursue the intimacy goals, or alternatively, to forgo connectedness and pursue self-protection goals that will shield them from the consequences of potential rejection.

Murray, Holmes, and Collins (2006) have posited the existence of a cognitive, behavioral and affective system that allows people to reconcile the motivational tension between connectedness and self-protection. This system is comprised of a series of procedural "if-then" rules that serve to shift priority from connectedness to self-protection goals as relationship circumstances dictate in order to maximize a person's sense of assurance that they are safe in their level of dependence. In situations in which this motivational tension is aroused, this regulatory system prioritizes connectedness goals or self-protection goals that in turn govern responses to these events.

Though this system operates normatively, chronic perceptions of a partner's regard play a critical role in determining which of these motivationally oppositional goals is prioritized in risky or threatening interpersonal situations. Extensive research by Murray and her colleagues (Murray et al., 1996, 2000, 2006, 2009; Murray, Derrick, Leder, & Holmes, 2008; Murray, Griffin, et al., 2006; Murray & Holmes, 2009) has demonstrated that those high and low in perceived regard differ drastically in their responses to relationship risk. Those who are chronically high in perceived regard (e.g., HSEs) respond to these situations by prioritizing connectedness goals. Confident that their partners care for them and will be responsive to them, HSEs draw closer to their partners in the face of threat. They cast aside rejection concerns and pursue connectedness in an effort to affirm their relationships. In contrast, those low in chronic perceived regard (e.g., LSEs) respond to relationship threat by prioritizing self-protection goals. They continually doubt their partners' valuation of them and readily forego connectedness to guard themselves against the pain of anticipated rejection.

These differences in self-regulation as a function of relationship threat have important effects on relationship functioning. In a series of experiments, Murray, Rose, Bellavia, Holmes, and Kusche (2002) activated rejection concerns by leading participants to believe that their romantic partners perceived faults in them or in the relationship. They then assessed participants' relationship evaluations on a variety of measures and found that responses varied as a function of chronic perceived regard. Relative to control participants, LSEs in the relationship threat condition rated their partners more negatively and were less optimistic about their future with that person. This relational devaluation reflected a self-protective motivation. By psychologically distancing themselves from their partners, LSEs sought to minimize the importance of the relationship and shelter themselves from the pain of anticipated rejection. HSEs, however, responded to rejection concerns in a radically different manner. Though they appeared to be less sensitive to relationship threats generally, an overall pattern emerged that HSEs made more *positive* relationship evaluations relative to control participants. Therefore, HSEs' chronic confidence in their partner's regard encouraged attempts to enhance their relationships despite the inherent risks.

This pattern of responding to acute relationship threats has also been observed in daily marital interactions. A 21-day daily diary study of married couples revealed that the way in which people responded to actual relationship stressors hinged on chronic perceived regard (Murray, Bellavia, Rose, & Griffin, 2003). Following days in which they felt hurt by their partners, participants who felt less valued behaved self-protectively. They distanced themselves from their partners by treating them in more critical and cold ways. In contrast, participants who felt valued by their partners reacted to perceived hurts by pursuing connectedness on the following day. That is, they compensated for feelings of vulnerability by drawing closer to their partners and by responding in a constructive manner.

The prioritization of self-protection or connectedness goals in response to interpersonal risk has important effects on relationship outcomes. An ironic consequence of self-protection goals is that they often bring about the very rejection they are meant to guard against. Repeated devaluation of a relationship is often exacerbated over time, as people (i.e., LSEs) become less charitable towards their partners on evaluations of both subjective qualities, such as warmth, and also on more objective traits such as attractiveness (Murray et al., 2000). Ultimately, this has a detrimental impact on relational well-being for both LSEs and their partners

(Murray et al., 2003) and greatly increases the likelihood of relationship dissolution. In contrast, prioritization of connectedness goals generally brings about positive outcomes in relationships, heightening commitment and satisfaction over time and enhancing relationship longevity (Murray et al., 2000; Wieselquist, Rusbult, Foster and Agnew, 1999). Though the pursuit of connectedness goals in the face of threat entails some degree of risk, evidence suggests that these responses to relationship threat are far more constructive in maintaining a satisfying romantic partnership.

To date, the primary focus of research on risk regulation processes has focused on exploring their relational impact. However, recent findings indicate that the impact of the risk regulation system is not limited to interpersonal contexts. Cavallo, Fitzsimons, and Holmes (2009) posited that the risk regulation system may be linked with a more fundamental motivational system that governs global approach and avoidance motivation and thereby affects self-regulation outside of relationship contexts as well. In this series of studies, HSE and LSE participants responded to relationship threats with shifts in global approach motivation that mirrored the regulatory shifts observed in prior risk regulation research. Following a relationship threat, LSEs inhibited their motivation to pursue positive outcomes. Relative to control participants, threatened LSEs were less willing to partake in rewarding but risky recreational activities (e.g., bungee jumping) and in another study, made more conservative decisions about financial investments. This concern for safety over reward mirrors the self-protective goal pursuit commonly observed in relationships. In contrast, HSEs in these studies appeared to bolster their approach motivation in response to relationship threat. Relative to control participants, those in the threat condition reported *greater* willingness to partake in risky recreational activities and a greater preference for a lucrative but highly risky investment strategy. They displayed heightened sensitivity to positive outcomes in the face of threat, a broad motivational response that may partially underlie HSEs' inclination to prioritize connectedness goals when confronted with relationship risk.

These findings imply that that the interpersonal risk regulation system reflects the activation of a broader motivational system that guides the pursuit of approach- and avoidance-directed goals. That is, the regulatory system that manages relationship-specific goals may have evolved from a more global system that governs pursuit of risk and rewards generally. If this is indeed the case, chronic perceived regard may alter the manner in which people pursue non-relational goals as well. It is possible that perceived regard's centrality to relationship functioning may "spill over" to other goal domains in ways that can significantly alter personal outcomes.

Taken together, research on the role of perceived regard in shaping relationship outcomes has revealed that it influences relationship self-regulation by altering sensitivity to rejection and ensuing responses to it. Whereas early research focused on identifying the impact of divergent risk regulation strategies on relationship well-being, recent work has begun to examine the precise operation of these strategies. Though the impact of perceived regard is pervasive in threatening relationship situations, situations in which it does *not* moderate responses are highly informative for understanding of relational self-regulation.

The Impact of Perceived Regard on Implicit and Explicit Responses to Relationship Threat

Much of the research we have presented in the preceding portion of the chapter has examined how people high or low in perceived regard think and act when rejection risk is salient. As might be expected, this work has primarily examined deliberative and explicit responses. More recently, research has explored how perceptions of a partner's regard influence relatively implicit or automatic responses to interpersonal risk. Studying risk regulation at this level of analysis has yielded several instances in which implicit and explicit responses diverge from one another. Perceived regard has little impact on implicit responses to threat, but it serves a highly important role in determining deliberative responses of the type we discuss earlier.

In a series of experimental studies, Murray, Derrick, Leder, and Holmes (2008) examined the activation of implicit connectedness and self-protection goals following relationship threat. They showed that interpersonal risk nonconsciously activated both of these goals equally among all participants, with chronic perceived regard having no bearing on implicit responses. When asked to consider a time in the past that they were hurt or disappointed by a close other who was not their partner, both HSEs and LSEs demonstrated heightened activation of connectedness goals, reflecting a motivation to draw closer to romantic partners in hopes

of alleviating feelings of vulnerability from sources external to the relationship (Murray et al., 2008). This adaptation reminds us of Bowlby's (1982) basic premise that even babies draw close to mothers when they are stressed by their environment. This finding is also consistent with recent work demonstrating that social threat motivates people to seek social belonging elsewhere (DeWall, Maner & Rouby, 2009; Maner, DeWall, Baumeister, & Schaller, 2007). However, another study revealed that more targeted relationship threats (e.g., about a recent time when people were hurt by their current partners) led to greater activation of *self-protection* goals in both HSEs and LSEs. This latter pattern of results was also observed when more global motivational orientations were examined. Relative to participants in a control condition, participants who experienced a relationship-specific threat showed activation of implicit domain-*general* avoidance goals that was not moderated by chronic perceived regard (Cavallo, Fitzsimons, & Holmes, 2010). Taken together, chronic perceived regard has little bearing on nonconscious, automatic responses to interpersonal risk. Why then, is perceived regard so influential in determining explicit responses?

To investigate the discrepancy between responses to explicit and implicit measures, Murray and her colleagues (2008) sought to detail the role that executive control plays in the operation of this regulatory system. Because connectedness and self-protection goals are oppositional, their concurrent activation in interpersonally risky situations presents a motivational conflict that must be resolved into a regulatory response (Cacioppo, Gardner, & Berntson, 1999). To do so, people must possess an executive control system that prioritizes one motivation over the other. Chronic perceived regard plays a critical role in the operation of this executive control system. People prioritize the situational motivation that best matches their chronic goal state, which differs as a function of stable beliefs about a partner's caring. Put another way, executive control processes override impulses that are incongruent with stable relationship goals.

People high in perceived regard are eminently confident in their partner's continued acceptance and have high expectations of the partner's benevolence. Because of their sense of safety, their chronic goal state is that of connectedness. When acute threats internal to the relationship activate self-protection goals, motivational conflict thus ensues. The executive control system then operates to overturn self-protective goals and prioritize situational connectedness goals that are congruent with their chronic motivational concerns. The resultant fit between dispositional and situational goals (cf. Higgins, 2005) likely reinforces connectedness goal strength and allows them to draw their partners closer in the face of threat.

This mechanism is similar for people low in perceived regard, though the outcomes are different. For these people, a partner's regard is perpetually in doubt and concerns about rejection (unwarranted though they may be) are ubiquitous. Consequently, self-protection goals are chronically active. When the conflicting impulse to connect with their partners is aroused by external threats, the executive control system prioritizes self-protection goals that are consistent with chronic motivations. Enhanced fit between situational goals and other goals drives low self-esteem people to "override" the impulse to connect and instead, distance themselves from their partners (Murray et al., 2008).

Recent studies have demonstrated how goal tension is resolved by prioritizing goals that are congruent with chronic relational motivations. In one such illustration, participants were implicitly primed with relationship-approach goals by completing a word-sorting task before rating closeness to their romantic partners on an explicit measure (Murray et al., 2008). For HSEs, the activation of situational relationship-approach goals was consistent with chronic connectedness goals and thus did not result in goal conflict. As such, HSEs reported feeling closer to their partner in the approach-priming condition than they did in the control condition. For LSE participants, however, the activation of relationship-promotion goals aroused a motivational conflict between these situational goals and more chronic self-protection goals. LSEs' executive control system served to "override" the implicitly primed connect goals and led participants in the approach-priming condition to report being *less* close to their partner than did control participants on the explicit rating scale, despite their lack of awareness of the relationship-promotion prime. Though this study illustrates the operation of the risk regulation system at its most basic level, similar evidence is seen using more elaborate methodologies.

Murray, Holmes, Aloni, Pinkus, Derrick, and Leder (2009) examined how people respond to heightened interdependence in their relationships. As romantic relationships develop, people experience restrictions on their autonomy as partners constrain each other's individual goal pursuits (cf. Fitzsimons & Shah, 2008). As such costs become apparent,

they present an internal risk to one's relationship and conflict with desires to maintain or heighten interdependence. In one experiment, autonomy costs were made salient by having participants list times in which their personal goals or desires were obstructed by their relationships (e.g., not being able to watch a TV show they wanted to). Next, participants provided both implicit and explicit evaluations of their relationship partners. Relative to participants in control conditions, participants who considered autonomy costs were more positive toward their partners on their implicit evaluations regardless of their chronic levels of perceived regard. Essentially, this compensatory response revealed an activation of connectedness goals in response to relationship threat among all participants. However, explicit ratings of partner valuing diverged as a function of self-esteem, reflecting different prioritization of goals by the executive control system.

High self-esteem participants prioritized connectedness goals over self-protection goals and provided explicit evaluations of their partners that were congruent with these goals. They set aside concerns about autonomy and continued to compensate on explicit measures. Low self-esteem participants, however, overrode their implicit positive feelings toward their partner and rated their partners more negatively on the deliberative self-report measures. This prioritization of self-protection goals over connectedness goals reflected a "correction" process that facilitates goal pursuit congruent with their chronic relational motivations.

Similarly, HSEs faced with motivational conflict also engage the executive control system to prioritize situational connectedness goals that fit with chronic relational motivations. This often leads to constructive responses to threat that serve to maintain healthy relationship functioning. Murray, Aloni, Holmes, Derrick, Stinson and Leder (2009) found that implicitly priming participants with the abstract concept of fairness in social exchange elicited feelings of anxiety about being inferior to their romantic partners. In turn, these participants attempted to protect themselves from potential rejection by heightening their partner's dependence on them. Relative to control participants, they sought to make themselves indispensable to their partners by assuming greater responsibility for their partner's daily functioning (e.g., keeping track of their partners' academic deadlines) and by narrowing their partners' social networks to elevate their importance to their partners. Such self-protective responses were observed among both HSE and LSE participants, again revealing that when risk is at the implicit level, perceived regard has minimal effect on relational goal pursuit.

However, when exchange concerns were *explicitly* primed, operation of the executive control system resulted in divergent responses among high and low self-esteem people. Low self-esteem participants again reported greater desire to promote their partners' dependence on them. They pursued self-protective goals in an attempt to heighten their importance to their partners and thus minimize the likelihood of rejection. High self-esteem participants, on the other hand, counteracted the impulse to self-protect and instead, displayed a similar level of connectedness goals as control participants. Specifically, they downplayed their anxiety about rejection and did not report any additional desire to heighten their partner's dependence. Thus, while all participants were motivated to protect themselves against rejection when inferiority concerns were activated implicitly, perceived regard moderated the extent to which people pursued these motivations when they were activated explicitly. Consistent with their chronic motivational orientations, low self-esteem participants pursued self-protection wholeheartedly, whereas high self-esteem participants instead overrode these motivations and behaved in relationship-promoting ways.

Is Executive Control Required For Risk Regulation?

Perceived regard exerts influence primarily on deliberative responses to interpersonal risk and has little bearing on automatic responses. However, research has only recently begun to examine the extent to which executive control is necessary for risk regulation and how differences between those high and low in perceived regard may be minimized or eliminated if people do not have full use of cognitive resources. Relationship dynamics shift when executive control is impaired, and current studies have provided insight into the importance of cognitive resources in the construction or erosion of relationship well-being.

In one investigation, all participants were exposed to a relationship threat (Cavallo, Holmes, Fitzsimons, Murray, & Wood, 2012). They were led to believe that they had overestimated their partners' regard for them and that they likely had exaggerated perceptions of how much their partners care about them. Next, participants completed a manipulation of cognitive load. Half the participants were asked to memorize a 3-digit string, whereas the other half

of the participants were instructed to memorize a 9-digit string—a difficult task that taxed participants' cognitive resources and undermined their capacity for executive control (Gilbert & Hixon, 1991). While doing this task, participants rated their relationship valuation on a number of measures. Among participants who had an easy digit rehearsal task (and therefore had full cognitive capacity), chronic perceived regard played a critical role. Participants high in perceived regard reported valuing their relationship greatly and were optimistic about their future with their partners, reflecting an emphasis on connectedness goals in the face of threat. In contrast, participants with low perceived regard were less positive in their evaluations, as they self-protectively derogated their relationships to buttress themselves from the threat of looming rejection.

Cognitive load undid these effects. High self-esteem participants were more conservative in their relationship evaluations relative to participants in the not-busy condition, presumably because diminished executive control rendered them less able to "override" conflicting self-protection goals activated by the threat manipulation with connection goals. That is, the positive cognitive constructions that supported their pursuit of connection goals were essentially removed. Conversely, low self-esteem participants made more generous evaluations of their relationships when cognitively busy. Demands on their cognitive control made them less inclined to set aside connectedness goals in pursuit of self-protection goals and consequently, and perhaps surprisingly, they were as positive about the future of their relationships as high self-esteem people were.

These findings mirror those observed in other recent risk regulation research. Murray and her colleagues (2008) found that when LSE participants' executive resources were depleted, they reported fewer concerns about rejection and a greater dependence on their partners as a source of happiness after a manipulation of interpersonal risk. This again revealed a lack of ability to enact self-protection goals that was not evident when LSE participants had ample regulatory resources. This particular finding informs our understanding of how perceived regard influences relationship outcomes and suggests ways in which interpersonal functioning can improve, particularly for low self-esteem people. Executive control allows LSEs the ability to implement procedural rules that serve to prioritize self-protection over connectedness in situations where these goals conflict. This leads to cognitions and behaviors that undermine relationship quality and ultimately heighten the likelihood of rejection (Murray et al., 2000). However, if this executive control is minimized in some way (e.g., by taxing self-regulatory ability in an unrelated domain), those low in perceived regard may be more inclined to pursue connectedness goals and thereby experience better outcomes. This research also suggests that rumination on negative events that is characteristic of LSEs (Heimpel, Wood, Marshall, & Brown, 2002) may be a contributing factor to disadvantageous risk regulation strategies. That is, with greater thought given to interpersonal risk, LSEs may override connectedness goals even more than the situation warrants.

These data also suggest that among high self-esteem people, relationship security is a constructive process. That is, people high in perceived regard do not passively experience positive relationship outcomes, but instead *create* them by using cognitive resources to pursue connectedness when the threat of rejection looms. Much as self-protection can be an effortful process for LSEs, HSEs must exert effort to set aside interpersonal risk and pursue connectedness. The threshold for detecting risk may be lower for HSEs (Murray et al., 2006), but it requires as much executive control to negotiate as it does for LSEs.

Future Directions

The relatively recent emergence of perceived regard as a core construct in relationship science has led to a more comprehensive understanding of the importance of feeling valued by romantic partners. However, there remain several avenues for future research that may further clarify and accentuate the role that perceived regard plays in determining romantic outcomes.

As discussed earlier in this chapter, the ways that beliefs about a partner's regard originate are still somewhat obscure despite recent advancements (e.g., Overall & Fletcher, 2010). More work examining perceived regard as an outcome of relationship processes, rather than as a predictor, would help to illuminate how such beliefs are crystallized. It may be particularly important to examine how prior relationship experience, not only with current partners, but also with previous partners, friends, and family members, influences perceptions of chronic perceived regard. It is likely that stable positive or negative beliefs about one's relational value are heavily influenced by prior relationships,

though the degree and nature of this influence is currently unclear.

Similarly, empirical study into perceived regard as an outcome of relationship processes may provide valuable insight into the dynamic nature of these beliefs. That is, the extent to which perceptions of a partner's regard are malleable and subject to change in the face of relationship events has not yet been fully explored. Because beliefs about perceived regard color interpretations of a partner's behavior (Murray et al., 2006), examining the types of relationship events that have the most direct influence on perceived regard may help inform means by which perceived regard may be made more positive and relationship stability thereby enhanced. Although the importance of perceived regard to romantic functioning seems readily apparent, future research into the psychological nature of these beliefs may contribute a great deal to understanding of the processes underlying this influence.

As alluded to in the latter portion of this chapter, it is important for researchers to continue to examine perceived regard's influence at the implicit level as well as the explicit level. Thus far, investigation at this level of analysis has attempted to identify how perceived regard influences implicit relationship processes and to reconcile these with previous results observed on explicit measures. Though such investigations have proved fruitful, they have primarily used explicit measures of perceived regard (often operationalized by reports of self-esteem) as the critical moderating variable. As such, less is known about the existence and nature of *implicit* beliefs about a partner's regard. Implicit beliefs about perceived regard may also play a crucial role in directing relationship behavior, and do so without conscious awareness. In one recent exploration, Murray, Holmes and Pinkus (2010) demonstrated that newlyweds' experience in conflict-of-interest situations predicted shifts in automatic attitudes (but not explicit ones) toward romantic partners several years later. They proposed that the outcomes of early interdependence experiences are registered nonconsciously and form the foundation of implicit attitudes about relationship partners. It is likely that implicit beliefs about a partner's regard are formed in a similar manner. That is, relationship experiences may contribute to the formation of automatic perceived regard without people's awareness, and these automatic beliefs may guide behavior or self-regulation to a similar extent that explicit beliefs do. Alternatively, such implicit attitudes toward romantic partners may actually serve as the foundation for explicit beliefs about a partner's regard. Beliefs about perceived regard may be, in fact, constructed from automatic partner attitudes. Although this link is admittedly speculative, further research into the implicit and explicit nature of perceived regard is warranted to provide a more thorough understanding of this highly important construct.

Conclusions

Perceptions of a partner's regard serve an instrumental role in shaping romantic relationships. Beliefs about the extent that one is valued by his/her romantic partner not only directly impact emotional well-being, but indirectly shape relationship outcomes by influencing goal pursuit. Feeling highly valued by one's romantic partner is associated with a host of positive outcomes and generally facilitates the pursuit of relationship intimacy, particularly in risky situations. Feeling less positively regarded, conversely, is highly detrimental to relationship and personal well-being and prompts engagement in self-protective goal pursuit that exacerbates relationship risk. Because perceived regard is of great importance to relationship science, it remains a promising avenue for future research. As scholars continue to investigate perceived regard and the cognitive processes underlying its impact of relationship outcomes, it will undoubtedly contribute a great deal to understanding relationship behavior. In addition, it may provide insight into how the detrimental impact of low perceived regard can be minimized. This may serve to improve relationship outcomes for those whose unwarranted negative beliefs often undermine their ability to fulfill fundamental needs to obtain intimacy and interdependence with romantic partners.

References

Baumeister, R. F., & Leary, M. R. (1995). The need to belong: Desire for interpersonal attachments as a fundamental human motivation. *Psychological Bulletin, 117*, 497–529.

Bowlby, J. (1982). *Attachment and Loss: Vol. 1. Attachment* (2nd ed.). New York, NY: Basic Books.

Cacioppo, J. T., Gardner, W. L., & Berntson, G. G. (1999). The affect system has parallel and integrative processing components: Form follows function. *Journal of Personality and Social Psychology, 76*, 839–855.

Cavallo, J. V., Fitzsimons, G. M., & Holmes, J. G. (2009). Taking chances in the face of threat: Romantic risk regulation and approach motivation. *Personality and Social Psychology Bulletin, 35*, 737–751.

Cavallo, J. V., Fitzsimons, G. M., & Holmes, J. G. (2010a). When self-protection overreaches: Relationship-specific threat activates domain-general avoidance motivation. *Journal of Experimental Social Psychology, 46*, 1–8.

Cavallo, J. V., Holmes, J. G., Fitzsimons, G. M., Murray, S. L., & Wood, J. V. (2012). Managing motivational conflict: How self-esteem and executive resources influence self-regulatory responses to risk. *Journal of Personality and Social Psychology, 103*, 430–451.

Cooley, C. H. (1902). *Human Nature and the Social Order*. New York: Scribner.

DeWall, C. N., Maner, J. K., & Rouby, D. A. (2009). Social exclusion and early-stage interpersonal perception: Selective attention to signs of acceptance following social exclusion. *Journal of Personality and Social Psychology, 96*, 729–741.

Fitzsimons, G. M., & Shah, J. Y. (2008). How goal instrumentality shapes relationship evaluations. *Journal of Personality and Social Psychology, 95*, 319–337.

Gilbert, D. T., & Hixon, J. G. (1991). The trouble of thinking: Activation and application of stereotypic beliefs. *Journal of Personality and Social Psychology, 60*, 509–517.

Heimpel, S. A., Wood, J. V., Marshall, M. A., & Brown, J. D. (2002). Do people with low self-esteem really want to feel better? Self-esteem differences in motivation to repair negative moods. *Journal of Personality and Social Psychology, 82*, 128–147.

Higgins, E. T. (2005). Value from regulatory fit. *Current Directions in Psychological Science, 14*, 209–213.

Holmes, J. G., & Cameron, J. (2005). An integrative review of theories of interpersonal cognition: An interdependence theory perspective. In M. W. Baldwin (Ed.), *Interpersonal Cognition* (pp. 415–447). New York: Guilford Press.

Impett, E. A., Gable, S. L., & Peplau, L. A. (2005). Giving up and giving in: The costs and benefits of daily sacrifice in intimate relationships. *Journal of Personality and Social Psychology, 89*, 327–344.

Laurenceau, J., Barrett, L. F., & Pietromonaco, P. R. (1998). Intimacy as an interpersonal process: The importance of self-disclosure, partner disclosure, and perceived partner responsiveness in interpersonal exchanges. *Journal of Personality and Social Psychology, 74*, 1238–1251.

Leary, M. R., & Baumeister, R. F. (2000). The nature and function of self-esteem: Sociometer theory. In M. P. Zanna (Ed.), *Advances in Experimental Social Psychology* (Vol. 32, pp. 1–62). San Diego: Academic Press.

Leary, M. R., Tambor, E. S., Terdal, S. K., & Downs, D. L. (1995). Self-esteem as an interpersonal monitor: The sociometer hypothesis. *Journal of Personality and Social Psychology, 68*, 518–530.

MacDonald, G., & Leary, M. R. (2005). Why does social exclusion hurt? The relationship between social and physical pain. *Psychological Bulletin, 131*, 202–223.

Maner, J. K., DeWall, C. N., Baumeister, R. F., & Schaller, M. (2007). Does social exclusion motivate withdrawal or reconnection? Resolving the "porcupine problem." *Journal of Personality and Social Psychology, 92*, 42–55.

Murray, S. L., Aloni, M., Holmes, J. G., Derrick, J. L., Stinson, D. A., & Leder, S. (2009). Fostering partner dependence as trust insurance: The implicit contingencies of the exchange script in close relationships. *Journal of Personality and Social Psychology, 96*, 324–348.

Murray, S. L., Bellavia, G. M., Rose, P., & Griffin, D. W. (2003). Once hurt, twice hurtful: How perceived regard regulates daily marital interactions. *Journal of Personality and Social Psychology, 84*, 126–147.

Murray, S. L., Derrick, J. L., Leder, S., & Holmes, J. G. (2008). Balancing connectedness and self-protection goals in close relationships: A levels-of-processing perspective on risk regulation. *Journal of Personality and Social Psychology, 94*, 429–459.

Murray, S. L., Griffin, D. W., Rose, P., & Bellavia, G. (2006). For better or worse? Self-esteem and the contingencies of acceptance in marriage. *Personality and Social Psychology Bulletin, 32*, 866–880.

Murray, S. L., & Holmes, J. G. (2009). The architecture of interdependent minds: A motivation-management theory of mutual responsiveness. *Psychological Review, 116*, 908–928.

Murray, S. L., Holmes, J. G., Aloni, M., Pinkus, R. T., Derrick, J. L., & Leder, S. (2009). Commitment insurance: Compensating for the autonomy costs of interdependence in close relationships. *Journal of Personality and Social Psychology, 97*, 256–278.

Murray, S. L., Holmes, J. G., & Collins, N. L. (2006). Optimizing assurance: The risk regulation system in relationships. *Psychological Bulletin, 132*, 641–666.

Murray, S. L., Holmes, J. G., & Griffin, D. W. (2000). Self-esteem and the quest for felt security: How perceived regard regulates attachment processes. *Journal of Personality and Social Psychology, 78*, 478–498.

Murray, S. L., Holmes, J. G., MacDonald, G., & Ellsworth, P. C. (1998). Through the looking glass darkly? When self-doubts turn into relationship insecurities. *Journal of Personality and Social Psychology, 75*, 1459–1480.

Murray, S. L., Holmes, J. G., & Pinkus, R. T. (2010). A smart unconscious? Procedural origins of automatic partner attitudes in marriage. *Journal of Experimental Social Psychology, 46*, 650–656.

Murray, S. L., Rose, P., Bellavia, G. M., Holmes, J. G., & Kusche, A. G. (2002). When rejection stings: How self-esteem constrains relationship-enhancement processes. *Journal of Personality and Social Psychology, 83*, 556–573.

Overall, N. C., & Fletcher, G. J. O. (2010). Perceiving regulation from intimate partners: Reflected appraisal and self-regulation processes in close relationships. *Personal Relationships, 17*, 433–456.

Overall, N. C., Fletcher, G. J. O., & Simpson, J. A. (2006). Regulation processes in intimate relationships: The role of ideal standards. *Journal of Personality and Social Psychology, 91*, 662–685.

Reis, H. T., Clark, M. S., & Holmes, J. G. (2004). Perceived partner responsiveness as an organizing construct in the study of intimacy and closeness. In D. J. Mashek, & A. P. Aron (Eds.), *Handbook of Closeness and Intimacy* (pp. 201–225). Mahwah, NJ: Lawrence Erlbaum Associates.

Rusbult, C. E., & Van Lange, P. A. M. (2003). Interdependence, interaction and relationships. *Annual Review of Psychology, 54*, 351–375.

Rusbult, C. E., Verette, J., Whitney, G. A., Slovik, L. F., & Lipkus, I. (1991). Accommodation processes in close relationships: Theory and preliminary empirical evidence. *Journal of Personality and Social Psychology, 60*, 53–78.

Van Lange, P. A. M., Rusbult, C. E., Drigotas, S. M., Arriaga, X. B., Witcher, B. S., & Cox, C. L. (1997). Willingness to sacrifice in close relationships. *Journal of Personality and Social Psychology, 72*, 1373–1395.

Wieselquist, J., Rusbult, C. E., Foster, C. A., & Agnew, C. R. (1999). Commitment, pro-relationship behavior, and trust in close relationships. *Journal of Personality and Social Psychology, 77*, 942–966.

Peer Rejection among Children and Adolescents: Antecedents, Reactions, and Maladaptive Pathways

Jaana Juvonen

Abstract

It is proposed that exclusion from peer interactions compromises development primarily through two defensive pathways involving aggression and social-withdrawal. Hostile attributional biases and anger expectations enable aggressive children to maintain positive self-views in the face of rejection, but place them at risk for continued problem behaviors. Although withdrawal from peer interactions helps nonaggressive children reduce rejection distress, lack of peer contact increases the risk of continued social problems. That is, social-cognitive biases together with peer feedback help account for the diverging developmental pathways and outcomes of aggressive vs. withdrawn rejected children. The implications of a developmental approach are discussed in terms of current debates about the effects and functions of rejection.

Key Words: aggression, development, emotional distress, hostile attributions, peer networks, self-blame, social-cognitive biases, withdrawal

Introduction

Repeated exclusion and bullying experiences in childhood and adolescence are associated with compromised development. For example, children repeatedly rejected by their classmates are at risk for a wide range of adjustment difficulties, including mental health problems and criminality by young adulthood (Asher & Coie, 1990). These findings are consistent with Harlow's experiments with Rhesus monkeys, which demonstrated that young monkeys deprived of peer contact showed signs of maladjustment later in life. Although the pathways or exact mechanisms by which earlier peer relationship problems compromise development are not fully understood, the assumption guiding developmental research is that social skills acquired through positive peer interactions are critical for adaptive interpersonal interaction and healthy emotional well-being (Baumeister & Leary, 1995; Ladd, 1999).

Most research on peer rejection among children and adolescents focuses on subtypes of socially marginalized youth. Specifically, aggression and social withdrawal have been linked to group-based peer rejection (dislike and avoidance) among children starting at age 4 (Wood, Cowan, & Baker, 2002). Nearly half of rejected children in elementary schools are aggressive (Parkhurst & Asher, 1992; Rubin, Bukowski, & Parker, 1998), whereas 10% to 30% are socially withdrawn. The two sets of behavioral correlates are particularly interesting inasmuch as aggressive-rejected children appear to be protected from distress, but they are at risk for subsequent conduct problems, including criminality (e.g., Coie, Terry, Lenox, Lochman, & Hyman, 1995). In contrast, socially withdrawn-rejected youth show signs of emotional distress both concurrently and over time (e.g., Rubin, LaMare, & Lollis, 1990).

Given the current debates in social psychology about whether rejection causes significant emotional distress and whether aggressive responses to threats of social isolation are defensive reactions (Blackhart, Nelson, Knowles, & Baumeister, 2009; Leary, Twenge, & Quinlivan, 2006; Williams, 2007), I review research on the two subtypes of rejected youth. My goal is to demonstrate the ways in which findings on naturally unfolding peer rejection complement the knowledge gained from laboratory studies. Because peer rejection in childhood and adolescence is studied by relying mainly on correlational methods, any conclusions about the effects of rejection are easily confounded by the causes of rejection (Juvonen & Gross, 2005). Yet in light of evidence suggesting that both hostile and submissive-withdrawn reactions to peer ridicule increase the risk of continued or repeated exclusion (Salmivalli, Karhunen, & Lagerspetz,1996), I consider aggression and social withdrawal not only as risk factors for peer rejection, but I propose that they also capture maladaptive (fight vs. flight) defenses to social exclusion.

Aggressive-Rejected Children

As mentioned above, aggressive-rejected children and adolescents do not report emotional distress following exclusion by their peers (e.g., Parkhurst & Asher, 1992). Yet, they are at risk for committing criminal acts later in life (e.g., Kupersmidt & Coie, 1990; Tremblay, Masse, Vitaro, & Dobkin, 1995), including interpersonal violence (Coie et al, 1995). If the aggression displayed is not only considered as behavior that increases the risk of peer rejection, but also as a response to rejection, then it is a maladaptive reaction inasmuch as the hostile responses do not facilitate positive interactions. However, if aggression is viewed as a defensive response to a threatened sense of belonging (Baumeister & Leary, 1995), then it can help protect positive self-views and explain why the hostile behavior is maintained.

Consistent with the defensiveness hypothesis, aggressive-rejected youth underestimate the degree to which they are disliked and they rate their social competencies as high as do their more liked and popular peers (Bovin & Begin, 1989; Hymel, Bower, & Woody, 1993; Patterson, Kupersmidt, & Griesler, 1990). Moreover, in experimental studies that rely on confederate responses, aggressive-rejected youth deflect disapproval cues more than other children do (Zakriski & Coie, 1996). Thus, aggressive-rejected youth appear to be particularly good at protecting themselves from negative social feedback. How are they able to do that?

Social Cognitions of Aggressive-Rejected Youth

Analyses of the ways in which aggressive and rejected youth focus their attention and construct their social experiences help us understand their positive self-views. For example, Schippell, Vasey, Cravens-Brown and Bretveld (2003) demonstrated that reactively aggressive adolescents displayed suppressed attention to rejection, ridicule, and failure cues. A meta-analysis by Orobio de Castro and colleagues (2002), in turn, shows that hostile attributional bias in reaction to ambiguously threatening behavior is very robust among aggressive children. Similar biases have been shown among rejected children (Feldman & Dodge, 1987), and hostile attributions about others' negative intent are especially pronounced among aggressive-rejected children (Dodge, 1993). Recent laboratory experiments with college students provide further evidence that rejection increases the likelihood that neutral stimuli are perceived hostile, and that hostile cognitions in turn mediate the association between exclusion and aggression (DeWall, Twenge, Gitter, & Baumeister, 2009). Thus, hostile attributional bias helps not only explain aggressive reactions (see Weiner, 1995), but combined with lack of attention to rejection cues, these social-cognitive biases also protect youth from emotional distress and negative self-views.

Focusing on defense mechanisms associated with exclusion among elementary school age girls, Sandstrom and Cramer (2003) found that low peer preference was associated with greater reliance on denial (cf. lack of attention to rejection cues) and projection (cf. hostile attribution bias). When experimentally manipulating exclusion with an unknown peer, girls who were not accepted by their classmates were more likely than their better-accepted peers to rely on these defense mechanisms. Taken together, the findings suggest that repeated rejection experiences foster coping responses that help youth protect themselves from the blows of social exclusion. But why do these defensive mechanisms not protect aggressive-rejected youth from subsequent maladjustment?

Positive Peer Feedback Reinforces Maladaptive Behaviors

Although it is imperative to understand intrapsychological processes related to experiences of exclusion, developmental research demonstrates that it is also critical to understand the role of the larger peer context in which peer rejection unfolds. Although rejected sociometric status (i.e., high proportion of classmates naming the same peer as someone who they dislike or with whom they do not want to play or "hang out") is an indicator of sentiments within a peer group, it does not necessarily provide information about how the rejected child is treated. Daily report data suggest that peers do not necessarily convey their negative sentiments the same way toward those who are aggressive vs. those who are equally disliked but withdrawn. When 10 to 13-year-old children documented their everyday social experiences with peers aggressive-rejected boys were significantly less likely to report negative peer treatment than their withdrawn-rejected counterparts (Sandstrom & Cillessen, 2003). These findings suggest that peer reactions to aggressive-rejected children are "kinder" than what was expected on the basis of the sentiments of the peer group members. This is understandable because it is self-protective not to convey one's dislike toward an aggressive peer (Juvonen & Galvan, 2009). However, this means that aggressive-rejected youth experience their social environment friendlier (or at least less hostile) than what their rejection rate conveys.

Not only might peers be reluctant to convey their dislike toward a peer who is aggressive, but they often also rate hostile peers as popular (e.g., Juvonen, Graham, & Schuster, 2003; Luthar & McMahon, 1996). For example, Juvonen et al. (2003) found that by the beginning of middle school when new social hierarchies are established, bullies were considered "cooler" than those identified as socially adjusted. Although bullies had prominent social status, they were also moderately rejected. In other words, dominant peers do not have to be liked (Juvonen & Galvan, 2009). These findings suggest that aggressive-rejected youth's views of their social success are not necessarily biased, but they also partly reflect their "distorted" reality.

Whereas the absence of negative feedback from peers may protect aggressive-rejected children from negative self-views, it also provides them with no reason to change their behavior (Juvonen & Gross, 2005). Moreover, aggressive tendencies are likely to be honed over time, inasmuch as hostile youth tend to affiliate with like peers. Cairns, Cairns, Neckerman, Gest, and Gariepy (1988) demonstrated that aggressive youth are not social isolates but they are as likely to be socially connected as their non-aggressive peers. However, Patterson, Capaldi and Bank (1991) point out that peer rejection limits aggressive children's options for typical (healthy) peer relationships, permitting them only to befriend similarly aggressive and rejected peers. Affiliation with other aggressive youth is likely to further encourage their hostile behavior patterns. Because interactions between antisocial youth facilitate "deviance training," whereby deviant youth encourage one another's problematic behavior (Dishion, Spracklen, Andrews, & Patterson, 1996), it is therefore not surprising that antisocial (including aggressive) youth are at greater risk for subsequent criminal behaviors (Dishion, McCord, & Poulin, 1999). Thus, the combination of the "kinder than expected" social feedback and friendships with other aggressive youth can help account why aggressive-rejected youth are at risk for increasingly violent behaviors.

In sum, research on aggressive-rejected children suggest hostile behavior can conceptualized as a defensive strategy that helps protect positive self-views (cf. Baumeister, Smart, & Boden, 1996). As depicted in Figure 10.1 below, suppressed attention to rejection cues and hostile attributions, lack of expressed negative peer sentiments, social prominence, and affiliations with other aggressive youth all help maintain positive self-views and the aggressive behaviors that enable these social dynamics. Moreover, the social feedback aggressive-rejected youth receive from their peers along with the specific ties with other aggressive youth are likely to

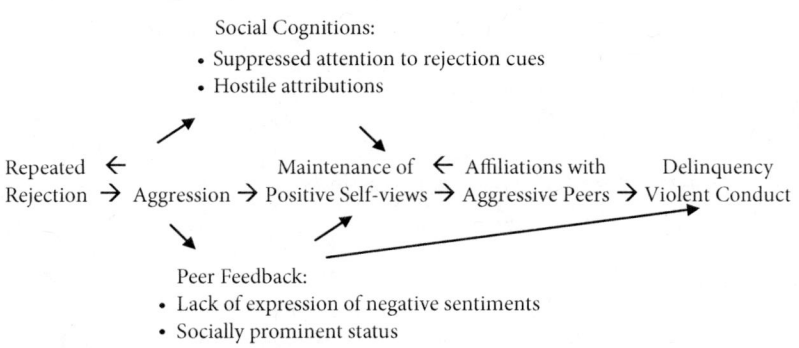

Figure 10.1 Developmental Pathway for Aggressive-Rejected Children.

also directly predict increasingly maladaptive hostile behaviors over time.

Withdrawn-Rejected Children

As mentioned earlier, there is a somewhat smaller group of rejected children who are socially withdrawn rather than aggressive. Unlike aggressive-rejected youth who seem to be able to protect themselves from the sting of exclusion, withdrawn-rejected youth show signs of emotional distress and are at risk for subsequent internalizing problems, such as depression and social anxiety (e.g., Rubin, LeMare, & Lollis, 1990; Burk, Dodge, & Price, 1995; Boivin, Hymel, & Bukowski, 1995). Their concerns over additional rejection experiences can isolate youth to the point that their subsequent mental health problems are likely to be due to lack of social contacts (e.g., Cacioppo & Hawkley, 2005). Thus, although withdrawal from peer interactions may alleviate rejection distress, lack of peer contact can have lasting impact on their well-being.

Compared to aggressive-rejected children, withdrawn-rejected children report greater loneliness, emotional distress, and have more negative self-perceptions (e.g., Boivin & Hymel, 1997; Volling, MacKinnon-Lewis, Rabiner, & Baradaran, 1993). The question is whether these differences merely reflect distinct psychological profiles or personalities of the two groups of rejected youth or whether we can document that negative social experiences independently contribute to the unfavorable self-views and distress of withdrawn-rejected youth. Addressing this question, Boivin, Hymel and Bukowski (1995) demonstrated that the aversive social experiences of socially withdrawn children indeed explained their feelings of loneliness and depression two years later. Also, studies on victims of bullying (most of who are submissive and withdrawn) show that negative social experiences largely account for their subsequent emotional distress (e.g., Kochenderfer & Ladd, 1996; Kochenderfer-Ladd & Wardrop, 2001).

Compared with aggressive-rejected youth, withdrawn-rejected youngsters' self-views are also more realistic. That is, unlike aggressive children, withdrawn-rejected children acknowledge their social difficulties and feel lonely (Hymel, Bowker, & Woody, 1993; Parkhurst & Asher, 1992). Awareness of problems is critical: rejected and bullied youth feel depressed and lonely only when they recognize their social plight (Panak & Graber, 1992; Graham & Juvonen, 2000; Graham, Bellmore, & Juvonen, 2003). Ironically, this realism does not serve them

well when depression and anxiety make them avoid peer interactions.

Observations of peer interactions in groups of unacquainted peers show that nonassertive boys become increasing withdrawn as the group's behavior is more coercive toward them (Schwartz, Dodge, & Coie, 1993). The most victimized boys spent less and less time in social play as they received increasing negative responses from their peers. Similarly, Dodge (1983) demonstrated that boys who were initially neither liked nor disliked by their classmates displayed high levels of withdrawn behavior in novel play groups only after they were rebuffed. Thus, aversive peer interactions not only contribute to emotional distress, they also contribute to subsequent avoidance of social situations.

Much like in the case of Harlow's monkeys, low level or lack of peer contact can result in long-term deficits in social interaction. These deficits can help explain why socially withdrawn-rejected youth are at risk for continued emotional problems. Hence, although social withdrawal can be conceptualized as a defensive "flight" response to repeated peer rejection, it does not protect in the long term. To understand the reactions of withdrawn-rejected children, it is helpful to examine how they construe their plight and how they are treated by peers compared with those who are aggressive.

Social Cognitions of Withdrawn-Rejected Youth

Once rejected children experience distress, they are likely to become increasingly sensitive to social threat cues (London, Downey, & Bonica, 2007). Based on interpretations of videotaped peer interactions, Bell-Dolan (1995) found that compared with their nonanxious peers, anxious children were more likely to misinterpret nonhostile interactions as hostile. Such bias likely captures anxiety-arousing expectations. That is, concerns about future rejection increase attention to rejection cues and such hypervigilance likely heightens sense of exclusion (Downey, Mougios, Ayduk, London, & Shoda, 2004). By relying on hypothetical vignettes, London, Downey, & Bonica (2010) showed that whereas anxious expectations of rejection predict elevated anxiety and social withdrawal, anger expectations predict increased aggression and decreased anxiety among young adolescents.

In addition to sensitivity to social cues and anxious expectations, attributional interpretations of social situations can help account for differential responses to aversive peer encounters. Unlike aggressive youth who tend to blame others, lonely children are more likely to attribute their social failures to internal and stable attributions (Hymel et al., 1983). Similarly, submissive victims of bullying are particularly likely to self-blame (Graham & Juvonen, 1998). Thus, in contrast to the hostile attribution bias implicating others (characteristic of aggressive-rejected youth), socially withdrawn youth who feel the emotional pain of rejection, blame themselves. Research on victims of bullying shows that internal and uncontrollable attributions mediate the associations between peer maltreatment and level of emotional distress (Graham & Juvonen, 1998). Hence, the ways aggressive versus withdrawn youth interpret their world allow us to explain their distinct ways of reacting to their rejection experiences.

Peer Responses Reinforce Maladaptive Thoughts and Behaviors

To comprehend how such diametrically opposite set of social-cognitions (other vs. self-blame; anxious vs. anger expectations) of aggressive-rejected and withdrawn-rejected children might develop, it is informative to examine the peer feedback that the two groups receive. As described earlier, daily reports of social experiences revealed that aggressive-rejected boys report significantly fewer negative peer encounters than do withdrawn-rejected youth (Sandstrom & Cillessen, 2003). Such differences can be understood when considering the likelihood of retaliation. That is, withdrawn-rejected peers are less of a threat compared to peers who are aggressive. Hence, timid children who feel lonely and distressed are safe targets.

Finally, by virtue of their problems, socially withdrawn-rejected youth are unlikely to be socially connected. Lack of friendship networks places them at risk for a host of negative peer interactions (Hodges, Malone, & Perry, 1997). Moreover, when socially withdrawn youth have friends, they are typically other socially insecure and marginalized peers (Rubin, Wojslawowicz, Rose-Krasnor, Booth-LaForce, & Burgess, 2006). Hence, similarly to the aggressive-rejected children, the peer socialization experiences of withdrawn-rejected youth are suboptimal and likely to reinforce maladaptive behaviors.

The developmental pathway of withdrawn-rejected youth is depicted in Figure 10.2. As shown in the figure, withdrawn children experiencing repeated rejection blame themselves for social failures and have anxious expectations. These maladaptive social-cognitions, in turn, elevate their level of distress and negative self-views. The distress and self-views are also affected by the negative peer feedback received (i.e., overt exclusion and anxious-withdrawn friends). Although avoidance of peer contact can protect youth from additional negative social experiences and emotional distress, avoidance of peer contact, combined with mainly negative peer feedback increases the risk of depression. Hence, social isolation helps explain why socially withdrawn-rejected youth are at risk for long-term emotional problems, such as depression.

Does Rejection Independently Contribute to Long-Term Maladjustment?

Because aggression and social withdrawal are nonnormative behaviors likely to elicit negative reactions from peers (see Juvonen & Gross, 2005), it is critical to know whether peer rejection independently contributes to subsequent problems or whether it merely functions as a marker of dysfunction (Parker & Asher, 1987). Indeed, evidence suggests that rejection contributes to subsequent maladjustment over and above behavioral risk factors.

Following up a large sample of African-American children from middle childhood to early adolescence, Coie, Lochman, Terry and Hyman (1992) demonstrated that childhood peer rejection contributed to

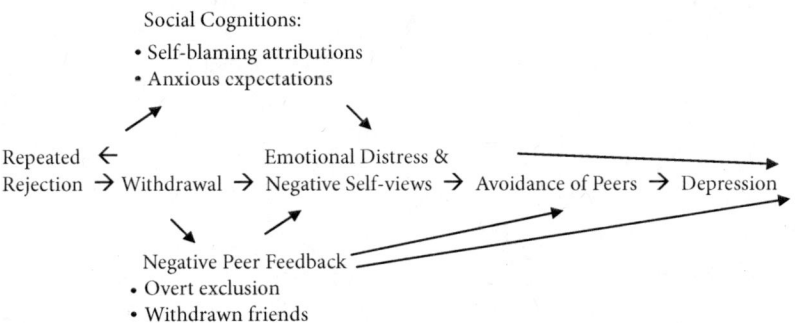

Figure 10.2 Developmental Pathway for Withdrawn-Rejected Children.

externalizing problems three years later, over and above childhood aggression. Subsequent analyses of the same sample revealed that the combination of childhood aggression and peer rejection not only predicted greater externalizing problems among boys seven years later better than either aggression or rejection alone, but that also the combination of aggression and rejection increased the risk of committing assaults by the second year in high school (Coie, et al., 1995). Focusing on an ethnically mixed sample of girls, Prinstein and La Greca (2004) showed that when aggressive girls were rejected (as opposed to not rejected), aggression remained stable across 6 years and predicted increased levels of substance use and risky sexual behaviors (cf. Bierman & Wargo, 1995). These findings suggest that rejection is not only a marker for problem behaviors, but it also increases the stability of behavior problems and amplifies the risk for subsequent delinquent and problem behaviors.

Whereas peer rejection seems to amplify the association between earlier signs of aggression and subsequent conduct problems, rejection experiences explain or account for the links between social withdrawal and emotional distress. As mentioned earlier, Boivin et al. (1995) showed that the association between earlier social withdrawal and subsequent emotional distress was mediated by negative peer status. In other words, the aversive social experiences of socially withdrawn children explained their feelings of loneliness and depression 2 years later. Additional studies on victims of bullying show even more clearly that the social experiences account for subsequent emotional distress (e.g., Kochenderfer & Ladd, 1996).

In sum, in spite of the problems associated with correlational research, there is adequate support for the fact that exclusion experiences negatively affect developmental trajectories. The ways in which rejection compromises subsequent well-being depend in part on the behavioral correlates of rejection. Whereas exclusion by peers amplifies the ways in which early aggression is associated with subsequent problems, exclusion confronted by socially withdrawn youth accounts for their subsequent distress. These findings are intriguing in the face of the experimental social psychological evidence suggesting that

some rejection manipulations are more effective in inducing distress than others (see Blackhart et al., 2010; Williams, 2009 for a review) and that aggressive responses to exclusion indicate insensitivity to negative social experiences that reflect a defensive response (e.g., DeWall, 2009).

Summary of the Developmental Sequence Stemming from Peer Rejection

The critical intrapsychological and interpsychological components of a developmental model of the consequences of repeated peer rejection are summarized in Figure 10.3. Consistent with social-cognitive information processing models (e.g., Dodge & Crick, 1990; Crick & Dodge, 1994), this author proposed that rejection elicits negative expectancies and social-cognitive (attentional as well as attributional) biases in the rejected. Depending on behaviors (i.e., aggression vs. withdrawal) that caused the rejection to happen, the social-cognitions vary. In the case of aggressive children, suppressed attention to rejection cues, inferences of hostile intent by others, and anger expectations help protect positive self-views and avoid emotional distress. In the case of submissive and socially withdrawn children, heightened attention to rejection cues, anxious expectations, and tendency to blame oneself, in turn, promote increased emotional distress and negative self-evaluations.

Emotional distress (or lack thereof) and self-views that are both shaped by the social cognitions of the rejected help us understand how youth react to their rejection experiences. Consistent with the above review, social-cognitions likely promote the very behavior patterns (e.g., aggression and social withdrawal) that elicited the rejection in the first place. Social perceptions, in turn, mediate the relation between the initial eliciting behavior and distress and related self-views. In sum, the proposed developmental model depicts an array of interpersonal and intrapersonal processes that are likely to propel rejected youth toward increasingly problematic future.

Beyond the Main Effects of Rejection

The above reviewed research suggests one reason why examination of the main effects of rejection

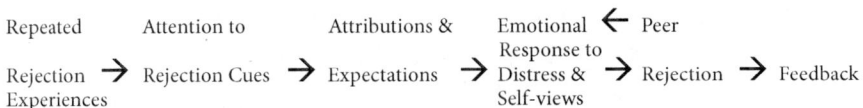

Figure 10.3 Developmental Sequence of the Consequences of Repeated Rejection Experiences.

reveals mixed and partly puzzling results. Based on an extensive meta-analysis of 192 studies, Blackhart et al. (2010) conclude that contrary to the compelling conceptual arguments about the need to belong (Baumeister & Leary, 1995), the evidence on rejection causing distress and low self-esteem is weaker than expected. Although several possible moderators were tested in this meta-analysis, individual differences, such as those examined by developmental psychologists were not included (after all, most studies included were laboratory investigations). Yet the current review, albeit much more limited in its scope and thoroughness than the meta-analysis, suggests that rejection experiences interact with the psyche of the target of rejection. Whether or not social exclusion is related to increased distress and negative self-evaluations depends on the psychological profile of the rejected. That is, individual differences (and particularly behaviors that increase the risk of rejection) likely amplify as a function of repeated rejection experiences (Juvonen & Gross, 2005) and other peer feedback. Unless individual differences are considered, the effects can indeed cancel one another out in any large-scale meta-analyses. But besides ignoring possible moderators, even more is at stake is when laboratory experiments are used to make conclusions about the group functions of rejection, to which I turn in the next section.

Group Function of Rejection

Consistent with the predominant approach to peer rejection in developmental psychology, the current review focused on peer rejection not as a dyadic encounter but as a plight of an individual within a group of (familiar) peers. Therefore it is pertinent to consider the function that rejection serves within the group. That is, why are some members of the group (e.g., classroom) shunned by others?

When the typical correlates of rejection are conceptualized as antecedents of (as opposed to reactions to) rejection, the findings suggest that any non-normative or deviant behaviors increase the likelihood of peer rejection (see Juvonen & Gross, 2005; Juvonen & Galvan, 2009 for review). That is, aggressive and socially withdrawn behaviors elicit peer rejection because they are deviant in most groups (Wright, Giammarino & Parad, 1986; Boivin, Dodge, & Coie, 1995). Thus, exclusion is an effective means of social control (e.g., Kerr et al. 2009). By excluding the one who does not fit in, the group can be more cohesive (cf. Gruter & Masters, 1986).

Although aggression and social withdrawal are almost universal predictors of rejection in childhood and adolescence, studies that manipulate the composition of peer groups show that this is not necessarily the case. Instead, those who stand out from the rest of the group are most likely to be rejected (Stormshak et al., 1999; Sentse Scholte, Salmivalli, & Voeten, 2007). If rejection captures the lack of fit between the child and the group, then a great number of laboratory experiments that examine the effects of rejection may be limited in informing us about the social functions of rejection. The findings about lack of emotional distress and low self-esteem as a result of experimentally manipulated rejection experience (Blackhart et al., 2010) may not only mask critical individual differences, but moreover fail to provide insights about the function that rejection serves within groups. Thus, when the effect of a social experience is not examined under conditions in which it typically occurs, but under artificially decontextualized situations, the conclusions about its social function are likely to be limited.

Future Directions

The social misfit hypothesis allows us to make predictions about the effects of rejection. If rejection is to "teach a lesson" to anyone who deviates from the group norms (Juvonen & Galvan, 2009), violations should be punished (see also Kerr et al, 2009). Although the initial goal of such punishment may be to correct the deviant behavior by increasing compliance to group norms, the research reviewed in this chapter shows that the effects of the punishment (i.e., exclusion) may not work. But aggression and social withdrawal likely represent extreme (defensive) reactions to rejection. The question is whether we can demonstrate that a threat of rejection promotes conformity to group norms?

This is a question that guided much of the earlier social psychology research on conformity and at least two more recent experimental investigations on rejection. For example, Williams, Cheung, and Choi (2000) showed that those who were ostracized in a virtual ball tossing game conformed to incorrect perceptual judgments of others in a new group situation immediately following the exclusion experience. DeWall (2010), in turn, demonstrated that participants whose future social status was threatened formed attitudes about policies that were consistent with the prevailing opinion of a novel peer group. In both sets of studies, there was anticipation of further contact with the group. Hence, anticipation of further contact might be critical in facilitating conformity, whereas aggressive reactions may be specifically targeted at experimenters who convey the threat of future social isolation.

Although conformity to group norms should indeed facilitate peer approval, there are likely to be other important reactions that can give us insights about the social functions of rejection. For example, DeWall, Maner, and Rouby (2009) demonstrated that a threat of exclusion increased attention to smiling faces (but not to faces conveying disapproval) among college students. Compared with participants who did not experience any threat of exclusion, those who did, fixated their attention more easily and longer on smiley faces and more quickly identified such positive expressions in the mix of others. The authors considered these "attentional attunements" as signs of approval seeking. These findings and other possible signs of the need to repair and facilitate acceptance by others enable us to gain insights to the non-defensive reactions to rejection that serve the group.

Conclusions

In sum, developmental research supports the conclusion that aggression is a defensive response to rejection that enables individuals avoid emotional distress and maintain positive self-views. But aggression is not the only defensive response to exclusion. Withdrawal from peer interactions allows individuals avoid the emotional distress that results from rejection when they blame themselves and come to expect negative social experiences. Hence, this author proposes that the two subtypes of chronically rejected children studied by developmental psychologists provide insights into defensive responses to exclusion. Although the social-cognitive mechanisms and peer feedback associated with each response shed light on the current debates about the effects of rejection, research on the nondefensive responses is needed to learn more about the function that rejection serves in groups and larger collectives.

References

Asher, S. R., & Coie, J. D. (Eds.) (1990). *Peer Rejection in Childhood. Cambridge Studies In Social And Emotional Development*. New York: Cambridge University Press.

Baumeister, R. F., & Leary, M. R. (1995). The need to belong: Desire for interpersonal attachments as fundamental human motivation. *Psychological Bulletin, 117*, 497–529.

Baumeister, R. F., Smart, L, & Boden, J. M. (1996). Relation of threatened egotism to violence and aggression: The dark side of self-esteem. *Psychological Review, 103*, 5–33.

Bell-Dolan, D. J. (1995). Social cue interpretation of anxious children. *Journal of Clinical Child Psychology, 24*, 2–10.

Bierman, K. L., & Wargo, J. B. (1995). Predicting the longitudinal course associated with aggressive-rejected, aggressive (nonrejected), and rejected (nonaggressive) status. *Development and Psychopathology, 7*, 669–682.

Blackhart, G. C., Nelson, B. C., Knowles, M. L., & Baumeister, R. F. (2009). Rejection elicits emotional reactions but neither causes immediate distress nor lowers self-esteem: A meta-analytic review of 192 studies on social exclusion. *Personality and Social Psychology Review, 4*, 269–309.

Boivin, M., Dodge, K. A., Coie, J. D. (1995). Individual-group behavioral similarity and peer status in experimental play groups of boys: the social misfit revisited. *Journal of Personality and Social Psychology, 62*, 269–279.

Boivin, M., & Hymel, S. (1997). Peer experiences and social self-perceptions: A sequential model. *Developmental Psychology, 33*, 135–145.

Boivin, M., Hymel, S., & Bukowski, W. M. (1995). The roles of social withdrawal, peer rejection, and victimization by peers in predicting loneliness and depressed mood in childhood. *Development & Psychopathology, 7*, 765–785

Cacioppo, J. T., & Hawkley, L. C. (2005). People thinking about people: The vicious cycle of being a social outcast in one's own mind. In K. D. Williams, J. P. Forgas, & W. von Hippel, (Eds.), *The Social Outcast: Ostracism, Social Exclusion, Rejection, and Bullying* (pp.91–108). New York: Psychology Press.

Cairns, R. B., Cairns, B. D., Neckerman, H. J., Gest, S. D., & Gariepy, J. L. (1988). Social networks and aggressive behavior: Peer support or peer rejection? *Developmental Psychology, 24*, 815–823.

Coie, J. D., Lochman, J. E., Terry, R., & Hyman, C. (1992). Predicting early adolescent disorder from childhood and peer rejection. *Journal of Consulting and Clinical Psychology, 60*, 783–792.

Coie, J. D., Terry, R., Lenox, K., & Lochman, J. (1995). Childhood peer rejection and aggression as predictors of stable patterns of adolescent disorder. *Development & Psychopathology, 7*, 697–713.

Crick, N. R., & Dodge, K. A. (1994). A review and reformulation of social information-processing mechanism in children's social adjustment. *Psychological Bulletin, 113*, 74–101.

Gruter, M., & Masters, R. D. (1986). Ostracism as a social and biological phenomenon: An introduction. *Ethology and Sociobiology, 7*, 149–158.

DeWall, C. N. (2010). Forming a basis for acceptance: Excluded people form attitudes to agree with potential affiliates. *Social Influence, 5*, 245–260.

DeWall, N. C. (2009). The pain of exclusion: Using insights from neuroscience to understand emotional and behavioral responses to social exclusion. In M. J. Harris (Ed.), *Bullying, Rejection, and Peer Victimization: A Social Cognitive Neuroscience Perspective* (pp. 201–224). New York: Springer Publishing Co.

DeWall, N. C., Maner, J. K., & Rouby, A. A. (2009). Social exclusion and early-stage interpersonal perception: Selective attention to signs of acceptance. *Journal of Personality and Social Psychology, 96*, 729–741.

DeWall, N. C., Twenge, J. M., Gitter, S. A., & Baumeister, R. F. (2009). It's the thought that counts: The role of hostile cognition in shaping aggressive responses to social exclusion. *Journal of Personality and Social Psychology, 96*, 45–59.

Dishion, T. J., McCord, J., & Poulin, F. (1999). When interventions harm: Peer groups and problem behavior. *American Psychologist, 54*, 755–764.

Dishion, T. J., Spracklen, K. M., Andrews, D. W., & Patterson, G. R. (1996). Deviancy training in male adolescent friendships. *Behavior Therapy*, 27, 373–390.

Dodge, K. A. (1983). Behavioral antecedents of peer social status. *Child Development*, 54, 1386–1399.

Dodge, K. A. (1993). Social-cognitive mechanisms in the development of conduct disorder and depression. *Annual Review of Psychology*, 44, 559–584.

Dodge, K. A., & Crick, N. R. (1990). Social information-processing bases of aggressive behavior in children. *Personality & Social Psychology Bulletin. Special Issue: Illustrating the Value Of Basic Research*, 16, 8–22.

Downey, G., Mougios, V., Ayduk, O., London, B., & Shoda, Y. (2004). Rejection sensitivity and the defensive motivational system: Insights from the startle response to rejection cues. *Psychological Science*, 15, 668–673.

Feldman, E., & Dodge, K. A. (1987). Social information processing and sociometric status: Sex, age, and situational effects. *Journal of Abnormal Child Psychology*, 15, 211–227.

Graham, S., Bellmore, A., & Juvonen, J. (2003). Peer victimization in middle school: When self- and peer views diverge. *Journal of Applied School Psychology*, 19, 117–137.

Graham, S., & Juvonen, J. (1998). Self-blame and peer victimization in middle school: An attributional analysis. *Developmental Psychology*, 31, 731–740.

Hodges, E. V. E., Malone, M. J., & Perry, D. G. (1997). Individual risk and social risk as interacting determinants of victimization in the peer group. *Developmental Psychology*, 33, 1032–1039.

Hymel, S., Bowker, A., & Woody, E. (1993). Aggressive versus withdrawn unpopular children: Variations in peer and self-perceptions in multiple domains. *Child Development*, 64, 879–896.

Hymel, S., Frigang, R., Franke, S., Both, L., Bream, L., & Borys, S. (*1983, June*). *Children's attributions for social situations: Variations as a function of social status and self-perception variables.* Paper presented at the annual meeting of the Canadian psychological Association, Winnipeg, Manitoba.

Juvonen, J., & Galvan, A. (2009). Bullying as a means to foster compliance. In M. J. Harris, (Ed.), *Bullying, Rejection, and Peer Victimization: A Social Cognitive Neuroscience Perspective.* (pp. 299–318). New York: Springer.

Juvonen, J., Graham S., & Schuster, M. (2003). Bullying among young adolescents: The strong, weak, and troubled. *Pediatrics*, 112, 1231–1237.

Juvonen, J., & Gross, E. F. (2005). The rejected and the bullied: Lessons about social misfits from developmental psychology. In K. D. Williams ., J. P. Forgas, & W. von Hippel . (Eds), *The Social Outcast: Ostracism, Social Exclusion, Rejection, and Bullying* (pp. 155–170). New York: Psychology Press.

Kerr, N. L., Rumble, A. C. Park, E. S., Ouwerkerk, J. W., Parks, C. D., Gallucci, M. P., & van Lange, P. A. M. (2009) "How many bad apples does it take to spoil the whole barrel?": Social exlusion and tolerance for bad apples. *Journal of Experimental Social Psychology*, 45, 603–613.

Kochenderfer, B. J., & Ladd, G. W. (1996). Peer victimization: Cause or consequence of school maladjustment? *Child Development*, 67, 1305–1317

Kochenderfer-Ladd, B. J., & Wardrop, J. L. (2001). Chronicity and instability of children's peer victimization experiences as predictors of loneliness and social satisfaction trajectories. *Child Development*, 72, 134–151.

Kupersmidt, J. B., & Coie, J. D. (1990). Preadolescent peer status, aggression, and school adjustment as predictors of externalizing problems in adolescence. *Child Development*, 61, 1350–1362.

Ladd., G. W. (1999). Peer relationships and social competence during early and middle childhood. *Annual Review of Psychology*, 50, 333–359.

Leary, M. R., Twenge, J. M., & Quinlivan, E. (2006). Interpersonal rejection as a determinant of anger and aggression. *Personality and Social Psychology Review*, 2, 111–132.

London, B., Downey, G., & Bonica, C. (2007). Social causes and consequences of rejection sensitivity. *Journal of Research on Adolescence*, 17, 481–506.

Luthar, S. S., & McMahon, T. J. (1996). Peer reputation among inner-city adolescents: Structure and correlates. *Journal of Research on Adolescence*, 6, 581–603.

Orobio de Castro, B., Veerman, J. W., Koops, W., Bosch, J. D., & Monshouwer, H. J. (2002). Hostile attribution of intent and aggressive behavior: A meta-analysis. *Child Development*, 73, 916–934.

Panak, W. F., & Garber, J. (1992). Role of aggression, rejection, and attributions in the prediction of depression in children. *Development and Psychopathology*, 7, 145–165.

Parker, J. G., & Asher, S. R. (1987). Peer relations and later personal adjustment: Are low-accepted children at risk? *Psychological Bulletin*, 102, 357–389.

Parkhurst, J. T., & Asher, S. R. (1992). Peer rejection in middle school: Subgroup differences in behavior, loneliness, and interpersonal concerns. *Developmental Psychology*, 28, 231–241.

Patterson, C. J., Kupersmidt, J. B., & Griesler, P. C. (1990). Children's perceptions of self and of relationships with others as a function of sociometric status. *Child Development*, 61, 1335–1349.

Patterson, G. R., Capaldi, D., & Bank, L. (1991). An early starter model for predicting delinquency. In D. J. Pepler & K. H. Rubin . (Eds.), *The Development and Treatment of Childhood Aggression* (pp. 139–168). Hillsdale, NJ: Lawrence Erlbaum Associates.

Prinstein, M. J., & La Greca, A. M. (2004). Childhood peer rejection and aggression as predictors of adolescent girls' externalizing and health risk behaviors: A 6-year longitudinal study. *Journal of Consulting and Clinical Psychology*, 72, 103–112.

Rubin, K. H., LeMare, L. J., & Lollis, S. (1990). Social withdrawal in childhood: Developmental pathways to peer rejection. In S. R. Asher, & J. D. Coie . (Eds.), *Peer Rejection in Childhood* (pp. 217–249). New York: Cambridge University Press.

Rubin, K. H., Wojslawowicz, J. C., Rose-Krasnor, L., Booth-LaForce, C., & Burgess, K. B. (2006). The best friendships of the withdrawn children: Prevalence, stability, and relationship quality. *Journal of Abnormal Child Psychology*, 34, 143–157.

Salmivalli, C., Karhunen, J., & Lagerspetz, K. M. J. (1996). How do victims respond to bullying? *Aggressive Behavior*, 22, 99–109.

Sandstrom, M. J., & Cillessen, A. H. N. (2003). Sociometric Status and Children's Peer Experiences: Use of the Daily Diary Method. *Merrill-Palmer Quarterly*, 49, 427–452.

Sandstrom, M. J., & Cramer, P. (2003). Girls use of defense mechanisms following peer rejection. *Journal of Personality*, 71, 605–627.

Schippell, P. L., Vasey, M. W., Cravens-Brown, L. M., and Bretveld, R. A. (2003). Suppressed attention to rejection, ridicule, and failure cues: A unique correlate of reactive but not proactive aggression in youth. *Journal of Clinical Child & Adolescent Psychology, 32*, 40–55.

Schwartz, D., Dodge, K. A., & Coie, J. D. (1993). The emergence of chronic peer vicitimization in boys' play groups. *Child Development, 64*, 1755–1772.

Sentse, M., Scholte, R., Salmivalli,C., & Voeten, M. (2007). Person-group dissimilarity in involvement in bullying and its relation with social status. *Journal of Abnormal Child Psychology, 35*, 1009–1019.

Stormshak, E. A., Bierman, K. L., Bruschi, C., Dodge, K. A., Coie, J. D., & the Conduct Problems Prevention Research Group. (1999). The relation between behavior problems and peer preference in different classroom contexts. *Child Development, 70*, 169–182.

Tremblay, R. E., Masse, L. C., Vitaro, F., & Dobkin, P. L. (1995). The impact of friends' deviant behavior on early onset of deliquency: Longitudinal data from 6 to 13 years of age. *Development & Psychopathology, 7*, 649–667.

Volling, B. L., MacKinnon-Lewis, C., Rabiner, D., & Baradaran, L. P. (1993). Children's social competence and sociometric status: Further exploration of aggression, social withdrawl, and peer rejection. *Development and Psychopathology, 5*, 459–483.

Weiner, B. (1995). *Judgments Of Responsibility: A Foundation for a Theory of Social Conduct.* New York: Guilford Press.

Williams, K. D. (2007). Ostracism. *Annual Review of Psychology, 58*, 425–452.

Williams, K. D., Cheung, C. K. T., Choi, W. (2000). Cyberostracism: Effects of being ignored over the Internet. *Journal of Personality and Social Psychology, 79*, 748–762.

Wood, J. J., Cowan, P. A., & Baker, B. L. (2002). Behavior problems and peer rejection in preschool boys and girls. *Journal of Genetic Psychology, 163*, 72–88.

Wright, J. C., Giammarino, M., & Parad, H. W. (1986). Social status in small groups: Individual-group similarity and the social "misfit." *Journal of Personality and Social Psychology, 5*, 523–536.

Zakriski, A. L., & Coie, J. D. (1996). A comparison of aggressive-rejected and no aggressive-rejected children's interpretations of self-directed and other-directed rejection. Child Development, *67*, 1048–1070.

PART 5

Individual Exlcusion: Behavior and Cognition

Rejection and Aggression: Explaining the Paradox

C. Nathan DeWall *and* Jean M. Twenge

Abstract

How does social rejection influence aggression? The need to belong operates in a similar manner as other motivations. Hungry people work hard to get food. Out of work, people go out of their way to find employment. Social rejected do what they need to regain a sense of belonging. Yet rejected people often engage in behaviors that will result in further rejection, such as aggression. This chapter discusses a decade's worth of experimental research on the relationship between social rejection and aggression, with an eye toward explaining why aggression occurs and how to prevent it.

Key Words: social exclusion, social rejection, ostracism, aggression, mass violence

Rejection and Aggression: Explaining the Paradox

Seung-Hui Cho had never been the aggressive type. Growing up, he had been diagnosed with major depression and social anxiety disorder. He had difficulty speaking, which may have drawn ridicule from his middle school classmates. His mental health deteriorated, leading those around him to suggest he receive medical treatment. While at Virginia Tech University, he had few, if any, positive and lasting relationships. He showed disturbing behavior in class. He stalked and harassed women.

On April 16, 2007, he opened fire, killing 32 people and wounding another 25. The shootings were the deadliest incident by a single gunman in U.S. history. During the attack, Cho took a break to mail a package to NBC News that contained a manifesto, pictures, and video recordings of himself. In the video recordings, Cho mentioned feeling rejected: "You just loved to crucify me. You loved inducing cancer in my head, terror in my heart and ripping my soul all this time." The Virginia Tech Review Panel (2008) concluded that Cho engaged in a fantasy where "he would be remembered as the savior of the oppressed, the downtrodden, the poor, and the rejected."

Why did Seung-Hui Cho, a person with no history of violence, feel compelled to murder so many people who he felt were responsible for his social rejection? Scholars will never know why people commit extreme acts of violence. But a growing body of research suggests that social rejection causes people—even those not inclined to lash out at others—to behave aggressively. Such behavior represents a paradox: rejected people crave new opportunities to make friends, but they engage in the very behavior that will scare new friends away. This chapter reviews research that helps explain why social rejection increases aggression.

This chapter is divided into seven sections. The first section discusses the starting point for much of this work: how social rejection relates to aggression outside of the laboratory. The second section reviews research that social rejection causes aggression in controlled, laboratory settings. Third, we review research that social rejection has implications for mass violence. Fourth, we offer some explanations about why rejection increases aggression. Fifth, we identify personality traits that heighten a rejected person's risk for behaving aggressively. Sixth, we identify factors that make rejected people resilient against aggression. The final section discusses future directions for research.

Rejection and Aggression Outside the Lab

April 20, 1999 started out like most other days at a high school near the American Rocky Mountains. Students were ushered into their classes, teachers began their lessons, and the office staff started their daily tasks. Midway through the day, two students who had experienced chronic social rejection, Eric Harris and Dylan Klebold, entered the high school carrying semiautomatic guns. They started shooting, eventually killing 13 people and injuring many others before they turned the guns on themselves. The Columbine High School massacre shocked the nation, leading many people to try to understand what causes such violent actions. Unfortunately, the Columbine High School massacre was not an isolated incident. Between 1995 and 2001, at least 15 school shootings occurred.

It is impossible to know why people engage in extreme acts of violence. But Leary and colleagues (2003) knew it was possible to examine common features that existed across a group of school shootings. They hypothesized that one reason why school shootings occur was that the perpetrators experienced social rejection. Because humans have a fundamental need for positive and lasting relationships (Baumeister & Leary, 1995), thwarting the need to belong may increase the likelihood that a person will perpetrate violence. Using case study methods, Leary and colleagues (2003) rated how much perpetrators of school shootings experienced chronic or acute social rejection. Their results were stunning: In all but two cases, school shooters experienced chronic or acute social rejection.

Several correlational studies also suggested a link between social isolation and aggressive or antisocial behavior. Aggressive children have fewer friends and are less accepted by peers (Coie, 1990; Newcomb, Bukowski, & Pattee, 1993). Single men commit more crimes than married men, even when age is controlled (Sampson & Laub, 1993).

These findings offer a useful starting point for understanding a relationship between social rejection and aggression. They show that thwarting the need to belong may increase aggression. To establish a causal relationship between social rejection and aggression, however, experiments were needed. The next section discusses some of the first laboratory experiments that tested the hypothesis that social rejection increases aggression.

Rejection Increases Aggression toward Other Individuals

Imagine arriving at a psychology laboratory for a study concerning group dynamics. You meet four or five strangers of the same gender, whom you get to know for about 15 minutes. Next, an experimenter leads you to an individual room, hands you a piece of paper, and asks you to write down the names of two people you just met who you like and respect. Your decision will help the experimenter form groups for a later activity. After about 5 minutes, the experimenter returns and lets you that know nobody picked you as a partner. Because nobody picked you, she can't get the groups together as she normally would. You will spend the rest of the hour alone.

This was precisely the situation that Twenge and colleagues (2001) used to induce feelings of social rejection. Half of the participants were given this social rejection feedback, whereas the other half received social acceptance feedback, namely that everyone chose them for the task. (Accepted participants were also told that the experimenter could not get the groups together because everyone had accepted them, and that they would spend the rest of the hour alone.) Next, participants received an opportunity to blast someone not involved in the rejection experience with white noise. In effect, participants had the opportunity to aggress toward an innocent bystander.

Consistent with the case study results, social rejection, compared to acceptance, caused people to blast an innocent bystander with intense and prolonged noise. The results were replicated in several other experiments that used different social rejection manipulations and measures of aggression, which suggests a robust relationship between social rejection and aggression. In over a decade since the publication of the Twenge et al. (2001) experiments, the relationship between social rejection and aggression has been replicated many times (see Leary, 2010; Williams, 2009, for reviews).

What this research leaves unanswered, however, is whether social rejection can increase mass violence. The next section reviews research that seeks to extend work on social rejection increasing aggression toward individuals by showing that socially rejected people will also behave aggressively toward groups of people.

Rejection Increases Aggression toward Groups

Why might social rejection increase mass violence? Rejected people behave aggressively toward both the people who reject them and innocent bystanders, but that does not explain why rejected people behave aggressively toward groups. Gaertner and colleagues (2008) proposed that one reason why rejection increases mass violence, as demonstrated in the Virginia Tech and Columbine High School massacres, is that rejected people associate rejection with an entire group instead of one individual. By associating an entire group with rejection, socially rejected people will retaliate against the entire group of individuals.

To test this hypothesis, Gaertner and colleagues (2008) created a situation in which half of the participants completed the experiment with three confederates who shared a common interest. This condition was labeled "high-entitative" because the three confederates comprised a cohesive unit. The other half of the participants completed the experiment with three confederates who did not share common interests (low-entitative group). Participants were then told that the experiment could only accommodate three people, which meant that one of the people in the room could not participate. For participants assigned to the social rejection condition, one of the confederates pointed at them and declared, "S/he should be the one who leaves!" Participants assigned to the control condition were told that they had been randomly selected not to participate in the experiment. All participants were then escorted outside of the room, where they received a surprise from the experimenter: They could deliver aversive blasts of noise to the three confederates.

Rejected participants behaved more aggressively toward the three confederates compared with non-rejected participants, but this effect only occurred when the aggression was directed at a group of people who shared a common identity. When the rejection was not associated with the entire group of confederates, rejected participants were no more likely to behave aggressively than nonrejected participants were. These results offer the first direct evidence that social rejection can increase mass violence by associating rejection with a group of people.

Why Does Social Rejection Increase Aggression?

Having shown a consistent relationship between social rejection and aggression, researchers began to ask *why* such aggression occurs. Understanding the mechanisms underlying the link between social rejection and aggression not only aids researchers in knowing why the effect occurs, but it is also a crucial element in designing interventions to reduce aggression. By targeting the causes of the relationship, researchers have a better understanding of how to reduce rejection-related aggression.

A plausible candidate was anger. Rejection increases anger (Leary, Twenge, & Quinlivan, 2006), which is an emotion that has a clear relationship to aggression (Berkowitz, 1990; Bushman & Huesmann, 2010; Carver & Harmon-Jones, 2009). To examine whether anger mediates the relationship between social rejection and aggression, Chow and colleagues (2008) conducted a pair of studies in which people were exposed to a social rejection manipulation. Instead of the group rejection manipulation mentioned earlier, Chow and colleagues led participants to believe that they were participating in a study that examined mental visualization. To that end, participants would complete a virtual ball-tossing game (Cyberball) with two other participants (Williams, Cheung, & Choi, 2000). In reality, the two other participants were preprogrammed to mimic a real person's actions. Half of the participants, who were randomly assigned to the social exclusion condition, received one toss from the other two participants and never received the ball again. The other half of the participants were assigned to the social acceptance condition, in which they received tosses from the other participants an equal number of times. Participants then reported how much anger and sadness they experienced during Cyberball.

Next, participants completed a measure of antisocial behavior, which took the form of choosing appealing (chocolate chip cookies, potato chips, and M&M candies) or unappealing (raisins, saltine crackers, and prunes) food for the other two Cyberball players to eat. Socially excluded participants felt angrier and gave more unappealing snacks to their Cyberball partners than did socially accepted participants. Crucially, the rise in anger among socially excluded participants helped explain their antisocial behavior. Sadness, which has a withdrawal motivational profile not frequently associated with aggression (Carver & Harmon-Jones, 2009), did not mediate the relationship between social exclusion and antisocial behavior. A second study replicated and extended this mediational pattern by showing that anger mediated the link between exclusion and antisocial behavior in situations wherein people perceived that they experienced exclusion unfairly. Thus, the more anger participants recalled experiencing during the social exclusion experience, the more they engaged in antisocial behavior.

Aggression and antisocial behavior are complex behaviors that operate through various mechanisms (Anderson & Bushman, 2002; DeWall, Anderson, & Bushman, 2011). Anger may offer one path through which social exclusion triggers aggression, but other mechanisms warrant consideration. We hypothesized that socially excluded people may adopt a hostile cognitive mindset, in which they perceived ambiguous situations as threatening. This hostile cognitive bias may, in turn, help explain why socially excluded people behave aggressively.

To test this hypothesis, DeWall and colleagues (2009) conducted a series of experiments in which participants were exposed to a social exclusion manipulation, completed a measure designed to assess a hostile cognitive mindset, and then were given the opportunity to behave aggressively. Across each experiment, socially excluded participants, compared with nonexcluded participants, showed evidence of a hostile cognitive bias: They completed more ambiguous word stems (R _ P _) with aggressive (RAPE) instead of neutral (ROPE) words; they perceived greater similarity between aggressive words (CHOKE) and neutral words (NIGHT); and they rated another person's ambiguous actions as extremely aggressive. This hostile cognitive bias helped explain why socially excluded people behaved aggressively.

Follow-up studies extended this research to aggression within romantic relationships (Pond, DeWall, McNulty, Finkenauer, et al., 2012). Feelings of social exclusion, whether experienced in general or directly from one's partner, predicted higher rates of intimate partner violence perpetration. Consistent with our previous studies, having a hostile cognitive bias toward one's romantic partner had a direct role in predicting aggression toward the partner.

These findings provide two answers regarding why socially excluded people engage in antisocial and even aggressive behavior. First, social exclusion increases anger, which in turn increases antisocial behavior. Second, socially excluded people begin to see the world through "blood-colored glasses," and this hostile cognitive bias has implications for greater aggression toward strangers and romantic partners. To be sure, there are likely other reasons why socially excluded people behave aggressively. In some ways, researchers have only begun to scratch the surface in terms of understanding mechanisms underlying the relationship between social exclusion and aggression.

Thus far, the reviewed research has examined how people generally respond to social rejection. Some people may be especially prone to aggression in the wake of social rejection. The next section discusses research that has identified traits that predispose rejected people to behave aggressively.

Who Is at Risk?

Not all socially excluded people behave aggressively. And of those that do, some people behave more aggressively than others. This begs the question: What factors heighten a person's risk for aggression in the wake of social exclusion? To date, researchers have identified two traits that function as risk factors for aggression: narcissism and rejection sensitivity.

Narcissism refers to a personality trait marked by an inflated sense of self-worth, which is marked by feelings of grandiosity and entitlement (Campbell, Rudich, & Sedikides, 2002). Narcissists, compared with nonnarcissists, have high levels of agentic traits such as intelligence, power, and dominance (Brown & Zeigler-Hill, 2004; Campbell et al. 2002). In terms of the Five-Factor Model, narcissists score high on extraversion and low on agreeableness (Miller & Campbell, 2008). Narcissists have high self-esteem, but their self-esteem is fragile (Sedikides et al., 2004). Given their high and unstable self-esteem, narcissists are prone to lash out at others when they feel threatened (Baumeister, Smart, & Boden, 1996; Bushman & Baumeister, 1998). Thus, narcissists might be at risk for behaving aggressively when they experience social exclusion.

Twenge and Campbell (2003) conducted four studies to test this hypothesis. When recalling a past social rejection experience, narcissism was associated with greater anger. This effect was replicated in a second experiment, in which participants actually experienced rejection. Social rejection also increased aggression more for narcissists than for nonnarcissists, regardless of whether the target was a rejector or an innocent bystander. Self-esteem did little to explain the link between social rejection and aggression, which suggests that simple positive self-views do not adequately explain the findings. These results confirm the hypothesis that narcissists, who have elevated but fragile self-esteem, are prone to aggression when they experience social rejection.

On the surface, rejection sensitivity resembles the flipside of narcissism. Rejection sensitive people anticipate rejection from others, whereas narcissists expect admiration from others. Rejection sensitive people worry that others will reject them, whereas narcissists remain confident that others will accept them. Why might rejection sensitivity heighten an excluded person's risk for aggression?

Ayduk and colleagues (2008) proposed that rejection sensitivity has cognitive and affective components that facilitate aggression. For example, high rejection sensitive people, compared to their low rejection sensitive counterparts, have stronger cognitive associations between rejection and hostility (Ayduk et al., 1999). Rejection sensitivity is also associated with a stronger hostile perceptual bias, in which people perceive others' ambiguous behavior as hurtful (Downey & Feldman, 1996). Just as a hostile perceptual bias can help explain why excluded people behave aggressively (DeWall et al., 2009), traits associated with such a bias may heighten an excluded person's risk for aggression.

To examine this possibility, Ayduk and colleagues (2008) conducted a two-part experiment. In the first session, participants completed a questionnaire that measured their rejection sensitivity. In the second session, participants arrived at the laboratory in pairs. The experimenter informed them that a third participant would select one of them as a partner for a chat room discussion. To help the third participant decide who to pick, both participants were instructed to write a short essay about themselves that would be emailed to the third participant. Approximately 10 minutes later, the experimenter returned to the room, led participants to individual rooms, and delivered the social rejection feedback. By random assignment, half of the participants were told that the third participant did not pick them (social rejection condition). The other half of the participants were told that the third participants picked them (social acceptance condition).

Next, participants had the opportunity to behave aggressively toward the third participant. They prepared a food sample for the third participant, who expressed a strong disliking for spicy food. On the basis of a rigged drawing, the food sample contained spicy hot sauce. The experimenter informed participants that the third participant would have to consume the entire food sample. Hence, the measure of aggression was the amount of hot sauce participants made the third participant eat (Lieberman et al., 1999). The hot sauce measure of aggression conforms to the standard definition of aggression (Bushman & Huesmann, 2010).

Social rejection increased hot sauce allocation, but this effect was moderated by rejection sensitivity. Among rejected people, rejection sensitivity was associated with greater aggression. In contrast, rejection sensitivity was unrelated to aggression among accepted people. These effects were independent of neuroticism, which ruled out the alternative explanation that general negative affect was driving the findings.

Together, these results offer a starting point for understanding risk factors for rejection-related aggression. Narcissism and rejection sensitivity combine with social rejection to produce extremely elevated levels of aggression. Future work will likely catalogue a litany of other risk factors for rejection-related aggression, much in the same way that scholars have done in others areas of aggression (e.g., alcohol-related aggression, intimate partner violence perpetration). For now, narcissism and rejection sensitivity represent two factors that researchers can target for understanding who is prone to behave aggressively when rejected.

Who Is Resilient?

Until this point, the chapter has focused on whether social rejection increases aggression (it does, toward both individuals and groups), why rejection increases aggression (anger and hostile cognitive bias), and what factors predispose rejected people to behave aggressively (narcissism and rejection sensitivity). This section discusses research on three factors that reduce the relationship between social exclusion and aggression: social connection, religiosity, and restoring control.

The need to belong operates through standard motivation patterns. When it is thwarted, the desire for affiliation becomes intensified (Maner et al., 2007). In most experiments that examine the relationship between social exclusion and aggression, excluded people receive no opportunity to satisfy their drive for renewed affiliation. By offering excluded people some satisfaction of their motivation for social reconnection, they may behave less aggressively.

A pair of recent investigations explored this possibility. In the first investigation (Twenge et al., 2007), excluded participants behaved aggressively, but this effect was eliminated if participants had a friendly (vs. neutral) social interaction, recalled childhood memories, or wrote about either a celebrity or a family member (vs. a recent meal). The second investigation systematically manipulated how many people accepted participants (zero to three or four, depending on the manipulation used), which allowed us to examine whether offering participants a small taste of acceptance was enough to reduce aggression (DeWall et al., 2010). Acceptance by no one produced the largest amount of aggression. But experiencing acceptance from just one person was enough to reduce aggression. Consistent with social impact theory (Latané, 1981), the relationship between the number of acceptors and aggression followed a power function: each additional acceptor had a decreasing incremental effect on reducing aggression. A little acceptance went a long way in reducing aggression.

Religiosity represents another factor that reduces rejection-related aggression. Karl Marx's famous claim that "religion is the opiate of the people" (Marx, 1844/1970) implies that religion creates an illusory world in which people are able to forget the actual pain and suffering in their worlds. Although Marx's statement is often used to personify his stance toward religion, it suggests that religiosity might relieve the negative consequences of social rejection. Freud (1930/1961) also argued that religion functions in part to reduce feelings of social exclusion and isolation. A recent series of studies examined not only whether socially excluded people turn to religion as a coping mechanism, but also whether bringing religious concepts to mind reduces rejection-related aggression (Aydin, Fischer, & Frey, 2010).

Chronic feelings of social exclusion related to higher levels of religious affiliation and religious behavior. More important, having religious participants write about their attitudes toward God, compared with writing about their attitudes toward environmental protection, reduced the relationship between social rejection and aggression. Similar effects occurred for both Christian and Muslim samples, suggesting that different forms of religiosity have a similar buffering effect (Aydin et al., 2010).

Restoring control is a third factor that can reduce or eliminate rejection-related aggression. According to Williams (2009), social exclusion threatens needs for control along with self-esteem, belonging, and meaningful existence. Therefore, when socially excluded people experience a loss of control, they may behave aggressively to restore their feelings of control. By restoring their sense of control, socially excluded people may behave less aggressively.

To test this hypothesis, Warburton and colleagues (2006) exposed participants to a social exclusion manipulation and then measured their aggression using the hot sauce paradigm. Between the social exclusion manipulation and aggression measure, participants completed a task designed to increase or decrease their feelings of control. In the control task, participants listened to unpleasant sounds through headphones. For participants in the restored control condition, participants could control when they heard the noise and how long the noise lasted. For participants in the diminished control condition, the compact disc player controlled when they heard the noise and how long it lasted.

Restoring control eliminated the relationship between social exclusion and aggression. Among participants in the restored control condition, social exclusion did not increase aggression. In contrast, social exclusion increased aggression among participants in the diminished control condition.

Together, these findings demonstrate three factors that can reduce rejection-related aggression. Offering socially excluded people opportunities to regain social connection, whether through a pleasant interaction or a small taste of acceptance, decreased their aggression. Among socially excluded religious people, bringing to mind their attitudes toward religion reduced their aggression. Last, giving socially excluded people control over their environment quenched their desire to restore their feelings of control, thereby decreasing their aggression.

Future Directions

In some ways, research on rejection-related aggression is in its infancy. Ample opportunities exist for future research. One avenue may examine the role of genetic polymorphisms that predispose socially rejected people to behave aggressively. Two of the most widely studied genes related to aggression are a polymorphism in the promoter of the monoamine oxidase A gene (MAOA) and genetic variations in the serotonin transporter gene (5-HT). The MAOA gene is commonly referred to as the "warrior gene" because of its robust relationship to aggression and antisocial behavior, whereas the 5-HT gene helps transport the "feel good" serotonin transmitter. When people do not feel good, they are more prone to behave aggressively. After a provocation, male participants with the low expression allele of the MAOA gene (MAOA-L), compared with male participants with the high expression allele (MAOA-H), doled out significantly more hot sauce to someone who expressed dislike for spicy foods (McDermott, Tingley, Cowden, Frazzetto, & Johnson, 2009). When rejected, MAOA-L carriers also show stronger brain activation in regions associated with emotion distress (dorsal anterior cingulate cortex) compared with MAOA-H carriers, which helps explain their higher levels of trait aggression (Eisenberger, Way, Taylor, Welch, & Lieberman, 2007). Hence, rejected MAOA-L carriers may behave more aggressively on laboratory tasks compared to rejected MAOA-H carriers. Social rejection may also modulate the expression of aggression most strongly among people with the low expression of the serotonin transporter gene (short-short) compared to people with higher expression (short-long, long-long). Future research may explore whether social rejection represents a specific adverse environmental factor that influences aggression as a function of serotonin expression.

Self-control processes may also moderate and mediate the relationship between social rejection and aggression. Theoretical and empirical work suggests that self-control is crucial in understanding aggression (Denson, DeWall, & Finkel, 2012; DeWall, Finkel, & Denson, 2011; Gottfredson & Hirschi, 1990). High trait self-control buffers people from situational factors that normally increase aggression (DeWall, Baumeister, Stillman, & Gailliot, 2007). Therefore, social rejection may not increase aggression among people with high self-control as much as it does among people with low self-control. Self-control differs not only between people, but it also fluctuates within people. Social rejected people become unwilling to control their impulses (Baumeister, DeWall, Ciarocco, & Twenge, 2005; DeWall, Baumeister, & Vohs, 2008; Oaten et al., 2008), which may also contribute to their higher aggression.

A final area of future research may examine whether extremely prolonged periods of social rejection, lasting months or even years, increase aggression. For example, Williams (2001) recounts the story of a woman whose husband ostracized her for decades. She became resigned to her life as an ostracized wife, but she did not lash out at the husband. If people experience prolonged social rejection, they may incorporate it into their daily life, making it unlikely that they would experience strong and frequent aggressive urges.

Conclusions

Over the past 10 years, more research has uncovered knowledge of the relation between social rejection and aggression than during any other period in the history of psychology. This chapter reviews that research, tracing its beginning to recent interventions aimed at reducing aggression. Far from reaching a plateau, research in this area will continue to explain why rejected people behave aggressively—and how such aggression can be reduced.

References

Anderson, C. A., & Bushman, B. J. (2002). Human aggression. *Annual Review of Psychology, 53,* 27–51.

Aydin, N., Fischer, P., & Frey, D. (2010). Turning to God in the face of ostracism: Effects of social exclusion on religiousness. *Personality and Social Psychology Bulletin, 36,* 742–753.

Ayduk, O., Downey, G., Testa, A., Yen, Y., & Shoda, Y. (1999). Does rejection elicit hostility in rejection sensitive women? *Social Cognition, 17,* 245–271.

Ayduk, O., Gyurak, A., & Luerssen A. (2008). Individual differences in the rejection–aggression link in the hot sauce paradigm: the case of rejection sensitivity, *Journal of Experimental Social Psychology, 44,* 775–782.

Baumeister, R. F., DeWall, C. N., Ciarocco, N. J., & Twenge, J. M. (2005). Social exclusion impairs self-regulation. *Journal of Personality and Social Psychology, 88,* 589–604.

Baumeister, R. F., & Leary, M. R. (1995). The need to belong: Desire for interpersonal attachments as a fundamental human motivation. *Psychological Bulletin, 117,* 497–529.

Baumeister, R. F., Smart, L., & Boden, J. M. (1996). Relation of threatened egotism to violence and aggression: The dark side of high self-esteem. *Psychological Review, 103,* 5–33.

Berkowitz, L. (1990). On the formation and regulation of anger and aggression: A cognitive-neoassociationistic analysis. *American Psychologist, 45,* 494–503.

Brown, R. P., & Zeigler-Hill, V. (2004). Narcissism and the non-equivalence of self-esteem measures: A matter of dominance? *Journal of Research in Personality, 38,* 585–592.

Bushman, B. J., & Baumeister, R. F. (1998). Threatened egotism, narcissism, self-esteem, and direct and displaced aggression: Does self-love or self-hate lead to violence? *Journal of Personality and Social Psychology, 75,* 219–229.

Bushman, B. J., & Huesmann, L. R. Aggression . In Fiske, S. T. Gilbert, D. T., & Lindzey, G. (Eds.) (2010). *Handbook of Social Psychology* (Vol. 2, 5th ed., pp. 833–863). Hoboken, NJ: John Wiley & Sons Inc.

Campbell, W. K., Rudich, E., & Sedikides, C. (2002). Narcissism, self-esteem, and the positivity of self-views: Two portraits of self-love. *Personality and Social Psychology Bulletin, 28,* 358–368.

Carver, C. S., & Harmon-Jones, E. (2009). Anger is an approach-related affect: Evidence and implications. *Psychological Bulletin, 135,* 183–204.

Chow, R. M., Tiedens, L. Z., & Govan, C. L. (2008). Excluded emotions: The role of anger in antisocial responses to ostracism. *Journal of Experimental Social Psychology, 44,* 896–903.

Coie, J. D., (1990). Toward a theory of peer rejection. In S. R. Asher & J. D. Coie (Eds.), *Peer Rejection in Childhood* (pp. 365–401). New York: Cambridge University Press.

Denson, T. F., DeWall, C. N., & Finkel, E. J. (2012). Self-control and aggression. *Current Directions in Psychological Science, 21,* 20–25.

DeWall, C. N., Anderson, C. A., & Bushman, B. J. (2011). The general aggression model: Theoretical extensions to violence. *Psychology of Violence, 1,* 245–25

DeWall, C. N., Baumeister, R. F., Stillman, T. F., & Gailliot, M. T. (2007). Violence restrained: Effects of self-regulation and its depletion on aggression. *Journal of Experimental Social Psychology, 43,* 62–76.

DeWall, C. N., Baumeister, R. F., & Vohs, K. D. (2008). Satiated with belongingness?: Effects of acceptance, rejection, and task framing on self-regulatory performance. *Journal of Personality and Social Psychology, 95,* 1367–1382.

DeWall, C. N., Finkel, E. J., & Denson, T. F. (2011). Self-control inhibits aggression. *Social and Personality Psychology Compass, 5,* 458–472.

DeWall, C. N., Twenge, J. M., Bushman, B. J., Im, C., & Williams, K. D. (2010). Acceptance by one differs from acceptance by none: Applying social impact theory to the rejection-aggression link. *Social Psychological and Personality Science, 1,* 168–174.

DeWall, C. N., Twenge, J. M., & Gitter, S. A., & Baumeister, R. F. (2009). It's the thought that counts: The role of hostile cognitions in shaping aggression following rejection. *Journal of Personality and Social Psychology, 96,* 45–59.

Downey, G., & Feldman, S. (1996). Implications of rejection sensitivity for intimate relationships. *Journal of Personality and Social Psychology, 70,* 1327–1134.

Eisenberger, N. I., Way, B. M., Taylor, S. E., Welch, W. T., & Lieberman, M. D. (2007). Understanding genetic risk for aggression: Clues from the brain's response to social exclusion. *Biological Psychiatry, 61,* 1100–1108.

Freud, S. (1961). *Civilization and its discontents* (J. Strachey, Trans.). New York: Norton. (Original work published 1930).

Gaertner, L., Iuzzini, J., O'Mara, E. M. (2008). When rejection by one fosters aggression against many: Multiple-victim aggression as a consequence of social rejection and perceived groupness. *Journal of Experimental Social Psychology, 44,* 958–970.

Gottfredson, M. R., & Hirschi, T. (1990). *A General Theory of Crime.* Stanford, CA: Stanford University Press.

Latané, B. (1981). The psychology of social impact. *American Psychologist, 36,* 343–356.

Leary, M. R. (2010). Affiliation, acceptance, and belonging. In S. T. Fiske, D. T. Gilbert, & G. Lindzey (Eds.), *Handbook of Social Psychology* (Vol. 2, 5th ed., pp. 864–897). New York: John Wiley & Sons.

Leary, M. R., Kowalski, R. M., Smith, L., & Phillips, S. (2003). Teasing, rejection, and violence: Case studies of the school shootings. *Aggressive Behavior, 29,* 202–214.

Leary, M. R., Twenge, J. M., & Quinlivan. E. (2006). Interpersonal rejection as a determinant of anger and aggression. *Personality and Social Psychology Review, 10,* 111–132.

Lieberman, J. D., Solomon, S., Greenberg, J., & McGregor, H. A. (1999). A hot new way to measure aggression: Hot sauce allocation. *Aggressive Behavior, 25,* 331–348.

Maner, J. K., DeWall, C. N., Baumeister, R. F., & Schaller, M. (2007). Does social exclusion motivate withdrawal or reconnection? Resolving the "porcupine problem." *Journal of Personality and Social Psychology, 92,* 42–55.

Marx, K. (1970). *Introduction to a contribution to the critique of Hegel's Philosophy of Right.* Oxford: Cambridge (Original work published in 1844).

McDermott, R., Tingley, D., Cowden, J., Frazzetto, G., & Johnson, D. D. P. (2009). Monoamine oxidase A gene (MAOA) predicts behavioral aggression following provocation. *Proceedings of the National Academy of Sciences, 106,* 2118–2123.

Miller, J. D., & Campbell, W. K. (2008). Comparing clinical and social-personality conceptualizations of narcissism. *Journal of Personality, 76,* 449–476.

Newcomb, A. F., Bukowski, W. M., & Pattee, L. (1993). Children's peer relations: A meta-analytic review of popular, rejected, neglected, controversial, and average sociometric status. *Psychological Bulletin, 113,* 99–128.

Oaten, M., Williams, K. D., Jones, A., & Zadro, L. (2008). The effects of ostracism of self-regulation in the socially anxious. *Journal of Social and Clinical Psychology, 27,* 471–504.

Pond, R. S., DeWall, C. N., McNulty, J. K., Finkenauer, C., Lambert, N. M.… Fincham, F. D. (2012). *Thwarted connection: Social disconnection predicts intimate partner violence through a hostile perceptual bias.* Manuscript in preparation.

Report of the Virginia Tech Review Panel (2008). Retrieved on February 2, 2012 from http://www.governor.virginia.gov/TempContent/techPanelReport.cfm

Sampson, R. J., & Laub, J. H. (1993) *Crime in the making: Pathways and turning points through life.* Cambridge, MA: Harvard University Press.

Sedikides, C., Rudich, E. A., Gregg, A. P., Kumashiro, M., & Rusbult, C. (2004). Are normal narcissists psychologically healthy?: Self-esteem matters. *Journal of Personality and Social Psychology, 87,* 400–416.

Twenge, J. M., Baumeister, R. F., Tice, D. M., & Stucke, T. S. (2001). If you can't join them, beat them: Effects of social exclusion on aggressive behavior. *Journal of Personality and Social Psychology, 81,* 1058–1069.

Twenge, J. M., & Campbell, W. K. (2003). "Isn't it fun to get the respect that we're going to deserve?" Narcissism, social rejection, and aggression. *Personality and Social Psychology Bulletin, 29,* 261–270.

Twenge, J. M., Zhang, L., Catanese, K. R., Dolan-Pascoe, B., Lyche, L. F., & Baumeister, R. F. (2007). Replenishing connectedness: Reminders of social activity reduce aggression after social exclusion. *British Journal of Social Psychology, 46,* 205–224.

Warburton, W. A., Williams, K. D., & Cairns, D. R. (2006). When ostracism leads to aggression: The moderating effects of control deprivation. *Journal of Experimental Social Psychology, 42,* 213–220.

Williams, K. D. (2001). *Ostracism: The Power of Silence.* New York: Guilford Press.

Williams, K. D. (2009). Ostracism: Effects of being excluded and ignored. In M. P. Zanna (Ed.), *Advances in Experimental Social Psychology* (Vol. 41, pp. 275–314). New York: Academic Press.

Williams, K. D., Cheung, C. K. T., & Choi, W. (2000). Cyberostracism: Effects of being ignored over the Internet. *Journal of Personality and Social Psychology, 79,* 748–762.

How and When Exclusion Motivates Social Reconnection

Daniel C. Molden *and* Jon K. Maner

Abstract

Because fulfilling needs for social connection is so fundamental to health and well-being, people should be highly motivated to restore social connections when they are threatened. This chapter begins by discussing three ways in which people seek to reconnect with others after experiencing social exclusion: (1) ingratiating social behavior, (2) attention toward and sensitivity for social cues, and (3) the activation, exaggeration, and even invention of perceived relationships to important individuals or groups. The chapter then considers how social anxiety and broader concerns with security can heighten people's focus on self-protection and suppress their willingness to pursue reconnection. The chapter concludes by discussing important directions for future research on how people balance motivations for reconnection and self-protection, as well as on how people regulate their level of social connection more generally.

Key Words: belonging regulation, cooperation, group identification, ingratiation, parasocial relationships, motivations for promotion and prevention, social anxiety, social sensitivity

Introduction

At the turn of the 20th century in the United States, the mortality rate for young infants admitted to hospitals was close to 40%. Appalled, the medical community rallied to address what they assumed was the primary culprit: a poor understanding of children's nutritional requirements. However, after a decade of improvements in this area, the mortality rate had barely changed. Infants admitted to hospitals were still dying in alarming numbers even when nourished in exactly the same way as those who were thriving outside of the hospital (Bakwin, 1942).

Doctors next turned their attention to potential problems with infection. They began to place infants in isolated rooms and attend to them in masks and hoods. Visits by parents were forbidden and a special apparatus was used with " ... inlet and outlet values and sleeve arrangements for the attendants ... " so that the infant could be cared

for "almost untouched by human hands" (Bakwin, 1942, p. 31). Yet, several years after these new policies were instituted, high rates of mortality and health problems for infants in hospitals remained; while there, they generally slept poorly, failed to gain weight, and were often listless and nonresponsive.

Finally, doctors began to consider the possibility of psychological rather than physical causes for these problems; that is, that the infants were suffering from a lack of social attention and social contact. To remedy these circumstances, hospital staff began to be charged with compensating for any lack of direct maternal care. In a reversal of previous policies, all staff were instructed to pick up and play with the infants, and in cases in which a particular infant was hospitalized for an extended period, one person was designated to provide regular contact. Moreover, instead of being barred from the wards, parents were welcomed and encouraged to hold and interact with their children. The results of these interventions were striking. Infant mortality sharply decreased, and did so to a much greater degree than could be explained by larger regional or national trends over the same time period (Bakwin, 1942).

These early findings on infant mortality dramatically illustrate that beyond basic physical needs for nourishment and shelter, humans also have fundamental needs for social contact and social connection (Bowlby, 1969/1981; Harlow, 1958; Maslow, 1954; for a review see Baumeister & Leary, 1995). So fundamental are these needs for *belonging* that prolonged experiences of social isolation are not only seriously detrimental to newborn infants, but they also diminish adult health, well-being, and even overall lifespan (Cacioppo, Hawkley, & Berntson, 2003; House, Landis, & Umberson, 1988). Indeed, even fleeting experiences or perceptions of social exclusion have powerful effects on people's emotions (MacDonald & Leary, 2005; see also chapter 16), thoughts (Williams, 2007; see also chapter 3), and behaviors (Leary, Twenge, & Quinlivan, 2006; see also chapters 11 and 13).

Given that needs for belonging are so fundamental, experiences of social exclusion should presumably motivate vigorous efforts toward reconnecting with others (Maner, DeWall, Baumeister, & Schaller, 2007; Pickett & Gardner, 2005). Yet, despite the simplicity of this proposal and the long history of research on needs for belonging, it is only recently that studies have systematically examined such efforts. The present chapter reviews this recent research and discusses what it reveals about how and under what circumstances people seek to reconnect with others in the wake of social exclusion.

As displayed in Figure 12.1, studies have revealed three different ways in which people seek to reconnect with others following exclusion. First, they ingratiate themselves with others and create opportunities for social connection. Second, they attend to and display sensitivity for social cues that might signal opportunities for social connection. Third, they activate, exaggerate, and even invent perceived social connections to personally important social groups. We begin by discussing each of these responses to exclusion. Next, we consider circumstances that may hinder people's ability or willingness to seek reconnection. In particular, we discuss variables such as social anxiety or generally heightened concerns with security that may lead people to prioritize self-protection over social reconnection in the wake of exclusion. Finally, we discuss some important future directions for research on when and how people cope with experiences of social exclusion and more generally regulate their belonging needs.

How Exclusion Motivates Efforts at Reconnection

Social exclusion can elicit conflicting social motivations (Smart Richman & Leary, 2009; see also chapter 5). On the one hand, people want to reconnect with people so as to restore their level of belonging. On the other hand, people also wish to avoid further rejection. Therefore, to the extent that people do seek reconnection following exclusion, they tend to do so in ways that are relatively indirect and circumspect so as to avoid opening themselves up to further social harm. That is, although people actively seek to repair social connections after exclusion, they prefer more cautious and judicious strategies to accomplish this goal. Indeed, this caution is evident in the three primary ways by which people have been found to pursue reconnection following exclusion illustrated in Figure 12.1 (ingratiation, being sensitive to social cues, and expanding their perceptions of social connection), all of which involve relatively passive efforts at engagement. The following sections describe each of these responses to exclusion in greater detail.

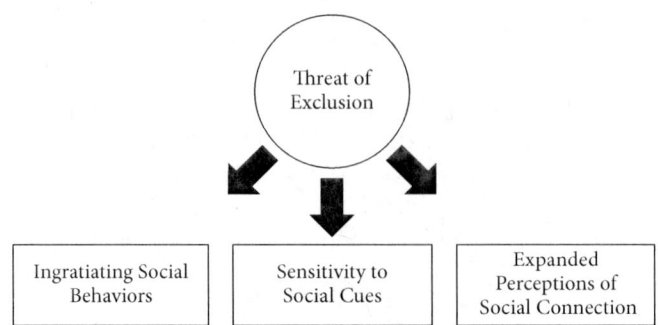

Figure 12.1 How People Attempt to Restore Feelings of Social Connection Following Experiences of Exclusion.

Exclusion and Ingratiating Social Behavior

Efforts at ingratiation following social exclusion can take many forms, including conformity, cooperation, and unconscious mimicry of nonverbal behaviors. For example, in one study, Williams and colleagues exposed participants to an episode of social exclusion by having them play a digital ball-toss game with two other individuals via computer (Williams, Cheung, & Choi, 2000). During this game of *Cyberball*, after initially sharing the ball with the participant, the two other players tossed the ball only to each other. After this experience of exclusion, participants then took part in what they believed was a separate computer task with a new group of individuals. This task involved a set of perceptual identification problems in which members of the group publicly shared their answers. As in the classic studies by Asch (1956), on several trials all of the other members of the group (who were actually confederates) endorsed a clearly wrong answer. As would be expected from those seeking to ingratiate themselves and expand their opportunities for social connection, excluded participants were much more likely to conform to the incorrect group opinion compared with participants in a control condition.

Additional evidence for ingratiation through conformity comes from a study by Kerr and colleagues (Kerr et al., 2009). Participants took part in a group decision-making task in which they decided how much of a $5 allotment they would keep for themselves and how much they would invest in a common account benefiting the entire group. Investments would always increase the collective outcome for other group members, but unless everyone else chose to invest all of their money as well, these investments would decrease participants' personal outcomes. Participants therefore faced relatively strong temptations to be self-serving and not invest in the common account. However, results showed that when all group members' decisions would be public and a vote would be held as to whether each member should be excluded from subsequent rounds of the task, participants invested a significantly greater amount of money to the common account, as long as they believed that at least a majority of the other group members had also invested in the common account, and (see also DeCremer & Leonardelli, 2003). Thus, similar to the Williams et al. (2000) study, when the threat of social exclusion was salient, participants chose to ingratiate themselves to the rest of the group by conforming to what they believed to be the normative, cooperative response, even when doing so detracted from their individual outcomes.

Another study by Williams and Sommer (1997) provides evidence for ingratiation in the wake of social exclusion by examining a different type of group dynamic. After undergoing exclusion in a live ball-toss game played with two confederates, participants learned that they would all be performing a brainstorming task in which they would each, on their own, generate as many creative uses for a knife as they could. Although participants in a control (nonexclusion) condition displayed *social loafing* by relaxing their individual effort on the task (Latane, Williams, & Harkins, 1979), women who had been excluded during the ball-toss game showed an opposite, *social compensation* effect. That is, excluded women dedicated significantly more effort to the brainstorming task and generated more uses for a knife, as is consistent with a desire to regain their standing in the group.

All of the studies reviewed thus far are consistent with the idea that social exclusion increases desires for reconnection and ingratiating behavior, but the evidence they present is somewhat indirect and open to other possible interpretations. Further studies by Maner and colleagues provide a more direct indication that people respond to exclusion with a desire for reconnection (Maner et al., 2007). For example, after writing about a time in which they felt rejected, participants expressed greater interest in a student service designed to help them connect with others socially. Similarly, after thinking about losing all of their social connections in the future, participants expressed greater desire to work with a partner, as opposed to alone.

Moreover, Maner and colleagues further showed that the desire for social reconnection following exclusion also translated into overt behaviors aimed at ingratiating oneself to a prospective partner (Maner et al., 2007). Participants interacted with a confederate who, after ostensibly watching a video of the participant, declined the opportunity for further interaction. After this perceived rejection, participants engaged in a workplace simulation exercise with a new partner. Consistent with the idea that rejection elicits efforts at ingratiation, participants who had been rejected rated their new partner's work as especially creative and, on the basis of that evaluation, rewarded the partner with a cash award. This generous behavior presumably was intended to pave the way for a pleasant interaction.

This direct evidence of efforts at reconnection following exclusion found by Maner and colleagues is further reinforced by research that has observed attempts at ingratiation by ethnic minorities during interracial interactions, in which expectations of rejection are often high. In two studies, Shelton and colleagues first measured or manipulated minority students' general anticipations of being stigmatized by others based on their ethnicity and then assessed both their verbal and nonverbal behavior during their interactions with white students (Shelton, Richeson, & Salvatore, 2005). They found that minority students with increased expectations of exclusion by their white partners made extra efforts at preventing this exclusion: These minority students talked more during the interaction, asked their partners more questions about themselves, and smiled and leaned forward more during the conversation.

Finally, in addition to all of these conscious efforts at reconnection when experiencing social exclusion, some studies have shown that exclusion can activate automatic and nonconscious pursuit of social connection as well. Much research has demonstrated that people mimic others' nonverbal behaviors during social interactions without awareness or intent. Furthermore, this nonconscious mimicry occurs more frequently when people are motivated to establish social connection (e.g., Lakin & Chartrand, 2003), and is effective at increasing feelings of social connection with others (van Baaren, Holland, Kawakami, & van Knippenberg, 2004). Lakin, Chartrand, and Arkin (2008) recently extended these findings by demonstrating that threats of exclusion increase such nonconscious affiliation seeking (see also Murray & Holmes, 2009; chapter 25). Participants were first excluded during a game of Cyberball, as detailed earlier, and then performed a joint task in which they sat at a table with a partner and described photographs that the partner could not see. During the interaction, the partner (who was actually a confederate) gently shook her foot. The primary measure of interest was how much the participant mimicked this behavior and shook his or her foot as well. Recordings of the interactions revealed that excluded participants engaged in almost twice as much mimicry as nonexcluded participants (see also Lakin & Chartrand, 2003). Moreover, no participants reported any awareness of the confederate's foot shaking, indicating that this subtle means of affiliation-seeking was indeed nonconscious and unintentional.

Thus, numerous studies demonstrate that people employ a wide variety of conscious and nonconscious strategies to ingratiate themselves with others when they are expecting, or have just experienced, some form of social exclusion. Furthermore, as noted at the outset, these strategies largely appear to involve relatively cautious and indirect means of pursuing social connection. Even in the Maner et al. (2007) studies, in which people rewarded and complemented interaction partners following exclusion, these behaviors did not take place face-to-face and may have represented people's efforts to indirectly set the stage for positive interactions with this partner in the future. By comparison, in another series of studies by Twenge and colleagues, in which participants (1) received direct requests to volunteer their time or donate money, (2) were confronted face-to-face with someone who needed assistance, or (3) directly participated in a social exchange with a less-than-completely-trustworthy partner, experiences of social exclusion *decreased* cooperation with others (Twenge, Baumeister, DeWall, Ciarocco, & Bartels, 2007). This further reinforces the idea that, although exclusion increases desires for reconnection, it also leads to greater wariness and caution in social situations. We later discuss this possibility in more detail when considering the specific circumstances in which pursuit of reconnection is most likely following exclusion.

Exclusion and Sensitivity for Social Cues

As noted, in addition to cautiously behaving in ingratiating ways following exclusion, people carefully analyze their social surroundings so as to identify opportunities for affiliation versus further exclusion. When needs for belonging are activated, these needs not only affect people's behaviors, but also influence their basic cognitive processes such as attention and perception (e.g., DeWall, Maner, & Rouby, 2009; see also chapter 17). Analogous to other fundamental motivations, such as concerns with maintaining self-worth, increased needs for belonging can thus influence information processing in ways that facilitate the identification of possibilities for social reconnection (see Molden & Higgins, 2012).

For example, Gardner, Pickett, and colleagues have demonstrated that both chronic loneliness and temporary experiences of or thoughts about exclusion increase attention to a range of socially significant stimuli. First, exclusion enhances attention to, and memory for, positive and negative social events (Gardner, Pickett, & Brewer, 2000; Gardner, Pickett, Jefferis, & Knowles, 2005; Hess & Pickett, 2010). Second, exclusion enhances attention to the positive or negative emotional tone of a speaker's voice, even when this tone interferes with the current goal of responding only to the valence of the words spoken (Gardner et al., 2005; Pickett, Gardner, & Knowles, 2004). Third, exclusion enhances the ability to identify subtle facial cues of specific positive and negative emotional expressions (Gardner et al., 2005; Pickett et al., 2004). Thus, experiences of exclusion and concerns with social connection may increase sensitivity to a range of information that could signal whether or not opportunities for reconnection exist.

Two additional studies using different measures of attention to social information further support this social sensitivity hypothesis. First, participants who had just relived an experience of social exclusion were better able to identify genuine smiles from "fake" (i.e., non-Duchenne) smiles than participants who had relived neutral experiences (Bernstein, Young, Brown, Sacco, & Claypool, 2008). That is, excluded participants showed a heightened ability to separate individuals who were showing true signs of affiliation from individuals who were displaying "masking" smiles that often signal an individual is actually experiencing negative emotions (see Ekman, Freisen, & O'Sullivan, 1988). Moreover, participants who had just relived an experience of social exclusion more frequently chose those displaying genuine smiles as someone with whom they would like to work on a joint project as compared with those displaying non-Duchenne smiles (Bernstein, Sacco, Brown, Young, & Claypool, 2010). Thus, experiences of exclusion do not appear to motivate people to optimistically interpret any potential signal of affiliation and perceive fake smiles as genuine (cf. Ditto, Scepansky, Munro, Apanovitch, & Lockhart, 1998); instead, such experiences increase people's sensitivity for distinguishing between true opportunities for affiliation versus the potential for negative interactions with others.

One final study in which sensitivity to social cues was measured independent of any emotional responses also provides evidence for broad increases in social sensitivity following exclusion (Wilkowski, Robinson, & Friesen, 2009). After reliving a past experience of exclusion, participants performed a task in which they fixed their attention upon a neutral-expressioned face that appeared in the center of a computer screen. Periodically, the face would shift its gaze to the right or left, and a short time later an asterisk would appear on either on the side of the screen toward which the face was looking or on the side of the screen opposite where the face was looking. The objective of the task was to respond as quickly as possible at the appearance of the asterisk. Participants who had relived an experience of exclusion were affected more by where the face was gazing (i.e., showed greater facilitation in their response time when the face gazed toward where the asterisk appeared) as compared with participants who had relived an experience of acceptance, suggesting an increased sensitivity to the social cues the face provided.

Although these previous findings suggest that exclusion may create a general sensitivity to both positive and negative social events, at the level of early-stage information processing, exclusion appears to focus people specifically on opportunities for social affiliation. In a series of studies, DeWall and colleagues investigated the influence of social exclusion on people's immediate attention to facial expressions involving various emotions (DeWall et al., 2009). Across a variety of methods (e.g., eye-tracking, visual search), the threat of exclusion selectively increased people's attention to smiling faces. This is consistent with the idea that people initially seek reconnection after exclusion because a smiling face typically serves as an unambiguous signal of social acceptance. In contrast, these studies provided no evidence for increased attention to angry faces, which signal social threat. Although excluded individuals may indeed eventually become vigilant to social threat (e.g., further rejection), results from these experiments suggest that at the level of initial social perception, attention to signs of affiliation trumps vigilance to potential social threat.

Overall, there is much evidence to suggest that basic mechanisms of attention and perception are influenced by feelings of social exclusion. Moreover, these effects reflect an increased sensitivity to others' social experiences and emotional states, which provide another way in which people can cautiously test their environment for opportunities to reconnect following exclusion.

Exclusion and Enhanced Perceptions of Social Connection

Beyond increasing their attention and sensitivity to cues in the environment that signal opportunities for social connection, excluded people may also strive to fulfill their needs for belonging by calling to mind their existing connections, exaggerating these connections, or even inventing them where they may not exist. That is, when immediate opportunities for directly pursuing reconnection do not exist or are felt to be too risky, people may seek more psychological or symbolic means of coping with exclusion (Gardner, Pickett, & Knowles, 2005; Park & Maner, 2009).

For example, the anticipation or experience of exclusion influences people's thoughts about their membership and status in the social groups with which they might identify. After reliving exclusionary experiences, as compared with experiences of acceptance or nonsocial negative outcomes such as physical pain, people are more likely to call to mind thoughts about their broad ethnic or gender identities, as well as the more specific clubs, teams, or family groups to which they belong (Knowles & Gardner, 2008). Reliving experiences of exclusion or receiving feedback about their differences from a typical member of an important social group (which presumably raises concerns about future exclusion) also leads people to rate the social groups to which they belong as larger, more inclusive, more cohesive, and more important (Knowles & Gardner, 2008; Pickett, Silver, & Brewer, 2002). For groups with which they are highly identified, increased concerns about possible exclusion can even lead people to self-identify with both positive and negative stereotypes about the group and present themselves to others in these more stereotypical ways (Pickett, Bonner, & Coleman, 2002). Moreover, not only does this increased attention to, altered perceptions of, and behavior in line with one's group memberships emerge in response to threats of social exclusion, but it also helps to protect against the negative affect and concerns about one's social competence that exclusion produces (Knowles & Gardner, 2008).

Similar results were observed by Maner and colleagues, who examined effects of exclusion on perceptions of new social interaction partners (Maner et al., 2007). In one study, participants who were made to feel excluded by a group of their peers were subsequently asked to judge a set of faces, all of whom were displaying perfectly neutral facial expressions. Instead of perceiving those people as neutral, however, participants who had been excluded perceived those individuals as displaying friendliness and warmth. That is, exclusion led participants to manufacture signs of positive social affiliation when essentially none existed. In another study, people who had been made to feel excluded by a partner who ostensibly refused to work with them subsequently judged a new prospective interaction partner based only on a photograph. A similar pattern emerged; excluded participants rated the new partner as more friendly, warm, and inviting. Seeing others in such a positive social light in the absence of any real information about them presumably reflects an enhanced desire for positive social contact.

In addition to simply calling to mind the larger social groups to which they belong or bolstering connections to other individuals, people who have experienced exclusion may even (consciously or unconsciously) attempt to manufacture a sense of social connection in clearly nonsocial domains. One way in which people accomplish this is by forming and perpetuating what can be termed *parasocial* relationships with fictional characters portrayed in novels or on television (Horton & Wohl, 1956). For example, after recalling conflicts with close others, people were found to spend more time ruminating about a television program featuring their favorite characters as compared with just watching television in general (Derrick, Gabriel, & Hugenberg, 2009; see also Knowles 2007; chapter 26). Furthermore, as with calling to mind one's actual social connections, these thoughts about favorite fictional characters actually protect against the negative affect, feelings of rejection, and loss of self-esteem that recalling experiences of social exclusion creates. Another way in which people can manufacture social connection is by ascribing social qualities to the inanimate objects and animal companions with which they interact. For example, both chronic feelings of social exclusion and current anticipation of exclusion led people to attribute qualities like emotion and intention to gadgets that respond to external stimuli (e.g., an alarm clock that "runs away" when the snooze button is pressed), and to see their pets as considerate and sympathetic (Epley, Akalis, Waytz, & Cacioppo, 2008; Epley, Waytz, Akalis, & Cacioppo, 2008; see also chapter 23). Thus, when people's basic needs for belonging are threatened, they may try to fulfill their social needs through nonsocial means by inventing connections toward pets and even inanimate objects.

Considered together, all of the research reviewed thus far demonstrates that attempting to restore social connection is a fundamental and widespread response to experiences of exclusion. However, as we have noted, the generally cautious way in which reconnection is pursued suggests that there are other concerns beyond belonging evoked by social exclusion as well (Smart Richman & Leary, 2009; Williams, 2007; see also chapters 3 and 5). Therefore, in certain circumstances, these additional concerns may interfere with people's desire to seek reconnection and lead to other responses such as withdrawal or even hostility (see chapter 11). The next section describes some of these concerns in detail and presents studies demonstrating their impact.

When Exclusion Motivates Efforts at Reconnection

Much research has shown that, in addition to a desire for social reconnection, exclusion can also evoke strong feelings of anxiety and distress (MacDonald & Leary, 2005; see also chapter 20). Although achieving reconnection would presumably alleviate these feelings, experiences of exclusion may be negative enough to compel people to seek a more immediate escape. That is, unless pursuing reconnection appears at least somewhat likely to succeed and unlikely to result in further exclusion, people would be expected to seek some other strategy of coping with the "hurt feelings" produced by exclusion.

Several of the studies by Maner and colleagues (2007) reviewed in the preceding sections directly examined whether the perceived likelihood of affiliation is a critical precondition for initiating efforts at social reconnection. In one of their studies, they manipulated whether or not participants expected to have an opportunity interact with a new partner after experiencing exclusion from a previous partner. When participants did expect to interact with their new partner, they responded to exclusion with increased generosity that presumably paved the way for a positive social interaction, as described earlier. However, when participants did not expect to actually meet their new partner face to face, the opposite occurred and they behaved in a less generous fashion. This suggests that people strive for reconnection, particularly (and perhaps only) when they perceive a high likelihood of having a positive social interaction.

Maner and colleagues have also examined how more general concerns about whether efforts at reconnection would actually just lead to further possibilities for exclusion can prevent people from seeking reconnection as well. Individuals who are high in social anxiety experience a pronounced fear of negative social evaluation and an exaggerated fear of rejection (Heimberg, Lebowitz, Hope, & Schneier, 1995). Consequently, these individuals tend to respond to exclusion not by seeking reconnection, but instead by withdrawing from others to avoid the potential for further rejection. That is, people high in social anxiety are more likely to generalize exclusion in one interaction to the potential for exclusion in other social interactions; unlike those low in social anxiety, those high in social anxiety do not see new interaction partners as providing new opportunities for social connection and, if anything, are less willing to ingratiate themselves to these partners following exclusion.

For example, Maner et al. (2007) showed that, whereas most people responded to rejection by seeing new interaction partners in a positive light (as friendly and warm), people high in social anxiety responded instead by seeing others as aggressive and threatening. Similarly, whereas most people responded to rejection by behaving in a generous way toward a new interaction partner, those high in social anxiety instead responded by withholding rewards from the partner (see also Murray & Holmes, 2009). Evidence from other studies further indicates that whereas most people respond to rejection by increasing nonverbal signals that invite affiliation (e.g., increased eye contact and positive vocal tone), those high in social anxiety instead respond with signs of avoidance (e.g., decreased eye contact) (Mallott, Maner, DeWall, & Schmidt, 2009). Finally, although in response to social exclusion, most people display increased levels of progesterone (a sign of social affiliative motivation), in these circumstances, those high in social anxiety display decreased levels of progesterone; such decreases are consistent with a desire for social withdrawal rather than social affiliation (Maner, Miller, Schmidt, & Eckel, 2010).

Social anxiety presumably suppresses people's impulses for reconnection following social exclusion by raising specific fears of further exclusion in response to attempts at reconnection. That is, such anxiety creates a more cautious, security-focused approach to coping with exclusion that encourages withdrawal from rather than reengagement in social contact (Clark & Wells, 1995). In a recent program of research, Molden, Lucas, Gardner, and colleagues extended this line of thinking by investigating whether general self-regulatory concerns with maintaining safety and security that are not directly tied to dispositional levels of social anxiety (see Higgins, 1997; Molden, Lee, & Higgins, 2008) can similarly attenuate people's pursuit of reconnection following exclusion (Lucas, Knowles, Gardner, Molden, & Jefferis, 2010; Molden, Lucas, Gardner, Dean, & Knowles, 2009).

Across three studies, Molden et al. (2009) examined self-regulatory concerns for safety and security (i.e., *prevention*) in the context of exclusion by exposing participants to (or having them relive) instances of exclusion in which they were actively and explicitly *rejected*. Such rejection was expected to communicate a distinct loss of social connection and activate more prevention-focused modes of goal pursuit. As is the case with individuals dispositionally high in social anxiety, participants who were actively rejected were indeed focused less on restoring social connections and more on withdrawing from social contact and ruminating about the mistakes they made that led to their exclusion. In contrast, participants who were instead exposed to or relived instances of exclusion in which they were more passively and implicitly *ignored* did seek reconnection; these experiences of exclusion, which were expected to communicate a failure to gain social connection and activate more growth-oriented, *promotion-focused* modes of goal pursuit (Higgins, 1997; Molden et al., 2008), led participants to actively seek to restore social connections and think about all of the actions they could have taken to achieve these connections.

Just as these studies suggest that broader prevention-focused concerns with safety and security can inhibit people's pursuit of reconnection following social exclusion, an additional series of studies by Lucas et al. (2010) further demonstrated that the interference of chronic anxiety about social connections with the pursuit of reconnection can be overcome by activating more promotion-focused modes of goal pursuit. Across three studies, whereas chronically lonely individuals were generally found to anticipate exclusion, report intentions for social avoidance, and show less affiliation-seeking (assessed by nonconscious behavioral mimicry as described earlier) (Lakin et al., 2008), both subtle and direct primes of their broader motivations for promotion decreased lonely individuals' concerns about exclusion, reduced their desires for avoidance, and even increased their behavioral mimicry. Indeed, when they were promotion focused, lonely individuals did not differ from nonlonely individuals in their social evaluations or pursuit of social connection.

On the whole, the research reviewed in this section indicates that one primary obstacle to the pursuit of reconnection following social exclusion is the larger concerns with safety and security that exclusion can activate (cf. Lucas, Molden, & Gardner, 2010). Whether these concerns arise from (1) doubts about the possibility of connecting with a particular individual (Maner et al. 2007), (2) general fears about negative evaluations by others (Mallot et al., 2009; Maner et al., 2007, 2010), or (3) the activation of broader modes of self-regulation (Lucas, Knowles, et al., 2010; Molden et al., 2009), they inhibit thoughts and behaviors aimed at reconnection and tend to instead produce withdrawal from and avoidance of social contact. These findings help to further illuminate why the types of ingratiating behaviors that are observed when people seek reconnection in the wake of exclusion are largely indirect. Concerns with security are rarely absent when exclusion is experienced; therefore, even when such concerns can be partially overcome and efforts toward reconnection are pursued, these efforts seem likely to still reflect a more cautious and measured approach (cf. Maner et al., 2007; Twenge et al., 2007).

Conclusions

When experiencing social exclusion, people appear highly motivated to alleviate the threats to belonging that arise. However, experiences of exclusion can also evoke powerful negative emotions that could instead lead people to withdraw from social contact. The research reviewed in this chapter suggests that both impulses for reconnection and for withdrawal are indeed prominent in people's reactions to social exclusion and that which one prevails may depend on a variety of factors.

In general, even when desires for reconnection win out following exclusion, they are still tempered by a wariness about the possibility of further exclusion. The behaviors that are observed in these contexts tend to be indirect and aimed at ingratiation rather than overt attempts at relationship formation. People seek out group settings (Maner et al., 2007); they adhere to group norms (Kerr et al., 2009; Williams et al., 2001) and contribute more to group efforts (Williams & Sommer, 1997); and they engage in verbal and nonverbal behaviors that subtly communicate desires for affiliation (Shelton et al., 2005), at times outside of conscious awareness (Lakin & Chartrand, 2003; Lakin et al., 2008). Furthermore, whenever people's anxiety over future experiences of exclusion or broad concerns with security in general are salient, even these cautious attempts at reconnection seem to disappear (Mallot et al., 2009; Maner et al., 2007; Molden et al., 2009).

However, even when people's anxieties and security concerns appear to restrain their efforts at ingratiation, the research reviewed here suggests that additional psychological mechanisms may still be available to help people achieve at least some sense of reconnection. First, exclusion increases people's attention to (DeWall et al., 2009; Gardner et al., 2000; Hess & Pickett, 2010; Wilkowski et al., 2009) and sensitivity in interpreting (Bernstein et al., 2008; Bernstein et al., 2010; Gardner, Pickett, Knowles, et al., 2005; Pickett et al., 2004) social information. Thus, following exclusion, people become increasingly interested in studying available social cues, presumably as a means of identifying opportunities for reconnection that exist and manage risks of further exclusion. In addition, exclusion enhances people's attention to and beliefs about the importance of those broader social connections they still do have; it brings to mind all of the different social groups of which they are a member (Knowles & Gardner, 2008), elevates the perceived cohesiveness and inclusiveness of these groups (Knowles & Gardner, 2008; Pickett et al., 2002), and increases both identification with and tendency to behave in line with group-based stereotypes (Pickett et al., 2001). Finally, exclusion can even at times compel people to manufacture human-like feelings of social connection to fictional characters (Derrick et al., 2009), pets (Epley, Akalis, et al., 2008; Epley, Waytz, et al., 2008), and inanimate objects (Epley, Akalis, et al., 2008). Therefore, even when people are reticent to engage in behaviors that might facilitate reconnection, their motivations to restore feelings of belonging following exclusion still have important effects on their thoughts and behavior.

One important question for future research, therefore, is that although increased concerns with security reduce ingratiating behaviors following exclusion, do these concerns also simultaneously increase social sensitivity and identification with larger social groups? That is, do feelings of social anxiety or prevention-focused motivations reduce people's willingness to engage in behaviors aimed at restoring social connections, but at the same time increase people's thoughts about and attention to the social environment? Some evidence consistent with this possibility is that whereas chronically lonely individuals are less likely to engage in subtle efforts at reconnection such as nonconscious mimicry (Lucas, Knowles, et al., 2010), these individuals show increased attention and sensitivity to social information (Gardner, Pickett, Knowles, et al., 2005), and a greater tendency to create human-like connections to their pets (Epley, Waytz, et al., 2008). Additional studies that simultaneously measure several of the ways in which people attempt to restore feelings of social connection depicted in Figure 12.1 could shed greater light on when people select one mechanism or another.

Another important question for future research is what additional factors beyond concerns with security might influence when people's desires for reconnection win out and lead to ingratiation following exclusion versus when their hurt feelings and desires to avoid further exclusion lead to withdrawal or even hostility? Smart Richman and Leary's (2009) recent multimotive model of exclusion (see also chapter 5) proposes some other possible determinants, such as the value of the relationship, the perceived availability of alternative relationships, and the perceived fairness of the exclusion itself. When relationships are valuable and other relationships are not readily available, then people may be compelled to engage in more ingratiation and efforts at reconnection, even if social anxiety or concerns with security are high (cf. Murray & Holmes, 2009). In contrast, when the exclusion is perceived as unfair, even if anxiety about further exclusion or concerns with security are low, people may be more likely to display withdrawal or hostility rather than ingratiation. These too are important topics for future research.

Models of social exclusion that incorporate multiple motives and specify multiple threats that can arise from experiences of exclusion (Molden et al., 2009; Murray & Holmes, 2009; Smart Richman & Leary, 2009; Williams, 2007) also raise questions concerning how these separate motives might have additive or interactive effects. For example, a study by Hess and Pickett (2010) demonstrated that following exclusion in a game of Cyberball, people not only showed increased attention to (and thus memory for) others' social behaviors, as is consistent with motives for reconnection, they also show decreased attention to their own social behaviors, as is consistent with motives for withdrawal from and avoidance of the hurt feelings evoked by exclusion. Additional studies that further illuminate how and when the different motivations activated by social exclusion can operate together rather than in opposition could provide further insight into the varied responses people display after experiencing exclusion.

Finally, a more general question that current research on social exclusion raises is to what extent do people's attempts to regulate their feelings of social connection operate in the same manner as their attempts to regulate their other basic needs? Although belonging regulation is bound to involve broad self-regulatory processes that are shared among all forms of goal pursuit (e.g., Carver & Scheier, 1990; Kruglanski et al., 2002), it might feature unique aspects as well. For example, although exclusion can threaten multiple needs, such as esteem, belonging, and control, all at once (Williams, 2007; see also chapter 3), addressing threats to belonging may take precedence over other needs (cf. Maslow, 1955). Indeed, recent studies by Knowles and colleagues (Knowles, Lucas, Molden, Gardner, & Jefferis, 2010) found that as compared with needs to maintain feelings of competence and esteem, belonging needs are less *substitutable*. That is, when people's esteem was threatened, they readily sought to affirm strengths in other domains to compensate for these threats (see Tesser, 2000); however, when people's belonging was threatened, as is consistent with the other findings reviewed here, they sought to reaffirm their strengths in the social domain rather than attempt to compensate for belonging threats through other means. Therefore, additional studies could examine whether there are other unique aspects of belonging regulation that separate this process from people's attempts to address their other basic needs.

To conclude, fulfilling needs for belonging is absolutely essential for health and well-being; therefore, when their social connections are threatened, people have strong motives to seek reconnection. Although efforts toward reconnection may at times be overshadowed by more immediate desires for self-protection and escape from the negative emotions associated with social exclusion, people appear to have a variety of behavioral and psychological strategies that allow them to overcome these protective impulses and cautiously seek to reestablish social bonds. For, like the hospitalized infants who were kept in isolation and removed from human contact, the only way for people to truly recover in the wake of exclusion is to rebuild their connections to the social world.

References

Asch, S. E. (1956) Studies of independence and conformity: A minority of one against a unanimous majority. *Psychological Monographs, 70*, 1–70

Bakwin, H. (1942). Loneliness in infants. *American Journal of Diseases in Children, 63*, 30–40.

Baumeister, R. F., & Leary, M. R. (1995). The need to belong: Desire for interpersonal attachments as a fundamental human motivation. *Psychological Bulletin, 117*, 497–529.

Bernstein, M. J., Young, S. G., Brown, C. M., Sacco, D. F., & Claypool, H. M. (2008). Adaptive responses to social exclusion: Social rejection improves detection of real and fake smiles. *Psychological Science, 19*, 981–983.

Bernstein, M. J., Sacco, D. F., Brown, C. M., Young, S. G., & Claypool, H. M. (2010). A preference for genuine smiles following social exclusion. *Journal of Experimental Social Psychology, 46*, 196–199.

Bowlby, J. (1969/1981). *Attachment (Attachment and Loss, Vol. 1)*. New York: Basic Books.

Cacioppo, J. T., Hawkley, L. C., & Berntson, G. G. (2003). The anatomy of loneliness. *Current Directions in Psychological Science, 12*, 71–74.

Carver, C. S., & Scheier, M. (1990). Principles of self-regulation: Action and emotion. In E. T. Higgins, & R. M. Sorrentino (Eds.) *Handbook of Motivation and Cognition: Foundations of Social Behavior* (Vol. 2., pp. 3–52). New York: Guilford Press.

Clark D. M., Wells A. (1995). A cognitive model of social phobia. In R. G Heimberg, M. Liebowitz, D. Hope, & F. Scheier (Eds.). *Social Phobia: Diagnosis, Assessment, and Treatment* (69–93). New York: Guilford.

DeCremer, D., & Leonardelli, G. J. (2003). Cooperation in social dilemmas and the need to belong: The moderating effect of group size. *Group Dynamics: Theory, Research, and Practice, 7*, 168–174.

Derrick, J. L., Gabriel, S., & Hugenberg, K. (2009). Social surrogacy: How favored television programs provide the experience of belonging. *Journal of Experimental Social Psychology, 45*, 352–362.

DeWall, C. N., Maner, J. K., & Rouby, D. A. (2009). Social exclusion and early-stage interpersonal perception: Selective attention to signs of acceptance. *Journal of Personality and Social Psychology, 96*, 729–741.

Ditto, P. H., Scepansky, J. A., Munro, G. D., Apanovitch, A. M., & Lockhart, L. K. (1998). Motivated sensitivity to preference-inconsistent information. *Journal of Personality and Social Psychology, 75*, 53–69.

Ekman, P., Friesen, W. V., & O'Sullivan, M. (1988). Smiles when lying. *Journal of Personality and Social Psychology, 54*, 414–420.

Epley, N., Akalis, S., Waytz, A., & Cacioppo, J. T. (2008). Creating social connection through inferential reproduction: Loneliness and perceived agency in gadgets, gods, and greyhounds. *Psychological Science, 19*, 114–120.

Epley, N., Waytz, A., Akalis, S., & Cacioppo, J. T. (2008). When we need a human: Motivational determinants of anthropomorphism. *Social Cognition, 26*, 143–155.

Gardner, W. L., Pickett, C. L., & Brewer, M. B. (2000). Social exclusion and selective memory: How the need to belong influences memory for social events. *Personality and Social Psychology Bulletin, 26*, 486–496.

Gardner, W. L., Pickett, C. L., Jefferis, V., & Knowles, M. (2005). On the outside looking in: Loneliness and social monitoring. *Personality and Social Psychology Bulletin, 31*, 1549–1560.

Gardner, W. L., Pickett, C. L., & Knowles, M. L. (2005). Social snacking and shielding: Using social symbols, selves, and surrogates in the service of belong needs. In K. D. Williams, J. P. Forgas, & W. von Hippel (Eds.). *The Social Outcast: Ostracism, Social Exclusion, Rejection, and Bullying* (pp. 243–262). New York: Psychology Press.

Harlow, H. F. (1958). The nature of love. *American Psychologist, 13*, 673–685.

Higgins, E. T. (1997). Beyond pleasure and pain. *American Psychologist, 52*, 1280–1300.

Heimberg, R., Liebowitz, M., Hope, D., & Schneier, F. (Eds.) (1995). *Social Phobia: Diagnosis, Assessment and Treatment*. New York: Guilford Press.

Hess, Y. D., & Pickett, C. L. (2010). Social rejection and self versus other awareness. *Journal of Experimental Social Psychology, 46*, 453–456.

Horton, D., & Wohl, R. R. (1956). Mass communication and para-social interaction: Observations on intimacy at a distance. *Psychiatry, 19*, 215–229.

House, J. S., Landis, K. R., & Umberson, D. (1988). Social relationships and health. *Science, 241*, 540–545

Kerr, N. L., Rumble, A. C., Park, E. S., Ouwerkerk, J. W, Parks, C. D., Gallucci, M., & van Lange, P. A. M. (2009). "How many bad apples does it take to spoil the whole barrel?"

Social exclusion and toleration for bad apples. *Journal of Experimental Social Psychology, 45,* 603–613

Knowles, M. L. (2007). *The Nature of Parasocial Relationships.* Unpublished doctoral dissertation. Evanston, IL: Northwestern University.

Knowles, M. L., & Gardner, W. L. (2008). Benefits of membership: The activation and amplification of group identities in response to social rejection. *Personality and Social Psychology Bulletin, 34,* 1200–1213.

Knowles, M. L., Lucas, M. G., Molden, D. C., Gardner, W. L., & Jefferis, V. E. (2010). There's no substitute for belonging: Self-affirmation following social and non-social threats. *Personality and Social Psychology Bulletin, 36,* 173–186.

Kruglanski, A., Shah, J., Fishbach, A., Friedman, R., Chun, W., & Sleeth- Keppler, D. (2002). A theory of goal systems. In M. Zanna (Ed.). *Advances in Experimental Social Psychology* (Vol. 34, pp. 331–378). San Diego: Academic Press.

Lakin, J. L., & Chartrand, T. L. (2003). Using nonconscious behavioral mimicry to create affiliation and rapport. *Psychological Science, 14,* 334–339.

Lakin, J. L., Chartrand, T. L., & Arkin, R. M. (2008). I am too just like you: Nonconscious mimicry as an automatic behavioral response to social exclusion. *Psychological Science, 19,* 816–822.

Latane, B., Williams, K., & Harkins, S. (1979). Many hands make light the work: The causes and consequences of social loafing. *Journal of Personality and Social Psychology, 37,* 822–832.

Leary, M. R., Twenge, J. M., & Quinlivan, E. (2006). Interpersonal rejection as a determinant of anger and aggression. *Personality and Social Psychology Review, 10,* 111–132.

Lucas, G. M., Knowles, M. L., Gardner, W. L., Molden, D. C., & Jefferis, V. E. (2010). Increasing social engagement among lonely individuals: The role of acceptance cues and promotion motivations. *Personality and Social Psychology Bulletin, 36,* 1346–1359.

Lucas, G. M., Molden, D. C., & Gardner, W. L. (2010). *Anxiety and Security-Focused Goal Pursuit: An Integrative Approach.* Unpublished manuscript. Evanston, IL: Northwestern University.

MacDonald, G., & Leary, M. R. (2005). Why does social exclusion hurt? The relationship between social and physical pain. *Psychological Bulletin, 131,* 202–223.

Mallot, M., Maner, J. K., DeWall, C. N., & Schmidt, N. B. (2009). Compensatory deficits following rejection: The role of social anxiety in disrupting affiliative behavior. *Depression and Anxiety, 26,* 438–446.

Maner, J. K., DeWall, C. N., Baumeister, R. F., & Schaller, M. (2007). Does social exclusion motivate interpersonal reconnection? Resolving the "porcupine problem." *Journal of Personality and Social Psychology, 92,* 42–55.

Maner, J. K., Miller, S. L., Schmidt, N. B., & Eckel, L. A. (2010). Endocrinology of exclusion: Rejection elicits motivationally tuned changes in progesterone. *Psychological Science, 21,* 581–588.

Maslow, A. (1954). *Motivation and Personality.* New York: Harper.

Molden, D. C., & Higgins, E. T. (2012). Motivated thinking. In K. J. Holyoak, & R. G. Morrison (Eds.), *The Oxford Handbook of Thinking and Reasoning* (pp. 390–409). New York: Oxford University Press.

Molden, D. C., Lee, A. Y., & Higgins, E. T. (2008). Motivations for promotion and prevention. In J. Shah, & W. Gardner (Eds.), *Handbook of Motivation Science* (pp.169–187). New York: Guilford.

Molden, D. C., Lucas, G. M., Gardner, W. L., Dean, K., & Knowles, M. L. (2009). Motivations for prevention or promotion following social exclusion: Being rejected versus being ignored. *Journal of Personality and Social Psychology, 96,* 415–431.

Murray, S. L., & Holmes, J. G. (2009). The architecture of interdependent minds: A motivation-management theory of mutual responsiveness. *Psychological Review, 116,* 908–928.

Park, L., & Maner, J. K. (2009). Does self-threat promote social connection? The role of self-esteem and contingencies of self-worth. *Journal of Personality and Social Psychology, 96,* 203–217.

Pickett, C. L., Bonner, B. L., & Coleman, J. M. (2002). Motivated self-stereotyping: Heightened assimilation and differentiation needs results in increased levels of positive and negative self-stereotyping. *Journal of Personality and Social Psychology, 82,* 543–562.

Pickett, C. L., & Gardner, W. L. (2005). The social monitoring system: Enhanced sensitivity to social cues as an adaptive response to social exclusion. In K. Williams, J. Forgas, & W. von Hippel (Eds.), *The Social Outcast: Ostracism, Social Exclusion, Rejection, and Bullying* (pp. 213–225). New York: Psychology Press.

Pickett, C. L., Gardner, W. L., & Knowles, M. (2004). Getting a cue: The need to belong and enhanced sensitivity to social cues. *Personality and Social Psychology Bulletin, 30,* 1095–1107.

Pickett, C. L., Silver, M. D., & Brewer, M. B. (2002). The impact of assimilation and differentiation needs on perceived group importance and judgments of ingroup size. *Personality and Social Psychology Bulletin, 28,* 546–558.

Shelton, J. N., Richeson, J. A., & Salvatore, J. (2005). Expecting to be the target of prejudice: Implications for interethnic interactions. *Personality and Social Psychology Bulletin, 31,* 1189–1202.

Smart Richman, L., & Leary, M. R. (2009). Reactions to discrimination, stigmatization, ostracism, and other forms of interpersonal rejection: A multimotive model. *Psychological Review, 116,* 365–383.

Tesser, A. (2000). On the confluence of self-esteem maintenance mechanisms. *Personality and Social Psychology Review, 4,* 290–299.

Twenge, J. M., Baumeister, R. F., DeWall, C. N., Ciarocco, N. J., & Bartels, J. M. (2007). Social exclusion decreases prosocial behavior. *Journal of Personality and Social Psychology, 92,* 56–66.

van Baaren, R. B., Holland, R. W., Kawakami, K., & van Knippenberg, A. (2004). Mimicry and prosocial behavior. *Psychological Science, 15,* 71–74.

Wilkowski, B. M., Robinson, M. D., & Friesen, C. K. (2009). Gaze-triggered orienting as a tool of the belongingness self-regulation system. *Psychological Science, 20,* 495–501.

Williams, K. D. (2007). Ostracism. *Annual Review of Psychology, 58,* 425–452.

Williams, K. D., Cheung, C. K. T., & Choi, W. (2000). Cyberostracism: Effects of being ignored over the internet. *Journal of Personality and Social Psychology, 79,* 748–762.

Williams, K. D., & Sommer, K. L. (1997). Social ostracism by one's coworkers: Does rejection lead to loafing or compensation? *Personality and Social Psychology Bulletin, 23,* 693–706.

Social Rejection Reduces Intelligent Thought and Self-Regulation

Tyler F. Stillman *and* Roy F. Baumeister

Abstract

This chapter reviews evidence that social rejection reduces intelligent thought and self-regulation. Correlational research has demonstrated that social rejection and low intellectual performance are related, as loneliness is associated with poor cognitive functioning. Experimental research has shed light on the correlational findings, as participants assigned to be rejected performed slowly and inaccurately on reasoning problems relative to participants assigned to control conditions. Hence, social rejection reduces intelligent thought. Evidence also indicates that rejection reduces self-control, as people who are rejected perform poorly on a wealth of self-control tasks.

Key Words: intelligence, ostracism, self-control, self-regulation, social rejection

Introduction

It is widely accepted that humans are social beings (e.g., Aronson, 1972; Baumeister & Leary, 1995). Of course, social creatures are not rare in nature, as a number of nonhuman beings are highly social (e.g., wolves, bees, or bonobos). However, humans relate to each other in ways that are qualitatively different from the ways in which other social animals relate to each other. Baumeister (2005) characterized this difference by describing humans as *cultural* beings. In particular, Baumeister argued that the distinctly human pattern of within-species interaction is not simply a matter of people being exceptionally social. Rather, human interaction relies on a shared system of meanings, or culture, and culture has been essential to humanity's biological success as a species. Many nonhuman animals are just as social as humans are, but no nonhuman animals approach the extent to which culture permeates human life.

The acquisition of food is illustrative of how culture enables humans to deal effectively with the problems that confront other species. Humans rarely get food directly from nature. Instead, most people get at least some of the food they consume from other people in a way that requires a shared system of meanings. This requires language and often involves money or barter, which requires a great deal of shared meanings. In short, Baumeister's (2005) argument is that culture is essential to the biological success of humanity.

The benefits of culture require that one be included in a larger group, making social exclusion a threat to both mental and physical well-being (see Baumeister & Leary, 1995; Gruter & Masters, 1986; Seligman, 1975; Williams, 2001; see also chapter 2). Consider the difficulty one would have in meeting one's need for shelter, food, and water alone and without any help from one's social and cultural relationships. Perhaps it would be possible for some people to survive, but clearly belonging to a social and cultural group improve one's chances of survival.

In addition to inclusion, the benefits of culture also require specific mental capacities, perhaps especially self-regulation and intelligent thought. One would be hard-pressed to benefit from shared systems of meaning without the intelligence to understand a shared system of meaning. Put differently, human culture makes use of highly intelligent thought. Likewise, human social and cultural life relies on self-regulation. For example, trading money or other goods for food requires that one inhibits aggressive and sexual impulses.

One implication of Baumeister's (2005) thesis is that the benefits of intelligent thought and self-regulation are indirect and occur via human social and cultural relationships. The extraordinary human intellect and capacity for self-regulation were not designed to function in the absence of social and cultural relationships. Consequently, rejection could reduce intelligence and self-regulation, as these capacities were meant to function within a social and cultural context. This chapter surveys some research supporting the notion that rejection reduces intelligent thought and self-regulation separately.

Rejection Reduces Intelligent Thought
Correlational Research

Low levels of belonging and low intelligence are both predictors of criminality and could be causally related. Evidence indicates that people with relatively low levels of social belonging are more likely to commit crimes and act aggressively. Children of single parents are more likely to end up in prison than children who are raised with two parents (Gottfredson & Hirschi, 1990). Likewise, unmarried men are more likely to commit crimes than their married counterparts (Sampson & Laub, 1990). Researchers have consistently found that people who commit crimes demonstrate low intelligence (e.g., Gottfredson & Hirschi, 1990; National Research Council, 1993; Walsh, Beyer, & Petee, 1987; Wilson & Herrnstein, 1985). These findings are consistent with the idea that social rejection reduces intelligence. Of course, one could offer alternative accounts for this patterns of results.

Research on academic performance is also informative regarding the relationship between belonging and intelligent thought. High school and middle school students categorized as having a learning disability are lonelier and less socially accepted than their peers (Valas, 1999). Again, this is consistent with the view that social rejection reduces intelligent thought and conflicts with the idea that rejection increases intelligent thought. To be sure, the reverse causation is highly plausible (as Valas emphasized); namely, that the stigma of having a learning disability elicited rejection and thereby caused loneliness. Bidirectional causation is also plausible.

A similar link between loneliness and poor cognitive functioning was found among elderly people (Martin, Hagberg, & Poon, 1997). Loneliness correlated with low intelligence (as measured by the Wechsler Adult Intelligence Scale; Wechsler, 1981) in a Swedish sample. (The effect was not significant among elderly participants in a US sample, although the measure of loneliness differed across the two samples.)

In short, correlational research suggests that loneliness and intelligence are related, with loneliness corresponding to poorer intelligence. Yet the direction of causation is unclear in these studies. To establish whether rejection can actually cause poor intellectual functioning, experimental research is required.

Experimental Findings

Williams and colleagues (2000) found that ostracism increased how much people conformed to the opinions of others. That is, people who were ignored subsequently adopted others' opinions readily. Conformity suggests a lack of thoughtful reflection, although it could also be a manifestation of the desire to connect with others (see DeWall, Baumeister, & Vohs, 2008; Maner, DeWall, Baumeister, & Schaller, 2007; Mead, Baumeister, Stillman, Rawn, & Vohs, 2011).

More direct evidence comes from experimental studies that specifically assessed the impact of rejection and exclusion on intellectual performance. A series of studies on precisely that question was reported by Baumeister, Twenge, and Nuss (2002). In the first experiment, participants completed a personality questionnaire and received feedback from the experimenter (see Twenge, Baumeister, Tice, & Stucke, 2001). Part of the feedback legitimately reflected participants' responses to the questionnaire (i.e., how introverted/extroverted they were), and part of the feedback was false. The false feedback constituted the manipulation of social rejection. Participants assigned to the rejection condition were led to believe that they would end up friendless and alone later in life, whereas participants in the belonging condition were led to believe that they would have rewarding relationships throughout life. However, the expected effects of rejection on intelligence between these two conditions could simply reflect the fact that some participants received bad news and others received good news. Therefore, the experimenters included a third condition in which participants receive bad news; namely, that their personality inventory indicated that they were accident prone and would likely suffer multiple broken bones. If participants who were rejected demonstrated decreased intelligence relative to those who received news of impending misfortune, then one could conclude that rejection, rather than bad news, reduces intelligence.

Consistent with the view that rejection impairs intelligent thought, performance on an accepted measure of intelligence (the General Mental Abilities Test; Janda, 1996; Janda, Fulk, Janda, & Wallace, 1995) varied as a function of personality feedback. Rejection led participants to work more slowly than participants in the acceptance and misfortune control conditions. Participants in the rejected condition also provided fewer correct responses than did participants in the acceptance condition. In short, rejection reduced both the accuracy and speed of responses.

In their next study, Baumeister et al. (2002) sought to determine whether the observed effects of rejection on IQ generalized to memory. Memory was assessed using a reading comprehension exercise from the GRE Verbal section, in which a passage of text is followed by questions about that text. As in Study 1, participants were assigned to receive personality feedback that predicted a future life filled with social acceptance, rejection, or nonsocial misfortune. However, the stage at which the feedback was administered varied as well, to shed light on whether the expected deficits in memory occurred during encoding or retrieval. That is, some participants were given the rejection feedback after having read the passage but before answering questions about it (which would affect retrieval but not encoding), whereas others were given the rejection feedback before having read the passage (which would affect encoding) and then debriefed before the questions (so retrieval should be relatively unaffected).

As expected, rejection impaired performance on the memory test. However, rejection did not demonstrably affect the encoding of information. Participants' responses did not vary due to rejection feedback when they received the rejecting feedback before reading the essay. In contrast, participants who received rejecting feedback after reading the essay—but before answering questions about it—demonstrated poorer recall relative to participants who received accepting or misfortune feedback. One could therefore conclude that rejection impairs information retrieval but not information encoding. Put simply, the rejected person seems capable of taking in new information just as effectively as

anyone else, but his or her capacity to retrieve and use that information was compromised.

There was, however, an alternative way of looking at the results on reading comprehension. Rejected people were in fact able to answer simple, easy questions about the material just as well as controls. These were questions that asked precisely what the person had read. The deficits were found on the more difficult questions that required the person not only to retrieve information, but also to make inferences, deductions, and other extrapolations from it. It is therefore possible that rejection affected not retrieval per se, but rather the sort of effortful thought that operates on information so as to proceed to novel conclusions and insights. To put this in other terms, the findings could be interpreted as indicating that rejection impairs controlled cognitive processing but leaves automatic processing largely intact.

A third study was designed to determine whether the effects of exclusion were specific to complex cognitive tasks and controlled processing or whether rejection would reduce performance on simple, relatively automatic tasks as well. Participants were again given false personality feedback to manipulate rejection. Next, they were either asked to solve logical reasoning questions from the GRE analytic section or asked to memorize a list of nonsense syllables (e.g., *fum*). For the analytical problems, rejection reduced both the number of correct responses and the number of problems attempted. In other words, rejection reduced both speed and accuracy (as it did in Study 1). Yet rejection had no effect on the simple cognitive task of recalling nonsense syllables. These findings are consistent with the view that rejection disrupts active reasoning and other controlled processes, but rejection does not seem to have a generalized effect on simple cognitive functions that depend mainly on automatic processes.

Indirect Learning and Emotion

There is a second way in which social rejection might reduce intelligent thought and learning. One important way in which people learn is via emotional experiences. Imagine a person who kicks the family dog while in a foul mood. Imagine further that this person immediately feels the sting of regret for hurting the family pet. The experience of regret could be sufficiently aversive that the offender would resolve never to hurt the dog again. This process has been described as *indirect emotional learning* (Baumeister, Vohs, DeWall, & Zhang, 2007; Stillman & Baumeister, 2010). According to this view, an important source of learning how to respond wisely and intelligently stems from experiencing emotions. Anything that would disrupt the normal process of experiencing emotions could interfere with the normal process of learning from emotions.

Although one might expect that being rejected would bring about a potent emotional reaction, this has not been borne out by experimental research. Across several studies and a number of social rejection manipulations, the emotional responses of socially rejected participants did not differ from those of accepted participants (e.g., Gardner, Pickett, & Brewer, 2000; Twenge, Baumeister, Tice, & Stucke, 2001; Twenge, Catanese, & Baumeister, 2002, 2003; Twenge & Campbell, 2003; Zadro, Williams, & Richardson, 2004). Some null results could be due to weak effects and small sample sizes. A meta-analysis by Blackhart et al. (2009) combining results from a large number of studies confirmed that rejected people overall feel worse than accepted ones and even slightly worse than participants in neutral control conditions. Still, the absolute level of emotion even among rejected persons was not negative, and if anything the mean emotional state in experimental rejection conditions is either at the neutral midpoint or slightly on the positive side (i.e., indicating more positive than negative emotion, although not much of either). Thus, contrary to intuition, laboratory manipulations of rejection do not cause palpable emotional distress.

Instead of acute emotionality, people seem to experience emotional numbness in the wake of social rejection. Indeed, social rejection causes people to become insensitive to both physical and emotional pain (DeWall & Baumeister, 2006). The numbness to physical pain has been more thoroughly documented in the animal literature than among humans (MacDonald & Leary, 2005). The emotional numbing that follows from social rejection may disrupt the correction of stupid behavior, such as kicking the family dog. In other words, the implication for intelligent thought is that emotionally numbed people are less likely to learn something from the kinds of emotional experience that would normally bring about improved behavior and smarter choices, although that is partly speculative.

Summary

Evidence points to the conclusion that social rejection has a negative impact on intelligence. Experimental findings indicate causality; specifically that rejection causes a decrease in intelligent

thought. Correlational research is helpful in demonstrating that the effects of social exclusion observed in the laboratory are not necessarily short-lived and are not dependent on a laboratory procedure. Future research might seek to determine whether affirming close relationships or one's place within a group might momentarily increase intelligent thought.

Rejection Impairs Self-Regulation
Limited-Resource Model

Self-regulation is the capacity to alter one's dominant response to meet a desired goal or standard. Passing up a tempting piece of chocolate cake to meet a health goal is an example of self-regulation. There are a number of empirical findings that are supportive of the view that rejection reduces self-regulation. Most such evidence is based on the limited-resource model of self-regulation (Baumeister, Bratslavsky, Muraven, & Tice, 1998). The limited-resource model holds that one's capacity to restrain impulses changes from moment to moment and from situation to situation. This variability in self-regulation reflects fluctuations in self-regulation resources. Put differently, self-regulation is dependent on a limited resource, such that exercising self-regulation temporarily depletes this limited resource and leaves an individual less able to exercise self-regulation successfully. For example, a person who resists a piece of delicious chocolate cake, thereby depleting self-regulation resources, may subsequently be more likely to lash out in anger in response to provocation.

Supportive Findings

Evidence that rejection impairs self-regulation can be found in studies that look at the effect of rejection on behaviors dependent on self-regulation. Depleting self-regulatory resources by prior acts of self-control leads to increases in aggressive behavior (DeWall, Baumeister, Stillman, & Gailliot, 2007; Stucke & Baumeister, 2006), so the effect of rejection on aggression has implications for how rejection affects self-regulation generally. Evidence indicates that rejection does cause people to behave aggressively (see chapter 11). For instance, in one study some participants were led to believe that a peer reported having a negative reaction to the prospect of working with them. Other participants believed the peer wanted to work with them. Those receiving the rejecting feedback rated themselves as wanting to behave aggressively toward the peer, including wanting to humiliate him or her (Buckley, Winkel, & Leary, 2004). Other experimental studies have similarly found that social rejection prompts aggressive acts (i.e., issuing loud blasts of unpleasant sounds), even against innocent (nonrejecting) people (Twenge, Baumeister, Tice, & Stucke, 2001).

The effect sizes of exclusion on aggression are generally quite large, although one could question whether these laboratory studies generalize outside the laboratory. An analysis of school shootings suggested that they do generalize (Leary, Kowalski, Smith, & Phillips, 2003). In nearly every school shooting, the perpetrator had been thoroughly socially excluded. A second question one could raise is whether the effects of rejection on aggression really depend on self-regulation, but empirical evidence indicates that stifling aggressive responding does require self-regulation (DeWall, Baumeister, Stillman, & Gailliot, 2007; Stucke & Baumeister, 2006). In short, evidence points to the conclusion that rejection increases aggression and that refraining from acting aggressively depends on self-regulation. This is consistent with the view that rejection decreases self-regulation, although alternative accounts are possible.

Rejection reduces the restraint of aggressive impulses, but does it affect help-giving behaviors? Helping people requires overriding one's selfish impulses, so the effect of rejection on helping also speaks to the relationship between rejection and self-regulation. Experimental findings demonstrate that rejection decreases helping and other prosocial behaviors (Twenge, Baumeister, DeWall, Ciarocco, & Bartels, 2007), which is consistent with the notion that rejection reduces self-regulation.

Rejection also seems to promote lethargy, which suggests an absence of active self-regulation. Williams (2001) anecdotally reported that several participants who had been in the ostracism condition sat and did nothing after the experiment had concluded. Researchers have also tested the effect of rejection on lethargy empirically (Twenge, Catanese, & Baumeister, 2003). When asked to explain the meaning of 10 proverbs, rejected participants wrote fewer words than participants in the control conditions, suggesting a preference not to exert effort (although one could also argue that this is due to a decrease in intelligent thought). Rejected participants also behaved more sluggishly than those in control conditions when playing a reaction-time game. In particular, rejected participants reacted more slowly than those in control conditions during an ostensibly competitive reaction-time game. Fast reaction times require that one be focused and attentive, so one implication of this finding is

that rejection reduces the regulation of focus and attention.

Direct Evidence That Rejection Impairs Self-Regulation

One could offer alternative explanations for the effects of rejection on aggression, helping, and lethargy that do not involve self-regulation. A direct test of the hypothesis that rejection impairs self-regulation was undertaken in six experiments by Baumeister, DeWall, Ciarocco, and Twenge (2005). The authors made use of two different means of manipulating social rejection. One procedure involved participants receiving false feedback from a personality questionnaire indicating that they would end up alone in life (described previously). In the second procedure, several participants met each other as a group, and those assigned to the rejection condition were subsequently told that none of the other participants wanted to work with him or her on an upcoming task. The effects of rejection were similar for both social rejection manipulations.

In Experiment 1, participants who were rejected drank fewer ounces of a healthy but unsavory drink relative to participants who were accepted or given negative news. Put differently, participants in the control condition persisted in drinking the unpleasant beverage, whereas rejected participants were quick to give in to the impulse not to continue drinking. In Experiment 2, participants were given the chance to eat unhealthy snacks. Rejected participants ate more cookies than control participants. Thus, rejection reduced participants' willingness to override their distaste for an unpleasant (but healthy) beverage in Experiment 1, and it reduced their willingness to override the impulse not to eat a tasty (but unhealthy) food in Experiment 2.

In Experiment 3, the researchers moved beyond measures of consumption and instead used a measure of persistence. In particular, they tested whether rejected participants would persist for less time on an unsolvable puzzle. As expected, participants in the control condition withstood the impulse to quit for longer than did rejected participants, who quickly abandoned the attempt to solve the puzzle. Experiment 4 assessed self-regulation in yet another way, namely, attention control. (See Baumeister, Heatherton and Tice, 1994, and Carver and Scheier, 1981, on the crucial nature of attention control to self-regulation success.) Participants heard different information presented simultaneously to both ears, and their task was to ignore what was said in one ear and record any words that included an *m* or a *p* in the other ear. Thus participants had to force their attention away from the information presented to one ear and focus it on the information presented to the other ear. Rejected participants demonstrated substantial decrements in the task, relative to control conditions.

The question addressed in Studies 5 and 6 was whether the self-regulation failure demonstrated by participants was due to an inability to exert self-regulation or an unwillingness to do so. If rejected participants who are given an incentive to self-regulate show no self-regulation deficits, then this suggests they are simply unwilling (and not unable) to self-regulate. Both studies followed the procedures of Study 4 in that self-regulation was measured by the dichotic listening task. In Study 5, participants were made self-aware (by placing a mirror in front of them), which stimulates self-regulation. In Study 6, participants were offered a cash incentive to perform well. In both studies, the heightened motivation to self-regulate eliminated the deficits normally caused by rejection. Apparently, people who are rejected have the ability to self-regulate; they simply are unwilling to do so.

Beyond a Linear Relationship between Rejection and Self-Regulation

Recent investigations have sought to clarify the conditions under which rejection impairs self-regulation. Might there be people for whom social rejection has an especially long-lasting effect on self-regulation? Researchers predicted that in the wake of social rejection people high in social anxiety would demonstrate poor self-regulation for substantially longer than other people (Oaten, Williams, Jones, & Zadro, 2008). To test this, some participants were ostracized and others were included in an online game. Results indicated that overall, ostracized participants ate more (unhealthy) cookies immediately following ostracism. Forty-five minutes after being ostracized, only participants high in social anxiety evinced poor self-regulation (again, by eating several cookies). Thus, as predicted, the effects of social rejection were found to last longer among the socially anxious.

A series of experiments illustrated that the way in which a self-control task is framed has important implications for the effect of rejection on self-regulation (DeWall, Baumeister, & Vohs, 2008). In one study, participants in the acceptance condition were led to believe that they could expect good close relationships in the future, whereas participants in the rejection condition were led to

believe that they would be alone. Next, participants played the game Operation, which requires slow, deliberate, controlled movements. As expected, rejected participants made more errors on the task relative to accepted participants. However, this was not the case when participants were led to believe that doing well at Operation was indicative of good social skills. When Operation was framed this way, rejected participants made fewer errors than accepted participants did. Thus, the decrements in self-regulation following rejection were eliminated when the self-regulation task was framed as being diagnostic of social skills. The implication is that when self-regulation is seen as a means of attaining social connection, excluded people can self-regulate effectively.

A second study assessed self-regulation by measuring how long participants could keep their arm submerged in ice water (1°C). Participants assigned to the acceptance condition were led to believe they were going to have fulfilling social relationships, whereas participants in the control condition were not given any feedback. For some participants, the ice water task was described as indicating the promise of social acceptance (as pain endurance, ostensibly, helps one endure difficult relationship episodes). Results indicated that socially accepted participants showed decrements in self-regulation relative to the control condition, but only when the ice water task was described portending good future relationships. When the task was not framed as diagnostic of social skills, social acceptance prompted a modest increase in self-regulation relative to the neutral control condition.

The authors conducted five additional studies, and found a similar pattern of results using different means of bringing about social rejection and different measures of self-regulation. The additional studies also found that accepted participants only demonstrated poor self-regulation on tasks that were ostensibly linked to social skills, but they demonstrated good self-regulation when the there was no motive (or, in one study, a financial motive) for good self-regulation. DeWall and colleagues (2008) concluded that the desire to belong socially conforms to the broad pattern observed in other motivations. Namely, that thwarting a desire (as social rejection thwarts the desire for social connection) causes people to strive to attain it, whereas satiating that desire (social acceptance) decreases the motivation to attain it. Social rejection causes people to strive to attain social inclusion, by exerting high levels of effort to perform well on tasks that they believe are linked to the promise of future social connection. When the self-regulation tasks are not framed as linked to possible future social connection, social rejection reduces self-regulation.

Family Inclusion Increases Self-Regulation

If rejection decreases self-regulation, might emphasizing familial inclusion improve self-regulation? In three studies, researchers found that thinking about family relationships increased self-regulation (Stillman, Tice, Fincham, & Lambert, 2009). In Study 1, participants who were subliminally primed with the names of family members demonstrated more persistence on a language task than participants primed with neutral words. In Study 2, subjects who were asked to write about a positive relationship with a family member demonstrated more persistence on math problems than those assigned to write about control topics. Study 3 sought to determine whether thinking about family relationships replenishes self-regulation resources that have been depleted. In this study, participants were first asked to control their attention (or not, in the neutral condition). Next, participants saw a picture of close family member (or not, in the control condition). Thus the design was a 2 (attention control or not) × 2 (family prime or not). Results indicated that participants in the neutral condition (not assigned to control attention) were affected by the picture of a loved one, such that having seen the picture decreased the number of unhealthy cookies eaten. However, participants whose self-regulation resources had been reduced by controlling their attention were unaffected by seeing the picture of a loved one. In sum, it seems that making belonging and social relationships salient has the opposite effect that rejection does, namely, increasing self-regulation. However, the effect does not seem to replenish lost resources, but rather to provide a temporary self-regulation boost.

Summary

The successful restraint of aggression, helping others, and acting in ambitious, nonlethargic way are signs of successful self-regulation. These faculties are impaired by rejection, suggesting that rejection may impair self-regulation. Six experiments (Baumeister et al., 2005) found direct evidence that rejection impaired self-regulation, as rejected participants drank less healthy beverage, ate more unhealthy food, gave up sooner on a persistence task, and performed poorer on an attention-control task than controls. Thus, rejection weakens self-regulation. The inverse is also true, as thinking about warm and close family relationships increased self-regulation. However, when a self-regulation task is framed as being diagnostic of social skills, socially rejected people actually demonstrate better self-regulation than socially accepted people do.

Conclusions

Humans have a remarkably high level of intelligence and capacity for self-regulation relative to nonhuman animals. These capacities help people address the problems common to other animals, such as providing food and protection. However, the benefits of intelligence and self-regulation are indirect and occur via culture, according to Baumeister's (2005) thesis. In other words, human intelligence and capacity for self-regulation are designed by nature to function within a social and cultural context. One extension of this argument is that self-regulation and intelligence were not designed to operate in the absence of social relationships. Consistent with this idea, rejection brings about a decrease in intelligent thought and self-regulation.

References

Aronson, E. (1972). *The Social Animal*. New York: Freeman

Baumeister, R. F. (2005). *The Cultural Animal: Human Nature, Meaning, and Social Life*. New York: Oxford University Press.

Baumeister, R. F., Bratslavsky, E., Muraven, M., & Tice, D. M. (1998). Ego depletion: Is the active self a limited resource? *Journal of Personality and Social Psychology, 74,* 1152–1165.

Baumeister, R. F., DeWall, C. N., Ciarocco, N. J., & Twenge, J. M. (2005). Social exclusion impairs self-regulation. *Journal of Personality and Social Psychology, 88,* 589–604.

Baumeister, R. F., Heatherton, T. F., & Tice, D. M. (1994). *Losing Control: How and Why People Fail at Self-Regulation*. San Diego, CA: Academic Press.

Baumeister, R. F., & Leary, M. R. (1995). The need to belong: Desire for interpersonal attachments as a fundamental human motivation. *Psychological Bulletin, 117,* 497–529.

Baumeister, R. F., Twenge, J. M., & Nuss, C. (2002). Effects of social exclusion on cognitive processes: Anticipated aloneness reduces intelligent thought. *Journal of Personality and Social Psychology, 83,* 817–827.

Baumeister, R. F., Vohs, K. D., DeWall, C. N., & Zhang, L. (2007). How emotion shapes behavior: Feedback, anticipation, and reflection, rather than direct causation. *Personality and Social Psychology Review, 11,* 167–203.

Blackhart, G. C., Nelson, B. C., Knowles, M. L., & Baumeister, R. F. (2009). Rejection elicits emotional reactions but neither causes immediate distress nor lowers self-esteem: A meta-analytic review of 192 studies on social exclusion. *Personality and Social Psychology Review, 13,* 269–309.

Buckley, K., Winkel, R., & Leary, M. (2004). Reactions to acceptance and rejection: Effects of level and sequence of relational evaluation. *Journal of Experimental Social Psychology, 40,* 14–28.

Carver, C. S., & Scheier, M. F. (1981). *Attention and Self-Regulation: A Control Theory Approach to Human Behavior*. New York: Springer-Verlag.

Ciarocco, N. J., Sommer, K. L., & Baumeister, R. F. (2001). Ostracism and ego depletion: The strains of silence. *Personality and Social Psychology Bulletin, 27*, 1156–1163.

DeWall, C. N., & Baumeister, R. F. (2006). Alone but feeling no pain: Effects of social exclusion on physical pain tolerance and pain threshold, affective forecasting, and interpersonal empathy. *Journal of Personality and Social Psychology, 91*, 1–15.

DeWall, C. N., Baumeister, R. F., Stillman, T. F., & Gailliot, M. T. (2007). Violence restrained: Effects of self-regulatory capacity and its depletion on aggressive behavior. *Journal of Experimental Social Psychology, 43*, 62–76.

DeWall, C. N., Baumeister, R. F., & Vohs, K. D. (2008). Satiated with belongingness? Effects of acceptance, rejection, and task framing on self-regulatory performance. *Journal of Personality and Social Psychology, 95*, 1367–1382.

DeWall, C. N. & Twenge, J. M. (2013). Aggression. In C. N. DeWall (Ed.), *The Oxford Handbook of Social Exclusion*. New York: Oxford University Press.

Gardner, W. L., Pickett, C. L., & Brewer, M. B. (2000). Social exclusion and selective memory: How the need to belong affects memory for social information. *Personality and Social Psychology Bulletin, 26*, 486–496.

Gottfredson, M. R., & Hirschi, T. (1990). *A General Theory of Crime*. Stanford, CA: Stanford University Press.

Gruter, M., & Masters, R. D. (1986). Ostracism as a social and biological phenomenon: An introduction. *Ethology and Sociobiology, 7*, 149–158.

Janda, L. (1996). *The Psychologists' Book of Self-Tests*. New York: Berkley.

Janda, L. H., Fulk, J., Janda, M., & Wallace, J. (1995). *The Development of a Test of General Mental Abilities*. Unpublished manuscript. Norfolk, VA: Old Dominion University.

Leary, M. R. (2013). Evolution of exclusion in humans. In C. N. DeWall (Ed.), *The Oxford Handbook of Social Exclusion*. New York: Oxford University Press.

Leary, M. R., Kowalski, R. M., Smith, L., & Phillips, S. (2003). Teasing, rejection, and violence: Case studies of the school shootings. *Aggressive Behavior, 29*, 202–214.

MacDonald, G., & Leary M. R. (2005). Why does social exclusion hurt? The relationship between social and physical pain. *Psychological Bulletin, 131*, 202–223.

Maner, J. K., DeWall, C. N., Baumeister, R. F., & Schaller, M. (2007). Does social exclusion motivate interpersonal reconnection? Resolving the "porcupine problem." *Journal of Personality and Social Psychology, 92*, 42–55.

Martin, P., Hagberg, B., & Poon, L. (1997). Predictors of loneliness in centenarians: A parallel study. *Journal of Cross-Cultural Gerontology, 12*, 203–224.

Mead, N. L., Baumeister, R. F., Stillman, T. F., Rawn, C. D., & Vohs, K. D. (2011). Social exclusion causes people to spend and consume in the service of affiliation. *Journal of Consumer Research, 37*, 902–919.

National Research Council. (1993). *Understanding and Preventing Violence*. Washington, DC: National Academy Press.

Oaten, M., Williams, K. D., Jones, A., & Zadro, L. (2008). The effects of ostracism on self-regulation in the socially anxious. *Journal of Social and Clinical Psychology, 27*, 471–504.

Sampson, R. J., & Laub, J. H. (1993). *Crime in the Making: Pathways and Turning Points through Life*. Cambridge, MA: Harvard University Press.

Seligman, M. E. P. (1975). *Helplessness: On Depression, Development, and Death*. San Francisco: Freeman.

Stillman, T. F., & Baumeister, R. F. (2010). Guilty, free, and wise. Belief in free will facilitates learning from negative emotions. *Journal of Experimental Social Psychology, 46*, 951–960.

Stillman, T. F., Tice, D. M., Fincham, F. D., & Lambert, N. M. (2009). The psychological presence of family improves self-control. *Journal of Social and Clinical Psychology, 28*, 498–529.

Stucke, T. S., & Baumeister, R. F. (2006). Ego depletion and aggressive behavior: Is the inhibition of aggression a limited resource? *European Journal of Social Psychology, 36*, 1–13.

Twenge, J. M., Baumeister, R. F., DeWall, C. N., Ciarocco, N. J., & Bartels, J. M. (2007). Social exclusion decreases prosocial behavior. *Journal of Personality and Social Psychology, 92*, 56–66.

Twenge, J. M., Baumeister, R. F., Tice, D. M., & Stucke, T. S. (2001). If you can't join them, beat them: Effects of social exclusion on aggressive behavior. *Journal of Personality and Social Psychology, 81*, 1058–1069.

Twenge, J. M., & Campbell, W. K. (2003). "Isn't it fun to get the respect that we're going to deserve?" Narcissism, social rejection, and aggression. *Personality and Social Psychology Bulletin, 29*, 261–272.

Twenge, J. M., Catanese, K. R., & Baumeister, R. F. (2002). Social exclusion causes self-defeating behavior. *Journal of Personality and Social Psychology, 83*, 606–615.

Twenge, J. M., Catanese, K. R., & Baumeister, R. F. (2003). Social exclusion and the deconstructed state: Time perception, meaninglessness, lethargy, lack of emotion, and self-awareness. *Journal of Personality and Social Psychology, 85*, 409–423.

Valas, H. (1999) Students with learning disabilities and low-achieving students: Peer acceptance, loneliness, and depression. *Social Psychology of Education, 3*, 173–192

Walsh, A., Beyer, J. A., & Petee, T. A. (1987). Violent delinquency: An examination of psychopathic typologies. *Journal of Genetic Psychology, 148*, 385–392.

Wechsler, D. (1981). *Wechsler Adult Intelligence Scale, Revised*. New York: Psychological Corporation.

Williams, K. D. (2001). *Ostracism: The Power of Silence*. New York: Guilford Press.

Williams, K. D., Cheung, C. K. T., & Choi, W. (2000). CyberOstracism: Effects of being ignored over the Internet. *Journal of Personality and Social Psychology, 79*, 748–762.

Wilson, J. O., & Herrnstein, J. Q. (1985). *Crime and Human Nature*. New York: Simon & Schuster.

Zadro, L., Williams, K. D., & Richardson, R. (2004). How low can you go? Ostracism by a computer lowers belonging, control, self-esteem, and meaningful existence. *Journal of Experimental Social Psychology, 40*, 560–567.

PART 6

Individual Exclusion: Physiological, Neural, and Emotional Responses

Cortisol Responses to Social Exclusion

Sally S. Dickerson *and* Peggy M. Zoccola

Abstract

Experiences of social exclusion, or contexts that create the potential for social exclusion, not only have potent psychological effects, but they can have physiological consequences as well. This chapter reviews research that has examined the effects of social exclusion, rejection, and social evaluation on cortisol, an important health-relevant hormone. Studies have demonstrated that acute experiences of social evaluation or interpersonal rejection can elicit cortisol reactivity, particularly when the evaluation is unambiguous and salient. Social evaluation or exclusion can also precipitate rumination, which could serve to maintain elevated cortisol levels in response to these threats. Chronic forms of social exclusion (e.g., loneliness, peer victimization) have been associated with dysregulated cortisol patterns. Prolonged experiences of social exclusion, evaluation, or rejection may lead to negative health consequences via extended exposure to cortisol or dysregulation in the system.

Key Words: cortisol, emotions, exclusion, rejection, rumination, self-conscious, social evaluation

Introduction

Experiences of social exclusion are intrinsically painful. Most people can vividly recall times in which they did not feel accepted by a valued social group or individual, experienced feelings of ostracism, or felt stigmatized or rejected by others. We often have intense emotional responses to these social exclusion events, such as feeling ashamed. These emotional responses can prompt maladaptive cognitive processes, like rumination. Experiences of social exclusion—or contexts that create the *potential* for social exclusion—can not only have potent psychological effects, but they can have physiological consequences as well. This chapter describes research that has examined the effects of social exclusion, rejection, and social evaluation on cortisol, an important health-relevant hormone.

Why might experiences of social exclusion elicit physiological changes? Humans have a fundamental need to be socially accepted by others (e.g., Baumeister & Leary, 1995; Williams, 2007).

Therefore, conditions that jeopardize this goal, such as those with the potential for social exclusion, ostracism, or rejection, are viewed as profound threats. Threats to other central goals—such as threats to physical self-preservation or survival, can elicit a range of emotional, physiological, and behavioral changes designed to adaptively respond to the situation. Like threats to physical self-preservation, we have proposed that threats to social self-preservation—conditions in which there is the potential for a loss of social acceptance, esteem, or status—also elicit psychobiological responses, including increases in cortisol (Dickerson, Gruenewald, & Kemeny, 2004; Dickerson, Gruenewald, & Kemeny, 2011; Gruenewald, Dickerson, & Kemeny, 2007).

Threats to the social self include conditions of social-evaluative threat (SET), in which the self could be negatively judged by others (Dickerson & Kemeny, 2004). Social-evaluative threat can occur in performance contexts in which valued attributes such as competence or intelligence are on the line (e.g., giving a presentation). Social-evaluative threat could also be experienced in contexts of negative interpersonal evaluation or rejection within close relationships or social interactions. It can also include situations in which one feels judged by others on the basis of a stigmatized characteristic or identity. Central to these contexts is a core component of social evaluation or rejection, which could result in social exclusion. Given that social exclusion can be a consequence of social evaluation, research on the physiological correlates of SET also examines the physiological correlates of social exclusion.

The hormone cortisol is an important biomarker to assess in the context of social exclusion or evaluation for several reasons. First, cortisol is an essential regulatory hormone that can influence a number of health outcomes. Cortisol is the end product of hypothalamic-pituitary-adrenocortical (HPA) axis activation. This process is initiated when the hypothalamus releases corticotrophin-releasing hormone (CRH), which in turn stimulates the anterior pituitary to secrete adrenocorticotropic hormone (ACTH). Adrenocorticotropic hormone triggers the adrenal cortex to release cortisol into the bloodstream. Once in circulation, cortisol can regulate or exert effects on a number of physiological systems (e.g., sympathetic nervous system, immune system). Cortisol plays an important role in metabolic functioning. It can mobilize energy resources by elevating glucose levels, which can provide fuel for the central nervous system and other peripheral systems (for review, see Sapolsky, Romero, & Munck, 2000). The release of cortisol in the context of an acute threat is thought to be adaptive, as cortisol could provide the metabolic resources to deal with the demands of the situation. However, if the threat is repeated or chronic, extended exposure to cortisol can contribute to multiple disease processes (e.g., McEwen, 1998).

Second, in nonhuman primates and other animals, both acute and chronic forms of social threat can be associated with increases in cortisol (for review, see Sapolsky, 2005). For example, subordinate baboons demonstrate elevations in the stress hormone relative to their dominant counterparts. In humans, social threats such as social evaluation or exclusion may elicit cortisol reactivity as well.

Acute Social-Evaluative Threat and Cortisol Responses

There is growing evidence that contexts characterized by SET or exclusion can elicit cortisol responses. We first examined this relationship in a meta-analysis of 208 acute psychological stressors that assessed cortisol as an outcome (Dickerson & Kemeny, 2004). We found that overall, stressors with a social-evaluative component (e.g., audience present) were associated with greater cortisol reactivity compared with those without social-evaluative elements. Indeed, the effect size for the social-evaluative stressors was more than four times the magnitude ($d = .67$) of those without social-evaluation ($d = .15$). Importantly, these effect size estimates controlled for other methodological factors that can influence cortisol responses (e.g., timing of assessment, time of day).

Furthermore, we found that this effect was heightened under uncontrollable SET. There is a theoretical overlap between social threat and uncontrollability. For example, Williams (2007) proposed that ostracism can threaten our sense of control, suggesting that uncontrollable and social-evaluative (or rejecting or ostracizing) contexts may often occur in concert. Stressors were coded as "uncontrollable" when nothing could be done to change the outcome of the situation (e.g., task was impossible, had unrealistic time constraints). Stressors with both uncontrollability and social-evaluation elicited strong, robust cortisol increases ($d = .92$), particularly when compared with stressors without either component ($d = -.06$). Uncontrollable, social-evaluative stressors were not only associated with greater reactivity, they also had longer times to recovery; in fact, the effects of the uncontrollable, social-evaluative stressors persisted on average for 40 minutes longer than other types of tasks. These findings demonstrate that a social-evaluative uncontrollable threat—in which others are present and failure is a likely outcome—are profound threats capable of eliciting robust, prolonged cortisol responses.

Subsequent experimental studies have corroborated and extended these meta-analytic findings. Gruenewald and colleagues (2004) manipulated SET in the laboratory by randomly assigning participants to undergo a speech and math stressor in the presence or absence of an evaluative audience. Those in the SET condition showed strong and substantial cortisol responses to the performance stressor; however, those in the non-SET condition showed no increases in cortisol. This effect has now been replicated in several studies using similar SET manipulations with performance stressor tasks (e.g., Dickerson, Mycek, & Zaldivar, 2008; Het, Rohleder, Schoofs, Kirschbaum, & Wolf, 2009) or physical stressors (i.e., cold pressor) (Schwabe, Haddad, & Schachinger, 2008).

Another study examined the effects of ballroom dancing competitions, a real-life social-evaluative manipulation (Rohleder, Beulen, Chen, Wolf, & Kirschbaum, 2007). They found that cortisol levels among the dancers were elevated on a social-evaluative competition day compared with a rehearsal day. Furthermore, those participants who reported feeling more stressed by the evaluators also showed greater cortisol reactivity, suggesting that perceptions of the intensity of social evaluation are associated with this physiological response. Taken together, the studies that manipulate SET either in the laboratory or in naturally occurring situations demonstrate that the SET context can elicit cortisol responses, particularly when compared with otherwise equivalent non-SET situations.

Components of the Social-Evaluative Context associated with Reactivity

Many components are often embedded in a social-evaluative situation: Others are present when it is typically/frequently videotaped and there are many evaluative cues from the audience members (e.g., facial expressions). A series of studies have begun to delineate the critical components of the social-evaluative context responsible for eliciting cortisol responses. For example, we compared whether the mere social presence of others is enough to elicit a cortisol response, or whether the individuals must be in an evaluative mode (Dickerson et al., 2008). We randomly assigned participants one of three conditions: an SET condition (two audience members present), a non-SET condition (no others present), or a presence condition, in which a research assistant was working on a computer in the room but not explicitly evaluating the participant. Consistent with past research, we found that the SET condition triggered large increases in cortisol, and the non-SET condition did not lead to changes in this parameter. Most interestingly, the presence condition was not associated with increases in cortisol either; the presence and non-SET conditions were equivalent. This finding demonstrates that just having others present may not responsible for eliciting cortisol under SET; instead, others may need to be in an explicitly evaluative mode to lead to increases in cortisol.

Other studies have examined whether the potential for subsequent evaluation is enough to elicit cortisol responses. Our meta-analytic review demonstrated that the presence of an audience or social comparison was associated with larger cortisol responses than studies that videotaped the performance, demonstrating that subsequent evaluation may not be as potent an elicitor of cortisol activity (Dickerson & Kemeny, 2004). Additional studies have corroborated this effect, showing that only videotaping the performance stressor (with an otherwise minimal social context) did not lead to increases in cortisol (Robbins, Dickerson, Epstein, & Zaldivar, 2012; Taylor et al., 2010). Taken together, these studies suggest that the potential for evaluation is not the critical component of the social-evaluative context leading to increases in cortisol levels. Rather, appraisals of real-time social evaluation may be necessary to bring about increases in cortisol.

A related question addresses whether evaluation that occurs remotely still triggers cortisol responses. In other words, do those evaluating the performance need to be in the same room, or can perceived social evaluation from another location elicit reactivity? A series of studies have shown that remote evaluation (e.g., through a one-way mirror) is indeed capable of eliciting cortisol levels. However, this type of evaluation is typically less robust than if there is "live" social evaluation in the same room as the participants (Het et al., 2009; Kelly, Matheson, Martinez, Merali, & Anisman, 2007; but see Andrews, Wadiwalla, Juster, Lord, Lupien, & Pruessner, 2007). For example, Kelly and colleagues (2007) found the presence of a live audience was associated with a cortisol response of approximately three times the magnitude compared with forms of remote evaluation. This suggests that remote evaluation can elicit cortisol levels, but "live" or real-time evaluation may lead to bigger increases.

Taken together, this body of research demonstrates that in general, larger cortisol changes are triggered under conditions in which the social evaluation is maximized; the real-time visual presence of an evaluative audience is a reliable way to elicit substantial increases in cortisol. When this evaluative context is diminished, cortisol changes tend to be minimized as well.

Emotional Correlates of Social-Evaluative Threat

Studies that have manipulated SET in the laboratory have provided the opportunity to examine the cognitive and emotional effects of social evaluation and how these psychological responses may be associated with the physiological responses observed. We have proposed that SET may trigger self-conscious cognitions and emotions, and that this specific class of appraisals and emotions may in turn be linked with the increases in corti-sol (Dickerson, Gruenewald, & Kemeny, 2004; Gruenewald, Dickerson, & Kemeny, 2007). This prediction is based on theoretical and empirical evidence that self-conscious emotions are triggered when one believes that others are judging one's social acceptability (e.g., Leary, 2007). Consistent with this premise, participants in a social-evaluative con-dition have shown greater increases in self-conscious emotions compared with those in a nonevaluative condition (Dickerson et al., 2008; Gruenewald et al., 2004). Additionally, although other emotions such as fear can increase during this type of performance task, we have found that increases in fear are simi-lar for SET and non-SET conditions. This could be because all of the participants completed a task that they rated as demanding, difficult, and effortful. The self-conscious emotions (e.g., ashamed, embar-rassed), however, appeared to be the most sensitive to social context of the emotions assessed.

We have also tested whether the experience of self-conscious emotions was associated with cor-tisol changes. For those in the social-evaluative conditions, those who showed the highest levels of self-conscious emotions also showed the larg-est increases in cortisol (Dickerson et al., 2008; Gruenewald et al., 2004). There were no significant correlations between other emotional states (e.g., fear, sadness) and the cortisol responses. These results demonstrated a unique association between self-conscious emotion and cortisol reactivity that was not found for other emotional states. This suggests that SET may trigger self-conscious emo-tions, which in turn are correlated with increases in cortisol.

Interpersonal Rejection/Exclusion and Cortisol Responses

The studies reviewed in the preceding section all used social-evaluative performance stressors to examine cortisol reactivity to threats to the social self. However, many experiences of social evaluation and criticism occur in the context of interpersonal interactions and relationships. A series of studies have examined the effects of interpersonal rejec-tion or exclusion on cortisol and other outcomes. For example, Gunnar and colleagues have examined acceptance and rejection among children (Gunnar, Sebanc, Tout, Donzella, & van Dulman, 2003). They found that children who were more disliked by their peers had elevated cortisol levels compared with those who were more socially accepted or liked.

Other studies have experimentally manipulated social exclusion/rejection. Blackhart and colleagues (2007) had participants engage in a 15-minute con-versation with four to six other individuals. After this period, participants randomly assigned to a rejection condition were told that "nobody wants to work with you" on a subsequent task. Those assigned to the acceptance condition were told "eve-ryone wants to work with you." They found that the rejection condition was associated with elevated cortisol levels compared with the acceptance condi-tion or a control condition. This was especially the case among those in the rejection condition who were also low in defensiveness.

Stroud and colleagues (2000) developed a rejec-tion paradigm in which the participant and two confederates engage in an interaction task (Yale Interpersonal Stressor; YIPS). Over the course of the task, the participant is gradually and systemat-ically excluded from conversation. Results showed that this exclusion experience led to increases in cor-tisol among the female participants; however, men did not show changes in cortisol in response to this form of interpersonal rejection.

A subsequent study used the YIPS protocol among women (Zwolinski, 2008) and found that, overall, there was not a significant increase in corti-sol in response to interpersonal exclusion. Instead, there was an interaction with menstrual cycle phase and relational victimization by peers. Women in the luteal phase of the menstrual cycle who reported high levels of relational victimization by others were the only ones to show increases in cortisol in response to interpersonal rejection. Taken together, these studies demonstrate that social exclusion manipu-lations can elevate cortisol levels, but only subsets of the participants may show this response. Future research will need to delineate the likely complex reasons for potential gender differences in cortisol responses to rejection. It is possible that women perceive the gradual rejection experience differently and make different evaluative appraisals compared with men. Men and women may also differ in their hypervigilance to their own and others emotions (e.g., Nolen-Hoeksema & Jackson, 2001), which could lead to differences in cortisol responses in this rejection context.

Ford and Collins (2010) examined cortisol responses to interpersonal rejection, and whether the individual difference of self-esteem moderated this response. In this study, male and female partici-pants were led to believe they would be engaging in an online chat with a potential dating partner. They were then told that the conversation would not occur because either the partner chose not to continue (rejection condition) or because he or she got sick (control condition). Although there was not a main effect of condition on cortisol, they found that self-esteem and condition interacted to predict cortisol. Specifically, those with low self-esteem in the rejection condition showed higher cortisol levels compared with those with high self-esteem in the rejection condition or participants in the control condition. Further, negative social self-appraisals and self-blame mediated the effects of self-esteem on cortisol responses. Those low in self-esteem made more negative social self-appraisals (e.g., that they were socially incompetent, not fun to be with) and blamed themselves more for their partner's rejection, which in turn led to elevated cortisol levels.

Other research has manipulated social rejection/exclusion through the standardized Cyberball task (Williams, Cheung, & Choi, 2000), in which the participant believes she or he is playing a game of "catch" on a computer with others remotely. In the social-exclusion condition, the participant receives three "tosses" from other players, but then does not receive the ball anymore. In the inclusion condition, the participant receives approximately every fourth ball. Contrary to hypotheses, the authors found no effect of condition on cortisol levels; in fact, there was no significant increase in cortisol in either group (Zoller, Maroof, Weik, & Deinzer, 2010).

It appears, however, that Cyberball can influence subsequent reactivity to social threat. In another Cyberball study (Weik, Maroof, Zöller, & Deinzer, 2010), male and female participants were randomly assigned to one of three conditions: social exclusion, exclusion attributed to technical default, or social inclusion. Results indicated that although cortisol levels did not change in response to the social exclusion task, cortisol responses did differ when participants later engaged in a social-evaluative performance stressor. These responses were moderated by sex. Women who were socially excluded had blunted cortisol responses to the stressor, but men did not. This study demonstrates that although Cyberball may not directly elicit increases in cortisol, the experience of social exclusion can influence subsequent responses to SET, at least among women. Future research should extend this interesting finding that repeated experiences of social rejection/social evaluation could alter cortisol reactivity.

Taken together, the results from these studies, which have examined the effects of social exclusion or rejection on cortisol, have been mixed. Although some have demonstrated increases in cortisol in response to rejection, the effects have typically emerged only in a subset of individuals (e.g., women, those low in self-esteem). Perhaps factors that seem to be associated with reactivity in social-evaluative performance situations, such as the salience of the audience, also play a part in reactivity to interpersonal rejection; the studies that used remote rejection (e.g., Cyberball) tended to not strongly activate the HPA axis.

Additionally, the cortisol effects in the social exclusion and rejection studies were generally smaller in magnitude than those observed for social-evaluative performance tasks. Indeed, one study compared the magnitude of cortisol changes for the YIPS and a social-evaluative performance stressor among children 7 to 17 years old (Stroud et al., 2009). Whereas the social-evaluative performance stressor resulted in substantial cortisol elevations, particularly among the adolescents, the interpersonal rejection paradigm led to less cortisol activation overall. Future studies that compare perceptions of evaluation and rejection among different types of interpersonal stressors could clarify the relationship between cortisol reactivity and interpersonal threats. There are many factors that differ between social-evaluative performance stressors and interpersonal rejection manipulations that could lead to differences in the magnitude of cortisol responses. For example, the panelists in the performance stressors provide sustained, explicit evaluation throughout the task, whereas in some of the rejection paradigms the evaluation may be more fleeting and ambiguous. Studies that manipulate these factors may provide insight into the differences in cortisol responses observed with social-evaluative performance stressors and certain rejection stressor contexts.

Rumination and Responses to Social Evaluation or Social Exclusion

The effects of social evaluation or exclusion on cortisol may extend beyond the immediate response. In addition to eliciting cortisol, situations characterized by SET can also lead to rumination. Mentally rehearsing past stressors through rumination may, in turn, prolong the acute stress response (Brosschot, Gerin, & Thayer, 2006).

Rumination has been defined in multiple ways, but it is broadly characterized by repetitive, unwanted, past-oriented thoughts about negative content (Watkins, 2008). Although there are individual differences in the tendency to ruminate (Nolen-Hoeksema, 1991), situational characteristics can also determine whether or not an individual ruminates. For instance, several theorists have argued that real or perceived threat to fundamental needs or goals can elicit and maintain rumination (e.g., Gold & Wegner, 1995; Martin & Tesser, 1996; Trapnell & Campbell, 1999). In addition, theorists have argued that shame may increase ruminative thoughts (Joireman, 2004; Trapnell & Campbell, 1999). Both are key features of SET and social exclusion.

Social-evaluative threat may be particularly likely to prompt ruminative thought for two reasons. First, it threatens individuals' fundamental needs for social acceptance and belongingness by preventing the satisfaction of the social self-preservation goal (Dickerson et al., 2004). Consistent with the theory that unattained goals drive rumination, this failure in goal attainment is expected to elicit rumination. Second, perceived negative evaluation by one's peers may create a discrepancy between one's actual self and one's ideal self (Higgins, 1987). In other words, negative social evaluation by others becomes negative self-evaluation and can result in the experience of shame. Moreover, when an individual perceives that others view him- or herself as worthless, or having lower relational value (i.e., lower social standing), he or she will experience shame (Dickerson et al., 2004).

Several lines of research support the notion that shame and rejection lead to rumination. Empirical work has shown that the experience of shame (Cheung, Gilbert, & Irons, 2004; Joireman, 2004; Orth, Berking, & Burkhardt, 2006), stigma-related stressors (Hatzenbuehler, Nolen-Hoeksema, & Dovidio, 2009), and rejection from a romantic partner (Perilloux & Buss, 2008) are positively associated with rumination. In addition, our work suggests that SET may lead to both shame and rumination (Dickerson, Mycek, & Zaldivar, 2008; Zoccola, Dickerson, & Zaldivar, 2008). Participants were randomly assigned to deliver a speech in one of three contexts: in front of an evaluative audience panel (SET), in the presence of an inattentive confederate, or alone in a room. Participants in the SET condition demonstrated greater self-conscious emotions and cognitions (e.g., ashamed, embarrassed) (Dickerson et al., 2008) and rumination (Zoccola et al., 2008), compared with those who performed the identical tasks without the evaluative component. Specifically, we found that those in the SET condition reported greater levels of negative thoughts about the speech in the 10-minute period immediately after the stressor. Our recent work has replicated this SET/rumination effect, and further found that the effects persisted hours and even days later (Zoccola, Dickerson, & Lam, 2012). Furthermore, we found evidence that self-conscious cognitions and emotions mediated the effect of SET on subsequent rumination. Social-evaluative threat triggered greater increases in self-conscious emotions, which in turn led to higher levels of rumination. Taken together, these studies suggest that situations characterized by SET and that induce self-conscious emotions are likely candidates for prompting rumination.

Rumination is thought to be maladaptive, as it focuses on past problems instead of solving problems for the future (Gold & Wegner, 1995). Moreover, rumination has been linked to a variety of negative mental and physical health outcomes, such as the development and exacerbation of depression (Nolen-Hoeksema, Morrow, & Frederickson, 1993), maintenance of social anxiety (Clark & Wells, 1995), and persistence of posttraumatic stress disorder (Michael, Halligan, Clark, & Ehlers, 2007). Relative to distraction, rumination can lead to greater negative mood (e.g., Nolen-Hoeksema & Morrow, 1993; Rusting & Nolen-Hoeksema, 1998), impairments in problem solving (e.g., Lyubomirsky, Tucker, Caldwell, & Berg, 1999), and displaced aggression (e.g., Bushman, Bonacci, Pedersen, Vasquez, & Miller, 2005).

Rumination may also extend physiological stress responses, and for those who ruminate after the experience of social evaluation or rejection, the cortisol stress response may be longer lasting. This could occur through delayed recovery of the stress response (i.e., longer time to turn off the response). For example, elevated levels of cortisol may continue to circulate in the body long after the rejecting situation has ended. In addition, subsequent recall of the situation could serve to reactivate the stress response later in time. For instance, thinking about yesterday's argument may trigger increases in cortisol again today. If repeated over time, delayed recovery and repeated reactivation of the stress response may lead to prolonged exposure to stress hormones and may affect health (Brosschot et al., 2006).

Emerging evidence supports the link between rumination and prolonged cortisol activation (for review, see Zoccola & Dickerson, 2012). In one such study, participants who ruminated on recent interpersonal transgressions (e.g., being wronged or hurt) had increases in basal salivary cortisol (McCullough, Orsulak, Brandon, & Akers, 2007). Two other studies demonstrated that rumination on stressors predicts greater cortisol reactivity and delayed recovery in response to laboratory performance stressors

(Zoccola et al., 2008; Zoccola, Quas, Yim, 2010). Additionally, for those with a tendency to ruminate, recalling a stressor in a SET context may also trigger a cortisol response (Zoccola et al., 2010). Two weeks after experiencing a SET laboratory stressor, participants returned for a surprise interview about the stressor from the first session, which was conducted in either a supportive or SET context. There was no increase in cortisol in response to the supportive stressor recall interview. In the SET interview condition, however, trait rumination predicted reactivation of the cortisol stress response. Together, these studies provide evidence that rumination may play a role in amplifying and prolonging the immediate cortisol stress response, particularly in the context of SET.

Chronic Interpersonal Rejection and Social Exclusion

Whereas the acute experience of social evaluation or rejection can elicit short-term changes in cortisol, more prolonged experiences could lead to dysregulation of the HPA axis. Indeed, a meta-analysis found that chronic stressors that were social in nature were associated with higher morning and evening cortisol levels when compared with stressors without a social element (Miller, Chen, & Zhou, 2007). Additionally, chronic stressors that were likely to elicit the emotion of shame were also associated with higher evening cortisol levels. Research on loneliness—which could result from feelings of social exclusion—has also demonstrated associations with heightened cortisol activity. Individuals reporting greater feelings of loneliness have shown higher morning and evening cortisol levels compared with those who feel less lonely (Pressman, Cohen, Miller, Barkin, Rabin, & Treanor, 2005). These elevations in cortisol may be particularly likely when loneliness is experienced in the context of interpersonal stressors. Those with high levels of interpersonal stress and reporting momentary feelings of loneliness have higher levels of cortisol than those experiencing loneliness coupled with lower levels of interpersonal stressors (Doane & Adam, 2010). Other work has found that trait loneliness is associated with larger cortisol responses to awakening (Steptoe, Owen, Kunz-Ebrecht, & Brydon, 2004). Also, the prior day's feelings of loneliness have predicted greater cortisol awakening responses in adolescents (Doane & Adam, 2010) and older adults (Adam, Hawkley, Kudielka, & Cacioppo, 2006). Taken together, chronic social stressors and feelings of loneliness have been associated with heightened cortisol activity.

The relationship between social exclusion, as conceptualized as repeated peer victimization, and cortisol activity has also been examined. Vaillancourt and colleagues (Vaillancourt, Duku, Decatanzaro, Macmillan, Muir, & Schmidt, 2008) compared daily cortisol levels of bullied and nonbullied 12 year olds. Results indicated that, overall, children who were verbally bullied either occasionally or frequently demonstrated reduced cortisol secretion, or hypocortisolism, compared with nonbullied children. However, results also revealed sex differences in cortisol levels among those occasionally verbally bullied. Boys had greater daily cortisol levels, whereas girls had lower levels. These findings suggest that dysregulation of the HPA axis (reduced daily secretion of cortisol) may result from chronic bullying. Notably, however, these results were not the same for males and females. Future studies should examine whether this type of social exclusion and rejection is perceived differently by males compared with females or if some other mechanism is responsible (e.g., sex hormones). Additionally, a meta-analysis demonstrated that factors such as duration of the stressor or time since stressor onset are important for understanding when hypercortisolism versus hypocortisolism emerges (Miller et al., 2007). Assessing these factors in future studies could shed light on when peer victimization or exclusion may result in heightened or blunted patterns of cortisol secretion.

Other research has found that cortisol reactivity is a moderator between peer victimization and depressive symptomology (Rudolph, Troop-Gordon, & Granger, 2010). Specifically, children with both high levels of peer victimization and who showed higher anticipatory cortisol levels before a social stressor subsequently reported higher levels of depressive symptoms 1 year later. Additionally, those exposed to victimization and had higher anticipatory cortisol levels also tended to engage in more rumination, providing a potential mechanism for these effects. This suggests that victimization coupled with high stress-related HPA axis activity may be a risk factor for negative outcomes such as depressive symptomology.

Conclusions

A large body of evidence demonstrates that cortisol is a hormone that is sensitive to social threats, including social evaluation, rejection, and exclusion. Acute experiences of social evaluation or interpersonal rejection can elicit cortisol reactivity, particularly when it is unambiguous and salient. Social exclusion or evaluation can also lead to rumination, which could serve to maintain cortisol responses to these forms of social threat. Chronic forms of social exclusion or rejection, such as perceptions of loneliness or peer victimization, have also been associated with dysregulated cortisol patterns. Prolonged exposure to social exclusion or evaluation, whether by repeated victimization or cognitive processes such as rumination, may lead to negative health consequences via prolonged exposure to cortisol or dysregulation in the HPA axis.

Cortisol is not the only physiological parameter that can be elicited by social evaluation and exclusion. Indeed, a number of studies have documented a range of physiological responses to these types of threats, including changes in cardiovascular and immunological parameters (for review, see Dickerson et al., 2011). Furthermore, social exclusion has been shown to affect a wide range of behaviors, including self-control, aggression, and the desire to connect with others. Future studies that incorporate the assessment of a range of physiological, neural, and behavioral responses to social exclusion will more fully document the potential negative impact of social exclusion across different parameters and systems, as well as the interactions between these outcomes.

References

Adam, E. K., Hawkley, L. C., Kudielka, B. M., & Cacioppo, J. T. (2006). Day-to-day dynamics of experience-cortisol association in a population-based sample of older adults. *Proceedings of the National Academy of Sciences, 103*, 17058–17063.

Andrews, J., Wadiwalla, M., Juster, R. P., Lord, C., Lupien, S. J., & Pruessner, J. C. (2007). Effects of manipulating the amount of social-evaluative threat on the cortisol stress response in young healthy men. *Behavioral Neuroscience, 121*(5), 871–876.

Baumeister, R. F., & Leary, M. R. (1995). The need to belong: desire for interpersonal attachments as a fundamental human motivation. *Psychological Bulletin, 117*, 497–529.

Blackhart, G. C., Eckel, L. A., & Tice, D. M. (2007). Salivary cortisol in response to acute social rejection and acceptance by peers. *Biological Psychology, 75*, 267–276.

Brosschot, J. F., Gerin, W., & Thayer, J. F. (2006). The perseverative cognition hypothesis: A review of worry, prolonged stress-related physiological activation, and health. *Journal of Psychosomatic Research, 60*, 113–124.

Bushman, B. J., Bonacci, A. M., Pedersen, W. C., Vasquez, E. A., & Miller, N. (2005). Chewing on it can chew you up: Effects of rumination on triggered displaced aggression. *Journal of Personality and Social Psychology, 88*(6), 969–983.

Cheung, M. S.-P., Gilbert, P., & Irons, C. (2004). An exploration of shame, social rank and rumination in relation to depression. *Personality and Individual Differences, 36*, 1143–1153.

Clark, D. M., & Wells, A. (1995). A cognitive model of social phobia. In R. G. Heimberg, M. Liebowitz, D. A. Hope, & F. R. Schneier (Eds.), *Social Phobia: Diagnosis, Assessment, and Treatment* (pp. 69–93). New York: Guilford Press.

Dickerson, S. S., Gruenewald, T. L., & Kemeny, M. E. (2004). When the social self is threatened: Shame, physiology, and health. *Journal of Personality, 72*, 1191–1216.

Dickerson, S. S., Gruenewald, T. L., & Kemeny, M. E. (2011). Physiological effects of social threat: Implications for health. In J. Cacioppo, & J. Decety (Eds.), *Handbook of Social Neuroscience*. New York: Oxford University Press.

Dickerson, S. S., & Kemeny, M. E. (2004). Acute stressors and cortisol responses: A theoretical integration and synthesis of laboratory research. *Psychological Bulletin, 130*(3), 355–391.

Dickerson, S. S., Mycek, P. M., & Zaldivar, F. P. (2008). Negative social evaluation, but not mere social presence, elicits cortisol responses to a laboratory stressor task. *Health Psychology, 27*, 116–121.

Doane, L. D., & Adam, E. K. (2010). Loneliness and cortisol: Momentary, day-to-day, and trait associations. *Psychoneuroendocrinology, 35*(3), 430–441.

Ford, M. B., & Collins, N. L. (2010). Self-esteem moderates neuroendocrine and psychological responses to interpersonal rejection. *Journal of Personality and Social Psychology, 98*, 405–419.

Gold, D. B., & Wegner, D. M. (1995). Origins of ruminative thought: Trauma, incompleteness, nondisclosure, and suppression. *Journal of Applied Social Psychology, 25*, 1245–1261.

Gruenewald, T. L., Dickerson, S. S., & Kemeny, M. E. (2007). A social function for the self-conscious emotions: Social-self preservation theory. In J. Tracy, R. Robins, & J. Tangney (Eds.), *Self-Conscious Emotions* (2nd ed.). New York: Guilford Press.

Gruenewald, T. L., Kemeny, M. E., Aziz, N., & Fahey, J. L. (2004). Acute threat to the social self: Shame, social self-esteem, and cortisol activity. *Psychosomatic Medicine, 66*, 915–924.

Gunnar, M. R., Sebanc, A. M., Tout, K., Donzella, B., & van Dulmen, M. M. H. (2003). Peer rejection, temperament, and cortisol activity in preschoolers. *Developmental Psychobiology, 43*, 346–358.

Hatzenbuehler, M. L., Nolen- Hoeksema, S., & Dovidio, J. (2009). How does stigma get under the skin? The mediating role of emotion regulation. *Psychological Science, 20*, 1282–1289.

Het, S., Rohleder, N., Schoofs, D., Kirschbaum, C., & Wolf, O. T. (2009). Neuroendocrine and psychometric evaluation of a placebo version of the "Trier Social Stress Test." *Psychoneuronendocrinology, 34*, 1075–1086.

Higgins, E. T. (1987). Self-discrepancy: A theory relating self and affect. *Psychological Review, 94*, 31–340.

Joireman, J. (2004). Empathy and the self-absorption paradox II: Self-rumination and self-reflection as mediators between shame, guilt, and empathy. *Self and Identity, 3*, 225–238.

Kelly, O., Matheson, M., Martinez, A., Merali, Z., & Anisman, H. (2007). Psychosocial stress evoked by a virtual audience: Relation to neuroendocrine activity. *CyberPsychology & Behavior, 10*(5), 655–662.

Leary, M. R. (2007). Motivational and emotional aspects of the self. *Annual Reviews of Psychology, 58*, 317–344.

Lyubomirsky, S., Tucker, K. L., Caldwell, N. D., & Berg, K. (1999). Why ruminators are bad problem solvers: Clues from the phenomenology of dysphoric rumination. *Journal of Personality and Social Psychology, 77*, 1041–1060.

Martin, L. L., & Tesser, A. (1996). Some ruminative thoughts. In R. S. Wyer (Ed.), *Advances in Social Cognition* (Vol. 9, pp. 1–47). Hillsdale, NJ: Lawrence Erlbaum Associates.

McCullough, M. E., Orsulak, P., Brandon, A., & Akers, L. (2007). Rumination, fear, and cortisol: An in vivo study of interpersonal transgressions. *Health Psychology, 26*, 126–132.

McEwen, B. S. (1998). Stress, adaptation, and disease. Allostatis and allostatic load. *Annals of the New York Academy of Sciences, 840*, 33–44.

Michael, T., Halligan, S. L., Clark, D. M., & Ehlers, A. (2007). Rumination in posttraumatic stress disorder. *Depression and Anxiety, 24*(5), 307–317.

Miller, G. E., Chen, E., & Zhou, E. (2007). If it goes up, must it come down? Chronic stress and the hypothalamic-pituitary-adrenocortical axis in humans. *Psychological Bulletin, 133*, 25–45.

Nolen-Hoeksema, S. (1991). Responses to depression and their effects on the duration of depressive episodes. *Journal of Abnormal Psychology, 100*, 569–582.

Nolen-Hoeksema, S., & Jackson, B. (2001). Mediators of the gender difference in rumination. *Psychology of Women Quarterly, 25*(1), 37–47.

Nolen-Hoeksema, S., & Morrow, J. (1993). Effects of rumination and distraction on naturally occurring depressed mood. *Cognition & Emotion, 7*(6), 561–570.

Nolen-Hoeksema, S., Morrow, J., & Fredrickson, B. L. (1993). Response styles and the duration of episodes of depressed mood. *Journal of Abnormal Psychology, 102*(1), 20–28.

Orth, U., Berking, M., & Burkhardt, S. (2006). Self-conscious emotions and depression: Rumination explains why shame but not guilt is maladaptive. *Personality and Social Psychology Bulletin, 32*, 1608–1619.

Perilloux, C. & Buss, D. M. (2008). Breaking up romantic relationships: Costs experienced and coping strategies deployed. *Evolutionary Psychology, 6*, 164–181.

Pressman, S. D., Cohen, S., Miller, G. E., Barkin, A., Rabin, B. S., & Treanor, J. J. (2005). Loneliness, social network size, and immune response to influenza vaccination in college freshman. *Health Psychology, 24*, 297–306.

Robbins, M. L., Dickerson, S. S., Epstein, E. B., & Zaldivar, F. (2012). *The potential for evaluation and cortisol: A preliminary investigation.* Manuscript in preparation.

Rohleder, N., Beulen, S. E., Chen, E., Wolf, J. M., & Kirschbaum, C. (2007). Stress on the dance floor: The cortisol stress response to social-evaluative threat in competitive ballroom dancers. *Personality and Social Psychology Bulletin, 33*, 69–84.

Rudolph, K. D., Troop-Gordon, W., & Granger, D. A. (2010). Individual differences in biological stress responses moderate the contribution of early peer victimization to subsequent depressive symptoms. *Psychopharmacology, 214*(1), 209–219.

Rusting, C. L., & Nolen-Hoeksema, S. (1998). Regulating responses to anger: Effects of rumination and distraction on angry mood. *Journal of Personality and Social Psychology, 74*(3), 790–803.

Sapolsky, R. M. (2005). The influence of social hierarchy on primate health. *Science, 308*, 648–652.

Sapolsky, R. M., Romero, L. M., & Munch, A. U. (2000). How do glucocorticoids influence stress responses? Integrating permissive, suppressive, stimulatory, and preparative actions. *Endocrine Reviews, 21*, 55–89.

Schwabe, L., Haddad, L., & Schachinger, H. (2008). HPA axis activation by a socially evaluated cold-pressor task. *Psychoneuroendocrinology, 33*, 890–895.

Steptoe, A., Owen, N., Kunz-Ebrecht, S. R., & Brydon, L. (2004). Loneliness and neuroendocrine, cardiovascular, and inflammatory stress responses in middle-aged men and women. *Psychoneuroendocrinology, 29*, 593–611.

Stroud, L. R., Foster, E., Papandonatos, G. D., Handwerger, K., Granger, D. A., Kivlighan, K. T., & Niaura, R. (2009). Stress response and the adolescent transition: Performance versus peer rejection stressors. *Development and Psychopathology, 21*, 47–68.

Stroud, L. R., Tanofsky-Kraff, M., Wilfley, D. E., & Salovey, P. (2000). The Yale Interpersonal Stressor (YIPS): Affective, physiological, and behavioral responses to a novel interpersonal rejection paradigm. *Annals of Behavioral Medicine, 22*, 204–213.

Taylor, S. E., Seeman, T. E., Eisenberger, N. I., Kozanian, T. A., Moore, A. N., & Moons, W. G. (2010). Effects of a supportive or unsupportive audience on biological and psychological responses to stress. *Journal of Personality and Social Psychology, 98*, 47–56.

Trapnell, P. D., & Campbell, J. D. (1999). Private self-consciousness and the five factor model of personality: Distinguishing rumination from reflection. *Journal of Personality and Social Psychology, 76*, 284–304.

Watkins, E. R. (2008). Constructive and unconstructive repetitive thought. *Psychological Bulletin, 134*, 163–206.

Weik, U., Maroof, P., Zöller, C., & Deinzer, R. (2010). Pre-experience of social exclusion suppresses cortisol response to psychosocial stress in women but not in men. *Hormones and Behavior, 58*(5), 891–897.

Williams, K. D. (2007). Ostracism. *Annual Review of Psychology, 58*, 425–452.

Williams, K. D., Cheung, C. K. T., & Choi, W. (2000). Cyberostracism: Effects of being ignored over the internet. *Journal of Personality and Social Psychology, 79*, 748–762.

Vaillancourt, T., Duku, E., Decatanzaro, D., Macmillan, H., Muir, C., & Schmidt, L. (2008). Variation in hypothalamic-pituitary-adrenal axis activity among bullied and non-bullied children. *Aggressive Behavior, 34*(3), 294–305.

Zoccola, P. M., & Dickerson, S. S. (2012). Assessing the relationship between rumination and cortisol: A review. *Journal of Psychosomatic Research, 73*, 1–9.

Zoccola, P. M., Dickerson, S. S., & Lam, S. (2012). Eliciting and maintaining ruminative thought: The role of social-evaluative threat. *Emotion*. Advance online publication. doi: 10.1037/a0027349.

Zoccola, P. M., Dickerson, S. S., & Zaldivar, F. P. (2008). Rumination and cortisol responses to laboratory stressors. *Psychosomatic Medicine, 70*, 661–667.

Zoccola, P. M., Quas, J. A., & Yim, I. S. (2010). Cortisol responses to a psychosocial laboratory stressor and later verbal recall of the stressor: The role of trait and state rumination. *Stress, 13*, 435–433.

Zoller, C., Maroof, P., Weik, U., & Deinzer, R. (2010). No effect of social exclusion on salivary cortisol secretion in women in a randomized controlled study. *Psychoneuroendocrinology, 35*, 1294–1298.

Zwolinski, J. (2008). Biopsychosocial responses to social rejection in targets of relational aggression. *Biological Psychology, 79*, 260–267.

Why Rejection Hurts: The Neuroscience of Social Pain

Naomi I. Eisenberger

Abstract

Although people often describe experiences of social rejection as being "painful," one is left to wonder whether these descriptions are primarily metaphorical or whether there is something truly painful about rejection experiences. This chapter reviews accumulating evidence showing that social pain—the painful feelings following social rejection, exclusion, or loss—relies on some of the same neural circuitry that is involved in processing physical pain. Moreover, building on this overlap in the neural circuitry underlying physical and social pain, this chapter reviews several consequences of this shared circuitry. Specifically, evidence is reviewed to show: (1) that individuals who are more sensitive to one kind of pain are also more sensitive to the other and (2) that factors that typically alter one type of pain (e.g., Tylenol reduces physical pain) can alter the other as well (e.g., Tylenol reduces social pain). Other possible consequences of this shared neural circuitry are discussed.

Key Words: anterior insula, dorsal anterior cingulate cortex, fmri, neuroimaging, physical pain, social exclusion, social neuroscience, social pain, social rejection

Introduction

If you listen closely to the ways in which individuals describe experiences of social rejection or exclusion, you will notice an interesting pattern. They use physical pain words to describe experiences of social pain, as illustrated by phrases like "that *hurt* my feelings" or "he *broke* my heart." Indeed, in the English language, we have no other means of expressing these painful social experiences other than with words typically reserved for physical pain. Moreover, this pattern is not unique to English speakers; languages across the globe—from Armenian to Mandarin—use pain words to describe these negative social experiences (MacDonald & Leary, 2005). Such widespread overlap in the terminology used to describe physical pain and social pain begs the question, why? Is the "pain" of social rejection truly comparable to physical pain or are individuals simply being metaphorical when they say that rejection "hurts?"

Accumulating research has suggested that the "pain" of social rejection may be more than just a figure of speech, and that part of the reason that individuals describe rejection as being painful is because experiences of rejection are processed by some of the same neural machinery that processes physical pain (Eisenberger, Lieberman, & Williams, 2003; Eisenberger & Lieberman, 2004, 2005; Eisenberger, 2012a, 2012b). In fact, it has been suggested that, because of the importance of social connection for human survival, the social attachment system—which ensures social connection—may have piggybacked onto the physical pain system, borrowing the pain signal to indicate when social relationships are threatened (Panksepp, 1998). Specifically, as a mammalian species, humans are born relatively immature without the capacity to feed or fend for themselves and must rely on the care and protection of a caregiver in order to survive. Later in life, being connected to close others as well as to a social group increases chances of survival by providing access to shared resources as well as protection from predators (Axelrod & Hamilton, 1981). Thus, over the course of evolutionary history, being separated from close others significantly decreased chances of survival. Consequently, if broken social ties are experienced as painful, an individual will be more likely to avoid situations that might threaten social ties or lead to rejection, hence increasing one's likelihood of inclusion in the social group and one's chances of survival. In short, to the extent that social rejection or exclusion is a threat to survival, feeling hurt by these experiences may be an adaptive way to prevent them.

In this chapter, I will review evidence that supports the notion that physical pain and social pain—the painful experience following social rejection or loss—rely on shared neural substrates. To do this, I will first review the neural regions involved in the distressing experience of physical pain and then show that socially painful experiences rely on some of these same neural regions. I will then review two consequences that can be expected

from a physical–social pain overlap. Specifically, I will first review evidence showing that individuals who are more sensitive to one kind of pain are also more sensitive to the other. I will then review evidence demonstrating that factors that alter (increase or decrease) one kind of pain experience alter the other in a congruent manner. (See Fig. 15.1 for a conceptual model.) Finally, I will discuss what this shared neural circuitry means for our experience and understanding of social pain.

Social Pain Relies on Physical Pain–Related Neural Regions

As primary support for the hypothesis that physical and social pain processes overlap, neuropsychological and neuroimaging research has shown that some of the same neural regions that are involved in physical pain are also involved in separation distress behaviors in nonhuman mammals and socially painful experiences in humans. I will first delineate the neural substrates underlying the affective or "distressing" component of physical pain and then review research demonstrating that certain social

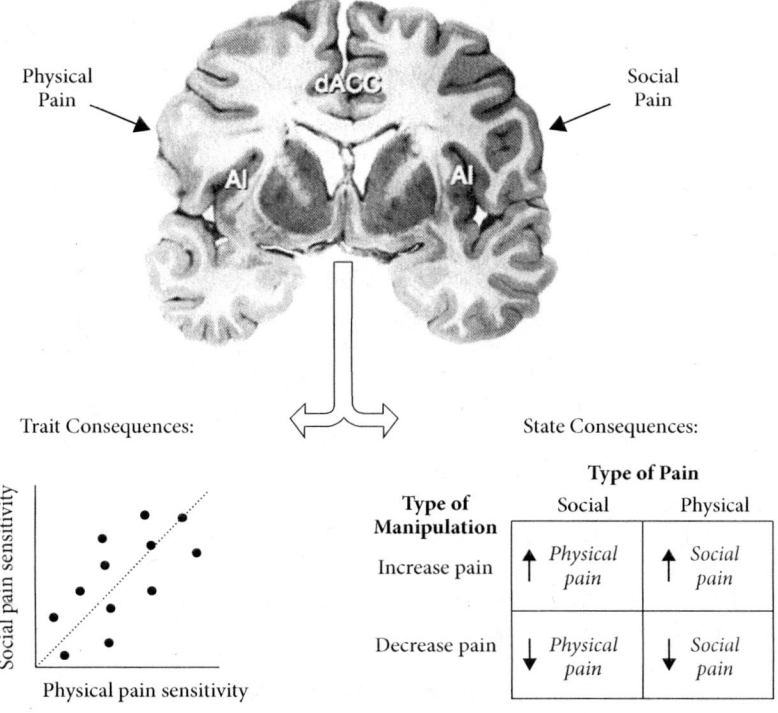

Figure 15.1 A model depicting the overlapping neural regions activated by physical and social pain (dorsal anterior cingulate cortex [dACC] and anterior insula [AI]) as well as the *trait* consequences of this overlap (individual differences in sensitivity to one kind of pain should relate to individual differences in sensitivity to the other) and the *state* consequences of this overlap (factors that increase or decrease one kind of pain should have a similar effect on the other type of pain).

Figure reprinted with permission from Eisenberger, N. I. (2012a). The neural bases of social pain: Evidence for shared representations with physical pain. *Psychosomatic Medicine, 74*, 126–135.

pain–related processes, such as separation-distress behaviors and experiences of social rejection or exclusion, rely on some of these same regions.

The Neural Correlates of Physical Pain

The neural underpinnings of physical pain have been fairly well delineated (Apkarian, Bushnell, Treede, & Zubieta, 2005; Peyron, Laurent, & Garcia-Larrea, 2000; Price, 2000; Rainville, 2002). Pain experience can be roughly divided into two subcomponents: (1) the sensory component, which codes for the discriminative aspects of pain (e.g., location, intensity) and (2) the affective component, which codes for the unpleasant or distressing experience associated with physical pain. Because social rejection does not involve any direct sensory contact, we have suggested that the affective component of pain and its underlying neural substrates may be more relevant for understanding social pain experience.

The affective component of physical pain is processed, in part, by the dorsal portion of the anterior cingulate cortex (dACC) and the anterior insula (Apkarian et al., 2005; Peyron et al., 2000; Price, 2000; Rainville, 2002). As evidence for this, patients with chronic pain conditions who have undergone cingulotomy—a surgery in which a portion of the dACC is removed (Richter et al., 2004)—report that they can still localize pain sensations (sensory component intact) but that the pain experience no longer "bothers" them (Foltz & White, 1968; Hebben, 1985). Similar effects have been observed following insular lesions (Berthier, Starkstein, Leiguardia, & Carrea, 1988). Thus, the dACC and anterior insula appear to play a role in the affective, or what is sometimes referred to as the "suffering," component of physical pain experience.

Neuroimaging studies parallel these neuropsychological findings, lending additional support to the notion that the dACC and anterior insula process the affective component of pain. In one study, subjects who were hypnotized to selectively increase the unpleasantness of painful stimuli (affective component) without altering the intensity (sensory component) showed increased activity in the dACC without increased activity in the primary somatosensory cortex, known to be involved in the sensory component of physical pain (Rainville, Duncan, Price, Carrier, & Bushnell, 1997). Moreover, other work has shown that self-reports of pain unpleasantness correlate specifically with activity in the dACC (Peyron et al., 2000; Tölle et al., 1999) and the anterior insula (Schreckenberger et al., 2005).

THE NEURAL CORRELATES OF SEPARATION DISTRESS VOCALIZATIONS

Interestingly, one of these two regions, the ACC, which is clearly implicated in pain distress, also contributes to separation distress vocalizations. Thus, in most mammalian species, infants emit distress vocalizations upon separation from the mother. These vocalizations are thought to reflect the distress of maternal-infant separation and serve the function of cueing the mother to retrieve the infant to end the separation. Along these lines it has been shown that lesioning the ACC (both dorsal and ventral portions) can reduce these distress vocalizations (Hadland, Rushworth, Gaffan, & Passingham, 2003; MacLean & Newman, 1988). Conversely, electrically stimulating the ACC leads to the spontaneous production of these vocalizations (Robinson, 1967; Smith, 1945). Although these same effects have not been observed for the anterior insula, other regions that play a role in pain processing—such as the periaqueductal gray (PAG)—are also known to contribute to distress vocalization production (Bandler & Shipley, 1994).

THE NEURAL CORRELATES OF SOCIAL PAIN IN HUMANS

Building on these prior findings, research has shown that the experience of social pain in humans relies on some of these same neural regions that contribute to pain distress in humans and separation distress behaviors in non-human mammals. In the first neuroimaging study of social exclusion (Eisenberger et al., 2003), participants were led to believe that they would be playing a virtual ball-tossing game ("Cyberball;" Williams et al., 2000) with two other individuals over the internet. In reality, participants played with a preset computer program. Over the course of the game, participants were included in one round of the game and excluded in another, when the two other "players" stopped throwing them the ball. When comparing neural activity during social exclusion with neural activity during social inclusion, participants showed significant activation in the dACC and anterior insula—regions often activated in response to the distress of physical pain. Moreover, individuals who reported feeling more social distress in response to the exclusion episode (e.g., "rejected," "disconnected") showed greater activity in the dACC, consistent with this region's role in tracking the subjective unpleasantness of physical pain experience.

Subsequent studies, using variations of the ball-tossing game described above, have produced similar findings. Thus, both our own group and others have found that greater self-reported social distress in response to social exclusion (using Cyberball) was associated with greater activity in the dACC (Eisenberger, Taylor, Gable, Hilmert, & Lieberman, 2007b; Onoda et al., 2009) and anterior insula (DeWall, Masten, Powell, Combs, Schurtz & Eisenberger, 2012; Masten, Eisenberger, Borofsky, Pfeifer, McNealy, & Dapretto, 2009). Moreover, individual difference factors that typically moderate responses to social exclusion (e.g., social support, anxious attachment, self-esteem) show the expected relationships with neural activity. Individuals with more social support or who spend more time with friends showed reduced activity in the dACC and anterior insula in response to social exclusion (Eisenberger et al., 2007b; Masten, Telzer, Fuligni, Lieberman, & Eisenberger, 2012). Conversely, individuals who scored higher in anxious attachment, the tendency to worry about rejection from close others, showed increased activity in the dACC and anterior insula in response to social exclusion (DeWall et al., 2012). Similarly, individuals with lower self-esteem (vs. higher self-esteem) reported feeling more hurt in response to social exclusion and showed greater activity in the dACC (Onoda et al., 2010). Finally, individuals who reported feeling more socially rejected or disconnected in their real-world social interactions (assessed daily across a 10-day period) showed greater activity in the dACC and PAG in response to social exclusion (Eisenberger, Gable, & Lieberman, 2007a), suggesting a link between real-world experiences of social rejection and pain-related neural activation.

Importantly, recent work has shown that social and physical pain experiences activate overlapping pain-related neural regions (Kross, Berman, Mischel, Smith, Wager, 2011). In this study, participants who were recently rejected by a romantic relationship partner completed two tasks in the functional MRI (fMRI) scanner: (1) a social pain task, in which they were asked to think back to their relationship rejection experience, and (2) a physical pain task, in which they received painful heat stimulation. Results demonstrated overlapping neural activity in the dACC and anterior insula in response to both the social and physical pain tasks. Interestingly, this study also demonstrated overlapping neural activity in regions known to process the sensory component of physical pain (secondary somatosensory cortex; posterior insula). Future work will be needed to further examine the extent

to which the sensory component of pain is involved in social pain experience.

In addition to social exclusion and rejection, negative social evaluation activates these pain-related regions as well. For example, in a recent study (Eisenberger, Inagaki, Muscatell, Haltom, & Leary, 2011), participants were told that they were in a study of first impressions and that another subject (who was actually a confederate) would serve as an evaluator—providing the participant with some feedback on an interview that he/she completed earlier. While participants were in the scanner, they viewed a display, which they believed was controlled by the evaluator. Every 10 seconds, participants saw a new feedback word appear on the screen to indicate the evaluator's ongoing impression of the participant's interview (the feedback was the same for each participant). These feedback words were preselected to be interpreted as rejecting (e.g., "boring"), neutral (e.g., "spontaneous"), or positive (e.g., "intelligent"). Participants were also asked to rate how they felt in response to each new feedback word by pressing one of four buttons ranging from 1-very bad to 4-very good. Results demonstrated, not surprisingly, that participants felt significantly worse following the rejecting feedback. Moreover, to the extent that participants reported feeling worse in response to the feedback words, they showed greater activity in both the dACC and bilateral insula.

In addition to studies examining the neural correlates underlying the experience of social exclusion or negative social evaluation, studies using rejection-themed images or facial expressions have shown similar effects. For example, in response to viewing rejection-themed images (paintings by Edward Hopper) versus acceptance-themed images (paintings by August Renoir), participants showed significant activation in both the dACC and anterior insula (Kross, Egner, Ochsner, Hirsch, & Downey, 2007). Moreover, in a separate study, individuals who scored higher in rejection sensitivity showed greater dACC activity in response to viewing videos of individuals making disapproving facial expressions—a potential cue of social rejection (Burklund, Eisenberger, & Lieberman, 2007). Thus, the dACC and anterior insula may be responsive, not only to the experience of rejection, but also to cues that represent or signal social rejection (or the possibility of social rejection).

Finally, other types of socially painful experiences, such as bereavement, also activate pain-related neural regions. Thus, bereaved participants who viewed pictures of their deceased first-degree relative (vs. pictures of a stranger) showed greater activity in the dACC and anterior insula (Gündel, O'Connor, Littrell, Fort, & Richard, 2003). A subsequent study replicated these findings, showing that bereaved individuals experiencing either normal or complicated grief evidenced greater activity in the dACC and anterior insula in response to viewing images of the deceased (O'Connor et al., 2008). Thus, various types of socially painful experiences—including bereavement—may activate pain-related neural regions as well.

SUMMARY

The research reviewed here provides initial support for the hypothesis that physical and social pain processes overlap by demonstrating that experiences of social pain activate neural regions involved in processing the unpleasantness of physical pain. A second way of investigating the physical–social pain overlap is by exploring some of the expected consequences of such an overlap.

Consequences of a Physical–Social Pain Overlap

To the extent that physical and social pain processes rely on shared neural substrates, there should be several consequences of this shared circuitry. First, because both physical and social pain are governed by some of the same underlying neural circuitry, individuals who are more sensitive to one kind of pain should also be more sensitive to the other. Second, because altering one type of pain should alter the underlying neural system that supports both types of pain experience, factors that either increase or decrease one type of pain should alter the other type of pain in a similar manner (see Fig. 15.1). Here, I will review evidence for each of these hypothesized consequences of a physical–social pain overlap. I will then discuss several other possible consequences of a physical–social pain overlap that have remained largely unexplored.

Consequence #1: Individuals who are more sensitive to one kind of pain should also be more sensitive to the other.

On the surface, physical pain sensitivity and social pain sensitivity seem like very different constructs; how much it hurts when we break a bone appears to share minimal similarity with how much our heart aches following a relationship breakup. However, to the extent that these pain processes rely on shared neural substrates, it should follow that individuals who are more sensitive to one kind of pain should

be more sensitive to the other as well. To examine this, we have explored whether baseline sensitivity to physical pain relates to self-reported sensitivity to social rejection (Eisenberger, Jarcho, Lieberman, & Naliboff, 2006). In this study, participant's baseline sensitivity to physical pain was assessed by asking participants to rate the temperature at which they perceived a painful heat stimulus delivered to their forearm to be very unpleasant ("pain threshold"). After this, participants played one round of the Cyberball game in which they were socially excluded and were then asked to rate how much social distress they felt in response. Consistent with our hypothesis, individuals who were more sensitive to physical pain at baseline (e.g., lower baseline pain thresholds) were also more socially distressed by the social exclusion episode. Moreover, this relationship remained significant after controlling for neuroticism, suggesting that this relationship cannot be explained solely by a general tendency to report higher levels of negative experience.

A second way that we have explored this consequence is by examining whether a genetic correlate of physical pain sensitivity, specifically the mu-opioid receptor gene (OPRM1), relates to social pain sensitivity as well (Way, Taylor, & Eisenberger, 2009). Previous research has shown that a polymorphism in the mu-opioid receptor gene (OPRM1; A118G) is associated with physical pain sensitivity, such that individuals with the variant G allele tend to experience more physical pain and need more morphine to deal with pain (Chou et al., 2006a-b; Coulbault et al., 2006). Here, we examined whether this polymorphism was also related to social pain sensitivity.

To do this, participants (n = 125) were genotyped for the OPRM1 gene and were asked to complete a self-report measure of trait sensitivity to rejection (Mehrabian Sensitivity to Rejection Scale; Mehrabian, 1976; e.g., "I am very sensitive to any signs that a person might not want to talk to me"). Following this, a subset of these participants (n = 30) completed the Cyberball game in the scanner; neural activity was assessed while they were socially included and then excluded. Results demonstrated that G allele carriers—previously shown to be more sensitive to physical pain—also reported significantly higher levels of rejection sensitivity. Moreover, neuroimaging analyses revealed that G allele carriers showed greater activity in the dACC and anterior insula in response to social exclusion. Thus, a genetic correlate of physical pain sensitivity related to both dispositional and neural sensitivity to social pain.

Consequence #2: Factors that increase or decrease one type of pain should affect the other in a similar manner.

A second consequence of a physical–social pain overlap is that factors that alter one type of pain experience should alter the other in a similar manner. Here, I review several studies that have examined: (1) *pain potentiation effects*, namely whether factors that increase social pain (e.g., social exclusion) also increase physical pain and whether factors that increase physical pain (e.g., inflammation) also increase social pain and (2) *pain regulation effects*, namely whether factors that reduce social pain (e.g., social support) also reduce physical pain and whether factors that reduce physical pain (e.g., Tylenol) also reduce social pain.

Social Pain Potentiation Effects

To begin to explore whether factors that increase social pain also increase physical pain, we investigated whether an experience of social exclusion increased sensitivity to experimental pain stimuli (Eisenberger et al., 2006). In this study, participants were randomly assigned to play a round of the Cyberball game in which they were either included or excluded. Then, while participants were either being included or excluded, an experimenter delivered three painful heat stimuli (customized to each participant's pain threshold) to their forearm and participants were asked to rate the unpleasantness of each stimulus. After the game concluded, participants rated how much social distress they felt in response to the Cyberball game. Although excluded individuals did not report higher pain ratings in response to the heat stimuli than included individuals, we found that, among excluded subjects, those who felt the most social distress also reported the highest pain ratings in response to the heat stimuli. Moreover, this effect remained after controlling for neuroticism, suggesting that the positive relationship between social distress and pain distress was not due solely to a greater tendency to report negative affect and could reflect a more specific relationship between physical and social pain processes. In addition, another study demonstrated increased physical pain sensitivity in response to being socially excluded (versus included) during a Cyberball game (Bernstein & Claypool, 2012). Thus, augmented sensitivity to one type of pain may relate to augmented sensitivity to the other.

It should be noted, however, that these findings are different from those of other studies that examined the effect of social exclusion (using a different manipulation) on physical pain sensitivity (Bernstein & Claypool, 2012; DeWall & Baumeister, 2006). Based on the observation that extreme pain or stress can result in temporary analgesia or numbness (Gear, Aley, & Levine, 1999), these studies examined whether extreme forms of social exclusion could lead to numbness, not only to negative social experiences but to physical pain as well. Indeed, in these studies, participants who were socially excluded by being told that they would be alone in the future (vs. those who were given no feedback or told that they would have satisfying relationships in the future) showed a reduction in physical pain sensitivity (Bernstein & Claypool, 2012; DeWall & Baumeister, 2006).

It is not yet clear why these studies observed different relationships between social exclusion and physical pain. One possible explanation for the difference might relate to the underlying nature of the pain system, such that mild pain (e.g., being excluded by strangers during the Cyberball game) augments pain sensitivity whereas more intense pain (e.g., being told that one will be alone in the future) leads to analgesia (Bernstein & Claypool, 2012; Gear et al., 1999; Price, 2000). Indeed there is some evidence for this possibility (Bernstein & Claypool, 2012). It is also possible that the "future alone" manipulation may have induced more depression-like affect, which in some cases has been associated with reduced experimental pain sensitivity (Adler & Gattaz, 1993; Dickens, McGowan, & Dale, 2003; Orbach, Mikulincer, King, Cohen, & Stein, 1997), whereas the Cyberball manipulation may have induced more anxiety-like affect, which has been linked with increased experimental pain sensitivity (Cornwall & Donderi, 1998; Lautenbacher & Krieg, 1994; Melzack & Wall, 1999). Future studies will be needed to determine the specific effects of experiences of social exclusion on physical pain.

Physical Pain Potentiation Effects

Few studies, to date, have investigated whether factors that increase physical pain also increase social pain, perhaps because of the counterintuitive nature of the hypothesis. However, we have recently investigated whether inflammatory activity, which is known to increase physical pain sensitivity, also increases social pain sensitivity. Inflammatory activity occurs in response to sickness or infection. Thus, upon detecting a foreign agent (e.g., bacteria), the immune system produces chemical messengers called proinflammatory cytokines, which both orchestrate an inflammatory response at the site of infection (signaling other immune cells to the area) and signal the brain to engage in certain behaviors to promote recovery and recuperation from illness (Maier & Watkins, 1998). One consequence of inflammatory activation is increased physical pain sensitivity, presumably to encourage rest and prevent further injury (Watkins & Maier, 2000).

To explore whether inflammatory activity also increases social pain experience, participants (n = 39) were randomly assigned to either receive placebo or endotoxin—a bacterial agent that safely increases inflammatory activity. Participants were then asked to report on their feelings of social disconnection (e.g., "I feel disconnected from others," "I feel overly sensitive around others [e.g., my feelings are easily hurt]") every hour for the next 6 hours. In addition, participants completed the Cyberball social exclusion task in the fMRI scanner during the time of peak cytokine response (2 hours post endotoxin infusion). Results revealed that participants exposed to endotoxin (vs. placebo) showed a greater increase over time in feelings of social disconnection (which resolved by the study's end) (Eisenberger, Inagaki, Mashal, & Irwin, 2010). Moreover, among subjects exposed to endotoxin, those who showed the largest increase in proinflammatory cytokines also showed the greatest neural activity in the dACC and anterior insula in response to social exclusion (Eisenberger, Inagaki, Rameson, Mashal, & Irwin, 2009), suggesting that heightened inflammatory activity is associated with heightened social pain sensitivity. Thus, inflammatory activation, known to increase physical pain sensitivity, also appears to increase feelings of social disconnection and social pain sensitivity.

Social Pain Regulation Effects

Although social support is typically assumed to reduce experiences of social pain (Eisenberger et al., 2007b; Masten et al., 2012), one direct corollary of the physical–social pain overlap is that social support may reduce physical pain as well. Indeed, a great deal of correlational research has already shown that individuals who have more social support tend to experience less physical pain across a wide array of domains, including during childbirth (Chalmers, Wolman, Nikodem, Gulmezoglu, & Hofmeyer, 1995; Kennell, Klaus, McGrath, Robertson, & Hinkley, 1991), following surgery (King, Reis, Porter, & Norsen, 1993; Kulik and Mahler, 1989), and during cancer (Zaza & Baine, 2002). However, from these correlational studies alone, it is not clear if social support directly reduces physical

pain or whether some third variable (e.g., extraversion) explains some of these effects. Thus, we have recently explored whether social support directly reduces pain experience in a causal manner.

To examine this question, female participants in long-term romantic relationships received a series of painful heat stimuli to their forearm as they completed several different experimental conditions, which included holding their partner's hand (social support) versus a stranger's hand or a squeezeball (control conditions) and viewing pictures of their partner (social support) versus pictures of a stranger or an object (control conditions). Analyses revealed that participants reported feeling significantly less pain in the social support conditions—when they were either holding their partner's hand or viewing a picture of their partner (Master, Eisenberger, Taylor, Naliboff, Shirinyan, & Lieberman, 2009). Indeed, this finding has now been replicated by our own group (Eisenberger, Master et al., 2011) as well as by independent investigators (Younger, Aron, Parke, Chatterjee, & Mackey 2010). Moreover, the pain relief associated with viewing pictures of a significant other was related to reduced activity in both the dACC and anterior insula (Eisenberger et al., 2011; Younger et al., 2010). Thus, simple reminders of one's social support figure may be capable of directly reducing the experience of physical pain, not just social pain.

Physical Pain Regulation Effects

Finally, we have examined whether factors that are typically thought to reduce physical pain, such as Tylenol, can also reduce social pain (DeWall et al., 2010). Here, participants were randomly assigned to take either a normal dose of Tylenol (1,000 mg) or placebo each day for 3 weeks. Every night, over this 3-week period, participants were asked to rate their daily "hurt feelings" (e.g., "Today, I rarely felt hurt by what other people said or did to me" (reverse-scored)). Results demonstrated that participants in the Tylenol condition showed a significant decrease in self-reported hurt feelings over time, whereas participants in the placebo condition showed no significant change. In fact, participants in the Tylenol group reported significantly lower daily hurt feelings than participants in the placebo group starting on Day 9 and continuing to the end of the study.

To further explore the neural mechanisms that might underlie these changes in self-reported hurt feelings, in a second study, participants were randomly assigned to take either Tylenol (this time

2,000 mg/day) or placebo each day for a 3-week period. Then, at the end of the 3 weeks, participants completed the Cyberball social exclusion task in the fMRI scanner. Consistent with the results from the first study, participants in the Tylenol condition showed significantly less activity in the dACC and anterior insula compared with subjects in the placebo condition, who showed normal increases in these regions. Thus Tylenol, typically thought of as a physical painkiller, appears to act as a "social painkiller" as well.

Other Consequences of a Physical–Social Pain Overlap?

There are several other possible consequences of a physical–social pain overlap that have not yet been directly explored through this lens. One of these may be the aggressive behaviors that are observed following both physical and social pain. One of the consequences of physical pain stimulation is aggressive behavior aimed at those presumably causing the pain, and this is well-documented in animals (Berkowitz, 1983, 1993). Indeed, aggressive responses to physical pain make sense as a way of protecting the self if one is in danger of being physically harmed. Interestingly, these same types of aggressive responses have also been documented in the context of social rejection (Leary, Twenge, & Quinlivan, 2006; Twenge, Baumeister, Tice, & Stucke, 2001), with individuals becoming more aggressive following social rejection. However, aggressive responses to rejection make less intuitive sense, as aggression is presumably not conducive to either protecting the self or mending social ties. One possible explanation for this counterintuitive finding, however, is that rejection-induced aggression may be a by-product of an adaptive response to physical pain, which was subsequently co-opted by the social pain system. In other words, although aggressive responses to rejection may be maladaptive in recreating social bonds, this response may reflect a conservation of a behavioral response that is adaptive following physical pain.

Another possible consequence of this overlap that has not yet been directly explored is the similar physiological stress responses that are observed in response to both physical threat and social threat. It is well known that physical threat induces physiological stress responses to mobilize energy and physical resources to deal with the threat (Taylor, 2003), and this makes good sense. Escaping a predator or navigating some other life-threatening situation may require a significant amount of physical energy

or it may require a redistribution of physiological responses to appropriately respond to the threat at hand (e.g., increased inflammatory activity to deal with possible injury or infection). However, recent work has shown that these same physiological stress responses are recruited in response to social threats as well, such as being socially evaluated (Dickerson, Gable, Irwin, Aziz, & Kemeny, 2009; Dickerson & Kemeny, 2004). Although this may not seem surprising to stress researchers who have witnessed these effects repeatedly, from a functional perspective, it makes little sense that the body would require significant energy resources or increased inflammatory activity to manage the stress of social evaluation. After all, how much physical energy is needed to give a public speech? Why would inflammatory activity be heightened in response to performing an evaluative task, which presumably carries little risk for infection or physical injury? However, if the threat of social rejection or social evaluation is interpreted by the brain in the same manner as the threat of physical harm, biological stress responses might be triggered to both for the simple reason that these two systems overlap.

Summary

The studies summarized here further support the hypothesis that physical and social pain processes overlap by shedding light on some of the expected functional consequences of such an overlap. Specifically, I have shown that individuals who are more sensitive to physical pain are also more sensitive to social pain and that factors that increase or decrease one type of pain increase or decrease the other in a parallel manner. In addition, as suggested here, there are likely many other functional consequences of such an overlap that have yet to be explored. Future research will be needed to further explore and uncover these effects.

Conclusions

The research reviewed here sheds light on why people use physical pain words to describe experiences of social pain. Indeed, there is now good evidence to suggest that the pain of social rejection may be more than just metaphorical, relying on some of the same neural circuitry that makes physical pain "distressing." One of the implications of these findings is that episodes of rejection or relationship dissolution can be just as damaging and debilitating to the person experiencing those events as episodes of physical pain. Thus, even though we may treat physical pain conditions more seriously and regard them as more valid ailments, the pain of social loss can be equally as distressing, as demonstrated by the activation of pain-related neural circuitry to social disconnection as well.

Of course, even though physical and social pain rely on shared neural circuitry, the neural substrates of physical and social pain certainly do not overlap completely. Intuitively, we know this to be true because we can differentiate between pain due to a relationship snub and pain due to physical injury. Moreover, research has identified specific differences between these two types of pain experience. For example, although individuals can easily relive the pain of previous relationship breakups or other socially painful events, it is much harder, and sometimes impossible to relive the pain of physical injury (Chen, Williams, Fitness, & Newton, 2008). Future work will be needed to further clarify the mechanisms that differentiate physical and social pain.

In the end, it is important to keep in mind that while painful in the short-term, feelings of distress and heartache following social exclusion or broken social relationships also serve an adaptive function, namely to ensure the maintenance of close social ties. Indeed, the inability to respond to broken social ties with pain-related responses may underlie certain disorders associated with social impairments, such as autism (Masten, Colich, Rudie, Bookheimer, Eisenberger, & Dapretto, 2011). Over the course of evolutionary history, avoiding social rejection and staying socially connected to others likely increased chances of survival. Hence, the experience of social pain, while distressing and hurtful in the short-term, is an evolutionary adaptation that promotes social bonding and ultimately survival.

References

Adler, G., & Gattaz, W. F. (1993). Pain perception threshold in major depression. *Biological Psychiatry, 15*, 687–689.

Apkarian, A. V., Bushnell, M. C., Treede, R.-D., & Zubieta, J.-K. (2005). Human brain mechanisms of pain perception and regulation in health and disease. *Journal of Pain, 9*, 463–484.

Axelrod, R., & Hamilton, W. D. (1981). The evolution of cooperation. *Science, 211*, 1390–1396.

Bandler, R., & Shipley, M. T. (1994). Columnar organization in the midbrain periaqueductal gray: Modules for emotional expression? *Trends in Neurosciences, 17*, 379–389.

Berkowitz, L. (1983). Aversively stimulated aggression: Some parallels and differences in research with animals and humans. *American Psychologist, 38*, 1135–1144.

Berkowitz, L. (1993). *Aggression: Its Causes, Consequences and Control.* Philadelphia: Temple University Press.

Bernstein, M. J., & Claypool, H. M. (2012). Social exclusion and pain sensitivity: Why exclusion sometimes hurts and sometimes numbs. *Personality and Social Psychology Bulletin, 38*, 185–196.

Berthier, M., Starkstein, S., Leiguardia, R., & Carrea, R. (1988). Asymbolia for pain: A sensory-limbic disconnection system. *Annals of Neurology, 24*, 41–49.

Burklund, L. J., Eisenberger, N. I., & Lieberman, M. D. (2007). Rejection sensitivity moderates dorsal anterior cingulate activity to disapproving facial expressions. *Social Neuroscience, 2*, 238–253.

Chalmers, B., Wolman, W. L., Nikodem, V. C., Gulmezoglu, A. M., & Hofmeyer, G. J. (1995). Companionship in labour: Do the personality characteristics of labour supporters influence their effectiveness? *Curationis, 18*, 77–80.

Chen, Z., Williams, K. D., Fitness, J., & Newton, N. (2008). When hurt won't heal: Exploring the capacity to relive social and physical pain. *Psychological Science, 19*, 789–795.

Chou, W.Y., Wang, C.-H., Liu, P.-H., Liu, C.-C., Tseng, C.-C., & Jawan, B. (2006b). Human opioid receptor A118G polymorphism, affects Intravenous patient-controlled analgesia morphine consumption after total abdominal hysterectomy. *Anesthesiology, 105*, 334–337.

Chou, W-Y., Yang, L.-C., Lu, H. F., Ko, J. Y., Wang, C. H., Lin, S. H. et al. (2006a). Association of mu-opiod receptor gene polymorphism (A118G) with variations in morphine consumption for analgesia after total knee arthroplasty. *Acta Anaesthesiol Scandanavica, 50*, 787–792.

Cornwall, A., & Donderi, D. C. (1988). The effect of experimentally induced anxiety on the experience of pressure pain. *Pain, 35*, 105–113.

Coulbault, L., Beaussier, M., Verstuyft, C., Weikmans, H., Dubert, L., Trégouet, D., et al. (2006). Environmental and genetic factors associated with morphine response in the postoperative period. *Pharmacogenetics and Genomics, 79*, 316–324.

DeWall, C. N., & Baumeister, R. F. (2006). Alone but feeling no pain: Effects of social exclusion on physical pain tolerance and pain threshold, affective forecasting, and interpersonal empathy. *Journal of Personality and Social Psychology, 91*, 1–15.

DeWall, C. N., MacDonald, G., Webster, G. D., Masten, C. L., Baumeister, R. F., Powell, C., Combs, D., Schurtz, D. R., Stillman, T. F., Tice, D. M., & Eisenberger, N. I. (2010). Tylenol reduces social pain: Behavioral and neural evidence. *Psychological Science, 21*, 931–937.

DeWall, C. N., Masten, C. L., Powell, C., Combs, D., Schurtz, D. R., & Eisenberger, N. I. (2012). Do neural responses to rejection depend on attachment style? An fMRI study. *Social Cognitive and Affective Neuroscience, 7*, 184–192.

Dickens, C., McGowan, L., & Dale, S. (2003). Impact of depression on experimental pain perception: a systematic review of the literature with meta-analysis. *Psychosomatic Medicine, 65*, 369–375.

Dickerson, S. S., Gable, S. L., Irwin, M. R., Aziz, N., & Kemeny, M. E. (2009). Social-evaluative threat and proinflammatory cytokine regulation: An experimental laboratory investigation. *Psychological Science, 20*, 1237–1244.

Dickerson, S. S., & Kemeny, M. E. (2004). Acute stressors and cortisol responses: A theoretical integration and synthesis of laboratory research. *Psychological Bulletin, 103*, 355–391.

Eisenberger, N. I. (2012a). The neural bases of social pain. Evidence for shared representations with physical pain. *Psychosomatic Medicine, 74*, 126–135.

Eisenberger, N. I. (2012b). The pain of social disconnection: examining the shared neural underpinnings of physical and social pain. *Nature Reviews Neuroscience, 13*, 421–434.

Eisenberger, N. I., Gable, S. L., & Lieberman, M. D. (2007a). fMRI responses relate to differences in real-world social experience. *Emotion, 7,* 745–754.

Eisenberger, N. I., Inagaki, T. K., Mashal, N. M., & Irwin, M. R. (2010). Inflammation and social experience: An inflammatory challenge induces feelings of social disconnection in addition to depressed mood. *Brain, Behavior, and Immunity, 24,* 558–563.

Eisenberger, N. I., Inagaki, T. K., Muscatell, K. A., Haltom, K. E. B., & Leary, M. R. (2011). The neural sociometer: Brain mechanisms underlying state self-esteem. *Journal of Cognitive Neuroscience, 23,* 3448–3455.

Eisenberger, N. I., Inagaki, T. K., Rameson, L., Mashal, N. M., & Irwin, M. R. (2009). An fMRI study of cytokine-induced depressed mood and social pain: The role of sex differences. *Neuroimage, 47,* 881–890.

Eisenberger, N. I., Jarcho, J. M., Lieberman, M. D., & Naliboff, B. D. (2006). An experimental study of shared sensitivity to physical pain and social rejection. *Pain, 126,* 132–138.

Eisenberger, N. I., & Lieberman, M. D. (2004). Why rejection hurts: The neurocognitive overlap between physical and social pain. *Trends in Cognitive Sciences, 8,* 294–300.

Eisenberger, N. I., & Lieberman, M. D. (2005). Broken hearts and broken bones: The neurocognitive overlap between social pain and physical pain. In K. D. Williams, J. P. Forgas, & von Hippel (Eds.), *The Social Outcast: Ostracism, Social Exclusion, Rejection, and Bullying* (pp. 109–127). New York: Cambridge University Press.

Eisenberger, N. I., Lieberman, M. D., & Williams, K. D. (2003). Does rejection hurt: An fMRI study of social exclusion. *Science, 302,* 290–292.

Eisenberger, N. I., Master, S. L., Inagaki, T. I., Taylor, S. E., Shirinyan, D., Lieberman, M. D., & Naliboff, B. (2011). Attachment figures activate a safety signal-related neural region and reduce pain experience. *Proceedings of the National Academy of Sciences, 108,* 11721–11726.

Eisenberger, N. I., Taylor, S. E., Gable, S. L., Hilmert, C. J., & Lieberman, M. D. (2007b). Neural pathways link social support to attenuated neuroendocrine stress responses. *Neuroimage, 35,* 1601–1612.

Foltz, E. L, & White, L. E., (1968). The role of rostral cingulotomy in "pain" relief. *International Journal of Neurology, 6,* 353–373.

Gear, R. W., Aley, K. O., & Levine, J. D. (1999). Pain-induced analgesia mediated by mesolimbic reward circuits. *The Journal of Neuroscience, 15,* 7175–7181.

Gündel, H., O'Connor, M.-F., Littrell, L., Fort, C., Richard, L. (2003). Functional Neuroanatomy of grief: An fMRI study. *Journal of Psychiatry, 160,* 1946–1953.

Hadland, K. A, Rushworth, M. F. S., Gaffan, D., & Passingham, R. E. (2003). The effect of cingulate lesions on social behaviour and emotion. *Neuropsychologia, 41,* 919–931.

Hebben, N. (1985). Toward the assessment of clinical pain. In G. M. Aronoff (Ed.), *Evaluation and Treatment of Chronic Pain.* Baltimore: Urban & Schwarzenburg (pp. 451–462).

Kennell, J., Klaus, M., McGrath, S., Robertson, S., & Hinkley, C. (1991). Continuous emotional support during labor in US hospital: A randomized control trial. *Journal of the American Medical Association, 265,* 2197–2201.

King, K. B., Reis, H. T., Porter, L. A., & Norsen, L. H. (1993). Social support and long-term recovery from coronary artery surgery: Effects on patients and spouses. *Health Psychology, 12,* 56–63.

Kulik, J. A., & Mahler, H. I. (1989). Social support and recovery from surgery. *Health Psychology, 8,* 221–238.

Kross, E., Berman, M. G., Mischel, W., Smith, E. E., & Wager, T. D. (2011). Social rejection shares somatosensory representations with physical pain. *Proceedings of the National Academy of Sciences, 108,* 6270–6275.

Kross, E., Egner, T., Ochsner, K., Hirsch, J., & Downey, G. (2007). *Journal of Cognitive Neuroscience, 19,* 945–956.

Lautenbacher, S., & Krieg, J. C. (1994). Pain perception in psychiatric disorders: a review of the literature. *Journal of Psychiatric Research, 28,* 109–122.

Leary, M. R., Twenge, J. M., & Quinlivan, E. (2006). Interpersonal rejection as a determinant of anger and aggression. *Personality and Social Psychology Review, 10,* 111–132.

MacDonald, G., & Leary, M. R. (2005). Why does social exclusion hurt? The relationship between social and physical pain. *Psychological Review, 131,* 202–223.

MacLean P. D., & Newman, J. D. (1988). Role of midline frontolimbic cortex in production of the isolation call of squirrel monkeys. *Brain Research, 45,* 111–123.

Maier, S. F., & Watkins, L. R. (1998). Cytokines for psychologists: Implications of bidirectional immune-to-brain communication for understanding behavior, mood, and cognition. *Psychological Review, 105,* 83–107.

Masten, C. L., Colich, N., Rudie, J., Bookheimer, S. Y., Eisenberger, N. I., & Dapretto, M. (2011). An fMRI investigation of responses to peer rejection in adolescents with autism spectrum disorders. *Developmental Cognitive Neuroscience, 1,* 260–270.

Masten, C. L., Eisenberger, N. I., Borofsky, L., Pfeifer, J. H., McNealy, K., & Dapretto, M. (2009). Neural correlates of social exclusion during adolescence: Understanding the distress of peer rejection. *Social Cognitive and Affective Neuroscience, 4,* 143–157.

Masten, C. L., Telzer, E. H., Fuligni, A., Lieberman, M. D. & Eisenberger, N. I. (2012). Time spent with friends in adolescence relates to less neural sensitivity to later peer rejection. *Social Cognitive and Affective Neuroscience, 7,* 106–114.

Master, S. L., Eisenberger, N. I., Taylor, S. E., Naliboff, B. D., Shirinyan, D., & Lieberman, M. D. (2009). A picture's worth: Partner photographs reduce experimentally induced pain. *Psychological Science, 20,* 1316–1318.

Mehrabian, A. (1976). Questionnaire measures of affiliative tendency and sensitivity to rejection. *Psychological Reports, 38,* 199–209.

Melzack, R., & Wall, D. (1999). *Textbook of Pain.* Edinburgh: Churchill Livingstone.

O' Connor, M. F., Wellisch, D. K., Stanton, A., Eisenberger, N. I., Irwin, M. R., & Lieberman, M. D. (2008). Craving love? Enduing grief activates brain's reward center. *NeruoImage, 42,* 969–972.

Onoda, K., Okamoto, Y, Nakashima, K, Nittono, H., Ura, M., & Yamawaki, S. (2009). Decreased ventral anterior cingulate cortex activity is associated with reduced social pain during emotional support. *Social Neuroscience, 4,* 443–454.

Onoda, K., Okamoto, Y., Nakashima, K, Nittoni, H., Yoshimura, S., Yamawaki, S., Yamaguchi, S., & Ura, M. (2010). Does low self-esteem enhance social pain? The relationships between trait self-esteem and anterior cingulate cortex activation induced by ostracism. *Social Cognitive and Affective Neuroscience, 5,* 383–391.

Orbach, I., Mikulincer, M., King, R., Cohen, D., Stein, D. (1997). Thresholds and tolerance of physical pain in suicidal and nonsuicidal adolescents. *Journal of Consulting and Clinical Psychology, 65*, 646–652.

Panksepp, J. (1998). *Affective Neuroscience.* New York: Oxford University Press.

Peyron, R., Laurent, B., & Garcia-Larrea, L. (2000). Functional imaging of brain responses to pain. A review and meta-analysis. *Neurophysiological Clinics, 30*, 263–288.

Price, D. D. (2000). Psychological and neural mechanisms of the affective dimension of pain. *Science, 288*, 1769–1772.

Rainville, P. (2002). Brain mechanisms of pain affect and pain modulation. *Current Opinion in Neurobilogy, 12*, 195–204.

Rainville, P., Duncan, G. H., Price, D. D., Carrier, B., & Bushnell, M. D. (1997). Pain affect encoded in human anterior cingulate but not somatosensory cortex. *Science, 277*, 968–971.

Richter, E. O., Davis, K. D., Hamani, C., Hutchison, W. D., Dostrovsky, J. O., Lozano, A. M. (2004). Cingulotomy for psychiatric disease: Microelectrode guidance, a callosal reference system for documenting lesion location, and clinical results. *Neurosurgery, 54*, 622–28.

Robinson, B. W., (1967). Neurological aspects of evoked vocalizations. In S. A. Altmann (Ed.), *Social Communication Among Primates* (pp. 135–147). Chicago: The University Press.

Schreckenberger, M., Siessmeier, T., Viertmann, A., Landvogt, C., Buchholz, H. -G., Rolke, R., et al. (2005). The unpleasantness of tonic pain is encoded by the insular cortex. *Neurology, 64*, 1175–1183.

Smith, W. (1945). The functional significance of the rostral cingular cortex as revealed by its responses to electrical excitation. *Journal of Neurophysiology, 8*, 241–255.

Taylor, S. E. (2003). *Health Psychology* (5th ed.). New York: McGraw Hill.

Tölle, T. R., Kaufmann, T., Siessmeier, T., Lautenbacher, S., Berthele, A., Munz, F., et al. (1999). Region-specific encoding of sensory and affective components of pain in the human brain: A positron emission tomography correlation analysis. *Annals of Neurology, 45*, 40–47.

Twenge, J. M., Baumeister, R. F., Tice, D. M., & Stucke, T. S, (2001). If you can't join them, beat them: Effects of social exclusion on aggressive behavior. *Journal of Personality and Social Psychology, 81*, 1058–1069.

Watkins, L. R., & Maier, S. F. (2000). The pain of being sick: Implications of immune-to-brain communication for understanding pain. *Annual Review of Psychology, 51*, 29–57.

Way, B. M., Taylor, S. E., & Eisenberger, N. I. (2009). Variation in the mu-opioid receptor gene (OPRM1) is associated with dispositional and neural sensitivity to social rejection. *Proceedings of the National Academy of Sciences, 106*, 15079–15084.

Williams, K. D., Cheung, C. K. T., & Choi, W. (2000). Cyberostracism: Effects of being ignored over the Internet. *Journal of Personality & Social Psychology, 79*, 748–762.

Younger, J., Aron, A., Parke, S., Chatterjee, N., & Mackey, S. (2010). Viewing pictures of a romantic partner reduces experimental pain: Involvement of neural reward systems. *PLoS One, 5*, e13309.

Zaza, C., & Baine, N. (2002). Cancer pain and psychosocial factors: A critical review of the literature. *Journal of Pain and Symptom Management, 24*, 526–542.

Social Pain

Terry K. Borsook *and* Geoff MacDonald

Abstract

The critical importance of social connectedness to human health and well-being is well established. There is now accumulating evidence that when a threat to this connectedness (i.e., social injury) occurs, a pain-like experience—social pain—can result. The first part of this chapter presents an up-to-date summary of animal and human brain imaging studies demonstrating an overlap in biological and neural systems mediating both social and physical pain. The second part reviews the literature examining the potential implications of this overlap, including the effect of reducing physical pain on social pain, the impact of social support on physical pain sensitivity, and the effects of socially painful events on physical pain perception. The chapter concludes with an exploration of what we believe are pressing issues and questions to be addressed in future research in the expanding field of social pain.

Key Words: exclusion, ostracism, pain, rejection, social

Introduction

Being socially excluded can feel awful. Being spurned by a love interest, turned down by a desired group, or grieving the loss of a loved one are all aversive experiences and can engender feelings of sadness, frustration, shame, and anger. But there is more to it. There is an element that distinguishes these types of experiences from other types of negative experiences: Social exclusion hurts. English speakers often use terms like "broken hearted," "hurt," and "wounded" to describe social disconnection. Indeed, across multiple languages, as diverse as Spanish, Hebrew, Mandarin, and Inuktitut, native speakers use terms that mean "hurt" or "injury" to describe the emotional reaction to social rejection (MacDonald and Leary, 2005).

If physical injury produces physical pain, then the result of social injury can be described as social pain (MacDonald, 2009). MacDonald and Leary (2005) define social pain as "a specific emotional reaction to the perception that one is being excluded from desired relationships or being devalued by desired relationship partners or groups. Exclusion may be a result of a number of factors, including rejection, death of a loved one, or forced separation." (p. 202). In other words, social pain is an emotionally aversive pain-like experience that occurs in reaction to a socially disconnecting event. But does the use of the word pain merely represent a convenient metaphor or are physical and social pain related more fundamentally?

The benefits of social connection and the repercussions of disconnection to human development, health, and survival are sweeping and profound. Beginning in infancy, all mammals depend on a bond with caregivers to survive (Bowlby, 1969) and many behavioral and regulatory functions critical to survival throughout life are forged in early years through interactions with caregivers and others in the child's social milieu (Bowlby, 1969; 1973; 1980; Schore, 1994, 2003). This social impact is by no means limited to the early years and continues throughout the lifespan. Numerous epidemiological studies have shown that socially isolated people are 2 to 3 times more likely to die in a given time period (Seeman, 1996; House, Landis, Umberson, 1988). People who perceive high levels of social support enjoy numerous health benefits (Uchino, 2006; Reblin & Uchino, 2008), including antibody response to flu immunization (Pressman et al., 2005), survival following myocardial infarction (Rodriguez-Artalajo et al., 2006; Schmaltz et al., 2007), and postoperative pain and recovery (Mitchinson et al., 2008). A recent review of data from the massive Framingham Heart Study showed that if a close friend becomes obese (or smokes), it increases the chance of becoming obese (or smoking) oneself by some 50%. Consider that the World Health Organization definition of health has encompassed the social sphere since 1948, stating that health is "a state of complete physical, mental and *social well-being* and not merely the absence of disease or infirmity" (italics added). It is perhaps because of the extensive influence of relationships on health and survival that the human need for belonging and acceptance is so strong (Baumeister & Leary, 1995). Humans evolved to depend not just on the operation of systems within the body but also on the interplay between the individual as a whole and the social systems surrounding the individual.

Given the immense and widespread impact of social factors on human health, social disconnection would pose a formidable menace. Therefore, some neurophysiological machinery may have evolved to efficiently recognize and react to threats of exclusion, as well as motivate measures aimed at preventing and repairing social injury. Because physical pain serves exactly this function in the case of physical injury, it seems that pain would make an ideal candidate for this purpose (Eisenberger & Lieberman, 2004; MacDonald & Leary, 2005; Panksepp, 1998, 2010).

This chapter investigates the notion of social pain by examining the evidence for links between the pain resulting from physical injury and the pain-like agony that can follow social exclusion. To understand why and how pain might serve as a regulator of social inclusion, it would be helpful to look more closely at the nature of pain. What is pain and what is its function?

What is Pain?

Pain is immensely powerful. It can cripple, paralyze, and instill raw fear. But it is also remarkably useful. Pain signals the presence or threat of injury and is a mechanism of self-preservation. Its considerable ability to capture attention makes it difficult to ignore, and its aversiveness strongly motivates reactions aimed at its reduction. So feared is pain that people may go to great lengths to avoid feelings of pain, even if it means also sacrificing considerable benefits, such as when individuals avoid going to the dentist although they know it is necessary (Berggren & Meynert, 1984). Although pain is unpleasant, it is difficult to imagine being able to survive without it. Individuals born without the ability to feel pain, or who feel pain sensation but experience it as nonaversive, suffer continual injuries, amputations of limbs, loss of vision, and a shortened lifespan (Nagasako, Oaklander, & Dworkin, 2003).

Pain is notoriously subjective and private and has so far proven very difficult to index with objective measures such as blood, urine, or even brain imaging tests. Even novel methods such as those that detect facial muscle activity (Craig, 1992) have been of limited use. Indeed, pain's inherently subjective and private nature can exacerbate feelings of isolation for those whose pain cannot be explained medically, potentially leading to social pain. Far from being a linear function of tissue damage, pain is a highly complex phenomenon, consisting of multiple facets, involving numerous neural circuits, as well as the endocrine and immune systems (Benarroch, 2001; Chapman, Tuckett, & Song, 2008). Pain is impacted by a plethora of contextual (e.g., beliefs, expectation), cognitive (e.g., attention), mood, chemical, memory, and genetic factors (Tracey & Mantyh, 2007), and prompts a multitude of protective (nocifensive), affective, cognitive, and behavioral responses.

A very widely cited current definition of pain states that "pain is an unpleasant sensory and emotional experience associated with actual or potential tissue damage, or described in terms of such damage" (Merskey & Bogduk, 1994, p. 210). The reference to "sensory and emotional experience" suggests that pain is regarded as having two components: sensory and affective. The sensory aspect refers to location and qualities of the sensation (e.g., throbbing or stabbing intense pain in the right big toe). The affective component refers to the emotional aspect of the experience—how unpleasant, irritating, or distressing the pain experience is. The distinctiveness of these two dimensions has been demonstrated in numerous ways. For example, each dimension can be impacted independently as a result of changes in nociceptive stimulus intensity and psychological factors (Price, Harkins, & Baker, 1987; Price, 1999). Second, hypnotic suggestions can separately target each dimension (Rainville, Carrier, Hofbauer,

Bushnell & Duncan, 1999). Finally, pain sensation and pain unpleasantness are reliably mediated by distinct neural systems (Rainville, Duncan, Price, Carrier, & Bushnell, 1997; Tölle et al., 1999).

Although the physical sensations associated with physical pain are often quite different from those associated with social pain, the affective component may be more similar. As a result, it is the emotional aspect of a socially distressing experience to which the term social pain has been applied. MacDonald and Leary (2005) have suggested that social pain is actually one form of emotional pain and that the affective responses to physical trauma are themselves a subcategory of emotional pain (MacDonald & Leary, 2005). Emotional pain can arise when some harm or loss has occurred to the individual. Just as physical pain arises from physical injury, social pain may arise from social injury. Social pain, then, has been conceptualized primarily as the emotional distress that arises in the event of social harm or loss. Although it is possible that social pain may be found to vary along sensory dimensions such as pain quality (throbbing, stabbing) and location (stomach, chest), the sensory component of social pain is currently poorly understood, and at the phenomenonological level, seemingly differs from the sensory aspect of physical pain. Further research is necessary to identify the contribution of sensory elements to the experience of social pain.

Among the first lines of evidence supporting the notion of social pain there is research showing that opioids, a key player in physical pain modulation systems, also play a pivotal role in modulating social distress. It is to this research that we turn next.

Overlapping Biochemical Systems—Opioids

The opioid system is intimately and extensively involved in regulating physical pain. For example, opiate drugs such as morphine, which mimic the action of endogenous opioids, are currently considered to be among the most powerful and effective analgesic drugs available for the treatment of moderate to severe pain (Bie & Pan, 2007; Fine & Portenoy, 2004).

Not long after the discovery of the opioid system in the brain, a series of studies by Jaak Panksepp and colleagues showed that the administration of morphine calmed distress cries emitted by socially separated animals (Herman & Panksepp, 1978; Panksepp, Herman, Conner, Bishop, & Scott, 1978; Panksepp, Vilberg, Bean, Coy, & Kastin, 1978; Panksepp, Herman, Vilberg, Bishop, &

DeEskinazi, 1980; but see Winslow and Insel, 1991). An opiate drug, long known as a physical pain analgesic, also dulled social pain. In one study, for example, Herman and Panksepp (1978) segregated infant guinea pigs from their mothers and placed the infants in a pen by themselves for 15 minutes each day over a period of 2 to 3 weeks. Such an involuntary separation from the mother typically provokes distress vocalizations (DVs) in young animals. When injected with the mu-opioid agonist morphine sulfate, however, the isolated guinea pigs emitted significantly fewer DVs compared with animals given a saline injection, while having no effect on overall activity. The effect was dose dependent; higher doses of opioids led to fewer DVs. These results were subsequently replicated in several studies (Herman & Panksepp, 1978, 1981; Keverne et al., 1997; Panksepp, 1998; Panksepp, Herman, Conner, Bishop, & Scott, 1978) and with different animals, including rats (Carden, Hernandez, & Hofer, 1996; Carden & Hofer, 1990b; Kehoe & Blass, 1986; Kehoe & Boylan, 1994), primates (Kalin, Shelton, & Barksdale, 1988; Keverne et al., 1989), dogs (Panksepp, Herman, Conner, Bishop, & Scott, 1978), and birds (Panksepp, Vilberg, Bean, Coy, & Kastin, 1978). Over the course of the evolutionary history of an organism, features that evolved to serve one function may later be co-opted to serve another, a process known as *exaptation*. Panksepp conjectured that systems mediating both physical and social pain overlapped and since socially complex mammals appeared relatively recently in evolutionary history, the social distress system may have exapted the more evolutionarily ancient physical pain system to signal social disconnection (Panksepp, 1998).

A different line of research has found that opioids are centrally involved in the diminished pain sensitivity (hypoalgesia) observed concomitant with social isolation (Kehoe & Blass, 1986b; Naranjo & Fuentes, 1985; Puglisi-Allegra & Oliverio, 1983). For example, in one study (Puglisi-Allegra & Oliverio, 1983), mice were either separated or housed in groups of six for a period of 8 weeks. In addition, some were subjected to immobilization stress or no stress and some received morphine or saline. The socially isolated mice demonstrated a higher nociceptive threshold (lower pain sensitivity) in response to painful heat stimuli than the grouped mice. This effect was diminished with injection of naloxone (a mu-opioid antagonist), implying that the isolation-induced hypoalgesia was opioid-mediated. Most importantly, administration of morphine had no effect on isolated mice though it did decrease pain sensitivity in the grouped mice. Taken together, social isolation modulates physical pain sensitivity via opioid systems and the chronic activation of the opioid system (induced by long-term social isolation) may reduce opioid receptor binding (Schenk, Britt, Atalay, & Charleson, 1982). If applicable to humans, these results have important clinical implications and suggest yet another way by which social and physical pain are linked: chronic social pain may induce changes in opioid receptor binding that may compromise both an individual's endogenous physical pain modulation system operation as well as responsiveness to opiate drugs such as morphine.

In sum, the finding that opiates can calm social distress in animals, together with the finding that opioids mediate social threat-induced hypoalgesia and that chronic exposure to social threats impairs responsiveness to opiate drugs administered to relieve physical pain, provide persuasive evidence that opioids play a key role in linking both types of pain experience. A biochemical overlap implies that a neural overlap is likely but more direct evidence is required. The next two sections explore this evidence.

Overlapping Neural Systems

Our understanding of how neural systems participate in the pain experience has expanded dramatically over the past decade with the application of technologies such as positron emission tomography and functional MRI that enable the relatively noninvasive observation of responses in the intact human brain (Perl, 2007). Studies employing these imaging systems have led to the discovery of a number of anatomically distinct brain regions that are reliably related to the processing of acute physical pain (Apkarian, Bushnell, Treede, & Zubieta, 2005; Peyron, Laurent, & Garcia-Larrea, 2000; Tracey & Mantyh, 2007). These areas include bilateral secondary somatosensory cortex (SII), anterior insular cortex (AIC), anterior cingulate cortex (ACC), contralateral thalamus, the primary somatosensory cortex (S1), and the dorsolateral prefrontal cortex. These findings are corroborated by results from studies employing pharmacologically-induced hypoalgesia, which have shown effects predominantly in these areas (Casey et al., 2000; Geha et al., 2007; Wagner et al., 2007; Wise et al., 2002, 2004). The numerous regions showing reliable links to acute physical pain episodes are often referred to collectively as the *pain matrix*, and reflect the rich and multidimensional nature of the pain experience.

Evidence in support of a social/physical pain neural overlap would therefore need to show that socially injurious events lead to neural responses that are similar to those occurring following physical injury. The first study examining neural responses to exclusion experiences in humans was work by Eisenberger, Lieberman, and Williams (2003). In their study, participants were asked to undergo fMRI brain scanning while playing a video ball-toss game (Cyberball) with two other players. Relative to periods of inclusion, exclusion from play midway through the game was associated with an increase in dorsal anterior cingulate cortex (dACC), insular cortex (IC), and right ventrolateral prefrontal cortex (RVPFC) activity. Higher levels of self-reported distress were associated with greater activity in the dACC and less activity in the RVPFC, but they were not related to IC activity. Meditational analyses showed that the RVPFC acts to diminish feelings of social distress through inhibition of dACC activity. A comparison condition in which participants were excluded due to a technical glitch (implicit exclusion) was associated with greater dACC activity but not with any change in RVPFC activity, perhaps because feelings of exclusion were not of sufficient magnitude to prompt self-regulatory responses. The researchers suggest that their results indicate an overlap in the neural circuitry serving both physical and social pain.

Eisenberger, Gable, and Lieberman (2007) asked participants to record how connected and accepted they felt during social interactions throughout the day over the course of 10 days. After this experience sampling period, participants engaged in a Cyberball task while being scanned with fMRI. The neural response to an exclusion experience in the scanner (exclusion from Cyberball play) was an excellent indicator of the tendency to experience social distress in daily living. Specifically, individuals who showed greater activity in the left dACC during the Cyberball game reported significantly higher levels of distress during daily social interactions (as well as greater distress in response to the Cyberball game). Greater activity in the amygdala and left periaqueductal gray also predicted daily social distress but not distress in response to the Cyberball game.

Burklund, Eisenberger, and Lieberman (2007) used fMRI to compare neural responses to brief video clips of disapproving, angry, and disgusted facial expressions in young, healthy adults. There was increased activity in the amygdala in response to exposure to all three facial expressions (compared with fixation), but disapproval faces provoked greater amygdala activity than anger, implying that disapproving faces can be as threatening as anger, if not more so. Contrary to their predictions, however, disapproval faces in general provoked no greater (or lesser) levels of dACC activity. The authors did find that people with higher scores on a measure of rejection sensitivity responded to disapproving (but not other) faces with greater dACC activation (but not other limbic areas), as well as reduced activation in the ventromedial prefrontal cortex (VMPFC; a region that has been associated with the regulation of responses to threatening situations).

In sum, advances in imaging brain function in the living human brain have provided the opportunity to peer in on the neural activity that occurs during exposure to painful events. The research discussed in this chapter provides some preliminary evidence that there are commonalities among neural circuits involved in mediating the experience of both acute physical and social pain. If there is in fact an overlap, one implication is that any interventions targeting one type of pain should also, by some means, act to influence the other type of pain. In the next section we examine evidence that a widely used over-the-counter analgesic may also quell the pain of social injury.

Effect of Reducing Physical Pain on Social Pain

One implication of an overlap in the neural substrates of both social and physical pain is that any factor that decreases one type of pain should decrease the other type. A recent study by DeWall et al. (2010) sought to investigate whether a widely used physical pain reliever, acetaminophen, would soothe the sting of social pain. In one experiment, DeWall et al (2010) randomly assigned participants to receive either 1,000 mg/day of acetaminophen (Tylenol) or placebo over a period of 21 days. Each evening participants recorded in a diary the degree to which they experienced social pain by answering questions such as "Today, being teased hurt my feelings" and "Today, I rarely felt hurt by what other people said or did to me." The researchers discovered that whereas individuals receiving the placebo reported no change in hurt feelings, individuals taking the acetaminophen reported a significant decline in hurt feelings over the course of the study. In a second experiment, participants were randomly assigned to consume 2,000 mg/day of acetaminophen or a placebo for 21 days, then were scanned using fMRI as they experienced social exclusion in the context of a Cyberball game. DeWall et al. found that, compared with those taking placebo, participants who had taken acetaminophen showed significantly less activity in the dACC and bilateral anterior insula during an exclusion event versus inclusion. Therefore, acetaminophen, a drug typically taken to ease physical pain, was found to calm the hurt brought on by everyday social events. Moreover, following an acute exclusion event, acetaminophen decreased neural activity in brain areas previously linked to social pain. This research has shown that interventions that typically calm physical pain have the potential to also calm the hurt of social disconnectedness. We next turn to the question of what happens to physical pain under conditions of strengthened social connectedness.

Social Support and Physical Pain Sensitivity

According to Panksepp (2010), social environments may be cause for pain but they also provide a powerful resource for coping with pain. There is evidence that feelings of social connectedness and support can have a beneficial impact on physical pain. For example, social support has been found to be negatively associated with the pain of childbirth (Klaus et al., 1986), postoperative pain (Kulik & Mahler, 1989; Mitchinson et al., 2008), and clinical opiate use (Mitchinson et al., 2008). Most of this research, however, is correlational and therefore it is not possible to know whether social support eases pain or people experiencing lower levels of pain are able to garner (or at least perceive) more social support.

In one of the first experimental studies examining the effects of social support on pain, Brown, Sheffield, and Robinson (2003) asked young adults to plunge an arm into painfully cold ice water (the cold-pressor task). Participants performed this task either alone or with the companionship of a friend or stranger. Companions were instructed to provide active support (engaging in the task as much as possible), passive support (quiet, making little eye contact), or interaction support (interacting with the partner as much or little as they wished). Brown and colleagues found that that recipients of active and passive support reported less physical pain than their counterparts performing the task either alone or with interaction support. The researchers suggest that the reason that the interaction support group failed to show a hypoalgesic effect similar to what was achieved under the active and passive support conditions is because negative transactions may have occurred that undermined the benefits of any positive support. The data support the conclusion that physically painful stimuli can be made less painful in the presence of a consistently socially supportive companion compared with the person who must endure it alone.

While Brown, Sheffield, Leary, and Robinson (2003) demonstrated the consequences of one type of socially connecting experience (the presence of a supportive companion) on physical pain processing, Master et al. (2009) extended this research by investigating the effects of two other forms of socially connecting experiences on physical pain. In their study, women in long-term romantic relationships were invited to the lab with their partners. Participants placed an arm behind an opaque curtain and this arm was then exposed to a series of thermal stimuli under several different conditions: while holding the hand of the partner (who sat behind a curtain), holding the hand of a male stranger, holding an object, viewing the partner's photo, viewing a photo of the male stranger, viewing photos of an object (chair), and viewing a fixation crosshair. Half the thermal stimulations induced low pain, whereas half induced high pain. Participants rated the unpleasantness of each stimulation. The researchers found that holding the partner's hand led to significantly lower pain ratings than holding an object or holding a stranger's hand. A similar pattern of findings emerged in the case of the photographs. Viewing a partner's photo led to significantly lower pain ratings compared with viewing photos of an object or of the stranger. Thus, being primed with photos of a loved one may be sufficient to activate associated mental representations of being loved and supported and thus reduce reactivity to pain.

In a somewhat different approach, Eisenberger, Taylor, Gable, Hilmert, and Lieberman (2007) used an experience sampling methodology to record the degree to which participants felt socially supported at several times throughout the day over a period of 10 days. Subsequently, participants were placed in an fMRI scanner and played a game of Cyberball in which they were excluded from play at a certain point. Cortisol reactivity to a social stressor (speech and mental arithmetic in front of an evaluative audience) was assessed prior to the daily experience sampling. The researchers found that during the Cyberball rejection event, two brain regions were related to daily levels of social support as well as cortisol reactivity. Specifically, higher levels of reported daily social support were associated with attenuated cortisol reactivity and with lower levels of activity in the dACC and B 8 (a subregion of the prefrontal cortex known to be associated with emotional

distress) within the context of the Cyberball social rejection. They further found that this relationship between high daily social support and cortisol reactivity in the face of the social stressor, was mediated by individual differences in dACC and BA 8 reactivity. The inverse relationship between social support and neural and neuroendocrine reactivity to a stressful event suggests that stressors somehow have a diminished effect in people who experience higher levels of social support compared with those with lower levels of social support.

In sum, these studies provide converging evidence that social support curtails both the experience of pain and neural signatures known to be positively associated with pain. The next section examines another way by which social experience influences physical pain, this time when social connectedness is threatened.

Effects of Acute Social Pain on Physical Pain Experience

With human health being so extensively influenced by social relationships, social injury (e.g., loss, rejection, failure to connect) may be processed as menacing in a fashion similar to physical injury. When facing an imminent threat, the body responds by discharging a host of physiological measures aimed at facilitating survival—the so-called flight-fight-freeze (FFF) response (Bracha et al, 2004). These measures include elevating heart rate, quickening respiration, dilating pupils, interrupting digestion, and increasing sweating. The FFF response also typically involves hypoalgesia, a reduction in pain sensitivity, because pain would be counterproductive if it prevents an organism from surviving a threat. For example, prey displaying behaviors reflecting injury would be preferred by predators. Evolution, therefore, may have favored animals that expressed stress-induced hypoalgesia under threatening situations (Butler & Finn, 2009). This phenomenon of threat-induced hypoalgesia has been very well established in the literature using animal models (e.g., Amit & Galina, 1986; Butler & Finn, 2009). Endogenous hypoalgesic responses have been witnessed in mice as a result of exposure to numerous nonsocial stressors such as foot shocks (Chesher & Chan 1977), food restriction (Wideman et al, 1996), and restraint (Costa et al, 2005). Threat-induced hypoalgesia has been observed in humans upon exposure to spiders among spider-phobics (Janssen & Arntz, 1996), virtual reality game playing (Hoffman et al, 2001), mental arithmetic (Flor & Grüsser, 1999), and electric shock (Rhudy & Meager, 2000, 2003). For example, Rhudy and Meager (2000) randomly assigned participants to three emotion-induction conditions: they provoked fear in some participants by exposing them to a painful electric shock, anxiety in others through the threat of shock, and did nothing to the third group. They found that the fear elicited by exposure to the shock caused a significant increase in pain threshold whereas the anxiety prompted by threat of shock led to an increase in pain reactivity.

For many social animals, especially humans, social defeat, loss, and exclusion may be among the most critical threats to safety of all. If so, such threats may well trigger FFF responses. Research on nonhuman animals has indeed revealed analgesic responses to a range of social stressors including social isolation (Puglisi-Allegra & Oliverio, 1983), defeat experiences (Kavaliers, 1988), and social conflict (Rodgers & Hendrie, 1983). Just as with FFF responses to physical threats, then, one response to exclusion may be the activation of endogenous pain modulation systems. Thus, we submit that the occurrence of a socially painful event presents a potent threat in and of itself, which is capable of provoking the same response that any acute threat would—the invocation of the body's stress response—with the result being the modulation of physical pain. In short, social injury should provoke a social threat-induced hypoalgesia.

Social threat has been shown to promote hypoalgesia in humans. Some participants in a study by DeWall and Baumeister (2006) were randomly assigned to receive false feedback that they would live a life marked by social isolation (friends would drift away, marriages would be short-lived). Other participants were either told that they would enjoy stable, rewarding relationships throughout life or that they would become increasingly accident prone. The group receiving the dire prediction of a life alone reported significantly higher pain thresholds and greater pain tolerance (i.e., lower pain sensitivity) relative to those not receiving this grim forecast. Although a reliable hypoalgesic effect of social disconnection was uncovered, the manipulation used in this study was arguably so severe that the results may not generalize to the kinds of experiences people are likely to encounter in daily life and therefore prompts the question, "Is such a strong shock required to produce hypoalgesia, or might reduced pain sensitivity occur as a consequence of somewhat more everyday social interactions?"

To investigate this question we asked healthy, pain-free undergraduates to work with a partner on a structured social task that entailed taking turns answering questions about themselves (Borsook & MacDonald, 2010). Though the partner posed as another participant, she was in fact an experimental confederate instructed to behave in one of two ways. For the participants randomly assigned to the negative encounter condition, the confederate's behavior was standoffish. She smiled infrequently, made little eye contact, used a closed body posture, and kept her answers brief. For the positive encounter group, the confederate showed great interest in the participant, used affirmative phrases ("I agree with you," "Absolutely true!"), smiled often and made frequent eye contact. A control group was asked to privately think about answers to the personal questions. We found that participants exposed to the negative social encounter with the confederate reported significantly lower pain intensity and unpleasantness after the exchange relative to baseline, whereas the positive exchange and no-interaction control groups presented no change in pain ratings. The social hypoalgesic effect observed in our study is consistent with prior research (e.g., DeWall & Baumeister, 2006) yet was achieved via a considerably more naturalistic social experience, suggesting that social hypoalgesia may be a relatively common event in daily life.

Given the extensive importance of the social network to human health and survival, it seems reasonable to expect that damage to this network may very well pose a considerable threat. Acute social injury and the resulting social pain should therefore be regarded as threats, potentially provoking a physiological response, including hypoalgesia, just as would any other perceived threat. Results from studies in our own lab as well as others have support this prediction.

Why Do Both Social Disconnection and Social Support Lead to Hypoalgesia?

We saw in the last section that socially disconnecting experiences had the effect of dulling pain sensitivity in both animals and humans. But earlier we saw evidence that cues of social support (Brown, Sheffield, Leary, and Robinson, 2003; Master et al., 2009) and positive affect (Rhudy et al., 2008) also prompted hypoalgesic effects. How can such diametrically opposed experiences both lead to the same hypoalgesic outcome? Furthermore, to the extent that socially threatening experiences induce negative affect (Buckley, Winkel & Leary, 2004; Williams, Cheung, & Choi, 2000; but see DeWall & Baumeister, 2006), negative affect has been shown to be related to an *increase* in pain sensitivity (Rhudy & Meagher, 2000; Rhudy et al., 2008). How can all these seemingly conflicting outcomes be reconciled?

One empirically-supported theory proposed by Rhudy and colleagues (see Rhudy et al., 2008) contends that the influence of emotions on pain experience depends on both emotional *valence* (positive or negative) and *arousal* level (mild, intense). Furthermore, the exact effect of increasing levels of arousal depends on whether affective valence is positive or negative. Rhudy and colleagues point to considerable research from their own lab and others showing that moderate levels of positive affect reliably produce moderate levels of hypoalgesia, with very intense positive affect (e.g., genital stimulation) producing profound pain inhibition. This hypoalgesic effect of positive affect provides one potential explanation for the findings of studies showing pain-inhibiting consequences of social support.

By what mechanisms social support (and the concomitant positive affect) provokes hypoalgesia is not known. However, one possibility is that social support works by way of a stress-buffering process. According to a widely regarded model of the stress response (Lazarus & Folkman, 1984), the recognition of a threat instigates a process of appraisal (consciously and/or subconsciously) that takes account of an individual's coping resources such as prior exposure to the threat, assessments of one's own capabilities, and past successes or failures. It is possible that social support is taken as a resource that can be brought to bear on a threat, thereby reducing its magnitude or enhancing the individual's perceived coping capacity (Cohen, Gottlieb & Underwood, 2000; Cohen & Wills, 1985). If we consider physical injury and/or the resulting pain to be the threats in the Brown, Sheffield, Leary, and Robinson (2003) and Master et al. (2009) studies, then perhaps social support diminished the perceived menace or enhanced the perceived manageability of the injury represented by the pain signal. With diminished danger, pain might abate as well. Another (related) possibility is that the positive affect generated by social support might facilitate an awareness of a broader array of creative possibilities for coping with pain. Extensive work by Fredrickson (2001, 2009) has shown that whereas negative emotions narrow one's focus to prepare the body to respond in particular ways, positive emotions can expand cognitive and behavioral repertoires, increasing the number of possible responses we can perceive. Recent evidence (Harmon-Jones & Gable, 2009)

has revealed that this broadening effect of positive affect is most likely to occur under conditions of a withdrawal motivation, which presumably would be the case under conditions of painful stimuli. With a broadened perspective and enhanced creative potential, it seems likely that any problem, even pain, may seem more manageable against a backdrop of an expanded canvas of possibilities.

Whatever the mechanism, if positive affect produces hypoalgesia, how is it possible that negative affect, presumably elicited during times of social exclusion, would similarly inhibit pain? Rhudy et al. (2008) point out that in most studies, negative emotions have the effect of *facilitating* pain sensitivity, and the degree of hyperalgesia increases as negative affect increases in intensity but only up to a point. At around the point of moderate arousal, there is a threshold at which the effect of negative affect on pain reverses and nociceptive reactions become *inhibited*. In one study, for example, Rhudy and Meagher (2001) found that merely threatening people with painful shocks led to hyperalgesia, whereas exposure to shocks led to hypoalgesia. Although both groups similarly reported negative affect, the shocked group reported significantly elevated arousal compared with the threatened-only group. Rhudy and colleagues suggest that the stress-induced hypoalgesic effects observed in numerous animal and human studies occur because the stressors employed are of sufficient intensity to surpass this reversal threshold point, often because they are inescapable (which is associated with strong arousal) and are especially threatening.

The participants in the DeWall and Baumeister (2006) and Borsook and MacDonald (in press) studies both demonstrated hypoalgesia, despite an apparently wide gap in the intensity of the manipulations (life spent alone vs. an unrewarding social encounter). The valence-arousal theory implies that the reason for these outcomes is that both manipulations (even the less intense one) provoked an arousal level that exceeded the reversal threshold. Given the vital importance of social connectedness to human health, it seems possible that seemingly minimal signs of social network weakening could be processed as a formidable threat, which would elicit intense arousal. This explanation accords with the fact that in animal studies socially disconnecting stressors (isolation, conflict, etc.) almost always elicit hypoalgesia.

In sum, cues of a supportive social environment would signal that valuable resources are available to cope with injury, thereby provoking pain inhibition systems. On the other hand, by virtue of the danger associated with social disconnection, cues of social injury would signal a formidable threat, likewise provoking pain inhibition processes. Thus, it may be that hypoalgesia is an appropriate response both during times of social disconnection and social support but that it occurs for different reasons and via different mechanisms.

Future Directions
What Are the Implications of Chronic Social Pain?

Although long distinguished from acute pain only by duration, chronic physical pain is now viewed as distinguishable on a number of factors. Chronic physical pain has been shown to be associated with structural and functional changes in cerebral tissue (Apkarian et al., 2004b; May, 2008), and spontaneous pain episodes in chronic pain patients are correlated with entirely different neural activation patterns than those seen during acute pain events (Apkarian et al., 2005). For example, whereas acute pain tends to be correlated with increased activity in the ACC, IC, S1, and Thalamus, spontaneous pain episodes in chronic pain patients are associated with elevated activity in prefrontal regions of the cortex (i.e., prefrontal cortex [PFC]; Apkarian et al., 2005). In sum, long-term pain leads to a process of pain *chronification*, which entails structural and functional changes that alter the brain's response to noxious stimuli. In some cases, this chronification process is associated with the persistence of pain long after an instigating injury has healed. Indeed, it can be said that acute pain is a symptom of a condition (injury), whereas chronic pain is a condition in and of itself.

With such differences between acute and chronic pain there are grounds to expect that these differences could be influential factors guiding the dynamics between social and physical pain. First, given the presumption of a neurophysiological overlap between social and physical pains, if chronic physical pain leads to particular patterns of structural and functional changes in the brain, might chronic social pain lead to similar changes? For example, people who endure chronic feelings of painful loneliness and disconnection may exhibit neural adaptations similar to those occurring for people enduring chronic physical pain. Eisenberger et al. (2003, 2007) have found elevated activity in the dACC in response to an acute episode of exclusion. Because the transition from acute to chronic pain (i.e., chronification) is associated with a shift

in activity from the classical pain matrix regions (e.g., ACC, IC, and S1) toward the PFC, would greater activity be observed in the PFC, instead of the dACC, in people suffering chronic social pain in response to, say, a task requiring them to recall/relive an episode of exclusion?

Second, if long-term social pain leads to neural changes that mirror chronic physical pain, would chronic social pain make the chronification of physical pain more likely or more rapid? Repeated exposure to stressful events has been found to alter pain responses in animals (Coutinho et al., 2002; Dickinson, Leach & Flecknell, 2009; Rivat et al., 2007). For example, Rivat et al. (2007) found that while naïve rats (who had no prior exposure to the experimental stressors or resulting physiological responses) displayed stress-induced hypoalgesia, experienced rats exhibited hyperalgesia, a phenomenon known as latent pain sensitization. Coutinho et al. (2002) examined the effects of separating infant rats from their mothers for 180 minutes daily. Pain reactions were significantly higher, and stressed induced hypoalgesia significantly lower in the maternally separated rats compared to their nonisolated counterparts. Altered pain responses resulting from early exposure to stressors have also been documented in humans. For example, Taddio, Katz, Ilerich, and Koren (1997) found that circumcision in newborn infants led to increased pain responses 4 to 6 months after surgery.

Third, chronic pain patients often struggle with feelings of disconnection, being misunderstood, frustration that their condition is invisible, and not being able to express their difficulties with pain for fear that they will not be accepted. Yet, remarkably few studies have tackled how such social realities impact the lives of people with chronic pain, including the pain experience itself and the ability to function in life.

What Are the Effects of Physical Pain On Social Perceptions?

The investigation of the dynamics between social experience and physical pain has been almost entirely one way: what influence does social experience have on physical pain? It is possible, however, that the arrow of influence points the other way as well; that the presence of physical pain may alter the perception of social experiences. The impact of physical pain on a wide range of cognitive and emotional tasks has already been documented (Apkarian, Sosa, Krauss, et al., 2004a) and there is considerable evidence that people in pain (at least chronic pain) exhibit information biases toward pain stimuli, selectively attending to and processing pain- and illness-related stimuli (Pincus & Morley, 2001). Therefore given the crucial importance of social connections there is reason to believe that social signals may be particularly vulnerable to the influence of physical pain.

How Can Brain Imaging Be Used to Expand Knowledge of the Neural Correlates of Social Pain?

The fMRI studies by Eisenberger and colleagues (Eisenberger et al., 2003, 2007) have offered a first glimpse at the neural consequences of social exclusion. However, the features of the most commonly used experimentally induced exclusion paradigm, Cyberball, may limit the generalizability of these studies' results, suggesting that future studies should employ alternative exclusion methodologies. First, Cyberball may confound rejection with expectation violation (i.e., surprise). The arbitrary exclusion during the game may well lead to feelings of social distress, but might also induce surprise and confusion. Eisenberger et al. (2003) found increased dACC activity in response to exclusion due to an ostensible technical glitch (implicit exclusion). We suggest that there might have been a degree of expectancy violation in this implicit condition as well as in the explicit condition. Whereas in the explicit condition the surprise was being suddenly excluded for no apparent reason in the middle of a game, the implicit condition may have provoked surprise that one was not able to play a game one was expecting to play. It appears, therefore, that both exclusion conditions may have entailed some degree of *surprise*. Because dACC activation has been linked to expectancy violation (Botvinick, Cohen, & Carter, 2004), the question arises as to whether the dACC activation observed by Eisenberger et al. (2003) mainly reflects expectancy violation or social pain. Using a paradigm that separated expectancy violation from social feedback (acceptance vs. rejection), Somerville, Heatherton, and Kelley (2006) found evidence suggesting that the dorsal region of the ACC (dACC) was sensitive to expectancy violation, with increasing activity when feedback did not match expectations, whereas the ventral region was sensitive to feedback type, showing greater activity when the participant was liked versus not liked. Future studies should employ a variety of exclusion methods[1] and attempt to distinguish between the effects of social distress and other psychological states (such as expectancy violation, surprise, frustration, etc.).

Second, activity in the ACC, as well as other regions associated with the "pain matrix" such as the AIC, thalamus, and prefrontal cortex (PFC) is by no means specific to pain and occurs under a wide array of conditions other than pain (Peyron, Laurent, & Garcia-Larrea, 2000; Wager, 2005). For example, dACC activity has been linked to numerous functions including effortful thinking (of the kind that occurs when learning a new skill; Allman et al., 2001), error detection (Gehring & Knight, 2000), performance monitoring (van Veen, Holroyd, Cohen, et al., 2004), reward assessment (Knutson et al., 2000), and expectancy violation (Botvinik, Cohen, & Carter, 2004). The existence of pain cannot be assumed, therefore, by dint of merely observing activity in these regions. Combining imaging data from numerous studies employing a wide array of exclusion methods, along with improved social pain measures, will help to boost confidence that neural correlates of exclusion experiences reflect predominantly pain, rather than other phenomena.

What Is the Best Way to Operationalize Social Pain?

An important issue in the social pain literature is the measurement of social pain. Several studies (Eisenberger et al., 2003, 2006, 2007; DeWall et al., 2010) have used a brief instrument that purportedly measures social distress. Items include "I felt liked," "I felt rejected," "I felt invisible" and "I felt powerful." The extent to which this instrument indexes the presence of pain, per se, is not known. The validity of this and other social pain measures has important implications for the interpretation of social pain research. For example, in the study by Eisenberger et al. (2006), sensitivity to physical pain related to sensitivity to exclusion and vice versa. But because mild to moderate negative affect prompts heightened pain sensitivity (Rhudy & Meagher, 2000, 2001, Rhudy et al., 2008), if social distress reflects general negative affect, then the positive correlation between social distress and physical pain may simply reflect the impact of negative affect on physical pain rather than any special relationship between social and physical pain. Future studies should include alternative measures that employ items relating to pain specifically ("hurts," "aches," "stings," "wounded," "upset," etc.) such as Leary and Springer's (2001) measure of hurt feelings proneness (e.g., DeWall et al., 2010).

Conclusion

A vast and growing literature has demonstrated that social connectedness can have an immense impact on human health and well-being. The importance of relationships to physical integrity is perhaps the reason why we evolved such a strong drive to be accepted, and may also be the key factor that prompted the exaptation of pain to signal social injury. Social pain is the emotionally aversive pain-like experience that can attend socially excluding events (and the memory of such events) and in this chapter we have explored evidence that social and physical pain share a number of phenomenological as well as biochemical and neural features. Some of the earliest evidence of this overlap comes from a series of studies showing that opioids, a peptide long known to be intimately involved in regulating physical pain, can also effectively ease social distress and modulate social-threat induced hypoalgesia, and that chronic exposure to social distress impairs opiate efficacy in reducing physical pain. We explored findings from recent brain imaging studies showing that cortical activity in people experiencing the distress of exclusion is similar to that of people receiving nociceptive stimuli, and that people's neural responses to an exclusion experience effectively predict the tendency to experience social distress in everyday life. We also looked at research reporting hypoalgesic responses under the opposing conditions of both social support and social threat and explored candidate mechanisms by which these responses occur. Finally, in spite of a growing body of evidence linking social and physical pain, there remain several outstanding issues that need to be addressed in future research and we identified three such issues. Being the highly social animals that we are, social exclusion feels awful. But more than that, exclusion can be as injurious to health as physical injury and as such, it can provoke a feeling that is remarkably pain-like, with consequences that parallel those of physical pain. We look forward to seeing understanding of the phenomenon of social pain and its relation to physical pain expand, ideally with increasing application in clinical settings to help people suffering from both types of pain.

Note

1. Especially those known to produce strong responses, such as the "life alone" (Twenge, Baumeister, Tice, & Stucke, 2001) and the "no one chose you" (Nezlek et al., 1997) methods. In the "life alone" approach, participants are told that, on the basis of a personality test, it can be predicted that they will experience a life of isolation (or a life filled with rewarding relationships). In the "no one chose you" paradigm, participants are asked to select whom they would like to work with on a task, from among a group of individuals they had just met, and then are subsequently informed that no one (or everyone) chose them as partners.

References

Allman, J. M., Hakeem, A., Erwin, J. M., Nimchinsky, E., & Hof, P. (2001). The anterior cingulate cortex. The evolution of an interface between emotion and cognition. *Annals of the New York Academy of Sciences*, *935*, 107–117.

Amit, Z., & Galina, Z. H. (1986). Stress-induced analgesia: Adaptive pain suppression. *Physiological Reviews*, *66*(4), 1091–1120.

Apkarian, A. V., Bushnell, M. C., Treede, R. D., & Zubieta, J. K. (2005). Human brain mechanisms of pain perception and regulation in health and disease. *European Journal of Pain (London)*, *9*(4), 463–484.

Apkarian, A. V., Sosa, Y., Krauss, B. R., Thomas, P. S., Fredrickson, B. E., Levy, R. E., et al. (2004a). Chronic pain patients are impaired on an emotional decision-making task. *Pain*, *108*(1–2), 129–136.

Apkarian, A. V., Sosa, Y., Sonty, S., Levy, R. M., Harden, R. N., Parrish, T. B., et al. (2004b). Chronic back pain is associated with decreased prefrontal and thalamic gray matter density. *The Journal of Neuroscience*, *24*(46), 10410–10415.

Baumeister, R. F., & Leary, M. R. (1995). The need to belong: desire for interpersonal attachments as a fundamental human motivation. *Psychological bulletin*, *117*, 497–529.

Benarroch, E. E. (2001). Pain-autonomic interactions: A selective review. *Clinical Autonomic Research*, *11*(6), 343–349.

Berggren, U., & Meynert, G (1984). Dental fear and avoidance: Causes, symptoms, and consequences. *Journal of the American Dental Association*, *109*, 2, 247–251.

Bie, B., & Pan, Z. Z. (2007). Trafficking of central opioid receptors and descending pain inhibition. *Molecular Pain*, *3*, 37.

Borsook, T. K., & MacDonald, G. (2010). Mildly negative social encounters reduce physical pain sensitivity. *Pain. 151*, 372–377.

Botvinick, M. M., Cohen, J. D., & Carter, C. S. (2004). Conflict monitoring and anterior cingulate cortex: An update. *Trends in Cognitive Sciences*, *8*(12), 539–546.

Bowlby, J. (1969). *Attachment and Loss: Vol. 1. Attachment*. New York: Basic Books.

Bowlby, J. (1973). *Attachment and Loss: Vol. 2. Separation, Anxiety and Anger*. New York: Basic Books.

Bowlby, J. (1980). *Attachment and Loss: Vol. 3. Loss, Sadness and Depression*. New York: Basic Books.

Bracha, H. S., Ralston, T. C., Matsukawa, J. M., Williams, A. E., & Bracha, A. S. (2004). Does "fight or flight" need updating? *Psychosomatics*, *45*(5), 448–449.

Brown, J. L., Sheffield, D., Leary, M. R., & Robinson, M. E. (2003). Social support and experimental pain. *Psychosomatic Medicine*, *65*(2), 276–283.

Buckley, K. E., Winkel, R. E., & Leary, M. R. (2004). Reactions to acceptance and rejection: Effects of level and sequence of relational evaluation. *Journal of Experimental Social Psychology*, *40*(1), 14–28.

Burklund, L. J., Eisenberger, N. I., & Lieberman, M. D. (2007). The face of rejection: Rejection sensitivity moderates dorsal anterior cingulate activity to disapproving facial expressions. *Social Neuroscience*, *2*(3–4), 238–253.

Butler, R. K., & Finn, D. P. (2009). Stress-Induced analgesia. *Progress in Neurobiology*, *88*(3), 184–202.

Carden, S. E., & Hofer, M. A. (1990). Socially mediated reduction of isolation distress in rat pups is blocked by naltrexone but not by Ro 15-1788. *Behavioral Neuroscience*, *104*(3), 457–463.

Carden, S. E., Hernandez, N., & Hofer, M. A. (1996). The isolation and companion comfort responses of 7- and 3-day-old rat pups are modulated by drugs active at the opioid receptor. *Behavioral Neuroscience, 110*(2), 324–330.

Casey, K. L., Svensson, P., Morrow, T. J., Raz, J., Jone, C., & Minoshima, S. (2000). Selective opiate modulation of nociceptive processing in the human brain. *Journal of Neurophysiology, 84*(1), 525–533.

Chapman, C. R., Tuckett, R. P., & Song, C. W. (2008). Pain and stress in a systems perspective: Reciprocal neural, endocrine, and immune interactions. *The Journal of Pain, 9*(2), 122–145.

Chesher, G. B., & Chan, B. (1977). Footshock induced analgesia in mice: Its reversal by naloxone and cross tolerance with morphine. *Life Sciences, 21*(11), 1569–1574.

Cohen, S., Gottlieb, B. H., & Underwood, L. G. (2000). Social relationships and health. In S. Cohen, B. H. Gottlieb, & L. G. Underwood (Eds.), *Social Support Measurement and Intervention: A Guide for Health and Social Scientists* (pp. 3–28). New York: Oxford Univ Press.

Cohen, S., & Wills, T. A. (1985). Stress, social support, and the buffering hypothesis. *Psychological Bulletin, 98*(2), 310–357.

Costa, A., Smeraldi, A., Tassorelli, C., Greco, R., & Nappi, G. (2005). Effects of acute and chronic restraint stress on nitroglycerin-induced hyperalgesia in rats. *Neuroscience Letters, 383*(1–2), 7–11.

Coutinho, S. V., Plotsky, P. M., Sablad, M., Miller, J. C., Zhou, H., Bayati, A. I., et al. (2002). Neonatal maternal separation alters stress-induced responses to viscerosomatic nociceptive stimuli in rat. *American Journal of Physiology, Gastrointestinal and Liver Physiology, 282*(2), G307–G316.

Craig, K. D. (1992). The facial expression of pain better than a thousand words? *APS Journal, 1*(3), 153–162.

DeWall, C. N., & Baumeister, R. F. (2006). Alone but feeling no pain: Effects of social exclusion on physical pain tolerance and pain threshold, affective forecasting, and interpersonal empathy. *Journal of Personality and Social Psychology, 91*(1), 1–15.

Dewall, C. N., Macdonald, G., Webster, G. D., Masten, C. L., Baumeister, R. F., Powell, C., et al. (2010). Acetaminophen reduces social pain: Behavioral and neural evidence. *Psychological Science, 21*(7), 931–937.

Dickinson, A. L., Leach, M. C., & Flecknell, P. A. (2009). Influence of early neonatal experience on nociceptive responses and analgesic effects in rats. *Laboratory Animals, 43*(1), 11–16.

Eisenberger, N. I., Gable, S. L., & Lieberman, M. D. (2007). Functional magnetic resonance imaging responses relate to differences in real-world social experience. *Emotion (Washington, DC), 7*(4), 745–754.

Eisenberger, N. I., & Lieberman, M. D. (2004). Why rejection hurts: A common neural alarm system for physical and social pain. *Trends in Cognitive Sciences, 8*(7), 294–300.

Eisenberger, N. I., Jarcho, J. M., Lieberman, M. D., & Naliboff, B. D. (2006). An experimental study of shared sensitivity to physical pain and social rejection. *Pain, 126*(1–3), 132–138.

Eisenberger, N. I., Lieberman, M. D., & Williams, K. D. (2003). Does rejection hurt? An FMRI study of social exclusion. *Science (New York), 302*(5643), 290–292.

Eisenberger, N. I., Taylor, S. E., Gable, S. L., Hilmert, C. J., & Lieberman, M. D. (2007). Neural pathways link social support to attenuated neuroendocrine stress responses. *Neuroimage, 35*(4), 1601–1612.

Fine, P. G., & Portenoy, R. K. (2004). The endogenous opioid systems. In P. G. Fine & R. K. Portenoy (Eds.), *A Clinical Guide to Opioid Analgesia* (pp. 9–15). New York: McGraw-Hill.

Flor, H., & Grüsser, S. M. (1999). Conditioned stress-induced analgesia in humans. *European Journal of Pain (London), 3*(4), 317–324.

Fredrickson, B. (2009). *Positivity: Groundbreaking Research Reveals How to Embrace the Hidden Strength of Positive Emotions, Overcome Negativity and Thrive.* New York: Crown Publishing.

Fredrickson, B. L. (2001). The role of positive emotions in positive psychology. *American Psychologist, 56*(3), 218–226.

Geha, P. Y., Baliki, M. N., Chialvo, D. R., Harden, R. N., Paice, J. A., & Apkarian, A. V. (2007). Brain activity for spontaneous pain of postherpetic neuralgia and its modulation by lidocaine patch therapy. *Pain, 128*(1–2), 88–100.

Gehring, W. J., & Knight, R. T. (2000). Prefrontal-cingulate interactions in action monitoring. *Nature Neuroscience, 3*(5), 516–520.

Harmon-Jones, E., & Gable, P. A. (2009). Neural activity underlying the effect of approach-motivated positive affect on narrowed attention. *Psychological Science, 20*(4), 406–409.

Herman, B. H., & Panksepp, J. (1978). Effects of morphine and naloxone on separation distress and approach attachment: Evidence for opiate mediation of social affect. *Pharmacology, Biochemistry, and Behavior, 9*(2), 213–220.

Herman, B. H., & Panksepp, J. (1981). Ascending endorphin inhibition of distress vocalization. *Science, 211*(4486), 1060–1062.

Hoffman, H. G., Garcia-Palacios, A., Patterson, D. R., Jensen, M., Furness, T., & Ammons, W. F. (2001). The effectiveness of virtual reality for dental pain control: A case study. *Cyberpsychology & Behavior: The Impact of the Internet, Multimedia and Virtual Reality on Behavior and Society, 4*(4), 527–535.

House, J. S., Landis, K. R., & Umberson, D. (1988). Social relationships and health. *Science, 241*(4865), 540.

Janssen, S. A., & Arntz, A. (1996). Anxiety and pain: Attentional and endorphinergic influences. *Pain, 66*(2–3), 145–150.

Kalin, N. H., Shelton, S. E., & Barksdale, C. M. (1988). Opiate modulation of separation-induced distress in non-human primates. *Brain Research, 440*(2), 285–292.

Kavaliers, M. (1988). Evolutionary and comparative aspects of nociception. *Brain Research Bulletin, 21*(6), 923–931.

Kehoe, P., & Boylan, C. B. (1994). Behavioral effects of kappa-opioid-receptor stimulation on neonatal rats. *Behavioral Neuroscience, 108*(2), 418–423.

Kehoe, P., & Blass, E. M. (1986). Opioid-Mediation of separation distress in 10-day-old rats: Reversal of stress with maternal stimuli. *Developmental Psychobiology, 19*(4), 385–398.

Keverne, E. B., Nevison, C. M., & Martel, F. L. (1997). Early learning and the social bond. *Annals of the New York Academy of Sciences, 807*, 329–339.

Keverne, E. B., Martensz, N. D., & Tuite, B. (1989). Beta-endorphin concentrations in cerebrospinal fluid of monkeys are influenced by grooming relationships. *Psychoneuroendocrinology, 14*(1–2), 155–161.

Klaus, M. H., Kennell, J. H., Robertson, S. S., & Sosa, R. (1986). Effects of social support during parturition on maternal and infant morbidity. *British medical journal (Clinical research ed.), 293*(6547), 585–587.

Knutson, B., Westdorp, A., Kaiser, E., & Hommer, D. (2000). FMRI visualization of brain activity during a monetary incentive delay task. *Neuroimage, 12*(1), 20–27.

Kulik, J. A., & Mahler, H. I. (1989). Social support and recovery from surgery. *Health Psychology, 8*(2), 221–238.

Lazarus, R. S., & Folkman, S. (1984). *Stress, Appraisal, and Coping.* New York: Springer.

Leary, M. R., & Springer, C. (2001). Hurt feelings: The neglected emotion. In R. M. Kowalski (Ed.), *Aversive Behaviors and Relational Transgressions* (pp. 151–175). Washington, DC: American Psychological Association.

MacDonald, G. (2009). *Social pain and hurt feelings. In The Cambridge Handbook of Personality Psychology* (pp. 541–555). New York: Cambridge University Press.

Macdonald, G., & Leary, M. R. (2005). Why does social exclusion hurt? The relationship between social and physical pain. *Psychological Bulletin, 131*(2), 202–223.

Master, S. L., Eisenberger, N. I., Taylor, S. E., Naliboff, B. D., Shirinyan, D., & Lieberman, M. D. (2009). A picture's worth: Partner photographs reduce experimentally induced pain. *Psychological Science 20*, 1316–1318.

May, A. (2008). Chronic pain may change the structure of the brain. *Pain, 137*(1), 7–15.

Merskey, H., & Bogduk, N. (1994). *Classification of Chronic Pain.* Seattle, WA: IASP Press.

Mitchinson, A. R., Kim, H. M., Geisser, M., Rosenberg, J. M., & Hinshaw, D. B. (2008). Social connectedness and patient recovery after major operations. *Journal of the American College of Surgeons, 206*(2), 292–300.

Nagasako, E. M., Oaklander, A. L., & Dworkin, R. H. (2003). Congenital insensitivity to pain: An update. *Pain, 101*(3), 213–219.

Naranjo, J. R., & Fuentes, J. A. (1985). Association between hypoalgesia and hypertension in rats after short-term isolation. *Neuropharmacology, 24*(2), 167–171.

Nezlek, J. B., Kowalski, R. M., Leary, M. R., Blevins, T., & Holgate, S. (1997). Personality moderators of reactions to interpersonal rejection: Depression and trait self-esteem. *Personality and Social Psychology Bulletin, 23*(12), 1235.

Panksepp, J. (2010). The neurobiology of social loss in animals: Some keys to the puzzle of psychic pain in humans. In G. MacDonald & L. Jensen-Campbell (Eds.), *Social Pain: Neuropsychological and Health Implications of Loss and Exclusion.* Washington, DC: APA Books.

Panksepp, J. (1998). *Affective Neuroscience: The Foundations of Human and Animal Emotions.* New York: Oxford University Press.

Panksepp, J., Herman, B., Conner, R., Bishop, P., & Scott, J. P. (1978). The biology of social attachments: Opiates alleviate separation distress. *Biological Psychiatry, 13*(5), 607–618.

Panksepp, J., Herman, B. H., Vilberg, T., Bishop, P., & DeEskinazi, F. G. (1980). Endogenous opioids and social behavior. *Neuroscience and Biobehavioral Reviews, 4*(4), 473.

Panksepp, J., Vilberg, T., Bean, N. J., Coy, D. H., & Kastin, A. J. (1978). Reduction of distress vocalization in chicks by opiate-like peptides. *Brain Research Bulletin, 3*(6), 663–667.

Perl, E. R. (2007). Ideas about pain, a historical view. *Nature Reviews. Neuroscience, 8*(1), 71–80.

Peyron, R., Laurent, B., & Garcia-Larrea, L. (2000). Functional imaging of brain responses to pain. A review and meta-analysis. *Neurophysiol Clin, 30*, 263–288.

Pincus, T. & Morley, S. (2001). Cognitive-Processing bias in chronic pain: A review and integration. *Psychological Bulletin, 127*(5), 599–617.

Pressman, S. D., & Cohen, S. (2005). Does positive affect influence health? *Psychological Bulletin, 131*(6), 925–971.

Pressman, S. D., Cohen, S., Miller, G. E., Barkin, A., Rabin, B. S., and Treanor, J. J. (2005). Loneliness, social network size, and immune response to influenza vaccination in college fresh-men. *Health Psychol.* 24: 297–306.

Price, D. D., Harkins, S. W., & Baker, C. (1987). Sensory-affective relationships among different types of clinical and experimental pain. *Pain, 28*(3), 297–307.

Price DD (1999) *Psychological Mechanisms of Pain and Analgesia.* Seattle, WA: IASP Press.

Puglisi-Allegra, S., & Oliverio, A. (1983). Social isolation: Effects on pain threshold and stress-induced analgesia. *Pharmacology, Biochemistry, and Behavior, 19*(4), 679–681.

Rainville, P., Carrier, B., Hofbauer, R. K., Bushnell, M. C., & Duncan, G. H. (1999). Dissociation of sensory and affective dimensions of pain using hypnotic modulation. *Pain, 82*(2), 159–171.

Rainville, P., Duncan, G. H., Price, D. D., Carrier, B., & Bushnell, M. C. (1997). Pain affect encoded in human anterior cingulate but not somatosensory cortex. *Science, 277*(5328), 968–971.

Reblin, M., & Uchino, B. N. (2008). Social and emotional support and its implication for health. *Curr Opinion in Psychiatry, 21*(2), 201–205.

Rhudy, J. L., Grimes, J. S., & Meagher, M. W. (2004). Fear-Induced hypoalgesia in humans: Effects on low intensity thermal stimulation and finger temperature. *The Journal of Pain, 5*(8), 458–468.

Rhudy, J. L., & Meagher, M. W. (2000). Fear and anxiety: Divergent effects on human pain thresholds. *Pain, 84*(1), 65–75.

Rhudy, J. L., & Meagher, M. W. (2001). The role of emotion in pain modulation. *Current Opinion in Psychiatry, 14*(3), 241.

Rhudy, J., & Meagher, M. (2003). Negative affect: effects on an evaluative measure of human pain. *Pain, 104*(3), 617–626.

Rhudy, J. L., Williams, A. E., McCabe, K. M., Russell, J. L., & Maynard, L. J. (2008). Emotional control of nociceptive reactions (ECON): Do affective valence and arousal play a role? *Pain, 136*(3), 250–261.

Rivat, C., Laboureyras, E., Laulin, J. P., Le Roy, C., Richebé, P., & Simonnet, G. (2007). Non-nociceptive environmental stress induces hyperalgesia, not analgesia, in pain and opioid-experienced rats. *Neuropsychopharmacology, 32*(10), 2217–2228.

Rodgers, R. J. & Hendrie, C. A. (1983). Social conflict activates status-dependent endogenous analgesic or hyperalgesic mechanisms in male mice: Effects of naloxone on nociception and behaviour. *Physiology & Behavior, 30*(5), 775–780.

Rodriguez-Artalejo, F., Guallar-Castillón, P., Herrera, M. C., Otero, C. M., Chiva, M. O., Ochoa, C. C., et al. (2006). Social network as a predictor of hospital readmission and mortality among older patients with heart failure. *Journal of Cardiac Failure, 12*(8), 621–627.

Schenk, S., Britt, M. D., Atalay, J., & Charleson, S. (1982). Isolation rearing decreases opiate receptor binding in rat brain. *Pharmacology, Biochemistry, and Behavior, 16*(5), 841–842.

Schmaltz, H. N., Southern, D., Ghali, W. A., Jelinski, S. E., Parsons, G. A., King, K. M., et al. (2007). Living alone, patient sex and mortality after acute myocardial infarction. *Journal of General Internal Medicine, 22*(5), 572–578.

Schore, A. (1994). *Affect Regulation and the Origin of the Self: The Neurobiology of Emotional Development.* Hillsdale, NJ: Lawrence Erlbaum Associates.

Schore, A. (2003). *Affect Regulation and the Repair of the Self.* New York: Norton.

Seeman, T. E. (1996). Social ties and health: The benefits of social integration. *Annals of Epidemiology, 6*(5), 442–451.

Somerville, L. H., Heatherton, T. F., & Kelley, W. M. (2006). Anterior cingulate cortex responds differentially to expectancy violation and social rejection. *Nature Neuroscience*, *9*(8), 1007–1008.

Taddio, A., Katz, J., Ilersich, A. L., & Koren, G. (1997). Effect of neonatal circumcision on pain response during subsequent routine vaccination. *Lancet*, *349*(9052), 599–603.

Tölle, T. R., Kaufmann, T., Siessmeier, T., Lautenbacher, S., Berthele, A., Munz, F., et al. (1999). Region-Specific encoding of sensory and affective components of pain in the human brain: A positron emission tomography correlation analysis. *Annals of Neurology*, *45*(1), 40–47.

Tracey, I., & Mantyh, P. W. (2007). The cerebral signature for pain perception and its modulation. *Neuron*, *55*(3), 377–391.

Twenge, J. M., Baumeister, R. F., Tice, D. M., & Stucke, T. S. (2001). If you can't join them, beat them: Effects of social exclusion on aggressive behavior. *Journal of Personality and Social Psychology*, *81*(6), 1058–1069.

Uchino, B. N. (2006). Social support and health: A review of physiological processes potentially underlying links to disease outcomes. *Journal of Behavioral Medicine*, *29*(4), 377–387.

van Veen, V., Holroyd, C. B., Cohen, J. D., Stenger, V. A., & Carter, C. S. (2004). Errors without conflict: Implications for performance monitoring theories of anterior cingulate cortex. *Brain and Cognition*, *56*(2), 267–276.

Wager, T. D. (2005). The neural bases of placebo effects in pain. Current Directions in *Psychological Science*, *14*(4), 175–179.

Wagner, K. J., Sprenger, T., Kochs, E. F., Tölle, T. R., Valet, M., & Willoch, F. (2007). Imaging human cerebral pain modulation by dose-dependent opioid analgesia: A positron emission tomography activation study using remifentanil. *Anesthesiology*, *106*(3), 548–556.

Wideman, C. H., Murphy, H. M., & McCartney, S. B. (1996). Interactions between vasopressin and food restriction on stress-induced analgesia. *Peptides*, *17*(1), 63–6.

Williams, K. D., Cheung, C. K., & Choi, W. (2000). Cyberostracism: Effects of being ignored over the internet. *Journal of Personality and Social Psychology*, *79*(5), 748–762.

Winslow, J. T., & Insel, T. R. (1991). Endogenous opioids: Do they modulate the rat pup's response to social isolation? *Behavioral Neuroscience*, *105*(2), 253–263.

Wise, R. G., Rogers, R., Painter, D., Bantick, S., Ploghaus, A., Williams, P., et al. (2002). Combining fmri with a pharmacokinetic model to determine which brain areas activated by painful stimulation are specifically modulated by remifentanil. *Neuroimage*, *16*(4), 999–1014.

Wise, R. G., Williams, P., & Tracey, I. (2004). Using fmri to quantify the time dependence of remifentanil analgesia in the human brain. *Neuropsychopharmacology*, *29*(3), 626–635.

PART 7

Exclusion across Individuals

Perceived Social Isolation within Personal and Evolutionary Timescales

John T. Cacioppo, Louise C. Hawkley, *and* Joshua Correll

Abstract

Evolutionary time and evolutionary forces operate at such a different scale of organization than we experience in everyday life that personal experience is not sufficient to understand the role of loneliness in human existence. Research over the past decade suggests a very different view of loneliness than suggested by personal experience, one in which loneliness serves a variety of adaptive functions in specific habitats. We outline an evolutionary theory of loneliness, with an emphasis on its potential adaptive value in an evolutionary timescale.

Key Words: collective identity, evolution, heritability, loneliness, selflessness, social isolation, social learning, social pain

Introduction

Robert Weiss (1973) conceptualized loneliness as perceived social isolation, which he described as a gnawing, chronic disease without redeeming features. On the scale of everyday life, it is understandable how something as personally aversive as loneliness could be regarded as a blight on human existence. However, evolutionary time and evolutionary forces operate at such a different scale of organization than we experience in everyday life that personal experience is not sufficient to understand the role of loneliness in human existence. Our research has suggested a very different view of loneliness than suggested by personal experience, one in which loneliness serves a variety of adaptive functions in specific habitats. Our goal here is to outline our evolutionary theory of loneliness to explore its potential adaptive value in an evolutionary timescale. For instance, we explain how loneliness draws attention to the prospect that our social connection to others is at risk or absent; motivates us to repair or replace the safe, collaborative social surroundings we need to ensure a genetic legacy; and provides

incentives for people to become more compassionate and empathie members of our quintessentially social species.

Evolutionary Context

The Earth is more than 4.5 billion years old, with the earliest forms of life dating back approximately 3.5 billion years (Schopf, 1999). The Phanerozoic Eon in which we presently live dates back approximately 545 million years and is the only period in which much animal life existed (Miller et al., 2005). Microbial life existed prior to this period, and the fossil record suggests that photosynthetic cyanobacteria (the oldest known bacteria dating back more than 3.5 billion years) during the Proterozoic Eon may have contributed substantially to stromatolite formations and to a substitution of oxygen for carbon dioxide in the Earth's atmosphere. The reduction in atmospheric carbon dioxide, in turn, contributed to long ice ages and a sharp reduction in microflora during the Proterozoic Eon (Knoll & Holland, 1995) and, ultimately, to an environment suitable for aerobic organisms and life as we know it (Lane, 2002).

Life is driven by self-preservation: finding food, avoiding becoming food, and—a signature feature of biological life—reproducing. Most of the species that inhabit the earth either are born in such large numbers that some survive long enough to reproduce, and/or are born with the capacity to find sustenance and avoid predation sufficiently well that some survive long enough to reproduce. It is the ability of such organisms to reproduce that determines what genes constitute the gene pool for the future generations of that species. These genes, in turn, shape the structure and function of the organisms that constitute the species. Environmental factors such as the availability of food, water, predators, toxins, and climate influence which offspring survive to reproduce. Natural selection refers to the process by which heritable characteristics (i.e., phenotypes, including behavioral predispositions) become more common in a population over successive generations to the extent that they increase the odds that an organism survives and reproduces in a specific habitat.

Moreover, natural selection unfolds in adjustments across several layers of organization including genes, gene expression, individuals, groups, cultures, species, and environments (Boyd & Richerson, 1985; Caporael & Brewer, 1995). These adjustments are achieved in evolutionary time through competition for survival between and within species such that, within species, some offspring survive long enough to reproduce and others do not.

Genetic variation among members of a species, in turn, constitutes an important engine of natural selection that contributes to the differential rates of survival and reproduction in specific habitats. It is important to note that natural selection acts on phenotypes in a habitat. Across generations, this selective pressure can contribute to a specialization of species, or populations within species, to different kinds of environments. For instance, Conover and Munch (2002) experimentally examined the effects of fishing large, small, or random-size captive adult fish. Within four generations, large-harvested fish evolved to a lower weight for a given age and small-harvested fish did the opposite. Thus, natural selection operating on a phenotype (i.e., size of fish) led to slower or faster rates of growth depending on the environment (Conover & Munch, 2002).

As environments change, the selective pressures can also change, leading to new challenges for self-preservation within an individual's lifetime and to potentially new adjustments in the population across generations.[1] A given phenotypic expression may be beneficial or deleterious at the level of the individual in a lifetime but nevertheless have adaptive value at the level of the population in evolutionary time.

Genes that promote behavior that increases the odds of the genes surviving within a specific environment are perpetuated across generations (Dawkins, 1976), and this notion has sometimes led justifiably to a focus on genes when explaining evolutionary mechanisms. Genes are a hereditary mechanism through which adaptive phenotypes in specific environments are sculpted across generations at the level of a population but, as we have noted, phenotypes rather than genes are the target of natural selection. Consequently, a given phenotype within a population today may not map in a one-to-one fashion into the underlying genotype. An evolutionary analysis requires a clear specification of the phenotype and an analysis of its adaptive value within specific environments at multiple levels of organization across the evolutionary timescale. The phenotype of loneliness may be viewed fruitfully within this context.

Loneliness within a Personal Timescale

The phenotypic expression of loneliness (perceived social isolation) within a personal timescale refers to processes that operate within individuals and within generations. Humans are a meaning-making species born to the longest period of dependency of any species and are dependent on conspecifics across the lifespan to survive and prosper. Perhaps not surprisingly, therefore, humans do not fare well, whether they live solitary lives (House, Landis, & Umberson, 1988) or simply *perceive* that they are socially isolated (i.e., lonely; e.g., Cole, et al., 2007; Hawkley, Masi, Berry, & Cacioppo, 2006; Penninx, et al., 1997; Seeman, 2000; Sugisawa, Liang, & Liu, 1994). Loneliness within a personal lifespan has also been associated with the progression of Alzheimer's Disease (Wilson, et al., 2007), obesity (Lauder, Mummery, Jones, & Caperchione, 2006), increased vascular resistance (Cacioppo, Hawkley, Crawford, et al., 2002), elevated blood pressure (Cacioppo, Hawkley, Crawford, et al., 2002; Hawkley et al., 2006), increased hypothalamic pituitary adrenocortical activity (Adam, Hawkley, Kudielka, & Cacioppo, 2006; Steptoe, Owen, Kunz-Ebrecht, & Brydon, 2004), less salubrious sleep (Cacioppo, Hawkley, Berntson, et al., 2002; Pressman, et al., 2005), diminished immunity (Kiecolt-Glaser, et al., 1984; Pressman, et al., 2005), reduction in independent living (Russell, Cutrona, de la Mora,

& Wallace, 1997; Tilvis, Pitkala, Jolkkonen, & Strandberg, 2000), alcoholism (Akerlind & Hornquist, 1992), depressive symptomatology (Cacioppo et al., 2006; Heikkinen & Kauppinen, 2004), suicidal ideation and behavior (Rudatsikira, Muula, Siziya, & Twa-Twa, 2007), and mortality in older adults (Penninx, et al., 1997; Seeman, 2000). Loneliness has even been associated with gene expression—specifically, the underexpression of genes bearing anti-inflammatory glucocorticoid response elements and overexpression of genes bearing response elements for proinflammatory NF-κB/Rel transcription factors (Cole, et al., 2007).

The physiological effects of social isolation in humans are clearly adverse for the individual in contemporary times, in which life expectancy now extends well into the eighth decade. Many of the most significant of these physiological costs are incurred with the onset and progression of the chronic diseases of aging (e.g., hypertension). In evolutionary times, humans did not live long enough for these physiological effects to be of much consequence for the individual or for the population.

That loneliness has an evolutionary basis is suggested by adoption and twin studies with children (Bartels, Cacioppo, Hudziak, & Boomsma, 2008; McGuire & Clifford, 2000) and with adults (Boomsma, Cacioppo, Muthen, Asparouhov, & Clark, 2007; Boomsma, Cacioppo, Slagboom, & Posthuma, 2006; Boomsma, Willemsen, Dolan, Hawkley, & Cacioppo, 2005). These studies indicate that loneliness has a sizeable heritable component. We will return to the heritable component in the next section, when we examine possible evolutionary mechanisms underlying loneliness, but it is important to emphasize that heritability does not preclude the operation of strong environmental influences on the expression of this phenotype. For instance, freshmen who leave family and friends behind often feel increased social isolation when they arrive at college even though they are surrounded by large numbers of other young adults (e.g., Cutrona, 1982; Russell, Peplau, & Cutrona, 1980). Lower levels of loneliness are associated with marriage (Hawkley, Browne, & Cacioppo, 2005; Pinquart & Sörensen, 2003), higher education (Savikko, Routasalo, Tilvis, Strandberg, & Pitkala, 2005), and higher income (Andersson, 1998; Savikko, et al., 2005), whereas higher levels of loneliness are associated with living alone (Routasalo, Savikko, Tilvis, Strandberg, & Pitkala, 2006), infrequent contact with friends and family (Bondevik & Skogstad, 1998; Hawkley,

Browne, & Cacioppo, 2005; Mullins & Dugan, 1990), dissatisfaction with living circumstances (Hector-Taylor & Adams, 1996), physical health symptoms (Hawkley et al., 2008), disabilities (Hughes, et al., 2010), chronic work and/or social stress (Hawkley et al., 2008), small social network (Hawkley, Browne, & Cacioppo, 2005; Mullins & Dugan, 1990), lack of a spousal confidant (Hawkley et al., 2008), marital or family conflict (Jones, 1992; Segrin, 1999), poor quality social relationships (Hawkley et al., 2008; Mullins & Dugan, 1990; Routasalo, et al., 2006), and divorce and widowhood (Dugan & Kivett, 1994; Dykstra & de Jong, 1999; Holmen, Ericsson, Andersson, & Winblad, 1992; Samuelsson, Andersson, & Hagberg, 1998).

Some of the effects of loneliness within personal time are summarized in Figure 17.1. An early and extended dependence on caregivers, and limited physical endowments across the lifespan, place humans at risk when they are isolated. As Brewer (2004) noted:

> Many of the evolved characteristics that have permitted humans to adapt to a wide range of physical environments, such as omnivorousness and tool making, create dependence on collective knowledge and cooperative information sharing. As a consequence, human beings are characterized by obligatory interdependence (Caporael & Brewer, 1995), and our evolutionary history is a story of co-evolution of genetic endowment, social structure, and culture (p. 107).

In this context, it is clearly adaptive to have an aversive signal that draws attention to the prospect that our social connection to others is at risk or absent and that motivates us to ensure or replace the safe, collaborative social surroundings we need to ensure a genetic legacy (Cacioppo, et al., 2006). Hunger, thirst, and pain, for instance, have evolved to prompt an organism to change its behavior in a way that protects the individual and promotes the likelihood his or her genes will make their way into the gene pool. We have proposed that the social pain of loneliness evolved to serve as a signal that one's connections to others are weakening and to motivate the repair and maintenance of the connections to others that are needed for our health and well-being as well as for the survival of our genes (Cacioppo, et al., 2006). That is, just as physical pain is an aversive signal that evolved to motivate one to take action that minimizes damage to one's physical body, loneliness is an aversive state that motivates us to take action that minimizes

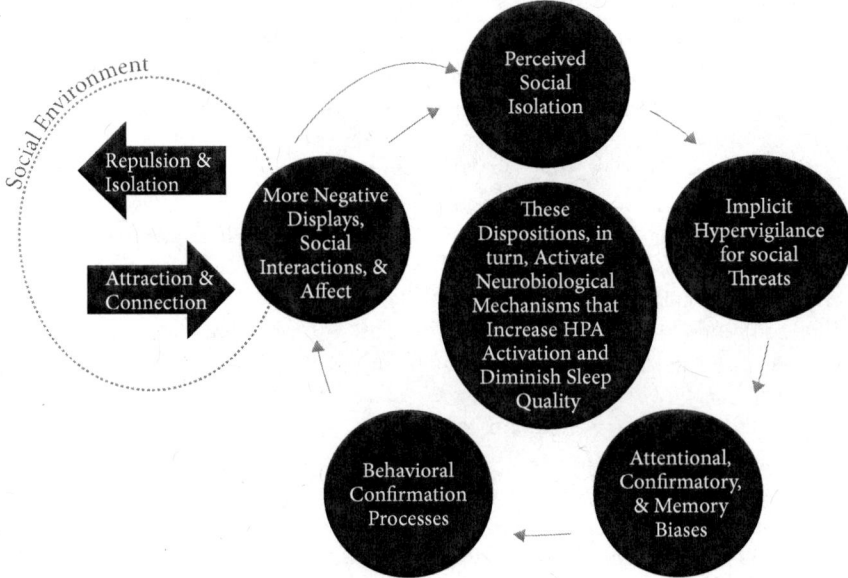

Figure 17.1 The Effects of Loneliness on Human Cognition

Reprinted with permission from Cacioppo, J. T., & Hawkley, L. C. (2009). Perceived social isolation. *Trends in Cognitive Sciences,13,* 447–454.

damage to one's social body (cf. Cacioppo, Fowler, & Christakis, 2009).

Humans are capable of duplicity and changing alliances, so being with others is not sufficient to ensure one is embedded in a safe social surrounding, especially in vulnerable times such as when one is asleep (Cacioppo, Hawkley, Berntson, et al., 2002). Accordingly, research has shown that it is the quality, not the quantity of one's social connections that predicts loneliness (i.e., perceived social isolation) across a lifetime (Cacioppo, et al., 2000; Wheeler, Reis, & Nezlek, 1983). In nonhuman social species, being shunned or ostracized is associated with high rates of mortality (Williams, 2003). In human beings, finding oneself uncertain that one can confide in, depend on, or trust others is not only an unhappy social environment, it can also be a profoundly unsafe social environment. Others with whom one once cooperated can no longer be counted on for cooperation, and strangers cannot be assumed to be friends rather than foes. Thus, we have posited that the perceived social isolation that motivates one to attend to and to seek connection with others also leads to additional effects.

First, loneliness increases explicit attention to social stimuli and increases implicit attention to social threats. Another basic motivational state, hunger, similarly increases an organism's attention to food. Not everything that appears edible is safe to eat by humans, however. Over an evolutionary timescale,

our taste buds have developed to be much more sensitive to bitter (e.g., concentrations of 1:2,000,000) than to sweet (e.g., concentrations of 1:200). Poisons tend to have a bitter taste, so this difference in sensitivity has evolved to protect the individual from dangers that arise as a result of the drive to find food. Given it is more costly to fall victim to a fatal assault than to forego a friendship, becoming more sensitive to social threats may be beneficial, especially in environments populated by dangerous foes.

The effects of loneliness on the motivation to connect and on implicit hypervigilance for social threats serve to increase the salience of social cues, produce a confirmatory bias toward seeing social dangers, and create negative memory biases for social information. For instance, lonely individuals not only tend to form more negative social impressions of others, but their memory for their interactions with others grows more negative over time (e.g., Duck, Pond, & Leatham, 1994). When an individual's negative social expectations elicit behaviors from others that validate these expectations, the expectations are buttressed and increase the likelihood of the individual behaving in ways that push away the very people to whom he or she most wants to be close to better fulfill their social needs (Downey & Romero-Canyas, 2005; Murray, Bellavia, Rose, & Griffin, 2003; Rotenberg, 1994). Consequently, lonely individuals may view themselves to be passive victims in their social world, but they are active contributors through their self-protective interactions with others (Cacioppo & Hawkley, 2005). These are largely counterproductive effects of loneliness when viewed within a personal timescale. For instance, the effects of loneliness on social cognition and self-preservation may produce paradoxically self-defeating behavior in safe and embracing social environments but the same effects may benefit the individual and/or the group in hostile and duplicitous environments.

Lonely people are viewed more negatively—in terms of their psychosocial functioning and in terms of their interpersonal attraction or acceptance—than are nonlonely people (Lau & Gruen, 1992; Rotenberg & Kmill, 1992). Once people in a lonely person's social environment form a negative impression, their behaviors toward that individual can reinforce his or her negative social expectancies (Rotenberg, Gruman, & Ariganello, 2002), promote hostile or antagonistic behavior, and sustain the lonely individual's isolated existence. For instance, (Rotenberg, et al., 2002) found that individuals rated opposite-gender partners who they expected to be lonely as less sociable, and behaved toward them in a less sociable manner than they did toward partners they expected to be nonlonely. The opposite social forces appear to preserve the superior life of individuals very low in loneliness, in that they are perceived and treated more positively and are more likely to be given a benefit of the doubt in uncertain or ambiguous situations.

Evidence from behavioral and functional magnetic resonance imaging (fMRI) studies also supports the notion that loneliness increases attention to negative social stimuli (e.g., social threats). Using a modified emotional Stroop task, lonely participants, relative to nonlonely participants, showed greater Stroop interference specifically for negative social relative to negative non-social words (Shintel, Cacioppo, & Nusbaum, 2006). No differences between lonely and nonlonely participants were found in Stroop interference for positive social relative to positive nonsocial words. Stroop interference is used to gauge the implicit processing of stimuli, so these results suggest that loneliness is associated with a heightened accessibility of negative *social* information. Similarly, Yamada, and Decety (2009) investigated the effects of subliminal priming on the detection of painful facial expressions. Using signal detection analyses, they found that, although the pain was more easily detected in dislikable than likable faces overall, lonely individuals were more sensitive (d') to the presence of pain in dislikable faces than were nonlonely individuals.

We have also found differences in the pattern of regional brain activation produced by lonely and nonlonely individuals when thinking about people (Cacioppo, Norris, Decety, Monteleone, & Nusbaum, 2009). Activation of the visual cortex to the presentation of unpleasant social, in contrast to nonsocial, pictures was directly related to the loneliness of the participant, indicative of greater visual attention to the negative social stimuli (see Fig. 17.2). These results are consistent with the

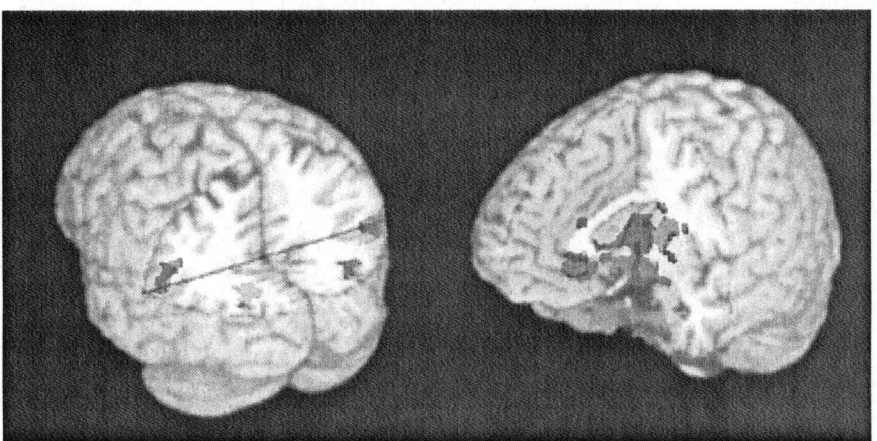

Figure 17.2 *Left Panel.* Clusters of voxels in the left and right visual cortices exhibited a positive relationship between loneliness and activation in the Unpleasant Social—Unpleasant Nonsocial contrast; whereas clusters of voxels in the left and right TPJ exhibited a negative relationship between loneliness and activation in the Unpleasant Social—Unpleasant Nonsocial contrast. *Right panel.* A cluster of voxels centered in the ventral striatum, but extending to the amygdala and portions of the anterior thalamus, showed an inverse relationship between loneliness and activation in the Pleasant Social—Pleasant Nonsocial contrast.

Reprinted with permission from Cacioppo, J. T., Norris, C. J., Decety, J., Monteleone, G., & Nusbaum, H. (2009). In the eye of the beholder: Individual differences in perceived social isolation predict regional brain activation to social stimuli. *Journal of Cognitive Neuroscience, 21*, 83–92.

behavioral data indicating that loneliness is related to an attentional bias for negative social stimuli.

A possible casualty of loneliness and the priming of social threats is that lonely individuals may be more likely to focus on their needs and their preservation in negative circumstances. To examine this possibility, activation in the temporoparietal junction (TPJ)—a region that has been found previously to be activated in theory of mind tasks and in tasks in which individuals take the perspective of another—was also examined (Cacioppo et al., 2009). Consistent with this reasoning, TPJ activation was observed when participants viewed unpleasant pictures of people versus objects, and loneliness was inversely related to amount of activation observed.

Recent research suggests that loneliness modulates the rudimentary reward system, as well. The ventral striatum, a key component of the mesolimbic dopamine system, is rich in dopaminergic neurons and is critical in reward processing and learning (Delgado, Miller, Inati, & Phelps, 2005; O'Doherty, 2004). The ventral striatum is activated by primary rewards such as stimulant drugs (Leyton, 2007), abstinence-induced cravings for primary rewards (Wang, et al., 2007), and secondary rewards such as money (Seymour, Daw, Dayan, Singer, & Dolan, 2007). Evidence that social reward also activates the ventral striatum has begun to accumulate in studies of romantic love (Aron, et al., 2005), social cooperation (Rilling, et al., 2002), social comparison (Fliessbach, et al., 2007), and punitive altruism (De Quervain, et al., 2004). We investigated how an individual's loneliness was related to the differential activation of the ventral striatum to pleasant social versus matched nonsocial images (Cacioppo et al., 2009). As depicted in Figure 17.2, lonely individuals showed weaker activation of the ventral striatum to pleasant pictures of people than of equally pleasant pictures of objects, whereas nonlonely individuals showed stronger activation of the ventral striatum to pleasant pictures of people than of objects.

There is a synergism between loneliness and affect, as well. Specifically, we have posited that loneliness has evolved to increase depressive symptomatology for two reasons. First, this lessens the likelihood individuals will try to force one's way back into a group. Second and more importantly, by acting on depressive symptomatology, loneliness increases the likelihood that an individual who feels socially isolated will evince sad facial and postural displays and audible crying, which function as a call for others to come to their aid and serve as a supportive connection (Allen & Badcock, 2003). Whether this passive mechanism for broaching a social divide succeeds and benefits the individual again depends on the social environment, such as the likelihood that a caring friend will see and be willing and able to respond to the distress cues.

Empirical evidence exists with regard to parts of this reasoning. For instance, loneliness and depressive symptoms are distinct states both by measures of statistical (Cacioppo et al., 2006) and functional independence (Adam, et al., 2006; Cole, et al., 2007; Hawkley et al., 2006). In addition, longitudinal studies have shown that loneliness predicts increases in depressive symptomatology above and beyond what can be explained by basal levels of depressive symptomatology (Cacioppo, Hughes, Waite, Hawkley, & Thisted, 2006; Heikkinen & Kauppinen, 2004; Wei, Russell, & Zakalik, 2005) and beyond what is predicted by associated psychosocial variables such as objective stress, perceived stress, social network size, neuroticism, and social support (Cacioppo, Hawkley, & Thisted, 2010). Finally, loneliness is related to stronger expectations of and motivations to avoid bad social outcomes and weaker expectations of and motivations to approach good social outcomes (Gable, 2006).

The effects of loneliness on dysphoria are not limited to the laboratory. An experience sampling study, in which participants were beeped randomly nine times per day for 7 days, confirmed that the social interactions of lonely, in contrast to nonlonely, individuals were more negative and less satisfying, and such interactions contributed subsequently to more negative moods and interactions (Hawkley, Preacher, & Cacioppo, 2007). A subsequent social network analysis of residents in Framingham, Massachusetts, further revealed that loneliness was contagious and led to a person being moved over time to the periphery of the social network (Cacioppo et al., 2009). Loneliness can clearly have detrimental effects on individuals when viewed within a personal timescale.

Loneliness has yet another cognitive consequence—it diminishes self-regulation. Social isolation in nonhuman animals has been found to increase the likelihood of a prepotent response (see Cacioppo & Hawkley, 2009b). Early evidence from young adults who performed a dichotic listening task suggested the same effect occurred in humans as a function of loneliness (Cacioppo, et al., 2000). Specifically, participants were asked to identify the consonant-vowel pair presented in the left or right ear. Typically, performance shows a right-ear advantage and performance is better for the ear to which participants have been instructed to attend. In this task, then, the prepotent response is a right-ear advantage. Lonely and nonlonely individuals showed an equivalent right ear advantage under the no-instruction condition and an equivalent attentional shift to the right ear when instructed to attend to the consonant-vowels presented in the right ear. However, lonely participants showed a weaker left-ear advantage (the non-prepotent response) when instructed to attend to this ear than did non-lonely participants, thereby demonstrating a stronger influence of the prepotent response when the non-prepotent response was required.

Poorer self-regulation when feeling isolated is not limited to attentional control. In cross-sectional and longitudinal research, lonely individuals have been found to have lower odds of engaging in regular exercise than nonlonely individuals, and the poorer emotional regulation of individuals when they felt lonely mediated the effect (Hawkley, Thisted, & Cacioppo, 2009). Experimental manipulations that lead people to believe they face a future of social isolation also decrease self-regulation. In an illustrative study, Baumeister and colleagues (Baumeister & DeWall, 2005) had the participants complete two questionnaires: an introversion/extraversion test and a personality inventory. Participants then were randomly assigned to receive no feedback (Control Group) or to receive feedback to induce feelings of a future of social isolation (Future Alone), social connection (Future Belonging), or general misfortune (Misfortune Control Group). Results revealed that the Future Alone group performed significantly worse than the other groups on the General Mental Ability Test of the Graduate Record Exam. Bad news itself was not enough to cause the disruption, only bad news about social connection.

In subsequent variations on this experimental paradigm, randomly assigned participants to the Future Alone Group, relative to the other groups, performed similarly on a rote memorization task but attempted the fewest problems and made the most mistakes on a logical reasoning task (Baumeister, DeWall, Ciarocco, & Twenge, 2005), consumed more delicious but unhealthy foods (Baumeister et al., 2005), and were more aggressive toward others (Twenge, Baumeister, Tice, & Stucke, 2001). A perceived future of social isolation, then, did not impair routine mental ability, only the higher order cognitive and self-regulatory processes that are characteristic of executive functioning. A brain scan conducted while participants performed moderately difficult math problems revealed that the brains of the future socially isolated participants were less active in the areas involved in the "executive control" of attention (Campbell et al., 2006). When one considers how unpleasant perceived social isolation is, it is perhaps understandable why individuals dealing with the misery of loneliness are less likely to deny themselves guilty pleasures or require of themselves the discipline and effort required to maintain good executive functioning.

In sum, loneliness can have beneficial and deleterious effects within a personal lifetime, with the balance between the two influenced to some extent by features of the environment. The remarkable fact may not be that loneliness can have positive and negative effects on an individual, but that most people do not feel lonely most of the time. The search for social connection may be slowed by the self-preservational biases outlined in Figure 1 but, ultimately, the motive to repair or replace one's frayed social connections is likely to succeed (Masi, Chen, Hawkley, & Cacioppo, 2011).

Multilevel models of evolution conceptualize fit in terms of embedded structures, genes within cells, cells within organ systems, organ systems within individuals, individuals within groups, groups within populations (Caporael & Brewer, 1991; Wilson, et al., 2007). The effects of loneliness on the hypothalamic pituitary adrenocortical axis (Cacioppo & Hawkley, 2009b; Hawkley & Cacioppo, 2009), for instance, serve to position individuals to respond to threats, with few long-term health consequences until the relatively recent expansion in the human lifespan. But loneliness certainly carries costs for individuals within a personal timescale. What are the costs and benefits of loneliness within an evolutionary timescale? We turn to this question next.

Loneliness within an Evolutionary Timescale

It is simple to forget that social species, by definition, form and live within superorganismal structures. As a general rule, members of social species fare poorly when forced to live solitary lives. This is not limited to humans. Isolation from conspecifics, for instance, decreases the lifespan of the fruit fly, *Drosophila melanogaster* (Ruan & Wu, 2008); promotes the development of obesity and Type 2 diabetes in mice (Nonogaki, Nozue, & Oka, 2007); delays the positive effects of running on adult neurogenesis in rats (Stranahan, Khalil, & Gould, 2006); increases the activation of the sympatho-adrenomedullary response to an acute immobilization or cold stressor in rats (Dronjak, Gavrilovic, Filipovic, & Radojcic, 2004); decreases the expression of genes regulating glucocorticoid response in the frontal cortex of piglets (Poletto, Steibel, Siegford, & Zanella, 2006); decreases open field activity, increases basal cortisol concentrations, and decreases lymphocyte proliferation to mitogens in pigs (Kanitz, Tuchscherer, Puppe, Tuchscherer, & Stabenow, 2004); increases the 24-hour urinary catecholamines levels and evidence of oxidative stress in the aortic arch of the Watanabe Heritable Hyperlipidemic rabbit (Nation et al., 2008); increases the morning rises in cortisol in squirrel monkeys (Lyons, Ha, & Levine, 1995); and disrupts psychosexual development in and the reproductive capacity of rhesus monkeys (Harlow, Dodsworth, & Harlow, 1965). From an evolutionary standpoint, one can ask what might be the benefits across generations of such deleterious responses to isolation.

Population Level Effects

When we move to the evolutionary timescale, the individual level effects manifest at the level of the population. This is so because the phenotypic expression of a trait (e.g., loneliness) within an evolutionary timescale refers to processes that operate between individuals and across generations. An organism's ability to reproduce has the potential to influence the genes that constitute the gene pool for the future generations of that species. These genes, in turn, shape the structure and function of the organisms that constitute the species. For most species, this means animals that survive to reproduce contribute their genes to the gene pool.

Reproduction is not the sole determinant of whether mammalian genes make their way to the gene pool. Mammals as infants require maternal, paternal, and/or collective care to survive so that they might reproduce. For instance, human infants are born in modal litter sizes of one and to the longest period of utter dependency of any species. Without the nurturance of caregivers, they would perish along with the genetic legacy of their parents. Ceteris paribus, therefore, a phenotype that increases the likelihood that a mammalian *offspring* would survive to reproduce would have a selective advantage. Therefore, social motivations (e.g., nurturance of dependents, reciprocity) are important for mammalian species generally and for human beings in particular.

Metaphorically speaking, the selfish gene under these conditions would need to add social connection and care to its repertoire. Ancestors who were inclined to form social connections—for instance, in order to avoid the pain of social disconnection and reinforced by the negative affect relief of reestablishing meaningful connections—were more likely to nurture their offspring, communicate and work together, share food and defense, and retaliate in the face of violations of social norms. Individuals with no such feelings of loneliness when separated from others may have roamed the earth better nourished than those who felt distressed by social separation, but the abandoned offspring—and the genetic predisposition of the parents—would have been less likely to survive (Cacioppo et al., 2006). In this section, therefore, we consider in more detail how, across generations, loneliness may have contributed to certain behavioral dispositions, and to the development of other dispositions, that promote our survival as a species.

Humans are both a species on which environments act and a powerful factor producing the environments (e.g., pollution, deforestation, housing, political and legal systems, culture) in which they exist. Many random factors determine survival of individuals, but genetic variation operates nonrandomly and generally more at the level of individual-selection processes than at the level of group-selection processes, whereas sociocultural variation operates nonrandomly and generally more at the level of group-selection processes than individual-selection processes. We therefore also consider briefly how loneliness may have contributed to human social behaviors and culture across generations.

Brewer (2004) suggests four propensities that are important for human sociality: cooperativeness, group loyalty, adherence to socially learned norms, and fear of social exclusion. Loneliness, as the pain of (perceived) social isolation, is a capacity with which humans are born that contributes to all four forms of sociality. As noted above, the aversiveness of loneliness can increase attention to one's position within the social environment, and the negative affect relief from re-establishing meaningful social connections serves to reinforce these social bonds.

The present model has features in common with Bowlby's (1969, 1982) emphasis on infant attachment, but the need to form attachments represents only a part of the story. Social pain in response to disconnections, the reward felt when those connections are reinstated, and individual differences in sensitivity to social pain and reward are also fundamental to our evolutionary model. According to our evolutionary model (Cacioppo & Hawkley,

2003) loneliness is thought to operate in part through social pain, which co-opts the physical pain system (Eisenberger, Lieberman, & Williams, 2003), and social reward, which co-opts the appetitive system (Rilling, et al., 2002), to protect the gene if not the individual. Specifically, the social pain of loneliness and the social reward of connecting with others motivate the person to repair and maintain social connections even when his or her immediate self-interests are not served by the sharing of resources or defense. In this way, loneliness promotes adaptive collective behavior to preserve the selfish molecules known as genes (Dawkins, 1976). Moreover, loneliness like physical pain and reward is posited to be influenced by situational factors but there are also stable individual differences in sensitivity.

Recent work by Eisenberger, Lieberman, and Williams (2003) and DeWall et al. (2010) on social pain and by Rilling et al (2002) on social reward is in accord with the notion that loneliness may have evolved to use the physical pain and reward systems to extend its protective function to include others. In a recent fMRI study in which participants were excluded from or included in a social situation (i.e., a ball tossing game), for instance, Eisenberger, Lieberman, and Williams (2003) found neural activation localized in a dorsal portion of the anterior cingulate cortex (ACC) that is implicated in the affective component of the pain response. The authors argue that the similarity in activation of the dorsal ACC to physical pain (e.g., Rainville, Duncan, Price, Carrier, & Bushnell, 1997) and to social pain suggests that the experiences of physical and social pain may share a common neuroanatomical basis. Furthermore, Eisenberger and her colleagues suggest that: "Because of the adaptive value of mammalian social bonds, the social attachment system … may have piggybacked onto the physical pain system to promote survival" (p. 291).

The Phenotype of Loneliness and Possible Underlying Evolutionary Mechanisms

Natural selection operates on phenotypes. It therefore can be useful to articulate the full phenotype of loneliness and to consider its adaptive function within an evolutionary timescale. Specifically, an explication of the phenotype of loneliness and a description of the adaptive function each aspect of this phenotype might be serving may help us understand the processes that operate between individuals and contribute to species survival across generations even though loneliness may be damaging in the short run to individuals who cannot rectify their isolation. That is, examining the possible evolutionary mechanisms underlying loneliness should add to our understanding of how loneliness sculpts us as a species.

The phenotypic expression of loneliness has been described as a strong sense of social pain, emptiness, isolation, sadness for lack of confidants, unimportance, and worthlessness (Weiss, 1973). Psychometric analyses reveal three basic dimensions underlying this phenotype, reflecting the degree of isolation (or connection) in three domains: intimate attachments, face-to-face relations, and social identities (Hawkley, Browne, & Cacioppo, 2005). These three dimensions are correlated but separable and robust. For instance, this factor structure has been identified in men as well as women; African Americans, Euro-Americans, and Latino-Americans; and in young adults as well as older adults in the United States (Hawkley, Browne, & Cacioppo, 2005) and in China (Hawkley, Gu, & Cacioppo, in preparation). If these different aspects of the phenotype have evolved, what is the adaptive function served by each across generations? Evolution provides more than a historical perspective, it is a continuous process that may shed light on who we are as a species and why certain behavioral tendencies operate as they do.

The first factor is *intimate isolation/connection*, or what Weiss (1973) termed emotional loneliness, and it refers to the perceived presence/absence of someone in your life who serves as a nurturing confidant, someone who affirms your value as a person. In a population-based study of middle-age and older adults, the best predictor of intimate isolation (net the other two factors that were identified) was marital status: participants who were married were, on average, lower in intimate isolation than were participants who were unmarried (Hawkley, Browne, & Cacioppo, 2005).

This facet of the phenotype of loneliness, with its emphasis on emotional aspects of loneliness and intimate connectedness, may be based on heritable differences in sensitivity to the pain of social disconnection (Cacioppo & Hawkley, 2009a). These individual differences can serve an important function in an evolutionary timescale. Individuals who are relatively insensitive to the pain of social disconnection may be more likely to serve as explorers but their insensitivity to social connection may not compel them return to share their discoveries. Individuals who are sensitive to the pain of social connection, in contrast, may be more likely to remain in or return to the group and contribute to the protection and maintenance of the group, but they may be less likely to make solitary journeys that reveal new territories, threats, or opportunities. Both types of predispositions can be important. A population consisting only of explorers may be characterized by sufficiently weak forces holding the group together that the group would splinter when pitted against oppositional forces. A population consisting only of people who are susceptible to loneliness, on the other hand, might be at risk for insecurities of other kinds, such as starvation or predation as a result of a slow rate of exploration and discovery. Note that the benefits of the population having individual differences in sensitivity to disconnection would accrue even if the group as a whole tended to peripheralize individuals who manifested loneliness. Most individuals who feel lonely resolve their loneliness before it becomes an extreme condition, and even those who fail to resolve loneliness before it becomes severe nevertheless tend to form new connections given sufficient time (Masi et al., 2011). These new connections may be with others who share a sense of isolation, which, through the process of assortive mating, contributes to the continuation of heritable individual differences in loneliness at the level of the population (Distel, et al., 2010).

What evidence is there that the heritability of loneliness reflects, at least in part, individual differences in sensitivity to social disconnection? Relevant evidence is available from a surprising source: Myron Hofer's (2009) research on the selective breeding of rats. A well-characterized response to maternal separation is the separation cry. In the rat, the separation cry is in the ultrasonic range (40–45 kHz). These ultrasonic vocalizations (USVs) to isolation are attenuated in a dose-related fashion by anxiolytics that act on benzodiazepine and serotonin receptors and are exaggerated by anxiogenics such as the benzodiazepine receptor partial inverse agonist FG7142 (e.g., Brunelli & Hofer, 2001). Neuroanatomical studies reviewed by Hofer (2009) point to the periaquaductal grey area as a neural substrate for these USVs in rats and the hypothalamus, amygdala, thalamus, and hippocampus and cingulate cortex as the neural substrates for isolation calls in primates. As Hofer notes:

> The evolution of such a response is clarified by the finding that infant rat USV is a powerful stimulus for the lactating rat, capable of causing her to interrupt an ongoing nursing bout, initiate searching outside the nest, and direct her search toward the source of

the calls … The mother's retrieval response to the pup's vocal signals then results in renewed contact between pup and mother. This contact, in turn, quiets the pup (Hofer, 2009, p. 20).

Hofer uses the concept of attachment to describe the emotional expression represented by the USVs and the reestablishment of the social bond by the maternal search for, renewed contact with, and comfort response of the rat pup.

Although the infant USV helps guide the mother to the infant, these USVs can also lead predators to the infant. Ultrasonic vocalizations may be beneficial or deleterious, depending on the presence of predators in the environment. As a consequence, no single level of intensity of USVs to isolation is universally best, and heritable individual differences in this predisposition exist in the population. Some rat pups, who might be characterized as sensitive to separation, cry frequently (albeit ultrasonically) when isolated, whereas others are less sensitive to separation and show less distress when isolated. Hofer and colleagues selectively bred adult rats that, as rat pups, showed either high or relatively low rates of USVs to separation (Brunelli & Hofer, 2007). After 25 generations of selective breeding, differences behavior between the two lines of rats were reminiscent of some of the differences observed in humans who are high or low in loneliness: the high, relative to low, USV line showed more distress to isolation as an infant; greater latency to play as an adolescent; and greater depression-like behaviors, greater anxiety-like behaviors, greater latency to social interactions, greater startle, and diminished learning as an adult. That is, the high USV line was anxious and passive, whereas the low USV line was exploratory, active, and aggressive (Hofer, 2009).

This work, then, supports a link between loneliness and attachment processes and points to a specific aspect of the phenotype (sensitivity to isolation) and evolutionary mechanisms for this phenotype. Note, however, that in this context the mother–infant attachment *builds* on heritable differences in sensitivity to isolation rather than the pain of isolation resulting from poor infant attachment behaviors by the mother.

The second factor is *relational isolation/connection*, or what Weiss (1973) termed social loneliness, and refers to the perceived presence/absence of quality friendships or family connections. The best predictor of relational isolation was the frequency of contact with friends and family: participants who had frequent contact with friends and family were lower in relational isolation even after statistically controlling for the two other loneliness factors (Hawkley, Browne, & Cacioppo, 2005). This factor is found in women as well as men, but it appears to be more heavily weighted in women than in men such that it plays a larger role in influencing degree of loneliness in women than in men.

The relational connectedness aspect of the phenotype of loneliness may have a different evolutionary basis than the intimate connectedness aspect. For instance, loneliness not only serves to signal the prospect that our social connection is at risk or absent and to motivate us to repair or restore the safe, collaborative social surround we need to ensure a genetic legacy, but it may also provide incentives to become more compassionate and empathic members of our social species. Consider the contemporary practice of time-out. When a child acts selfishly or socially inappropriately, a common practice is to isolate the child from the others for approximately one minute per year of age. This enforced social isolation is typically painful for the child and may be associated with displays of sadness or general negative affect, which we noted serves as an appeal for connection and support by anyone in the vicinity. Upon reintegration to the group following the time-out, the child tends to act in a more empathic, less narcissistic fashion—that is, the existence of the aversive state of loneliness can contribute to our socialization and culture.

Although time-out is a recent innovation, it is illustrative of a more general principle in which an individual in a social setting who is made to feel isolated is compelled to change his or her behavior toward others. The "silent treatment" between close social others, workplace expulsion, teasing, being excluded or ignored in social circumstances, and countless other passive or active rejection behaviors, whether enacted for virtuous or malicious reasons, are potent elicitors of social pain (Williams, Suchy, & Rau, 2009) and can also serve to promote other-oriented social motives. Evidence of shunning and ostracism can be found in nonhuman social species as well as in various cultures across human history. Ostracism in most social species is associated with an early death (Williams, 2001). In humans, the chronic feeling of social isolation, even when the person remains among the protective embrace of others, is associated with significant adverse mental and physical outcomes (Hawkley & Cacioppo, 2009; Patterson & Veenstra, 2010). Because humans need to be able to work together to survive and prosper, the effects of time-out,

shunning, and related methods of interpersonal rejection on people's social skills (e.g., reduced selfishness, increased perspective taking and empathy) benefit the individual and contribute to social adhesion and resilience.

Humans are especially adept in observational learning—extracting information about the environment based on their observations of the costs and benefits of those with whom they are connected or about whom they care. Social learning, in turn, promotes the development of common knowledge and practices, that is culture, adding to the centripetal forces banding individuals together to form adaptable, cooperative groups (Rendell, et al., 2010). The effect of loneliness on people's attention to interpersonal information may, therefore, have the additional benefit of promoting social learning.

But isn't selfishness the law of our genes? The notion of "selfish genes" (and, by extension, selfish organisms) was popularized in Richard Dawkins' 1976 book by that title. Not long afterwards, an article appeared in *Science* that presented evidence that the most vicious members of a warlike tribe in South America had the most wives and children. The underlying notion was one of (genetic) survival of the fittest: Those warriors who were particularly vicious were more likely to contribute their genes to the gene pool. Methodological objections have left this an open question, however, and new evidence now exists that calls this interpretation into question. Beckerman and colleagues (Beckerman, et al., 2009) found that the most aggressive warriors may have more children but they have *lower* indices of reproductive success than their milder brethren in part perhaps because the most aggressive warriors and their offspring are also more likely to be the targets of revenge killings. These data are consistent with the notion that the content of the human gene pool is influenced by interpersonal connections and the reproductive success of one's offspring, not simply to one's own reproductive success.

The third factor is *collective isolation/connection*, an aspect that Weiss (1973) did not identify in his qualitative studies. Collective isolation refers to the perceived presence/absence of a meaningful connection with a group or social entity beyond the level of individuals (e.g., school, team, nation). The best predictor found in middle-age and older adults for collective isolation was the number of voluntary groups to which participants belonged: the more voluntary associations to which participants belonged, the lower their collective isolation, again even after statistically controlling for the two other factors (Hawkley, Browne, & Cacioppo, 2005). This factor is also found in women as well as men, but it is more heavily weighted in men than in women.

Given humans are adapted for group living, an aspect of the phenotype of loneliness that represents superorganismal structures, collective identities, and in-group biases may also have evolved due to their unique adaptive function in certain habitats. For instance, warfare among ancestral hunter-gatherers appears to have contributed to selection for human social behaviors, especially altruistic behaviors (Bowles, 2009; LeVine & Campbell, 1972; Wilson, et al., 2007). As Darwin (1871) noted:

> A tribe including many members who, from possessing a high degree of the spirit of patriotism, fidelity, obedience, courage, and sympathy, were always ready to aid one another, and to sacrifice themselves for the common good would be victorious over most other tribes; and this would be natural selection (p. 166).

Generally in the animal kingdom, if males compete, coalitions tend to form (de Waal & Pollick, 2005). Competition between groups promotes hierarchies and cooperation within groups, an effect demonstrated in the classic study of boys at summer camps by Sherif, Harvey, White, Hood, and Sherif (1961) and in recent research on chimpanzees:

> Chimpanzee males conduct warfare against neighboring groups and do so in a highly consolidated fashion; if they did not, then foreign groups would invade their territories. We see how competition and cooperation are not mutually exclusive aspects of society, be it human or ape (de Waal & Pollick, 2005, p. 40).

Recent anthropological investigations of *Ardipithecus ramidus* (who lived approximately 4.4 million years ago) has led to the conclusion that certain adaptations exhibited by this early hominin species (i.e., diminution of male canine size, upright walking, and absence of ovulatory signaling) reduced intrasexual conflict among males and fostered pair bonding and greater male parental investment (de Waal & Pollick, 2005; Lovejoy, 2009). In the human pair bond and nuclear family, the members are part of a larger collective within which the nuclear family is fully integrated. Indeed, the human pair bond may have evolved hand in hand with the group. For instance, heterosexual pair bonding in humans raises the certitude of paternity, thereby increasing the parental investment in dependent offspring. In addition, it lessens rivalry for sexual partners among males, with the consequent reduction in sexual rivalry lessening the competition among males, promoting cooperation in hunting and warfare, and altering the organization and operation of the population to make it more resilient. As de Waal and Pollick (2005) note: "Human families are part and parcel of the society ... In evolutionary terms, there first must have been the larger society, within which developed the human family" (p. 34).

Social hierarchies in the Macaque are rigid and matriarchal. In chimpanzees and human beings, in contrast, social hierarchies reflect alliances and coalitions based on cooperative agreements. Typically, physical might and recognizing the shifting status of friends and foes may not be sufficient to achieve and maintain a position of status and power in these hierarchies. One also needs to be able to represent and navigate complex social hierarchies, social norms, and cultural developments; subjugate self interests to the interests of the group in exchange for long-term benefits; and recruit support to sanction individuals who violate social norms—that is, to be perceived as serving the interests of the group or at least much of the group. Moreover, individual reciprocity promotes cooperative arrangements between individuals; network reciprocity promotes cooperation and prosocial behavior at the level of the group. When prosocial behavior and cooperation can be assumed based on group membership rather than personal friendship, the transaction costs of interactions within the group can be reduced significantly, and a strong connection to the group benefits the individual members and increases the ability of the group to adapt to new challenges and to martial an effective defense.

In sum, people have self-interests as well as group interests, and these interests can be in conflict. Within such circumstances, identification with and investments in the group increase the likelihood of the continuity of the group as a whole and the survival of its members (Brewer, 2004). Ceteris paribus, the pain of collective isolation and the rewarding feeling of collective identity and connection serve to promote group interests in such circumstances, where deleterious effects at the level of the individual within a lifetime can be offset by the beneficial effects within an evolutionary timescale. Research on social dilemmas has shown that people are more likely to act for the common good rather than selfishly when a collective social identity is available (Kramer & Brewer, 1984; Swann, Gomez, Dovidio, Hart, & Jetten, 2010). When people perceive themselves to be part of a valued group (collective connection), they are also more inclined to agree with other group members, even on beliefs that may seem irrational, than when they think of themselves as unique individuals. This tendency can result in poorer decisions in some circumstances, but the cooperation and collective investments it promotes can also be beneficial in other circumstances. The emergence of a collective connectedness factor underlying loneliness, therefore, suggests that we have evolved the capacity for and motivation to form relationships not only with other individuals but also to groups (e.g., a Chicago Cubs or Boston Red Sox fan), with the consequence being the promotion of cooperation in adverse conditions (e.g., hunting, warfare).

Conclusions

We have argued that loneliness may have deleterious consequences for an individual, but it is a heritable individual difference that evolved because of the important functions it serves for individuals in our species. Natural selection operates across generations, and it is a process that continues. Understanding how natural selection operates to produce the capacity for humans to feel loneliness may contribute to our understanding of who we are as a species and why certain behavioral tendencies continue to operate as they do.

Loneliness is distinct from but nevertheless often conflated with related constructs, such as depressive symptomatology, insecure attachment style, empathy, need to belong, shyness, poor social skills, and introversion. For instance, an individual might have a strong or weak affiliative need, but it is whether this need is satisfied that determines whether the individual is lonely or not. Our goal in this chapter has been to outline an evolutionary theory of loneliness to explore its potential adaptive value in an evolutionary timescale. We have argued that loneliness serves to promote and protect a fundamental property of our species—our connection to others. For instance, loneliness draws attention to the prospect that our social connection to others is at risk or absent; motivates us to repair or replace the safe, collaborative social surround we need to ensure a genetic legacy; provides incentives for people to become more compassionate and empathic members of our quintessentially social species; and keeps us attuned to our social identities, thereby increasing social adhesion, cooperation, and network reciprocity.

Brewer (2004) notes that: "If humans are adapted to live in groups and depend on group effectiveness for survival, then our motivational systems should be tuned to the requirements for group effectiveness" (p. 111). Loneliness may feel like a painfully miserable, hopeless, and unwanted state, but different *aspects* of this motivational phenotype may each have an important adaptive value (and a distinct evolutionary origin) for a complex social species such as our own wherein our genetic survival depends on caregiving, trust and cooperation, and group living, especially when alliances and allegiances can change dramatically as situations shift. If this reasoning is correct, then loneliness may well be a polygenic trait subject to epigenetic influences.

The capacity for feeling loneliness, when viewed from an evolutionary perspective as an adaptive biological capacity, is not so much about a dysfunctional property of humankind that produces personal misery as it is about promoting the resilience of social groups, with significant benefits to the individual members of those groups. More specifically, social resilience is increased to the extent that the pain of loneliness and the reward of meaningful connection contribute to members of the group interacting in ways that minimize each member's feelings of loneliness. Let us explain.

Resilience as a property of a substance refers to its ability to recoil or spring back into shape after bending, stretching, or being compressed. People can also be more or less resilient, and in this context resilience refers to a person's ability to withstand or recover quickly from difficult conditions. A person's resilience is not a capacity that, akin to intelligence or musical talent, is relatively invariant across contexts, but rather it is like the resilience of physical substances, which can vary a great deal across contexts. For instance, water in a warm environment (i.e., when it is in a liquid state) is much more resilient than water in a frozen environment (i.e., when it is in the solid state of ice).

Similarly, an individual's resilience can vary dramatically as a function of the social context. Social resilience is an inherently multilevel construct, revealed by capacities of individuals *and* groups to foster, engage in, and sustain positive social relationships and to endure and recover from stressors and social isolation (Cacioppo, Reis, & Zautra, 2011). Emergent levels of organization, ranging from dyads, families, and groups to cities, civilizations, and international alliances have long been apparent in human existence, but identifying the features of individuals, relationships, and group structures and norms that promote social resilience remains an important challenge.

Social resilience is more than fulfilling friendships and the comfortable exchange of ideas, however. Social resilience is not equivalent to warm hugs, unconditional positive regard, and anticompetition sentiments. Both science and the Olympics rest on competition as well as cooperation, both involve intense training and criticism, and both enterprises are high in social resilience. We again see that it is not the presence of cooperation *or* competition but it is the dynamics of cooperation and competition, inclusion and exclusion, and interdependence and independence that contributes to social resilience. Loneliness contributes to this dynamic interplay by providing an alarm when the threat of social disconnection begins to rise as well as individual differences in sensitivity to such threats.

Social resilience recognizes that, as a social species, we work, think, and excel as groups/teams as well as individuals. Wolves and lions hunt in teams, and by doing so they are able to bring down prey that would be impossible to conquer alone. Human civilizations rest on the specialization, differentiation, and orchestration of human expertise so that we, as a collective, can achieve more than we could by our solitary efforts. Social resilience is an emergent (but not a magical) property. People who have diverse interests, skills, and resources and who can work together make it more likely the group as a whole can respond adaptively to unforeseen problems and challenges. The functions each person serves in such adverse circumstances may not be defined a priori by the knowledge or "skills" of the individuals per se. Instead, how these individuals are combined can fundamentally change the capacities/functions the group can achieve to address a novel challenge. When individuals feel rejected, isolated, distrusted, devalued, or simply disliked, they cannot work effectively as part of the unit, and they are less likely to adapt creatively as a unit as required by the challenges they confront.

Social resilience implies not merely acceptance of diversity, but rather a value in diversity and the intention to incorporate diverse perspectives into group activity for the creative adaptations that such diversity predisposes. Surrounding oneself with a lot of "mini-mes" can be self-affirming but it does little to help one adapt to new challenges and problems or to withstand or recover quickly from very difficult conditions. People are not unique in this regard. Homogenous gene pools are at greater risk than their heterogeneous counterparts for extinction when exposed to new environmental challenges. Given recent research demonstrating that making people feel affiliated increases dehumanization of out-group members whereas loneliness has the opposite effect (Waytz & Epley, 2009), loneliness

may serve an adaptive function in homogeneous social environments by encouraging the inclusion of those different from the modal member and contributing to migrations to other groups.

Acknowledgment

This work was supported by National Institute of Aging Program Project Grant No. PO1 AG18911 & RO1 AG034052-01 and by a grant from the John Templeton Foundation. Address correspondence to John T. Cacioppo, Center for Cognitive and Social Neuroscience, University of Chicago, Chicago, IL 60637, Cacioppo@uchicago.edu.

Note

1. Whereas natural selection acts nonrandomly on phenotypes in a specific environment, genetic drift and mutation acts randomly on genotypes. As genetic drift represents the change in relative frequency of alleles in a population due to random sampling, its influence on the population genotype is greater for small than for large populations (Futuyma, 1998). Genetic drift and mutations contribute nonsystematic genetic variation on which natural selection can then operate across generations at the level of phenotypes to improve the fit of a species to the environment.

References

Adam, E. K., Hawkley, L. C., Kudielka, B. M., & Cacioppo, J. T. (2006). Day-to-day dynamics of experience—cortisol associations in a population-based sample of older adults. *Proceedings of the National Academy of Science of the United States of America*, 103(45), 17058–17063. doi: 0605053103 [pii] 10.1073/pnas.0605053103 [doi]

Akerlind, I., & Hornquist, J. O. (1992). Loneliness and alcohol abuse: A review of evidences of an interplay. *Social Science and Medicine*, 34(4), 405–414.

Allen, N. B., & Badcock, P. B. T. (2003). The social risk hypothesis of depressed mood: evolutionary, psychosocial, and neurobiological perspectives. *Psychological Bulletin*, 129(6), 887–913.

Andersson, L. (1998). Loneliness research and interventions: a review of the literature. *Aging & Mental Health*, 2(4), 264–274.

Aron, A., Fisher, H., Mashek, D. J., Strong, G., Li, H., & Brown, L. L. (2005). Reward, motivation, and emotion systems associated with early-stage intense romantic love. *Journal of Neurophysiology*, 94(1), 327–337. doi: 00838.2004 [pii] 10.1152/jn.00838.2004 [doi]

Bartels, M., Cacioppo, J. T., Hudziak, J. J., & Boomsma, D. I. (2008). Genetic and environmental contributions to stability in loneliness throughout childhood. *American Journal of Medical Geneticss. Part B: Neuropsychiatric Genetics*, 147(3), 385–391. doi: 10.1002/ajmg.b.30608 [doi]

Baumeister, R., & DeWall, N. (2005). The inner dimension of social exclusion: Intelligent thought and self-regulation among rejected persons. In K. D. Williams, J. P. Forgas, & W. von Hippel (Eds.), *The Social Outcast: Ostracism, Social Exclusion, Rejection, and Bullying*. (pp. 53–76). New York: Psychology Press.

Baumeister, R. F., DeWall, C. N., Ciarocco, N. J., & Twenge, J. M. (2005). Social exclusion impairs self-regulation. *Journal of Personality and Social Psychology, 88*(4), 589–604. doi: 2005-02948-001 [pii] 10.1037/0022-3514.88.4.589 [doi]

Beckerman, S., Erickson, P. I., Yost, J., Regalado, J., Jaramillo, L., Sparks, C., et al. (2009). Life histories, blood revenge, and reproductive success among the Waorani of Ecuador. *Proceedings of the National Academy of Sciences of the United States of America, 106*(20), 8134–8139. doi: 0901431106 [pii] 10.1073/pnas.0901431106 [doi]

Bondevik, M., & Skogstad, A. (1998). The oldest old, ADL, social network, and loneliness. *Western Journal of Nursing Research, 20*(3), 325–343.

Boomsma, D., Cacioppo, J., Slagboom, P., & Posthuma, D. (2006). Genetic linkage and association analysis for loneliness in dutch twin and sibling pairs points to a region on chromosome 12q23–24. *Behavior Genetics, 36*(1), 137–146.

Boomsma, D., Willemsen, G., Dolan, C., Hawkley, L., & Cacioppo, J. (2005). Genetic and environmental contributions to loneliness in adults: The Netherlands Twin Register Study. *Behavior Genetics, 35*(6), 745–752.

Boomsma, D. I., Cacioppo, J. T., Muthen, B., Asparouhov, T., & Clark, S. (2007). Longitudinal genetic analysis for loneliness in Dutch twins. *Twin Res Hum Genet, 10*(2), 267–273. doi: 10.1375/twin.10.2.267 [doi]

Bowlby, J. (1969). *Attachment.* New York: Basic Books.

Bowlby, J. (1982). *Attachment and Loss. Vol.1, Attachment.* London: Hogarth.

Bowles, S. (2009). Did warfare among ancestral hunter-gatherers affect the evolution of human social behaviors? *Science, 324*(5932), 1293–1298. doi: 324/5932/1293 [pii] 10.1126/science.1168112 [doi]

Boyd, R., & Richerson, P. J. (1985). *Culture and the Evolutionary Process.* Chicago: University of Chicago Press.

Brewer, M. B. (2004). Taking the social origins of human nature seriously: toward a more imperialist social psychology. *Personality & Social Psychology Review, 8*(2), 107–113.

Brunelli, S. A., & Hofer, M. A. (2001). Selective breeding for an infantile phenotype (isolation calling): A window on developmental processes. In Blass (Ed.), *Handbook of Behavioral Neurobiology* (pp. 433–482). New York: Plenum Press.

Brunelli, S. A., & Hofer, M. A. (2007). Selective breeding for infant rat separation-induced ultrasonic vocalizations: Developmental precursors of passive and active coping styles. *Behavioural Brain Research., 182*(2), 193.

Cacioppo, J. T., Ernst, J. M., Burleson, M. H., McClintock, M. K., Malarkey, W. B., Hawkley, L. C., et al. (2000). Lonely traits and concomitant physiological processes: the MacArthur social neuroscience studies. *International Journal of Psychophysiology, 35*(2–3), 143–154.

Cacioppo, J. T., Fowler, J. H., & Christakis, N. A. (2009). Alone in the crowd: The structure and spread of loneliness in a large social network. *Journal of Personality and Social Psychology, 97*(6), 977–991. doi: 10.1037/a0016076

Cacioppo, J. T., & Hawkley, L. C. (2003). Social isolation and health, with an emphasis on underlying mechanisms. *Perspectives in Biology and Medicine, 46*(3 supplement), s39–s52.

Cacioppo, J. T., & Hawkley, L. C. (2005). People thinking about people: The vicious cycle of being a social outcast in one's own mind. In K. D. Williams, J. P. Forgas, & W. von Hippel (Eds.), *The Social Outcast: Ostracism, Social Exclusion, Rejection, and Bullying* (pp. 91–108). New York: Psychology Press.

Cacioppo, J. T., & Hawkley, L. C. (2009a). *Loneliness. Handbook of Individual Differences In Social Behavior* (pp. 227–240). New York: Guilford.

Cacioppo, J. T., & Hawkley, L. C. (2009b). Perceived social isolation and cognition. *Trends in Cognitive Sciences, 13*(10), 447–454. doi: 10.1016/j.tics.2009.06.005

Cacioppo, J. T., Hawkley, L. C., Berntson, G. G., Ernst, J. M., Gibbs, A. C., Stickgold, R., et al. (2002). Do lonely days invade the nights? Potential social modulation of sleep efficiency. *Psychological Science, 13*(4), 384–387.

Cacioppo, J. T., Hawkley, L. C., Crawford, L. E., Ernst, J. M., Burleson, M. H., Kowalewski, R. B., et al. (2002). Loneliness and health: potential mechanisms. *Psychosom Med, 64*(3), 407–417.

Cacioppo, J. T., Hawkley, L. C., Ernst, J. M., Burleson, M., Berntson, G. G., Nouriani, B., et al. (2006). Loneliness within a nomological net: An evolutionary perspective. *Journal of Research in Personality, 40*(6), 1054–1085.

Cacioppo, J. T., Hawkley, L. C., & Thisted, R. A. (2010). Perceived social isolation makes me sad: Five year cross-lagged analysis of loneliness and depressive symptomatology in the Chicago Health, Aging, and Social Relations study. *Psychology and Aging, 25*(2), 453–463. doi: 10.1037/a0017216

Cacioppo, J. T., Hughes, M. E., Waite, L. J., Hawkley, L. C., & Thisted, R. A. (2006). Loneliness as a specific risk factor for depressive symptoms: cross-sectional and longitudinal analyses. *Psychology and Aging, 21*(1), 140–151. doi: 2006-03906-014 [pii] 10.1037/0882-7974.21.1.140 [doi]

Cacioppo, J. T., Norris, C. J., Decety, J., Monteleone, G., & Nusbaum, H. (2009). In the eye of the beholder: individual differences in perceived social isolation predict regional brain activation to social stimuli. *Journal of Cognitive Neuroscience, 21*(1), 83–92. doi: 10.1162/jocn.2009.21007

Cacioppo, J. T., Reis, H. T., & Zautra, A. J. (2011). Social resilience: The value of social fitness with an application to the military. *American Psychologist, 66*, 43–51. doi: 10.1037/a0021419

Campbell, W. K., Krusemark, E. A., Dyckman, K. A., Brunell, A. B., McDowell, J. E., Twenge, J. M., et al. (2006). A magneto-encephalography investigation of neural correlates for social exclusion and self-control. *Social Neuroscience, 1*(2), 124–134. doi: 759346796 [pii] 10.1080/17470910601035160 [doi]

Caporael, L. R., & Brewer, M. B. (1991). Reviving evolutionary psychology: biology meets society. *Journal of Social Issues, 47*(3), 187–195.

Caporael, L. R., & Brewer, M. B. (1995). Hierarchical evolutionary theory: There is an alternative, and it's not creationism. *Psychological Inquiry, 6*(1), 31–34.

Cole, S. W., Hawkley, L. C., Arevalo, J. M., Sung, C. Y., Rose, R. M., & Cacioppo, J. T. (2007). Social regulation of gene expression in human leukocytes. *Genome Biology, 8*(9), R189.181-R189.113. doi: gb-2007-8-9-r189 [pii] 10.1186/gb-2007-8-9-r189 [doi]

Conover, D. O., & Munch, S. B. (2002). Sustaining fisheries yields over evolutionary time scales. *Science, 297*(5578), 94.

Cutrona, C. E. (1982). Transition to college: Loneliness and the process of social adjustment. In L. A. Peplau & D. Perlman (Eds.), *Loneliness: A Sourcebook of Current Theory, Research, and Therapy* (pp. 291–309). New York: John Wiley & Sons.

Darwin, C. (1871). *The Descent of Man and Selection in Relation to Sex*. London: Murray.

Dawkins, R. (1976). *The Selfish Gene*. New York: Oxford University Press.

De Quervain, D. J. F., Fischbacher, U., Treyer, V., Schellhammer, M., Schnyder, U., Buck, A., et al. (2004). The neural basis of altruistic punishment. *Science, 305*(5688), 1254–1258.

de Waal, F. B. M., & Pollick, A. S. (2005). The biology of family values: Reproductive strategies of our fellow primates. In S. M. Tipton & J. Witte (Eds.), *Family Transformed: Religion, Values, and Society in American Life* (pp. 34–51). Washington, DC: Georgetown University Press.

Delgado, M. R., Miller, M. M., Inati, S., & Phelps, E. A. (2005). An fMRI study of reward-related probability learning. *Neuroimage, 24*(3), 862–873. doi: S1053-8119(04)00592-0 [pii] 10.1016/j.neuroimage.2004.10.002 [doi]

DeWall, C. N., MacDonald, G., Webster, G. D., Masten, C. L., Baumeister, R. F., Powell, C., et al. (2010). Acetaminophen reduces social pain: Behaviorall and neural evidence. *Psychological Science, 21*, 931–937.

Distel, M. A., Rebollo-Mesa, I., Abdellaoui, A., Derom, C. A., Willemsen, G., Cacioppo, J. T., et al. (2010). Familial resemblance for loneliness. *Behavior Genetics, 40*(4), 480–494.

Downey, G. D., & Romero-Canyas, R. (2005). Rejection sensitivity as a predictor of affective and behavioral responses to interpersonal stress: A defensive motivational system. In K. D. Williams, J. P. Forgas & W. von Hippel (Eds.), *The Social Outcast: Ostracism, Social Exclusion, Rejection, and Bullying*. New York: The Psychology Press.

Dronjak, S., Gavrilovic, L., Filipovic, D., & Radojcic, M. B. (2004). Immobilization and cold stress affect sympatho-adrenomedullary system and pituitary-adrenocortical axis of rats exposed to long-term isolation and crowding. *Physiology and Behavior, 81*(3), 409–415. doi: 10.1016/j.physbeh.2004.01.011 [doi] S0031938404000356 [pii]

Duck, S., Pond, K., & Leatham, G. (1994). Loneliness and the evaluation of relational events. *Journal of Social and Personal Relationships, 11*(2), 253.

Dugan, E., & Kivett, V. R. (1994). The importance of emotional and social isolation to loneliness among very old rural adults. *Gerontologist, 34*(3), 340–346.

Dykstra, P. A., & de Jong, G. J. (1999). [Differential indicators of loneliness among elderly. The importance of type of partner relationship, partner history, health, socioeconomic status and social relations]. *Tijdschrift Voor Gerontologie En Geriatrie, 30*(5), 212–225.

Eisenberger, N. I., Lieberman, M. D., & Williams, K. D. (2003). Does rejection hurt? An fMRI study of social exclusion. *Science, 302*(5643), 290–292.

Fliessbach, K., Weber, B., Trautner, P., Dohmen, T., Sunde, U., Elger, C. E., et al. (2007). Social comparison affects reward-related brain activity in the human ventral striatum. *Science, 318*(5854), 1305–1308. doi: 10.1126/science.1145876

Futuyma, D. J. (1998). Evolutionary biology, 3rd ed. Sunderland, MA: Sinauer.

Gable, S. L. (2006). Approach and avoidance social motives and goals. *Journal of Personality, 74*(1), 175–222. doi: JOPY373 [pii] 10.1111/j.1467-6494.2005.00373.x [doi]

Harlow, H. F., Dodsworth, R. O., & Harlow, M. K. (1965). Total social isolation in monkeys. *Proceedings of the National Academy of Sciences of the United States of America, 54*(1), 90–97.

Hawkley, L. C., Berntson, G. G., Engeland, C. G., Marucha, P. T., Masi, C. M., & Cacioppo, J. T. (2005). Stress, aging, and resilience: Can accrued wear and tear be slowed? *Canadian Psychology-Psychologie Canadienne, 46*(3), 115–125.

Hawkley, L. C., Browne, M. W., & Cacioppo, J. T. (2005). How can I connect with thee? Let me count the ways. *Psychological Science, 16*(10), 798–804. doi: doi:10.1111/j.1467-9280.2005.01617.x

Hawkley, L. C., & Cacioppo, J. T. (2009). Loneliness. In H. Reis & S. Sprecher (Eds.), *Encyclopedia of Human Relationships* (pp. 985–990). Thousand Oaks, CA: Sage Press.

Hawkley, L. C., Gu, Y., Luo, Y., & Cacioppo, J. T. (in press). The mental representation of social connectiosn: Generaizability extended to Beijing adults. *PLOS ONE*.

Hawkley, L. C., Hughes, M. E., Waite, L. J., Masi, C. M., Thisted, R. A., & Cacioppo, J. T. (2008). From social structure factors to perceptions of relationship quality and loneliness: The Chicago Health, Aging, and Social Relations Study. *The Journal of Gerontology. Series B, Psychological Sciences and Social Sciences, 63*, S375–384.

Hawkley, L. C., Masi, C. M., Berry, J. D., & Cacioppo, J. T. (2006). Loneliness is a unique predictor of age-related differences in systolic blood pressure. *Psychology and Aging, 21*(1), 152–164. doi: 2006-03906-015 [pii] 10.1037/0882-7974.21.1.152 [doi]

Hawkley, L. C., Preacher, K. J., & Cacioppo, J. T. (2007). Multilevel modeling of social interactions and mood in lonely and socially connected individuals: The MacArthur social neuroscience studies. In A. D. Ong & M. van Dulmen (Eds.), *Oxford Handbook of Methods in Positive Psychology* (pp. 559–575). New York: Oxford University Press.

Hawkley, L. C., Thisted, R. A., & Cacioppo, J. T. (2009). Loneliness predicts reduced physical activity: Cross-sectional & longitudinal analyses. *Health Psychology, 28*(3), 354–363. doi: 10.1037/a0014400

Hector-Taylor, L., & Adams, P. (1996). State versus trait loneliness in elderly New Zealanders. *Psychological Reports, 78*(3 Pt 2), 1329–1330.

Heikkinen, R.-L., & Kauppinen, M. (2004). Depressive symptoms in late life: a 10-year follow-up. *Archives of Gerontology and Geriatrics, 38*(3), 239–250.

Hofer, M. A. (2009). Developmental neuroscience. In G. G. Berntson & J. T. Cacioppo (Eds.), *Handbook of Neuroscience for the Behavioral Sciences* (pp. 12–31). Hoboken: Wiley.

Holmen, K., Ericsson, K., Andersson, L., & Winblad, B. (1992). Subjective loneliness—a comparison between elderly and relatives. *Vard i Norden, 12*(2), 9–13.

House, J. S., Landis, K. R., & Umberson, D. (1988). Social relationships and health. *Science, 241*(4865), 540–545.

Jones, D. C. (1992). Parental divorce, family conflict and friendship networks. *Journal of Social and Personal Relationships, 9*(2), 219–235. doi: 10.1177/0265407592092004

Kanitz, E., Tuchscherer, M., Puppe, B., Tuchscherer, A., & Stabenow, B. (2004). Consequences of repeated early isolation in domestic piglets (Sus scrofa) on their behavioural, neuroendocrine, and immunological responses. *Brain, Behavior, and Immunity, 18*(1), 35–45.

Kiecolt-Glaser, J. K., Ricker, D., George, J., Messick, G., Speicher, C. E., Garner, W., et al. (1984). Urinary cortisol levels, cellular immunocompetency, and loneliness in psychiatric inpatients. *Psychosomatic Medicine, 46*(1), 15–23.

Knoll, A. H., & Holland, H. D. (1995). Oxygen and proterozoic evolution: an update. In National Research

Council (Ed.), *Effects of Past Global Change on Life: Studies in Geophysics* (pp. 21–33). Washington, DC: National Academy Press.

Kramer, R. M., & Brewer, M. B. (1984). Effects of group identity on resource use in a simulated commons dilemma. *Journal of Personality and Social Psychology, 46*(5), 1044–1057.

Lane, N. (2002). *Oxygen: The Molecule that Made the World.* Oxford; New York: Oxford University Press.

Lau, S., & Gruen, G. E. (1992). The social stigma of loneliness: effect of target person's and perceiver's sex. *Personality and Social Psychology Bulletin, 18*(2), 182–189. doi: 10.1177/0146167292182009

Lauder, W., Mummery, K., Jones, M., & Caperchione, C. (2006). A comparison of health behaviors in lonely and non-lonely populations. *Psychology, Health & Medicine, 11*(2), 233–245.

LeVine, R. A., & Campbell, D. T. (1972). *Ethnocentrism: Theories of Conflict, Ethnic Attitudes, and Group Behavior.* New York: John Wiley.

Leyton, M. (2007). Conditioned and sensitized responses to stimulant drugs in humans. *Progress in Neuro-Psychopharmacology and Biological Psychiatry, 31*(8), 1601–1613. doi: S0278-5846(07)00311-9 [pii] 10.1016/j.pnpbp.2007.08.027 [doi]

Lovejoy, C. O. (2009). Reexamining human origins in light of Ardipithecus ramidus. *Science, 326*(5949), 74–748. doi: 10.1126/science.1175834

Lyons, D. M., Ha, C. M., & Levine, S. (1995). Social effects and circadian rhythms in squirrel monkey pituitary-adrenal activity. *Hormones and Behavior, 29*(2), 177–190. doi: S0018-506X(85)71013-6 [pii] 10.1006/hbeh.1995.1013 [doi]

Masi, C. M., Chen, H.-Y., Hawkley, L. C., & Cacioppo, J. T. (2011). A meta-analysis of interventions to reduce loneliness. *Personality and Social Psychology Review, 15*, 219–266. PM ID number: 20716644; doi: 10.1177/1088868310377394.

McGuire, S., & Clifford, J. (2000). Genetic and environmental contributions to loneliness in children. *Psychological Science, 11*(6), 487–491.

Miller, K. G., Kominz, M. A., Browning, J. V., Wright, J. D., Mountain, G. S., Katz, M. E., et al. (2005). The phanerozoic record of global sea-level change. *Science, 310*(5752), 1293–1298. doi: 10.1126/science.1116412

Mullins, L. C., & Dugan, E. (1990). The influence of depression, and family and friendship relations, on residents' loneliness in congregate housing. *Gerontologist, 30*(3), 377–384.

Murray, S. L., Bellavia, G. M., Rose, P., & Griffin, D. W. (2003). Once hurt, twice hurtful: How perceived regard regulates daily marital interactions. *Journal of Personality and Social Psychology, 84*(1), 126–147.

Nation, D. A., Gonzales, J. A., Mendez, A. J., Zaias, J., Szeto, A., Brooks, L. G., et al. (2008). The effect of social environment on markers of vascular oxidative stress and inflammation in the Watanabe heritable hyperlipidemic rabbit. *Psychosom Med, 70*(3), 269–275. doi: PSY.0b013e3181646753 [pii] 10.1097/PSY.0b013e3181646753 [doi]

Nonogaki, K., Nozue, K., & Oka, Y. (2007). Social isolation affects the development of obesity and type 2 diabetes in mice. *Endocrinology, 148*(10), 4658–4666. doi: 10.1210/en.2007-0296

O'Doherty, J. P. (2004). Reward representations and reward-related learning in the human brain: insights from neuroimaging. *Current Opinion in Neurobiology, 14*(6), 769–776. doi: S0959-4388(04)00168-0 [pii] 10.1016/j.conb.2004.10.016 [doi]

Patterson, A. C., & Veenstra, G. (2010). Loneliness and risk of mortality: A longitudinal investigation in Alameda County, California. *Social Science and Medicine, 71*(1), 181–186.

Penninx, B. W., van Tilburg, T., Kriegsman, D. M., Deeg, D. J., Boeke, A. J., & van Eijk, J. T. (1997). Effects of social support and personal coping resources on mortality in older age: the Longitudinal Aging Study Amsterdam. *American Journal of Epidemiology, 146*(6), 510–519.

Pinquart, M., & Sörensen, S. (2003). Risk factors for loneliness in adulthood and old age—A meta-analysis. In S. P. Shohov (Ed.), *Advances in Psychology Research* (Vol. 19, pp. 111–143). Hauppauge, NY: Nova Science Publishers, Inc.

Poletto, R., Steibel, J. P., Siegford, J. M., & Zanella, A. J. (2006). Effects of early weaning and social isolation on the expression of glucocorticoid and mineralocorticoid receptor and 11beta-hydroxysteroid dehydrogenase 1 and 2 mRNAs in the frontal cortex and hippocampus of piglets. *Brain Research, 1067*(1), 36–42. doi: S0006-8993(05)01380-6 [pii] 10.1016/j.brainres.2005.10.001 [doi]

Pressman, S. D., Cohen, S., Miller, G. E., Barkin, A., Rabin, B. S., & Treanor, J. J. (2005). Loneliness, social network size, and immune response to influenza vaccination in college freshmen. *Health Psychol, 24*(3), 297–306. doi: 2005-04818-009 [pii] 10.1037/0278-6133.24.3.297 [doi]

Rainville, P., Duncan, G. H., Price, D. D., Carrier, B., & Bushnell, M. C. (1997). Pain affect encoded in human anterior cingulate but not somatosensory cortex. *Science., 277*(5328), 968.

Rendell, L., Boyd, R., Cownden, D., Enquist, M., Eriksson, K., Feldman, M. W., et al. (2010). Why copy others? Insights from the Social Learning Strategies Tournament. *Science, 328*(5975), 208–213. doi: 10.1126/science.1184719

Rilling, J., Gutman, D., Zeh, T., Pagnoni, G., Berns, G., & Kilts, C. (2002). A Neural basis for social cooperation. *Neuron, 35*, 395–504.

Rotenberg . (1994). Loneliness and interpersonal trust. *Journal of Social and Clinical Psychology, 13*(2), 152–173.

Rotenberg, Gruman, J. A., & Ariganello, M. (2002). Behavioral confirmation of the loneliness stereotype. *Basic & Applied Social Psychology, 24*(2), 81–89.

Rotenberg, & Kmill, J. (1992). Perception of lonely and non-lonely persons as a function of individual differences in loneliness. *Journal of Social and Personal Relationships, 9*(2), 325–330. doi: 10.1177/0265407592092009

Routasalo, P. E., Savikko, N., Tilvis, R. S., Strandberg, T. E., & Pitkala, K. H. (2006). Social contacts and their relationship to loneliness among aged people—a population-based study. *Gerontology, 52*(3), 181–187. doi: GER2006052003181 [pii] 10.1159/000091828 [doi]

Ruan, H., & Wu, C. F. (2008). Social interaction-mediated lifespan extension of Drosophila Cu/Zn superoxide dismutase mutants. *Proceedings of the National Academy of Sciences of the United States of America, 105*(21), 7506–7510. doi: 0711127105 [pii] 10.1073/pnas.0711127105 [doi]

Rudatsikira, E., Muula, A. S., Siziya, S., & Twa-Twa, J. (2007). Suicidal ideation and associated factors among school-going adolescents in rural Uganda. *BMC Psychiatry, 7*, 67. doi: 1471-244X-7-67 [pii] 10.1186/1471-244X-7-67 [doi]

Russell, D., Peplau, L. A., & Cutrona, C. E. (1980). The revised UCLA Loneliness Scale: concurrent and discriminant validity evidence. *Journal of Personality and Social Psychology, 39*(3), 472–480.

Russell, D. W., Cutrona, C. E., de la Mora, A., & Wallace, R. B. (1997). Loneliness and nursing home admission among rural older adults. *Psychology and Aging, 12*(4), 574–589.

Samuelsson, G., Andersson, L., & Hagberg, B., 4, 361–378. (1998). Loneliness in relation to social, psychological and medical variables over a 13-year period: A study of the elderly in a Swedish rural district. *Journal of Mental Health and Aging, 4*, 361–378.

Savikko, N., Routasalo, P., Tilvis, R. S., Strandberg, T. E., & Pitkala, K. H. (2005). Predictors and subjective causes of loneliness in an aged population. *Archives of Gerontology and Geriatrics, 41*(3), 223–233.

Schopf, J. W. (1999). *Cradle of Life: The Discovery of Earth's Earliest Fossils.* Princeton, NJ: Princeton University Press.

Seeman, T. (2000). Health promoting effetcs of friends and family on health outcomes in older adults. *American Journal of Health Promotion, 14*(6), 362–370.

Segrin, C. (1999). Social skills, stressful events, and the development of psychosocial problems. *Journal of Social & Clinical Psychology, 18*, 14–34.

Seymour, B., Daw, N., Dayan, P., Singer, T., & Dolan, R. (2007). Differential encoding of losses and gains in the human striatum. *Journal of Neuroscience, 27*(18), 4826–4831. doi: 27/18/4826 [pii] 10.1523/JNEUROSCI.0400-07.2007 [doi]

Sherif, M., Harvey, O. J., White, B. J., Hood, W. R., & Sherif, G. W. (1961). *Intergroup Conflict and Cooperation: The Robbers Cave Experiment.* Norman. OK: University Book Exchange.

Shintel, H., Cacioppo, J. T., & Nusbaum, H. (2006). *Accentuate the negative, eliminate the positive? Individual differences in attentional bias to positive and negative information.* Paper presented at the 47th Annual Meeting of the Psychonomic Society, Houston, TX.

Steptoe, A., Owen, N., Kunz-Ebrecht, S. R., & Brydon, L. (2004). Loneliness and neuroendocrine, cardiovascular, and inflammatory stress responses in middle-aged men and women. *Psychoneuroendocrinology, 29*(5), 593–611.

Stranahan, A. M., Khalil, D., & Gould, E. (2006). Social isolation delays the positive effects of running on adult neurogenesis. *Nature Neuroscience, 9*(4), 526–533. doi: nn1668 [pii] 10.1038/nn1668 [doi]

Sugisawa, H., Liang, J., & Liu, X. (1994). Social networks, social support, and mortality among older people in Japan. *Journal of Gerontology, 49*(1), S3–13.

Swann, W. B., Gomez, A., Dovidio, J. F., Hart, S., & Jetten, J. (2010). Dying and killing for one's group. *Psychological Science.* doi: 10.1177/0956797610376656

Tilvis, R. S., Pitkala, K. H., Jolkkonen, J., & Strandberg, T. E. (2000). Social networks and dementia. *Lancet, 356*(9223), 77–78.

Twenge, J. M., Baumeister, R. F., Tice, D. M., & Stucke, T. S. (2001). If you can't join them, beat them: Effects of social exclusion on aggressive behavior. *Journal of Personality and Social Psychology, 81*(6), 1058–1069.

Wang, Z., Faith, M., Patterson, F., Tang, K., Kerrin, K., Wileyto, E. P., et al. (2007). Neural substrates of abstinence-induced cigarette cravings in chronic smokers. *Journal of Neuroscience, 27*(51), 14035–14040. doi: 10.1523/jneurosci.2966-07.2007

Waytz, A., & Epley, N. (2009). *Social Affiliation Increases Dehumanization.* Chicago: University of Chicago.

Wei, M., Russell, D. W., & Zakalik, R. A. (2005). Adult attachment, social self-efficacy, self-disclosure, loneliness, and subsequent depression for freshman college students: A longitudinal study. *Journal of Counseling Psychology, 52*(4), 602–614.

Weiss, R. S. (1973). *Loneliness: The Experience of Emotional and Social Isolation.* Cambridge, MA: MIT Press.

Wheeler, L., Reis, H., & Nezlek, J. (1983). Loneliness, social interaction, and sex roles. *Journal of Personality and Social Psychology, 45*(4), 943–953.

Williams, D. R. (2003). The Health of Men: Structured inequalities and opportunities. *American Journal of Public Health, 93*(5), 724–731.

Williams, K. D. (2001). *Ostracism: The Power of Silence.* New York: Guilford Press.

Williams, P. G., Suchy, Y., & Rau, H. K. (2009). Individual differences in executive functioning: implications for stress regulation. *Annals of Behavioral Medicine, 37*(2), 126–140. doi: 10.1007/s12160-009-9100-0 [doi]

Wilson, R. S., Krueger, K. R., Arnold, S. E., Schneider, J. A., Kelly, J. F., Barnes, L. L., et al. (2007). Loneliness and risk of Alzheimer disease. *Archives of General Psychiatry, 64*(2), 234–240.

Yamada, M., & Decety, J. (2009). Unconscious affective processing and empathy: An investigation of subliminal priming on the detection of painful facial expressions. *Pain, 143*(1–2), 71–75.

The Social Stigma of Identity- and Status-Based Rejection Sensitivity

Bonita London *and* Lisa Rosenthal

Abstract

Drawing on research and theory from the social identity, stereotyping, stress and coping, and personality literatures, we review research that uses a common theoretical framework (rejection sensitivity; RS) to explore the mechanisms through which stigmatization on the basis of race, gender, sexual orientation, and age affects and shapes the life experiences of targets of stigmatization. Rejection Sensitivity is conceptualized as a cognitive-affective processing dynamic borne out of past experiences of rejection and maltreatment, and leading to situationally activated anxious expectations of rejection in current contexts. Applied to the context of identity-based stigmatization, we present a review of empirical research aimed at exploring the underlying mechanism by which exposure to cues of identity-based marginalization activates the RS dynamic and leads to variations in perceptions and coping with threat among members of stigmatized groups. We review the RS literature applied to African Americans, Asian Americans, women, gay men, and the elderly.

Key Words: gender, race/ethnicity, rejection, rejection sensitivity, sexual orientation, social identity

Introduction

In his book, *Stigma-Notes on the Management of a Spoiled Identity*, Goffman (1963) defined *stigma* as an attribute that reduces an individual to someone considered tainted and discounted. A stigmatized person, according to Crocker, Major, and Steele (1998), "possess(es) some attribute or characteristic that conveys a social identity that is devalued in a particular social context" (p. 505). Often, the devalued status of a group is rooted in immutable characteristics, such as gender, race, sexual orientation, or physical disability, so that the source of one's rejection is ever present for as long as that attribute is devalued in that context. Yet despite the typically static nature of stigma, research suggests that the impact of a stigmatizing attribute or identity is not uniform (e.g., Lazarus & Folkman, 1984; London, Downey, Bolger, & Velilla, 2005). Although some members of a stigmatized group might experience heightened distress when encountering bias as a result of their stigma, others may experience distress to a lesser degree. An individual might feel anxiety when approaching a negatively stereotyped domain related to his or her identity, but may feel no anxiety when approaching a non-stereotyped domain. Some may show impairment in performance under the threat of judgment, whereas others may be mobilized to engage further and prove the "doubter" wrong. The threat of gender stigmatization may make an individual withdraw or self-silence, but the same individual might respond to race stigmatization by confronting the perpetrator. This chapter reviews research that uses a common theoretical framework (rejection sensitivity) to explore the mechanisms through which stigmatization on the basis of race, gender, sexual orientation, and age affects and shapes the life experiences of targets of stigmatization.

Drawing on the basic definitions of stigma (e.g., Goffman, 1963; Crocker et al., 1998), a growing body of work in psychology has explored the consequences of holding a stigmatized identity for the psychological and physical health, and academic and career success of the stigmatized, as well as for intergroup relations (see Major & O'Brien, 2005 for a review). Members of stigmatized or marginalized groups often report heightened stress and compromised physical and mental health outcomes as a result of exposure to discrimination (e.g., Clark, Anderson, Clark, & Williams, 1999; Goodwin, Williams, & Carter-Sowell, 2010; Landrine, Klonoff, Gibbs, Manning, & Lund, 1995; Mays, Cochran, & Barnes, 2007; Okazaki, 2009), self-doubt and lower achievement outcomes when under the threat of evaluation in stereotyped domains (e.g., Crocker & Major, 1989; Steele & Aronson, 1995), and strained intergroup relations (e.g., West, Shelton, & Trail, 2009).

The experience of stigmatization and social exclusion is impactful not just because rejection hurts, but also because acceptance helps. As social creatures dependent upon one another for survival, human beings are naturally inclined to seek acceptance and avoid rejection (e.g., Baumeister & Leary, 1995; DeWall, Maner, & Rouby, 2009; Downey & Feldman, 1996; Williams, 2001). Feelings of belonging and acceptance can lower depression, act as a protective buffer against chronic physical pain issues, and promote a sense of comfort, investment, and engagement in institutions (e.g., Bailis, Chipperfield, & Helgason, 2008; McLaren, Jude, & McLachlan, 2007; Mendoza-Denton, Downey, Purdie, Davis, & Pietrzak, 2002). Alternatively, the stress and strain of social rejection and marginalization can result in decreased self-esteem (e.g., Williams, Shore, & Grahe, 1998), diminished cognitive performance (e.g., Baumeister & Twenge, 2001), and increased depression (McLaren et al., 2007), among numerous other consequences. As evidence of the primal relevance of social exclusion, Eisenberger, Lieberman, and Williams (2003) used fMRI data to show that the same brain regions activated in response to physical pain are also activated in response to social exclusion, but not to social inclusion. Thus, being accepted or rejected by others has broad implications for nearly every life consequence and may be rooted deeply in the human psyche.

Overt versus Subtle Cues of Status-Based Rejection

Over recent decades in the United States, there have been considerable social and structural reforms to address the historic inequities in domains like educational achievement, hiring and evaluation policies, and health care between members of some traditionally marginalized groups (e.g., African Americans and Latinos) and majority groups (e.g., European Americans, men) (e.g., Zirkel, 2008). In addition to these structural advancements, changing social norms have made overt expressions of prejudice and bias less socially acceptable (e.g., Fazio, Jackson, Dunton, & Williams, 1995; Gaertner & Dovidio, 2005). Yet despite shifts in overt discrimination and explicit stigmatization of some groups, research suggests that more subtle, covert forms of bias persist (e.g., Greenwald & Banaji, 1995; Greenwald, McGhee, & Schwartz, 1998).

To observe and measure subtle cues of bias and their impact, researchers have often used reaction-time and physiological studies to demonstrate that negative implicit attitudes toward historically marginalized groups, and physiological arousal consistent with threat during intergroup interactions with outgroup members exist (e.g., Blascovich, Mendes, Hunter, Lickel, & Kowai-Bell, 2001; Greenwald & Banaji, 1995). For example, Mendes, Gray, Mendoza-Denton, Major, and Epel (2007) reported that white interviewees with higher implicit racial bias toward blacks showed greater stress reactions (e.g., neuroendocrine responses) when being interviewed by a black interviewer compared with white interviewees with low implicit racial bias toward blacks. Using an attentional bias paradigm, Richeson and Trawalter (2008) demonstrated that white participants with a high motivation to appear non-prejudiced toward blacks still show a tendency to attend to neutral black faces presented in short durations, consistent with threat monitoring theories (e.g., Downey, Mougios, Ayduk, London, & Shoda, 2004). Thus, for targets of stigmatization, rejection, marginalization, and bias continue to be real and relevant threats in their social world—both through overt forms of bias and discrimination, and more subtle forms of marginalization and exclusion.

Although seemingly counterintuitive, several studies have demonstrated that subtle cues of rejection can have just as substantial costs for the health, well-being, and achievement of the rejected as do overt cues of rejection. For targets of stigma, subtle or ambiguous marginalization may result in greater stress because the uncertainty of whether one is being excluded or ignored unintentionally versus intentionally because of one's social group membership can cause anxiety and distress (e.g., Crocker,

Voelkl, Testa, & Major, 1991; Lazarus & Folkman, 1984; Mendoza-Denton et al., 2002). Consistent with this theory, Cheryan, Plaut, Davies, and Steele (2009) proposed and demonstrated that the effects of "ambient" cues of marginalization (i.e., "social symbolic objects that embody and communicate group member stereotypes," p. 1046) can undermine women's interest and sense of belonging in domains in which women have been historically excluded. These ambient cues can be as subtle as the stereotypic male-themed posters or decorations in an office space that help to convey the presence and value of men rather than women in the environment, yet also provide messages of rejection that lead women to disengage from domains in which gender rejection is possible. Similarly, Mendoza-Denton, Shaw-Taylor, Chen, and Chang (2009) demonstrated that women have impaired performance on an academic task following exposure to subtle cues of the potential for gender bias compared with overt cues. Other researchers have also demonstrated that uncertainty or ambiguity disrupts performance for stigmatized groups more so than even cues of blatant bias (e.g., Salvatore & Shelton, 2007).

Other evidence suggests that the negative impact of exposure to ambiguous prejudice is unique to traditionally marginalized groups—nonstigmatized majority group members aren't as negatively affected by subtle cues that they may be targets of unfair treatment. In contrast to a finding that traditionally marginalized group members show greater impairment to ambiguous compared with blatant prejudice, Salvatore and Shelton (2007) also showed that white participants had greater cognitive impairment following blatant prejudice against their own group compared with nonprejudice or ambiguous prejudice cues. Studies demonstrating the negative consequences of ambiguity and subtle bias for traditionally stigmatized groups highlight the new dilemma for targets of stigma—whereas overt social identity–based exclusion is troubling because of its blatant rejection message, subtle, covert, or ambiguous forms of rejection are equally as troubling because of their ambiguity.

The stress and coping literature can also lend insight into yet another layer of the social rejection dilemma for traditionally marginalized groups— why and how encountering subtle or ambiguous cues of marginalization might be experienced differently by different individuals or in different instances within the same individual. As described earlier, two members of the same stigmatized group can have vastly different perceptions of and reactions to experiences of bias. The stress and coping literature suggests that how an event is perceived, appraised, and coped with determines its stressful impact on the individual (Lazarus & Folkman, 1984; London et al., 2005). Given the prevalence of subtle forms of rejection discussed earlier, the process of perceiving, appraising, and coping with rejection cues may be highly variable from individual to individual. Experiencing the negative consequences of social marginalization or bias first requires the individual to detect the subtle or ambiguous cues of rejection in a given situation. Detection or perception of rejection often requires some level of perceptual sensitivity or attunement to the subtle cues—a skill in which there may be great individual differences. Appraisal of the cue as threatening often involves an assessment of the situation as being important or self-relevant (e.g., Higgins, 1996), such that the threat has meaning. And finally, the outcome of the situation depends on how it is coped with (e.g., through avoidance or confrontation). Taken together, the social cues of rejection in a given situation and the individual's appraisal and response to those cues converge to inform the process of status-based rejection and its consequences.

Rejection Sensitivity: A Person X Situation Dynamic
Interpersonal Rejection Sensitivity

Building on the idea that situations differ in (1) whether they are accepting or rejecting, (2) how rejection is conveyed (subtle or overt), (3) the relevance of the situation to the individual (e.g., their gender, race, personality), and (4) one's attunement, perceptions, and responses to such cues—several researchers have adopted the common theoretical framework of RS to understand the process underlying status-based rejection experiences. Downey and Feldman (1996) first proposed the RS framework to address the Person by Situation dynamic (e.g., Mischel & Shoda, 1995) inherent in the social rejection process. They first applied their theory and research to understanding rejection in interpersonal relationships (Personal RS) (Downey & Feldman, 1996). The RS model was then used to explain rejection expectations in children (e.g., London, Downey, Bonica, & Paltin, 2007). Recently, several researchers have used the model to explore the antecedents, processes, and consequences of status- and identity-based rejection.

Rejection sensitivity (Personal RS) is conceptualized as a cognitive-affective processing dynamic borne out of past experiences of rejection and maltreatment in previous relationships (Downey & Feldman, 1996; Downey, Freitas, Michaelis, & Khouri, 1998). The Personal RS model posits that (1) past experiences of rejection give rise to (2) the anxious expectation of similar rejection in current interpersonal interactions, (3) facilitating a readiness to perceive rejection, particularly in ambiguous situations, and (4) intense reactions when rejection is perceived. The model theorizes that experiences of rejection or exclusion from important others early in life create an internal working model for expectations of how others will treat you in subsequent relationships. These anxious expectations can become activated in interpersonal situations (e.g., when asking someone to do a favor for you, or in dating relationships) and can sensitize the individual to recognize the subtle cues of rejection present when seeking acceptance.

Over several studies (using cross-sectional, experimental, and longitudinal experience sampling methodologies), Downey and colleagues demonstrated that individuals high in Personal RS are more likely to retrospectively report maltreatment from caregivers in their past (Feldman & Downey, 1994), and show higher levels of internalizing disorders, loneliness (London, Downey, Bonica, & Paltin, 2007), depression (Ayduk, Downey, & Kim, 2001), social avoidance (Downey, Feldman & Ayduk, 2000), and hostile reactions in response to rejection (Downey & Feldman, 1996). Taken together, the dozens of studies using the Personal RS framework have provided support for the tenets of the model, and insight into the vast consequences of rejection sensitivity for well-being and interpersonal relationships. The Personal RS framework (as originally defined), taps into general, nonspecific rejection concerns but does not capture the unique and specific rejection concerns of members of traditionally stigmatized groups.

Expanding the Rejection Sensitivity Model to Account for Status-Based Rejection

Identifying the need for a theoretical model that captures similar processes of concerns, expectations, perceptions, and responses to subtle cues of rejection—but on the basis of one's stigmatized social identities—Mendoza-Denton et al. (2002) adapted the Personal RS framework for race-based rejection concerns (Race RS). Mendoza-Denton and colleagues (2002) hypothesized that, like the Personal RS dynamic in which some individuals with past histories of rejection develop anxious expectations of interpersonal rejection, members of traditionally

marginalized groups may also develop concerns and expectations of rejection based on prior experiences of discrimination. In the case of marginalized groups, the past experiences of rejection that lead to anxious expectations of rejection need not be direct, personal encounters only. The common history and cultural knowledge of marginalization that members of traditionally stigmatized social groups share provide additional information on which to base their rejection expectations and concerns. As an example from the United States, knowledge of racial profiling by police against African-American males may result in a young African-American male approaching a police roadblock with great anxiety and expectations that he may be unfairly stopped because of his race, even if he has never yet himself been pulled over by police (Mendoza-Denton et al., 2002).

Other researchers have similarly applied the Personal RS model to the social identity–based rejection experiences of other stigmatized groups. In addition to African Americans, Chan and Mendoza-Denton (2008) applied the Race RS model to the experiences of Asian Americans in the United States. London, Downey, Romero-Canyas, Rattan, and Tyson (2012; London & Downey, 2007: London, Downey, & Mace, 2007) expanded the Personal and status-based RS models by conceptualizing the unique interpersonal and situational triggers, responses, and outcomes associated with gender-based rejection in women. Similarly, Pachankis, Goldfriend, and Ramrattan (2008) extended the model to status-based rejection in gay men, and two researchers extended the model to age-based marginalization (Chow, Au, & Chiu, 2008; Kang & Chasteen, 2009). Although bonded by the common conceptualization of the Personal RS framework (e.g., Downey & Feldman, 1996), these varying status-based instantiations of the RS model each provide unique and novel contributions to the literature. Although each model operationalizes status-based RS as the level of anxious expectations of status-based rejection, the specific situations that trigger the activation of the rejection concerns and the coping responses and outcomes differ based on the social identity activated.

Measuring Status-Based Rejection Sensitivity

Important to the conceptualization of status-based RS is the idea of situational specificity. Although there may be some underlying similarities in the mechanisms involved in the multiple forms of rejection sensitivity within an individual (e.g., the general tendency to be concerned about how one is perceived and treated by others), there is also important independence among the various constructs of rejection sensitivity. For example, given biases against women in the business world, a Latina woman in a corporate office may interpret experiences in which her contributions or ideas are dismissed through the lens of her gender identity. The same Latina woman may attribute an encounter with a stranger who doesn't expect her to speak or understand English through the lens of her Latina identity. Further, individuals high in one form of status-based RS are not believed to be globally and indiscriminately sensitive to rejection in all forms. For example, a woman who is high in sensitivity to gender-based rejection (Gender RS) given personal experiences of bias because of her gender may not be high in sensitivity to race-based rejection (Race RS), even if she is also a member of a traditionally stigmatized racial/ethnic group. Finally, the status-based RS dynamic is likely to show individual differences in perceptions of threat in situations in which the cues of threat are subtle or ambiguous. In overt situations of discrimination, there is little need for interpretation, but in subtle situations, differences in attunement to and perceptions of the ambiguous cues determine their impact.

All of the status-based RS questionnaires (race, gender, sexual orientation, age) present a series of brief scenarios depicting situations in which members of the target group might expect status-based rejection because of their stigmatized identity. For example, one scenario in the Race RS questionnaire used with African Americans is: "Imagine you have just finished shopping for new clothes, and you are leaving the store carrying several bags. It's closing time and several people are filing out of the store at once. Suddenly, the alarm begins to sound, and a security guard comes over to investigate" (Mendoza-Denton et al., 2002). This scenario capitalizes on the concerns some African Americans may feel that they will be treated as criminals and not respected by authorities. The scenarios are typically designed to present an ambiguous situation so as to capture the variability in individuals' perceptual attunement to rejection cues. Following each scenario, participants are asked to indicate the extent to which they are anxious/concerned about the possibility of being rejected/treated negatively in the scenario, and then to indicate the extent to which they believe rejection is likely. The status-based RS measures are typically on a continuum based on the anxiety by expectations product score, ranging from 1 to 36, with higher numbers reflecting high anxiety/concern about being rejected as well as high expectations that rejection is likely in the situations described. Thus, the status-based RS questionnaires capture the expectation of threat weighted by its personal relevance and salience to the individual.

Overview of Status-Based Rejection Sensitivity Models

Mendoza-Denton et al. (2002) identified the specific situational triggers or cues that activate concerns of race marginalization for African Americans. The triggers or situations identified reflect the specific content of stereotypes related to African Americans. Chan and Mendoza-Denton (2008) developed a model of Asian Race RS in which the situations that trigger concerns of rejection are based on the stereotypes associated with Asian Americans (e.g., situations in which strangers do not expect an Asian American to speak or understand English). For women, power and status become triggers of gender-based rejection (e.g., Vescio, Gervais, Snyder, & Hoover, 2005), such as not being taken seriously in a corporate boardroom (London, Downey, Romero-Canyas, Rattan, & Tyson, 2012). For the aging, situations in which their cognitive ability or physical skills are required may trigger concerns of age-based bias. For gay men, concerns of being "outed," or being physically aggressed against because of their sexual orientation may emerge in specific situations.

Across the many forms of status-based RS, research demonstrates the uniqueness of the situational cues of threat for each social identity group. Further, the outcomes associated with the activation of threat also differ based on the social identity group. For example, whereas London et al. (2012) and Chan and Mendoza-Denton (2008) show that self-silencing and internalization are common responses for women and Asian Americans high in Gender and Race RS, respectively, Aronson and Inzlicht (2004) show that confidence and overestimation of one's skills in the face of stereotype threat may occur for African Americans high in Race RS.

RACE REJECTION SENSITIVITY: AFRICAN AMERICAN AND ASIAN AMERICAN

In a series of three studies, Mendoza-Denton et al. (2002) developed and validated a Race RS questionnaire for African Americans. They examined the consequences of being high in Race RS for African-American college students at a university in which academic achievement pressures were high and the students, faculty, and staff were predominantly European American (a context in which race might be most salient and thus activate concerns of rejection). To capture the situational quality of the Race RS dynamic, Mendoza-Denton et al. (2002) identified (through focus groups and pretesting) the types of situations that African Americans encounter in which subtle cues suggest that they may be devalued, discriminated against, or rejected. The situations identified include both academic domains (e.g., applying for a scholarship) and general social interactions (e.g., being watched while shopping in a store). Consistent with the theory that certain situations are relevant for particular social identity groups but not others, Mendoza-Denton et al. demonstrated that the situations reflected in the Race RS questionnaire were viewed as potentially threatening for African Americans but not for European American students. Thus, subsequent studies exploring the effects of Race RS on psychological well-being and academic achievement were conducted only with African Americans.

Given the pervasiveness of negative stereotypes about the lack of academic ability of African Americans (e.g., Steele & Aronson, 1995), much of the research on Race RS (specifically for African Americans) has centered on uncovering how Race RS interferes with academic self-efficacy, confidence, and sense of belonging in academic environments. Mendoza-Denton et al. (2002) conducted a daily diary study of first-year African-American students entering a competitive, predominantly white university during their first 3 weeks of their first semester of college. Research suggests that transitions are a time in which individuals may look to both overt and covert cues in their interaction with others to determine their sense of fit, inclusion, and acceptance in a new environment (London et al., 2005; Ruble & Seidman, 1996).

During the first 3 weeks of the transition to college, Mendoza-Denton et al. (2002) found that African Americans higher in Race RS reported a greater frequency of negative experiences that they attributed to their race, and greater feelings of alienation and rejection following those negative race-related experiences compared with those lower in Race RS. Thus, the context of the predominantly white institution seemed to activate the concerns of race bias for the high Race RS African-American students. The high Race RS African-American undergraduates also reported a lower sense of belonging at the university, and less positive feelings toward roommates and professors than low Race RS African Americans during the first 3 weeks of college. Further, these negative effects persisted over time—African-American undergraduates who were high in Race RS at the beginning of college reported greater feelings of anxiety about approaching professors for help during their second and third year in college, and even demonstrated a decline in GPA across the first five semesters of college. These latter findings highlight an important process by which Race RS may be associated with achievement differences in African-American compared with European-American students. For African Americans high in Race RS in a predominantly white institution, their engagement and success in college may be threatened by perceptions of bias, increased feelings of alienation, and avoidance of support seeking from those in the predominantly white academic institutions that are deemed threatening.

Although the decrease in support-seeking from academic resources may protect the self from potentially biased social and academic interactions (e.g., Crocker et al., 1991), it may also leave high Race RS students without the opportunity to gain valuable information about their academic progress from unbiased university professors and teaching assistants (e.g., Cohen, Steele, & Ross, 1999; London & Downey, 2007). These findings highlight the power of the individual differences approach by demonstrating that the same academic environment may hold differing levels of threat among African-American students. Mendoza-Denton et al. (2002) also demonstrated that their findings remained significant even while controlling for the effect of Personal RS, suggesting that Race RS contributes to academic and psychological outcomes in African Americans beyond what can be explained by the more general tendency to expect interpersonal rejection.

Aronson and Inzlicht (2004) expanded the notion that the threat high Race RS African-American undergraduates perceive in academic environments can undermine their academic success by drawing on the attributional ambiguity literature (see Crocker et al., 1991). Previously, Crocker and colleagues (1991) demonstrated that when members of negatively stereotyped groups receive critical feedback on their work from majority group members, they can experience uncertainty about whether the feedback they received was based on their actual work quality or negative stereotypes held by majority group members about their ability. Aronson and Inzlicht

(2004) hypothesized that having to discount academic feedback because of the potential for racial bias (e.g., Cohen et al., 1999; Crocker et al., 1991), and avoiding help-seeking because of concerns of biased treatment (e.g., Mendoza-Denton et al., 2002) may leave African-American students with a level of uncertainty about their academic strengths and weaknesses.

Consistent with this theorizing, Aronson and Inzlicht (2004) found that among African-American students, Race RS was negatively associated with performance on a verbal task (evidence of greater vulnerability to stereotype threat), and positively associated with inaccuracy, particularly overestimation, in predicting how well they would do on the verbal task. High Race RS African Americans may overestimate their skills, possibly because of the need to discount feedback from potentially biased sources, which interferes with accurate self-knowledge. But, low Race RS African Americans did not differ in their skill estimations from European-American students. In a second study, participants completed a diary twice a day for 8 days. Aronson and Inzlicht (2004) found that among African Americans, Race RS was positively associated with instability (greater changes across the 16 time points) in academic self-efficacy, but not in athletic self-efficacy or self-esteem. These findings suggest that Race RS is activated in, and interferes most with performance and confidence in stereotype-relevant domains for African Americans (e.g., academics) but not non-negatively stereotyped domains (e.g., athletics).

Mendoza-Denton, Pietrzak, and Downey (2008) also examined the interaction between Race RS and ethnic identification (i.e., feeling a sense of pride, respect, and connection to one's ethnic group) among African-American college students. They theorized that both constructs might affect sense of belonging and inclusion for African Americans in a predominantly white institution. Although much of the literature on ethnic identification indicates that stronger positive ethnic identity can act as a protective buffer against threatening environments for African Americans (e.g., Phinney, Cantu, & Kurtz, 1997), within the context of a predominantly white institution, it may also make race salient in a way that activates concerns of discrimination for those who are high in Race RS. Consistent with this notion, Mendoza-Denton et al. (2008) found that African-American students who were both high in Race RS and high in ethnic identification showed the lowest identification with their predominantly

white university. For these students, the group that they identify with strongly (their ethnic group) is the basis for their experiences of social rejection and thus undermines their connection to the environment in which rejection is experienced. For low Race RS African-American students, ethnic identification was not associated with identification with the predominantly white university.

Chan and Mendoza-Denton (2008) applied the Race RS model to Asian Americans by identifying situational cues/triggers that signal the potential for bias, discrimination, and marginalization specific to Asian-American identity. The Race RS model suggests that both the trigger situations and the consequences associated with the activation of RS differ based on the identity. Therefore, Chan and Mendoza-Denton (2008) hypothesized that activation of Asian-American Race RS would result in internalizing symptomatology (e.g., depression, lowered self-esteem, avoidance, and shame)—consistent with prevalence rates of these issues within the Asian-American community (e.g., Twenge & Crocker, 2002)—rather than the academic disidentification and poorer academic performance found in studies of Race RS activation for African Americans (e.g., Aronson & Inzlicht, 2004; Mendoza-Denton et al., 2002). In three studies, Chan and Mendoza-Denton found that being higher in Asian-American Race RS was associated with greater depressive symptoms, lower self-esteem, avoidance, and anxiety among Asian Americans. Additionally, they found that being higher in Asian-American Race RS was associated with greater feelings of shame and lower self-esteem after a simulated rejection scenario, and that feelings of shame mediated the relationship between Asian-American Race RS and self-esteem. Thus, for Asian Americans, the fear of social rejection because of their ethnicity may lead to social withdrawal and feelings of shame that put them at risk for depression and low self-esteem. This reaction is markedly different from high Race RS African Americans who showed no drops in self-esteem, and increased confidence/overestimation of their skills under race threat conditions (Aronson & Inzlicht, 2004).

Page-Gould, Mendoza-Denton, and Tropp (2008) demonstrated one mechanism through which Race RS might be diminished. Drawing on friendship-building paradigms (e.g., Aron, Melinat, Aron, Vallone, & Bator, 1997), Page-Gould et al. (2008) had pairs of European-American and Latino/a students build a cross-group friendship through self-disclosure tasks during three consecutive meetings in a lab. They assessed cortisol reactivity (an indicator of stress level) at each session to determine whether increasing closeness/friendship with outgroup members reduces the stress and anxiety associated with intergroup interactions—particularly for high Race RS Latino/a Americans. To the extent that expectations of rejection from outgroup members might be replaced by expectations of acceptance in high Race RS individuals, the feelings of mistrust, alienation, and intergroup anxiety that high Race RS marginalized group members feel may be diminished. Consistent with hypotheses, Page-Gould et al. (2008) found that successive contact with cross-race friends in the lab led to reductions in cortisol reactivity, particularly among high Race RS Latino/a students. They further found that the amount of prior cross-race contact moderated the association between Race RS and cortisol reactivity in Latinos/as. Finally, in a real-world application of the cross-race friendship hypothesis, Page-Gould et al. (2008) found that, particularly among high Race RS Latino/a students, those who made cross-race friendships showed low anxious affect in a daily diary study. This work demonstrates that Race RS in traditionally marginalized groups may be diminished through successive experiences of positive, acceptance-based interactions with previously rejecting outgroup members. The acceptance from others may replace the working model of rejection held by high Race RS individuals.

Gender Rejection Sensitivity

Although women have made substantial gains in many domains considered traditionally exclusionary to women (e.g., law, medicine, business), the prevalence of sexism, marginalization, and bias against women across many fields persists (e.g., Swim, Hyers, Cohen, & Ferguson, 2001). Further, cultural values continue to dictate the specific prescriptive and proscriptive norms appropriate for women, setting the stage for experiences of rejection when one violates those norms (e.g., Glick & Fiske, 1996). Research on sexism has demonstrated variability in the form gender-based rejection can take, from direct and overt sexist or sexual comments to subtle and ambiguous innuendos of perceived incompetence (e.g., Swim et al., 2001). Further, research has demonstrated the substantial costs of exposure to sexism for women's academic achievement (e.g., stereotype threat effects showing the underperformance of women in stereotyped domains) (Spencer, Steele, & Quinn, 1999) and psychological health (e.g., higher rates of psychiatric illnesses of women

who report greater frequency of exposure to sexism) (Klonoff & Landrine, 1995; Klonoff, Landrine, & Campbell, 2000). This work highlights the need to further understand the mechanism(s) through which perceptions of threat vary across individuals, and subsequently lead to differences in vulnerability to the negative achievement and well-being outcomes associated with sexism exposure. London et al. (2012) applied the RS theoretical framework to the issue of sexism—through work on Gender RS.

Similar to the conceptualization of Race RS, London et al. (2012; London, Downey & Mace, 2007) hypothesized that women with past experiences of or exposure to gender bias, marginalization, discrimination, or rejection would be more likely to develop greater attunement to cues that signal the potential for threat in gender-relevant situations. In a correlational study, London et al. (2012) demonstrated that Gender RS was positively correlated with higher retrospective reports of past experiences of sexism in women. To demonstrate the situational specificity of the Gender RS model, London et al. (2012) presented female participants with scenarios depicting ambiguous gender stereotype rejection cues (e.g., interviewing for a job in corporate finance), race stereotype rejection cues (e.g., approaching a police checkpoint), and interpersonal relationship cues (e.g., asking your romantic partner to move in with you). Women high in Gender RS were significantly more likely to attribute rejection to their gender in the gender-relevant scenarios compared with scenarios in which cues signaled race or personal rejection relevance. This finding suggests that concerns of rejection are situational—present when specific cues about a specific identity are present. Finally, consistent with the notion that Gender RS is not simply a marker of hypersensitivity and psychopathology, London et al. (2012) found that Gender RS was unrelated to measures of psychopathology such as social avoidance, social anxiety, depression, and low self-esteem (particularly when controlling for the general effects of Personal RS).

Across several studies, London and colleagues (2012) demonstrate that women high in Gender RS are more likely to perceive cues of gender bias in competitive academic environments in which women have been historically excluded. In an experimental study, they explored whether a common academic experience—having one's writing evaluated/graded by a university professor—can be particularly threatening for high Gender RS women. Participants in this study had their writing evaluated by a fictitious male university professor who conveyed his power, status, and rigid expectations of performance in a biographical statement. After writing an essay and submitting it online for evaluation by the professor, high Gender RS women reported higher levels of self-doubt in their ability to complete the task successfully and expectations that they would receive a grade on their writing lower than what they believe they deserved from an evaluator they viewed as potentially biased. When all women received feedback in which the professor conveyed criticisms of the work quality, high Gender RS women were more likely to attribute the feedback to gender bias, and were less willing to meet with the professor for additional feedback on their work than women low in Gender RS. This was the case even if avoiding the professor compromised their opportunity to receive a valuable academic benefit (publication of one's essay in a student journal). These findings demonstrated that high Gender RS women were more likely than low Gender RS women to anticipate gender bias when cues of its potential were present, perceive bias in the critical feedback of someone deemed threatening, and respond by avoiding further contact with the threat despite missing out on opportunities for advancement. Highlighting the importance of the situational cues of threat, when being evaluated by a female professor, Gender RS was not associated with negative anticipatory mood, lower evaluation expectations, self-doubts, or unwillingness to meet with the female professor (London, Downey, Romero-Canyas, Rattan, & Tyson, 2012).

Using the Gender RS (London et al., 2012) measure, Mendoza-Denton et al. (2009) demonstrated that ambiguous threat cues are particularly harmful to high Gender RS women, compared with explicit prejudice cues and explicit egalitarianism. In an experimental study, women were told that their performance on a task would be evaluated by a male graduate student. They were led into one of three graduate student offices that was decorated with materials meant to convey the attitudes of their graduate evaluator: a chauvinistic attitude (e.g., pictures of women in bikinis), a progressive or egalitarian attitude (e.g., breast cancer awareness posters), or an ambiguous attitude (the evaluator's gender was apparent but his attitudes toward women were not clear). Women then performed an SAT-style test of logic. Mendoza-Denton et al. (2009) found that high Gender RS women performed more poorly on the test when exposed to ambiguous cues about their evaluator compared with cues of a blatantly chauvinistic or a blatantly egalitarian evaluator. This

finding underscores the theory that ambiguity and uncertainty activate threat to a greater degree than even explicit bias for high status–based RS individuals. The uncertainty of whether one will be treated fairly is anxiety provoking and threatening.

Additionally, although the options for responding to anticipated or perceived threat are vast (e.g., approaching or confronting the source of the threat, or withdrawing and disengaging from the context), high Gender RS women tend to cope with anticipated or perceived threat by self-silencing, including not speaking up about perceived injustice, avoiding conflict, and outwardly pretending they are okay despite feelings of threat. Self-silencing may undermine academic success if women avoid academic help-seeking when encountering academic difficulty, and may undermine psychological well-being if women avoid mental health help-seeking despite distress owing to frequent exposure to sexism. Further, London et al. (2012) found that self-silencing coping mediated the relationship between Gender RS and self-reported academic disengagement in a competitive academic institution.

Consistent with the hypothesis that Gender RS is activated in contexts in which gender stereotypes are salient, the model has been tested in domains in which women have been historically and are currently marginalized—such as women in competitive law schools (London, Downey, & Mace, 2007) and women in science, technology, engineering, and mathematics (STEM) fields (Ahlqvist, London, & Rosenthal, in preparation). In law schools, women continue to report being exposed to, perceiving, and being academically, professionally, and personally affected by gender stereotypes and discrimination to a greater degree than their male counterparts (Krakauer & Chen, 2003). The culture of many top law schools is characterized by the Socratic method, which often entails the assertive, public questioning of one's logic and reasoning to show the flaws in one's thinking. This academic culture is often experienced as highly stressful by most students, both male and female (e.g., Sturm, 1999; Guinier, Fine, & Balin, 1997; London, Downey, & Mace, 2007; London, et al, 2012). Competitive law schools are also characterized by competition for a high class rank on the grade curve and for the limited leadership positions of law student organizations (e.g., Guinier et al., 1997). In sum, many competitive law school environments provide cues that the characteristics that are valued, supported, and respected are most consistent with masculine stereotypes of assertion, competition, and social comparison, and are less compatible with prescriptive norms for women. Thus, law schools may generate feelings of threat and alienation for those women who are high in Gender RS.

In a daily diary study of women and men entering a competitive law school, London et al. (2012) demonstrate that high Gender RS women began law school with the same level of previous academic achievement, engagement in their undergraduate courses, and expectations about engagement and success in law school as men and low Gender RS women. Yet, over the course of the first 3 weeks in law school, high Gender RS women began identifying cues of gender-based threat that interfered with their sense of belonging, confidence, and performance in law school. Men and low Gender RS women showed greater increases in self-confidence across the transition into law school than high Gender RS women. Further, high Gender RS women reported greater feelings of alienation following a negative gender-related rejection experience and reported lower confidence in their performance in their law classes than men and low Gender RS women. Finally, in response to academic conflict, high Gender RS women used more self-silencing coping strategies than either low Gender RS women or men. Taken together, these findings demonstrate the real-world consequences of perceiving gender rejection for high Gender RS women: low confidence, alienation, and undermining of academic performance (London et al., 2012). Across the 3 years of law school, these initial differences in confidence, belonging, and engagement may translate into larger differences in grades and subsequently access to career opportunities and earning potential.

SEXUAL ORIENTATION REJECTION SENSITIVITY

Pachankis et al. (2008) extended the status-based RS model to another historically stigmatized group—gay men. Past work has demonstrated higher rates of hostility and aggression experienced by gay men compared with lesbian and bisexual women, and the dire consequences of such negativity for health and well-being. For example, Remafedi, French, Story, Resnick, and Blum (1998) reported that 28.1% of gay or bisexual male youths compared with 4.2% of heterosexual male, 20.5% lesbian/bisexual female and 14.5% heterosexual female youth, have attempted suicide at least once in their lives. Thus, Pachankis et al. (2008) theorized that developing a model of status-based RS for gay men might provide insight into the complex array of antecedents

and consequences associated with marginalization for sexual minorities. Consistent with the Race RS and Gender RS models, Pachankis and colleagues identified the specific trigger situations that signal the devaluation and exclusion of gay men on the basis of their sexual identity (Gay RS; e.g., being laughed at by other men in a public setting, having hospital workers show hesitation in taking blood from you, being ignored by family members when with your significant other).

Drawing on retrospective research demonstrating the antecedents of Personal RS by Downey and Feldman (1996), Pachankis et al. (2008) determined that gay men high in Gay RS were more likely to report intolerance and rejection from their parents than gay men low in Gay RS. This finding provided some preliminary evidence of how rejection from important others such as caregivers might contribute to the development of Gay RS. Further, Pachankis et al. (2008) also found evidence that the relationship between perceived parental rejection and the level of Gay RS in gay men was mediated by internalized homophobia (endorsement of the negative attitudes held by society about gay men). Pachankis and colleagues also demonstrated the consequences of being high in Gay RS for well-being—high Gay RS men reported greater fear of negative evaluation, lower self-esteem, lower assertiveness, greater perceived discrimination, internalized homophobia, and interpersonal sensitivity than low Gay RS men. Being higher in Gay RS was also significantly associated with less assertive interpersonal behavior, even when controlling for parental rejection and internalized homophobia, suggesting Gay RS may have an important relationship with coping and behavioral responses.

AGE REJECTION SENSITIVITY

Chow et al. (2008), and Kang and Chasteen (2009) developed and validated two different measures of age-based rejection sensitivity (Age RS) among older adults. Drawing on research demonstrating that life transitions are typically stressful periods where individuals begin to question their existing identities, skills, and relationships (e.g., London et al., 2005; Mendoza-Denton et al., 2002; Ruble & Seidman, 1996), Chow et al. (2008) suggested that transitioning to old age may highlight the loss of one's previous skills and abilities and lead to concerns of bias and rejection from others based on age. Given the stress associated with aging, Chow et al. (2008) hypothesized that those individuals with heightened concerns about being rejected on the basis of their age (high Age RS) might suffer greater vulnerability to psychological health issues as a result of the added stress of perceived bias. The Age RS measure was created and normed on a sample of Chinese older adults (mean age of 70.09 years).

Chow et al. (2008) reported that adults high in Age RS reported higher levels of depression, lower social functioning, greater loneliness, and lower life satisfaction. In addition to the psychological outcomes, higher Age RS was associated with poorer physical health, including less physical functioning, more bodily pain, lower general health, and lower vitality. Chow et al. (2008) further explored whether discriminative facility, or the ability to choose situation-appropriate coping strategies, moderated the effect of Age RS on psychological or physical health functioning. Their findings demonstrate that, particularly when discriminative facility was low, Age RS was significantly associated with greater depression and lower social functioning. These associations were not significant when discriminative facility was high. Thus, Age RS may have negative consequences both psychologically and physically for older adults. Yet, discriminative facility may be an important buffer in reducing the negative consequences of Age RS for health and well-being outcomes.

Kang and Chasteen (2009) developed and validated a different Age RS measure using an adult sample greater than age 60. Consistent with Chow and colleagues (2008), Kang and Chasteen (2009) demonstrated a positive relationship between Age RS and lower perceived physical health and self-esteem. Further, Kang and Chasteen (2009) show that Age RS is positively related to perceptions of ageism and age-based stigma consciousness, demonstrating a link between Age RS and perceiving and being attuned to ageism.

Other Rejection Sensitivity Models: Sensitivity to Appearance-Based Rejection

In addition to the status-based RS models described in the preceding, there has also been a growing body of work addressing the issue of physical appearance-based RS. Park (2007) first developed and validated a measure of appearance-based rejection sensitivity (Appearance RS), defined as the level of anxious expectations of interpersonal rejection on the basis of one's physical appearance. Park (2007) conceptualizes Appearance RS as a specific form of Personal RS, rather than a form of status-based RS. Yet, to the extent that Appearance RS may capture some level of stigma rejection concerns related to obesity or physical anomalies (e.g., facial birthmarks), then it may reflect status-based rejection expectations similar to race, gender, age, and sexual orientation concerns. Findings from a series of studies demonstrate that Appearance RS is significantly related to higher appearance contingencies of self-worth, insecure attachment styles, neuroticism, as well as lower self-esteem and perceived attractiveness. Appearance-RS was also associated with greater disordered eating behaviors and greater social comparisons based on appearance, even when controlling for gender, self-esteem, appearance contingencies of self-worth, and Personal RS, among other constructs.

In an experimental study, Park (2007) found that participants experimentally exposed to appearance-based threat (i.e., asked to think about the aspects of their bodies they do not like) felt more alone and rejected if they were also high in Appearance RS, compared with participants in a control condition. In another study, results revealed that in a high-threat situation, reliving acceptance (e.g., being reminded about a personal strength or a close, caring relationship) improved state self-esteem, feelings of rejection, and mood for people high in Appearance RS (but not for people low in Appearance RS). These findings suggest that Appearance RS has important consequences for mental and physical health, but can be buffered by positive affirmation experiences—similar to the effect of cross-race friendships reported by Page-Gould et al. (2008).

Highlighting the importance of gender in appearance concerns, Park, DiRaddo, and Calogero (2009) determined that women score significantly higher in Appearance RS than men, and women's Appearance RS concerns were more contingent on peer acceptance of their physical looks than men. Park and Pinkus (2009) also demonstrated that being high in Appearance RS was associated with a greater desire to avoid social contact with both strangers and close others such as a friend after an appearance-based rejection experience, but not after appearance-based acceptance or intelligence-based rejection experiences. Finally, in a daily diary study, they determined that high trait Appearance RS was related to greater social avoidance, particularly on the days during which state Appearance RS was also high. These effects remained significant after controlling for other influential variables, such as self-esteem, self-rated attractiveness, Personal RS, social anxiety, gender, and relationship status.

Conclusions

Taken together, these various instantiations of status-based RS (applied to race, gender, sexual orientation, age, and appearance) provide insight into the processes involved in and consequences of status-based rejection for health and well-being, sense of belonging, academic performance, and self-knowledge, among other important life outcomes. Race and Gender RS show similar patterns of being positively related to heightened alienation and rejection following an identity-related rejection experience, avoidance of university resources deemed potentially threatening, and lower sense of belonging within the academic community. Findings from work on Race RS for Asian Americans, and Gender RS show patterns of self-silencing and internalization of affect that may subsequently undermine psychological well-being and health. Gay RS findings demonstrate the relationship among parental acceptance, internalization of negative attitudes toward the self, and RS levels. The activation of Age RS concerns is also associated with heightened stress and impairment of performance. Findings from research on Age RS suggests the importance of discriminative facility in coping efficacy, whereas findings from work in Race RS and Appearance RS highlights the importance of feelings of acceptance through cross-race friendships and general positive relationships, respectively. These models importantly highlight a process approach to understanding social exclusion and rejection, and demonstrate the importance of exploring individual differences in the expectations, perceptions, and responses to status-based rejection for understanding life outcomes ranging from academic achievement to mental health and well-being.

References

Ahlqvist, S., London, B., & Rosenthal, L. (in preparation). Gender-based Rejection Sensitivity and Identity fluctuations among women in STEM.

Aron, A., Melinat, E., Aron, E. N., Vallone, R., & Bator, R. (1997). The experimental generation of interpersonal closeness: A procedure and some preliminary findings. *Personality and Social Psychology Bulletin, 23*, 363–377.

Aronson, J., & Inzlicht, M. (2004). The ups and downs of attributional ambiguity: Stereotype vulnerability and the academic self-knowledge of African American students. *Psychological Science, 15*, 829–836.

Ayduk, O., Downey, G., & Kim, M. (2001). Rejection sensitivity and depressive symptoms in women. *Personality and Social Psychology Bulletin, 27*, 868–877.

Bailis, D.S., Chipperfield, J. G., & Helgason, T. R. (2008). Collective self-esteem and the onset of chronic conditions and reduced activity in a longitudinal study of aging. *Social Science and Medicine, 66*, 1817–1827.

Baumeister, R. F., & Leary, M. R. (1995). The need to belong: desire for interpersonal attachments as a fundamental human motivation. *Psychological Bulletin, 117*, 497–529.

Baumeister, R. F., & Twenge, J. M. (2001). Personality and social behavior. In N. J. Smelser, & P. B. Baltes, (Eds.), *International Encyclopedia of the Social & Behavioral Sciences*, Vol. 16. (pp. 11276–11281). New York: Elsevier.

Blascovich, J., Mendes, W. B., Hunter, S. B., Lickel, B., & Kowai- Bell, N. (2001). Perceiver threat in social interactions with stigmatized others. *Journal of Personality and Social Psychology, 80*, 253–267.

Chan, W. Y., & Mendoza-Denton, R. (2008). Status-based rejection sensitivity among Asian Americans: Implications for psychological distress. *Journal of Personality, 76*, 1317–1346.

Cheryan, S., Plaut, V. C., Davies, P., & Steele, C. M. (2009). Ambient belonging: How stereotypical environments impact gender participation in computer science. *Journal of Personality and Social Psychology, 97*, 1045–1060.

Chow, D. S., Au, E., & Chiu, C-Y. (2008). Predicting the psychological health of older adults: Interaction of age based rejection sensitivity and discriminative facility. *Journal of Research in Personality, 42*, 169–182.

Clark, R., Anderson, N. B., Clark, V. R., & Williams, D. R. (1999). Racism as a stressor for African Americans: A biopsychosocial model. *American Psychologist, 54*, 805–816.

Cohen, G. L., Steele, C. M., & Ross, L. D. (1999). The mentor's dilemma: Providing critical feedback across the racial divide. *Personality & Social Psychology Bulletin, 25*, 1302–1318.

Crocker, J., & Major, B. (1989). Social Stigma and self-esteem: The self protective properties of stigma. *Psychological Review, 98*(4), 608–630.

Crocker, J., Major, B., & Steele, C. M. (1998). Social stigma. In Gilbert, D., Fiske, S. T., & Lindzey, G. (Eds.), *The Handbook of Social Psychology* (4th ed., Vol. 2, pp. 504–553). New York: McGraw-Hill.

Crocker, J., Voelkl, K., Testa, M., & Major, B. (1991). Social Stigma: The affective consequences of attributional ambiguity. *Journal of Personality and Social Psychology, 60*(2), 218–228.

DeWall, C. N., Maner, J. K., & Rouby, D. A. (2009). Social exclusion and early-stage interpersonal perception: Selective attention to signs of acceptance. *Journal of Personality and Social Psychology, 96*, 729–741.

Downey, G., & Feldman, S. (1996). Implications of rejection sensitivity for intimate relationships. *Journal of Personality and Social Psychology, 70*(6), 1327–1343.

Downey, G., Feldman, S., & Ayduk, O. (2000). Rejection sensitivity and male violence in romantic relationships. *Personal Relationships, 7*, 45–61.

Downey, G., Freitas, A. L., Michaelis, B., & Khouri, H. (1998). The self-fulfilling prophecy in close relationships: Rejection sensitivity and rejection by romantic partners. *Journal of Personality and Social Psychology, 75*, 545–560.

Downey, G., Mougios, V., Ayduk, O., London, B., & Shoda, Y. (2004). Rejection sensitivity and the defense motivational system: Insights from the startle response to rejection cues. *Psychological Science, 15*, 668–673.

Eisenberger, N. I., Lieberman, M. D., & Williams, K. D. (2003). Does rejection hurt? An fMRI study of social exclusion. *Science, 302*, 290–292.

Fazio, R. H., Jackson, J. R., Dunton, B. C., Williams, C. J. (1995). Variability in automatic activation as an unobtrusive measure of racial attitudes: A bona fide pipeline? *Journal of Personality and Social Psychology, 69*, 1013–1027.

Feldman, S., & Downey, G. (1994). Rejection sensitivity as a mediator of the impact of childhood exposure to family violence on adult attachment behavior. *Development and Psychopathology*, 6, 231–247.

Gaertner, S. L., & Dovidio, J F. (2005). Categorization, recateogrization and intergroup bias. In J. F. Dovidio, P. Glick & L. Rudman . *Reflecting on the Nature of Prejudice*. Philadelphia: Psychology Press.

Glick, P., & Fiske, S. T. (1996). The Ambivalent Sexism Inventory: Differentiating hostile and benevolent sexism. *Journal of Personality and Social Psychology*, 70, 491–512.

Goffman, E. (1963). *Stigma: Notes on the Management of Spoiled Identity*. Englewood Cliffs, NJ: Prentice-Hall.

Goodwin, S. A., Williams, K. D., & Carter-Sowell, A. R. (2010). The psychological sting of stigma: The costs of attributing ostracism to racism. *Journal of Experimental Social Psychology*, 46, 612–618

Greenwald, A. G., & Banaji, M. R. (1995). Implicit social cognition: Attitudes, self-esteem, and stereotypes. *Psychological Review*, 102, 4–27.

Greenwald, A. G., McGhee, D. E., & Schwartz, J. L. K. (1998). Measuring individual differences in implicit cognition: The Implicit Association Test. *Journal of Personality and Social Psychology*, 74, 1464–1480.

Guinier, L., Fine, M., & Balin, J. (1997). *Becoming gentleman: Women, law school, and institutional change*. Boston: Beacon Press.

Higgins, E. T. (1996). Knowledge activation: Accessibility, applicability and salience. In E. T. Higgins, & A. W. Kruglanski (Eds.), *Social Psychology: Handbook of Basic Principles*. (pp. 136–168). New York: Guilford Press.

Kang, S. K., & Chasteen, A. L. (2009). The development and validation of the age-based rejection sensitivity questionnaire. *The Gerontologist*, 49, 303–316.

Klonoff, E. A., & Landrine, H. (1995). The Schedule of sexist events: A measure of lifetime and recent sexist discrimination in women's lives. *Psychology of Women Quarterly*, 19, 439–472.

Klonoff, E. A., Landrine, H., & Campbell, R. (2000). Sexist discrimination may account for well-known gender differences in psychiatric symptoms. *Psychology of Women Quarterly*, 24, 93–99.

Krakauer, L., & Chen, C. P. (2003). Gender barriers in the legal profession: Implications for career development of female law students. *Journal of Employment Counseling*, 40, 65–79.

Landrine, H., Klonoff, E. A., Gibbs, J., Manning, V., & Lund, M. (1995). Physical and psychiatric correlates of gender discrimination. *Psychology of Women Quarterly*, 19, 473–492.

Lazarus, R., & Folkman, S. (1984). *Stress, Appraisal and Coping*. New York: Springer.

London, B., Anderson, V., & Downey, G (2007). Studying Institutional Engagement: Utilizing social psychology research methods to study law student engagement. *Harvard Journal of Law and Gender*, 30(2), 389–407.

London, B., Anderson, V., & Downey, G. (2012). Status based rejection sensitivity and the transition to higher education. In S. Weinberg, & L. Stulberg (Eds.), *Diversity in American Higher Education*. New York: Routledge.

London, B., Downey, G., Bolger, N., & Velilla, E. (2005). A framework for studying social identity and coping with daily stress during the transition to college. In G. Downey, J. Eccles, & C. Chatman (Eds.). *Navigating the Future: Social Identity, Coping, and Life Tasks* (pp. 45–64). New York: Russel Sage Foundation Press.

London, B., Downey, G., Bonica, C., & Paltin, I. (2007). Social causes and consequences of rejection sensitivity in adolescents. *Journal of Research on Adolescence*, 17(3), 481–506.

London, B., Downey, G., & Mace, S. (2007). Psychological Theories of Educational Engagement: A multi-method approach to studying individual engagement and institutional change. *Vanderbilt Law Review*, 60(2), 455–481.

London, B., Downey, G., Romero-Canyas, R., Rattan, A., & Tyson, D. (2012). Gender Rejection Sensitivity: Implications for Women's Well-Being and Achievement in Gender Stereotyped Contexts. *Journal of Personality and Social Psychology*, 102(5), 961–979.

Major, B. N., & O'Brien, L. T. (2005). The social psychology of stigma. *Annual Review of Psychology*, 56, 393–421.

Mays, V. M., Cochran, S. D., & Barnes, N. W. (2007). Race, race-based discrimination, and health outcomes among African Americans. *Annual Review of Psychology*, 58, 201–225.

McLaren, S., Jude, B., & McLachlan, A. J. (2007). Sexual orientation, sense of belonging and depression in Australian men. *International Journal of Men's Health*, 6, 259–272.

Mendoza-Denton, R., Downey, G., Purdie, V., Davis, A., & Pietrzak, J. (2002). Sensitivity to status-based rejection: Implications for African-American students college experiences. *Journal of Personality and Social Psychology*, 83, 896–918.

Mendoza-Denton, R., Pietrzak, J., & Downey, G. (2008). Distinguishing institutional identification from academic goal pursuit: Interactive effects of ethnic identification and race- based rejection sensitivity. *Journal of Personality and Social Psychology*, 95, 338–351.

Mendes, W. B., Gray, H. M., Mendoza-Denton, R., Major, B., & Epel, E. S. (2007). Why egalitarianism might be good for your health: Physiological thriving during stressful intergroup encounters. *Psychological Science*, 18, 991–998.

Mendoza-Denton, R., Shaw-Taylor, L., Chen, S., & Chang, E. (2009). Ironic effects of explicit gender prejudice on women's test performance. *Journal of Experimental Social Psychology*, 45, 275–278.

Mischel, W., & Shoda, Y. (1995): A cognitive-affective system theory of personality: reconceptualizing situations, dispositions, dynamics, and invariance in personality structure. *Psychological review*, 102, 246–268.

Okazaki, S. (2009). Impact of racism on ethnic minority mental health. *Perspectives on Psychological Science*, 4, 103–107.

Pachankis, J. E., Goldfried, M. R., & Ramrattan, M. (2008). Extension of the rejection sensitivity construct to the interpersonal functioning of gay men. *Journal of Consulting and Clinical Psychology*, 76, 306–317.

Page-Gould, E., Mendoza-Denton, R., & Tropp, L. R. (2008). With a little help form my cross-group friend: Reducing anxiety in intergroup contexts through cross-group friendship. *Journal of Personality and Social Psychology*, 95,1080–1094.

Phinney, J. S., Cantu, C. L., & Kurtz, D. A. (1997). Ethnic and American identity as predictors of self-esteem among African American, Latino, and White adolescents. *Journal of Youth and Adolescence*, 26, 165–185.

Park, L. E. (2007). Appearance-based rejection sensitivity: Implications for mental and physical health, affect, and motivation. *Personality and Social Psychology Bulletin*, 33, 490–504.

Park, L. E., DiRaddo, A., & Calogero, R. M. (2009). Sociocultural influence and appearance-based rejection sensitivity among college students. *Psychology of Women Quarterly*, *33*, 108–119.

Park, L. E., & Pinkus, R. T. (2009). Interpersonal effects of appearance-based rejection sensitivity. *Journal of Research in Personality*, *43*, 602–612.

Remafedi, G., French, S., Story, M., Resnick, M. D., & Blum, R. (1998). The relationship between suicide risk and sexual orientation: Results of a population-based study. *American Journal of Public Health*, *88*, 57–60.

Richeson, J. A., & Trawalter, S. (2008). The threat of appearing prejudiced and race-based attentional biases. *Psychological Science*, *19*, 98–102.

Ruble, D. N., & Seidman, E. (1996). Social transitions: Windows into social psychological processes. In E. T. Higgins, & A. Kruglanski (Eds.), *Handbook of Social Processes* (pp. 830–856). New York: Guilford.

Salvatore, J., & Shelton, J. N. (2007). Cognitive costs of exposure to racial prejudice. *Psychological Science*, *18*, 810–815.

Spencer, S. J., Steele, C. M., & Quinn, D. M. (1999). Stereotype threat and women's math performance. *Journal of Experimental Social Psychology*, *35*, 4–28.

Steele, C. M., & Aronson, J. (1995). Stereotype threat and the intellectual test performance of African Americans. *Journal of Personality and Social Psychology*, *65*, 797–811.

Sturm, S. (1999) Rethinking race, gender, and the law in the twenty first century workplace. *Performance Improvement Quarterly*, *12*, 20–51.

Swim, J. K., Hyers, L. L., Cohen, L. L., & Ferguson, M. J. (2001). Everyday sexism: Evidence for its incidence, nature, and psychological impact from three daily diary studies. *Journal of Social Issues*, *57*, 31–53.

Twenge, J. M., & Crocker, J. (2002). Race and self-esteem: Meta-analyses comparing Whites, Blacks, Hispanics, Asians, and American Indians and comment on Gray-little and Hafdahl (2000). *Psychological Bulletin*, *128*, 371–408.

Vescio, T, Gervais, S. J., Snyder, M., & Hoover, A. (2005). Power and the creation of patronizing environments: The stereotype-based behaviors of the powerful and their effects on female performance in masculine domains. *Journal of Personality and Social Psychology*, *88*, 658–672.

West, T., Shelton, J. N., & Trail, T. (2009). Relational anxiety and interracial interactions. *Psychological Science*, *20*, 298–292.

Williams, K. D. (2001). *Ostracism.* New York: Guilford Press.

Williams, K. D., Shore, W. J., & Grahe, J. E. (1998). The silent treatment: Perceptions of its behaviors and associated feelings. *Group Processes and Intergroup Relations*, *1*, 117–141.

Zirkel, S. (2008). Creating more effective multiethnic schools. *Social Issues and Policy Review*, *2*, 187–241.

Depression and Suicide: Transactional Relations with Rejection

Kimberly A. Van Orden *and* Thomas E. Joiner, Jr.

Abstract

This chapter provides an overview of empirical data supporting the notion of a transactional relationship between depression and rejection, suggesting that rejection is both a cause and consequence of depression. Peer and family rejection in childhood and marital discord in adulthood are all associated with increased risk of developing a depressive disorder. Interpersonal processes involved in depression, such as self-verification striving, excessive reassurance-seeking, blame maintenance, and stress generation cause rejection and are key factors in the maintenance and recurrence of depressive symptoms. Rejection is also associated with increased risk of suicide. In particular, social isolation and family discord are associated with elevated risk of suicide. Many evidence-based psychotherapies for depression and suicidal behaviors target interpersonal functioning. These therapies help clients change their interactions with others to prevent rejection and skillfully manage emotional pain that results when rejection occurs. Thus, although rejection is associated with both depression and suicide, psychotherapy can halt the downward cycle.

Key Words: blame maintenance, depression, excessive reassurance seeking, psychotherapy, rejection, self-verification, stress generation, suicide

Introduction

Depression occurs in an interpersonal context in which rejection plays a prominent role. At first glance, it seems that the depression–rejection association would begin with maladaptive interpersonal processes that cause rejection, which in turn cause depression (and indeed this pathway is supported by data, as discussed later). However, the causal pathway runs in the reverse direction as well, with depression leading to interpersonal rejection. A first-hand account appearing in *The New York Times Magazine* illustrates the latter scenario:

The real question was why no one ever seemed to figure this grim scenario out on her own, just by looking at you. This was enraging in and of itself— the fact that severe depression, much as it might be treated as an illness, didn't send out clear signals for others to pick up on; it did its deadly dismantling

work under cover of normalcy. The psychological pain was agonizing, but there was no way of proving it, no bleeding wounds to point to. How much simpler it would be all around if you could put your mind in a cast, like a broken ankle, and elicit murmurings of sympathy from other people instead of skepticism ('You can't really be feeling as bad as all that') and in some cases outright hostility ('Maybe if you stopped thinking about yourself so much … ') (Merkin, 2009)

As Merkin points out, depression can lead to rejection, which can then deepen depression. The association between interpersonal rejection and depression is thus a transactional one: Rejection is one of many causes of depression and depression is one of the many causes of rejection. This chapter reviews and integrates the literature that describes the vicious cycle between rejection and depression with an emphasis on the interpersonal processes proposed to account for the association. Given that depression substantially elevates risk for suicide, it also discusses the associations between rejection and suicide in this chapter. However, given that depression is only one mental disorder that elevates risk for suicide, it discusses suicide separately at the end of the chapter.

Depression

Depression is a heterogeneous construct that can refer to normal states of sad, down, or blue moods as well as a class of mental disorders for which depressed mood is the key feature (Wakefield, 2009). In this chapter, the focus is on the latter definition of depression, namely, the depressive disorders. Mental health professionals use the *Diagnostic and Statistical Manual of Mental Disorders* (DSM) (American Psychiatric Association, 2000) to classify and diagnosis depressive disorders. According to the DSM, several disorders involve depression. In this chapter, *depression* refers to the presence of either major depressive disorder (MDD) or dysthymia. Major depressive disorder has two cardinal symptoms (i.e., at least one of these must be present for the diagnosis), sad or depressed mood and an absence of pleasure and enjoyment (i.e., anhedonia). To receive a diagnosis of MDD, an individual must experience at least one of the two cardinal symptoms for at least 2 weeks plus at least four additional symptoms— and these symptoms must be present for most of the day during those 2 weeks. The additional symptoms include sleep disturbances (i.e., sleeping too little or too much), appetite disturbances (i.e., eating too little or too much), impaired concentration, decreased energy, psychomotor disturbances (i.e., marked motoric agitation or slowing), feelings of worthlessness, and suicidal thoughts. The typical course of MDD is persistent (i.e., episodes that last far longer than the 2-week minimum) and recurrent (i.e., most individuals experience more than one episode of depression) (T. E. Joiner, Jr., 2000). A depressive disorder with a course marked by chronicity is dysthymia, which involves sad or depressed mood more days than not for at least 2 years and two additional depressive symptoms, such as low energy or sleep problems.

This aspect of the epidemiology of depressive disorders—recurrent and persistent course—is especially relevant to the association between rejection and depression because interpersonal processes play a key role in both the etiology and maintenance of depression (Joiner, 2000). Both are discussed in turn. First, rejection is discussed as an etiological factor in the onset of depression. Next, interpersonally based depressive processes that lead to rejection and thereby maintain depression are discussed.

Rejection as a Risk Factor for Depression

A large literature has documented robust associations between peer rejection among youth and the development of both internalizing problems, including loneliness and sadness, and externalizing problems, including acting out behaviors (McDougall, Hymel, Vaillancourt, & Mercer, 2001; Parker & Asher, 1987). Rejection experiences with parents are associated with depression: The experience of frequent rejection from primary caregivers during childhood leads to an insecure attachment style that persists into adulthood and increases the risk for depression (Hammen, Burge, Burney, & Adrian, 1990). The experience of childhood maltreatment is an especially severe form of rejection that is associated with depression both in childhood and into adulthood (J. Brown, Cohen, Johnson, & Smailes, 1999). In adulthood, marital discord is a form of rejection that has been robustly linked to depression (Fincham, Beach, Harold, & Osborne, 1997).

The preceding examples discuss relations between objective forms of rejection and depression. However, perceived rejection is also a strong predictor of depression, regardless of whether or not others actually engage in rejection. Rejection sensitivity is a cognitive-affective schema that leads individuals to be hypervigilant for signs of rejection and readily expect and perceive signs of rejection, even when there may be no objective signs of rejection. This cognitive style increases the risk for depression (Ayduk, Downey, & Kim, 2001) and actual rejection from others (Downey, Freitas, Michaelis, & Khouri, 1998).

Depression as a Risk Factor for Rejection

The remaining portion of this discussion is devoted to depression as a risk factor for rejection. Although data do suggest that rejection is likely one form of negative life event associated with increased risk for depression, it is only one of such types of life events involved in a much more complex, multifactorially based etiological process. In contrast, the evidence linking interpersonal processes, including the experience of and reaction to rejection in the maintenance and recurrence of depression, suggests that rejection and related interpersonal processes may be key factors at these later stages in the disorder. Thus, a proportionally greater part of the discussion is devoted to this aspect of the depression–rejection link.

This section discusses several interpersonal processes—self-verification striving, excessive reassurance-seeking, blame maintenance, and stress generation—that have been termed *self-propagatory processes* (Joiner, 2000). This means that these processes "take on a life of their own" and serve to maintain and/or exacerbate depressive symptoms. Transactional relationships exist between these processes and depression such that the processes fuel depression, which further fuels the process. Joiner (2000) likens the process to climbing a mountain covered with scree (i.e., loose rock debris). The metaphor might look like this. Imagine that normal, nondepressed mood is at the top of a mountain. Depression involves falling off the slope to the bottom into the "agonizing pain" (Merkin, 2009). Once at the bottom of the mountain—once depression has set in—it is tough to get to the top and feel better again (i.e., depression is persistent) because the path up to normal functioning is covered with scree. When trying to climb up scree, climbers continually slip back down toward the bottom because there is not any solid ground to grab hold of. Climbing up scree is not impossible, but for most people, it isn't easy. So too for individuals struggling to gain footing on their journey to recovery from depression. The interpersonal processes we discuss in the following tend to elicit rejection and thereby maintain depression. Therefore, rejection functions as a source of scree on the mountain.

Coyne's (1976) interpersonal model of depression describes the interpersonal context in which depression develops and is maintained. The first step in the model involves the presence of an intrapersonal vulnerability—self-doubt—in combination with dysphoric mood (i.e., a milder form of depressed mood) and a stressful life event. The depressogenic cascade is set in motion by the person's desire to assuage the dysphoric mood and dampen self-doubts, which manifests behaviorally as seeking reassurance from others about his or her self-worth. Initially, others often provide the solicited reassurance, but there is a catch: The reassurance clashes with the person's self-doubts, so the reassurance is not accepted as "true." This leaves the person in a state of dysphoria and self-doubts, which impels him or her to try again and seek more reassurance. But no amount of reassurance will ever be adequate. Joiner and colleagues (T. E. Joiner, Alfano, & Metalsky, 1993) suggest why this might be the case by integrating Coyne's model with self-verification theory (Swann, 1990), which posits that individuals seek both self-enhancing and self-confirming feedback. In the case of individuals with an intrapersonal vulnerability of self-doubt (as in Coyne's model), two types of feedback are sought—positive feedback about the self that disconfirms self-doubts as well as negative feedback about the self that confirms self-doubts. Joiner and colleagues (1993) propose that although seeking reassurance may function to disconfirm self-doubts temporarily, doing so will also likely activate needs for self-confirmation and thus the reassurance from others will be discounted as false. These competing motives leave the individual, as well as the people in his or her life, trapped in a vicious cycle that culminates in rejection of the reassurance-seeker whereby mild dysphoric mood becomes depressed mood.

Joiner and colleagues (T. E. Joiner, Jr., Metalsky, Katz, & Beach, 1999) propose that the key depressogenic interpersonal process in Coyne's (1976) model is the repetitive reassurance-seeking behavior of the self-doubting individual, which they term *excessive reassurance-seeking*. This construct is also the proximal cause of rejection: In short, excessive reassurance-seeking is interpersonally aversive, meaning it annoys and irritates other people, thereby increasing the likelihood that the excessive reassurance-seeker will be rejected by others. One of the items from the Reassurance-Seeking subscale of the Depressive Interpersonal Relationships Inventory (T. E. Joiner, Jr. & Metalsky, 2001), a commonly used assessment tool for excessive reassurance-seeking, illustrates this process. "Do the people you feel close to sometimes get 'fed up' with you for seeking reassurance from them about whether they *really* care about you?" Empirical studies have found that when others get "fed up," rejection is more likely to occur. The presence of excessive reassurance seeking functions as a moderator of the association between depression and rejection such that the association is strongest when excessive reassurance seeking is present (T. E. Joiner, Alfano, & Metalsky, 1992; Katz, Beach, & Joiner, 1998).

The presence of both depression and excessive reassurance seeking appears to be a key condition under which rejection will occur. Another interpersonal process that increases the likelihood that rejection will occur is termed *negative feedback seeking*. This construct is based on self-verification theory. Recall that this theory proposes that individuals are motivated to seek feedback about the self that confirms their own self-perceptions; doing so fosters a sense that one understands the self and the world and can make accurate predictions. Negative feedback seeking occurs when these self-views are negative and involves the tendency for individuals with negative self-views (i.e., low self-esteem) to seek out negative feedback from others. Data suggest that the presence of depression and both excessive reassurance seeking and negative feedback seeking is a condition under which rejection is likely to occur. Joiner, Alfano, and Metalsky (1993) found that mildly depressed students were more likely to be rejected by their roommates when they excessively sought reassurance *and* engaged in negative feedback seeking (T. E. Joiner et al., 1993). A prospective test of rejection as a result of the aforementioned constructs found that male roommates were most rejecting toward roommates who engaged in excessive reassurance seeking and negative feedback and had elevated levels of depressive symptoms. In fact, the association did not hold if the roommate was not depressed, suggesting that the association between the interpersonal processes and rejection is specific to the interpersonal context of depression. Why might these processes in the context of depression elicit rejection? Katz, Beach, and Joiner (1998) suggest rejection occurs for two reasons. First, interaction partners become overwhelmed with pleas for help to end personal distress. Second, partners are given the message that they are part of the problem or their relationship is no longer satisfying.

Reassurance seeking and negative feedback seeking represent transactional interpersonal processes that fuel a downward cycle of depression that originate with the depressed individual. *Blame maintenance,* in contrast, originates with the interaction partners of the depressed person. Blame maintenance describes the tendency to continue to expect once-depressed individuals to remain depressed and engage in interpersonally aversive behaviors. These expectations often persist despite the fact that interpersonally aversive behaviors largely remit, and more positive and adaptive behaviors of the once-depressed individual go unnoticed (T. E. Joiner, Jr., 2000). Blame maintenance creates relational turmoil and can be conceptualized as a form of rejection. Blame maintenance predicts recurrence of depression (Hooley & Teasdale, 1989). A related construct is *expressed emotion,* which refers to the tendency of relational partners of individuals with mental disorders, including depression, to express high levels of criticism to the depressed person. This form of rejection of someone who is depressed predicts high levels of depression relapse and recurrence (Butzlaff & Hooley, 1998).

Our discussion of the transactional relationship between rejection and depression highlights that individuals often enter a downward spiral of sorts in which depression is maintained by interpersonal processes that resulted from—or were exacerbated by—depression. This characterization begs the question, How does someone exit this downward spiral? One way this can occur is for the depressed person to receive treatment for depression in the form of psychotropic medication and/or psychotherapy proven to be efficacious for depression. A discussion of psychotherapy appears at the end of this chapter.

Suicide

Suicide was the 11th leading cause of death (across all ages) in the United States in 2006 (Heron et al., 2009), with approximately 30,000 individuals in the United States dying by suicide each year, and approximately 1 million worldwide (World Health Organization, 2008). These statistics refer to lethal suicidal behavior; however, nonlethal suicidal behaviors (i.e., suicide attempts) are much more common, with approximately 25 suicide attempts for every fatal suicide (McIntosh, 2008). Thoughts about suicide (i.e., suicidal ideation) are even more common, with approximately 3.3% of Americans seriously considering suicide each year (Kessler, Berglund, Borges, Nock, & Wang, 2005). As the preceding findings illustrate, one of the most striking aspects of the epidemiology of suicide is the finding replicated worldwide and over time that only a small subset of people who think about suicide go on to attempt, and even fewer will die by suicide (World Health Organization, 2008). Most theoretical models of suicide are inconsistent with this fact; however, the interpersonal theory of suicide (T. Joiner, 2005; Van Orden et al., 2010) proposes that to understand and predict suicide, the distinction must be made between desire for suicide and the capability to engage in suicidal behavior. Suicide is a frightening and physically painful act—even among those with a strong desire to die, not all are capable of engaging in suicidal behaviors. Consistent with the interpersonal theory of suicide, we propose that social rejection is primarily associated with suicidal desire, rather than capability for suicide. Thus, we conceptualize rejection as one form of an interpersonal negative life event that may contribute to desire for suicide.

A great deal of the literature on suicide involves investigation of risk factors for suicide—those factors associated with an increased probability of suicide occurring. However, suicide is inherently difficult to study: It is a low base rate event (i.e., relatively rare); individuals who experience the event of interest—suicide—cannot be interviewed; and it cannot be experimentally induced in the laboratory, for obvious ethical reasons. Thus, research on suicide relies on methods such as population-based studies, psychological autopsy studies that involve interviewing family members and friends of the person who died, and longitudinal studies of high-risk samples. Findings from studies using these diverse methodologies and using samples across the life span indicate the most consistent and strongest support for the following risk factors: mental disorder, past suicide attempts, social isolation, family conflict, unemployment, and physical illness (Van Orden et al., 2010). Two of these risk factors are particularly relevant to the association between rejection and suicide—social isolation and family conflict. Thus, this discussion focuses on the different manifestations of these risk factors and their relations with suicide. When possible, studies that specifically examined forms of rejection rather than its precursors or sequelae are examined. Although the theoretical basis for proposing a link between rejection and suicide is strong, the majority of the research on suicide has been conducted in an atheoretical context. Little research has specifically examined rejection as a life event that may increase risk for suicide.

Social isolation is arguably the strongest and most reliable predictor of suicidal ideation, attempts, and lethal suicidal behavior across the life span (T. E. Joiner & Van Orden, 2008; Trout, 1980). Empirical studies have demonstrated that social isolation is a pernicious risk factor for lethal suicidal behavior among youth (Hawton, Fagg, & Simkin, 1996) and adults (Appleby, Cooper, Amos, & Faragher, 1999), including the elderly (Conwell, 1997). Social isolation also elevates risk for nonlethal suicide attempts (Darke et al., 2007; Hall-Lande, Eisenberg, Christenson, & Neumark-Sztainer, 2007), and suicidal ideation (Bearman & Moody, 2004; Dutra, Callahan, Forman, Mendelsohn, & Herman, 2008; Haw & Hawton, 2008; Skodlar, Tomori, & Parnas, 2008). Thus, to the extent that rejection results in social isolation, it functions as a risk factor for suicide.

Indices of various facets of social isolation have been implicated in suicidal behavior. First, the affective state central to the construct of social isolation—loneliness—predicts suicidal ideation and behavior among samples varying in age, nationality, and clinical severity (Bonner & Rich, 1987; Butterworth, Fairweather, Anstey, & Windsor, 2006; D'Augelli, Grossman, Hershberger, & O'Connell, 2001; Koivumaa-Honkanen et al., 2001). Rejection also causes feelings of loneliness (McDougall et al., 2001), suggesting that rejection that results in severe feelings of loneliness may lead to suicidal ideation.

Rejection often reduces the number of people that an individual feels close to, which may also function as a mechanism that may lead to desire for suicide. The number of supportive individuals in a person's life is related to suicide risk, with marriage, children, and greater number of friends/family decreasing risk for suicidal behavior (Duberstein, Conwell, Conner, Eberly, Evinger, et al., 2004; Hoyer & Lund, 1993; Kposowa, 2000; Miller, 1978; Qin & Nordentoft, 2005; Stack, 2000; Turvey et al., 2002; Wingate et al., 2005). Living alone and having few social supports also elevates risk for suicidal behavior (Bartels et al., 2002; Conner, Duberstein, & Conwell, 1999; De Leo et al., 2001; Gove & Hughes, 1980; Nickel et al., 2006; Vanderhorst & McLaren, 2005). One study found that rejection resulting in the loss of friends after disclosing one's sexual orientation is associated with increased risk for suicide attempts among gay, lesbian, and bisexual youth (Hershberger, Pilkington, & D'Augelli, 1997).

The interpersonal theory of suicide proposes that all of the indicators of social isolation described in the preceding are associated with risk for suicide because they indicate that the human need for belongingness is unmet (Baumeister & Leary, 1995). A thwarted need to belong is posited by this theory to be a proximal cause of desire for suicide.

Poor relationship quality—in the form of family, marital, and peer conflict—is a robust precipitant of suicidal behavior across the life span (Beautrais, 2002; David A. Brent et al., 1994; Dervic, Brent, & Oquendo, 2008; Gould, Fisher, Parides, Flory, & Shaffer, 1996; Hershberger et al., 1997; Kaltiala-Heino, Rimpela, Marttunen, Rimpela, & Rantanen, 1999; Rubenowitz, Waern, Wilhelmson, & Allebeck, 2001). In particular, indices of family conflict are robust risk factors for lethal suicidal behavior. Studies have documented an association between family discord and lethal suicide attempts in both middle-age adults (M. Heikkinen, Aro, & Lönnqvist, 1994) and elder adults (Duberstein, Conwell, Conner, Eberly, & Caine, 2004; M. E. Heikkinen & Lonnqvist, 1995; Rubenowitz et al., 2001; Waern, Rubenowitz, & Wilhelmson, 2003). A particularly severe form of familial conflict, domestic violence, elevates risk for lethal suicidal behavior in adults (Gururaj, Isaac, Subbakrishna, & Ranjani, 2004; Samaraweera, Sumathipala, Siribaddana, Sivayogan, & Bhugra, 2008). In children and adolescents, discord with parents elevates risk for lethal suicidal behavior (David A. Brent et al., 1994; D. A. Brent et al., 1994; Gould et al., 1996; Hawton et al., 1996), as does familial stress (Brent, Baugher, Bridge, Chen, & Chiappetta, 1999). The interpersonal theory of suicide proposes that family conflict elevates risk for suicide because it indicates the presence of perceptions that one is a burden on others.

The construct of perceived burdensomeness is a proximal cause of suicidal desire according to the interpersonal theory of suicide. This construct involves the belief (almost always erroneous) that others in the person's life would be better off if the target person were dead. This construct involves a form of perceived rejection. In support of the relation between perceived burdensomeness and suicide, a psychological autopsy study of terminal cancer patients who died by suicide indicated that self-perceptions of being a burden on others was a key characteristic likely contributing to desire for suicide (Filiberti et al., 2001). In a comparison of suicide notes of individuals who made lethal versus nonlethal attempts, the presence of perceptions of burdensomeness on others differentiated between individuals who attempted and survived and individuals who attempted and died—with perceptions of burdensomeness characterizing the notes of those who died (T. Joiner et al., 2002). In addition, in the same study, greater perceptions of burdensomeness in the notes predicted the use of more lethal means among the sample of notes from individuals who died. Another study examining suicide notes found that the theme "a burden to others" was significantly more common among elders who died by suicide (compared with younger individuals), suggesting that this risk factor may be especially potent among older adults (Foster, 2003). A prospective study following psychiatric patients at high risk for suicide found that statements about feeling like a burden on others significantly elevated risk for suicide during a 60-day follow-up period after an evaluation (Motto & Bostrom, 1990). A final example of how perceptions of burdensomeness on others elevate risk for lethal suicidal behavior comes from a traditional practice of ritual suicide in the Yuit Eskimos of St. Lawrence Island (Leighton & Hughes, 1955). The belief underlying this practice is that becoming too

sick, infirm, or old could threaten the survival of the group. In this society, as in many others across history and cultures, ritual suicide became an explicit and socially sanctioned response to perceptions that one's existence burdened the group.

Self-perceptions that one is a burden on others also differentiate between individuals with histories of suicide attempts versus no attempts (R. M. Brown, Dahlen, Mills, Rick, & Biblarz, 1999; Van Orden, Lynam, Hollar, & Joiner, 2006) and are also associated with suicidal ideation (R. Brown et al., 2009; de Catanzaro, 1995; Van Orden et al., 2006). Similar to perceiving that one is a burden, the desire to "make others better off" is a more common reason given for suicide attempts versus episodes of self-harm without suicidal intent (M. Z. Brown, Comtois, & Linehan, 2002). The belief that someone wishes one dead was shown to differentiate between suicidal and nonsuicidal individuals (Rosenbaum & Richman, 1970). Another additional related construct, perceptions of expendability, also characterize suicidal adolescents (Woznica & Shapiro, 1990). Similarly, suicidal preschoolers (compared with preschoolers with behavior problems) have been shown to be more likely to be unwanted by their parents (Rosenthal & Rosenthal, 1984). Thus, perceiving that the self is so flawed as to be a liability for family and friends represents a form of perceived rejection that increases risk for suicide across the life span.

Treatment

Numerous psychotherapies are effective in treating depression, including some that specifically focus on modifying the interpersonal functioning of depressed individuals. One such therapy is interpersonal psychotherapy. In this therapy, the therapist helps the client choose one domain of interpersonal functioning to focus on—grief, interpersonal skills deficits, interpersonal disputes, or role transitions—and improve functioning in that area through the use of various techniques (e.g., eliciting affect, role plays, and analysis of specific situations) (Weissman, Markowitz, & Klerman, 2007). Another therapy, Cognitive Behavioral Analysis System of Psychotherapy (CBASP) is effective for treating chronic depression (McCullough, 2000). One of the key aspects of CBASP is teaching the client to engage in "situational analysis" that involves a detailed examination of a specific interpersonal situation with regard to whether the clients' thoughts and behaviors helped or hurt him or her in getting what he or she wanted out of the situation. Clients are helped to modify thoughts and behaviors to increase the likelihood of the situation turning out how they would have liked, and with practice, clients' interpersonal functioning improves and their mood lifts.

Dialectical behavior therapy (DBT) (Linehan, 1993), which strongly emphasizes the need to help suicidal clients improve their interpersonal functioning, is highly efficacious in the prevention of suicide attempts. Dialectical behavior therapy does so by teaching behavioral interpersonal skills and using the therapeutic relationship, as well as a skills group, to practice those skills. The core treatment target of DBT is emotion regulation—a set of behavioral responses that involve recognizing, modulating, and tolerating emotions. Emotion regulation is a necessary component of a skill repertoire that allows individuals to reduce the chances of rejection and/or skillfully tolerate the painful feelings that accompany rejection when it occurs. In this way, evidence-based psychotherapies that place strong emphasis on interpersonal functioning may help break the deleterious link between rejection and both depression and suicide.

Conclusions

This chapter described evidence that rejection is both a cause and consequence of depression. Peer and family rejection in childhood, and marital discord in adulthood, are all associated with increased risk of developing a depressive disorder. Interpersonal processes involved in depression, such as self-verification striving, excessive reassurance-seeking, blame maintenance, and stress generation cause rejection and are key factors in the maintenance and recurrence of depressive symptoms. Rejection is also associated with increased risk of suicide. In particular, social isolation and family discord are associated with elevated risk of suicide. The interpersonal theory of suicide proposes that when rejection, and perceived rejection, associated with social isolation and family discord cause thwarted belongingness and perceived burdensomeness, desire for suicide results. Evidence-based psychotherapies for depression and suicidal behaviors, including IPT, CBASP, and DBT, target interpersonal functioning. These therapies help clients change their interactions with others to prevent rejection and skillfully manage emotional pain that results when rejection occurs. Thus, although rejection is associated with both depression and suicide, psychotherapy can halt the downward cycle.

References

American Psychiatric Association. (2000). *Diagnostic and Statistical Manual of Mental Disorders* (4th ed., text revision ed.). Washington, DC: Author.

Appleby, L., Cooper, J., Amos, T., & Faragher, B. (1999). Psychological autopsy study of suicides by people aged under 35. *The British Journal of Psychiatry : The Journal of Mental Science, 175*, 168–174.

Ayduk, O., Downey, G., & Kim, M. (2001). Rejection sensitivity and depressive symptoms in women. *Personality and Social Psychology Bulletin, 27*(7), 868–877.

Bartels, S. J., Coakley, E., Oxman, T. E., Constantino, G., Oslin, D., Chen, H., et al. (2002). Suicidal and death ideation in older primary care patients with depression, anxiety, and at-risk alcohol use. *The American Journal of Geriatric Psychiatry: Official Journal of the American Association for Geriatric Psychiatry, 10*(4), 417–427.

Baumeister, R. F., & Leary, M. R. (1995). The need to belong: Desire for interpersonal attachments as a fundamental human motivation. *Psychological Bulletin, 117*(3), 497–529.

Bearman, P. S., & Moody, J. (2004). Suicide and friendships among American adolescents. *American Journal of Public Health, 94*(1), 89–95.

Beautrais, A. L. (2002). A case control study of suicide and attempted suicide in older adults. *Suicide & Life Threatening Behavior, 32*(1), 1–9.

Bonner, R. L., & Rich, A. R. (1987). Toward a predictive model of suicidal ideation and behavior: Some preliminary data in college students. *Suicide and Life-Threatening Behavior, 17*(1), 50–63.

Brent, D. A., Baugher, M., Bridge, J., Chen, T., & Chiappetta, L. (1999). Age- and sex-related risk factors for adolescent suicide. *Journal of the American Academy of Child & Adolescent Psychiatry, 38*(12), 1497–1505.

Brent, D. A., Perper, J. A., Moritz, G., Baugher, M., Schweers, J., & Roth, C. (1994). Suicide in affectively ill adolescents: A case-control study. *Journal of Affective Disorders, 31*(3), 193–202.

Brent, D. A., Perper, J. A., Moritz, G., Liotus, L., Schweers, J., Balach, L., et al. (1994). Familial risk factors for adolescent suicide: A case-control study. *Acta Psychiatrica Scandinavica, 89*(1), 52–58.

Brown, J., Cohen, P., Johnson, J. G., & Smailes, E. M. (1999). Childhood abuse and neglect: specificity of effects on adolescent and young adult depression and suicidality. *Journal of the American Academy of Child and Adolescent Psychiatry, 38*(12), 1490–1496.

Brown, M. Z., Comtois, K. A., & Linehan, M. M. (2002). Reasons for suicide attempts and nonsuicidal self-injury in women with borderline personality disorder. *Journal of Abnormal Psychology, 111*(1), 198–202.

Brown, R., Brown, S., Johnson, A., Olsen, B., Melver, K., & Sullivan, M. (2009). Empirical support for an evolutionary model of self-destructive motivation. *Suicide & Life Threatening Behavior, 39*(1), 1–12.

Brown, R. M., Dahlen, E., Mills, C., Rick, J., & Biblarz, A. (1999). Evaluation of an evolutionary model of self-preservation and self-destruction. *Suicide and Life-Threatening Behavior, 29*(1), 58–71.

Butterworth, P., Fairweather, A. K., Anstey, K. J., & Windsor, T. D. (2006). Hopelessness, demoralization and suicidal behaviour: The backdrop to welfare reform in Australia.

The Australian and New Zealand Journal of Psychiatry, 40(8), 648–656.

Butzlaff, R. L., & Hooley, J. M. (1998). Expressed emotion and psychiatric relapse. *Archives of General Psychiatry, 55*(6), 547–552.

Conner, K. R., Duberstein, P. R., & Conwell, Y. (1999). Age-related patterns of factors associated with completed suicide in men with alcohol dependence. *The American Journal on Addictions, 8*(4), 312–318.

Conwell, Y. (1997). Management of suicidal behavior in the elderly. *Psychiatric Clinics of North America, 20*(3), 667–683.

Coyne, J. C. (1976). Toward an interactional description of depression. *Psychiatry: Journal for the Study of Interpersonal Processes, 39*(1), 28–40.

D'Augelli, A. R., Grossman, A. H., Hershberger, S. L., & O'Connell, T. S. (2001). Aspects of mental health among older lesbian, gay, and bisexual adults. *Aging & Mental Health, 5*(2), 149–158.

Darke, S., Ross, J., Williamson, A., Mills, K. L., Havard, A., & Teesson, M. (2007). Patterns and correlates of attempted suicide by heroin users over a 3-year period: findings from the Australian treatment outcome study. *Drug and Alcohol Dependence, 87*(2–3), 146–152.

de Catanzaro, D. (1995). Reproductive status, family interactions, and suicidal ideation: Surveys of the general public and high-risk groups. *Ethology & Sociobiology, 16*(5), 385–394.

De Leo, D., Padoani, W., Scocco, P., Lie, D., Bille-Brahe, U., Arensman, E., et al. (2001). Attempted and completed suicide in older subjects: Results from the WHO/EURO Multicentre Study of Suicidal Behaviour. *International Journal of Geriatric Psychiatry, 16*(3), 300–310.

Dervic, K., Brent, D. A., & Oquendo, M. A. (2008). Completed suicide in childhood. *Psychiatric Clinics of North America, 31*(2), 271–291.

Downey, G., Freitas, A. L., Michaelis, B., & Khouri, H. (1998). The self-fulfilling prophecy in close relationships: Rejection sensitivity and rejection by romantic partners. *Journal of Personality and Social Psychology, 75*(2), 545–560.

Duberstein, P. R., Conwell, Y., Conner, K. R., Eberly, S., & Caine, E. D. (2004). Suicide at 50 years of age and older: perceived physical illness, family discord and financial strain. *Psychological Medicine, 34*(1), 137–146.

Duberstein, P. R., Conwell, Y., Conner, K. R., Eberly, S., Evinger, J. S., & Caine, E. D. (2004). Poor social integration and suicide: fact or artifact? A case-control study. *Psychological Medicine, 34*(7), 1331–1337.

Dutra, L., Callahan, K., Forman, E., Mendelsohn, M., & Herman, J. (2008). Core schemas and suicidality in a chronically traumatized population. *The Journal of Nervous and Mental Disease, 196*(1), 71–74.

Filiberti, A., Ripamonti, C., Totis, A., Ventafridda, V., De Conno, F., Contiero, P., et al. (2001). Characteristics of terminal cancer patients who committed suicide during a home palliative care program. *Journal of Pain and Symptom Management, 22*(1), 544–553.

Fincham, F. D., Beach, S. R., Harold, G. T., & Osborne, L. N. (1997). Marital satisfaction and depression: Different causal relationships for men and women? *Psychological Science, 8*(5), 351–357.

Foster, T. (2003). Suicide note themes and suicide prevention. *International Journal of Psychiatry in Medicine, 33*(4), 323–331.

Gould, M. S., Fisher, P., Parides, M., Flory, M., & Shaffer, D. (1996). Psychosocial risk factors of child and adolescent completed suicide. *Archives of General Psychiatry, 53*(12), 1155–1162.

Gove, W. R., & Hughes, M. (1980). Reexamining the ecological fallacy: A study in which aggregate data are critical in investigating the pathological effects of living alone. *Social Forces, 58*, 1157–1177.

Gururaj, G., Isaac, M. K., Subbakrishna, D. K., & Ranjani, R. (2004). Risk factors for completed suicides: A case-control study from Bangalore, India. *International Journal of Injury Control and Safety Promotion, 11*(3), 183–191.

Hall-Lande, J. A., Eisenberg, M. E., Christenson, S. L., & Neumark-Sztainer, D. (2007). Social isolation, psychological health, and protective factors in adolescence. *Adolescence, 42*(166), 265–286.

Hammen, C., Burge, D., Burney, E., & Adrian, C. (1990). Longitudinal study of diagnoses in children of women with unipolar and bipolar affective disorder. *Archives of General Psychiatry, 47*(12), 1112–1117.

Haw, C., & Hawton, K. (2008). Life problems and deliberate self-harm: Associations with gender, age, suicidal intent and psychiatric and personality disorder. *Journal of Affective Disorders, 109*(1–2), 139–148.

Hawton, K., Fagg, J., & Simkin, S. (1996). Deliberate self-poisoning and self-injury in children and adolescents under 16 years of age in Oxford, 1976–1993. *British Journal of Psychiatry, 169*(2), 202–208.

Heikkinen, M., Aro, H., & Lönnqvist, J. (1994). Recent life events, social support and suicide. *Acta psychiatrica Scandinavica. Supplementum, 377*, 65–72.

Heikkinen, M. E., & Lonnqvist, J. K. (1995). Recent life events in elderly suicide: A nationwide study in Finland. *International Psychogeriatrics, 7*, 287–300.

Heron, M. P., Hoyert, D. L., Murphy, S. L., Jiaquan, X., Kochanek, K. D., & Tejada-Vera, B. (2009). Deaths: Final data for 2006. *National Vital Statistics Reports, 57*(14), 1–135.

Hershberger, S. L., Pilkington, N. W., & D'Augelli, A. R. (1997). Predictors of suicide attempts among gay, lesbian, and bisexual youth. *Journal of Adolescent Research, 12*(4), 477–497.

Hooley, J. M., & Teasdale, J. D. (1989). Predictors of relapse in unipolar depressives: Expressed emotion, marital distress, and perceived criticism. *Journal of abnormal Psychology, 98*, 229–235.

Hoyer, G., & Lund, E. (1993). Suicide among women related to number of children in marriage. *Archives of General Psychiatry, 50*(2), 134–137.

Joiner, T. (2005). *Why People Die by Suicide*. Cambridge, MA: Harvard University Press.

Joiner, T., Pettit, J. W., Walker, R. L., Voelz, Z. R., Cruz, J., Rudd, M. D., et al. (2002). Perceived burdensomeness and suicidality: Two studies on the suicide notes of those attempting and those completing suicide. *Journal of Social & Clinical Psychology, 21*(5), 531–545.

Joiner, T. E., Alfano, M. S., & Metalsky, G. I. (1992). When depression breeds contempt: Reassurance seeking, self-esteem, and rejection of depressed college students by their roommates. *Journal of Abnormal Psychology, 101*(1), 165–173.

Joiner, T. E., Alfano, M. S., & Metalsky, G. I. (1993). Caught in the crossfire: Depression, self-consistency, self-enhancement, and the response of others. *Journal of Social & Clinical Psychology, 12*(2), 113–134.

Joiner, T. E., Jr. (2000). Depression's vicious scree: Self-propagating and erosive processes in depression chronicity. *Clinical Psychology: Science and Practice, 7*(2), 203–218.

Joiner, T. E., Jr., & Metalsky, G. I. (2001). Excessive reassurance seeking: Delineating a risk factor involved in the development of depressive symptoms. *Psychological Science, 12*(5), 371–378.

Joiner, T. E., Jr., Metalsky, G. I., Katz, J., & Beach, S. R. (1999). Depression and excessive reassurance-seeking. *Psychological Inquiry, 10*(4), 269–278.

Joiner, T. E., & Van Orden, K. A. (2008). The interpersonal psychological theory of suicidal behavior indicates specific and crucial psychotherapeutic targets. *International Journal of Cognitive Therapy, 1*(1), 80–89.

Kaltiala-Heino, R., Rimpela, M., Marttunen, M., Rimpela, A., & Rantanen, P. (1999). Bullying, depression, and suicidal ideation in Finnish adolescents: School survey. *British Medical Journal, 319*(7206), 348–351.

Katz, J., Beach, S. R., & Joiner, T. E., Jr. (1998). When does partner devaluation predict emotional distress? Prospective moderating effects of reassurance-seeking and self-esteem. *Personal Relationships, 5*(4), 409–421.

Kessler, R. C., Berglund, P., Borges, G., Nock, M., & Wang, P. S. (2005). Trends in suicide ideation, plans, gestures, and attempts in the United States, 1990–1992 to 2001–2003. *Journal of the American Medical Association, 293*(20), 2487–2495.

Koivumaa-Honkanen, H., Honkanen, R., Viinamäki, H., Heikkilä, K., Kaprio, J., & Koskenvuo, M. (2001). Life satisfaction and suicide: A 20-year follow-up study. *The American Journal of Psychiatry, 158*(3), 433–439.

Kposowa, A. J. (2000). Marital status and suicide in the National Longitudinal Mortality Study. *Journal of Epidemiology and Community Health, 54*(4), 254–261.

Linehan, M. M. (1993). *Cognitive-behavioral treatment of borderline personality disorder.* New York: Guilford.Leighton, A. H., & Hughes, C. C. (1955). Notes on eskimo patterns of suicide. *Southwestern Journal of Anthropology, 11,* 327–338.

McCullough, J. P., Jr. (2000). *Treatment for Chronic Depression: Cognitive Behavioral Analysis System of Psychotherapy (CBASP).* New York: Guilford Press.

McDougall, P., Hymel, S., Vaillancourt, T., & Mercer, L. (2001). The consequences of childhood peer rejection. In M. R. Leary (Ed.), *Interpersonal Rejection* (pp. 213–247). New York: Oxford University Press.

McIntosh, J. L. (2008). U.S.A. Suicide: 2005 Official Data Retrieved September 29, 2008 from http://www.suicidology.org/associations/1045/files/2005datapgs.pdf.

Merkin, D. (May 10, 2009). A journey through darkness: My life with chronic depression. *The New York Times Magazine.*

Miller, M. (1978). Geriatric suicide: The Arizona study. *The Gerontologist, 18*(5, Pt 1), 488–495.

Motto, J. A., & Bostrom, A. (1990). Empirical indicators of near-term suicide risk. *Crisis, 11*(1), 52–59.

Nickel, C., Simek, M., Moleda, A., Muehlbacher, M., Buschmann, W., Fartacek, R., et al. (2006). Suicide attempts versus suicidal ideation in bulimic female adolescents. *Pediatrics International: Official Journal of the Japan Pediatric Society, 48*(4), 374–381.

Parker, J. G., & Asher, S. R. (1987). Peer relations and later personal adjustment: are low-accepted children at risk? *Psychological Bulletin, 102*(3), 357–389.

Qin, P., & Nordentoft, M. (2005). Suicide risk in relation to psychiatric hospitalization. *Archives of General Psychiatry, 62*(4), 427–432.

Rosenbaum, M., & Richman, J. (1970). Suicide: The role of hostility and death wishes from the family and significant others. *American Journal of Psychiatry, 126*(11), 1652–1655.

Rosenthal, P. A., & Rosenthal, S. (1984). Suicidal behavior by preschool children. *American Journal of Psychiatry, 141*(4), 520–525.

Rubenowitz, E., Waern, M., Wilhelmson, K., & Allebeck, P. (2001). Life events and psychosocial factors in elderly suicides—a case-control study. *Psychological Medicine, 31*(7), 1193–1202.

Samaraweera, S., Sumathipala, A., Siribaddana, S., Sivayogan, S., & Bhugra, D. (2008). Completed suicide among Sinhalese in Sri Lanka: A psychological autopsy study. *Suicide and Life-Threatening Behavior, 38*(2), 221–228.

Skodlar, B., Tomori, M., & Parnas, J. (2008). Subjective experience and suicidal ideation in schizophrenia. *Comprehensive Psychiatry, 49*(5), 482–488.

Stack, S. (2000). Suicide: A 15-year review of the sociological literature. Part II: modernization and social integration perspectives. *Suicide & Life Threatening Behavior, 30*(2), 163–176.

Swann, W. B., Jr. (1990). To be adored or to be known? The interplay of self-enhancement and self-verification. In E. T. Higgins (Ed.), *Handbook of Motivation and Cognition: Foundations of Social Behavior* (Vol. 2, pp. 408–448). New York: Guilford Press.

Trout, D. L. (1980). The role of social isolation in suicide. *Suicide and Life-Threatening Behavior, 10*(1), 10–23.

Turvey, C. L., Conwell, Y., Jones, M. P., Phillips, C., Simonsick, E., Pearson, J. L., et al. (2002). Risk factors for late-life suicide: A prospective community-based study. *American Journal of Geriatric Psychiatry. Special Issue: Suicidal Behaviors in Older Adults, 10*(4), 398–406.

Vanderhorst, R. K., & McLaren, S. (2005). Social relationships as predictors of depression and suicidal ideation in older adults. *Aging & Mental Health, 9*(6), 517–525.

Van Orden, K. A., Lynam, M. E., Hollar, D., & Joiner, T. E., Jr. (2006). Perceived Burdensomeness as an Indicator of Suicidal Symptoms. *Cognitive Therapy and Research, 30*(4), 457–467.

Van Orden, K. A., Witte, T. K., Cukrowicz, K. C., Braithwaite, S. R., Selby, E. A., & Joiner Jr, T. E. (2010). The interpersonal theory of suicide. *Psychological Review, 117*(2), 575–600.

Waern, M., Rubenowitz, E., & Wilhelmson, K. (2003). Predictors of suicide in the old elderly. *Gerontology, 49*(5), 328–334.

Wakefield, J. C. (2009). Definition of depression. In R. E. Ingram (Ed.), *The International Encyclopedia of Depression* (pp. 207–208). New York: Springer.

Weissman, M. M., Markowitz, J. C., & Klerman, G. L. (2007). *Clinician's Quick Guide to Interpersonal Psychotherapy.* New York: Oxford University Press.

Wingate, L. R., Bobadilla, L., Burns, A. B., Cukrowicz, K. C., Hernandez, A., Ketterman, R. L., et al. (2005). Suicidality in African American men: The roles of southern residence, religiosity, and social support. *Suicide and Life-Threatening Behavior, 35*(6), 615–629.

World Health Organization. (2008). Suicide statistics: Introduction. Retrieved January 2, 2008 from http://www.who.int/mental_health/prevention/suicide/suicideprevent/en/print.html.

Woznica, J. G., & Shapiro, J. R. (1990). An analysis of adolescent suicide attempts: The expendable child. *Journal of Pediatric Psychology, 15*(6), 789–796.

Individual Differences in Responses to Social Exclusion: Self-Esteem, Narcissism, and Self-Compassion

Michelle R. vanDellen, Ashley Batts Allen, *and* W. Keith Campbell

Abstract

Experiences of social exclusion disrupt people's feelings of belongingness. Because self-esteem is connected to how socially connected people feel to important others, such experiences lower state self-esteem. The authors suggests that these situations evoke self-regulatory processes aimed at bringing state self-esteem back in line with standards for trait self-esteem. This chapter focuses on three individual differences, each related to self-views, that may be related to reactions to social exclusion: trait self-esteem, narcissism, and self-compassion. Trait self-esteem is generally associated with heightened reactions to social exclusion that are aimed at restoring immediate self-feelings; narcissism is associated with aggressive responses to social exclusion; and self-compassion is associated with stable responses that are unmarked by extreme negative affect or externalizing. The authors concludes with suggestions for interventions aimed at reducing aggression in response to social exclusion.

Key Words: narcissism, self-compassion, self-esteem, rejection

Introduction

Experiences of social exclusion interrupt individuals' desires to feel like they belong to important groups, communities, and societies. Furthermore, these experiences indicate that people may not have the kind of community support that they both want and need to survive (Baumeister & Leary, 1995). According to sociometer theory, state self-esteem serves as an indicator of how much acceptance people experience at any given moment (i.e., relational valuation) (Leary, Terdal, Tambor, & Downs, 1995). In this view, self-esteem fluctuates in direct response to experiences of social rejection and acceptance, with relational devaluation leading to larger drops in state self-esteem than relational valuation (Leary, Haupt, Strausser, & Chokel, 1998). Not only does social exclusion lead to decreased self-esteem, but rejection experiences also lead to neurological and physiological reactions

similar to those of physical pain (DeWall et al., in press; Eisenberger, Lieberman, & Williams, 2003; MacDonald & Leary, 2005).

This chapter examines how individual differences affect these reactions to social exclusion. First, it discusses social exclusion as a situational trigger of the regulation of state self-esteem. Second, it examines how trait self-esteem, or enduring views about one's worth, affects reactions to social exclusion. Third, it highlights how the individual differences of narcissism and self-compassion, two constructs that are both related to self-esteem but that lead to vastly different responses to negative experiences, affect reactions to social exclusion. Finally, the chapter concludes with recommendations for how interventions might decrease aggression and other negative behaviors by focusing on building self-compassion and suggest future directions for research along these lines.

Social Exclusion and the Regulation of State Self-Esteem

Although people may immediately respond to social rejection with emotional shock (e.g., DeWall & Baumeister, 2006), after time, they tend to report increased negative affect and decreased positive affect compared with people who were not rejected (Blackhart, Nelson, Knowles, & Baumeister, 2009). The connection between social exclusion and self-regulation lies here, where negative affect is incited. In self-regulatory models, negative affect develops when undesired discrepancies occur between people's standards and their current state of affairs. Although people may not be aware of these discrepancies, negative affect serves as a trigger for self-regulation, a relatively automatic process by which people either change their standards or begin effortful progress aimed at reducing the present discrepancy (Carver & Scheier, 1981, 1990; Higgins, 1987; Rothbaum, Weisz, & Snyder, 1982).

In the case of social exclusion, negative affect arises because a desired state of being (i.e., feeling positive about oneself) is not being met (vanDellen, Bradfield, & Hoyle, 2010). The negative affect that results is a trigger for the regulation of state self-esteem. This self-regulation occurs in response to the specific standard of high trait self-esteem being violated. Although not everyone has high trait self-esteem, we assume that all people do *want* to have positive self-views (Gibbons & McCoy, 1991; Pyszczynski, Greenberg, Arndt, & Schimel, 2004; Sedikides & Strube, 1997), and as a result, experiences of social rejection that decrease state self-esteem and incite negative affect incite a discrepancy between a desired standard and one's current state. As a result, people engage in responses that may either bolster their self-esteem or change their standards for self-esteem (Rothbaum et al., 1982). Given the current cultural centrality—at least in Western societies—and perceived importance of self-esteem (Campbell & Foster, 2006), we assume that most people desire to respond in ways that bolster their esteem. An important component of this framework is the experience of negative affect. If negative affect is strong, self-regulation of state self-esteem will be more likely and more dominant (Higgins, 1987). If negative affect is weak, or can be quickly reframed as personally irrelevant, regulation of state self-esteem is less likely.

Some mechanisms of regulating state self-esteem in response to social exclusion are relatively innocuous. For instance, after social exclusion, people may shift their attention to domains in which they feel competent as a way of reminding themselves that they still have value (Steele, Spencer, & Lynch, 1993). Other work suggests that people shift their attention to positive social information and become more empathetic and better at detecting emotions in others (DeWall, Maner, & Rouby, 2009; Gardner, Pickett, & Brewer, 2000; Pickett, Gardner, & Knowles, 2004). These responses to social exclusion involve internalizing behaviors, such as attentional shifts and cognitive focus. However, some responses to social exclusion involve externalizing behaviors. These behaviors include aggression, which has the potential to affect not only the individual who was excluded, but also others (Leary, Twenge, & Quinlivan, 2006; Twenge, Baumeister, Tice, & Stucke, 2001).

Because responses to social exclusion likely entail the regulation of state self-esteem, we would expect that certain trait variables would be associated with different patterns of responses. Specifically, individual differences associated with self-perception should affect the magnitude and type of responses that people evidence after social exclusion. This chapter focuses on trait self-esteem (i.e., consistent patterns of self-evaluation), narcissism (i.e., inflated patterns of self-evaluation associated with dominance and entitlement), and self-compassion (i.e., patterns of self-perception that minimize the importance of state experiences and focus on the common humanity in one's experience).

Trait Self-Esteem

Although trait self-esteem—enduring views about one's personal worth (Rosenberg,1965)—appears to have little direct effect on behavior (Baumeister, Campbell, Krueger, & Vohs, 2003), it is an important moderator of behaviors. That is, specific situations may affect people with high self-esteem differently than they affect people with low self-esteem. One potential class of situations that may influence people differently is when state self-esteem is threatened. Recently, we conducted a meta-analysis in which we examined how trait self-esteem influenced reactions to both general threats and relational devaluation (vanDellen, Campbell, Hoyle, & Bradfield, 2011). In that paper, we focused on whether high trait self-esteem was associated with increased, decreased, or unchanged esteem-restorative reactions to threats compared with low trait self-esteem. For the purposes of this chapter, we use the same dataset to examine whether experiences of relational devaluation lead to similar or different reactions among people with high and low trait self-esteem.

The dataset includes 29 relevant studies that contained either a group of people with premeasured low self-esteem, premeasured high self-esteem, or both groups of low and high self-esteem as well as an indicator of relational devaluation. Of these studies, seven included a direct measure of relational devaluation (e.g., participants were rejected from a group; participants were exposed to exclusion priming conditions) and 22 included an indirect measure of relational devaluation (e.g., participants were given information that their personality lacked socially desirable qualities). We expected that direct manipulations of relational devaluation would lead to stronger negative affective reactions than indirect manipulations, but that both might be useful for understanding how trait self-esteem moderates reactions to social exclusion.

Effect sizes were calculated using Cohen's d to represent the difference between participants who were relationally devalued and participants who were not relationally devalued. Each study produced at least two independent effect sizes: one for participants with relatively high self-esteem and one for people with relatively low self-esteem. Positive effect sizes represent movement towards immediately restoring self-esteem (e.g., aggression, shifting attention to other positive self-thoughts, attributing the failure to an external source) and negative effect sizes represent movement toward self-change (e.g., increased negative affect, decreased state self-esteem, attributing the failure to an internal source). Effect sizes that do not differ significantly from zero are assumed to represent resistance that may be either passive (e.g., the participants did not notice the threat or did not notice it was self-relevant) or active (e.g., the participants engaged in behaviors that restored their self-esteem to its original level but did not overcorrect for the threat).

Overall, relational devaluation led to reactions consistent with the immediate restoration of self-esteem, d (k = 29) = 0.19, $p < .0001$. Significant heterogeneity of effect sizes existed within the sample, Q (28) = 184.05, $p < .0001$, and so we examined whether any potential moderators might explain this variability. First, we found that trait self-esteem moderated the relationship between relational devaluation and immediate restoration of self-esteem, Q (1) = 19.50, $p < .0001$. The mean effect size for participants with high self-esteem was d (k = 29) = 0.31, $p < .0001$, whereas the mean effect size for participants with low self-esteem was d (k = 27) = 0.07, $p > .05$. In our dataset, participants with high self-esteem were more likely to engage in efforts to immediately restore self-esteem after relational devaluation than were participants with low self-esteem.

The studies that we included in the analysis varied in how directly they socially excluded participants. Some studies directly excluded people (e.g., participants were told that other participants did not choose to work with them on a task), whereas others indirectly excluded participants (e.g., they received feedback that they may have an unpleasant personality or poor social skills). We compared these types of exclusion manipulations and found that the average effect sizes they produced differed, Q (1) = 43.52, $p < .0001$. People responded to indirect devaluation with attempts to restore self-esteem, d (k = 22) = 0.26, $p < .0001$, but they responded to direct devaluation with breaking responses, d (k = 7) = −0.28, $p < .0001$. Furthermore, the directness of the devaluation influenced both participants with high self-esteem, Q (1) = 12.38, $p < .0001$, and participants with low self-esteem, Q (1) = 35.33, $p < .0001$. As Table 20.1 shows, direct and indirect devaluations affected people with low and high self-esteem somewhat differently. Direct devaluations led to negative responses to the situation, although this effect was only significant for people with low self-esteem. Indirect devaluations, however, led to esteem-restorative responses by both people with low and high self-esteem.

These results suggest that trait self-esteem significantly affects responses to social exclusion. We find that people with high trait self-esteem are better equipped to restore self-esteem immediately after experiencing devaluation than people with low self-esteem. This is consistent with a view of self-esteem as a cognitive resource, one that may provide people with a reminder that their positive self-feelings may still be valid despite situational evidence that others might not value them (Campbell & Lavallee, 1993; Spencer, Josephs, & Steele, 1993; vanDellen et al., 2011).

Narcissism and Self-Compassion

The results of the meta-analysis suggest that trait self-esteem might be a good thing for coping with

Table 20.1 Cohen's d across Level of Self-Esteem and Type of Devaluation

Level of Self-Esteem	Direct Devaluation	Indirect Devaluation
Low	−0.54*	0.16*
High	−0.04	0.36*

*$p < .0001$.

social exclusion. People with high self-esteem seem more prepared and better able to respond to social exclusion. However, high self-esteem is not always a good thing. In fact, increased self-esteem is associated with higher self-serving biases (Campbell & Sedikides, 1999; Fein & Spencer, 1997) and increased aggression, particularly after provocation (Baumeister, Smart, & Boden, 1996; Bushman & Baumeister, 2002). The remainder of this chapter focuses attention on two variables—narcissism and self-compassion—that are both correlated with self-esteem and provide interesting directions for future research on the role of individual differences in reacting to social exclusion.

Although both narcissism and self-compassion are positively correlated with self-esteem, when the effect of trait self-esteem is controlled, they are not correlated with each other (Leary, Tate, Adams, Allen, & Hancock, 2007; Neff, 2003a; Neff &Vonk, 2009). Consequently, we expect that they relate to different patterns of responses in reaction to social exclusion. Narcissism is often linked with preferences toward dominance and entitlement (e.g., Campbell, Bonacci, Shelton, Exline, & Bushman, 2004), whereas self-compassion, a relatively new individual difference variable, is associated with stability of responses, even when situations are threatening to the self (Neff & Vonk, 2009). Although research clearly links these individual differences with responding to self-threats, the reasons for these patterns are unclear. Next is discussed what is known about narcissism, self-compassion, and social exclusion. We highlight what potential mechanisms may be explaining their associations with responding to social exclusion and suggest important areas for future research.

NARCISSISM

There is a clear relationship between narcissism and responding to self-threats. Narcissism increases defensive reactions to threat. These defensive reactions tend to be aggressive. For instance, when responding to threats about competence, narcissists are more likely to deliver unpleasantly loud and long-lasting noise blasts to those who have negatively evaluated them (Bushman & Baumeister, 1998). Our own work has confirmed that narcissists similarly respond to experiences of social exclusion with aggression (Twenge & Campbell, 2003). In a series of studies, narcissists were more likely than non-narcissists to experience anger after rejection and deliver higher-intensity noise blasts to people who had not previously rejected them.

Social rejection, especially for narcissists, is a complicated phenomenon that involves thwarting both dominance (e.g., social control) and belongingness motivations. To date, it is unclear whether it is dominance or belonging motivation (or both) that leads to these aggressive responses. Several studies on the mitigation of aggression after threats suggest that both motivations may be involved. For instance, providing a self-esteem boost mitigated the aggressive responses of narcissists in response to ego-threats (Thomaes, Bushman, Orobio de Casto, Cohen, & Denissen, 2009). This self-esteem boost plausibly could have restored feelings of dominance, suggesting that when the dominance motivation is not threatened, narcissists do not engage in aggression. However, similar research has also shown that manipulating perceived closeness and communal goals increases commitment in relationships and, more importantly, decreases aggressive responses after threats (Finkel, Campbell, Buffardi, Kumashiro, & Rusbult, 2009; Konrath, Bushman, & Campbell, 2006). Future research is needed to understand the complex motivational threats that narcissists receive when they experience social exclusion.

The fact that social exclusion triggers aggression in narcissists is somewhat surprising given their low level of commitment to their social and romantic relationships (Campbell & Foster, 2002). Narcissists tend to engage in game playing, evidence higher levels of infidelity, and otherwise appear to be minimally invested in their relationships (e.g., Campbell, Foster, & Finkel, 2002). When these relationships end or encounter problems, we would expect narcissists not to be affected by exclusion. This is clearly not the pattern of responses we see among narcissistic reactions to exclusion. Rather, narcissists tend to become increasingly hostile—both in their affect and their behavior—after being rejected. Two possibilities for this pattern of responses exist. One possibility is that narcissists may be complacent about relationships up to a point, but when a certain threshold of perceived importance is surpassed, the loss of that relationship is viewed as a large threat. Possibly this threshold represents the integration of the partner into the self. When this threshold is met, it is possible that negative experiences in that relationship lead to aggression. Daily diary studies reveal that narcissists tend to be hypersensitive to the behaviors of others, perceiving more often that other people have wronged them in some way (McCullough, Emmons, Kilpatrick, & Mooney, 2003). Concerning this vulnerability hypothesis, one possibility is that this reactive interpersonal behavior is itself moderated by the form or type of narcissism (Zeigler-Hill, Clark, & Pickard, 2008). Specifically, more vulnerable forms of narcissism might be related to more reaction to social exclusion. Vulnerable narcissism is characterized by a cold or disagreeable interpersonal style but also higher levels on neuroticism and insecure attachment (Miller, Dir, Gentile, Wilson, Pryor, & Campbell, 2010). A second possibility is that narcissists perceive social exclusion as a threat to their competence or achievement. New diary evidence, for example, shows that direct dominance and achievement threats are linked with more extreme reactions from narcissists than social rejection threats (Zeigler-Hill, Myers, & Clark, 2010). Possibly, this increased importance placed on dominance and achievement threats leads ambiguous threats (e.g., social exclusion) to be perceived as threats to competence or dominance.

In sum, narcissism predicts externalizing reactions to social exclusion. What is less clear is the mechanism underlying these externalizing reactions. We speculate that (1) narcissism could predict reactivity to social exclusion when a certain threshold of attachment or connection is met, (2) narcissism with more vulnerable components could result in stronger reactions to social threats, or (3) narcissists overinterpret social exclusion as a dominance or achievement threat.

SELF-COMPASSION

Although self-compassion is a central component of eastern philosophy, it has only recently gained attention as a psychological construct. As defined by Neff (2003a), self-compassion involves, "being open to and moved by one's own suffering, experiencing feelings of caring and kindness toward oneself, taking an understanding, nonjudgmental attitude toward one's inadequacies and failures, and recognizing that one's experience is part of the common human experience" (p. 224). Studies of young adults show that self-compassion correlates highly with indicators of mental health and adjustment, including lower anxiety, lower depression, and higher life satisfaction (Neff, 2003b). Additionally, self-compassion is positively associated with other indicators of well-being, including happiness, optimism, and positive affect (Neff, Kirkpatrick, & Rude, 2007). Recent work with older adults also shows that self-compassion moderates the relationship between physical health and well-being, such that older adults who are suffering physically are more likely to maintain higher well-being if they

are highly self-compassionate (Allen, Goldwasser, & Leary, in press).

Unlike self-esteem, self-compassion is not a result of self-evaluation. Although self-esteem and self-compassion are highly correlated, a person could have low self-esteem and high self-compassion (or vice versa). In many respects, self-compassion is most valuable when one's self-esteem has been threatened or damaged. Whereas self-esteem is contingent upon the successful attainment of one's goals, self-compassion comes into play when those goals have been thwarted. Neff and Vonk (2009) collected data on 2,187 participants at 12 different time points across a period of 8 months. The primary goal of the study was to identify the ways in which self-esteem and self-compassion differentially related to ego-focused reactivity over time. Self-compassion negatively predicted self-worth instability, self-worth contingency, social comparison, public self-consciousness, self-rumination, and need for cognitive closure over and above self-esteem. Furthermore, when compared directly, self-compassion was a stronger negative predictor of these constructs than trait self-esteem. In terms of stability, self-compassion predicted more stability in state feelings of self-worth across the 8-month period than trait self-esteem. Thus, self-compassion is equally as beneficial (if not more so) as trait self-esteem without many of the downsides.

For example, unlike self-esteem, self-compassion does not lead one to think more highly of themselves than they ought to. In fact, self-compassion is associated with taking more responsibility for negative events; however, this admittance of responsibility is not accompanied by negative self-thoughts or excessive overreactions. Because self-compassionate people are forgiving of their faults and inadequacies, self-compassion is not associated with narcissism. Narcissism involves a process of self-evaluation that does not characterize self-compassion, and their positive correlation is the result of their mutual relationship with self-esteem (Neff, 2003a; Neff & Vonk, 2009). Whereas narcissism is associated with increasingly extreme emotional and self-serving reactions to devaluation, self-compassion protects people from experiencing intense negative emotions and negative self-feelings when experiencing a negative social event such as exclusion.

Although research on self-compassion is still in its beginning stages, some studies have addressed the relationship between self-compassion and signs of social exclusion. Specifically, Leary et al. (2007) conducted a series of studies assessing self-compassion and reactions to unpleasant events. They found that self-compassion, self-esteem, and narcissism differentially predicted emotional reactions after imagining embarrassing social events and that self-compassion accounted for the most unique variance in predictions of emotion. Self-compassion also predicted less catastrophizing, less personalizing, and more equanimity in factor analyzed thought patterns. Self-esteem did not predict any of the thought patterns and narcissism had a positive relationship with a humorous thought pattern. Leary et al. (2007) also examined the relationship between self-compassion and social exclusion by assessing reactions to neutral (often taken as negative) feedback. Self-compassion buffered low self-esteem participants from experiencing a sharp increase in negative affect following the neutral feedback. Additionally, participants who were higher in self-compassion were less likely to attribute the neutral feedback to being a reflection of their personality and they reported liking the other participant more than low self-compassion participants.

These studies show that self-compassion can buffer people against the negative emotional and cognitive effects of embarrassment and rejection. We suspect that these effects are driven by the recognition that social exclusion is part of the common human experience as well as the mindful awareness of one's emotional reactions inherent in self-compassion. Although little is known about the processes underlying the self-compassionate mindset, a recent review of self-compassion and coping showed that self-compassion is most closely related to positive cognitive restructuring (Allen & Leary, 2010). As a means of coping with a negative event such as being socially excluded, the self-compassionate individual is more likely to respond by evaluating the situation honestly with an effort toward focusing on the positive aspects so as to learn from the situation.

Conclusions

Not all people react to social exclusion in the same way. Here, we have summarized research about the influence of trait self-esteem, narcissism, and self-compassion on reactions to social exclusion. We reported findings from a meta-analysis on trait self-esteem and reactions to social exclusion. In this analysis, we found that people high in trait self-esteem tend to engage in activities that are aimed at immediately restoring positive self-feelings. People high in narcissism likewise tend to engage in esteem-restoring activities, particularly when these activities involve externalizing. We discussed the need for future research to identify the extent to which these reactions are owing to the fact that social exclusion thwarts a social motivation or a dominance/achievement motivation.

Finally, the chapter discussed new research on the trait of self-compassion. Unlike people who are high in self-esteem and narcissism, people high in self-compassion tend to be stable in response to threat. Because self-compassion promotes a calm, understanding, and objective reaction to negative life events, self-compassionate people are less likely to respond with aggression following social exclusion and other negative self-relevant experiences. A great deal of attention has been focused on building self-esteem so as to increase life satisfaction and well-being. However, current research suggests that self-compassion may have the benefits of self-esteem without many of the costs, and focusing on self-compassion interventions could be worthwhile. Two experimental laboratory investigations with college students have shown that increasing self-compassion temporarily results in changes in participants' emotional reactions. Leary et al. (2007) showed that asking participants to think about a negative event and then respond in a self-compassionate way, led participants to take greater responsibility for the negative event, experience less negative affect, and report more similarity with other people who experienced similar things. Adams and Leary (2007) induced self-compassion in a group of highly restrictive eaters who had just engaged in an unhealthy eating behavior. Consequently, highly restrictive eaters who received the self-compassion induction ate less in subsequent tasks than those who had not received the self-compassion induction.

Two longer self-compassion interventions have also shown positive results. Neff, Kirkpatrick, and Rude (2007) used a Gestalt two-chair technique that lowers feelings of self-criticism and helps people show themselves more compassion (Greenberg, 1983; Safran, 1998). Results from this study showed that levels of self-compassion increased over a 1-month period as participants experienced less anxiety, depression, rumination, and thought suppression. The most long-lasting effects of teaching people to be more self-compassionate come from a group-based therapy intervention developed by Gilbert and Procter (2006) called compassionate mind training. This therapy involves cognitive restructuring so as to teach self-critical individuals how to be more self-compassionate and has resulted in a significant decrease in depression, feelings of inferiority, submissive behavior, shame, and self-attacking tendencies. Future research is needed to investigate how self-compassion may be used in interventions for those who are victimized by peers or who are victims of other forms of chronic rejection.

Together, these findings point to the notion that self-compassion is a viable construct for use in interventions. Furthermore, the effect of even simple or short-term inductions of self-compassion may be long-lasting. We suggest that future research aimed at decreasing the negative responses to social exclusion focus on self-compassion as a mechanism for reducing externalizing behaviors such as aggression. One method of decreasing the negative effects, particularly the aggressive/antisocial effects, of social exclusion may be to focus our time and energy in developing more large scale self-compassion interventions with an effort toward engaging populations who are most vulnerable to social exclusion first.

References

Adams, C. E., & Leary, M. R. (2007). Promoting self-compassionate attitudes toward eating among restrictive and guilty eaters. *Journal of Social and Clinical Psychology*, *26*, 1120–1144.

Allen, A. B., Goldwasser, E. R., & Leary, M. R. (in press). Self-compassion an well-being among older adults. *Self & Identity*.

Allen, A. B., & Leary, M. R. (2010). Self-compassion, stress, and coping. *Social and Personality Psychology Compass*, *4*, 107–118.

Baumeister, R. F., Campbell, J. D., Krueger, J. I., & Vohs, K. D. (2003). Does high self-esteem cause better performance, interpersonal success, happiness, or healthier lifestyles? *Psychological Science in the Public Interest*, *1*, 1–44.

Baumeister, R. F., & Leary, M. R. (1995). The need to belong: Desire for interpersonal attachments as a fundamental human motivation. *Psychological Bulletin*, *117*, 497–529.

Baumeister, R. F., Smart, L., & Boden, J. M. (1996). Relation of threatened egotism to violence and aggression: The dark side of high self-esteem. *Psychological Review*, *103*, 5–33.

Blackhart, G. C., Nelson, B. C., Knowles, M. L., & Baumeister, R. F. (2009). Rejection elicits emotional reactions about neither causes immediate distress nor lowers self-esteem: A meta-analytic review of 192 studies on social exclusion. *Personality and Social Psychology Review*, *13*, 269–309.

Bushman, B. J., & Baumeister, R. F. (1998). Threatened egotism, narcissism, self-esteem, and direct and displaced aggression: Does self-love or self-hate lead to violence? *Journal of Personality and Social Psychology*, *75*, 219–229.

Bushman, B. J., & Baumeister, R. F. (2002). Does self-love or self-hate lead to violence? *Journal of Research in Personality*, *36*, 543–545.

Campbell, J. D., & Lavallee, L. F. (1993). Who am I? The role of self-concept confusion in understanding the behavior of people with low self-esteem. In R. F. Baumeister (Ed.), *Self-Esteem: The Puzzle of Low Self-Regard* (pp. 3–20). New York: Plenum.

Campbell, W. K., Bonacci, A. M., Shelton, J., Exline, J. J., & Bushman, B. J. (2004). Psychological entitlement: Interpersonal consequences and validation of a new self-report measure. *Journal of Personality Assessment*, *83*, 29–45.

Campbell, W. K., & Foster, C. A. (2002). Narcissism and commitment in romantic relationships: An Investment Model analysis. *Personality and Social Psychology Bulletin*, *28*, 484–495.

Campbell, W. K., Foster, C. A., & Finkel, E. J. (2002). Does self-love lead to love for others? A story of narcissistic game playing. *Journal of Personality and Social Psychology*, *83*, 340–354.

Campbell, W. K., & Foster, J. D. (2006). Self-esteem: Evolutionary roots and historical cultivation. In M. Kernis (Ed). *Self-Esteem: Issues and Answers* (pp. 340–346). New York: Psychology Press.

Campbell, W. K., & Sedikides, C. (1999). Self-threat magnifies the self-serving bias: A meta-analytic integration. *Review of General Psychology*, *3*, 23–43.

Carver, C. S., & Scheier, M. F. (1981). *Attention and Self-Regulation: A Control-Theory Approach to Human Behavior*. New York: Springer-Verlag.

Carver, C. S., & Scheier, M. F. (1990). Origins and functions of positive and negative affect: A control-process view. *Psychological Review*, *97*, 19–35.

DeWall, C. N., & Baumeister, R. F. (2006). Alone but feeling no pain: Effects of social exclusion on physical pain tolerance and pain threshold, affective forecasting, and interpersonal empathy. *Journal of Personality and Social Psychology*, *91*, 1–15.

DeWall, C.N., MacDonald, G., Webster, G. D., Masten, C., Baumesiter, R. F., Powell, C., Combs, D., Schurtz, D. R., Stillman, T. F., Tice, D. M., & Eisenberger, N. I. (in press). Tylenol reduces social pain: Behavioral and neural evidence. *Psychological Science*.

DeWall, C. N., Maner, J. K., & Rouby, D. A. (2009). Social exclusion and early-stage interpersonal perception: Selective attention to signs of acceptance. *Journal of Personality and Social Psychology*, *96*, 45–59.

Eisenberger, N. I., Lieberman, M. D., & Williams, K. D. (2003). Does rejection hurt? An fMRI study of social exclusion. *Science*, *302*, 290–292.

Fein, S., & Spencer, S. J. (1997). Prejudice as self-image maintenance: affirming the self through derogating others. *Journal of Personality and Social Psychology*, *73*, 31–44.

Finkel, E. J., Campbell, W. K., Buffardi, L. E., Kumashiro, M., & Rusbult, C. E. (2009). The metamorphosis of Narcissus: Communal activation promotes relationship commitment among narcissists. *Personality and Social Psychology Bulletin*, *35*, 1271–1284.

Gardner, W. L., Pickett, C. L., & Brewer, M. B. (2000). Social exclusion and selective memory: How the need to belong influences memory for social events. *Personality and Social Psychology Bulletin*, *26*, 486–496.

Gibbons, F. X., & McCoy, S. B. (1991). Self-esteem, similarity, and reactions to active versus passive downward comparisons. *Journal of Personality and Social Psychology*, *60*, 414–424.

Gilbert, P., & Procter, S. (2006). Compassionate mind training for people with high shame and self-criticism: Overview and pilot study of a group therapy approach. *Clinical Psychology & Psychotherapy*, *13*, 353–379.

Greenberg, L. S. (1983). Toward a task analysis of conflict resolution in Gestalt therapy. *Psychotherapy: Theory, Research, and Practice*, *20*, 190–201.

Higgins, E. T. (1987). Self-discrepancy: A theory relating self and affect. *Psychological Review, 94*, 319–340.

Leary, M. R., Haupt, A. L., Strausser, K. S., & Chokel, J. T. (1998). Calibrating the sociometer: The relationship between interpersonal appraisals and state self-esteem. *Journal of Personality and Social Psychology, 74*, 1290–1299.

Leary, M. R., Tate, E. B., Adams, C. E., Allen, A. B., & Hancock, J. (2007). Self-compassion and reactions to unpleasant self-relevant events: The implications of treating oneself kindly. *Journal of Personality and Social Psychology, 92*, 887–904.

Leary, M. R., Terdal, S. K., Tambor, E. S., & Downs, D. L. (1995). Self-esteem as an interpersonal monitor: The sociometer hypothesis. *Journal of Personality and Social Psychology, 68*, 518–530.

Leary, M. R., Twenge, J. M., & Quinlivan, E. (2006). Interpersonal rejection as a determinant of anger and aggression. *Personality and Social Psychology Review, 10*, 111–132.

Konrath, S., Bushman, B. J., & Campbell, W. K. (2006). Attenuating the link between threatened egotism and aggression. *Psychological Science, 17*, 995–1001.

MacDonald, G., & Leary, M. R. (2005). Why does social exclusion hurt? The relationship between social and physical pain. *Psychological Bulletin, 131*, 202–223.

McCullough, M. E., Emmons, R. A., Kilpatrick, S. D., & Mooney, C. N. (2003). Narcissists as "victims": The role of narcissism in the perception of transgressions. *Personality and Social Psychology Bulletin, 29*, 885–893.

Miller, J. D., Dir, A., Gentile, B., Wilson, L., Pryor, L. R., & Campbell, W. K. (2010). Searching for a vulnerable dark triad: Comparing factor 2 psychopathy, vulnerable narcissism, and borderline personality disorder. *Journal of Personality. Journal of Personality, 78*, 1529–1564.

Neff, K. D. (2003a). The development and validation of a scale to measure self-compassion. *Self and Identity, 2*, 223–250.

Neff, K. D. (2003b). Self-compassion: An alternative conceptualization of a healthy attitude toward oneself. *Self and Identity, 2*, 85–101.

Neff, K. D., Kirkpatrick, K. L., & Rude, S. S. (2007). Self-compassion and adaptive psychological functioning. *Journal of Research in Personality, 41*, 139–154.

Neff, K. D., & Vonk, R. (2009). Self-compassion versus global self-esteem: Two different ways of relating to oneself. *Journal of Personality, 77*, 23–50.

Pickett, C. L., Gardner, W. L., & Knowles, M. (2004). Getting a cue: The need to belong and enhanced sensitivity to social cues. *Personality and Social Psychology Bulletin, 30*, 1095–1107.

Pyszczynski, T., Greenberg, J., Arndt, J., & Schimel, J. (2004). Why do people need self-esteem: A theoretical and empirical review. *Psychological Bulletin, 130*, 435–446.

Rosenberg, M. (1965). *Society and the Adolescent Self-Image.* Princeton, NJ: Princeton University Press.

Rothbaum, F., Weisz, J. R., & Snyder, S. S. (1982). Changing the world and changing the self: A two-process model of perceived control. *Journal of Personality and Social Psychology, 42*, 5–37.

Safran, J. D. (1998). *Widening the Scope of Cognitive Therapy: The Therapeutic Relationship, Emotion, and the Process of Change.* Northvale, NJ: Jason Aronson.

Sedikides, C., & Strube, M. J. (1997). Self-evaluation: To thine own self be good, to thine own self be sure, to thine own self be true, and to thine own self be better. In M. P. Zanna (Ed.), *Advances in Experimental Social Psychology* (Vol. 29, pp. 209–269). New York: Academic Press.

Spencer, S. J., Josephs, R. A., & Steele, C. M. (1993). Low self-esteem: The uphill struggle for self-integrity. In R. F. Baumeister (Ed.), *Self-Esteem: The Puzzle of Low Self-Regard* (pp. 21–36). New York: Plenum.

Steele, C. M., Spencer, S. J., & Lynch, M. (1993). Self-image resilience and dissonance: The role of affirmational resources. *Journal of Personality and Social Psychology, 64*, 885–896.

Thomaes, S., Bushman, B. J., Orobio de Casto, B., Cohen, G. L., & Denissen, J. J. A. (2009). Reducing narcissistic aggression by buttressing self-esteem: An experimental field study. *Psychological Science, 20*, 1536–1542.

Twenge, J. M., Baumeister, R. F., Tice, D. M., & Stucke, T. S. (2001). If you can't join them, beat them: Effects of social exclusion on aggressive behavior. *Journal of Personality and Social Psychology, 81*, 1058–1069.

Twenge, J. M., & Campbell, W. K. (2003). Isn't it fun to get the respect that we're going to deserve? Narcissism, social rejection, and aggression. *Personality and Social Psychology Bulletin, 29*, 261–272.

vanDellen, M. R., Bradfield, E. K., & Hoyle, R. H. (2010). Self-regulation of state self-esteem following threat: Moderation by trait self-esteem. In R. H. Hoyle (Ed.) *Handbook of Personality and Self-Regulation.* Malden, MA: Blackwell.

vanDellen, M. R., Campbell, W. K., Hoyle, R. H., & Bradfield, E. K. (2011). Compensating, resisting, and breaking: A meta-analytical investigation of reactions to threat. *Personality and Social Psychology Review, 15*, 51–74.

Zeigler-Hill, V., Clark, C. B., & Pickard, J. D. (2008). Narcissistic subtypes and contingent self-esteem: Do all narcissists base their self-esteem on the same domains? *Journal of Personality, 76*, 753–774.

Zeigler-Hill, V., Myers, E.M., & Clark, C.B. (2010). Narcissism and self-esteem reactivity: The role of negative achievement events. *Journal of Research in Personality, 44*, 285–292.

Attention-Deficit/Hyperactivity Disorder and the Challenges of Social Exclusion

Amori Yee Mikami

Abstract

Attention-Deficit/Hyperactivity Disorder (ADHD) is a prevalent diagnosis among school-age children and symptoms frequently persist into adolescence and adulthood. This chapter describes the high levels of social exclusion faced by individuals with ADHD. Distinctions are made between children and adults with this disorder, as well as between males and females, when possible. In addition, ways in which ADHD subtype and comorbidity impact social relationships are also considered. Reasons why individuals with ADHD tend to be excluded by their peers, and the effectiveness of existing interventions for social problems in ADHD, are next summarized. The chapter concludes with suggestions for future research directions, including speculation regarding ways to improve the treatment of social exclusion.

Key Words: ADHD, behavior problems, disorders, intervention, psychopathology, treatment

Introduction

Attention-Deficit/Hyperactivity Disorder (ADHD) is one of the most prevalent disorders, beginning in childhood but often continuing to impair functioning across the life span. It has been well-established that youth with ADHD are at high risk for maladjustment in multiple areas including delinquency and conduct problems; school failure; substance abuse; depression and anxiety; and poor interpersonal relationships with family, teachers, and peers (Barkley, 2002; Mannuzza & Klein, 2000). Although each domain of impairment merits attention, this chapter focuses primarily on the social exclusion from peers faced by individuals with ADHD.

It is estimated that ADHD affects 3% to 7% of elementary school-aged children in the United States (American Psychiatric Association, 2000; Jensen et al., 1995). To receive a diagnosis of ADHD, individuals must display developmentally inappropriate, clinically significant symptoms of (a) inattention, and/or (b) hyperactivity/impulsivity.

Symptoms must have been present prior to age 7 and are required to cause impairment. Furthermore, symptoms must show themselves in more than one setting (e.g., both home and school).

The current chapter begins by summarizing the magnitude of social exclusion that individuals with ADHD experience, with consideration of individuals' age, gender, and ADHD subtype. Next, reasons for this social exclusion are discussed. Third, interventions for individuals with ADHD that target social exclusion from peers are reviewed. The chapter concludes with recommendations for future research and suggestions for improving the effectiveness of interventions for social exclusion in ADHD.

Magnitude of Social Exclusion in ADHD

It is difficult to overstate the level of social exclusion from peers that individuals with ADHD typically face. In fact, social exclusion is so extreme in magnitude that, although interpersonal difficulties are not currently part of the diagnostic criteria for

ADHD, some have argued that they should be included (Greene, Biederman, Faraone, Sienna, & Garcia-Jetton, 1997; Whalen & Henker, 1985; Wheeler & Carlson, 1994).

Among elementary school-aged children, the age group in which ADHD is typically diagnosed and most commonly studied, it is estimated that over 50% of children with ADHD are peer-rejected, relative to peer rejection base rates of 10% to 15% in typical classrooms (Hoza, Mrug et al., 2005). The definition of being peer- rejected is that the majority of peers name this child, during confidential sociometric interviews, as being someone whom they dislike, whereas few peers name the child as being someone whom they like (Coie, Dodge, & Coppotelli, 1982). Although children with ADHD are also rated by parents and teachers as being peer-rejected (Solanto, Pope-Boyd, Tyron, & Stepak, 2009), having peers directly report on their liking and disliking preferences to assess rejection is considered the gold standard in defining peer rejection.

Another study using peer sociometric measures found that 82% of a sample of 49 children with ADHD scored one standard deviation above their classroom average of being disliked by peers (Pelham & Bender, 1982). Fully 60% of children with ADHD scored two standard deviations above the average of being disliked, that is, in the top 2.5% of their class (Pelham & Bender, 1982). Some research suggests that children with ADHD are more actively disliked (e.g., nominated by peers as someone they do not want to be around) than are children with Conduct Disorder or depressive disorders, but not ADHD (Asarnow, 1988).

Social rejection of children with ADHD happens extremely quickly—occurring within less than one day (Erhardt & Hinshaw, 1994) or even within one hour of meeting unfamiliar peers (Hodgens, Cole, & Boldizar, 2000; Mikami, Jack, Emeh, & Stephens, 2010). Further, once established, the rejection of children with ADHD tends to be highly stable. Correlations between nominations of being disliked by peers are as high as $r = .7–.8$ over six weeks among an ADHD sample (Blachman & Hinshaw, 2002).

Yet, it is relatively unknown the extent to which peers' affective disliking of children with ADHD manifests itself in behavioral forms of social exclusion, such as observable ostracism or victimization. Although it has been established that peer rejection typically increases the likelihood of subsequent victimization more than vice versa (Schwartz, McFayden-Ketchum, Dodge, Pettit, & Bates, 1999), these studies have not been specific to ADHD populations. Despite the peer rejection of children with ADHD being well documented, the literature on behavioral ostracism or victimization among ADHD youth is not as advanced, particularly when multimeasure assessment procedures are involved. Nonetheless, there are suggestions that children with ADHD are more likely to be victimized, based on self-report, teacher report, and parent report, relative to comparison youth (Shea & Wiener, 2003; Wiener & Mak, 2009). However, children with ADHD may also have elevated rates of being bullies and bully-victims, as well as victims (Wiener & Mak, 2009). It is unknown whether the predictors of victimization are similar for children with ADHD relative to comparison children. To summarize, the rejection of children with ADHD has been extremely well established, but an area for future research is the ways in which this affective dislike may be behaviorally displayed in bullying and ostracism.

ADHD Subtype and Comorbidity

Children with ADHD are not a homogenous group, and their social behaviors and type of social exclusion faced may differ depending on ADHD subtype and patterns of comorbidity with other disorders. The DSM-IV-TR criteria specify that individuals with ADHD can be classified into three subtypes (American Psychiatric Association, 2000). The Combined Type (ADHD-C) is designated for individuals with both inattention and also hyperactivity/impulsivity. The Predominantly Inattentive Type (ADHD-I) is appropriate for the presence of inattention without hyperactivity/impulsivity, and the Predominantly Hyperactive/Impulsive Type (ADHD-HI) for hyperactivity/impulsivity without inattention. The majority of the research to date has involved participants with ADHD-C. The most common subtype in epidemiological studies is ADHD-I, but children with this subtype are underdiagnosed and underreferred for treatment (Robison, Sclar, Skaer, & Galin, 2004), and ADHD-HI is most salient for children younger than school-age (Lahey et al., 1998).

Evidence suggests that elementary school-age children with ADHD-C tend to have an intrusive, aggressive interpersonal style that may lead to them being rejected by peers, that is, actively disliked. By contrast, children with ADHD-I may behave passively or seem apathetic during peer interactions, which contributes to them being more neglected and ignored by their peers as opposed to actively rejected (Hodgens et al., 2000; Mikami, Huang-Pollock, Pfiffner, McBurnett, & Hangai, 2007; Milich, Balentine, & Lynam, 2001). This suggests that the nature of social exclusion may be different for the two subtypes; it may be purposeful for youth with ADHD-C but accidental for youth with ADHD-I.

To date, the different types of social exclusion experienced by youth with ADHD-C versus ADHD-I have been conceptualized to *result* from pre-existing differences in interpersonal behaviors between the two subtypes. Unstudied is whether the impact of active exclusion (rejection) versus passive exclusion (neglect) may also *contribute* to subsequent differential functioning among youth with ADHD-C versus ADHD-I. Recent work, using a college undergraduate sample, suggests that active exclusion experiences lead to participants reporting increased agitation, thoughts about actions one should not have taken, and withdrawal from contact; by contrast, passive exclusion experiences may evoke dejection, thoughts about actions one should have taken, and increased engagement in social contact (Molden, Lucas, Gardner, Dean, & Knowles, 2009). Whether these processes would apply to children with ADHD and their naturalistic exclusion experiences, and potentially exacerbate behavioral differences between the two subtypes, remains unknown.

Confounded with subtype is comorbidity. Half of children with ADHD have comorbid disruptive behavior problems (e.g., Oppositional Defiant Disorder, Conduct Disorder), and about 25% to 33% are estimated to have comorbid internalizing disorders such as anxiety or depression (Jensen, Martin, & Cantwell, 1997). Children with ADHD-C are more likely to have comorbid disruptive behavior disorders than are children with ADHD-I, and the presence of comorbid aggression exacerbates peer rejection (Milich et al., 2001; Pfiffner, Calzada, & McBurnett, 2000). Less studied are internalizing comorbidities with ADHD, but these are suggested to be equal among ADHD subtypes (Power, Costigan, Eiraldi, & Leff, 2004), and to be associated with peer neglect (Karustis, Power, Rescorla, Eiraldi, & Gallagher, 2000). However, some children with ADHD have both disruptive and internalizing comorbidities (Jensen et al., 1997), and little is known about the compounding effect of both types of comorbidities on peer relationships.

To summarize, the social relationships of children with ADHD appear to differ based on subtype and comorbidity, suggesting the importance of considering these factors when depicting interpersonal functioning. Collectively, evidence suggests that children who have ADHD-C and disruptive comorbidities are most at risk for being actively rejected. By contrast, children who have ADHD-I and internalizing comorbidities may be more neglected by peers.

Adolescents and Young Adults

The current ADHD literature has an under-representation of participants past elementary school age. Nonetheless, all available evidence suggests that adolescents and adults with ADHD remain impaired socially with peers (Bagwell, Molina, Pelham, & Hoza, 2001) and in their romantic relationships (Canu & Carlson, 2003). Notably missing from this work, however, is research that links behavioral forms of exclusion with these relationship difficulties among adolescents and adults with ADHD. In adult peer groups, social exclusion may take more subtle forms (e.g., coworkers don't invite a colleague to lunch; college classmates are hesitant to work with the student) that are more difficult to measure. However, these forms of ostracism may be relevant for adults with ADHD. In conclusion, extremely little is known about how adults with ADHD may experience social exclusion. However, because work suggests continuing interpersonal impairment among adults with this disorder, the social exclusion of adults with ADHD may represent a valuable topic for future study.

Gender Differences

The existing ADHD literature also has an under-representation of girls with the disorder relative to boys. Males outnumber females 3:1 in community samples, and up to 9:1 in clinical samples (Lahey et al., 1994). However, the research that does exist suggests that girls with ADHD face at least the same level of social exclusion from peers as do boys, if not more (Blachman & Hinshaw, 2002; Gaub & Carlson, 1997). For instance, rates of peer rejection among girls with ADHD far exceed those found for girls without ADHD (Hoza, Mrug et al., 2005). Similar to boys who have this disorder, the rejection of girls with ADHD is established very quickly in previously unfamiliar groups of peers (Blachman & Hinshaw, 2002).

Interestingly, it is possible that girls with ADHD may have additional trouble socially, relative to their male counterparts, because ADHD symptoms and conduct problems commonly associated with ADHD are more norm violating among girls (Mikami & Lorenzi, 2011). Further, inattentive and hyperactive/impulsive behaviors may interfere with the greater verbal give-and-take that characterizes female peer groups (Keenan & Shaw, 1997). Thus, although little research has been conducted among girls with ADHD, social exclusion is likely quite salient for females with this disorder.

Reasons for Social Difficulties in ADHD
Deficits among Individuals with ADHD

To date, the vast majority of the research on reasons for social exclusion has focused on problem behaviors enacted by youth with ADHD that are off-putting to peers. One of the main findings is that the core symptoms of ADHD interfere with appropriate social behavior. Among children, inattention not only affects schoolwork, but it also may compromise ability to read social cues, to attend to the rules of a game, and to follow fast-paced conversations with peers. Hyperactivity and impulsivity may interfere with the ability to wait one's turn in line or in a game, to listen to peers' concerns patiently, and to be a good sport by restraining impulses to be upset when losing (Landau, Milich, & Diener, 1998).

In addition, children with ADHD have deficient social-cognitive skills, which may also contribute to their peer problems. During peer interactions, children with ADHD have social goals of "winning"; by contrast, comparison youth are more likely to have the goal of "having fun and making a new friend" (Melnick & Hinshaw, 1996). Children with ADHD may struggle with taking the perspective of a peer, as is reflected in their difficulty giving directions to a peer who is prevented from seeing the same information as the child with ADHD (Whalen & Henker, 1992; Whalen, Henker, Collins, McAuliffe, & Vaux, 1979). Finally, children with ADHD may be more likely than comparison youth to interpret ambiguous peer provocations as hostile in intent, and less likely to propose adaptive strategies to solve hypothetical social conflicts (Matthys, Cuperus, & van England, 1999; Mikami, Lee, Hinshaw, & Mullin, 2008). Collectively, these behaviors on the part of children with ADHD are thought to cause their social exclusion from peers. In fact, children with ADHD have been called "negative social catalysts" (Whalen & Henker, 1985, 1992), reflecting the perspective that they possess characteristics that they bring to every interpersonal situation, which cause their relationship problems.

Biases of the Peer Group

Although children with ADHD do have behavior problems that contribute to their ostracism by peers, peer rejection does not occur in a vacuum in which only the behaviors of the child with ADHD are important. Rather, social exclusion is a mutual, reciprocal process that also involves the behaviors and values of the larger peer group that excludes the child with ADHD (Mikami, Lerner, & Lun, 2010).

One factor that may influence peer relationships above and beyond deficits within the child with ADHD is the extent to which the peer group views a child with ADHD as deviant and not like themselves. Research in developmental and social psychology, not specific to ADHD, supports this hypothesis. Even after accounting for a rejected child's behaviors, the magnitude that a child is disliked increases if his/her behavior is more deviant from whatever the norm is in that particular peer group (Boivin, Dodge, & Coie, 1995; Stormshak et al., 1999; Wright, Giammarino, & Parad, 1986). Thus, aggressive children are more rejected in peer groups in which aggressive behavior is unusual than those in which others also behave aggressively; similarly, withdrawn children are more rejected in peer groups in which withdrawal is unusual than those in which withdrawal is common. As an example of the robustness of this relationship, in one study of 4,650 children, the peer group norm of aggression accounted for 19% of the between-group variation in the association between peer rejection and aggressive behavior (Chang, 2004). These findings demonstrate that there is no set path between any particular behavior and rejection, and that rejection depends on the interpretations and values of the larger peer group.

Children may also be marginalized by peers if they are atypical demographically, not just behaviorally, demonstrating the strength of children's tendencies to reject individuals who violate group norms in a variety of ways (including harmless ways). Children who are a racial minority in their classroom are more likely to be disliked than are children in the majority (Jackson, Barth, Powell, & Lochman, 2006). Specifically, African-American children are more peer-rejected in predominantly white relative to predominantly black classrooms, but white children are more likely to be rejected in predominantly black relative to predominately white classrooms (Kistner, Metzler, Gatlin, & Risi, 1993). In sum, a body of literature suggests that simply being *different* from the group norm may encourage rejection from that peer group.

The peer group may also have cognitive biases against disliked children that perpetuate these children's rejected status (Hymel, Wagner, & Butler, 1990). Peers interpret the ambiguous behaviors of children whom they dislike as hostile in intent while interpreting the ambiguous behaviors of children whom they like as benign (Peets, Hodges, Kikas, & Salmivalli, 2007; Peets, Hodges, & Salmivalli, 2008). Peers selectively remember disliked children's negative behavior while forgetting their positive behaviors (Flannagan & Bradley, 1999), and attribute the negative behavior of a disliked child to internal, stable traits, while attributing positive behavior to situational causes; these attributions are reversed to favor popular children (Guerin, 1999; Hymel, 1986). Even children as young as preschool to first grade have been found to possess these cognitive biases (Denham & Holt, 1993; Mrug & Hoza, 2007). Collectively these findings suggest that peers are disposed to give the benefit of the doubt to their friends, whereas the identical actions by a disliked child are interpreted in such a way as to maintain that child's negative reputation and peer-rejected status.

Although the aforementioned research has not specifically focused on youth with ADHD, there is reason to believe that factors in the peer group affect the social status of children with this disorder. Children with ADHD engage in behaviors that may tax the patience of even the most inclusive peer group. However, behavior change among youth with ADHD is a necessary but probably not sufficient condition for improvements in social exclusion to occur. There are two reasons for this. First, even if child-focused treatment succeeds in reducing the most noxious disruptive and aggressive behaviors common among children with ADHD, clinicians often comment that many treated children remain awkward, odd, prone to daydreaming, or persist in engaging in socially off-time behaviors (Landau et al., 1998). Peer groups that are tolerant of harmless, but still deviant, behaviors such as these may be more likely to accept a child with ADHD, or the magnitude of the social rejection faced by a child with ADHD may be less extreme among such peers than it would be in a less tolerant peer group. Recent work has suggested that the correlation between ADHD symptoms and sociometrically-assessed peer rejection varies across classrooms, and may be attenuated when teachers personally like children with ADHD (McAuliffe, Hubbard, & Romano, 2009; Mikami, Griggs, Reuland, & Gregory, 2012).

Second, the tenacity of the negative reputations of children with ADHD is also likely to be just as strong, if not stronger, than for typically developing children. Therefore, even when a child with ADHD displays more positive behaviors, the peer group may be resistant to altering their impressions about that child. This may occur because peers' awareness that a child has the disorder of ADHD evokes rejection in and of itself. Merely labeling a target as "ADHD" (even if s/he does not in fact have ADHD) has been shown to create a stereotype such that unfamiliar peers make negative judgments about the target that extend beyond the information provided (Whalen, Henker, Dotemoto, & Hinshaw, 1983), and report lowered desire to be friends with the target (Canu, Newman, Morrow, & Pope, 2008). In another study, peers were told that certain children with whom they were about to interact had ADHD. In reality, the label of ADHD was falsely applied to randomly selected children who were unaware that their peers had been given this information. During the interaction afterwards, peers were more likely to reject children whom they thought had ADHD, and children labeled as ADHD were judged by observers to have poorer social skills than were children not labeled as ADHD (Harris, Milich, Corbitt, Hoover, & Brady, 1992).

Interventions for Social Exclusion in ADHD

To date, existing interventions for peer problems largely attempt to remediate deficits within the child with ADHD, but they have made only circumscribed progress towards improving peer relationships (Landau et al., 1998; Mrug, Hoza, & Gerdes, 2001). The first-line treatments for ADHD, stimulant medication and behavior management, are well validated for ameliorating the core symptoms of the disorder (MTA Cooperative Group, 1999), yet their usefulness for peer problems is modest. These treatments do reduce children's intrusive and disruptive behaviors (Chronis, Jones, & Raggi, 2006; Hinshaw, Henker, Whalen, Erhardt, & Dunnington, 1989; Murphy, Pelham, & Lang, 1992), and may result in improved social skills as rated by adults (Klein & Abikoff, 1997). Unfortunately, a corresponding reduction in peer exclusion (as assessed on sociometric measures wherein peers name their liking, disliking and friendship preferences) often does not follow (Hoza, 2007; Hoza, Gerdes et al., 2005). Because peer reports have greater validity in predicting subsequent adjustment than do adult informant ratings of social skills (Parker & Asher, 1987) gains on peer-reported acceptance and friendship are the desirable standard.

Some exceptions exist whereby, in small samples, children receiving stimulant medication (Whalen et al., 1989) and behavioral management (Pelham & Bender, 1982) may improve in peer-reported acceptance after treatment. Nonetheless, in both these studies, peer relationships were far from normalized. These positive outcomes must also be considered in light of a larger collection of null effects on peer-reported measures (Hoza, Gerdes et al., 2005; Landau et al., 1998; Landau & Moore, 1991; Mrug et al., 2001). For example, in the Multimodal Treatment Study of Children with ADHD (MTA Cooperative Group, 1999), both intensive medication and behavioral management failed to increase peer reports of acceptance or friendship at the immediate conclusion of the 14-month active treatment period (though treatments produced gains in adult informant-reported social skills). Relative to a matched sample of comparison youth, children with ADHD remained profoundly socially impaired, no matter which treatment they had received (Hoza, Gerdes et al., 2005). As discussed by the authors, it is notable that even the state-of-the-art treatments, delivered under ideal circumstances, did not improve peer relationships significantly.

Although social skills training is a widely used treatment for children with ADHD (Mrug et al., 2001; Nixon, 2001; Stormont, 2001), its efficacy for improving peer-assessed acceptance has received inconsistent empirical support (Gresham, Cook, Crews, & Kern, 2004; Mikami & Pfiffner, 2006; Pfiffner et al., 2000). In a study of 103 children with ADHD, Abikoff et al. (2004) found no added benefit of receiving social skills training plus stimulant medication over medication alone on adult-informant ratings or observations of social skills, either at the end of a 1-year intensive treatment period or a 2-year follow-up wherein treatment was provided less frequently. Although this study lacks a comparison condition of unmedicated children, other investigations have compared short-term, less intensive social skills training to no treatment and failed to find improvement in peer relationships, particularly when peer reports of liking are used to assess effectiveness (Abikoff et al., 2004; Antshel & Remer, 2003; Kolko, Loar, & Sturnick, 1990). Although some social skills training programs appear promising, especially when parents are involved to encourage generalization (Frankel, Myatt, Cantwell, & Feinberg, 1997; Pfiffner & McBurnett, 1997; Pfiffner et al., 2007), multiple investigators have concluded that social skills training is not as useful for children with ADHD as originally hoped (Abikoff, 1985; Barkley, 2004; de Boo & Prins, 2007; Guevremont & Dumas, 1994; Mrug et al., 2001; Pelham, Wheeler, & Chronis, 1998).

One reason why medication, behavioral management, and social skills training interventions may have circumscribed effectiveness on peer relationships is because none of these interventions consider factors in the peer group that contribute to social status. To the extent that these treatments reduce disruptive behaviors among youth with ADHD (MTA Cooperative Group, 1999), this may explain findings that adult informants report improvements in children's social skills. However, improvements in sociometrically-assessed peer exclusion may not always follow from such interventions (Hoza, Gerdes et al., 2005; Mikami & Pfiffner, 2006) because these treatments do nothing to encourage the peer group to be more tolerant of a child with ADHD who remains socially awkward after treatment in harmless ways, to eliminate the stigma associated with this diagnosis, or to make the peer group notice positive behavior changes resulting from treatment that would alter their impressions. In support of this hypothesis, Mikami et al. (in press) found that children with ADHD who received an intervention that supplemented behavioral management with procedures to increase the inclusiveness of the peer group displayed better peer sociometric acceptance relative to those children who receive behavioral management alone.

In sum, more research is needed to improve the efficacy of interventions for social exclusion among ADHD populations. Including novel targets of intervention, such as addressing the biases among the peer group that rejects the child with ADHD, is a potentially worthwhile direction.

Conclusions

The social exclusion from peers that children with ADHD face is pronounced, and may persist into adolescence and adulthood. Peer rejection occurs for both boys and girls with ADHD, which may be exacerbated if other comorbid disorders are present. Research has traditionally focused on deficits within youth with ADHD that are off-putting to peers and contribute to their ostracism. However, factors in the peer group may also be relevant in determining the extent to which children with ADHD are socially excluded. Interventions most commonly attempt to remediate deficits within children with ADHD, but peer rejection is often resistant to treatment. It is possible that, in addition to focusing on behavior change in the child with ADHD, other interventions may be needed to encourage the peer group to be more inclusive and accepting.

Future Directions

Overall, the social exclusion of individuals with ADHD is profound and does not fully remediate in response to existing treatments. Future studies would benefit from incorporation of understudied populations, in particular, adolescents and adults with ADHD. All available evidence suggests that individuals this age with ADHD continue to struggle with social relationships, but the nature of social exclusion may change and be more difficult to measure in adulthood relative to in childhood. This may be because of the fact that adults' social networks are not confined to a single classroom. The field is in need of studies with sensitive, developmentally appropriate measures of social exclusion in ADHD populations past childhood. In addition, girls with ADHD, the Inattentive Type of ADHD, and youth with ADHD and internalizing comorbidities, are all understudied groups in the existing research. Incorporation of these populations would lead to a more complete understanding of how social exclusion operates for individuals with ADHD.

Because peer relationship problems may exacerbate maladjustment in ADHD populations (Mikami & Hinshaw, 2006), treatments for social exclusion have high public health significance. Yet the limited effectiveness of existing interventions suggests that the field is in need of alternative ways to facilitate peer relationships among youth with ADHD. Although speculative, interventions that also target the peer group to be more accepting of youth with ADHD, and to notice positive behavior changes among youth with ADHD, may be a promising direction.

References

Abikoff, H. B. (1985). Efficacy of cognitive training intervention with hyperactive children: A critical review. *Clinical Psychology Review, 5*, 479–512.

Abikoff, H. B., Hechtman, L., Klein, R. G., Gallagher, R., Fleiss, K., Etcovitch, J., et al. (2004). Social functioning in children with ADHD treated with long-term methylphenidate and multimodal psychosocial treatment. *Journal of the American Academy of Child and Adolescent Psychiatry, 43*, 820–829.

American Psychiatric Association. (2000). *Diagnostic and Statistical Manual of Mental Disorders* (4th ed., text revision). Washington, DC: Author.

Antshel, K. M., & Remer, R. (2003). Social skills training in children with Attention Deficit Hyperactivity Disorder: A randomized-controlled clinical trial. *Journal of Clinical Child and Adolescent Psychology, 32*, 153–165.

Asarnow, J. R. (1988). Peer status and social competence in child psychiatric inpatients: A comparison of children with depressive, externalizing, and concurrent depressive and externalizing disorders. *Journal of Abnormal Child Psychology, 16*, 151–162.

Bagwell, C., Molina, B. S. G., Pelham, W. E., & Hoza, B. (2001). Attention-deficit hyperactivity disorder and problems in peer relations: Predictions from childhood to adolescence. *Journal of the American Academy of Child and Adolescent Psychiatry, 40*, 1285–1292.

Barkley, R. A. (2002). ADHD: Long-term course, adult outcome, and comorbid disorders. In P. S. Jensen & J. R. Cooper (Eds.), *Attention-Deficit/Hyperactivity Disorder: State of the Science and Best Practices* (pp. 4-1–4-12). Kingston, NJ: Civic Research Institute.

Barkley, R. A. (2004). Adolescents with attention-deficit/hyperactivity disorder: An overview of empirically based treatments. *Journal of Psychiatric Practice, 10*, 39–56.

Blachman, D. R., & Hinshaw, S. P. (2002). Patterns of friendship among girls with and without attention-deficit/hyperactivity disorder. *Journal of Abnormal Child Psychology, 30*, 625–640.

Boivin, M., Dodge, K. A., & Coie, J. D. (1995). Individual-group behavioral similarity and peer similarity and peer status in experimental play groups of boys: The social misfit revisited. *Journal of Personality & Social Psychology, 69*, 269–279.

Canu, W. H., & Carlson, C. L. (2003). Differences in heterosocial behavior and outcomes of ADHD-symptomatic subtypes in a college sample. *Journal of Attention Disorders, 6*, 123–133.

Canu, W. H., Newman, M. L., Morrow, T. L., & Pope, D. L. W. (2008). Social appraisal of adult ADHD: Stigma and influences of the beholder's Big Five personality traits. *Journal of Attention Disorders, 11*, 700–710.

Chang, L. (2004). The role of classroom norms in contextualizing the relations of children's social behaviors to peer acceptance. *Developmental Psychology, 40*, 691–702.

Chronis, A. M., Jones, H. A., & Raggi, V. L. (2006). Evidence-based psychosocial treatments for children and adolescents with attention-deficit/hyperactivity disorder. *Clinical Psychology Review, 26*, 486–502.

Coie, J. D., Dodge, K. A., & Coppotelli, H. (1982). Dimensions and types of social status: A cross-age perspective. *Developmental Psychology, 18*, 557–570.

de Boo, G. M., & Prins, P. J. M. (2007). Social incompetence in children with ADHD: Possible moderators and mediators in social skills training. *Clinical Psychology Review, 27*, 78–97.

Denham, S., & Holt, R. W. (1993). Preschoolers' likeability as a cause or consequence of their social behavior. *Developmental Psychology, 29*, 271–275.

Erhardt, D., & Hinshaw, S. P. (1994). Initial sociometric impressions of attention-deficit hyperactivity disorder and comparison boys: Predictions from social behaviors and from nonbehavioral variables. *Journal of Consulting and Clinical Psychology, 62*, 833–842.

Flannagan, D., & Bradley, L. (1999). Judging the behaviors of friends and unfamiliar peers: Patterns associated with age and gender. *Journal of Early Adolescence, 19*, 389–404.

Frankel, F., Myatt, R., Cantwell, D. P., & Feinberg, D. (1997). Parent-assisted transfer of children's social skills training: Effects on children with and without attention-deficit hyperactivity disorder. *Journal of the American Academy of Child and Adolescent Psychiatry, 36*, 1056–1064.

Gaub, M., & Carlson, C. L. (1997). Gender differences in ADHD: A meta-analysis and critical review. *Journal of the American Academy of Child and Adolescent Psychiatry, 36*, 1036–1045.

Greene, R. W., Biederman, J., Faraone, S. V., Sienna, M., & Garcia-Jetton, J. (1997). Adolescent outcome of boys with attention-deficit/hyperactivity disorder and social disability: Results from a 4-year longitudinal follow-up study. *Journal of Consulting and Clinical Psychology, 65*, 758–767.

Gresham, F. M., Cook, C. R., Crews, S. D., & Kern, L. (2004). Social skills training for children and youth with emotional and behavioral disorders: Validity considerations and future directions. *Behavioral Disorders, 30*, 32–46.

Guerin, B. (1999). Children's intergroup attribution bias for liked and disliked peers. *Journal of Social Psychology, 139*, 583–589.

Guevremont, D. C., & Dumas, M. C. (1994). Peer relationship problems and disruptive behavior disorders. *Journal of Emotional and Behavioral Disorders, 2*, 164–172.

Harris, M. J., Milich, R., Corbitt, E. M., Hoover, D. W., & Brady, M. (1992). Self-fulfilling effects of stigmatizing information on children's social interactions. *Journal of Personality and Social Psychology, 63*, 41–50.

Hinshaw, S. P., Henker, B., Whalen, C. K., Erhardt, D., & Dunnington, R. E. (1989). Aggressive, prosocial, and nonsocial behavior in hyperactive boys: Dose effects of methylphenidate in naturalistic settings. *Journal of Consulting and Clinical Psychology, 57*, 636–643.

Hodgens, J. B., Cole, J., & Boldizar, J. (2000). Peer-based differences among boys with ADHD. *Journal of Child Clinical Psychology, 29*, 443–452.

Hoza, B. (2007). Peer functioning in children with ADHD. *Journal of Pediatric Psychology, 32*, 655–663.

Hoza, B., Gerdes, A. C., Mrug, S., Hinshaw, S. P., Bukowski, W. M., Gold, J. A., et al. (2005). Peer-assessed outcomes in the Multimodal Treatment Study of children with Attention Deficit Hyperactivity Disorder. *Journal of Clinical Child and Adolescent Psychology, 34*, 74–86.

Hoza, B., Mrug, S., Gerdes, A. C., Bukowski, W. M., Kraemer, H. C., Wigal, T., et al. (2005). What aspects of peer relationships are impaired in children with Attention-deficit/Hyperactivity Disorder? *Journal of Consulting and Clinical Psychology, 73*, 411–423.

Hymel, S. (1986). Interpretations of peer behavior: Affective bias in childhood and adolescence. *Child Development, 57*, 431–445.

Hymel, S., Wagner, E., & Butler, L. J. (1990). Reputational bias: View from the peer group. In S. R. Asher & J. D. Coie (Eds.), *Peer Rejection in Childhood* (pp. 156–186). New York: Cambridge University Press.

Jackson, M. F., Barth, J. M., Powell, N., & Lochman, J. E. (2006). Classroom contextual effects of race on children's peer nominations. *Child Development, 77*, 1325–1337.

Jensen, P. S., Martin, D., & Cantwell, D. P. (1997). Comorbidity in ADHD: Implications for research, practice, and DSM-V. *Journal of the American Academy of Child and Adolescent Psychiatry, 36*, 1065–1079.

Jensen, P. S., Watanabe, H. K., Richters, J. E., Cortes, R., Roper, M., & Liu, S. (1995). Prevalence of mental disorder in military children and adolescents: A two-stage community survey. *Journal of the American Academy of Child and Adolescent Psychiatry, 34*, 1514–1524.

Karustis, J. L., Power, T. J., Rescorla, L. A., Eiraldi, R. B., & Gallagher, P. R. (2000). Anxiety and depression in children with ADHD: Unique associations with academic and social functioning. *Journal of Attention Disorders, 4*, 133–149.

Keenan, K., & Shaw, D. S. (1997). Developmental and social influences on young girls' early problem behavior. *Psychological Bulletin, 121*, 95–113.

Kistner, J. A., Metzler, A., Gatlin, D., & Risi, S. (1993). Classroom racial proportions and children's peer relations: Race and gender effects. *Journal of Educational Psychology, 85*, 446–452.

Klein, R. G., & Abikoff, H. B. (1997). Behavior therapy and methylphenidate in the treatment of children with ADHD. *Journal of Attention Disorders, 2*, 89–114.

Kolko, D. J., Loar, L. L., & Sturnick, D. (1990). Inpatient social-cognitive skills training with conduct disordered and attention deficit disordered children. *Journal of Child Psychology & Psychiatry, 31*, 737–748.

Lahey, B. B., Applegate, B., McBurnett, K., Biederman, J., Greenhill, L. L., Hynd, G. W., et al. (1994). DSM-IV field trials for attention deficit/hyperactivity disorder in children and adolescents. *American Journal of Psychiatry, 151*, 1673–1685.

Lahey, B. B., Pelham, W. E., Stein, M. A., Loney, J., Trapani, C., Nugent, K., et al. (1998). Validity of DSM-IV attention-deficit/hyperactivity disorder for younger children. *Journal of the American Academy of Child and Adolescent Psychiatry, 37*, 695–702.

Landau, S. L., Milich, R., & Diener, M. B. (1998). Peer relations of children with attention-deficit hyperactivity disorder. *Reading and Writing Quarterly, 14*, 83–105.

Landau, S. L., & Moore, L. A. (1991). Social skills deficits in children with Attention-Deficit Hyperactivity Disorder. *School Psychology Review, 20*, 235–251.

Mannuzza, S., & Klein, R. G. (2000). Long term prognosis in attention-deficit/hyperactivity disorder. *Child and Adolescent Psychiatric Clinics of North America, 9*, 711–726.

Matthys, W., Cuperus, J. M., & van England, H. (1999). Deficient social problem-solving in boys with ODD/CD, with ADHD, and with both disorders. *Journal of the American Academy of Child and Adolescent Psychiatry, 38*, 311–321.

McAuliffe, M., Hubbard, J., & Romano, L. (2009). The role of teacher cognition and behavior in children's peer relations. *Journal of Abnormal Child Psychology, 37*(5), 665–677.

Melnick, S. M., & Hinshaw, S. P. (1996). What they want and what they get: The social goals of boys with ADHD and comparison boys. *Journal of Abnormal Child Psychology, 24*, 169–185.

Mikami, A. Y., Griggs, M. S., Lerner, M. D., Emeh, C. C., Reuland, M. M., Jack, A., & Anthony, M. R. (in press). A randomized trial of a classroom intervention to increase peers' social inclusion of children with Attention-Deficit/Hyperactivity Disorder. *Journal of Consulting and Clinical Psychology.*

Mikami, A. Y., Griggs, M. S., Reuland, M. M., & Gregory, A. (2012). Teacher practices as predictors of children's classroom social preference. *Journal of School Psychology, 50*(1), 95–111.

Mikami, A. Y., & Hinshaw, S. P. (2006). Resilient adolescent adjustment among girls: Buffers of childhood peer rejection and attention-deficit/hyperactivity disorder. *Journal of Abnormal Child Psychology, 34*, 823–837.

Mikami, A. Y., Huang-Pollock, C. L., Pfiffner, L. J., McBurnett, K., & Hangai, D. (2007). Social skills differences among Attention-Deficit/Hyperactivity Disorder subtypes in a chat room assessment task. *Journal of Abnormal Child Psychology, 35*, 509–521.

Mikami, A. Y., Jack, A., Emeh, C. C., & Stephens, H. F. (2010). Parental influences on children with ADHD: I. Parental behaviors associated with children's peer relationships. *Journal of Abnormal Child Psychology, 38*, 721–736.

Mikami, A. Y., Lee, S. S., Hinshaw, S. P., & Mullin, B. C. (2008). Relationships between social information processing and aggression among adolescent girls with and without ADHD. *Journal of Youth and Adolescence, 37*, 761–771.

Mikami, A. Y., Lerner, M. D., & Lun, J. (2010). Social context influences on children's rejection by their peers. *Child Development Perspectives, 4*, 123–130.

Mikami, A. Y., & Lorenzi, J. (2011). Gender and conduct problems predict peer functioning among children with attention-deficit/hyperactivity disorder. *Journal of Clinical Child & Adolescent Psychology, 40*, 777–786.

Mikami, A. Y., & Pfiffner, L. J. (2006). Social skills training for youth with disruptive behavior disorders: A review of best practices. *Emotional and Behavioral Disorders in Youth, 6*, 3–23.

Milich, R., Balentine, A., & Lynam, D. (2001). ADHD combined type and ADHD predominantly inattentive type are distinct and unrelated disorders. *Clinical Psychology: Science and Practice, 8*, 463–488.

Molden, D. C., Lucas, G. M., Gardner, W. L., Dean, K., & Knowles, M. L. (2009). Motivations for prevention or promotion following social exclusion: Being rejected versus being ignored. *Journal of Personality and Social Psychology, 96*, 415–431.

Mrug, S., & Hoza, B. (2007). Impression formation and modifiability: Testing a theoretical model. *Merrill-Palmer Quarterly, 53*, 631–659.

Mrug, S., Hoza, B., & Gerdes, A. C. (2001). Children with Attention-Deficit/Hyperactivity Disorder: Peer relationships and peer-oriented interventions. *New Directions for Child and Adolescent Development, 91*, 51–77.

MTA Cooperative Group. (1999). A 14-month randomized clinical trial of treatment strategies for attention-deficit/hyperactivity disorder. *Archives of General Psychiatry, 56*, 1073–1086.

Murphy, D. A., Pelham, W. E., & Lang, A. R. (1992). Aggression in boys with Attention-Deficit/Hyperactivity Disorder: Methylphenidate effects on naturalistically observed aggression, provocation, and social information processing. *Journal of Abnormal Child Psychology, 20*, 451–466.

Nixon, E. (2001). The social competence of children with Attention Deficit Hyperactivity Disorder: A review of the literature. *Child Psychology and Psychiatry Review, 6*, 172–180.

Parker, J. G., & Asher, S. R. (1987). Peer relations and later personal adjustment: Are low-accepted children at risk? *Psychological Bulletin, 102*, 357–389.

Peets, K., Hodges, E. V. E., Kikas, E., & Salmivalli, C. (2007). Hostile attributions and behavioral strategies in children:

Does relationship type matter? *Developmental Psychology, 43*, 889–900.

Peets, K., Hodges, E. V. E., & Salmivalli, C. (2008). Affect-congruent social-cognitive evaluations and behaviors. *Child Development, 79*, 170–185.

Pelham, W. E., & Bender, M. E. (1982). Peer relationships in hyperactive children: Description and treatment. In K. D. Gadow & I. Bailer (Eds.), *Advances in Learning and Behavioral Disabilities* (Vol. 1, pp. 365–436). Greenwich, CT: JAI Press.

Pelham, W. E., Wheeler, T., & Chronis, A. M. (1998). Empirically supported psychosocial treatments for attention deficit hyperactivity disorder. *Journal of Child Clinical Psychology, 27*, 190–205.

Pfiffner, L. J., Calzada, E., & McBurnett, K. (2000). Interventions to enhance social competence. *Child and Adolescent Psychiatric Clinics of North America, 9*, 689–709.

Pfiffner, L. J., & McBurnett, K. (1997). Social skills training with parent generalization: Treatment effects for children with attention deficit disorder. *Journal of Consulting and Clinical Psychology, 65*, 749–757.

Pfiffner, L. J., Mikami, A. Y., Huang-Pollock, C. L., Easterlin, B., Zalecki, C. A., & McBurnett, K. (2007). A randomized controlled trial of integrated home-school behavioral treatment for ADHD, Predominantly Inattentive Type. *Journal of the American Academy of Child and Adolescent Psychiatry, 46*, 1041–1050.

Power, T. J., Costigan, T. E., Eiraldi, R. B., & Leff, S. S. (2004). Variations in anxiety and depression as a function of ADHD subtypes defined by DSM-IV: Do subtype differences exist or not? *Journal of Abnormal Child Psychology, 32*, 27–37.

Robison, L. M., Sclar, D. A., Skaer, T. L., & Galin, R. S. (2004). Treatment modalities among U.S. children diagnosed with attention-deficit hyperactivity disorder: 1995–1999. *International Clinical Psychopharmacology, 19*, 17–22.

Schwartz, D., McFayden-Ketchum, S., Dodge, K. A., Pettit, G. S., & Bates, J. E. (1999). Early behavior problems as a predictor of later peer group victimization: Moderators and mediators in the pathways of social risk. *Journal of Abnormal Child Psychology, 27*, 191–201.

Shea, B., & Wiener, J. (2003). Social exile: the cycle of peer victimization for boys with ADHD. *Canadian Journal of School Psychology, 18*, 55–90.

Solanto, M. V., Pope-Boyd, S. A., Tyron, W. W., & Stepak, B. (2009). Social functioning in predominantly inattentive and combined subtypes of children with ADHD. *Journal of Attention Disorders, 13*, 27–35.

Stormont, M. (2001). Social outcomes of children with AD/HD: Contributing factors and implications for practoce. *Psychology in the Schools, 38*, 521–531.

Stormshak, E. A., Bierman, K. L., Bruschi, C., Dodge, K. A., Coie, J. D., & Conduct Problems Prevention Research Group. (1999). The relation between behavior problems and peer preference in different classroom contexts. *Child Development, 70*, 169–182.

Whalen, C. K., & Henker, B. (1985). The social worlds of hyperactive (ADDH) children. *Clinical Psychology Review, 5*, 447–478.

Whalen, C. K., & Henker, B. (1992). The social profile of attention-deficit hyperactivity disorder: Five fundamental facets. *Child and Adolescent Psychiatric Clinics of North America, 1*, 395–410.

Whalen, C. K., Henker, B., Buhrmester, D., Hinshaw, S. P., Huber, A., & Laski, K. (1989). Does stimulant medication improve the peer status of hyperactive children? *Journal of Consulting & Clinical Psychology, 57*, 545–549.

Whalen, C. K., Henker, B., Collins, B. E., McAuliffe, S., & Vaux, A. (1979). Peer interaction in a structured communication task: Comparisons of normal and hyperactive boys and of methylphenidate (Ritalin) and placebo effects. *Child Development, 50*(388–401).

Whalen, C. K., Henker, B., Dotemoto, S., & Hinshaw, S. P. (1983). Child and adolescent perceptions of normal and atypical peers. *Child Development, 54*, 1588–1598.

Wheeler, J., & Carlson, C. L. (1994). The social functioning of children with ADD with hyperactivity and ADD without hyperactivity: A comparison of peer relations and social deficits. *Journal of Emotional and Behavioral Disorders, 2*, 2–12.

Wiener, J., & Mak, M. (2009). Peer victimization in children with attention-deficit/hyperactivity disorder. *Psychology in the Schools, 46*, 116–131.

Wright, J. C., Giammarino, M., & Parad, H. W. (1986). Social status and small groups: Individual-group similarity and the social "misfit." *Journal of Personality & Social Psychology, 50*, 523–536.

Attachment Orientations and Reactions to Ostracism in Close Relationships and Groups

Phillip R. Shaver *and* Mario Mikulincer

Abstract

Attachment theory is one of the most useful contemporary conceptual frameworks for understanding emotion regulation and mental health. In his exposition of attachment theory, John Bowlby explained how the sense of attachment security (confidence that one is lovable and that caregivers are available and supportive when needed) in relationships helps a person deal with threats, losses, and negative emotions and how attachment-related insecurities interfere with the regulation of negative emotions and recovery from rejections, losses, and setbacks throughout life. In the present chapter, we wish to explore the possibility that attachment security or insecurity in adulthood can help to explain individual differences in cognitive, emotional, and behavioral reactions to social rejection in both close relationships and groups. We review literature relevant to this proposal and also present data from a preliminary study of the buffering of one effect of ostracism—loss of meaning in life—by attachment security.

Key Words: attachment, interpersonal relationships, meaning in life, security, social rejection

Introduction

Although Bowlby (1973, 1980, 1982), the originator of attachment theory, did not focus on broad social processes and reactions to social inclusion or exclusion in groups, he did attempt to understand how and why disapproval, rejection, and social ostracism are so painful. His focus was on relationships between young children and their parents or other care providers, and the effects of these relationships on personality development and behavior in subsequent close relationships. The titles of the three volumes in his theoretical treatise—*Attachment, Separation,* and *Loss*—indicate how much emphasis he placed on separation, rejection, and bereavement. He saw these painful social experiences as major contributors to core security or insecurity throughout life. Attachment theory is an attempt to explain how security in relationships helps a person deal with threats, losses, and negative emotions and how attachment-related insecurities interfere with

the regulation of negative emotions and recovery from rejections, losses, and setbacks throughout life (Shaver & Mikulincer, 2002). In the present chapter, we wish to explore the possibility that attachment security or insecurity in adulthood can help to explain individual differences in cognitive, emotional, and behavioral reactions to social rejection in both close relationships and groups. We review literature relevant to this proposal and also present data from a preliminary study of the buffering of one effect of ostracism—loss of meaning in life—by attachment security.

Overview of Attachment Theory

Bowlby (1982) claimed that human beings are born with an innate psychobiological system (which he called the *attachment behavioral system*) that motivates them to seek proximity to supportive others (*attachment figures*) in times of need. He also delineated important individual differences in attachment-system functioning, which he attributed mainly to experiences in intimate relationships (Bowlby, 1973). Interactions with attachment figures who are available, sensitive, and responsive in times of need promote the normal development and operation of the attachment system and encourage the development of a stable sense of security. This sense of security is based on implicit beliefs that the world is generally safe and that other people are "well-intentioned and kind-hearted" (Hazan & Shaver, 1987). These beliefs are rooted in positive mental representations of self and others, which Bowlby (1973) called *internal working models*. Unfortunately, when a person's attachment figures have not been reliably available, sensitive, and supportive, the person has not found that seeking proximity to them relieves distress. Moreover, he or she is not likely to have developed a core sense of security, and negative working models of self (as not sufficiently lovable) and others (as unaccepting, unreliable, and unresponsive if not downright abusive or cruel) are likely to have developed, accompanied by distorted affect-regulation strategies (called *secondary attachment strategies*, conceptualized in terms of attachment-related *anxiety* and *avoidance*).

When studying individual differences in attachment-system functioning in adults, we have focused mainly on *attachment style*—a person's chronic pattern of relational expectations, emotions, and behaviors resulting from the internalization and memory of a particular attachment history (Fraley & Shaver, 2000). Beginning with Ainsworth, Blehar, Waters, and Wall's (1978) studies of infant attachment, and followed by hundreds of adult attachment studies, researchers have found that attachment styles can be measured along two orthogonal dimensions of *anxiety* and *avoidance* (Brennan, Clark, & Shaver, 1998). Attachment *anxiety* reflects the degree to which a person worries that relationship partners will not be available in times of need and is afraid of being rejected or abandoned. Attachment-related *avoidance* reflects the extent to which a person distrusts relationship partners' goodwill and strives to maintain independence and emotional distance from partners. People who score low on both dimensions are said to be secure, or secure with respect to attachment. The two dimensions can be measured with reliable and valid self-report scales (e.g., Brennan et al., 1998) and are associated in theoretically predictable ways with many aspects of personal well-being and relationship quality (see Mikulincer & Shaver, 2007a, for a review).

Although attachment orientations are initially formed in relationships with caregivers during childhood (Cassidy & Shaver, 2008), Bowlby (1988) claimed that important interactions with relationship partners can alter a person's working models and move the person from one region of the two-dimensional (anxiety by avoidance) space to another. Moreover, although a person's attachment style is often conceptualized as a single global orientation toward relationships, it is actually an emergent property of a complex network of cognitive and affective processes and mental representations, which includes many episodic, context-specific, and relationship-anchored memories and schemas (Mikulincer & Shaver, 2003). In fact, many studies indicate that a person's attachment orientation can change depending on current context and recent experiences (Mikulincer & Shaver, 2007b), making it possible to study the effects of experimentally primed senses of security and insecurity.

We have proposed that a person's location in the two-dimensional space defined by attachment anxiety and avoidance reflects both the person's sense of attachment security and the ways in which he or she deals with threats and stressors (Mikulincer & Shaver, 2003, 2007a). People who score low on these dimensions are generally secure and tend to employ constructive and effective affect-regulation strategies. In contrast, people who score high on either attachment anxiety or avoidance, or both (a condition called fearful avoidance), suffer from attachment insecurities. These insecure people tend to use secondary attachment strategies that we, following Cassidy and Kobak (1988), characterize as "hyperactivating" or "deactivating" the attachment behavioral system in an effort to cope with threats.

People who score high on attachment anxiety rely on hyperactivating strategies—energetic attempts to achieve proximity, support, and love combined with a lack of confidence that these resources will be provided and with feelings of sadness or anger when they are in fact not provided (Cassidy & Kobak, 1988). These reactions occur in relationships in which an attachment figure is sometimes responsive but unreliably so, placing the needy person on a partial reinforcement schedule that rewards exaggeration and persistence in proximity-seeking attempts when these efforts sometimes succeed. In contrast, people who score high on avoidant attachment tend to use deactivating strategies: trying not to seek proximity to others when threatened, denying vulnerability and a need for other people, and avoiding closeness and interdependence in relationships. These strategies develop in relationships with attachment figures who disapprove of and punish frequent bids for closeness and expressions of need (Ainsworth et al., 1978).

With these ideas in mind, we can characterize the attachment system in terms of emotion-regulation processes (Cassidy, 1994; Shaver & Mikulincer, 2007a). Perceived threats, including threats of rejection and ostracism, automatically activate the attachment system (Bowlby, 1982; Mikulincer, Gillath, & Shaver, 2002), which causes a threatened individual to seek proximity to protective others (or evoke comforting mental representations of them) as a means of managing the threat and restoring emotional balance. Current indications or memories of attachment-figure availability facilitate coping with threats and restore emotional balance, whereas indications of attachment-figure unavailability amplify distress and interfere with effective coping. For this reason, Bowlby (1988) viewed attachment insecurity as a risk factor for clinically significant emotional problems, a view that has been supported by research (see Mikulincer & Shaver, 2007a, for a review).

Attachment Orientations and Rejection in the Context of Close Relationships

According to attachment theory, explicit or implicit rejection within a close relationship (a phenomenon that Feeney, 2004, called *relationship denigration*) can destroy a person's sense of safety and security, evoke intense hurt feelings, and ruin a relationship (Shaver, Mikulincer, Lavy, & Cassidy, 2009). There are, however, attachment-related differences in the ways in which people appraise and react to potentially painful experiences.

Because of their histories of kind treatment in close relationships and their development of positive working models of self, relatively secure individuals do not need to depend as much as insecure people on a partner's continuous approval and validation. They are, of course, not completely invulnerable to relationship denigration and hurt feelings, but they can generally withstand challenges to their well-grounded positive beliefs and sense of value without being deeply hurt or resentful. Studies indicate that secure people are more likely than their insecure counterparts to excuse a partner's occasional unkind behavior and not attribute it to cruel intentions or an absence of love (e.g., Collins, 1996). Moreover, they can fairly easily forgive a partner following experiences of relationship denigration (e.g., Mikulincer, Shaver, & Slav, 2006).

Secure individuals' resilience in the face of provocations is also made possible by automatic activation of security-enhancing mental representations (Mikulincer & Shaver, 2004). Unlike infants and children, who are almost completely dependent on caregivers' sensitivity and responsiveness to cope with social disapproval or rejection, secure adults do not necessarily need to engage in actual support seeking when coping with such experiences. Rather, they can activate soothing and comforting mental representations of relationship partners who have regularly provided care and protection, or they can recall past supportive and loving interactions (e.g., Mikulincer et al., 2002). Moreover, secure people can mobilize caring qualities within themselves— qualities modeled on those of their supportive attachment figures—as well as representations of being loved and valued (Mikulincer & Shaver, 2004). These cognitive-affective mental representations provide genuine comfort, bolster the inner sense of safety and security, and help a secure person remain unperturbed by threats of interpersonal rejection and ostracism (e.g., Mikulincer, Hirschberger, Nachmias, & Gillath, 2001). In other words, calling upon a broad and deep set of security-enhancing mental representations when one is rejected and ostracized by a partner can reduce the damage to one's sense of security and thereby reduce pain and distress.

We saw interesting examples of these phenomena in a recent study of young adults' dreams (Mikulincer, Shaver, & Avihou-Kanza, 2011). Participants were asked to recall their dreams each morning for a month and write a brief account of each one, which was then analyzed by two independent coders. Dreams reported by participants who scored relatively high on attachment anxiety included significantly more representations of the self as anxious, helpless, unaccepted, or unloved. Those reported by relatively avoidant participants contained more representations of the self as unreceptive to others (i.e., more distant, uncooperative, emotionally unexpressive, or angry). Participants who scored relatively low on both insecurity dimensions (i.e., those who were relatively secure) had dreams indicating that they could cope assertively and effectively with social threats, and interestingly, in some dreams the psychological roots of this stance in long-term relationships with parents were revealed. For example:

> I was sitting in my elementary school library reading a book ... I spoke with friends and teachers, and

the place was just as it used to be. The principal came in and started yelling at us, saying we were barbaric children. At first I thought we might have been noisy and deserved this, but I told him that despite whatever we had done, we didn't deserve such treatment and he had overlooked my many good qualities. Despite being a little girl, I had enough self-confidence to tell him he was wrong. So I got up and told him I was not a barbarian and I came to the library to read good books. He then apologized. I felt proud of myself. At that instant, my mom appeared, hugged me, and said I was okay and she was proud of me. (I don't know how my mom got there.)

We do not mean to imply that secure people are completely immune to rejection, disapproval, or ostracism. Persistent or severe relationship denigration from an important relationship partner can surely shatter even a secure person's sense of safety and well-being, at least in the short run; it would be maladaptive for anyone to accept and calmly put up with such assaults. Nevertheless, in many unpleasant situations secure individuals use constructive regulatory strategies to resolve conflicts and misunderstandings, or to terminate destructive relationships if necessary, while retaining a sense of personal worth and emotional stability (e.g., Campbell, Simpson, Boldry, & Kashy, 2005; Simpson, Rholes, & Phillips, 1996).

Avoidant people also tend to report being relatively immune to relationship denigration, but their immunity is not due to an underlying sense of security and self-worth. Rather, avoidant people's resistance to the pain of rejection stems from deactivation of attachment-related wishes, goals, and concerns, and reliance on themselves for protection in times of need (Bowlby, 1980). Moreover, avoidant individuals try not to depend on a partner's support, care, or love. As a result they care less, at least at a conscious level, about rejection or ostracism. We have found (e.g., Mikulincer, Dolev, & Shaver, 2004) that this equanimity relies on suppression of negative feelings and memories, as well as self-doubts, which can be temporarily knocked off balance by an experimentally induced cognitive load. However, under normal conditions, suppression seems to allow avoidant people to keep their vulnerabilities and self-doubts suppressed (Fraley & Shaver, 1997; Mikulincer et al., 2004).

In contrast, attachment anxiety is associated with being vulnerable to a partner's disapproval, rejection, or neglect. Anxious individuals react strongly with hurt feelings, self-denigration, and anger toward the partner (Feeney, 2004). They have learned, in a history of interactions with self-preoccupied, unreliable, and unpredictable caregivers, to hyperactivate their attachment systems, maintaining constant vigilance for signs of impending separation or abandonment and exaggerating the importance of a partner's approval, support, and protection (Mikulincer & Shaver, 2007a; Shaver & Mikulincer, 2007). As a result of a history of hurtful, frustrating interactions with unreliable attachment figures, they have maintained ready access to painful memories, which causes a current relationship partner's rejection to amplify past hurt feelings (Mikulincer & Orbach, 1995).

People who score high on attachment anxiety tend to base their self-concepts on unstable, conditional sources of self-worth, such as others' immediate approval and validation (e.g., Park, Crocker, & Mickelson, 2004). Being overly reliant on others for a sense of value causes them, almost obsessively, to seek reassurance from relationship partners (Shaver, Schachner & Mikulincer, 2005), leaving them vulnerable to rejection, and perhaps sometimes even bringing it about, as a self-fulfilling prophecy, by annoying or exhausting the partner with intrusive vigilance and jealous suspicion (Collins, 1996). They feel exceptionally good, briefly, when a partner is affectionate or offers praise, but exceptionally bad when a partner is rejecting or neglectful (e.g., Campbell et al., 2005; Feeney, 2002).

Research confirms that attachment-anxious individuals are especially sensitive to rejection (e.g., Downey & Feldman, 1996) and are quicker than nonanxious individuals to recognize rejection-related words in lexical decision tasks (Baldwin & Kay, 2003; Baldwin & Meunier, 1999). Moreover, such people have difficulty inhibiting thoughts of rejection (Baldwin & Kay, 2003; Baldwin & Meunier, 1999). Baldwin and Kay (2003) exposed study participants to tones paired with photographs of rejecting (frowning) or accepting (smiling) faces, and then administered a lexical decision task in which rejection-related words were paired with each of the tones. Secure participants were slower to react to rejection-related words even when paired with rejection tones (as compared with a neutral tone), and anxious participants reacted faster to these words even in the presence of the acceptance tone. This implies that anxious individuals are so hypervigilant with respect to relationship denigration that they entertain rejection-related thoughts even in the presence of an accepting interpersonal context.

Research has also shown that people who score high on attachment anxiety react with greater distress than less anxious people to episodes of relationship denigration. Feeney (2004, 2005) asked people to recall and describe an event in which a romantic partner said or did something that hurt their feelings, finding that attachment-anxious people reacted to such experiences with exceptionally high distress, fear, and shame. In contrast, study participants who scored relatively high on avoidant attachment reported lower levels of hurt feelings and distress. Other researchers have also noted that attachment-anxious people experience strong negative emotions in response to either real or imagined partner infidelity (e.g., Guerrero, 1998; Knobloch, Solomon, & Cruz, 2001). And there is evidence that such people experience greater than average distress during conflicts with relationship partners (e.g., Feeney, 1994; Simpson et al., 1996). They also tend to be overwhelmed by negative feelings and catastrophic thoughts in response to real or imagined separations or abandonment (e.g., Meyer, Olivier, & Roth, 2005; Mikulincer, Florian, Birnbaum, & Malishkevich, 2002).

In two studies of reactions to a relationship partner's betrayal of trust (e.g., Jang, Smith, & Levine, 2002; Mikulincer, 1998), insecure people, as compared to secure ones, were less likely to talk openly with their partner about the betrayal. In addition, more anxious people were likely to ruminate about their partner's betrayal, talk around the problem, avoid discussing the partner's deception, and react with strong negative emotions. Avoidant people, in contrast, increased their distance from the transgressing partner and denied the importance of the incident.

Studies focusing on associations between attachment insecurities and forgiveness within couple relationships add to the body of evidence on hurt feelings. In two correlational studies of dating and married couples, Kachadourian, Fincham, and Davila (2004) found that anxious or avoidant people were less likely to forgive their romantic partners. In a diary study of daily fluctuations in the tendency to forgive a partner, Mikulincer et al. (2006) found that both attachment anxiety and avoidance predicted lower levels of forgiveness across 21 consecutive days. Moreover, whereas secure people were more likely to forgive their spouse on days when they perceived more positive spousal behavior, anxious or avoidant people reported little forgiveness even on days when they perceived their spouse to be available, attentive, and supportive.

In a recent laboratory experiment, Cassidy, Shaver, Mikulincer, and Lavy (2009) examined the influences of both dispositional attachment insecurities and experimental priming of the sense of attachment security on cognitive and emotional reactions to hurtful experiences in close relationships. Participants completed the Experiences in Close Relationships inventory (ECR; Brennan et al., 1998), a measure of dispositional attachment anxiety and avoidance, and then wrote a description of an incident in which a close relationship partner criticized, disapproved, rejected, or ostracized them. Participants then completed a short computerized task in which they were repeatedly exposed subliminally (for 22 milliseconds) to either a security-enhancing prime word (love, secure, affection) or a neutral prime (lamp, staple, building). Immediately after the priming trials, participants were asked to think again about the hurtful event they had described and to rate how they would react to such an event if it happened in the future: how rejected they would feel, how they would feel about themselves (using a list of positive and negative self-descriptive adjectives), and how well each of nine action descriptions fit the way they would react (various defensive and hostile reactions, various constructive reactions, and crying).

In the neutral priming condition, the findings conformed to the usual deactivating and hyperactivating strategies of avoidant and anxious people (e.g., as reported by Feeney, 2005). Avoidance scores were associated with less negative appraisals of the relationship denigration, less intense feelings of rejection, less crying, and more defensive/hostile reactions. In the neutral priming condition, attachment anxiety was associated with more intense feelings of rejection, more crying, and more negative emotions. These typical correlational findings were dramatically reduced in size (most approached zero) in the security-priming condition. In other words, security priming reduced the tendency of avoidant people to rely on deactivating defenses and the tendency of anxious people to react hyperactively to relationship denigration, suggesting, in line with attachment theory, that insecurity underlies both patterns of defense.

These findings support the hypothesized role of attachment security in regulating reactions to relationship denigration. When a person is already secure, based on a history of supportive relationships, he or she can deal constructively with hurtful experiences. When a person has a history of unreliable, unpredictable attachment figures and is dispositionally anxious as a result, he or she is likely to intensify distress and cope badly with perceived neglect or rejection. But this habitual response can be notably softened by a brief, unconscious augmentation of felt security. When a person has dealt with cool, consistently unsupportive attachment figures and developed a defensively avoidant pattern of relating to others, he or she is somewhat protected from the pain and distress of rejection and ostracism, but this benefit comes at the expense of considerable denial and interpersonal distance. This habitual protective armor can be at least temporarily softened by an infusion of felt security that seems to allow an avoidant person to become more "open to inner pain" (Cassidy, 2004), which could provide an opening for greater closeness in a relationship or, in clinical cases, greater openness to psychotherapy.

Attachment and Social Exclusion

Although attachment theory has been applied mostly to the study of close interpersonal relationships, recent studies have extended it and its associated measures into the domain of group dynamics (e.g., Rom & Mikulincer, 2003; Smith, Murphy, & Coats, 1999). According to Rom and Mikulincer (2003), relationships with a group as whole or with individual members of the group can fulfill some of the definitional criteria for attachment bonds. First, a group can be a target of proximity seeking. Many studies have shown that people prefer their own groups when stressed and tend to seek proximity to group members in times of need (see Devine, 1995; Dovidio & Gartner, 1993; for reviews). Second, a group can be a source of support, comfort, and relief—in attachment theory's terms, a safe haven in a storm of stresses and strains (e.g., Hogg, 1992). Third, a group can facilitate exploration and skill acquisition by, in the language of attachment theory, providing a secure base for exploration (e.g., Forsyth, 1990).

In support of this idea, Smith et al. (1999) showed that people can develop feelings or orientations of attachment anxiety or avoidance toward a group. Moreover, higher scores on measures of attachment anxiety and avoidance were related to lower identification with groups, stronger negative emotions related to groups, and lower perceived support from groups. Rom and Mikulincer (2003) pursued this line of research and found that attachment anxiety was associated with negative representations of oneself as a group member, appraising group interactions as threatening, more negative emotional reactions to experiences in groups,

greater endorsement of love and security goals in groups (e.g., being loved and accepted by group members), and poorer performance on group tasks. Avoidant attachment was associated with more negative appraisals of group members and group interactions, placing higher priority on self-reliance goals during group interactions, and contributing less to the promotion of closeness among group members. Rom and Mikulincer (2003) also found that group cohesiveness reduced the detrimental effects of attachment anxiety, but not of avoidance, on contributing to group performance.

These findings suggest that attachment theory may be useful as a framework for studying individual differences in group-related cognitions, emotions, and behavior. Moreover, they imply that warm, accepting interactions in groups can soothe at least some group members' anxieties and provide a sense of safety and security. They also suggest that rejection by or exclusion from a group might damage a person's sense of security and activate internal working models and habitual attachment-related strategies for dealing with distress. As a result, people with different attachment orientations may react to rejection or ostracism by a group in the same way they react to close relationship denigration.

Because attachment researchers have devoted most of their attention to studies of close dyadic relationships, there has not yet been a systematic program of research on links between attachment insecurities and reactions to rejection or ostracism by a group. There is, however, one recently published study that examined whether and how people with different attachment orientations differ in their reactions to messages of group respect or disrespect (Erez et al., 2009). In this study, Dutch university students were told they would participate in a study of team work; they then completed the ECR (Brennan et al., 1998), measuring attachment anxiety and avoidance, and were assigned to a four-member group. However, before meeting the other group members and beginning to work with them as a team, participants were asked to disclose some personal information about positive and negative life experiences by typing brief descriptions on a computer, ostensibly for the purpose of getting to know one another better. They then received descriptions of the other group members and were asked to rate the respect they felt toward each group member based on the descriptions each of them had ostensibly provided. Actually, of course, all of the participants received standardized, preprogrammed descriptions containing disclosures that had been rated as equally positive or equally negative in a pilot study.

Participants were randomly assigned to one of three experimental conditions, which determined the kind of average respect scores they had supposedly received from the other three group members. In the low respect condition, participants were informed that, on average, the other three group members had rated them lower than the neutral point and that their score was lower than the average respect scores received by the other three group members. In the average respect condition, participants were informed that, on average, the other three group members had rated them near the neutral point and that their respect score was quite similar to the scores received by the other three group members. In the high respect condition, participants were informed that their average respect score was higher than the neutral point and higher than the respect scores of the other three group members.

Following this experimental manipulation, participants reported on their commitment to the group and their worries concerning acceptance and approval by the other group members. In addition, Erez et al. (2009) assessed group-related behavior in two ways. First, participants were asked to work on a group task (a "speed and effort" task), and their actual effort expenditure on behalf of the group was assessed. Second, participants received a small amount of money (10 Euros) and were asked to decide how much of it they wished to share with the other group members.

Attachment anxiety was associated with more intense reactions to both the group respect and the group disrespect manipulations. That is, high group respect (as compared to average respect) resulted in higher reports of commitment to the group and more effort expenditure on the group's behalf—mainly among participants scoring high on attachment anxiety. Moreover, group disrespect (as compared to average respect) led to more group-related worries, lower group commitment, more money donated to the group, and higher effort expenditure on behalf of the group, again mainly among participants scoring high on attachment anxiety. These effects of group respect or disrespect were not significant among nonanxious (more secure) participants, and there were no significant effects of attachment-related avoidance.

As expected, then, when attachment-anxious individuals felt respected by their group, they became more committed to the group, expended more effort on behalf of the group, and shared more money with group members. When they felt disrespected, they became less committed but, presumably because of their strong need for others' approval, still worked hard for the group and contributed more money to its members. That is, attachment anxiety seemed to be associated with a tendency to continue investing in a possibly disrespectful group in hopes of being accepted and then feeling better about oneself. The same tendency has been observed in close relationships, wherein anxiously attached people seem more reluctant than secure ones to end unsatisfying relationships (Davila & Bradbury, 2001) and remain sexually and emotionally involved with abusive or rejecting partners (Davis, Shaver, & Vernon, 2003; Henderson, Bartholomew, & Dutton, 1997).

Although these findings indicate that attachment orientations moderate a person's reactions to group disrespect, they cannot be confidently extrapolated to experiences of social exclusion or ostracism. That is, receiving negative evaluative feedback from unfamiliar group members is not the same as being ostracized by a group to which one has belonged. Therefore, we cannot be confident that attachment-related insecurities will explain reactions to ostracism. We therefore conducted a study especially for this chapter to examine more directly the influence of attachment orientations on one previously studied reaction to social exclusion—loss of meaning in life (Stillman et al., 2009).

Sixty Israeli undergraduates completed the ECR measures of attachment anxiety and avoidance during a lecture class and were invited to participate in a social interaction experiment 3 to 4 weeks later. Upon arrival at the laboratory, participants were invited to play Cyberball, an interactive ball-tossing computer game designed to manipulate ostracism (Williams & Jarvis, 2006). Participants thought they were connected via the internet to two fellow students involved in the same exercise. In fact, there were no other students, and the throwing behavior of the other two players was controlled by the Cyberball program. Participants were randomly assigned to one of two conditions: ostracism and control. In the ostracism condition ($N = 30$), none of the computer-controlled players threw the ball to the participant after doing so briefly at the beginning of the exercise. That is, participants in the ostracism condition were given a small taste of social inclusion and were then ignored and excluded from the game. In the control condition ($N = 30$), the other two players tossed the ball to each other and to the participant with about equal frequencies.

After the game, all participants completed a distracting filler questionnaire about life habits, followed by a 20-item questionnaire concerning current thoughts and feelings. Five items tapped current feelings about life's meaning and purpose (e.g., "Right now, how meaningful does your life feel?" "Right now, how much do you feel your life has a purpose?"). These items were taken from the Presence subscale of the Meaning in Life Scale (Steger, Frazier, Oishi, & Kaler, 2006). Participants rated the extent to which each item described them at that moment using a 7-point scale ranging from 1 (*not at all*) to 7 (*absolutely*). Cronbach's alpha for these 5 items was .87. At the end of the experiment, participants completed a suspicion probe concerning the Cyberball game, were fully debriefed, and were thanked for participating.

A hierarchical regression analysis replicated Stillman et al.'s (2009) finding: Participants in the ostracism condition reported having a lower sense of meaning and purpose than participants in the control condition, $\beta = -.27$, $p < .05$. However, this effect was qualified by a significant interaction between experimental condition and attachment anxiety, $\beta = -.24$, $p < .05$. Simple slope tests revealed that ostracism (as compared to the control condition) caused participants to have a lower sense of meaning when attachment anxiety was relatively high (+1SD), $\beta = -.51$, $p < .01$, but not when it was relatively low (-1SD), $\beta = -.03$. In addition, attachment anxiety was significantly associated with lower meaning scores in the ostracism condition, $\beta = -.37$, $p < .05$, but not in the control condition, $\beta = .11$.

In summary, attachment anxiety was associated with feeling that life was less meaningful following an experience of social exclusion. Stated in the other direction, dispositional attachment security (indicated by low scores on the attachment anxiety scale) buffered the negative effect of ostracism on the sense of meaning and purpose in life. In fact, only the relatively high scorers on the attachment anxiety dimension reacted to social exclusion with a loss of meaning in life.

Conclusions

Although attachment theory was not created to explain reactions to social ostracism, but was instead created to explain negative long-term effects of early rejection, neglect, separation, or abandonment from caregivers in childhood, the constructs in the theory and measures that have been developed to test the theory's implications are useful in conceptualizing the effects of criticism and ostracism more broadly.

The theory and its associated research literature are likely to be useful in assessing the role of individual differences—particularly differences in dispositional and situationally manipulated security and insecurity—in reactions to rejection and ostracism. We have been involved with two recent studies, one published and one conducted for this chapter, which confirm our belief that attachment theory can help the field achieve a deeper understanding of the effects of rejection and ostracism, both within close relationships and in groups of various kinds. We look forward to learning more about this potential elaboration of attachment theory.

References

Ainsworth, M. D. S., Blehar, M. C., Waters, E., & Wall, S. (1978). *Patterns of Attachment: Assessed in the Strange Situation and at Home*. Hillsdale, NJ: Erlbaum.

Baldwin, M. W., & Kay, A. C. (2003). Adult attachment and the inhibition of rejection. *Journal of Social and Clinical Psychology, 22*, 275–293.

Baldwin, M. W., & Meunier, J. (1999). The cued activation of attachment relational schemas. *Social Cognition, 17*, 209–227.

Bowlby, J. (1973). *Attachment and Loss: Vol. 2. Separation: Anxiety and Anger*. New York: Basic Books.

Bowlby, J. (1980). *Attachment and Loss: Vol. 3. Sadness and Depression*. New York: Basic Books.

Bowlby, J. (1982). *Attachment and Loss: Vol. 1. Attachment* (2nd ed.). New York: Basic Books. (Original ed. 1969)

Bowlby, J. (1988). *A secure base: Clinical Applications of Attachment Theory*. London: Routledge.

Brennan, K. A., Clark, C. L., & Shaver, P. R. (1998). Self-report measurement of adult romantic attachment: An integrative overview. In J. A. Simpson & W. S. Rholes (Eds.), *Attachment Theory and Close Relationships* (pp. 46–76). New York: Guilford Press.

Campbell, L., Simpson, J. A., Boldry, J., & Kashy, D. A. (2005). Perceptions of conflict and support in romantic relationships: The role of attachment anxiety. *Journal of Personality and Social Psychology, 88*, 510–531.

Cassidy, J. (1994). Emotion regulation: Influences of attachment relationships. *Monographs of the Society for Research in Child Development, 59*, 228–283.

Cassidy, J. (2004). *Remaining open to the pain*. Invited address at a research conference on attachment, University of California, Davis.

Cassidy, J., & Kobak, R. R. (1988). Avoidance and its relationship with other defensive processes. In J. Belsky & T. Nezworski (Eds.), *Clinical Implications of Attachment* (pp. 300–323). Hillsdale, NJ: Erlbaum.

Cassidy, J., & Shaver, P. R. (Eds.) (2008). *Handbook of Attachment: Theory, research, and Clinical Applications* (2nd ed.). New York: Guilford Press.

Cassidy, J., Shaver, P. R., Mikulincer, M., & Lavy, S. (2009). Experimentally induced security influences responses to psychological pain. *Journal of Social and Clinical Psychology, 28*, 463–478.

Collins, N. L. (1996). Working models of attachment: Implications for explanation, emotion, and behavior. *Journal of Personality and Social Psychology, 71*, 810–832.

Davila, J., & Bradbury, T. N. (2001). Attachment insecurity and the distinction between unhappy spouses who do and do not divorce. *Journal of Family Psychology, 15,* 371–393.

Davis, D., Shaver, P. R., & Vernon, M. L. (2003). Physical, emotional, and behavioral reactions to breaking up: The roles of gender, age, emotional involvement, and attachment style. *Personality and Social Psychology Bulletin, 29,* 871–884.

Devine, P. G. (1995). Prejudice and out-group perception. In A. Tesser (Ed.), *Advanced Social Psychology* (pp. 466–524). New York: McGraw-Hill.

Dovidio, J. F., & Gaertner, S. L. (1993). Stereotypes and evaluative intergroup bias. In D. M. Mackie & D. L. Hamilton (Eds.), *Affect, Cognition, and Stereotyping* (pp. 167–193). San Diego: Academic Press.

Downey, G., & Feldman, S. I. (1996). Implications of rejection sensitivity for intimate relationships. *Journal of Personality and Social Psychology, 70,* 1327–1343.

Erez, A., Sleebos, E., Mikulincer, M., van IJzendoorn, M. H., Ellemers, N., & Koonenberg, P. M. (2009). Attachment anxiety, intra-group (dis)respect, actual efforts, and group donation. *European Journal of Social Psychology, 39,* 734–746.

Feeney, J. A. (1994). Attachment style, communication patterns, and satisfaction across the life cycle of marriage. *Personal Relationships, 1,* 333–348.

Feeney, J. A. (2002). Attachment, marital interaction, and relationship satisfaction: A diary study. *Personal Relationships, 9,* 39–55.

Feeney, J. A. (2004). Hurt feelings in couple relationships: Towards integrative models of the negative effects of hurtful events. *Journal of Social and Personal Relationships, 21,* 487–508.

Feeney, J. A. (2005). Hurt feelings in couple relationships: Exploring the role of attachment and perceptions of personal injury. *Personal Relationships, 12,* 253–271.

Forsyth, D. R. (1990). *Group Dynamics* (2nd ed.). Pacific Grove, CA: Brooks/Cole.

Fraley, R. C., & Shaver, P. R. (1997). Adult attachment and the suppression of unwanted thoughts. *Journal of Personality and Social Psychology, 73,* 1080–1091.

Fraley, R. C., & Shaver, P. R. (2000). Adult romantic attachment: Theoretical developments, emerging controversies, and unanswered questions. *Review of General Psychology, 4,* 132–154.

Guerrero, L. K. (1998). Attachment-style differences in the experience and expression of romantic jealousy. *Personal Relationships, 5,* 273–291.

Hazan, C., & Shaver, P. R. (1987). Romantic love conceptualized as an attachment process. *Journal of Personality and Social Psychology, 52,* 511–524.

Henderson, A. J. Z., Bartholomew, K., & Dutton, D. G. (1997). He loves me; he loves me not: Attachment and separation resolution of abused women. *Journal of Family Violence, 12,* 169–191.

Hogg, M. A. (1992). *The Social Psychology of Group Cohesiveness: From Attraction to Social Identity.* New York: Harvester Wheatsheaf.

Jang, S. A., Smith, S. W., & Levine, T. R. (2002). To stay or to leave? The role of attachment styles in communication patterns and potential termination of romantic relationships following discovery of deception. *Communication Monographs, 69,* 236–252.

Kachadourian, L. K., Fincham, F., & Davila, J. (2004). The tendency to forgive in dating and married couples: The role of attachment and relationship satisfaction. *Personal Relationships, 11,* 373–393.

Knobloch, L. K., Solomon, D.-H., & Cruz, M. G. (2001). The role of relationship development and attachment in the experience of romantic jealousy. *Personal Relationships, 8,* 205–224.

Meyer, B., Olivier, L., & Roth, D. A. (2005). Please don't leave me! BIS/BAS, attachment styles, and responses to a relationship threat. *Personality and Individual Differences, 38,* 151–162.

Mikulincer, M. (1998). Attachment working models and the sense of trust: An exploration of interaction goals and affect regulation. *Journal of Personality and Social Psychology, 74,* 1209–1224.

Mikulincer, M., Dolev, T., & Shaver, P. R. (2004). Attachment-related strategies during thought-suppression: ironic rebounds and vulnerable self-representations. *Journal of Personality and Social Psychology, 87,* 940–956.

Mikulincer, M., Florian, V., Birnbaum, G., & Malishkevich, S. (2002). The death-anxiety buffering function of close relationships: Exploring the effects of separation reminders on death-thought accessibility. *Personality and Social Psychology Bulletin, 28,* 287–299.

Mikulincer, M., Gillath, O., & Shaver, P. R. (2002). Activation of the attachment system in adulthood: Threat-related primes increase the accessibility of mental representations of attachment figures. *Journal of Personality and Social Psychology, 83,* 881–895.

Mikulincer, M., Hirschberger, G., Nachmias, O., & Gillath, O. (2001). The affective component of the secure base schema: Affective priming with representations of attachment security. *Journal of Personality and Social Psychology, 81,* 305–321.

Mikulincer, M., & Orbach, I. (1995). Attachment styles and repressive defensiveness: The accessibility and architecture of affective memories. *Journal of Personality and Social Psychology, 68,* 917–925.

Mikulincer, M., & Shaver, P. R. (2003). The attachment behavioral system in adulthood: Activation, psychodynamics, and interpersonal processes. In M. P. Zanna (Ed.), *Advances in Experimental Social Psychology* (Vol. 35, pp. 53–152). New York: Academic Press.

Mikulincer, M., & Shaver, P. R. (2004). Security-based self-representations in adulthood: Contents and processes. In W. S. Rholes & J. A. Simpson (Eds.), *Adult Attachment: Theory, Research, and Clinical Implications* (pp. 159–195). New York: Guilford Press.

Mikulincer, M., & Shaver, P. R. (2007a). *Attachment in Adulthood: Structure, Dynamics, and Change.* New York: Guilford Press.

Mikulincer, M., & Shaver, P. R. (2007b). Boosting attachment security to promote mental health, prosocial values, and inter-group tolerance. *Psychological Inquiry, 18,* 139–156.

Mikulincer, M., Shaver, P. R., & Avihou-Kanza, N. (2011). Individual differences in adult attachment are systematically related to dream narratives. *Attachment and Human Development, 13,* 105–123.

Mikulincer, M., Shaver, P. R., & Slav, K. (2006). Attachment, mental representations of others, and gratitude and forgiveness in romantic relationships. In M. Mikulincer & G. S. Goodman (Eds.), *Dynamics of Romantic Love: Attachment, Caregiving, and Sex* (pp. 190–215). New York: Guilford Press.

Park, L. E., Crocker, J., & Mickelson, K. D. (2004). Attachment styles and contingencies of self-worth. *Personality and Social Psychology Bulletin, 30,* 1243–1254.

Rom, E., & Mikulincer, M. (2003). Attachment theory and group processes: The association between attachment style and group-related representations, goals, memories, and functioning. *Journal of Personality and Social Psychology, 84*, 1220–1235.

Shaver, P. R., & Mikulincer, M. (2002). Attachment-related psychodynamics. *Attachment and Human Development, 4*, 133–161.

Shaver, P. R., & Mikulincer, M. (2007). Adult attachment theory and the regulation of emotion. In J. J. Gross (Ed.), *Handbook of Emotion Regulation* (pp. 446–465). New York: Guilford Press.

Shaver, P. R., Mikulincer, M., Lavy, S., & Cassidy, J. (2009). Understanding and altering hurt feelings: An attachment-theoretical perspective on the generation and regulation of emotions. In A. Vangelisti (Ed.), *Feeling Hurt in Close Relationships* (pp. 92–121). New York: Cambridge University Press.

Shaver, P. R., Schachner, D. A., & Mikulincer, M. (2005). Attachment style, excessive reassurance seeking, relationship processes, and depression. *Personality and Social Psychology Bulletin, 31*, 1–17.

Simpson, J. A., Rholes, W. S., & Phillips, D. (1996). Conflict in close relationships: An attachment perspective. *Journal of Personality and Social Psychology, 71*, 899–914.

Smith, E. R., Murphy, J., & Coats, S. (1999). Attachment to groups: Theory and management. *Journal of Personality and Social Psychology, 77*, 94–110.

Steger, M. F., Frazier, P., Oishi, S., & Kaler, M. (2006). The Meaning in Life Questionnaire: Assessing the presence of and search for meaning in life. *Journal of Counseling Psychology, 53*, 80–93.

Stillman, T. F., Baumeister, R. F., Lambert, N. M., Crescioni, A. W., DeWall, C. N., & Fincham, F. D. (2009). Alone and without purpose: Life loses meaning following social exclusion. *Journal of Experimental Social Psychology, 45*, 686–694.

Williams, K. D., & Jarvis, B. (2006). Cyberball: A program for use in research on interpersonal ostracism and acceptance. *Behavior Research Methods, 38*, 174–180.

PART 8

Combating Social Exclusion

Social Connection and Seeing Human

Adam Waytz

Abstract

Given that the motivation to affiliate with others is one of the most fundamental and important motivations, humans have developed a variety of strategies to cope with lack of affiliation following experiences of social exclusion. One strategy is anthropomorphism, whereby people create social connection by treating nonhumans as human-like agents capable of social support. This chapter reviews evidence that social exclusion increases the tendencies to anthropomorphize and to seek social connection with nonhumans. It also addresses three questions that follow from people's tendency to anthropomorphize as a means to attain social connection: (1) Is social connection with nonhumans effective? (2) Does connection with nonhumans diminish interest in connections with humans? (3) Could increases in social connection in fact increase dehumanization of other people? In attempting to answer these questions, this chapter provides avenues for future research on the relationship between social connection and *seeing human*.

Key Words: agency, anthropomorphism, dehumanization, mind perception, motivation, social exclusion,

Introduction

Imagination is undoubtedly one of humans' most valuable capacities. It enables a hungry person to conjure up the taste and scent of a delicious filet mignon, a bored child to envision a majestic fortress in a stack of couch cushions, or a frigid ice fisherman to visualize, and perhaps even feel, the warmth of a tropical island. Just as humans use their powers of imagination in attempts to remedy problems like hunger, boredom, and cold, so too do they use these powers to try to solve the problem of social exclusion. People are adept at creating social connection in nonhuman agents ranging from spiritual deities like God and the souls of ancestors, to technological gadgets like one's laptop or car, to one's pet dog or parakeet, to natural entities like trees and lakes.

This process of social substitution resembles how people fulfill other psychological motives through compensatory means. For example, people

need to feel good about themselves, and if their sense of integrity is threatened in a personally important domain (e.g., academic performance), they may restore their self-worth by affirming themselves in another personal domain (e.g., athletic performance; Steele, 1988). Similarly, people need to feel in control of their environment. When people experience a loss of personal control, they may attempt to regain a sense of mastery by seeking and upholding sources of external control like God, or the government (Kay, Gaucher, Napier, Callan, & Laurin, 2008). This compensatory means of attaining control operates similarly for people's motivation to attain existential meaning. When confronted with the psychological terror of death, people resolve this existential angst by striving for symbolic immortality or by bolstering their cultural worldview (Pyszczynski, Greenberg, & Solomon, 1999).

The flexibility and creativity that people display in attempts to satiate motivations for self-worth, control, and existential meaning, also emerges in their attempts to satisfy their desire for affiliation with others. When complete connection with others is lacking, people will seek pieces of social information and show a greater willingness to engage in social opportunities. For example, when people feel socially excluded, they will attend to the social and emotional cues of others (DeWall, Maner, & Rouby, 2009; Pickett, Gardner, & Knowles, 2004), express greater desire to work with others (Maner, DeWall, Baumeister, & Schaller, 2007; Williams & Sommer, 1997), and focus on symbolic reminders of loved ones such as mementos and photographs (Gardner, Pickett, & Knowles, 2005). All of these behaviors suggest that social disconnection increases attempts at substituting a novel source of connection for a recently lost one.

Attempts at social substitution extend to nonhumans as well. In the absence of human connection, people try to counteract feelings of social exclusion through anthropomorphism and seeking affiliation with nonhuman agents (Epley, Waytz, & Cacioppo, 2007). God, in particular, is one such agent that people seek when they feel socially disconnected. People high in loneliness or need to belong are more likely to seek a connection with God (Burris, Batson, Alstaedten, & Stephens, 1994; Maio & Gebauer, 2012; Rokach & Brock, 1998), and "singles" compared with people in committed relationships are more likely to perceive personal relationships with God (Granqvist & Hagekull, 2000). Experimental manipulations of social exclusion similarly increase religiosity (Aydin, Fischer, & Frey, 2010). In addition, people coping with the death of a close other often show an increase in spiritual belief (e.g., Glick, Weiss, Parks, 1974; McIntosh, Silver, & Wortman, 1993; Spilka, Hood, Gorsuch, 1985; Wuthnow, Christiano, Kuzlowski, 1980). These findings suggest that social deprivation—in this case the actual loss of a social affiliate—increases the pursuit of nonhuman sources of social affiliation. Of course, spiritual agents serve additional psychological functions such as providing control and meaning, but their capacity for social support likely also motivates people to turn to them after a social loss.

Like people who experience loneliness or the loss of a loved one, people with insecure interpersonal attachment styles who fear rejection and crave acceptance are particularly likely to form attachments with God compared with people who feel securely attached to their partners (Kirkpatrick & Shaver, 1990; Kirkpatrick, 1997, 1998). People who report an insecure attachment style in their interpersonal relationships also are more likely than securely attached people to report seeking and forming bonds with parasocial characters (Cole & Leets, 1999), fictional or real people who appear on television (see chapter 26, this volume). In another set of studies, people's self-reported loneliness correlated with the tendency to talk to themselves and to seek social support from watching television (Jonason, Webster, & Lindsey, 2008). Finally, loneliness correlates with the tendency to describe one's pets in terms of mental and socially supportive traits (Epley, Waytz, Akalis, Cacioppo, 2008) or to attribute mental states to technological gadgets (Epley, Akalis, Waytz, & Cacioppo, 2008) and to celestial bodies (Waytz, Cacioppo, Epley, 2007).

Experimental studies also demonstrate socially excluded people's proclivity to create social connection with nonhuman agents (Epley, Akalis et al., 2008). In one experiment, people who were led to anticipate a bleak social future marred by frequent exclusion and rejection, compared with people who were led to anticipate a future filled with social acceptance, expressed significantly higher belief in supernatural agents. Anticipating rejection from humans increased the tendency to affirm the existence of nonhuman supernatural agents.

In a second experiment, participants watched one of three separate video clips designed to induce different emotional experiences—fear, loneliness, or neutral feelings. Following this manipulation, participants again rated their belief in various supernatural agents and also selected three traits that best described a pet that they owned or one they knew well. People made to feel lonely reported significantly higher belief in supernatural agents than participants in the other two conditions *and* were more likely to describe their pets in mental and socially supportive traits (e.g. considerate, thoughtful, sympathetic) versus traits that were purely behavioral (e.g. active, lethargic) or traits that were mental, but not necessarily supportive (e.g. devious, creative). These results further suggest that the experience of social exclusion causes individual to seek connection with nonhuman agents through anthropomorphism. Given that this tendency was more pronounced for participants who experienced loneliness versus participants who experienced fear, these findings also suggest that social disconnection in particular, and not merely negative emotion, increases anthropomorphism.

Cross-sectional and experimental designs demonstrate that the experience of chronic loneliness, the experience of social loss in real life, or experimental manipulations of loneliness increase the tendency to humanize and pursue connection with nonhuman agents, exemplifying a demonstrable link between social exclusion and anthropomorphism. In doing so, this research also raises three interrelated questions: (Q1) Is anthropomorphism effective in satiating the motivation for social connection? (Q2) Does forming connections with nonhumans diminish people's desire to affiliate with humans? (Q3) Do increases in social connection—either with humans or nonhumans—increase dehumanization (just as decreases in social connection increase humanization)? What follows are attempts to provide answers to these questions.

Q1: Is Anthropomorphism Effective in Satiating the Motivation for Social Connection?

Harry Harlow (1958) famously demonstrated that infant monkeys who were isolated from their mothers were capable of forming connections surrogate "mothers" made from terrycloth and wires, clinging to these surrogates when frightened or distressed, and seeking comfort from them. Although the monkeys raised with surrogate mothers did not fare as well as monkeys raised with real mothers, monkeys raised with the terrycloth mothers grew up healthier and more well-adjusted than did monkeys raised without any source of affiliation. These findings suggest that social substitutes can provide some degree of meaningful affiliation. How much social substitution is effective for humans, and the degree to which anthropomorphism can satiate social connection still remains a matter of some debate.

Indeed a number of studies demonstrate that connection with a real, live, human being may not be the only way to achieve social connection. Indeed, recalling a positive social experience or experiencing nostalgia reduces loneliness and counteracts some of the consequences of social exclusion (Twenge, Zhang, Catanese, Dolan-Pascoe, Lyche, & Baumeister, 2007; Zhou, Sedikides, Wildschut, & Gao, 2008), suggesting that conjuring up the image of another person may be sufficient. In the realm of nonhuman connection, one set of studies demonstrated that turning to favored television programs buffered people against the threats of social rejection and reduced people's feelings of loneliness (Derrick, Gabriel, & Hugenberg, 2009). Other studies have shown that maintaining a pet as a human-like companion confers a variety of health and psychological benefits from improved cardiovascular functioning

to decreased anxiety (see McConnell, Brown, Shoda, Stayton, & Martin, 2011; Serpell, 2003). One study showed that animal assisted therapy for elderly residents of a nursing home also reduced loneliness (Banks & Banks, 2002). Another recent study with an elderly population found that providing seniors with an anthropomorphic robot dog even offered the same benefits to psychological well-being that an actual dog did (Banks, Willoughby, & Banks, 2008). Nursing home residents who interacted with a robotic seal called Paro, designed to provide companionship, also showed more positive mood and diminished stress (Wada, Shibata, Saito, & Tanie, 2004). Forming a relationship with God may benefit well-being as well. People who construe God as a partner or collaborator cope with stress and illness better than do people who do not construe God as a partner or collaborator (Pargament, 1997).

What remains unclear, however, is whether a relationship with a nonhuman entity is as socially satisfying as a relationship with another person. Nonhuman agents such as computers and avatars compare to real humans in their capacities for persuasion, ostracism, and social influence (Bailenson & Yee, 2005; Nass & Moon, 2000; Zadro, Williams, & Richardson, 2004), but it remains unknown whether they can provide social connection. Although connection with a nonhuman is better than no connection at all, there is no substitute for other people. Psychologist and loneliness expert, John Cacioppo, has noted that engaging in computer-mediated relationships to satisfy social connection is "like starving people eating celery. It's better than nothing, but there's no long-term sustenance" (Goldman, 2010). Indeed, one recent study showed an association between Internet use and increased loneliness (Stepanikova, Nie, & He, 2010).

Numerous factors likely moderate the effectiveness of nonhuman connections for satiating social needs. People's ability and willingness to anthropomorphize, for example, should influence how much nonhumans appear capable of support. For example, pets might function as satisfactory social companions for animal-lovers, but not for people who dislike animals and do not treat them as human-like. God may also boost feelings of connection for religious believers, but the presence of this spiritual agent likely does not affect atheists, who rarely consider the presence of a human-like God. In addition, nonhuman entities that more easily lend themselves to anthropomorphism are more likely to provide social connection. Compared to slugs, cats and dogs are far more morphologically similar to humans, are more readily anthropomorphizeable, and are likely to serve as better social companions. Future research may test how much these factors influence the effectiveness of anthropomorphism as satisfying means to attain social connection.

Q2: Does Affiliation with Nonhumans Diminish the Desire to Affiliate with Humans?

A second question that arises from people's tendency to anthropomorphize as a means to find social connection is whether people may come to *prefer* connection with nonhumans compared to humans. Because nonhuman entities such as pets are less evaluative and judgmental than humans, people may view them as favorable companions. One study demonstrated that when performing a difficult task, pet owners experienced less threat and reduced cardiovascular activity when accompanied by their pets than in the presence of their spouses (Allen, Blascovich, & Mendes, 2002). Following prolonged experiences of social exclusion, people may in fact find that connection with nonhumans is easier than connection with humans regardless of the actual benefits for physical and mental well-being. In support of this idea, people low in trust of others preferred simulated activities—interacting with media (watching a television show, seeing a movie, using the Internet)—compared with real social activities such as hanging out with friends (Green & Brock, 1998). A similar set of studies demonstrated that people felt simulated activities compared to real activities are less costly in terms of risks for rejection (Green & Brock, 2008). People particularly susceptible to rejection or people who are particularly distrustful of others may prefer the company of nonevaluative nonhuman agents compared with human ones. This is a question that awaits future research.

Q3: Do Increases in Social Connection Increase Dehumanization?

The need for social connection is similar to a fundamental drive state like thirst or hunger (Baumeister & Leary, 1995), and people can satiate sociality motivation like they can quench their thirst or satisfy their hunger. Increased feelings of intimacy in close relationships or belongingness in a group decreases the motivation to pursue new connections with others (Brewer, 1991 Reis, 1990). Being made to feel socially accepted also reduces performance on tasks related to forming new relationships (DeWall, Baumeister, & Vohs, 2008), suggesting that people become relatively less inclined to

seek social connection when this motivation is sated. Consistent with this reasoning, evolutionary theory suggests that there is a limited number of social relationships that people can maintain (Dunbar, 1992) and that when one reaches this limit, both the capacity and thus the desire to form new connections weakens. Considering others' interests, attitudes, feelings, and preferences are critical for connecting with them. Diminishing the motivation to connect with others may diminish the motivation to recognize, think about, or consider others' mental states as well.

Some evidence supports the idea that social connection increases dehumanization. First, the clearest examples of dehumanization arise in intergroup settings in which in-group members dehumanize out-group members (Goff, Eberhardt, Williams, & Jackson, 2006; Leyens et al., 2003). Second, research has identified other features of the collective that increase antisocial behavior, providing support for philosopher Reinhold Niebuhr's (1934, p. 35) observation that "the proportion of reason to impulse becomes increasingly negative when we proceed from the life of individuals to that of social groups." The sense of deindividuation one feels when surrounded by others can increase aggression (Zimbardo, 1969). The diffusion of responsibility that increases in the presence of a group likewise diminishes sensitivity to the suffering of others (Bandura, Underwood, & Fromson, 1975; Darley & Latané, 1968). Groups that are especially cohesive and homogeneous in nature tend to prevent people from expressing dissenting opinions in favor endorsing immoral action that they would not endorse in private (Janis, 1972). Third, many of history's most severe acts of violence have been committed by the most highly affiliated groups (Cohen, Montoya, & Insko, 2006), with evidence that in-group altruism and out-group hostility evolved jointly (Choi & Bowles, 2007).

My colleagues and I have also begun directly testing the hypothesis that social connection increases dehumanization (Waytz & Epley, 2012). In a series of studies, we manipulated social connection by having people write about someone with whom they feel closely connected (versus a stranger) or completing the study materials in the room with a close friend (versus a stranger). People who wrote about someone close to them or who completed the study in the company of a friend (compared to participants in comparable control groups) denied more basic mental states (e.g. pain, complex thought) and expressed more willingness to describe others as unfeeling savages. In one study, the experience of social connection increased participants' endorsement of harm toward a dehumanized group—terrorists responsible for the September 11, 2001 attacks on the United States. These findings suggest that although social connection is undoubtedly beneficial for one's *own* physical and mental well-being, social connection may have negative consequences for people outside one's immediate social circle.

Conclusions

The relationship between social connection and anthropomorphism suggests that social connection and the tendency to *see human* are inversely related. This relationship provides insight to how people attempt to solve the problem of social exclusion, and also speaks to the profundity of the need to belong. In the absence of actual human connection, people will attempt to make do with just about anything as a social substitute.

As technology advances, the possibilities for the development of sophisticated nonhuman social substitutes will be limitless. Already devices exist such as the "boyfriend pillow" (a pillow in the shape of a man's arm providing a hug) or "Huggy Pajamas" (pajamas that enable an individual to "send" a hug to another person from a remote distance by hugging an interface). Personalized humanoid robots that operate in service of providing social support are developing rapidly as well, and now hold capacities for social interaction, emotional responsiveness, and even sex. Such advancements speak to the power of human imagination and ingenuity in attempts to remedy the problem of social exclusion. However, future research will determine how effective anthropomorphism is as a solution to the problem of social exclusion, and whether there can ever be anything as good as the real thing.

References

Allen, K. M., Blascovich, J., & Mendes, W. B. (2002) Cardiovascular reactivity and the presence of pets, friends, and spouses: the truth about cats and dogs. *Psychosomatic Medicine, 64*, 727–739.

Aydin, N., Fischer, P., & Frey, D. (2010). Turning to God in the face of ostracism: Effects of social exclusion on religiousness. *Personality and Social Psychology Bulletin, 36*, 742–753.

Bailenson, J. N., & Yee, N. (2005). Digital Chameleons: Automatic assimilation of nonverbal gestures in immersive virtual environments. *Psychological Science, 16*, 814–819.

Bandura, A., Underwood, B., & Fromson, M. E. (1975). Disinhibition of aggression through diffusion of responsibility and dehumanization of victims. *Journal of Research in Personality, 9*, 253–269.

Banks, M. R., and Banks, W. A. (2002). The effects of animal-assisted therapy on loneliness in an elderly population in long-term care facilities. *The Journals of Gerontology Series A: Biological Sciences and Medical Sciences, 57*, 428–432.

Banks, M. R., Willoughby, L. M., & Banks, W. A. (2008). Animal–assisted therapy and loneliness in nursing homes: Use of robotic versus living dogs. *Journal of the American Medical Directors Association, 9*, 173–177.

Baumeister, R.F., & Leary, M.R. (1995). The need to belong: Desire for interpersonal attachments as a fundamental human motivation. *Psychological Bulletin, 117*, 497–529.

Brewer, M. B., (1991). The social self: On being the same and different at the same time. *Personality and Social Psychology Bulletin, 17*, 475–482.

Burris, C. T., Batson, C. D., Altstaedten, M., & Stephens, S. K. (1994). What a friend: Loneliness as a motivator of intrinsic religion. *Journal for the Scientific Study of Religion, 33*, 326–334.

Choi, J-K., & Bowles, S. (2007). The coevolution of parochial altruism and war. *Science, 318*, 636–640

Cohen, T. R., Montoya, R. M., & Insko, C. A. (2006). Group morality and intergroup relations: Cross-cultural and experimental evidence. *Personality and Social Psychology Bulletin, 32*, 1559–1572.

Cole, T., & Leets, L. (1999). Attachment styles and intimate television viewing. Insecurely forming relationships in a parasocial way. *Journal of Social and Personal Relationships, 16*, 495–511.

Darley, J. M., & Latané, B. (1968). Bystander intervention in emergencies: Diffusion of responsibility. *Journal of Personality and Social Psychology, 8*, 377–383.

Derrick, J. L., Gabriel, S., & Hugenberg, K. J. (2009). Social surrogacy: How favored television programs provide the experience of belonging. *Journal of Experimental Social Psychology, 45*, 352–362.

DeWall, C. N., Baumeister, R. F., & Vohs, K. D. (2008). Satiated with belongingness? Effects of acceptance, rejection, and task framing on self-regulatory performance. *Journal of Personality and Social Psychology, 95*, 1367–1382.

DeWall, C. N., Maner, J. K., & Rouby, D. A. (2009). Social exclusion and early-stage interpersonal perception: Selective attention to signs of acceptance. *Journal of Personality and Social Psychology, 96*, 729–741.

Dunbar, R. (1992). Coevolution of neocortex size, group size and language in humans. *Behavioral and Brain Sciences, 16*, 681–735.

Epley, N., Akalis, S., Waytz, A., & Cacioppo, J. T. (2008). Creating social connection through inferential reproduction: Loneliness and perceived agency in gadgets, gods, and greyhounds. *Psychological Science, 19*, 114–120.

Epley, N., Waytz, A., Akalis, S., & Cacioppo, J. T. (2008). When I need a human: Motivational determinants of anthropomorphism. *Social Cognition, 26*, 143–155.

Epley, N., Waytz, A., & Cacioppo, J. T. (2007). On seeing human: A three-factor theory of anthropomorphism. *Psychological Review, 114*, 864–886.

Gardner, W.L., & Pickett, C.L., & Knowles, M.L. (2005). Social "snacking" and social "shielding": The satisfaction of belonging needs through the use of social symbols and the social self. In K. Williams, J. Forgas, and W. von Hippel (Eds.), *The Social Outcast: Ostracism, Social Exclusion, Rejection, and Bullying* (pp. 227–242). New York: Psychology Press.

Glick, I. D., Weiss, R. S., & Parkes, C. M. (1974). *The First Year of Bereavement*. New York: John Wiley.

Goff, P. A., Eberhardt, J. L., Williams, M., & Jackson, M. C. (2008). Not yet human: Implicit knowledge, historical dehumanization, and contemporary consequences. *Journal of Personality and Social Psychology, 94*, 292–306.

Goldman, A. (2010). Look at all the lonely people [Electronic version]. *Las Vegas Weekly*. Retrieved March 31, 2010, from http://www.lasvegasweekly.com/news/2010/mar/04/look-all-lonely-people/

Granqvist, P., & Hagekull, B. (2000). Religiosity, adult attachment, and why "singles" are more religious. *International Journal for the Psychology of Religion, 10*, 111–123.

Green, M. C., & Brock, T. C. (1998). Trust, mood, and outcomes of friendship predict preferences for real versus ersatz social capital. *Political Psychology, 19*, 527–544.

Green, M. C., and Brock T. C. (2008). Antecedents and civic consequences of choosing real versus ersatz social activities. *Media Psychology, 11*, 5676–592.

Harlow, H. (1958). The nature of love. *American Psychologist, 13*, 573–685.

Janis, I. (1972). *Victims of Groupthink*. Boston, MA: Houghton-Mifflin.

Jonason, P. K., Webster, G. D., & Lindsey. A. E. (2008). Solutions to the problem of diminished social interaction. *Evolutionary Psychology, 6*, 637–651.

Kay, A. C., Gaucher, D., Napier, J. L., Callan, M. J., & Laurin, K. (2008). God and the Government: Testing a compensatory control mechanism for the support of external systems. *Journal of Personality and Social Psychology, 95*, 18–35.

Kirkpatrick, L. A. (1997). A longitudinal study of changes in religious belief and behavior as a function of individual differences in adult attachment style. *Journal for the Scientific Study of Religion, 36*, 207–217.

Kirkpatrick, L. A. (1998). God as a substitute attachment figure: A longitudinal study of adult attachment style and religious change in college students. *Personality and Social Psychology Bulletin, 24*(9), 961–973.

Kirkpatrick, L. A., & Shaver, P. R. (1990). Attachment theory and religion: Childhood attachments, religious beliefs, and conversion. *Journal for the Scientific Study of Religion, 29*(3), 315–334.

Knowles, M. (2013). Belonging regulation through the use of (para) social surrogates. In C. N. Dewall (Ed.), *The Oxford Handbook of Social Exclusion*. New York: Oxford University Press.

Leyens, J. Ph ., Cortes, B. P., Demoulin, S., Dovidio, J. F., Fiske, S. T., Gaunt, R., et al., (2003). Emotional prejudice, essentialism, and nationalism. *European Journal of Social Psychology, 33*, 704–717.

Gebauer, J. E., & Maio, G. R. (2012). The need to belong can motivate belief in God. *Journal of Personality, 80*, 465–501.

Maner, J. K., DeWall, C. N., Baumeister, R. F., & Schaller, M. (2007). Does social exclusion motivate interpersonal reconnection? Resolving the "porcupine problem." *Journal of Personality and Social Psychology, 92*, 42–55.

McConnell, A. R., Brown, C. M., Shoda, T. M., Stayton, L. E., & Martin, C. E. (2011) Friends with benefits: On the positive consequences of pet ownership. *Journal of Personality and Social Psychology, 101*, 1239–1252.

McIntosh, D. N., Silver, R. C., & Wortman, C. B. (1993). Religion's role in adjustment to a negative life event: Coping with the loss of a child. *Journal of Personality & Social Psychology, 65*, 812–821.

Nass, C., & Moon, Y. (2000). Machines and mindlessness: Social responses to computers. *Journal of Social Issues, 56*, 81–103.

Niebuhr, R. (1934). *Moral Man and Immoral Society*. New York: Charles Scribner's Sons.

Pargament, K. (1997). *The Psychology of Religious Coping*. New York: Guilford.

Pickett, C. L., Gardner, W. L., & Knowles, M. (2004). Getting a cue: The need to belong and enhanced sensitivity to social cues. *Personality and Social Psychology Bulletin, 30*, 1095–1107.

Pyszczynski, T. ; Greenberg, J., & Solomon, S. (1999). A dual process model of defense against conscious and unconscious death-related thoughts: An extension of terror management theory. *Psychological Review, 106*, 835–845.

Reis, H. T. (1990). The role of intimacy in interpersonal relationships. *Journal of Social and Clinical Psychology, 9*, 15–30.

Rokach, A., & Brock, H. (1998). Coping with loneliness. *Journal of Psychology: Interdisciplinary and Applied, 192*(1), 107–127.

Serpell, J. A. (2003). Anthropomorphism and anthropomorphic selection—beyond the "cute response." *Society & Animals, 11*, 83–100.

Spilka, B., Hood, R., and Gorsuch, R. (1985). *The psychology of Religion: An Empirical Approach*. Englewood Cliffs, NJ: Prentice-Hall.

Steele, C.M. (1988). The psychology of self affirmation: Sustaining the integrity of the self. In L. Berkowitz (Ed.), *Advances in Experimental Social Psychology, 21*, 261–301.

Stepanikova, I., Nie, N., & He, X. (2010). Time on the Internet at home, loneliness, and life satisfaction: Evidence from panel time-diary data. *Computers in Human Behavior, 26*, 329–338.

Twenge, J. M., Zhang, L., Catanese, K. R., Dolan-Pascoe, B., Lyche, L. F., & Baumeister, R. F. (2007). Replenishing connectedness: Reminders of social activity reduce aggression after social exclusion. *British Journal of Social Psychology, 46*, 205–224.

Wada, K., Shibata, T., Saito, T., & Tanie, K. (2004). Effects of robot assisted activity for elderly people and nurses at a day service center. *Proceedings of the IEEE, 92*, 1780–1788.

Waytz, A., Cacioppo, J. T., & Epley, N. (2007). [Loneliness and anthropomorphism]. Unpublished raw data.

Waytz, A., & Epley, N. (2012). Social connection enables dehumanization. *Journal of Experimental Social Psychology, 48*, 70–76.

Williams, K.D, & Sommer, K.L. (1997). Social ostracism by coworkers: Does rejection lead to loafing or compensation? *Personality and Social Psychology Bulletin, 23*, 693–706.

Wuthnow, R., Christiano, K., and Kuzlowski, J. (1980). Religion and bereavement. A conceptual framework. *Journal for the Scientific Study of Religion,19*, 408–430.

Zadro, L., Williams, K. D., & Richardson, R. (2004). How low can you go? Ostracism by a computer lowers belonging, control, self-esteem, and meaningful existence. *Journal of Experimental Social Psychology, 40*, 560–567.

Zhou, X., Sedikides, C., Wildschut, T., & Gao, D-G. (2008). Counteracting loneliness: On the restorative function of nostalgia. *Psychological Science, 19*, 1023–1029.

Zimbardo, P. G. (1969). The human choice: Individuation, reason, and order vs. deindividuation, impulse and chaos. In W. J. Arnold & D. Levine (Eds.), *Nebraska Symposium on Motivation* (Vol. 17, pp. 237–307). Lincoln, NE: University of Nebraska Press.

Attentional Retraining for Anxiety

Norman B. Schmidt

Abstract

Cognitive models of psychopathology, particularly disorders involving anxiety symptoms, emphasize information processing biases in their development and maintenance. Research has consistently shown that anxious individuals (including patients with anxiety disorders) show an attentional bias in favor of threat cues (i.e., a threat bias). For example, patients with social anxiety disorder may show an attentional bias relating to signs of social rejection such as toward angry or disapproving faces. Recent evidence suggests that it is possible to modify patterns of attention allocation to threat and the resulting changes alter affective responses to stress. This chapter reviews the literature supporting the view that it is possible to modify attentional bias to threat cues, and such attentional "retraining" procedures may offer novel, efficacious treatments for those suffering from anxiety psychopathology.

Key Words: anxiety, attention, cognitive bias, information processing, treatment

Introduction

During the past 30 years, cognitive models of psychopathology, particularly disorders involving anxiety and mood symptoms have emphasized the role that information processing anomalies may play in the development and maintenance of these conditions (Beck & Clark, 1997; Mogg & Bradley, 1998; Wells & Matthews, 1994; Williams, Watts, MacLeod, & Mathews, 1997). Research relevant to these models indicates that anxious and depressed individuals may show various types of attentional, interpretive, and/or memory bias (cf., Mathews & MacLeod, 2005). Very recently, research in this area has led to the development of novel, information-processing approaches, sometimes referred to as cognitive bias modification, that offer a completely new avenue for treatment of psychopathology. In this chapter, my intent is to focus on what appears to be the best established research domain within the cognitive bias modification: so-called attentional retraining, that has been applied to the anxiety disorders. More specifically, this chapter will illustrate how cognitive bias modification may be relevant to our understanding of social exclusion as that relates to one particular anxiety condition, social anxiety disorder.

Background

Anxiety-related psychopathology represents one of the most prevalent and debilitating forms of mental illness (Kessler, Berglund, et al., 2005). Extrapolating from epidemiological studies, it may be conservatively estimated that 25% of the population will suffer from clinically significant anxiety at some point in their lives, with a 12-month prevalence rate of approximately 18% (Kessler, Chiu, Demler, Merikangas, & Walters, 2005). When untreated, anxiety disorders generally maintain a chronic course (Pine, Cohen, Gurley, Brook, &

Ma, 1998) and result in substantial impairment across the lifespan (Ferdinand, van der Reijden, Verhulst, Nienhuis, & Giel, 1995). In addition to the immense personal suffering created by clinically significant anxiety syndromes, these disorders create a considerable public expense that includes treatment costs, lost work time, and mortality (Greenberg et al., 1999). Anxiety psychopathology is also associated with increased utilization of nonpsychiatric medical services (Greenberg et al., 1999), further amplifying the associated public health burden.

Despite the high prevalence and impairment created by anxiety psychopathology, the evolution in psychological and pharmacological treatments has made tremendous strides in the past few decades. Fortunately, efficacious treatments for anxiety are available including several types of pharmacotherapy as well as cognitive behavioral therapy (CBT) (Schmidt, Koselka, & Woolaway-Bickel, 2001). Antidepressants such as monoamine oxidase inhibitors, tricyclic antidepressants, and selective serotonin reuptake inhibitors (SSRIs) are among the psychotropic medications that have demonstrated the highest levels of efficacy in the treatment of anxiety disorders (see Sammons & Schmidt, 2001, for a review).

Although existing treatments benefit many individuals with anxiety psychopathology, there is substantial room for improvement. For example, CBT is often beneficial, but it is not equally effective for all individuals (Schmidt & Keough, 2010). Medication is an alternative treatment to CBT, but it has other limitations including a generally lower overall response rate relative to CBT when treatment dropout and long-term response are considered (Hofmann et al 2009).

Cognitive behavioral therapy protocols do not produce remission for all and, disturbingly, these rates do not appear to be improving over time (Ost 2008). Therefore, it is critical that we continue to innovate our treatments for anxiety. In this area, we generally have not seen very significant strides. In the area of optimizing treatment efficacy, it is worth highlighting that many studies in this area have focused on the use of various combinations of pharmacotherapy and CBT. This research focus has intuitive appeal, given that some of the more common forms of pharmacotherapy (i.e., SSRIs and increasingly the serotonin-norepinephrine reuptake inhibitors [SNRIs]) and CBT have demonstrated efficacy as well as presumed different mechanisms of action. Unfortunately, reviews of various combinations of medications and CBT have generally suggested that despite some short-term advantage of combined treatment (Hofmann Sawyer, Korte, & Smits, 2009), there does not appear to be long-term facilitation effects, and the combination of CBT plus benzodiazepines may have deleterious effects (Schmidt et al. 2001). Therefore, new approaches to treatment or new adjuncts to extant treatments are needed if we wish to help nonresponders. Alternative forms of treatment that target durable diatheses for the disorder may (1) provide improved efficiency relative to existing treatments or (2) in combination with CBT, they may increase the efficacy of extant treatments and the percentage of patients who return to relatively asymptomatic functioning subsequent to treatment.

In sum, anxiety and its disorders are common and often debilitating with high costs to both the individual and society. Thus, there is a clear need to develop highly effective and efficient treatments for these conditions. In this regard, cognitive bias modification offers a clear opportunity to expand treatment methods in novel areas to help address this pressing public health issue.

Cognitive Models of Anxiety

As I have noted, the overwhelming majority of psychological research on anxiety is derived from cognitive models describing these conditions. A good case example would be to examine one of the anxiety disorders, referred to as Generalized Anxiety Disorder (GAD). The defining feature of GAD is excessive, chronic, and uncontrollable worry (APA, 2000). This worry takes the form of catastrophic predictions about low-probability negative events (Borkovec, Shadick, & Hopkins, 1991) that are readily accessible in individuals with GAD. Although hypervigilance for threat-relevant cues is one explanation for worry (e.g., MacLeod, Mathews, & Tata, 1986; Mathews, 1990), contemporary cognitive models of GAD highlight at least three other factors that may be involved in persistent pathological worry. These include: intolerance of uncertainty (Dugas, Gagnon, Ladouceur, & Freeston, 1998), avoidance of unpleasant internal experiences (e.g., thoughts, images, emotions; Borkovec & Roemer, 1995), and negative metacognitive beliefs about the consequences of worry (e.g., Wells, 1999). According to these theories, attention is readily captured by a wide range of external and internal stimuli in GAD.

Recent accounts of the impact of anxiety on cognitive processing highlights a possible unifying explanation for these theoretical positions and relevant empirical findings. Namely, anxious individuals may exhibit a deficit in *attention control* resulting from undue influence of the stimulus-driven (bottom-up) attention system at the expense of the goal-directed (top-down) attention system (Eysenck, 1997). This idea is based on a growing body of research suggesting that anxiety impairs cognitive processing efficiency because it reduces attention control. That is, anxiety interferes with central executive function through: (a) inhibition of automatic responses in relation to threat-relevant distracters, and (b) shifting between task-relevant and task-irrelevant stimuli related to threat (see Eysenck, 2007 for a review). For example, using a rapid serial visual presentation task, Most, Scholl, Clifford, and Simons (2005) found that providing participants with specific knowledge about a target stimuli's features (i.e., top-down attention control) aided participants in focusing attention and ignoring irrelevant negative stimuli, but only for participants low in harm avoidance (a trait associated with anxiety). In contrast, participants high in harm avoidance did not benefit from this additional information, suggesting that they were not able to recruit the top-down attention systems in the context of emotional distracters.

Reduced flexibility in attention suggests less attention control is associated with reduced autonomic variability, a characteristic of individuals with anxiety disorders (Thayer, Friedman, Borkovec, Johnsen, & Molina, 2000). Finally, anxious individuals may employ compensatory strategies when their processing becomes inefficient (Eysenck et al., 1997) by searching for more evidence before responding to task demands, a behavioral tendency characteristic of people with GAD (e.g., Tallis, Eysenck, & Mathews, 1991). These findings support the role of basic attentional control deficits in GAD, and similar arguments can be made for the other anxiety disorders. Moreover, there is some indication that attention bias toward threat is proximal to the basic genetic predisposition for anxiety. For example, the short allele in a variable repeat sequence of the promoter region of the serotonin transporter gene (5-HTTLPR) is correlated with stronger activation in brain regions involved in processing emotional stimuli. Compared with participants with two long alleles, carriers of the short 5-HTTLPR allele exhibit a stronger attention bias for threat-relevant information, but they do not exhibit a stronger attention bias for depression related words (Beevers, et al., 2007).

In sum, the perception of threat in GAD is diffuse and results in increased likelihood that attention in these patients is captured by a wide array of potentially threatening stimuli. Furthermore, people with GAD are relatively ineffective at controlling their worries. This may be the consequence of deficits in attentional control resulting from excessive influence of the stimulus-driven attention system in the presence of potential threat and correlated with genes involved with anxiety. Therefore, attention control may be particularly important when developing new treatments for GAD because attention selectively facilitates the early processing of threat, thereby influencing subsequent cognitive, behavioral, and emotional processes related to worry (e.g,. Mathews, 1990; Wells & Matthews, 1994). To the extent that anxiety and worry interfere with central executive functioning via deficits in attention control, individuals with GAD are likely to display impairments in disengaging their attention from threat, accessing sources of nonthreat.

Possible candidate treatments for intervention in anxiety psychopathology are likely to emerge from basic experimental psychopathology research. For example, as McNally (2007) has pointed out, few would argue that animal learning research did *not* have a major impact on the beginnings of behavior therapy. However, the learning perspective became "cognitive" decades ago as it incorporated inferences about underlying information processing mechanisms. No such "evolution" occurred in clinical application of learning theory. Indeed, as Reiss (1980) noted long ago, our behavioral interventions are based on models that were outdated when they were first used.

How do we begin to establish a link between basic research and treatment? The treatment would have to rely on findings in basic research that have identified mechanisms thought to be involved in the maintenance of anxiety. Such mechanisms would ideally have the following four characteristics. *First*, they should evolve from reliable findings in the experimental psychopathology literature. *Second*, the purported mechanism underlying anxiety symptoms should be normalized after treatment. *Third*, the mechanism should predict anxiety symptoms in longitudinal studies. *Fourth*, modification of the mechanism should lead to changes in anxiety symptoms. There are very few mechanisms that satisfy all the above requirements. Indeed, I propose that attention bias to threat-relevant information comes closest to meeting these criteria. In the following sections I will present preliminary evidence for each of the above criteria.

Is There an Attention Bias to Threat in Anxiety Psychopathology?

Researchers have used a wide range of methods borrowed from cognitive psychology to examine attention bias to threat. These include the dichotic listening paradigm (Mathews & MacLeod, 1986), modified Stroop color-naming tasks (Mathews & MacLeod, 1985), the probe detection task (MacLeod, Mathews, & Tata, 1986), and continuous eye-tracking methods (Mogg, Millar, & Bradley, 2000). In general, research using these methods has consistently produced evidence that patients with anxiety preferentially attend to threat stimuli over neutral stimuli when the two compete for processing priority.

Two recent reviews provide clear evidence for the role of attention bias in anxiety. Mogg and Bradley (2005) reviewed 10 studies using the probe detection task and concluded that individuals with anxiety show an attention bias for threat that is absent in nonanxious controls. A meta-analysis conducted by Bar-Haim, et al., (2007) examined attention bias across 172 studies (N = 2263 anxious, N = 1768 nonanxious) and concluded that this bias is a consistent and reliable finding across a variety of paradigms. In summary, there is reason to believe that patients with anxiety psychopathology have an attention bias to threat relevant information that is not present in nonanxious individuals. If so, then an intervention designed to change attention bias may be useful in treating these conditions.

Does Attention Bias to Threat Normalize after Successful Treatment?

Although the previous summary suggests that attention bias to threat-relevant information may be a relevant mechanism in the genesis or maintenance of anxiety, it is not clear whether this role is causal or simply correlational. Cross-sectional group comparisons are at best helpful in identifying potential mechanisms for study. Once such mechanisms have been identified, other designs (e.g., experimental, prospective) need to be utilized to gather evidence regarding the causal role of attention bias to threat in the maintenance of the disorder.

Indirect evidence for the causal role of attention bias to threat in anxiety disorders can be gleaned from treatment outcome studies. That is, if attention bias to threat is a necessary condition for anxiety, then amelioration of the disorder should be associated with a reduction of attention bias to threat. Empirical investigations of this question have generally supported this hypothesis. For example,

Mathews, Mogg, Kentish, and Eysenck (1995) examined the impact of anxiety-management training on attention bias in GAD patients. Relative to nonclinical controls, individuals with GAD showed an attention bias toward threat cues before treatment. However, following the anxiety-reducing treatment, the GAD group showed a significant decline in this bias, which was maintained 3-months after treatment. Moreover, the magnitude of attention bias to threat in these "recovered" individuals no longer differed significantly from that observed in non-anxious controls. Mogg, Bradley, Millar, and White (1995) replicated and extended these findings by showing that successful treatment again normalized attentional bias. Moreover, reduction in anxious thoughts experienced by patients subsequent to treatment was substantially correlated (r = .77) with reduction in attention bias to threat-relevant stimuli, suggesting that treatment gains may be mediated by change in attention.

In summary, there is evidence that successful treatment for anxiety may lead to a normalization of attention bias for threat. This finding is consistent with the view that attention bias to threat-relevant information plays a role in the maintenance of anxiety problems. However, it is difficult to draw inferences regarding the causal role of attention bias to threat-relevant information in anxiety psychopathology. This is because alternative explanations can account for the obtained results. For example, this bias for threat could also be normalized if it were a consequence rather than a cause of anxiety. Additionally, treatment may impact some underlying factor that causes both the threat bias and anxiety. One way to resolve this ambiguity is to determine if threat bias predicts negative affective responses to stress above and beyond measures of trait anxiety.

Does Attention Bias to Threat Predict Anxiety Response?

More direct evidence for the causal role of attention bias to threat in anxiety comes from prospective studies. For example, MacLeod and Hagan (1992) administered a measure of attention bias (Stroop color naming task of threat words) to women scheduled to undergo a cervical examination. The researchers also administered various self-report measures of psychopathology. Eight weeks later, they interviewed a subset of women whose tests indicated cervical pathology and who underwent surgery. The measure of attention bias to threat, collected 8 weeks earlier, was a significant predictor of anxiety and dysphoria as a result of learning their test results. Two particular aspects of this relationship were noteworthy. First, attention bias to threat was a stronger predictor of negative response to stress than self-report measures of distress. Second, the relationship between attention bias to threat and later response was significant even after the baseline levels of anxiety were partialled out. In a follow-up study, van den Hout, Tenney, Huygens, Merckelbach, and Kindt (1995) found that the same measure of attention bias for threat words was the strongest predictor of the intensity of participants' negative affect in response to naturally occurring life stressors.

In summary, there is evidence for the predictive value of attention bias for threat over and above self-report data in determining response to negative life events and stressors. However, because of the naturalistic nature of these designs, it is not possible to rule out alternative explanations (e.g., maturity effect) in these studies. Conclusions regarding the causal role of attention bias in determining response to stress can only be drawn from experimental studies in which subjects are randomly assigned to conditions. We now turn to this source of evidence.

Does the Modification of Attention Bias to Threat Lead to Change in Anxiety Response?

Groundbreaking research by MacLeod, Rutherford, Campbell, Ebsworthy, and Holker (2002) suggests it may be possible to eliminate the attentional bias directly through a process of attentional retraining and thereby test this causal view directly. Macleod et al. (2002) conducted two studies, both of which found that experimental modification of attention allocation patterns with regard to threat cues produced expected changes in the intensity of participants' negative affective responses to an experimental stressor. Specifically, these authors selected subjects who were neither high nor low in trait anxiety and thus were expected to show neither a pattern of heightened nor reduced attention to threat cues. These subjects were randomly assigned to be trained either to increase or reduce attention to threat words relative to neutral words.

The training procedure used by MacLeod et al. (2002) closely resembled the typical visual attention task used in past studies of the attentional bias for threat cues. In this task, each trial consists of the presentation of two words on a computer monitor, one above the other, such that they compete for attention. On critical trials, one word is threat-relevant and the other is neutral in content.

The words appear for a brief interval and, subsequent to their disappearance, one of the words is replaced by one of two visual probes. Subjects are instructed to press one of two buttons to indicate which type of probe appeared. However, whereas probes follow threat-relevant and neutral words with equal frequency (i.e., there is no contingency between probes and either type of word) in the typical version of this task, Macleod et al.'s training tasks built in a strong contingency between probes and either neutral words (i.e., the "Attend Neutral" condition in which the location of the neutral word signals the location of the probe on most trials) or threat-relevant words (i.e., the "Attend Threat" condition in which threat words signal the position of the probe on most trials). In both studies, the two training conditions produced the intended attentional biases for supraliminally-presented stimuli.

Several minutes subsequent to attentional training, subjects completed an impossible anagram task, which was presented as a test of intelligence and thus served as an experimental stressor. In both studies, consistent with predictions, subjects in the Attend Threat condition reported significantly more negative affect in response to the anagram task than did those in the Attend Neutral condition. Thus, these studies provide the strongest initial support for the hypothesis that individual differences in the allocation of attention to threat cues are causally related to differences in vulnerability to heightened negative affect in response to stress.

Based on their findings, MacLeod et al. (2002) suggested that it may be possible to utilize such attentional training procedures to treat anxiety and related problems. However, changing biases in highly anxious individuals is likely to be considerably more difficult than changing patterns of attention in normal individuals. Indeed, MacLeod et al. suggest that their single session training procedure may produce only fairly transient changes in patterns of attention allocation for threat cues. In contrast to the subjects in MacLeod et al.'s study, who were unlikely to have a pre-existing threat bias, anxious individuals are likely to have a pre-existing bias. With anxious individuals, it is likely to require substantially more training sessions than the single session used by MacLeod and colleagues. Furthermore, the biases trained by MacLeod and colleagues produced their effects over a fairly brief time interval but their durability over longer intervals is unclear. Also, although MacLeod et al. showed that changes in attention allocation led to changes in negative affective response to a contrived laboratory stressor as measured by visual analog scale ratings, it remains unclear whether such attentional retraining can produce changes on clinical indicators of anxiety symptoms in daily life.

After a bit of a lull in published research in this area, there has been a flurry of recent studies For example, in the most recent work from the Australian group, the authors addressed whether attentional bias manipulation contributed to anxiety vulnerability in response to naturalistic stressful events (See, MacLeod, & Bridle, 2009). In this study, a home-based attentional training program was used to experimentally manipulate biased attentional response to emotionally negative stimuli. Findings suggested that this attentional manipulation served to reduce trait anxiety scores and to attenuate state anxiety responses to subsequent naturalistic stressors.

The application of these procedures to clinical samples emerged in 2009 in three studies. In the first attention retraining paradigm to be used with a clinical sample, Hazen, Vasey, & Schmidt (2009) tested the efficacy of five sessions of retraining, compared with sham training, on 24 adult participants with high levels of pathological worry. Approximately 40% of the sample met DSM criteria for GAD, with another 20% showing subclinical GAD symptoms. In this study, the intervention sessions were approximately 20 minutes in length, and the interval between sessions was approximately 6 days.

The treatment group completed the retraining procedure, which was designed to train a pattern of reduced attention to threat cues. Because MacLeod et al. (2002) did not show any effect of training on preattentive threat bias, subliminal training trials were not included in this procedure. The words used in this procedure were identical to those used by MacLeod et al. (2002). The task was similar to a typical probe discrimination task with the critical difference that probes followed the neutral word on nearly all trials. The procedure consisted of 216 trials in each session, all of which included one threat and one neutral word matched for length and word frequency.

On 204 (94.4%) of these trials, the probes appeared in the position of the neutral word. By virtue of the fact that the position of the probe was predicted by the position of the neutral word in most trials, it was expected that participants would learn to ignore the threat words and focus on the neutral words. The placebo group completed a procedure, which was identical to the treatment procedure except that probes appeared with equal frequency in the position of threat-relevant and neutral words. Findings were consistent with predictions in suggesting that, compared to the placebo group, the active retraining program produced significant reductions in both attention bias to threat and symptoms among this group of individuals with elevated worry symptoms.

Amir, Beard, Burns, & Bomyea (2009) tested the hypothesis that an 8-session attention modification program, similar to that described in Hazen et al. (2009), would change symptoms among a true clinical sample. In this study, participants included 27 treatment seeking patients diagnosed with GAD. Participants completed a probe detection task by identifying letters (E or F) replacing one member of a pair of words. Similar to previous work, the authors trained attention by including a contingency between the location of the probe and the nonthreat word in the active treatment group and not in the other (control condition). Once again, similar to Hazen et al. (2009), participants in the treatment group showed a decrease in attention bias to threat as well as a decrease in anxiety, as indicated by both self-report and interviewer measures. However, the control condition did not show change on attention bias to threat or symptoms.

One limitation of both the Hazen et al. (2009) and Amir et al. (2009) trials is that they failed to include a follow-up assessment to gauge whether the significant changes in anxiety persisted beyond the posttreatment evaluation. Moreover, these trials focused on GAD, so it is unclear whether these procedures may affect other anxiety conditions. A report by Schmidt, Richey, Buckner, and Timpano (2009) addresses both of these limitations.

In this study, patients ($N = 36$) with the generalized form of Social Anxiety Disorder (SAD) were randomized to either an attention training condition or a control dot-probe task condition. The SAD condition is marked by debilitating levels of social anxiety, which is reflected in a tendency to experience anxiety and worry in the context of social interactions. Highly anxious people tend to display hypervigilance to possible embarrassment or rejection and thus tend to avoid social interaction (Barlow, 2002). The negative effects of social exclusion are especially pronounced among socially anxious individuals (Oaten, Williams, Jones, & Zadro, 2008). Socially anxious individuals tend to generalize from a single instance of rejection to other potential partners, leading them to view even novel partners as sources of further rejection, rather than as sources of potential affiliation (Maner et al., 2007). In response to rejection, highly anxious individuals display interpersonal deficits reflecting a tendency toward social withdrawal (Mallott, Maner, DeWall, & Schmidt, 2009). Thus, relative to nonanxious people, socially anxious individuals are expected to have exaggerated concerns regarding social exclusion.

Participants completed 8 sessions delivered across 4 weeks. The retraining procedures in this study were very similar to those already described, except instead of using words, the modified dot-probe task used faces. The faces either portrayed a look of disgust (which is a potential social threat) or they were neutral. As predicted, patients in the attention training condition exhibited significantly greater reductions in social anxiety and trait anxiety, compared with patients in the control condition. In fact, patients received a diagnostic interview at posttreatment and these data were fairly remarkable in indicating that 72% of patients in the active treatment condition, relative to 11% of patients in the control condition, no longer met diagnostic criteria for SAD. Moreover, at a 4-month follow-up, patients in the attention training condition continued to maintain their clinical improvement, and the diagnostic differences across conditions persisted.

Conclusions

In summary, evidence from several lines of research is consistent with the hypothesis that attention bias to threat-relevant information may be a candidate as a mechanism involved in the maintenance of anxiety. Specifically, attention bias to threat is a reliable finding in experimental psychopathology, it normalizes after treatment, and it predicts anxiety symptoms in longitudinal studies. Early work in the cognitive bias manipulation literature suggests that attentional bias can be manipulated to produce change in affective responses to stress. More recent, clinical extensions of this work are consistent in suggesting that a similar intervention delivered to a diagnosed, treatment-seeking sample can positively impact anxiety symptoms and that these improvements are maintained over time.

Future Directions

Findings from attention training for clinical samples suggest a surprisingly effective treatment. Can we really expect that such a simple intervention could lead to such dramatic clinical effects? In this regard, it is worth considering that attention training has been used effectively to produce clinical changes

in other settings, such as neuropsychological rehabilitation. Research suggests that that attention training improves memory, learning, and some aspects of executive control (Ruff, Baser, Johnston, & Marshall, 1989). However, it is also clear that much more work is needed clearly establish the efficacy of these interventions for anxiety. Moreover, there are a number of anxiety diagnoses that have yet to be evaluated with these procedures. It will be important to determine whether attention retraining shows comparable benefits for panic disorder, posttraumatic stress disorder, and obsessive-compulsive disorder.

Pursuing this novel treatment direction is worthwhile in several regards. First, current treatments for anxiety have good efficacy, but a significant percentage of patients do not benefit from treatment either due to dropout or low responsiveness to therapy (Fedoroff & Taylor, 2001). Second, access to therapists trained in CBT for SAD is limited, and some patients do not want to take medications for their anxiety problems (Huppert, Franklin, Foa, & Davidson, 2003). Attention retraining is likely to have several advantages over traditional approaches because of the ease of delivery of the treatment. Some of the specific advantages that may make attention retraining treatment particularly appealing include little therapist contact and an intervention that requires little effort or motivation from clients. Furthermore, the computer-based interface of the attention retraining intervention opens up the possibility and the potential of reaching clients that do not have access to CBT or medication through web-based protocols. Expanding the deliverability of efficacious treatments in such a way would potentially greatly reduce the societal impact of anxiety disorders.

Cognitive bias modification, including attention retraining, is a relatively new but intriguing area of research. Much additional work is required, but these techniques appear to offer great possibilities both in the theoretical as well as in applied areas.

Note

Address requests for information and reprints to Norman B. Schmidt, Department of Psychology, Florida State University, Tallahassee FL 32306–4301 (e-mail: schmidt@psy.fsu.edu).

References

American Psychiatric Association. (2000). *Diagnostic and Statistical Manual of Mental Disorders (4th ed.)*. Washington, DC: American Psychiatric Association.

Amir, N., Beard, C., Burns, M., & Bomyea, J. (2009). Attention modification program in individuals with generalized anxiety disorder. *Journal of Abnormal Psychology, 118*, 28–33.

Bar-Haim, Y., Lamy, D., Pergamin, L., Bakermans-Kranenburg, M. J., van IJzendoorn, M. H. (2007). Threat-related attentional bias in anxious and nonanxious individuals: A meta-analytic study. *Psychological Bulletin, 133,* 1–24.

Barlow, D. H. (2002). *Anxiety and Its Disorders: The Nature and Treatment of Anxiety and Panic* (2nd ed.). New York, NY: Guilford Press.

Beck, A. T., & Clark, D. A. (1997). An information processing model of anxiety: Automatic and strategic processes. *Behaviour Research & Therapy, 35,* 49–58.

Beevers, C. G., Gibb, B. E., McGeary, J. E., Miller, I. W. (2007). Serotonin transporter genetic variation and biased attention for emotional word stimuli among psychiatric inpatients. *Journal of Abnormal Psychology, 116,* 208–212.

Borkovec, T.D., Shadick, R., Hopkins, M. (1991). The nature of normal and pathological worry. In R. R. Rapee & D. H. Barlow (Eds.). *Chronic Anxiety: Generalized Anxiety Disorder and Mixed Anxiety-Depression* (pp. 29–51). New York: Guilford Press.

Borkovec, T. D., & Roemer, L. (1995). Perceived functions of worry among generalized anxiety disorder subjects: Distraction from more emotionally distressing topics? *Journal of Behavior Therapy and Experimental Psychiatry, 26,* 25–30.

Dugas, M.J., Gagnon, F., Ladouceur, R., Freeston, M.H. (1998). Generalized anxiety disorder: A preliminary test of a conceptual model. *Behaviour Research and Therapy, 36,* 215–226.

Eysenck, M. W. (1997). *Anxiety and Cognition: A Unified Theory.* Hove, UK: Psychology Press.

Fedoroff, I. C., & Taylor, S. (2001) Psychological and pharmacological treatments of social phobia: A meta-analysis. *Journal of Clinical Psychopharmacology, 21,* 311–324.

Ferdinand, R. F., van der Reijden, M., Verhulst, F. C., Nienhuis, J., Giel, R. (1995). Assessment of the prevalence of psychiatric disorder in young adults. *British Journal of Psychiatry, 166,* 480–488.

Greenberg, P. E., Sisitsky, T., Kessler, R. C., Finkelstein, S. N., Berndt, E. R., Davidson, J. R., (1999). The economic burden of anxiety disorders in the 1990s. *Journal of Clinical Psychiatry, 60,* 427–435.

Hazen, R.A., Vasey, M.W., Schmidt, N.B. (2009). Attentional retraining: A randomized clinical trial for pathological worry. *Journal of Psychiatric Research, 43,* 627–633.

Hofmann, S. G., Sawyer, A. T., Korte, K. J., Smits, J. A. J. (2009). Is it beneficial to add pharmacotherapy to cognitive-behavioral therapy when treating anxiety disorders? A meta-analytic review. *International Journal of Cognitive Therapy, 2,* 162–178.

Huppert, J.D., Franklin, M.E., Foa, E.B., Davidson, J.R.T. (2003). Study refusal and exclusion from a randomized treatment study of generalized social phobia. *Journal of Anxiety Disorders, 17,* 683–693.

Kessler, R. C., Berglund, P., Demler, O., Jin, R., Merikangas, K. R., & Walters, E. E. (2005). Lifetime prevalence and age-of-onset distributions of DSM-IV disorders in the National Comorbidity Survey Replication. *Archives of General Psychiatry, 62,* 593–602.

Kessler, R. C., Chiu, W. T., Demler, O., Merikangas, K. R., Walters, E. E. (2005). Prevalence, severity, and comorbidity of 12-month DSM-IV disorders in the National Comorbidity Survey Replication. *Archives of General Psychiatry 62,* 617–627.

MacLeod, C., & Hagan, R. (1992). Individual differences in the selective processing of threatening information, and

emotional responses to a stressful life-event. *Behaviour Research and Therapy, 30,* 151–161.

MacLeod, C., Mathews, A., Tata, P. (1986). Attentional bias in emotional disorders. *Journal of Abnormal Psychology, 95,* 15–20.

MacLeod, C., Rutherford, E., Campbell, L., Ebsworthy, G., Holker, L. (2002). Selective attention and emotional vulnerability: Assessing the causal basis of their association through the experimental manipulation of attentional bias. *Journal of Abnormal Psychology, 111,* 107–123.

Mallott, M., Maner, J. K., DeWall, C. N., & Schmidt, N. B. (2009). Compensatory deficits following rejection: The role of social anxiety in disrupting affiliative behavior. *Depression and Anxiety, 26,* 438–446.

Maner, J. K., DeWall, C. N., Baumeister, R. F., Schaller, M. (2007). Does social exclusion motivate interpersonal reconnection? Resolving the "porcupine problem." *Journal of Personality and Social Psychology, 92,* 42–55.

Mathews, A. (1990). Why worry? The cognitive function of anxiety. *Behaviour Research and Therapy, 28,* 455–468.

Mathews, A., & MacLeod, C. (1985). Selective processing of threat cues in anxiety states. *Behaviour Research and Therapy, 23,* 563–569.

Mathews, A., & MacLeod, C. (1986). Discrimination of threat cues without awareness in anxiety states. *Journal of Abnormal Psychology, 95,* 131–138.

Mathews, A., & MacLeod, C. (2005). Cognitive vulnerability to emotional disorders. *Annual Review of Clinical Psychology, 1,* 167–195.

Mathews, A., Mogg, K., Kentish, J., Eysenck, M. (1995). Effect of psychological treatment on cognitive bias in generalized anxiety disorder. *Behaviour Research & Therapy, 33,* 293–303.

McNally, R. J. (2007). Mechanisms of exposure therapy: How neuroscience can improve psychological treatments for anxiety disorders. *Clinical Psychology Review, 27,* 750–759.

Mogg, K., & Bradley, B. P. (1998). A cognitive-motivational analysis of anxiety. *Behaviour Research & Therapy, 36,* 809–848.

Mogg, K., & Bradley, B. P. (2005). Attentional bias in generalized anxiety disorder versus depressive disorder. *Cognitive Therapy and Research, 29,* 29–45.

Mogg, K., Bradley, B. P., Millar, N., White, J. (1995). Cognitive bias in generalized anxiety disorder: A follow-up study. *Behaviour Research & Therapy, 33,* 927–935.

Mogg, K., Millar, N., Bradley, B.P. (2000). Biases in eye movements to threatening facial expressions in generalized anxiety disorder and depressive disorder. *Journal of Abnormal Psychology, 109,* 695–704.

Most, S.B., Scholl, B.J., Clifford, E.R., Simons, D.J. (2005). What you see is what you set: Sustained inattentional blindness and the capture of awareness. *Psychological Review, 112,* 217–242.

Oaten, M. R., Williams, K. D., Jones, A., & Zadro, L. (2008). The effects of ostracism on self-regulation in the socially anxious. *Journal of Social and Clinical Psychology, 27,* 471–504.

Ost, L.G. (2008). Cognitive behavior therapy for anxiety disorders: 40 years of progress. *Nordic Journal of Psychiatry, 62,* 5–10

Pine, D. S., Cohen, P., Gurley, D., Brook, J., Ma, Y. (1998). The risk for early-adulthood anxiety and depressive disorders in adolescents with anxiety and depressive disorders. *Archives of General Psychiatry, 55,* 56–64.

Reiss, S. (1980). Pavlovian conditioning and human fear: An expectancy model. *Behavior Therapy, 11,* 380–396.

Ruff, R. M., Baser, C. A., Johnston, J. M., Marshall, L. F. (1989). Neuropsychological rehabilitation: An experimental study with head injured patients. *The Journal of Head Trauma Rehabilitation, 4*, 20–36.

Sammons, M. T., & Schmidt, N. B. (2001). *Combined Behavioral and Pharmacological Treatments For Mental Distress.* Washington, DC: American Psychological Association.

Schmidt, N. B., & Keough, M. E. (2010). Treatment of panic. *Annual Review of Clinical Psychology, 6*, 241–256.

Schmidt, N. B., Koselka, M., & Woolaway-Bickel, K. (2001). Cognitive behavioral and pharmacological treatment strategies for phobic anxiety disorders (pp. 81–110). In M. T. Sammons, N. B. Schmidt (Eds.), *Rational Psychopharmacology: Combined Behavioral and Pharmacological Treatments for Mental Distress.* Washington, DC: American Psychological Association.

Schmidt, N. B., Richey, J. A., Buckner, J. D., Timpano, K. R. (2009). Attention training for generalized social anxiety disorder. *Journal of Abnormal Psychology, 118*, 5–14.

See, J., MacLeod, C., Bridle, R. (2009). The reduction of anxiety vulnerability through the modification of attentional bias: A real-world study using a home-based cognitive bias modification procedure. *Journal of Abnormal Psychology, 118*, 65–75.

Tallis, F., Eysenck, M., Mathews, A. (1991). Worry: A critical analysis of some theoretical approaches. *Anxiety Research, 4*, 97–108.

Thayer, J.F., Friedman, B.H., Borkovec, T.D., Johnson, B.H., Molina, S. (2000). Phasic heart period reactions to cued threat and nonthreat stimuli in generalized anxiety disorder. *Psychophysiology, 37*, 361–368.

Wells, A. (1999). A cognitive model of generalized anxiety disorder. *Behavior Modification, 23*, 526–555.

Wells, A., & Matthews, G. (1994). *Attention and Emotion: A Clinical Perspective.* Hove, UK: Erlbaum.

Williams, J. M. G., Watts, F. N., MacLeod, C., Mathews, A. (1997). *Cognitive Psychology and Emotional Disorders* (2nd ed.). Chichester: Wiley.

van den Hout, M., Tenney, N., Huygens, K., Merckelbach, H., Kindt, M. (1995). Responding to subliminal threat cues is related to trait anxiety and emotional vulnerability: a successful replication of MacLeod and Hagan (1992). *Behaviour Research and Therapy, 33*, 451–454.

Behavioral Mimicry as an Affiliative Response to Social Exclusion

Jessica L. Lakin *and* Tanya L. Chartrand

Abstract

The nonconscious behavioral mimicry and social exclusion literatures are merged to explore whether mimicking the behaviors of others could be a possible affiliative behavior that follows social exclusion. Behavioral mimicry has been linked to liking, affiliation, and the development of rapport, and typically operates outside of conscious awareness, making it an especially attractive way to recover from the negative effects of rejection. Data consistent with this argument are reviewed, and future directions for a fruitful continued merging of these literatures are discussed.

Key Words: affiliation, chameleon effect, exclusion, imitation, nonconscious behavioral mimicry, rejection

Introduction

As many of the chapters in this book reveal, people's responses to social exclusion experiences are quite complex (see also Richman & Leary, 2009; Williams, 2009; Williams, Forgas, & von Hippel, 2005). Emotionally, social exclusion may make people feel anger and frustration, sadness, or numbness, resignation and indifference. Cognitively, social exclusion causes a shift in time perspective, impairment in self-regulation, and reductions in complex cognitive abilities. And behaviorally, rejection leads people to engage in self-defeating behavior, increases interest in short-term gains, causes hostility and aggression, and often motivates behaviors that would ultimately serve to reconnect people with others (e.g., conformity, helping).

Understanding the consequences of social exclusion is further complicated by the circumstances surrounding the exclusion (Richman & Leary, 2009; Williams, 2009; Williams & Zadro, 2005), including the type of exclusion that occurs, the setting in which the exclusion occurs, the characteristics of the excluders, and individual differences in personality variables that are relevant to social exclusion experiences (e.g., need to belong, rejection sensitivity). Thankfully, the intense interest in this topic and the extensive amount of research on it over the past decade have allowed the literature in this field to develop to a point where these complexities are both recognized and appreciated.

One way to understand these multifaceted responses to social exclusion, especially with regard to its behavioral consequences, is to recognize that rejection threatens multiple fundamental needs, including the need to belong, the need for self-esteem, the need to have control over one's environment, and the need to have a sense of meaningful existence (Williams, 2001, 2009). When rejection occurs, then, addressing these threatened needs occurs in different ways depending on timing (e.g., when the outcome is assessed, the duration of the exclusion) and available situational alternatives. Specifically, Williams (2007a, 2007b, 2009) hypothesizes both an immediate reflexive response to rejection as well as a more reflective stage that, presumably, reflects people's responses to rejection when they have had more time to think (sometimes consciously) about them.

This two-step response system does much to explain the seeming inconsistencies within the exclusion literature. For example, although there was much debate about the existence and magnitude of emotional responses to exclusion experiences (see Blackhart, Nelson, Knowles, & Baumeister, 2009), Williams's model suggests that one might feel really bad immediately after exclusion, but that if the exclusion is prolonged, or if one is reflecting on a lifetime of exclusion, resignation may ultimately occur. This model is also important because it identifies moderators to exclusion experiences that can explain why rejection sometimes leads to behaviors designed to increase acceptance, and at other times, leads to behaviors that are clearly not going to serve this important need (e.g., aggression). In other words, at the reflective stage of responding, one can take into account attributions for the exclusion (e.g., was I excluded because of a something over which I have control?), characteristics of the excluders (e.g., was I excluded by someone important to me?), and situational variables (e.g., is there a possibility that I could affiliate with someone?) that ultimately determine behavioral responses (see Richman & Leary, 2009, for a more lengthy discussion of possible moderators).

Prosocial Behavioral Responses to Exclusion

At this point, we understand that both antisocial and prosocial responses to social exclusion can occur, and the determining factors seem to be individuals' appraisals of their current situation and situational constraints. For example, individuals often respond to exclusion by getting angry and aggressing against others (Twenge, Baumeister, Tice, & Stucke, 2001), but this aggressive response decreases or disappears entirely if participants experience feelings of control in an unrelated task (Warburton, Williams, & Cairns, 2006) or are reminded of a social connection (Twenge, Zhang, Catanese, Dolan-Pascoe, Lyche, & Baumeister, 2007). Individuals also have difficulty self-regulating after exclusion (Baumeister, DeWall, Ciarocco, & Twenge, 2005), but self-regulation can occur quite easily if it serves the larger goal of affiliation (DeWall, Baumeister, & Vohs, 2008).

Although anti-social responses to exclusion can and do occur in certain circumstances, prosocial responses to exclusion also make theoretical sense. Humans and other animals have a strong need to belong (Baumeister & Leary, 1995; see also Leary & Baumeister, 2000), and every type of exclusion threatens this fundamental need to some degree.

Thus, when one has been excluded, it would be both physically and socially adaptive to respond to that exclusion by trying to affiliate with others (Brewer, 1997; Caporael, 2001). To the extent that there are opportunities available for affiliation, then, it would make evolutionary sense to take advantage of them (Lakin, Jefferis, Cheng, & Chartrand, 2003).

Not surprisingly, there are a number of studies that demonstrate possible affiliative, prosocial responses to social exclusion. In one, participants were more likely to conform to the clearly incorrect answers of others in an Asch-like figure-judging task if they had recently been excluded in a ball-tossing game (Williams, Cheung, & Choi, 2000). Conformity is certainly not always a positive behavior, but it does serve to create similarity, which is strongly related to liking (Byrne, 1971). The threat of social exclusion also increases compliance to a request for a monetary donation (Carter-Sowell, Chen, & Williams, 2008) and reduces people's tendency to experience negative social influence; when uncooperative behavior was followed by the threat of social exclusion, cooperative behaviors increased (Kerr et al., 2009). Whether these particular affiliative responses are reflexive or reflective is an open question; regardless, it is clear that yielding to social influence is one possible way that people could affiliate with others after exclusion or rejection.

There is growing evidence that there are clear automatic and reflexive affiliative behaviors that happen after exclusion as well. For example, after rejection, people become more interested in social information (Gardner, Pickett, & Brewer, 2000; see also Pickett & Gardner, 2005), are more attuned to social opportunities (Maner, DeWall, Baumeister, & Schaller, 2007), and have better memory for social information, especially when it involves social behaviors of others (Hess & Pickett, 2010). This interest in affiliation even extends to perceptual processing of stimuli that might lead to social acceptance; the threat of exclusion causes people to pay more attention to and devote more time to processing smiling faces than disapproving faces (DeWall, Maner, & Rouby, 2009) and to show more interest in others who display genuine smiles as opposed to deceptive smiles (Bernstein, Sacco, Brown, Young, & Claypool, 2010). The postexclusion interest in affiliation even occurs when pursuing social connections might not be in a person's economic or personal best interests; for example, excluded participants were more likely than nonexcluded participants to spend money on a personally unappealing item to please a peer and to express interest in trying an illegal drug when it would facilitate a social connection (Mead, Baumeister, Stillman, Rawn, & Vohs, 2011).

Our work has focused on another possible automatic affiliative response to social exclusion: nonconscious behavioral mimicry. Specifically, given the strong link between mimicry of other people's behaviors and affiliation and rapport (see later), we were interested in whether the automatic tendency to imitate the mannerisms of others might occur after social exclusion as a way to help people to affiliate, albeit automatically, with others. We begin with a brief review of the mimicry literature to highlight the importance of this behavior in creating affiliation and rapport with others, and then discuss the specific links to the social exclusion literature. We end by discussing unanswered questions that will drive this literature in the next decade.

Nonconscious Behavioral Mimicry

Nonconscious behavioral mimicry occurs when an individual unwittingly imitates the mannerisms or behaviors of another person (Chartrand & Bargh, 1999; Chartrand, Maddux, & Lakin, 2005; Lakin et al., 2003). The idea of behavior matching has a long history in the field of psychology (e.g., James, 1890), but there has been a resurgence of interest in this topic over the past several decades. Almost without exception, this literature has revealed strong links, both correlational and causal, between behavioral mimicry and liking, affiliation, and rapport (interested readers can consult a number of recent review articles [e.g., Chartrand & Lakin, in press; Chartrand & van Baaren, 2009; Lakin, in press] for a more thorough understanding of the behavioral mimicry literature).

There is evidence that people imitate the behaviors of those with whom they have ongoing relationships: parents (Bernieri, Reznick, & Rosenthal, 1988; Jones, 2007), therapists (Charney, 1966; Maurer & Tindall, 1983), and teachers (Bernieri, 1988; LaFrance, 1979; LaFrance & Broadbent, 1976). But behavioral mimicry also occurs under the most minimal conditions; even neonates imitate the facial movements of complete strangers (e.g., Meltzoff & Moore, 1977). More recently, Chartrand and Bargh (1999, Experiment 1) had participants interact with two unfamiliar confederates who engaged in different nonverbal behaviors. Participants mimicked the mannerisms of the confederates—they shook their foot more when they were with a foot-shaker than when they were with a face-rubber, and rubbed their face more when they

were with a face-rubber than when they were with a foot-shaker. At the conclusion of the experiment, participants were asked about the mannerisms of the confederate, and about their own mannerisms, and none noticed either. The fact that participants unwittingly change their mannerisms and behaviors to blend in with their social environments is why this mimicry behavior has been called the "chameleon effect."

Nonconscious Behavioral Mimicry and Affiliation

The fact that people imitate others who are close to them suggests the importance of this behavior for establishing and maintaining relationships (Lakin et al., 2003). Indeed, the behavioral mimicry literature is now filled with examples linking mimicry to the development of liking. Chartrand and Bargh (1999, Experiment 2) manipulated behavioral mimicry and found that when a confederate mimicked the behavior of participants (as opposed to engaging in neutral, nondescript mannerisms), participants reported liking the confederate more, and that the interaction had been more smooth and harmonious. This general finding has been replicated a number of times (see Chartrand and Lakin, in press, or Lakin, in press, for a review), and has even been demonstrated with interpersonal synchrony rather than mimicry (Hove & Risen, 2009) and when avatars mimic the facial expressions of human participants (Bailenson & Yee, 2005). People who are mimicked are also more likely to help others, even others who were not involved in the interaction where mimicry first occurred (van Baaren, Holland, Kawakami, & van Knippenberg, 2004), have an easier time understanding the emotions of others (Stel & van Knippenberg, 2008), are more trustful of others (Maddux, Mullen, & Galinsky, 2008), and report feeling closer to others more generally (Ashton-James, van Baaren, Chartrand, Decety, & Karremans, 2007).

One of the most interesting aspects of people's tendency to imitate automatically others' behaviors is that this mimicry appears to be used strategically, albeit unconsciously, in situations where people are interested in trying to affiliate. Indirect evidence to support this idea was provided by Cheng and Chartrand (2003), who explored the relationship between self-monitoring and behavioral mimicry. High self-monitors are particularly interested in controlling their public image and behaving in a socially appropriate manner (Snyder, 1987), which Cheng and Chartrand argued would include trying to affiliate with similar or powerful targets. In their first study, college-student participants interacted with a confederate whom they believed to be a high school student, a fellow college student, or a graduate student. Low self-monitors did not differentially mimic the confederate in the three different description conditions, but high self-monitors exhibited greater mimicry in the fellow college student condition than in either the high school or graduate student conditions. A second study replicated this effect: High self-monitors mimicked an interaction partner who was described as being higher in status (i.e., a leader rather than a worker) to a greater degree than when their partner was lower in status, whereas low self-monitors didn't differentially mimic their partners. Cheng and Chartrand concluded that high self-monitors were especially sensitive to affiliative situational cues that suggested they should create liking, and nonconscious mimicry was the "tool" through which they accomplished their objective.

More directly, Lakin and Chartrand (2003) explored whether people who have an affiliation goal would be more likely to mimic the behaviors of interaction partners. In a first study, participants were given a conscious affiliation goal (i.e., they were told to affiliate with a future interaction partner), a nonconscious affiliation goal (i.e., they were subliminally primed with words like *friend* and *together*), or no affiliation goal. Participants were then surreptitiously videotaped while watching another participant (actually a confederate) who was touching her face while engaging in routine clerical tasks. The video tapes were later coded to determine how much participants were touching their own faces while watching the confederate. Regardless of whether the affiliation goal was conscious or nonconscious, participants with an active goal mimicked the behaviors of the potential interaction partner more than participants who did not have an affiliation goal.

A second study extended this initial finding by showing an increase in mimicry in a situation where there was even more pressure to create rapport with an unknown person: recent failure at an affiliation goal (Lakin & Chartrand, 2003, Experiment 2). Participants were subliminally primed with an affiliation goal or not, and then participated in an ostensibly unrelated second experiment. The second experiment involved two interviews with different confederates. The first interview was either successful (i.e., the confederate was friendly and polite) or unsuccessful (i.e., the confederate was unfriendly

and abrupt), leading participants to succeed or fail at their affiliation goal (if they had one). During the second interview, the second confederate shook her foot throughout the interaction, and participants were again surreptitiously videotaped so we could code the extent to which participants shook their own feet. Participants who were primed with an affiliation goal and were not able to accomplish this goal in a first interaction (i.e., they failed at their goal by interacting with an unfriendly, terse confederate) mimicked the behaviors of the second interaction partner more than participants who did not have an affiliation goal or participants who had an affiliation goal and succeeded in the first interaction. Presumably, participants who failed in a first attempt to achieve their goal continued to pursue their active goal with a newly introduced interaction partner by mimicking that person's behaviors.

In sum, this work sets the stage for linking social exclusion experiences to nonconscious behavioral mimicry. As the Cheng and Chartrand (2003) and Lakin and Chartrand (2003) studies reveal, people are more than able to use mimicry in situations wherein it is personally beneficial. In situations in which people want, or need, to affiliate, behavioral mimicry is one strategy for accomplishing this goal.

Nonconscious Behavioral Mimicry and Social Exclusion

Our recent work has attempted to merge the nonconscious behavioral mimicry literature with the social exclusion literature. Specifically, given the links between behavioral mimicry and affiliation, and between social exclusion and the need to restore feelings of belongingness, we have argued that one way in which people might be able to recover from social exclusion is by mimicking the behaviors of new interaction partners. Because behavioral mimicry often occurs nonconsciously (and may be more successful to the extent that it does, see Bailenson, Yee, Patel, & Beall, 2008), it should be a particularly common postexclusion affiliative behavior: it requires few, if any, taxed regulatory resources (Baumeister et al., 2005). Data from two studies that test this idea directly support our claim (Lakin, Chartrand, & Arkin, 2008; see also Lakin & Chartrand, 2005).

In the first study, participants completed two unrelated tasks. The first task involved playing a virtual ball-tossing game, Cyberball, with three other participants (actually confederates; Williams et al., 2000; Williams & Jarvis, 2006). Participants were not given any information about their fellow players. Half of the participants were excluded during the ball-tossing game, whereas the other half were included. In the second task, participants described a set of photographs to a new partner, someone who had not played Cyberball and therefore knew nothing of the exclusion or inclusion experience. This confederate shook her foot throughout her interaction with participants, and surreptitious video recordings of the participants were later coded to determine how much they mimicked this nonverbal behavior. Controlling for the amount of foot-shaking that occurred during a baseline period, participants who had been excluded while playing Cyberball mimicked the foot-shaking behavior of the confederate significantly more than participants who had been included. The participants' mimicry behavior had the desired effect too. When the confederate (who was blind to condition) was asked to evaluate her interactions with each participant, she reported that the interactions with excluded participants had gone more smoothly than her interactions with included participants.

A second experiment was conducted to explore whether affiliation needs resulting from exclusion could be addressed by mimicking the behaviors of *any* interaction partner. That is, we wondered whether mimicry of an interaction partner's behaviors would still occur if the interaction partner did not share a salient characteristic with the excluding group. We reasoned that mimicry of a partner who shared a commonality with participants and with their excluders would be especially likely to address any threatened belongingness needs that arose from the earlier exclusion.

The procedure for the second study was similar to that of the first, but this time, participants had more information about their fellow Cyberball players. Specifically, the female participants were excluded by either three males (i.e., an out-group) or three females (i.e., an in-group). Their subsequent interaction was still with a novel person who had not played Cyberball and knew nothing about it, but the confederate either shared a group membership with the participant (i.e., the confederate was female too) or not (i.e., the confederate was male).

We expected that participants who had been excluded by in-group members and then interacted with an in-group confederate would mimic the foot-shaking behavior of that confederate more than participants in any of the other conditions. Analyses revealed a significant interaction consistent with our prediction. Participants in the female

exclusion condition mimicked the female confederate more than the male confederate, but there were no differences between mimicry of the female and male confederates in the male exclusion condition or a control condition where participants did not play Cyberball. A planned contrast comparing the female exclusion/female confederate condition to the other conditions was also significant. The increase in mimicry observed in this condition was expected to be mediated by threatened belongingness needs; a correlational analysis indicated that belongingness needs were a stronger predictor of mimicry in the in-group exclusion/in-group confederate condition than in any of the other conditions.

In both of these experiments, the increase in mimicry by excluded participants occurred despite the fact that they reported no conscious awareness of the confederate's behaviors or the fact that their own behaviors were affected by the confederate. This suggests that the behavioral mimicry that occurred was indeed nonconscious. Use of mimicry in situations where people want to affiliate is functional, as it gives people an opportunity to pursue their affiliation goals without spending limited cognitive resources on determining the best way to do so. Given that being excluded can cause regulatory difficulties (Baumeister et al., 2005), automatic affiliative behaviors should be an attractive (unconscious) option after rejection occurs.

While the Lakin et al. (2008) studies are the only published ones to date that have directly linked being socially excluded to an increase in nonconscious behavioral mimicry, Over and Carpenter (2009) have recently replicated the conceptual link between ostracism and imitation more generally. Specifically, they primed 5-year-old children with a minimal display of ostracism: the children watched two short videos, each of which depicted a group of shapes moving away from a single shape. After watching the ostracism or control videos (where no rejection occurred), all the children watched an experimenter play with a new toy, which was actually a box, a ball, and three small tools. The experimenter interacted with the toy in a scripted manner and then passed all of the materials to the child, who was allowed to do whatever he or she wanted to do with them. An imitation score was calculated based on the extent to which the children engaged with the toy in a similar manner to that of the experimenter. As expected, children who had watched the ostracism videos imitated the experimenter's behaviors to a greater extent than the children who watched the control videos.

Over and Carpenter's (2009) data further support imitation as an affiliative behavior that occurs after exclusion (or the idea of exclusion). The fact that this link has been demonstrated in children is consistent with the idea that there is evolutionary significance to the mimicry/affiliation relationship (Lakin et al., 2003). Recent research with nonhuman primates, although not in the context of exclusion, further supports this claim. When capuchin monkeys were imitated by humans, the monkeys demonstrated more positive interest in interacting with the imitator compared to the nonimitator (e.g., they spent more time looking at the imitator; Paukner, Suomi, Visalberghi, & Ferrari, 2009). The authors conclude that imitation promotes affiliation even in nonhuman primates (see also de Waal & Ferrari, 2010).

Future Directions

The nonconscious behavioral mimicry findings of Lakin et al. (2008) and the imitation findings of Over and Carpenter (2009) are both consistent with the body of literature demonstrating affiliative behavioral consequences of social exclusion (e.g., Kerr et al., 2009; Williams et al., 2000). Because behavioral mimicry is often automatic, the Lakin et al. findings are probably most consistent with other research demonstrating an increased sensitivity to social information and opportunities after social exclusion. Just as people are interested in new chances to find positive interaction partners (Maner et al., 2007), engage in early perceptual processing of social information (Bernstein et al., 2010; DeWall et al., 2009), and pay more attention to and remember more social information (Gardner et al., 2000; Hess & Pickett, 2010) after being rejected, people also affiliate by automatically and nonconsciously tuning their behaviors to those of their interaction partners. This behavioral similarity creates liking and rapport, and results in smoother and more harmonious interactions (Chartrand et al., 2005).

As the social exclusion literature continues to develop, there are a number of questions that still need to be addressed to gain a fuller understanding of possible affiliative responses to exclusion. Studying nonconscious behavioral mimicry in this context also provides an opportunity to extend the mimicry literature.

First, the social exclusion literature provides a natural context in which one could study behavioral mimicry of in-group and out-group members, a topic that has been understudied in the imitation literature (see Yabar, Johnston, Miles, & Peace, 2006, for one exception to this statement). A related issue concerns how people feel about and respond to exclusion by out-group members. As the second study of Lakin et al. (2008) demonstrates, people were more likely to mimic the behaviors of an in-group partner following in-group exclusion. Does this finding hold for exclusion by other groups, particularly groups that are not based on sex? If exclusion is threatening to core social motives like the need to belong (even when it is exclusion from a disliked out-group like the KKK; Gonsalkorale & Williams, 2007), are there circumstances under which affiliating with someone, even if that person is an out-group member, would be better than affiliating with no one? In other words, future research will need to determine the limits to behavioral mimicry following exclusion: is it an all-or-none phenomenon, or is the automatic affiliative response subject to situational moderators as well? And, if so, identifying those moderators would be a meaningful contribution to both the social exclusion and behavioral mimicry literatures.

Second: Is an increase in behavioral mimicry a response unique to social exclusion, or is it a common response in other situations in which group-related concerns are activated? A related question is whether different types of exclusion experiences (e.g., active vs. passive) would all result in an increase in mimicking the behaviors of others (see Molden, Lucas, Gardner, Dean, & Knowles, 2009, for an argument about why this might not be the case). In other words, because of its link to affiliation, is behavioral mimicry an effective response to any type of group-related threat? There is some preliminary evidence that something as simple as feeling different from a group motivates behavioral mimicry (Uldall, Hall, & Chartrand, 2012), but this issue has not been fully explored. It is not yet clear whether and to what extent behavioral mimicry would address these types of perceived threats, or threats that result from different types of exclusion experiences.

Finally, one of the most important questions that has yet to be addressed concerns if and how the link between behavioral mimicry and social exclusion can be utilized to help people who experience rejection, particularly people like the socially anxious who seem to experience the consequences of rejection much more intensely (e.g., Oaten, Williams, Jones, & Zadro, 2008). This is a tricky topic. On the one hand, it seems that behavioral mimicry would be a simple and low-effort affiliative response to exclusion. It's automatic, and therefore happens unintentionally and without expenditure of limited cognitive resources (Chartrand et al., 2005). On the other hand, it is not clear the extent to which it can be taught, and if it can be taught, if it is as effective as when it happens spontaneously (but see Stel & Vonk, 2010). Given the fact that social exclusion is, at best, disheartening, and at worst, devastating, continuing to explore the link between nonconscious behavioral mimicry and rejection will be fruitful for both basic and applied reasons.

Conclusions

In this chapter, we have attempted to merge the literatures on behavioral mimicry and affiliative responses to social exclusion. Specifically, because behavioral mimicry is known to be related to affiliation, and because social exclusion threatens fundamental belongingness needs and therefore often motivates attempts to affiliate, we hypothesized that behavioral mimicry would be a low-cost, efficient response to social exclusion. Our own data, along with data from several others, support our theorizing: Mimicking others after exclusion restores feelings of belongingness, albeit outside of conscious awareness.

References

Ashton-James, C., van Baaren, R. B., Chartrand, T. L., Decety, J., & Karremans, J. (2007). Mimicry and me: The impact of mimicry on self-construal. *Social Cognition*, 25, 518–535. doi:10.1521/soco.2007.25.4.518

Bailenson, J. N., & Yee, N. (2005). Digital chameleons: Automatic assimilation of nonverbal gestures in immersive virtual environments. *Psychological Science*, 16, 814–819. doi:10.1111/j.1467-9280.2005.01619.x

Bailenson, J. N., Yee, N., Patel, K., & Beall, A. C. (2008). Detecting digital chameleons. *Computers in Human Behavior*, 24, 66–87. doi:10.1016/j.chb.2007.01.015

Baumeister, R. F., DeWall, C. N., Ciarocco, N. J., & Twenge, J. M. (2005). Social exclusion impairs self-regulation. *Journal of Personality and Social Psychology*, 88, 589–604. doi:10.1037/0022-3514.88.4.589

Baumeister, R. F., & Leary, M. R. (1995). The need to belong: Desire for interpersonal attachments as a fundamental human motive. *Psychological Bulletin*, 117, 497–529. doi:10.1037/0033-2909.117.3.497

Bernieri, F. J. (1988). Coordinated movement and rapport in teacher-student interactions. *Journal of Nonverbal Behavior*, 12, 120–138. doi:10.1007/BF00986930

Bernieri, F. J., Reznick, J. S., & Rosenthal, R. (1988). Synchrony, pseudosynchrony, and dissynchrony: Measuring the entrainment process in mother-infant interactions. *Journal of Personality and Social Psychology*, 54, 243–253. doi:10.1037/0022-3514.54.2.243

Bernstein, M. J., Sacco, D. F., Brown, C. M., Young, S. G., & Claypool, H. M. (2010). A preference for genuine smiles following social exclusion. *Journal of Experimental Social Psychology*, 46, 196–199. doi:10.1016/j.jesp.2009.08.010

Blackhart, G. C., Nelson, B. C., Knowles, M. L., & Baumeister, R. F. (2009). Rejection elicits emotional reactions but neither causes immediate distress nor lowers self-esteem: A meta-analytic review of 192 studies on social exclusion. *Personality and Social Psychology Review*, 13, 269–309. doi:10.1177/1088868309346065

Brewer, M. B. (1997). On the social origins of human nature. In C. McGarty & S. A. Haslam (Eds.), *The Message of Social Psychology: Perspectives on Mind in Society* (pp. 54–62). Cambridge, MA: Blackwell Publishers.

Byrne, D. (1971). *The Attraction Paradigm*. New York: Academic Press.

Caporael, L. R. (2001). Parts and wholes: The evolutionary importance of groups. In C. Sedikides & M. B. Brewer (Eds.), *Individual Self, Relational Self, Collective Self* (pp. 241–258). Philadelphia: Psychology Press.

Carter-Sowell, A. R., Chen, Z., & Williams, K. D. (2008). Ostracism increases social susceptibility. *Social Influence*, 3, 143–153. doi:10.1080/15534510802204868

Charney, E. J. (1966). Psychosomatic manifestations of rapport in psychotherapy. *Psychosomatic Medicine*, 28, 305–315.

Chartrand, T. L., & Bargh, J. A. (1999). The chameleon effect: The perception-behavior link and social interaction. *Journal of Personality and Social Psychology*, 76, 893–910. doi:10.1037/0022-3514.76.6.893

Chartrand, T. L., & Lakin, J. L. (in press). The antecedents and consequences of human behavioral mimicry. *Annual Review of Psychology*. doi: 10.1146/annurev-psych-113011-143754

Chartrand, T. L., Maddux, W. W., & Lakin, J. L. (2005). Beyond the perception-behavior link: The ubiquitous utility and motivational moderators of nonconscious mimicry. In R. R. Hassin, J. S. Uleman, & J. A. Bargh (Eds.), *The New Unconscious* (pp. 334–361). New York: Oxford University Press.

Chartrand, T. L., & van Baaren, R. B. (2009). Human mimicry. In M. P. Zanna (Ed.), *Advances in Experimental Social Psychology* (pp. 219–274). San Diego, CA: Academic Press. doi:10.1016/S0065-2601(08)00405-X

Cheng, C. M., & Chartrand, T. L. (2003). Self-monitoring without awareness: Using mimicry as a nonconscious affiliation strategy. *Journal of Personality and Social Psychology*, 85, 1170–1179. doi:10.1037/0022-3514.85.6.1170

de Waal, F. B., & Ferrari, P. F. (2010). Towards a bottom-up perspective on animal and human cognition. *Trends in Cognitive Science*, 14, 201–207. doi:10.1016/j.tics.2010.03.003

DeWall, C. N., Baumeister, R. F., & Vohs, K. D. (2008). Satiated with belongingness: Effects of acceptance, rejection, and task framing on self-regulatory performance. *Journal of Personality and Social Psychology*, 95, 1367–1382. doi:10.1037/a0012632

DeWall, C. N., Maner, J. K., & Rouby, D. A. (2009). Social exclusion and early-stage interpersonal perception: Selective attention to signs of acceptance. *Journal of Personality and Social Psychology*, 96, 729–741. doi:10.1037/a0014634

Gardner, W. L., Pickett, C. L., & Brewer. M. B. (2000). Social exclusion and selective memory: How the need to belong influences memory for social events. *Personality and Social Psychology Bulletin*, 26, 486–496. doi:10.1177/0146167200266007

Gonsalkorale, K., & Williams, K. D. (2007). The KKK won't let me play: Ostracism even by a despised outgroup hurts. *European Journal of Social Psychology*, 37, 1176–1186. doi:10.1002/ejsp.392

Hess, Y. D., & Pickett, C. L. (2010). Social rejection and self- versus other-awareness. *Journal of Experimental Social Psychology, 46*, 453–456. doi:10.1016/j.jesp.2009.12.004

Hove, M. J., & Risen, J. L. (2009). It's all in the timing: Interpersonal synchrony increases affiliation. *Social Cognition, 27*, 949–961. doi:10.1521/soco.2009.27.6.949

James, W. (1890). *Principles of Psychology*. New York: Holt.

Jones, S. S. (2007). Imitation in infancy: The development of mimicry. *Psychological Science, 18*, 593–599. doi:10.1111/j.1467-9280.2007.01945.x

Kerr, N. L., Rumble, A. C., Park, E. S., Ouwerkerk, J. W., Parks, C. D., Gallucci, M., & van Lange, P. A. M. (2009). "How many bad apples does it take to spoil the whole barrel?": Social exclusion and toleration for bad apples. *Journal of Experimental Social Psychology, 45*, 603–613. doi:10.1016/j.jesp.2009.02.017

La France, M. (1979). Nonverbal synchrony and rapport: Analysis by the cross-lag panel technique. *Social Psychology Quarterly, 42*, 66–70. doi:10.2307/3033875

La France, M., & Broadbent, M. (1976). Group rapport: Posture sharing as a nonverbal indicator. *Group and Organization Studies, 1*, 328–333. doi:10.1177/105960117600100307

Lakin, J. L. (in press). Behavioral mimicry and interactional synchrony. In J. L. Hall, & M. L. Knapp (Eds.), *Handbook of Communication Science*. Berlin: Mouton de Gruyter.

Lakin, J. L., & Chartrand, T. L. (2003). Using nonconscious behavioral mimicry to create affiliation and rapport. *Psychological Science, 14*, 334–339. doi:10.1111/1467-9280.14481

Lakin, J. L., & Chartrand, T. L. (2005). Exclusion and nonconscious behavioral mimicry. In K. D. Williams, J. P. Forgas, & W. von Hippel (Eds.), *The Social Outcast: Ostracism, Social Exclusion, Rejection, and Bullying* (pp. 279–295). New York: Psychology Press.

Lakin, J. L., & Chartrand, T. L., & Arkin, R. M. (2008). I am too just like you: Nonconscious behavioral mimicry as an automatic behavioral response to social exclusion. *Psychological Science, 19*, 816–822. doi:10.1111/j.1467-9280.2008.02162.x

Lakin, J. L., Jefferis, V. E., Cheng, C. M., & Chartrand, T. L. (2003). The Chameleon Effect as social glue: Evidence for the evolutionary significance of nonconscious mimicry. *Journal of Nonverbal Behavior, 27*, 145–162. doi:10.1023/A:1025389814290

Leary, M. R., & Baumeister, R. F. (2000). The nature and function of self-esteem: Sociometer theory. In M. Zanna (Ed.), *Advances in Experimental Social Psychology, 32*, (pp. 1–62). San Diego, CA: Academic Press.

Maddux, W. W., Mullen, E., & Galinsky, A. D. (2008). Chameleons bake bigger pies and take bigger pieces: Strategic behavioral mimicry facilitates negotiation outcomes. *Journal of Experimental Social Psychology, 44*, 461–468. doi:10.1016/j.jesp.2007.02.003

Maner, J. K., DeWall, C. N., Baumeister, R. F., & Schaller, M. (2007). Does social exclusion motivate interpersonal reconnection? Resolving the "porcupine problem." *Journal of Personality and Social Psychology, 92*, 42–55. doi:10.1037/0022-3514.92.1.42

Maurer, R. E., & Tindall, J. H. (1983). Effect of postural congruence on client's perception of counselor empathy. *Journal of Counseling Psychology, 30*, 158–163. doi:10.1037/0022-0167.30.2.158

Mead, N. L., Baumeister, R. F., Stillman, T. F., Rawn, C. D., & Vohs, K. D. (2011). Social exclusion causes people to spend and consume strategically in the service of affiliation. *Journal of Consumer Research, 37*, 902–919. doi:10.1086/656667

Meltzoff, A. N., & Moore, M. K. (1977). Imitation of facial and manual gestures by human neonates. *Science, 198*, 75–78. doi:10.1126/science.198.4312.75

Molden, D. C., Lucas, G. M., Gardner, W. L., Dean, K., & Knowles, M. L. (2009). Motivations for prevention or promotion following social exclusion: Being rejected versus being ignored. *Journal of Personality and Social Psychology, 96*, 415–431. doi:10.1037/a0012958

Oaten, M., Williams, K. D., Jones, A., & Zadro, L. (2008). The effects of ostracism on self-regulation in the socially anxious. *Journal of Social and Clinical Psychology, 27*, 471–504. doi:10.1521/jscp.2008.27.5.471

Over, H., & Carpenter, M. (2009). Priming third-party ostracism increases affiliative imitation. *Developmental Science, 12*, F1-F8. doi:10.1111/j.1467-7687.2008.00820.x

Paukner, A., Suomi, S. J., Visalberghi, E., & Ferrari, P. F. (2009). Capuchin monkeys display affiliation toward humans who imitate them. *Science, 325*, 880–883. doi:10.1126/science.1176269

Pickett, C. L., & Gardner, W. L. (2005). The social monitoring system: Enhanced sensitivity to social cues as an adaptive response to social exclusion. In K. D. Williams, J. P. Forgas, & W. von Hippel (Eds.), *The Social Outcast: Ostracism, Social Exclusion, Rejection, and Bullying* (pp. 213–226). New York: Psychology Press.

Richman, L. S., & Leary, M. R. (2009). Reactions to discrimination, stigmatization, ostracism, and other forms of interpersonal rejection. *Psychological Review, 116*, 365–383. doi:10.1037/a0015250

Snyder, M. (1987). *Public Appearances, Private Realities: The Psychology of Self-Monitoring*. New York: Freeman.

Stel, M., & van Knippenberg, A. (2008). The role of facial mimicry in the recognition of affect. *Psychological Science, 19*, 984–985. doi:10.1111/j.1467-9280.2008.02188.x

Stel, M., & Vonk, R. (2010). Mimicry in social interaction: Benefits for mimickers, mimickees, and their interaction. *British Journal of Psychology, 101*, 311–323. doi:10.1348/000712609X465424

Twenge, J. M., Baumeister, R. F., Tice, D. M., & Stucke, T. S. (2001). If you can't join them, beat them: Effects of social exclusion on aggressive behavior. *Journal of Personality and Social Psychology, 81*, 1058–1069. doi:10.1037/0022-3514.81.6.1058

Twenge, J. M., Zhang, L., Catanese, K. R., Dolan-Pascoe, B., Lyche, L. F., & Baumeister, R. F. (2007). Replenishing connectedness: Reminders of social activity reduce aggression after social exclusion. *British Journal of Social Psychology, 46*, 205–224. doi:10.1348/014466605X90793

Uldall, B. R., Hall, C. E., & Chartrand, T. L. (2012). *Social Chameleons: Effects of Social Identity Motives on Nonconscious Mimicry*. Manuscript in preparation.

van Baaren, R. B., Holland, R. W., Kawakami, K., & van Knippenberg, A. (2004). Mimicry and prosocial behavior. *Psychological Science, 15*, 71–74. doi:10.1111/j.0963-7214.2004.01501012.x

Warburton, W. A., Williams, K. D., & Cairns, D. R. (2006). When ostracism leads to aggression: The moderating effects of control deprivation. *Journal of Experimental Social Psychology, 42*, 213–220. doi:10.1016/j.jesp.2005.03.005

Williams, K. D. (2001). *Ostracism: The Power of Silence*. New York: Guilford Press.

Williams, K. D. (2007a). Ostracism. *Annual Review of Psychology*, *58*, 425–452. doi:10.1146/annurev.psych.58.110405.085641

Williams, K. D. (2007b). Ostracism: The kiss of social death. *Social and Personality Psychology Compass*, *1*, 236–247. doi:10.1111/j.1751-9004.2007.00004.x

Williams, K. D. (2009). Ostracism: A temporal need-threat model. In M. P. Zanna (Ed.), *Advances in Experimental Social Psychology* (pp. 275–314). doi:10.1016/S0065-2601(08)00406-1

Williams, K. D., Cheung, C. K. T., & Choi, W. (2000). Cyberostracism: Effects of being ignored over the Internet. *Journal of Personality and Social Psychology*, *79*, 748–762. doi:10.1037/0022-3514.79.5.748

Williams, K. D., Forgas, J., & von Hippel, W. (Eds.). (2005). *The Social Outcast: Ostracism, Social Exclusion, Rejection, and Bullying*. New York: Psychology Press.

Williams, K. D., & Jarvis, B. (2006). Cyberball: A program for use in research on interpersonal ostracism and acceptance. *Behavior Research Methods*, *38*, 174–180.

Williams, K. D., & Zadro, L. (2005). Ostracism: The indiscriminate early detection system. In K. D. Williams, J. P. Forgas, & W. von Hippel (Eds.), *The Social Outcast: Ostracism, Social Exclusion, Rejection, and Bullying* (pp. 19–34). New York: Psychology Press.

Yabar, Y., Johnston, L., Miles, L., & Peace, V. (2006). Implicit behavioral mimicry: Investigating the impact of group membership. *Journal of Nonverbal Behavior*, *30*, 97–113. doi:10.1007/s10919-006-0010-6

Belonging Regulation through the Use of (Para)social Surrogates

Megan L. Knowles

Abstract

If belonging is a fundamental human need, then social exclusion should motivate reconnection or another means of fulfilling one's belonging needs. Consistent with this premise, research reveals that individuals utilize myriad means of regaining a sense of belonging after social threat (Belonging Regulation Model; Gardner, Pickett, & Knowles, 2005). This chapter briefly surveys the nature of and evidence for these belonging maintenance strategies and details one of the strategies most far removed from the real world—the use of parasocial attachment figures as social surrogates. Research within and beyond psychology reveals that many individuals form parasocial, or one-sided, attachments to media figures such as television characters. Much like real relationships, these parasocial attachments can be drawn upon in order to maintain a subjective sense of connection. Indeed, exposure to parasocial attachment figures mitigates the negative consequences of exclusion. Last, this chapter raises questions about the boundary conditions of these phenomena.

Key Words: belonging needs, belonging regulation, parasocial attachments, social exclusion, social monitoring, social motivation, social surrogacy, television,

Introduction

According to Williams (2013), social exclusion threatens multiple human needs including the need to belong. A wealth of social psychological theories and research establishes that belonging is a fundamental motive to form and maintain positive, long-lasting relationships and group memberships (Baumeister & Leary, 1995; Maslow, 1954), and as such, individuals should respond to threats to their belonging by seeking out social connection. Accumulated knowledge—of both an anecdotal and empirical nature—confirms the assumption that thwarted belonging needs motivate people to repair them. In fact, individuals faced with social threats such as rejection, exclusion, or ostracism may avail themselves of myriad reparative strategies. Some reparative strategies foster reconnection directly whereas other strategies allow individuals to feel at least a subjective sense of connection. The current chapter begins by reviewing multiple reparative strategies within the context of a broader model of belonging regulation (Gardner et al., 2005). The latter portion of the chapter focuses on the use of parasocial relationships, or one-sided attachments to media figures, as a social surrogate—providing social succor when other social resources are not available.

Belonging Regulation Model
Social Monitoring System
SELECTIVE MEMORY AND ATTENTION

If individuals are motivated to maintain a sense of belonging, they should (1) pay particular attention to social information and (2) show selective retention of this social information when their belonging needs are heightened. Gardner and colleagues tested the selective attention hypothesis in a study using a vocal Stroop task. Specifically, participants were asked to categorize semantically positive (e.g., *pretty*) and negative (e.g., *bitter*) words in terms of word meaning (positive vs. negative) while ignoring the positive or negative vocal tone in which the word was spoken (Pickett, Gardner, & Knowles, 2004). Consistent with the selective attention hypothesis, participants' dispositional belonging needs predicted greater interference on the task—suggesting that individuals who are dispositionally high in belonging needs are more likely to spontaneously attend to social cues than those low in belonging needs.

Examining the selective memory hypothesis, Gardner and colleagues manipulated exclusion using a chat room paradigm, asked participants to read the diary entries of a same-sex student, and later gave participants a surprise recall test pertaining to the entries (Gardner, Pickett, & Brewer, 2000). In comparison to included participants, those who were excluded in the chat room recalled significantly more social entries (e.g., going out with a roommate) but not nonsocial entries (e.g., buying a lottery ticket). These studies and others provide convergent evidence of selective memory and attention for social information after social exclusion and among individuals with dispositionally high belonging needs.

DECODING ACCURACY

Are individuals with unfulfilled belonging needs any better at recognizing subtle social cues than those whose needs are satiated? Research has revealed that individuals with chronically high belonging needs are more accurate in recognizing facial displays of emotion, identifying the valence of vocal tones, and inferring others' thoughts and feelings than those low in belonging needs (Pickett et al., 2004). Moreover, their performance cannot be attributed to general motivation because belonging needs do not predict performance on nonsocial tasks such as math tests.

SOCIAL MONITORING AMONG THE LONELY

Given that dispositional belonging needs and social exclusion activate the social monitoring system, one might think that lonely people—those who lack sufficient social bonds—would also engage in similar social monitoring. Yet, lonely individuals are often thought to have insufficient social skills that hinder their attempts at relationship formation (Inderbitzen-Pisaruk, Clark, & Solano, 1992; Jones, Hobbs, & Hockenbury, 1982; Segrin, 1999; Solano & Koester, 1989; Spitzberg & Hurt. 1987;

Wittenberg & Reis, 1986). Contrary to the social deficit view of loneliness, research shows that lonely individuals more accurately decode social cues such as emotional facial expressions than nonlonely individuals, and they demonstrate greater incidental social memory than nonlonely individuals (Gardner, Pickett, Jefferis, & Knowles, 2005). In other words, individuals who are lonely resemble individuals who have dispositionally or acutely heightened belonging needs.

If lonely individuals are just as good as—if not better than—nonlonely individuals in decoding social cues, then why do lonely individuals underperform in social situations? Recent research has provided an initial explanation for this divergence: lonely individuals' social monitoring skills may not translate into behavior because they choke in actual social interactions (Knowles, Lucas, Gardner, & Baumeister, 2013). In other words, lonely individuals underperform in social situations despite their desire and striving for successful interactions. When social monitoring tasks are framed in a social way—as indicative of social success, lonely individuals typically perform worse than nonlonely individuals. But this is not the case when social monitoring tasks are framed in a nonsocial way—as indicative of academic success. That is, lonely individuals choke on tasks when their social implications are made salient. Furthermore this choking effect may be mediated by anxiety, given the outcome of a misattribution study (Knowles et al., 2013, Study 4). When lonely individuals' social stress was misattributed to a benign beverage, they again outperformed their nonlonely counterparts—suggesting that lonely individuals feel anxious about performing socially relevant tasks, and this stress impedes their performance.

JUDGMENTS OF SOCIAL DISTANCE

Individuals with chronically or acutely heightened belonging needs may be particularly accurate in recognizing facial displays of emotion, but these individuals may not be more accurate than their socially embedded counterparts in making other social judgments. In circumstances under which the accuracy of social judgments does not impact reconnection, rejected individuals should not necessarily perform better than the accepted. Whereas accurate social monitoring facilitates reconnection, accurate recollection of social distance, for instance, would have little impact on subsequent social interactions. In fact, recent evidence suggests that rejected individuals are less accurate than accepted individuals in recalling social distance (Knowles, Green, &

Weidel, 2013). Across three studies, my colleagues and I found that individuals are more likely to underestimate their physical distance to a friendly confederate after exclusion but not after inclusion. We surmise that excluded individuals want to draw friendly others near and distance themselves from unfriendly others in order to regain a sense of connection. Importantly, exclusion does not influence estimates of distance to nonsocial targets. Thus, exclusion does not impair individuals' ability to estimate distance, in general, but instead, exclusion seems to elicit an underestimation of one's distance to social targets, in particular.

Direct Repair via Reconnection

Rejected individuals' consistent underestimation of social distance suggests that they have a desire to reconnect with others, but other research provides much clearer evidence of this drive to regain a sense of belonging after social exclusion. In particular, work by Williams and colleagues revealed that ostracized individuals try to regain a sense of belonging by conforming on a group task (Williams, Cheung, & Choi, 2000) and by working particularly hard on a group task (Williams & Sommer, 1997). More recently, Maner, DeWall, Baumeister, and Schaller (2007) revealed that exclusion motivates individuals to form new friendships, generate favorable impressions of others, work with others rather than in isolation, and demonstrate their generosity to ingratiate themselves to others. Whereas Maner et al. (2007) found that excluded others who feared negative evaluation were less likely to engage in prosocial, affiliative behavior than those who did not fear negative evaluation, Romero-Canyas, Downey, Reddy, Rodriguez, Cavanaugh, and Pelayo (2010) found that individuals high in rejection sensitivity were more likely to do so. Specifically, Romero-Canyas and colleagues observed that individuals high in rejection sensitivity ingratiated themselves to their rejectors more so than those low in rejection sensitivity. Moreover, endocrinological responses to rejection parallel these divergent behavioral responses. Whereas socially anxious individuals show a drop in progesterone, a hormone associated with social affiliative behavior, following exclusion, individuals high in rejection sensitivity show an increase in progesterone instead (Maner, Miller, Schmidt, & Eckel, 2010). Although dispositional and situational factors moderate the release of progesterone and associated affiliative behaviors after rejection, research, on the whole, suggests that when friendly others are available, excluded individuals often perform affiliative behaviors in order to repair their belonging needs directly—by forming new or repairing old or broken social bonds.

Use of Tangible and Intangible Social Representations

USE OF CONCRETE SOCIAL SNACKS

When friendly others are not available to serve as sources of immediate connection, rejected individuals have to resort to other, less direct, means of regaining a sense of belonging. Among other strategies, socially isolated individuals may derive a sense of connection and belonging from concrete reminders of their social relationships or group memberships. These socially symbolic objects can take many forms. Wedding rings may make married people feel loved, college sweatshirts may make students feel socially embedded, and photographs of friends and family can make people feel connected. Preliminary evidence suggests that individuals who report feeling lonely prefer to engage in symbolically social activities like looking at family photographs, reading old emails, or daydreaming about friends over similar nonsocial activities such as looking at magazines, surfing the web, or daydreaming about fun, nonsocial activities (Gardner et al., 2005). Moreover, exposure to photographs may even have some protective value.

More recently, research has examined the use of social media as a means of social snacking. This work reveals that individuals with chronically high belonging needs spend more time on Facebook than those with low belonging needs (Knowles, 2009). Moreover, lonely individuals seem to use Facebook more than the nonlonely as a coping strategy (Sheldon, Abad, & Hinsch, 2011). In a recent study from my own lab, college-aged students engaged in more symbolically social behaviors such as checking their Facebook page and reading their text messages after being excluded from a group task than after being included (Knowles, 2009). Moreover, a follow-up study suggests that Facebook use may even foster recovery after rejection. Indeed, spending time on Facebook appears to mitigate rejection-induced aggression but comparably enjoyable activities such as reading comics online do not lessen the sting of rejection. Thus, social media seems to serve as a useful source of connection for individuals with chronically or acutely high belonging needs.

USE OF INTANGIBLE SOCIAL REPRESENTATIONS

Viewing concrete social reminders such as photographs of friends and family in one's wallet or

Facebook page may promote a sense of belonging, but these social reminders need not be concrete at all. In fact, the intangible social representations that we carry around in mind may serve a similar function. Research has revealed that individuals do draw upon social representations following social exclusion. Specifically, rejected individuals demonstrate greater activation of group-related constructs, social identities, and idiosyncratic than non-rejected individuals (Knowles & Gardner, 2008). Furthermore, rejected individuals who drew upon these intangible social resources reported better mood and higher self-esteem than those who failed to do so—suggesting that these representations had protective value.

Of course, people vary in the extent to which social representations are readily accessible. In particular, individuals with interdependent self-construals—those who fundamentally define the self in terms of their social relationships, identities, and group memberships—have social representations that are chronically salient (Cross, Bacon, & Morris, 2000; Markus & Kitayama, 1991). Given the heightened accessibility of these social representations, it appears that interdependent individuals are less susceptible to rejection-induced negative mood, cognitive deficits, aggressive tendencies, and low self-esteem than independent individuals (Gardner, Knowles, & Jefferis, 2006). Implicit activation of the social self appears to mediate these effects, suggesting that salient social representations—whether they are tangible or intangible in nature, serve as a resource—snacks, if you will—in lieu of a full social meal.

Inflating or Constructing Attachments

People who have chronically high belonging needs and those who experience social rejection or ostracism attempt to fortify their belonging in both direct and indirect ways. They try to regain or maintain social connection by forming new or repairing old social bonds. They try to bolster a subjective sense of connection by social snacking on symbolically social reminders or reflecting upon group memberships, relationships, and identities. The question remains: Will individuals distort the way they see their social world in order to regain a sense of belonging? The work pertaining to perceptions of interpersonal distance suggests that rejection influences social perceptions (Knowles et al., 2013), but the process by which this affiliative bias occurs is unknown. Other research provides more definitive evidence of attachment-enhancement.

ENTITATIVITY AND IMPORTANCE OF GROUPS

Past research by Knowles and Gardner (2008) revealed that individuals primed with rejection consider groups to which they belong to be more meaningful, cohesive entities (i.e., more entitative, or group-like) than groups to which they do not belong. In contrast, individuals primed with a nonsocial ego threat (i.e., failure) did not differentiate between their own groups and other groups in terms of meaningfulness. Similarly, only individuals primed with rejection perceived their own social groups to be more important than others' social groups. These findings suggest that individuals respond to rejection by inflating their group attachments.

BELONGING-ENHANCING ATTRIBUTIONS

In line with the group entitativity and importance findings, social rejection also produces a belonging-enhancing bias analogous to self-serving attributions (e.g., Miller & Ross, 1975). In one study by Knowles and Gardner (2005), participants relived a past rejection or a control experience (i.e., acceptance and failure). Participants then recalled a past group task such as a class project, a sporting event, or a social group's event, reported the extent to which the group's outcome was a success or a failure, and attributed that outcome to either teamwork or their own personal efforts. Results revealed that participants in the control groups made self-enhancing attributions by attributing group success to individual efforts and failure to teamwork; conversely, participants in the rejection group made attachment-enhancing attributions instead by attributing group success to teamwork and failure to individual efforts. In other words, rejected participants inflated their attachment to a group rather than their personal self—a reflection of a belonging illusion similar to Taylor and Brown's (1994) positive illusions.

NONTRADITIONAL ATTACHMENTS

Evidence suggests that heightened belonging needs motivate individuals to reconstrue their social world in order to regain or maintain at least an illusion of belonging. Indeed, rejected individuals inflate the meaningfulness and importance of their groups and bolster their attachments to their groups by making attachment-enhancing attributions. Will they go so far as to make social connections out of thin air? Suggesting the affirmative, work by Waytz and colleagues reveals that lonely individuals imbue pets (Epley, Waytz, Akalis, & Cacioppo, 2008), technological gadgets and tools (Epley, Akalis, Waytz, & Cacioppo, 2008), angels, and spirits with mental states and socially supportive traits in order to derive a sense of connection from them (see Waytz, 2013, for a review).

If nonhuman targets (e.g., pets and gadgets) and incorporeal beings (e.g., angels) serve as sources of social connection, can other nontraditional targets serve a similar function? For over 50 years, scholars have wondered whether media figures such as television characters can provide individuals with a sense of companionship and company. These one-sided "relationships" were first identified as *parasocial relationships* by Horton and Wohl (1956), who speculated that these nontraditional attachments could provide a sort of social compensation for the lonely, isolated, and rejected. We will address this question of social compensation, but first we must examine the nature of these parasocial attachment figures.

Parasocial Attachments

Of the flickering forms that appear on our television screens, many depict people—some of whom act as themselves in talk shows, reality shows, and news broadcasts, and many more of whom embody fictional characters who reside in Manhattan, Sunnydale, glossy suburbs, or far away galaxies. In none of these cases do media figures materialize in our living rooms, and with only rare exceptions, do we ever have a chance to meet them in person. In fact, we will never meet the fictional characters that populate the majority of television shows—from soap operas to sitcoms. Given these circumstances, how do we experience favorite television characters? Are these characters simply an incorporeal composition of pixels, or are they 2-D representations of people that are as human-like to us as friends and family seen in home movies and photographs?

Perceiving Characters as Real

In a controversial paper, Kanazawa (2002) argued that we are unable to distinguish television characters from real people because TV exposure is not a part of our evolutionary history. He did not provide compelling evidence to support this claim (Freese, 2003), but other research indicates that favorite television characters are seen as "real" to some degree.

SELF-REPORTED REALNESS

Initial efforts to understand the nature of parasocial attachments and individuals' perceptions of favorite television characters relied on self-report measures of "realness." Correlational studies have revealed a relationship between the strength of parasocial attachments to characters and the realness of their associated shows. For instance, viewers form stronger parasocial attachments to characters in realistic soap operas (Rubin & Perse, 1987) and to newscasters in realistic news broadcasts (Perse, 1990). Given the design of these studies, we cannot determine whether realistic shows are more conducive to the formation of attachments or if attachments cultivate a sense of character realness. Perhaps there is truth in each causal pathway.

Assessing the realness of characters rather than their environments, Wendi Gardner and I asked participants to report the extent to which either a favorite character or a nonfavorite character on the same show seem like real people (Gardner & Knowles, 2008, Study 1). We found that favorite TV characters were considered more human-like than other characters despite the fact that they were equally familiar with and knowledgeable of the others characters. Moreover, collapsed across all characters, liking predicted perceptions of realness. That is, to the extent participants liked a character, that character seemed more real to them.

SOCIAL FACILITATION EFFECTS

Given the limitations inherent in self-report measures, we ran a second experiment measuring behavioral outcomes associated with real audiences (Gardner & Knowles, 2008, Study 2). Specifically, we exposed individuals to a picture of their favorite TV character or a control character and asked them to complete well-learned and novel tasks, that is, copying words using their dominant hand and doing so with their nondominant hand, respectively. Consistent with classic social facilitation findings using audiences comprised of conspecifics (e.g., Zajonc, 1965), participants exposed to their favorite TV character performed better on the well-learned task and worse on the novel task than those exposed to a nonfavorite character. Thus, favorite TV characters functioned like a traditional audience of conspecifics. In other words, we see humans when we look at favorite TV characters.

SIMILARITY TO REAL RELATIONSHIPS

Parasocial relationships resemble real-world relationships in a variety of ways. For instance, the attachment literature suggests that individuals respond to parasocial relationships as they do real relationships. Reflecting the attachment behavior within the real world, research reveals that individuals with an anxious-ambivalent attachment style are the most likely to form parasocial relationships to their favorite TV personalities, followed by those with secure attachment styles, and finally, those with avoidant attachment styles (Cole & Leets, 1999). Like the anxious-ambivalent undergraduates in the study by Cole and Leets (1999), adolescent girls who have preoccupied attachment styles are particularly likely to become emotionally attached to their favorite media figure (Theran, Newberg, & Gleason, 2010). Similarly, mirroring real world breakups, individuals anticipating the end of their favorite TV character's show were more upset to the extent they had a strong attachment to the character (Cohen, 2004). Moreover, individuals with an anxious-ambivalent attachment reacted the most negatively to the expected dissolution of their parasocial relationships.

If parasocial relationships resemble real-life relationships such as friendships, one would expect favorite characters to elicit behaviors and affective responses consistent with friendship. To get at this question, I ran three studies in which I primed participants with their favorite TV character or a control target and assessed feelings of empathy and a desire to self-disclose (Knowles, 2008). As expected, I found that among participants primed with their favorite characters, attachment strength predicted self-disclosure and empathy. No significant relationships emerged among individuals primed with a control target. These studies suggest that strong parasocial attachments resemble real life friendships in that parasocial "friends" elicit responses commonly associated with friendship despite the fact these relationships are, by nature, nonreciprocal.

In sum, research suggests that favorite television characters are seen as human-like, at the very least. Even further, favorite television characters and other media figures may resemble friends or relationship partners that activate affective and behavioral patterns associated with real-world social bonds. Yet, we still do not know what motivates individuals to form parasocial attachments and what functions they serve.

Parasocial Attachments as Social Surrogates

Drawing upon theories of media uses and gratifications (Katz, Gurevitch, & Haas, 1973; Levy, 1979; Rosengren & Windahl, 1972; Rubin, 2002; Rubin & Rubin, 1985), many researchers have tried to determine the function that parasocial attachments serve for television viewers. Taking into account the research showing especially high media use among individuals who report being lonely or

having problems in their relationships (Armstrong & Rubin, 1989; Perlman, Gerson, & Spinner, 1978; Perse & Rubin, 1990), many researchers initially thought that lonely individuals would compensate for their dearth of actual attachments by forming parasocial ones (McCourt & Fitzpatrick, 2001; Rubin et al., 1985). In the words of Horton and Wohl (1956, p. 222),

> This function of the para-social then can properly be called compensatory, inasmuch as it provides the socially and psychologically isolated with a chance to enjoy the elixir of sociability.

Yet, contrary to expectations, there is little evidence that individuals with social deficits actively seek out media outlets to compensate for their lack of relationships. In fact, research suggests that lonely individuals watch more television than nonlonely individuals because they are in a more passive state; they are mainly using television to pass time (Perse & Rubin, 1990; Tsao, 1996). Regarding parasocial attachments in particular, numerous studies have failed to find an association between loneliness and the strength of parasocial attachments (Chory-Assad & Yanen, 2005; McCourt & Fitzpatrick, 2001; Rubin et al., 1985). Individuals with strong parasocial attachments appear no more likely to lack positive, meaningful relationships than those without parasocial attachments. If people do not form parasocial attachments to compensate for the lack of real ones, why do people form these one-sided relationships?

DISPOSITIONAL BELONGING NEEDS

Some research suggests that individuals do not necessarily seek out parasocial relationships to compensate for a lack of relationships or to directly replace failed relationships, but instead, individuals with chronically elevated belonging needs are particularly likely to form these nontraditional relationships (Knowles, 2007). In other words, people with a large "social appetite" who have dispositionally high needs for social inclusion and acceptance are more likely to form strong parasocial relationships than people with lower belonging needs.

This hypothesis was tested in a pair of studies assessing individuals' chronic need to belong and the strength of their parasocial attachments. Self-report measures of dispositional belonging needs (i.e., the Need to Belong Scale; Leary, Kelly, Cottrell, & Schreindorfer, 2007) and parasocial attachment strength (i.e., the Parasocial Interaction Scale; Rubin, Perse, & Powell, 1985) were distributed to hundreds of participants in a nationally representative sample

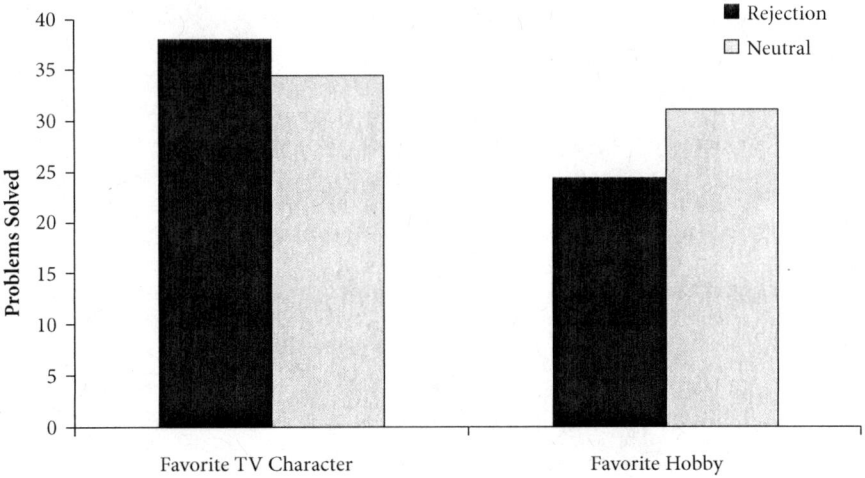

Figure 26.1 Number of Math Problems Solved Correctly as a Function of Reliving Task and Prime in Study 1
From Knowles & Gardner, 2012.

of Americans and multiple undergraduate samples (Knowles, 2007). Consistent with expectations, findings reveal a positive correlation between the measures such that individuals who reported high belonging needs were significantly more likely to form strong parasocial attachments to their favorite television character than those with low belonging needs.

PROTECTIVE VALUE AFTER REJECTION

If parasocial attachments are motivated, at least in part, by dispositional belonging needs, perhaps these attachments can serve belonging. Indeed, my colleagues and I have suggested that parasocial attachments can serve as social surrogates, protecting

individuals from the negative effects of social rejection (Gardner et al., 2005; Knowles, 2007). Wendi Gardner and I tested this social surrogacy hypothesis in a series of four studies (Knowles & Gardner, 2012). In three studies, we manipulated rejection via a reliving task, asked participants to write about either their favorite television character or control constructs (e.g., a hobby, favorite travel destination, or friend), and assessed negative outcomes associated with rejection. As expected, these studies revealed that priming individuals with favorite television characters or actual friends protected them from rejection-induced cognitive deficits (Fig. 26.1), drops in self-esteem (Fig. 26.2), and

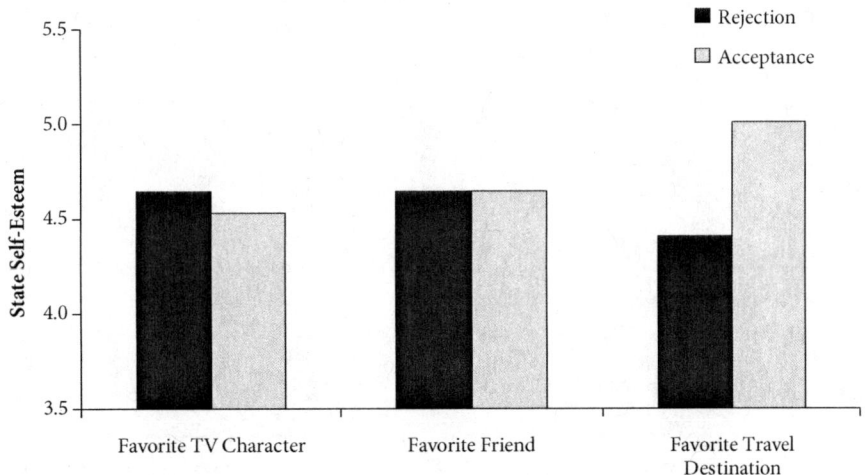

Figure 26.2 State Self-Esteem as a Function of Reliving Task and Prime in Study 2
From Knowles & Gardner, 2012.

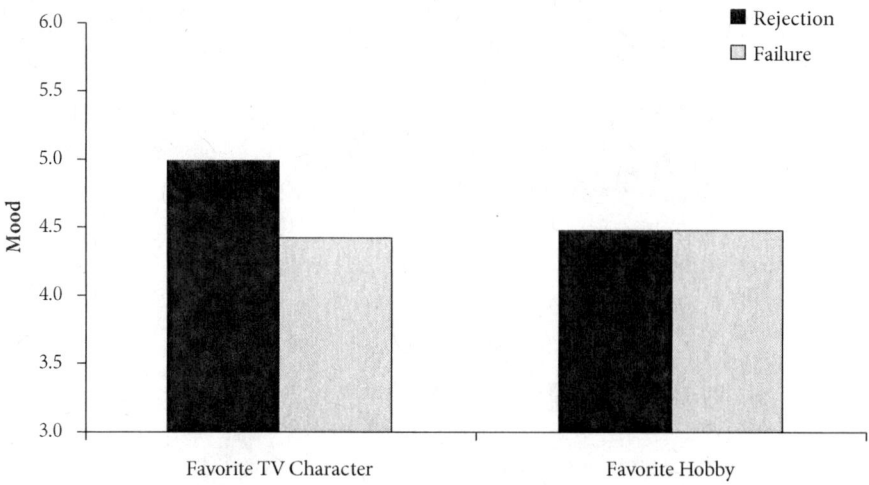

Figure 26.3 Mood as a Function of Reliving Task and Prime in Study 3
From Knowles & Gardner, 2012.

lowered mood (Fig. 26.3). Conversely, positive, nonsocial primes did not serve a comparable function. In the third study, we also assessed feelings of belongingness and found that favorite TV characters boosted rejected individuals' sense of belonging (see Fig. 26.4), and feelings of belongingness mediated the effect of the TV character prime on mood following rejection (Fig. 26.5).

Last, in the final study, we manipulated exclusion using Cyberball, exposed participants to images of their own or another participant's favorite television character, and assessed postrejection self-protective cognitions (i.e., perceptions of in-group entitativity). Consistent with previous research showing that individuals inflate the meaningfulness of their in-groups after rejection (Knowles & Gardner, 2008), excluded participants exposed to a control character described their in-groups as significantly more meaningful than their out-groups. Conversely, excluded participants exposed to their favorite TV characters did not show this self-protective cognition; they considered their in-groups and out-groups to be comparably meaningful and cohesive. In other words, excluded participants no longer needed to bolster their sense of belonging if they had been exposed to their favorite TV character. Across four studies, one's own favorite television character appeared to serve as a social surrogate, protecting individuals from the adverse impact of a social rejection.

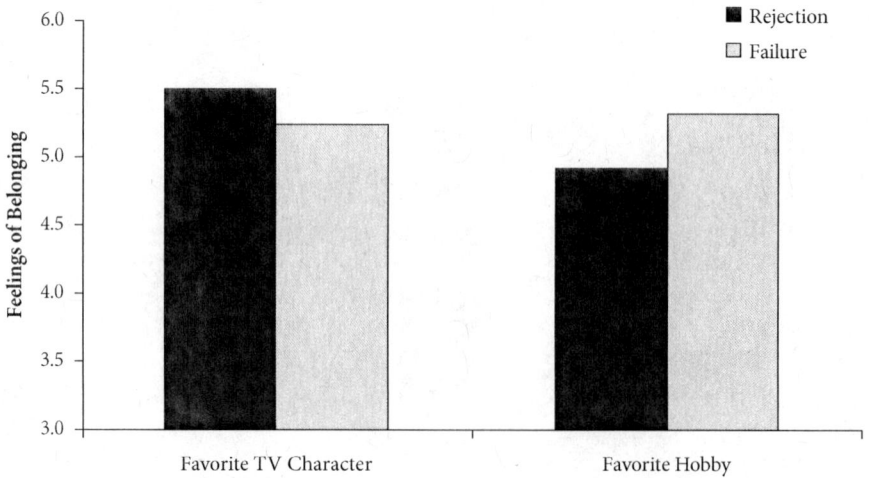

Figure 26.4 Feelings of Belonging as a Function of Reliving Task and Prime in Study 3
From Knowles & Gardner, 2012.

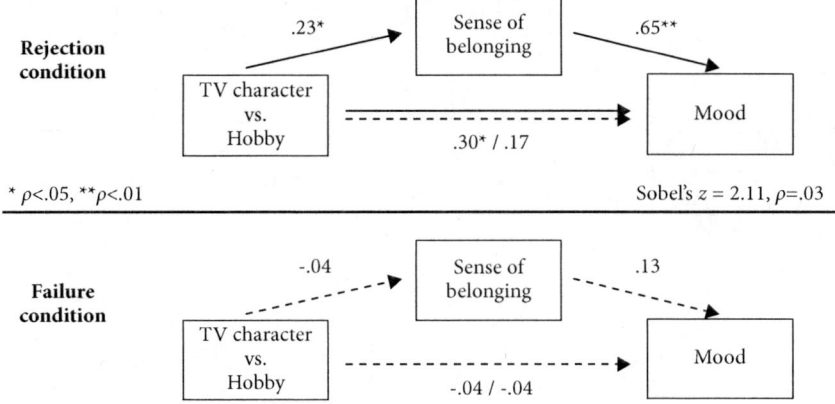

Figure 26.5 Tests of Mediation in Study 3
From Knowles & Gardner, 2012.

Expanding the focus from favorite television characters to favorite television programs, Derrick, Gabriel, and Hugenberg (2009) also put the social surrogacy hypothesis to the test. Consistent with prior research, they found that parasocial relationships within favorite television shows fostered a sense of belonging and buffered individuals against the negative consequences of exclusion. Specifically, their participants reported feeling less lonely when watching their favorite TV show. Also, exposure to a favorite TV show protected individuals against rejection-induced drops in self-esteem and mood and reduced the accessibility of the exclusion construct (measured via a word stem completion task). Moreover, participants who relived a negative interpersonal experience (i.e., a fight with a friend) demonstrated greater immersion in a favorite TV show than those who relived a neutral experience. Altogether, this work reveals that favorite television characters and their programs can serve as a resource when faced with social exclusion.

Conclusions

In sum, individuals with chronically or acutely heightened belonging needs may regain or maintain a sense of belonging by using one or more belonging regulation strategies such as direct repair of broken bonds, social snacking using socially symbolic reminders, reflecting upon intangible social representations, and inflating their attachments to groups. Perhaps most surprisingly, these individuals will form parasocial attachments to favorite television characters, and these characters act as social surrogates—buffering individuals from the sting of rejection. Much research needs to be done to fully understand the nature of the parasocial attachments

and the ways in which these attachments form and function in individuals' lives.

Future Directions

Q1: Because TV characters are not responsive to the viewer, does exposure to favorite television characters actually exacerbate feelings of rejection for some individuals? In particular, individuals who are high in rejection sensitivity (London-Thompson, 2013; Downey & Feldman, 1996) may find that TV characters reinforce feelings of loneliness and isolation. Having associated eye aversion with rejection and ostracism (Wirth, Sacco, Hugenberg, & Williams, 2010), individuals—especially those high in rejection sensitivity—may be particularly attuned to TV characters' eyes that are almost always averted from the camera, and consequently, the viewer. Perhaps an individual high in rejection sensitivity would even feel hostility toward a TV character who seems to be ignoring the aggrieved viewer and exacerbating his/her feeling of isolation (Ayduk, Downey, Testa, Yen, & Shoda, 1999; Downey, Freitas, Michaelis, & Khouri, 1998).

Q2: What is the value of a parasocial relationship in comparison to a real relationship? Given that individuals with strong parasocial attachments often report having lower self-esteem than those with no strong parasocial attachments, one might speculate that forming a parasocial attachment is not conducive to mental health and well-being, but the causal link (if any) between parasocial attachments and self-esteem is unknown. It may be the case that parasocial relationships provide one with the great relational flexibility that could prove advantageous, but at the same time, the one-sided nature of parasocial relationships does not allow for reciprocity found in the real world. A person may care about the health and well-being of his favorite television character, but that character will not reciprocate his concern and interest.

Q3: Do different parasocial attachments serve different functions? Can I derive a sense of connection from Buffy and her friends, identify with Rory Gilmore, and pass time with the Simpsons?

Q4: If some individuals view their favorite TV characters as friends, do these characters have the same influence over their lives than friends do? For instance, real-world friends influence what we like and dislike, according to Heider's Balance Theory (Heider, 1958). Similarly, do the sentiments of parasocial "friends" also influence our liking and disliking of objects? If I'm attached to Phoebe Buffay, who frequently sings of a "Smelly Cat," do I similarly grow fond of smelly cats?

Q5: What are the limits to the salve of the parasocial relationship? Surely parasocial attachments are not sufficient to relieve the pain of some social losses. It would be difficult to imagine how a television character could fill up the social want left by a deceased confidante or a divorced spouse.

Q6: Can attachments to favorite TV characters improve real world relationships? A lonely newcomer to a job may find that he has colleagues with similar viewing interests, and immediately, he has "shared history" with these strangers. Provided an individuals' favorite TV character is well functioning and socially appropriate, he or she could actually model social behavior for the socially unskilled.

References

Armstrong, C. B., & Rubin, A. M. (1989). Talk radio as interpersonal communication. *Journal of Communication, 39,* 84–94.

Ayduk, Ö., Downey, G., Testa, A., Yen, Y., & Shoda, Y. (1999). Does rejection elicit hostility in rejection sensitive women? *Social Cognition, 17,* 245–271.

Baumeister, R. F., & Leary, M. R. (1995). The need to belong: Desire for interpersonal attachments as a fundamental human motivation. *Psychological Bulletin, 117,* 497–529.

Chory-Assad, R. M., & Yanen, A. (2005). Hopelessness and loneliness as predictors of older adults' involvement in favorite television performers. *Journal of Broadcasting & Electronic Media, 49,* 182–201.

Cohen, J. (2004). Parasocial break-up from favorite television characters: The role of attachment styles and relationship intensity. *Journal of Social and Personal Relationships, 21,* 187–202.

Cole, T., & Leets, L. (1999). Attachment styles and intimate television viewing: Insecurely forming relationships in a parasocial way. *Journal of Social and Personal Relationships, 16,* 495–511.

Cross, S. E., Bacon, P. L., & Morris, M. L. (2000). The relational-interdependent self-construal and relationships. *Journal of Personality and Social Psychology, 78,* 791–808.

Derrick, J. D., Gabriel, S., & Hugenberg, K. (2009). Social surrogacy: How favored television programs provide the experience of belonging. *Journal of Experimental Social Psychology, 45,* 352–362.

Downey, G., & Feldman, S. I. (1996). Implications of rejection sensitivity for intimate relationships. *Journal of Personality and Social Psychology, 70,* 1327–1343.

Downey, G., Freitas, A. L., Michaelis, B., & Khouri, H. (1998). The self-fulfilling prophecy in close relationships: Rejection sensitivity and rejection by romantic partners. *Journal of Personality and Social Psychology, 75,* 545–560.

Epley, N., Akalis, S., Waytz, A., & Cacioppo, J. T. (2008). Creating social connection through inferential reproduction: Loneliness and perceived agency in gadgets, gods, and greyhounds. *Psychological Science, 19,* 114–120.

Epley, N., Waytz, A., Akalis, S., & Cacioppo, J. Y. (2008). When I need a human: Motivational determinants of anthropomorphism. *Social Cognition, 26,* 143–155.

Freese, J. (2003). Imaginary imaginary friends? Television viewing and satisfaction with friendships. *Evolution and Human Behavior, 24,* 65–69.

Gardner, W. L., & Knowles, M. L. (2008) Love makes you real: Favorite television characters are perceived as "real" in a social facilitation paradigm. *Social Cognition, 26,* 156–168.

Gardner, W. L., Knowles, M. L., & Jefferis, V. E. (2006). *Never alone: The interdependent self as a buffer from rejection.* Unpublished manuscript.

Gardner, W. L., Pickett, C. L., & Brewer, M. B. (2000). Social exclusion and selective memory: How the need to belong influences memory for social events. *Personality and Social Psychology Bulletin, 26,* 486–496.

Gardner, W. L., Pickett, C. L., Jefferis, V., & Knowles, M. L. (2005). On the outside looking in: Loneliness and social monitoring. *Personality and Social Psychology Bulletin, 31,* 1549–1560.

Gardner, W. L., Pickett, C. L., & Knowles, M. L. (2005). Social snacking and shielding: Using social symbols, selves, and surrogates in the service of belonging needs. In K. D. Williams, J. P. Forgas, & von Hippel, W. (Eds.), *The Social Outcast: Ostracism, Social Exclusion, and Bullying* (pp. 227–241). New York: Psychology Press.

Heider, F. (1958). *The Psychology of Interpersonal Relations.* New York: Wiley.

Horton, D., & Wohl, R. R. (1956). Mass communication and para-social interaction. *Psychiatry: Journal for the Study of Interpersonal Processes, 19,* 215–229.

Inderbitzen-Pisaruk, H., Clark, M. L., & Solano, C. H. (1992). Correlates of loneliness in midadolescence. *Journal of Youth Adolescence, 21,* 151–167.

Jones, W. H., Hobbs, S. A., & Hockenbury, D. (1982). Loneliness and social skill deficits. *Journal of Personality and Social Psychology Bulletin, 42,* 682–689.

Kanazawa, S. (2002). Bowling with our imaginary friends. *Evolution and Human Behavior, 23,* 167–171.

Katz, E., Gurevitch, M., & Haas, H. (1973). On the use of the mass media for important things. *American Sociological Review, 38,* 164–181.

Knowles, M. L. (2007). *The nature of parasocial relationships.* (Unpublished doctoral dissertation). Northwestern University, Evanston, IL.

Knowles, M. L. (2008, October). *Behavioral and affective consequences of exposure to a parasocial "friend."* Poster presentation at the meeting of the Society for Southeastern Social Psychologists, Greenville, SC.

Knowles, M. L. (2009, January). *Social media in response to chronic and acute belonging needs.* Poster presented at the meeting of the Society for Personality and Social Psychology, Las Vegas, NV.

Knowles, M. L., & Gardner, W. L. (2005). *But my other relationships are fabulous: The buffering effects of belonging illusions on rejection distress.* Unpublished manuscript, Department of Psychology, Northwestern University, Evanston, IL.

Knowles, M. L., & Gardner, W. L. (2012). *I'll be there for you . . . : Favorite television characters as social surrogates.* Manuscript in preparation.

Knowles, M. L., & Gardner, W. L. (2008). Benefits of membership: The activation and amplification of group identities in response to social rejection. *Personality and Social Psychology Bulletin, 34,* 1200–1213.

Knowles, M. L., Green, A., & Weidel, A. (2013). *Drawing others near: Judgments of interpersonal distance following social rejection.* Manuscript under review.

Knowles, M. L., Lucas, G. M., Gardner, W. L., & Baumeister, R. F. (2013). *Social monitoring among the lonely: Choking under social pressure.* Manuscript under review.

Leary, M. R., Kelly, K. M., Cottrell, C. A., & Schreindorfer, L. S. (2007). *Individual differences in the need to belong: Mapping the nomological network.* Unpublished manuscript, Department of Psychology and Neuroscience, Duke University.

Levy, M. R. (1979). Watching TV news as para-social interaction. *Journal of Broadcasting, 23,* 69–80.

London-Thompson, B. (2013). Rejection sensitivity. In C. N. DeWall (Ed.), *The Oxford Handbook Of Social Exclusion.* New York: Oxford University Press.

Maner, J. K., DeWall, C. N., Baumeister, R. F., & Schaller, M. (2007). Does social exclusion motivate interpersonal reconnection? Resolving the "Porcupine Problem." *Journal of Personality and Social Psychology, 92,* 42–55.

Maner, J. K., Miller, S. L., Schmidt, N. B., & Eckel, L. A. (2010). The endocrinology of exclusion: Rejection elicits motivationally tuned changes in progesterone. *Psychological Science, 21,* 581–588.

Markus, H. R., & Kitayama, S. (1991). Culture and the self: Implications for cognition, emotion, and motivation. *Psychological Review, 98,* 224–253.

Maslow, A. (1954). *Motivation and Personality.* New York: Harper.

McCourt, A., & Fitzpatrick, J. (2001). The role of personal characteristics and romantic characteristics in parasocial relationships: A pilot study. *Journal of Mundane Behavior, 2,* 1–12.

Miller, D. T., & Ross, M. (1975). Self-serving biases in attribution of causality: Fact or fiction? *Psychological Bulletin, 82,* 213–225.

Perlman, D., Gerson, A. C., & Spinner, B. (1978). Loneliness among senior citizens: An empirical report. *Essence, 2,* 239–248.

Perse, E. M. (1990). Media involvement and local news effects. *Journal of Broadcasting & Electronic Media, 34,* 17–36.

Perse, E. M., & Rubin, A. M. (1990). Chronic loneliness and television use. *Journal of Broadcasting & Electronic Media, 34,* 37–53

Pickett, C., Gardner, W. L. & Knowles, M. L. (2004). Getting a cue: The need to belong influences attention to subtle social cues. *Personality and Social Psychology Bulletin, 30,* 1095–1107.

Romero-Canyas, R., Downey, G., Reddy, K. S., Rodriguez, S., Cavanaugh, T. J., & Pelayo, R. (2010). Paying to belong: When does rejection trigger ingratiation? *Journal of Personality and Social Psychology, 99,* 802–823.

Rosengren, K. E., & Windahl, S. (1972). Mass media consumption as a functional alternative. In D. McQuail (Ed.), *Sociology of Mass Communication* (pp. 166–194). Middlesex, UK: Penguin Books.

Rubin, A. M. (2002). The uses-and-gratifications perspective of media effects. In J. Bryant & D. Zillman (Eds.), *Main effects: Advances in Theory and Research* (2nd ed., pp. 525–548). Mahwah, NJ: Lawrence Erlbaum Associates.

Rubin, A. M., & Perse, E. M. (1987). Audience activity and soap opera involvement: A uses and effects investigation. *Human Communication Research, 14,* 246–268.

Rubin, A. M., Perse, E. M., & Powell, R. A. (1985). Loneliness, parasocial interaction, and local news viewing. *Human Communication Research, 12,* 155–180.

Rubin, A. M., & Rubin, R. B. (1985). Interface of personal and mediated communication: A research agenda. *Critical Studies in Mass Communication, 2,* 36–53.

Segrin, C. (1999). Social skills, stressful life events, and the development of psychosocial problems. *Journal of Social and Clinical Psychology, 18,* 14–34

Sheldon, K. M., Abad, N, & Hinsch, C. (2011). A two-process view of Facebook use and relatedness need-satisfaction: Disconnection drives use, and connection rewards it. *Journal of Personality and Social Psychology, 100,* 766–775.

Solano, C. H., & Koester, N. H. (1989). Loneliness and communication problems: Subjective anxiety or objective skills? *Personality and Social Psychology Bulletin, 15,* 126–133.

Spitzberg, B. H., & Hurt, H. T. (1987). The relationship of interpersonal competence and skills to reported loneliness across time. *Journal of Social Behavior and Personality, 2,* 157–172.

Taylor, S. E., & Brown, J. D. (1994). Positive illusions and well-being revisited: Separating fact from fiction. *Psychological Bulletin, 116,* 21–27.

Theran, S. A., Newberg, E. M., & Gleason, T. R. (2010). Adolescent girls' parasocial interaction with media figures. *The Journal of Genetic Psychology: Research and Theory on Human Development, 17,* 270–277.

Tsao, J. (1996). Compensatory media use: An exploration of two paradigms. *Communication Studies, 47,* 89–109.

Waytz, A. (2013). Social connection and seeing human. In C. N. DeWall (Ed.), *The Oxford Handbook of Social Exclusion.* New York: Oxford University Press.

Williams, K. D. (2013). Ostracism and stages of coping. In C. N. DeWall (Ed.), *The Oxford Handbook of Social Exclusion.* New York: Oxford University Press.

Williams, K. D., Cheung, C. K. T., & Choi, W. (2000). Cyberostracism: Effects of being ignored over the internet. *Journal of Personality and Social Psychology, 79,* 748–762.

Williams, K. D., & Sommer, K. L. (1997). Social ostracism by coworkers: Does rejection lead to loafing or compensation? *Personality and Social Psychology Bulletin, 23,* 693–706.

Wirth, J. H., Sacco, D. F., Hugenberg, K., Williams, K. D. (2010). Eye gaze as relational evaluation: Averted eye gaze leads to feelings of ostracism and relational devaluation. *Personality and Social Psychology Bulletin, 36,* 869–882.

Wittenberg, M. T., & Reis, H. T. (1986). Loneliness, social skills, and social perception. *Personality and Social Psychology Bulletin, 12,* 121–130.

Zajonc, R. B. (1965). Social facilitation. *Science, 149,* 269–274..

The Birth and Death of Belonging

Jeff Schimel *and* Jeff Greenberg

Abstract

Terror management theory (TMT) (Greenberg, Pyszczynski, & Solomon, 1986) offers an evolutionary–existential–psychoanalytic perspective on the human motive to belong. According to this view, the evolution of sophisticated intellect allowed for consideration of the past and future in decision making, thereby freeing human beings from fixed response patterns. However, it also made humans uniquely aware of the inevitability of their own death. To manage potentially debilitating anxiety resulting from this awareness, humans have had to give up some of this freedom so as to feel securely embedded in a cultural meaning system (a cultural worldview) that provides meaning, self-worth, and a sense of immortality. Because other people are an important source of self-esteem and validation for cultural worldview beliefs, social connections with similar others are maintained to mitigate existential fear. A large empirical literature supporting this theoretical account is reviewed. Ensuing discussion considers how a TMT perspective can lend understanding to the multifarious reactions people have to social exclusion.

Key Words: belonging, cultural worldview, death, evolution, existential, freedom, self-esteem, social exclusion, terror management

The Birth and Death of Belonging

Recent theorizing has posited that four fundamental needs are threatened by social exclusion: a desire to feel accepted by others, self-esteem, control, and the need for a meaningful existence (Williams, 2007; Williams & Zadro, 2005). The attainment of these needs has long been hypothesized to play a vital role in managing existentially based fear (e.g., Becker, 1962/1971), yet very little research or discussion has been devoted to an understanding of the existential function of belonging. According to terror management theory (TMT) (Greenberg, Pyszczynski, & Solomon, 1986), social connections with other like-minded individuals provide people with self-esteem and validation for their core beliefs about the nature of reality, which in turn function to protect people from uniquely human concerns about death. The purpose of this chapter is to use TMT to enhance understanding of the human motive to belong and thereby shed light on the complexities of reactions to social exclusion.

Terror Management Theory
Primate Evolution and the Rise of Human Intellect

Terror management theory is based on the evolutionary–existential–psychoanalytic account of human motivation provided by Ernest Becker (1962/1971, 1973). From an evolutionary perspective a key difference between homo sapiens and other organisms, even our closest relatives the chimpanzees and great apes, is the size and complexity of the brain. The basis for human intellect began with a change that took place in the mammalian line. In contrast to insects and reptiles, mammal offspring are born helpless and dependent, unable to survive on their own without nourishment and protection from adult caregivers. The prolonged immaturity of young mammals had several far-reaching consequences. First, a premature arrival means that the brain continues to develop for an extended time after birth. Also, the young must remain in close contact with the mother. The result is that mammal offspring are now in a position to learn or model behaviors from their caregivers. This means too that mammals tend to develop a greater sensitivity to other members of their species, resulting in animals that are intrinsically social. Broadly construed, this need for a close mother–offspring tie to ameliorate the helpless vulnerability of the young could be considered the "birth" of mammalian and eventually human, belonging.

But a slower rate of maturation also laid the foundation for animals with higher mental complexity to evolve because now part of the development of the brain takes place outside the womb. This change allows the brain to develop in the context of the environment, which leads to greater adaptation through learning experiences (as opposed to hard-wired instinctual programming) and a higher degree of behavioral flexibility. Apparently, environmental pressures continued to favor animals with slower rates of maturation because looking across the mammalian line, and especially within the primate lineage, there is a steady progression such that the more cognitively complex the species, the more social, and the longer the period of dependence of the young. Becker (1962/1971) proposed that the need for intimate cooperation and social organization among primates and early humans increased an already high premium on delayed maturation; natural selection therefore continued to favor increases in brain size, eventually leading to the sophisticated ways of thinking among modern humans. These intellectual abilities include: (1) temporal thought—the ability to ponder the past and consider what might happen in the future, (2) symbolic thought—the capacity to reason using arbitrary symbols (the pinnacle of which is language), and (3) self-reflective thought—the ability to reflect on aspects of one's own existence. To be sure, these new ways of thinking provided human beings with unparalleled command over their world; but they also led to two important existential complexities.

Two Important Consequences of Human Intellect

FREEDOM

These cognitive capabilities bestowed human beings with a relatively high degree of freedom from fixed response patterns. According to Mithen (1996), language in particular allowed for a kind of cognitive fluidity or meta-representation (Karmiloff-Smith, 1992), in which highly specialized domains of knowledge that were previously isolated or "locked-up" in different parts of the brain to be combined to form new ideas and abstract concepts. Therefore, the development of language led to an abrupt shift from a highly specialized, domain specific kind of mentality to a generalized type of mentality that allowed for flexibility and creativity in adapting to environmental challenges. In combination with language and future-oriented thought, the capacity for self-awareness afforded humans even greater freedom from rigid response patterns because it allowed them to step back from a stimulus, bring relevant knowledge and memories to bear, anticipate future consequences, and choose a course of action. In other words, humans can pull themselves away from momentary sensory experience and engage in complex goal-directed behavior, a phenomenon called *self-regulation* (Carver & Scheier, 1981; Duval & Wicklund, 1972). Clearly, these intellectual abilities have led to a tremendous degree of flexibility in dealing with challenges and have allowed modern humans, relative to their primate cousins, to invent the means to prosper in a wide variety of environments across the globe.

DREAD

In addition to many benefits, these intellectual abilities also introduced two unfortunate consequences. Along with innumerable possibilities, freedom brings the burden of choosing, and of responsibility and guilt over the consequences of one's choices. This burden has important implications for human relations, but ones that would require a chapter devoted entirely to them (see Greenberg, Koole, & Pyszczynski, 2004). Here we will focus on the other burden of human intellect: awareness of the inevitability of death. The capacity to ponder one's existence (i.e., self-awareness), when combined with the ability to think about the future, became highly problematic because it made human beings aware that they are merely flesh-and-blood animals that will eventually decay and die. Most other animals only experience fear when they are faced with a clear and present danger. However, because humans can anticipate all kinds of future threats, self-awareness creates the potential for ever-present anxiety and dread.

According to TMT, this existentially based fear (an inadvertent byproduct of evolved human intellect), if experienced unchecked, would undermine many of the adaptive benefits of self-awareness by interfering with effective thought and action (i.e., self-regulation). Thus, to function with relative equanimity, humans used the same sophisticated cognitive abilities that created the problem of the awareness of death in the first place to construct and maintain cultural belief systems (i.e., cultural worldviews) that provide people with the sense that human existence is more meaningful and enduring than that of mere "animals." Cultural worldviews are humanly created shared symbolic conceptions of reality that give meaning, order, and predictability to human existence and provide a sense of literal or symbolic immortality to those who believe in the worldview and live up to its standards of value. Literal immortality refers to the notion that the faithful will continue to exist in the hereafter, whereas symbolic immortality (Lifton, 1979) refers to culturally esteemed symbols of the self (e.g., family, children, group identifications, creative achievements) that live on in the culture after one's physical death. Thus, self-esteem is the sense that one is on a path toward immortality by attaining symbolic value among those who share one's cultural worldview, a psychological structure that is theoretically eternal as long as generations of "believers" are able to perpetuate it. Next we consider how self-esteem developed into a device for managing existential fear.

Socialization and the Development of the Self-Esteem Motive

Despite the extreme state of vulnerability that lasts for many years after birth, the human child must go about the business of learning and exploring its environment so that the brain can develop into a complex organ. Thus, the child has a dilemma: It is vulnerable and needs to feel safe and secure through close contact with caregivers, but is compelled to explore and learn about the environment, which takes the child away from close proximity to caregivers. The attachment mechanism therefore evolved to provide a balance between the need for security versus exploration (Becker, 1962/1971; Bowlby, 1969). When the infant gets too far away from an attachment figure or is approached by strangers, it experiences an influx of anxiety, which motivates the infant to seek close contact with attachment figures so as to reduce this anxiety. Thus, early on in development, pain and anxiety is reduced by close, soothing contact with attachment figures.

However, as the child gets older, he or she realizes that the mere expression of bodily urges and intrinsic desires no longer bring the unconditional support of attachment figures. The parents begin to place expectations on the child to act in certain ways. When the child goes against these expectations, the parents may express disapproval, withdraw signs of affection, and perhaps even dispense punishment. Similarly, when the child is successful in curbing behavior to be in line with parental standards, the parents offer warm praise and affection, which attenuates feelings of anxiety. The end result of this processes is that the child, in large part, is forced to give up his or her own physical reality (the free expression of intrinsic desires coupled with automatic parental support), in exchange for a new social–symbolic reality, in which the child must abide by arbitrary codes of behavior laid down by the parents to receive the same feeling of love and support. Through this process, children learn that being "good" and meeting social standards leads to safety, protection, and the abatement of anxiety, whereas being bad and breaking these standards leads to vulnerability and heightened anxiety (Becker, 1971; Mikulincer & Shaver, 2007). This progression from attachment to socialization, in which the child internalizes parental standards of value to maintain parental love, denotes the emergence of self-esteem as a symbolic, standard-based psychological structure that functions to control the child's basic fears and anxieties.

This switch from *close contact with others* to a *self-esteem system* for managing anxiety broadens the child's source of security and allows for greater independence. Through the socialization of self-esteem, the child no longer needs to be in direct contact with Mom and Dad to feel safe and secure, he or she can now manage anxiety from a distance by maintaining an image of oneself as "good" in the parents' eyes. In addition to living up to internalized social standards, the other way children maintain their status as *loved from a distance* is by punishing themselves when they fail to live up to standards, which is the experience of guilt. Thus, by sharing in the symbols of the parents and society, children acquire a broader, more "portable" method of handling anxiety, and likewise gain autonomy from basic organismic fears that were once governed by the more rigid attachment mechanism. However, there is another source of anxiety brewing that calls for an even broader sense of protection.

Self-Consciousness and the Death of Belonging

Later in development, with increasing cognitive complexity and the acquisition of language, the child becomes fully self-aware. With the emergence of self-awareness, the child develops a mature understanding of the concept of death as biological, universal, and inevitable (Lonetto, 1980; Speece & Brent, 1996). The child now has the capacity to imagine threats around every corner and lethal threats that have yet to happen. Moreover, the child comes to realize that the parents (like the child) are made of physical matter that is not immune to death and decay and are therefore incapable of protecting the child from the many dangers in the world. This new source of fear prompts questions about the meaning of life, such as, "Where do babies come from?" and "What happens to animals when they die?" or the more pointed version of these questions, "Where did I come from?" and "What's going to happen to me when I die?" (Webb, 2002).

According to TMT, these questions reflect a budding awareness of human mortality made possible by the cognitive capacity for self-awareness, which triggers the need for a broader, more permanent source of protection beyond that provided by the parents. This point denotes the final shift from a basic desire for belonging and acceptance from others to a motive to live according to the ideals and teachings of the cultural worldview; that is, people strive to attain culturally valued occupations, roles, titles, group identifications, and achievements, and in so doing secure their place as valuable contributors to a meaningful, immortality procuring, cultural worldview. Although a basic sense of acceptance from others is still an important source of self-esteem and security in its own right, this final shift to investment in the cultural system of ideas allows for the broadest form of security, capable of shielding people from the overriding fear of death.

The Role of Others in Worldview Defense and Self-Esteem Maintenance

This analysis implies that other people play an important role in both the construction and maintenance of one's self-esteem and faith in the cultural worldview. Because the socialization process involves the internalization of symbolic codes of behavior laid down by the parents and society, the particular contingencies that constitute one's bases for self-worth are largely an accident of the culture into which one is born. Furthermore, because cultural worldviews (and the set of standards for

self-esteem they prescribe) are to some extent arbitrary, fictional accounts of reality, the only way these psychological structures can seem "real" is if people come together and reinforce each others' belief in their validity. One's faith in the correctness of the cultural worldview is therefore utterly dependent on consensual validation by others and one's vital sentiment of self-worth is likewise dependent on continual feedback from others that one is meeting the standards of the worldview.

Therefore, we suggest along with Becker (1962/1971), that compared with our primate cousins, the evolution of sophisticated intellectual abilities—especially the capacity for symbolic thought and self-awareness—released human beings from an instinctually programmed drive to belong to groups. However, because these same intellectual abilities (i.e., the capacity to be self-aware and anticipate the future) gave rise to an exponentially increased capacity for terror, humans re-socialized back into groups just as firmly and solidly as before. Now, the need for social connections is propelled by the motive to acquire meaning and self-worth so as to reduce existential fear, which explains why, unlike zebras and apes, people do not want inclusion in any group of conspecifics; they want to be included in groups of like-minded individuals that provide much-needed validation and support for their death-denying illusions. In fact, as the forthcoming literature review shows, when existential concern is high, people sometimes distance themselves from important social groups and relationships when these social identifications could potentially undermine self-esteem or faith in their cultural worldview. Ultimately, what people want is not to belong per se, but to be valued contributors to a meaningful symbolic reality. We seek belonging and social connection to the extent it serves that motive and we are perturbed by exclusion to the extent that it threatens our anxiety-buffering view of self and the world.

Empirical Evidence for a Terror Management Theory Perspective on Inclusion and Exclusion

To date, research supporting TMT (for reviews, see Greenberg, Solomon, & Arndt, 2008; Pyszczynski, Greenberg, Solomon, Arndt, & Schimel, 2004) comes from more than 400 experiments spanning at least 15 different countries (e.g., Japan, Iran, the United States, Canada, Italy, China, India, Germany, Israel). These studies show that worldview and self-esteem bolstering buffers anxiety and reduces concerns about mortality. Furthermore, reminding people of their mortality (mortality salience; MS) causes them to engage in symbolic defenses; that is, people show greater adherence to and defense of their cultural worldview and cling more fervently to attitudes, groups, and relationships that provide them with self-esteem. Moreover, substantial bodies of evidence have found these effects to be specific to heightened accessibility of death-related thought and different from the effects of thinking of other aversive topics (e.g., uncertainty, social exclusion, intense physical pain, a looming exam) (Martens, Burke, Schimel, & Faucher, 2011). Another line of evidence uniquely supporting TMT has shown that when people experience a potent threat to the symbols that provide them with meaning, self-worth, and faith in their cultural worldview, thoughts about death (but not other aversive thoughts) become more accessible to consciousness (see Hayes, Schimel, Arndt & Faucher, 2010 for a review).

A TMT perspective on belonging and interpersonal relationships emphasizes the role that social connections play in providing people with self-esteem and validation for their core beliefs about reality, which function to manage deeply rooted existential terror. Accordingly, MS should generally increase people's identification with important groups and close relationships. Furthermore, threatening these symbolic identifications should allow death thoughts to become more accessible. Finally, because social connections ultimately reduce existential fear by way of providing people with meaning and self-worth, MS should cause people to withdraw from social connections that have negative implications for self-esteem and faith in the cultural worldview, and approach social connections that have positive implications for these psychological structures. Next we will summarize research assessing these three general hypotheses.

Evidence for a Terror Management Function of Group Affiliations

Numerous studies have shown that reminders of death increase people's liking and support of the groups to which they belong, but decrease liking and support for opposing groups. For example, Greenberg et al. (1990) reminded Christian participants of their own death (versus control) and then had them evaluate a fellow Christian and a Jewish target. Mortality salience led Christians to show greater affection for the Christian target and decreased liking for the Jewish target. In another study, Greenberg et al. (1990) replicated the same pattern of results among Americans who evaluated an essay written by a foreigner that either praised or criticized America. Mortality salience also increases people's investment in their ethnic identities. For instance, Greenberg, Schimel, Martens, Solomon, and Pyszczynski (2001) found that white participants judged a white person who expressed pride in his group to be especially racist, relative to a black person (i.e., African American) who expressed the same sentiments. However, when placed under MS, white participants' evaluations completely reversed: The individual with white pride was judged to be less racist than the person who expressed black pride.

Effects of MS on in-group bias also apply to behavioral measures of aggression, helping, and affiliation. For example, McGregor et al. (1998) put research participants in charge of allocating a batch of super spicy hot sauce to another participant to try, knowing full well that the participant disliked spicy foods. McGregor et al. (1998) found that participants doled out much more hot sauce to the target (i.e., acted aggressively) when they had been reminded of death and the target opposed their political affiliation. Likewise, Jonas, Schimel, Greenberg, and Pyszczynski (2002) found that American participants led to think about their own death (versus control) donated more money to an in-group charity, but not to an out-group charity. Similarly, Ochsmann and Mathy (1994) found that following an MS induction, German participants sat closer to a German confederate and further away from a Turkish confederate.

A number of additional studies have found that MS increases perceptions of the cohesiveness of one's group, which contributes to a sense of group entitativity, the belief that one's group constitutes a real entity, possessing a real existence (see Castano & Dechesne, 2005 for a review). For example, among a sample of Italian participants, Castano, Yzerbyt, Paladino, and Sacchi (2002) found that MS led them to identify more strongly with Italy, judge Italians more favorably, and score higher on a measure of group entitativity. Similar research found that a reminder of death increased participants' ratings of overlap between the identity of themselves with their group of close friends. In a related vein, Castano (2004) had Scottish participants take part in an in-group–out-group categorization task in which they had to classify pictures of individuals as Scottish or English. They found that MS (versus control) led Scottish participants to classify more individuals as English, thereby increasing the perception of a cohesive, homogenous ingroup.

If group identifications serve a terror management function, then threats to these identifications should increase death thought accessibility (DTA). To assess this idea, Schimel et al. (2007) exposed Canadian participants who were heavily invested in their Canadian identity to materials that trivialized Canadian achievements or the achievements of another group (Australians). As expected, Canadians had higher DTA only when their Canadian identity was attacked. In a second study, Schimel et al. (2007) found that if the participants had an opportunity to defensively dismiss the threat before reading it, DTA remained low (Study 2). And in two follow-up studies, threatened nationalism on DTA was not due to the accessibility of negative or neutral thoughts in general (Study 3), nor was it the result of increases in general anxiety or anger. Rather, the more participants found the material "personally offensive" and "offensive to them as Canadians," the higher their DTA.

Evidence for a Terror Management Function of Close Relationships

Close relationships have been posited to serve a terror management function for multiple reasons. First, relationships are an important source of self-esteem; it is a tremendous boost to be loved and of primary value to another human being, someone who sees one's positive attributes when others do not, accepts one's flaws, and considers one to be attractive (Cox & Arndt, 2012). Moreover, both friends and romantic partners offer validation and support for one's core beliefs (worldview) and personal characteristics (bases for self-esteem) and help reframe failure experiences and negative events for each other in ways that seem less threatening (Cohen, 2004). As many theorists have suggested, close relationships are also an extension of an early attachment mechanism, and may therefore have some anxiety buffering properties in their own right (Becker, 1962/1971; Bowlby, 1969; Hart, Shaver, & Goldenberg, 2005). Finally, romantic partnerships provide people with protection from existential fear because they facilitate procreation and the raising of offspring, reinforcing a sense of immortality through one's progeny.

A growing empirical literature shows that close relationships protect people from concerns about death, particularly for people with a secure attachment style (see Mikulincer et al., 2003, for a review). Studies have shown that after MS, participants report a higher desire for intimacy with their partner, more commitment to their romantic relationship, more activation of thoughts that facilitate rather than inhibit social connectivity (i.e., good social skills versus fear of rejection), and more willingness to initiate social interactions. Additional studies have demonstrated that making romantic commitment salient reduces the use of other symbolic defenses in response to MS (Florian, Mikulincer, & Hirschberger, 2002; Study 2).

Further evidence for an existential function of relationships shows that threatening relational bonds increases DTA. Indeed, Mikulincer, Florian, Birnbaum, and Malishkevish (2002) found that having participants imagine separation from a romantic partner led to higher DTA among participants who were also high in attachment anxiety, presumably because such individuals are more insecure about their relationships (Mikulincer & Florian, 2000). Indeed, participants who evidenced the most DTA also reported the highest levels of distress in their contemplation of separation. However, among participants in a committed romantic relationship, contemplation of *real* problems in their relationship or of fear of intimacy increased DTA regardless of attachment style (Florian et al., 2002). In a related vein, Bassett (2005) found that disparaging the institution of marriage led participants to dissociate the self from concepts pertaining to death.

The results from MS studies and DTA studies show clear support for the idea that people rely on close relationships to manage death-related fear. From a TMT perspective, part of the reason for these effects is because relationships are a significant source of self-esteem. Some direct support for this idea was recently obtained by Cox and Arndt (2012). Across two studies, they found that MS led participants to exaggerate how positively their romantic partners (relative to an average person) viewed them on a number of trait adjectives. In another study, they found that participants' belief that their partners' held them in high regard mediated the effect of MS on increased commitment to the relationship, suggesting that relationships are indeed a self-esteem resource under existential threat. In addition, Kosloff, Greenberg, Sullivan, and Weise (2010) found that in the context of short-term relationships, MS led to increased preference for a self-esteem–enhancing dating prospect.

According to TMT, relationships are an important source of self-esteem, consensus for one's beliefs, and, in the case of some relationships, symbolic immortality, which shield people from existential fear. This analysis suggests that under conditions of existential threat, if people expect that a given relationship may not meet these needs, they may withdraw from the relationship or shift their investment to other relationships or psychological structures that offer a more reliable source of security. To test this idea, Strachman and Schimel (2006) had participants complete an online study in which they were primed to think about how they were different from or similar to their current partner on one important demographic variable. Mortality salience led participants primed to think about a dissimilar value to report being less committed to their relationship than those in a pain control condition. Complementing this finding, Kosloff et al. (2010) have shown that when contemplating long-term relationship prospects, MS increases preference for a worldview validating potential partner.

Theory and research suggests that in addition to romantic attachments and close friendships, the *parent–child relationship* may also buffer both children and parents from concerns about death. From the perspective of the parents, it seems likely that the parent–child bond would be an important source of security. As mentioned earlier, part of the reason why romantic relationships may provide existential security is because these partnerships are an important link in the chain toward the production of children, which provides a sense of symbolic immortality. Moreover, children shower their parents with love and are sources of great pride to them. Thus, consistent with a terror management function of children, research has shown that MS increases the desire for offspring (e.g., Wisman & Goldenberg, 2005) and that threats to the bond with one's child increased DTA among first-time mothers of children 3 to 12 months old (Taubman-Ben-Ari & Katz-Ben-Ami, 2008).

Research on the other side of the parent–child bond shows that parents provide psychological security against death concerns even for their adult children. Across three different studies, Cox et al. (2008) found that among young adults, priming thoughts of one's parent in response to MS reduced DTA and worldview defense, and increased implicit self-esteem. In two additional studies Cox et al. (2008) found that MS led young adults to have less difficulty recalling positive maternal interactions and greater difficulty recalling negative maternal interactions and caused participants to sit closer to a stranger if they were led to believe that the person was similar to a parental figure.

Building on the work of Mikulincer and colleagues (see Mikulincer et al., 2003) Cox et al. (2008) also hypothesized that securely attached individuals might come to rely more on their romantic relationships for existential security, whereas insecurely attached individuals might rely more on the older parent–child bond. To test this idea, Cox et al. (2008) had participants indicate the number of minutes (out of 100) on a phone card they would spend in a given week to call each of the following relationship partners: parent, sibling, romantic partner, and close friend. They found that MS led insecurely attached individuals to spend more minutes calling their parents, whereas MS led securely attached individuals to spend more minutes calling their romantic partners. In a related study, Cox et al. (2012) found that MS led securely attached individuals to exaggerate how positively their partners viewed them, whereas MS led insecurely attached individuals to exaggerate how positively their parents viewed them. Apparently, whether one withdraws from a particular relationship or draws closer to it seems to depend on one's prior attachment experiences that foster expectations about the types of relationships that are most likely to provide one with existential security. In other words, when concerns about death are heightened it is the implications that social connections have for people's sense of meaning and self-worth that determine whether they choose to increase or decrease such connections. Research investigating this idea more directly is discussed in the next section.

Effects of Mortality Salience on Group Affiliations Depend on Implications for Worldview Validation and Self-Esteem

According to TMT, people do not want any kind of belonging; they want group affiliations and relationships that provide a reliable source of meaning and self-worth. This means that when social identifications or interpersonal relationships reduce one's ability to maintain positive self-appraisals and faith in their worldview, heightened existential concerns should cause them to withdraw from those identities. A growing number of studies support this view.

For example, Dechesne, Greenberg, Arndt, and Schimel (2000) showed that MS increased Dutch participants' favorability toward their local soccer team and displayed greater optimism about an upcoming match between their team and a German team. In a second study, Dechesne et al. (2000a) replicated this effect with American college students, who tended to identify more strongly with their university football team after MS. However, after the football team lost an important game, MS participants were less likely to affiliate with the team than were non-MS participants and shifted their identification more toward the university basketball team.

Arndt, Greenberg, Schimel, Pyszczynski, and Solomon (2002) obtained similar results with gender and ethnic identity. In a first study, for women who were not under stereotype threat, MS led to greater identification with other women. However, placing women under stereotype threat completely eliminated this tendency. In two additional studies, Arndt et al. (2002) showed that death-related concerns affect people's ethnic identification. First, they showed that after reading about positive behaviors of Hispanic individuals (charity work), MS led Hispanic participants to evaluate paintings by Hispanic artists more favorably, but MS led to more negative evaluations of the paintings if they first read about a negative behavior of Hispanic individuals (i.e., drug dealing). In a follow-up study, Arndt et al. (2002) found that MS led Hispanic participants to skew their personalities to be more similar to the target (another Hispanic person) when primed with positive instances of the in-group, whereas MS led them to distort their personalities to be more discrepant from the target when they were primed with negative exemplars of the ingroup. Thus, across each of the three studies reported by Arndt et al. (2002), when MS led individuals to be particularly concerned about maintaining a favorable self-image, they were more likely to embrace an important social identity when it reflected positively on the self, whereas they tended to withdraw from that social identity when it reflected negatively on the self.

Continuing this line of research, Dechesne, Janssen, and van Knippenberg (2000) reasoned that because people with a high (versus low) need for closure tend to place more value on their group identity, they should be more likely to "fight rather than switch" when existential concerns are high and their group identification comes under attack. To test this idea, Dechesne et al. (2000b) exposed University of Nijmegen students to subliminal death primes or neutral primes, had them read a biting criticism of their university, and then measured their evaluation of the critic and their identification with the university. In support of their hypothesis, participants subliminally primed with death who were also high in need for closure were more likely to derogate the critic and did not disidentify with their university, whereas participants low in need for closure were less derogatory toward the critic and

were more likely to disidentify. In a second study, Dechesne et al. (2000) tested the idea that people would tend to disidentify when group identification was perceived as permeable, but defend when group identification was perceived as impermeable. To this end, the authors replicated the procedures of Study 1, but instead of categorizing participants according to need for closure they exposed half the participants to an essay stating that university identification stays with people their whole lives (impermeable), whereas the other half read an essay stating that people jump from one university to another more frequently (permeable). As expected, they found that when group identity seemed impermeable to participants, MS led them to derogate the critic, but when group identity seemed permeable MS led them to disidentify instead. These studies suggest that defending against criticism of one's group and distancing from that group can serve the same function; reminders of death activate concerns with protecting self-esteem, which leads people to either faithfully defend their group identifications or disengage from them, depending on factors that affect their level of investment in those groups.

Another variable that moderates the extent to which people desire affiliation with others or to remain separate from them is the extent to which they feel especially similar to or distinct from members of their group. People desire both to fit into a larger collective and stand out as special (Brewer, 1991; Rank, 1932/1989) and both contribute to feeling enduringly significant. Thus the desire for optimal distinctiveness, as Brewer (1991) labeled it, is likely to be intensified by MS, and may lead to movement toward or away from a group depending on whether the individual feels too distinct or not distinct enough. Simon et al. (1997) showed that when participants were given feedback that they were highly similar to other students, MS led them to distance themselves from fellow students on a measure of perceived similarity. However, when participants were given feedback that they were especially different from other students, MS led them to report greater similarity to fellow students.

In a related line of research, Walsh and Smith (2007) posited that the motive to be similar to or distinct from one's group may depend on the particular set of cultural values that are salient. According to Walsh and Smith (2007), American women may hold two opposing cultural standards. On the one hand, the American worldview prescribes being self-reliant and independent, but gender norms for women prescribe being communal and interpersonally sensitive. Whereas for American men, both cultural and gender norms prescribe the same value: Be a self-reliant individual. Given TMT's proposition that living up to cultural values reduces existential fear, Walsh and Smith reasoned that MS may lead women to increase their social identification with other women when their gender identity is primed, but to decrease their gender identification when the self (i.e., individualism) is primed. In a first study, that was exactly what they found. In a second study, Walsh and Smith (2007) added men to their sample, a neutral prime condition, a measure of students' identification with their university, and separate measures of a general desire for affiliation and uniqueness. As in Study 1, they found that MS led women to increase their gender identification in the gender prime condition and decrease their identification in the self-prime condition. Women's scores on the general measures of desire for affiliation and uniqueness were also consistent with this pattern. Men, on the other hand, did not report differences in gender identification as a function of the manipulations, but they did show a greater desire for uniqueness when primed with the self and MS.

In sum, research has shown that important groups and close relationships buffer individuals from death-related fear. Indeed, MS caused research participants to increase the favorability of their groups, identify with them more strongly, behave less aggressively and more charitably toward them, and increase the perception that their groups are cohesive entities. Similarly, MS intensified participants' commitment and desire for intimacy in close relationships, how much they felt positively evaluated by close others, and their desire to form new relationships. Research also demonstrated that threatening important group identifications and attachments increased DTA, suggesting that these social connections do indeed offer protection from existential fear. Additionally, MS caused participants to gravitate toward groups and relationships that had positive implications for their self-esteem and withdraw from these identifications when they had negative implications for self-esteem. These results uniquely support a TMT view of belonging because death thoughts (but not other types of aversive thoughts) motivated participants' belonging preferences, and death thoughts (but not negative thoughts in general) were activated when important social connections were threatened. Moreover, this research supports a TMT view concerning what types of groups and relationships people want and the particular conditions that foster such preferences that goes beyond a simple need for affiliation in any group or relationship.

Implications of a Terror Management Theory Analysis of the Desires for Inclusion and the Threat of Exclusion: Why Can't We All Just Get Along?

If cultural worldviews hinge in large part on consensual validation from others to seem real, then exposure to cultures of people with alternate worldviews, especially those that are diametrically opposed to one's own, should undermine one's faith in the worldview and the psychological protection it provides. What is even more disturbing about the existence of "different" others is that, despite the diagnosis that they are primitive, naive, or ignorant, these people with strange ways are usually quite happy with their beliefs. They are also just as unimpressed with our values and ideals as we are with theirs, which further implies that our own way of life may not be the one, true way. Thus, contact with others who define reality in different ways undermines consensus for people's death-denying ideologies, which may explain why people with different worldviews throughout history have had such a difficult time getting along. Indeed, a large volume of research based on TMT shows that when reminders of death increase people's need for faith in their cultural worldview, they are more hostile, derogatory, and aggressive toward those who do not share one's fundamental beliefs and values (e.g., McGregor et al., 1998; Pyszczynski et al., 2006).

The need for continual feedback from others as evidence that one is living up to cultural standards of value can also explain why people, even when they share similar cultural values, have trouble getting along in the drama of everyday life. Owing largely to the capacity for language and self-awareness, humans have an abundant storehouse of rich interior life (e.g., deep desires, individual perceptions, intentions, goals, and a rich life history). Yet human beings are rarely able to communicate these self-complexities effectively to others. This means that people spend much of their lives bumping up against others with their exterior selves, never realizing the rich interiors of the people around them, what makes them feel valued and important, what particular identities they have carved out for themselves, and what achievements really matter to them. Because people often have very different ways of deriving self-esteem, it is incredibly easy to offend someone—either purposely or inadvertently—by ignoring a photo album, not laughing at a joke, forgetting a name, or failing to send an invitation. Depending on the particular identities and achievements on which one's self-esteem is based, all of these seemingly trivial actions have the potential to undermine validation for one's self-worth, prompting insecurity and the need to defend.

Why Is Social Exclusion Psychologically Problematic?

From the perspective of TMT, the need for ongoing validation from others that one's life is meaningful and worthwhile is precisely why the experience of social exclusion is psychologically problematic. One of the most direct ways of negating one's self-esteem is to socially exclude the person. Not only does rejection send the clear message that one is inadequate, but it also undercuts consensual validation for one's general sense of "worth." We therefore suggest that what is largely at stake when individuals experience social exclusion is their self-esteem. Although numerous studies investigating the effects of social exclusion (curiously) do not invoke the concept of self-esteem, the various procedures that have been used to manipulate social exclusion would undoubtedly have negative implications for individuals' feelings of self-worth. For example, social exclusion has been operationally defined as personality feedback that one's marriages and relationships will all fail and that one will end up alone later in life, feedback that everyone else rated the person as the one individual in the group that they would least like to work with, and recollection of prior instances of being ostracized or rejected (see Williams, 2007). In all of these experimental contexts, the negative implications for one's self-esteem are clear: There is something about me that is basically inadequate or fundamentally flawed, so much so that other people would actively leave me (i.e., divorce), exclude me from a group activity, or just not want to be around me.

Another paradigm for studying social exclusion that has emerged in recent years has used a computer-simulated ostracism paradigm in which research participants are led to believe they are tossing a Cyberball to three or four other people over a computer network. In these rather minimal experiences of ostracism, excluded (versus included) participants report lower self-esteem, reduced belief that their lives are meaningful, and a lack of control, even though they have been excluded by complete strangers that cannot be seen or heard (see Williams,

2001, 2007). In one of the more striking demonstrations of this effect, participants indicate distress even when those who exclude them are thought to be members of a despised group (i.e., the Ku Klux Klan) (Gonsalkorale & Williams, 2006). It might be tempting to think that self-esteem needs could not possibly be at stake in this demonstration because the excluding persons are themselves disliked. However, there would still be negative implications for one's self-esteem because of what the rejection implies about the self. Williams (2007) posits that people initially respond to rejection reflexively, and this implies that participants may be reacting at first without considering who is doing the rejecting. However, the Cyberball procedure involves being ignored over several trials, giving participants plenty of time to process how they are being treated. Indeed, video recordings of participants seem to show a shift over trials from initial reactions of hurt and anger to sadness and dejection. Therefore, in response to repeated rejections by KKK members, one might have such thoughts as, "Even though these people are racists, they don't know me, so how do they know I'm not a racist too? The KKK would be lucky to have me and should feel that way even though I have no interest in joining these clowns. They don't even think I'm worthy to toss a ball with them based on superficial characteristics. Maybe there is something fundamentally wrong with me." Thus, even in minimal situations of rejection like this, people may indeed experience a blow to self-esteem, not because of their desire to be liked by a group of cyber-strangers (who wants to join the KKK?) or research participants per se (they have no control over one's actual fortunes), but because the rejection implies some deficiency that may impede success in contexts that matter down the road.

Exclusion from the Cultural Drama Hurts too

Another implication of a TMT analysis of social exclusion is that feeling disconnected from the cultural drama should be just as problematic (if not more so) than rejection by a specific person or group. If feeling as though one is a valuable contributor to a meaningful worldview protects people from deeply rooted fears about human mortality, then feeling like an insignificant member of the worldview should be associated with anxiety and despair even if one feels accepted and supported by friends and family. For example, take a family man in his fifties who gets laid off from the local aerospace plant because his duties can be performed more easily and cost-effectively by machines. Despite being inundated with social support from his wife, friends, and children, he may still feel like a failure and struggle with depression and anxiety because he is unable to participate in the cultural drama by filling his role as "provider."

This analysis also implies that one can feel protected and secure, at least to some extent, with very few social contacts and relationships as long as one can play a heroic role in the cultural drama. Indeed, one can be an isolated hermit, but feel as though one is changing the world in a significant way by bringing comfort to the poor (e.g., William Gillespie, Chuck Feeney, Ruth Lilly, Clarence Day, William Bingham), being a revolutionary political figure (e.g., Ayatollah Ali Khamenei, Vladimir Lenin), or creating great works of art (e.g., Vincent van Gogh, J. D. Salinger, Emily Dickinson). Although, from the perspective of TMT, even the isolated heroes of the world would still need at least some social validation for their contributions so as to feel as though their life's work is meaningful and impactful. For example, van Gogh clearly struggled with the general lack of enthusiasm for his work (de Leeuw, 1996), and the socially reclusive philosopher Arthur Schopenhauer was said to have spent his lonely life scanning the footnotes of journals to see whether there would ever be recognition of his work (Becker, 1962/1971).

Of course, the most optimal circumstance for psychological functioning would be to feel as though one is making a valuable contribution to cultural life while also having a close network of friends, family, and associates who validate one's claims to self-worth. Indeed, a large research literature shows that social support is generally linked to better overall physical and emotional health (e.g., Cohen, 2004; House, Landis, & Umberson, 1988). According to Cohen, social relationships buffer people from the negative effects of stress by validating people's identities, providing them with self-esteem and a sense of purpose, and helping them interpret adverse events in ways that seem less threatening. Thus, at least a minimal level of social relationships might be necessary for optimal physical health and psychological equanimity.

Merging Evolutionary Perspectives on Belonging and Social Exclusion with Terror Management Theory

Most theoretical perspectives explaining why people need to belong have emphasized the simple notion that a desire for ongoing interpersonal attachments constitutes a fundamental human need because belonging to groups was important for survival and reproduction (Baumeister & Leary, 1995). A sense of belonging is therefore desirable for its own sake, and when that desire is thwarted people should act in ways to restore it (Twenge, 2006). Theorists have further claimed that because ostracism from the group would have ultimately led to death, our ancestors must have developed a detection system to alert them to potential exclusion so they can act in ways to increase social ties with members of the group when minimal signs of rejection are detected (Williams, 2001). Current theorizing further explains that because of the dire costs of social exclusion, the social attachment system may have piggybacked onto the preexisting physical pain system that originally evolved to alert organisms to danger. Thus, the "hurt feelings" or "pain" that people experience in response to social rejection is a borrowed signal from the general pain system, which functions to alert the individual to maintain their social connections (Eisenberger & Lieberman, 2005).

We concur that some of the anxiety people experience when socially rejected might be an outgrowth of the attachment mechanism that evolved to keep primate infants in close proximity to caregivers. It is a long observed fact that primates and human infants experience fear in response to separation and strangers, which prompts proximity seeking to alleviate the distress (Bowlby, 1969). This notion is entirely consistent with TMT's developmental analysis, as stated earlier (see also Pyszczynski et al., 2004). However, the idea that human beings evolved an ostracism detection device to alert the individual to exclusion and then motivate inclusion seeking seems inconsistent with a large empirical literature showing that social exclusion threats cause people to think and act in ways that would do little to garner any kind of social approval. Indeed, following social exclusion threats, research participants have been shown to procrastinate more, eat more snack foods, and drink more alcohol, engage in selfish, impulsive behaviors, avoid self-awareness (a state associated with civilized behavior), and show less empathy toward others (Baumeister & DeWall, 2005; Twenge, 2006). Although a few studies have shown that under some circumstances people are more prosocial and conforming in response to exclusion (Williams, Cheung, & Choi, 2000; Williams & Sommer, 1997; but see Twenge, 2006 for an alternative explanation), the vast majority of the research shows that people become less prosocial and more hostile and aggressive toward others when they feel rejected (e.g., Leary, Kowalski, Smith, & Phillips, 2003; Twenge et al., 2007; see Twenge, 2006 for a review).

Instead of positing that social exclusion innately causes pain, which prompts people to seek inclusion specifically, we suggest as mentioned previously, that social exclusion hurts because it damages self-esteem. Indeed, it seems likely that people experience the same kind of hurt feelings when their self-esteem is threatened in situations that are relatively anonymous and removed from the evaluations of others (Greenberg & Pyszczynski, 1985). From this vantage point, social exclusion threatens people's self-esteem, the social–symbolic structure that developed on the heels of the attachment mechanism to control anxiety. Threats to this anxiety-buffering structure prompt people to engage in defenses to protect it.

In contrast with an evolved mechanism for managing social inclusion, we posit that a more functional ostracism–detection–device might be the experience of guilt. According to TMT's developmental analysis, one's moral conscience or superego develops out of the socialization process in which the child must internalize the standards of the parents and society to feel secure. Once the development of the superego is complete, children keep themselves in line with societal standards by punishing themselves. The tendency to torment oneself with guilt may therefore be the mechanism that keeps one in the good graces of society when the person fails to live up to social standards. Perhaps the reason why social exclusion often leads to hostile, defensive behaviors rather than a tendency to "tend and befriend" is because in most experiments investigating the effects of social exclusion (Twenge, 2006; Williams, 2007) as well as cases of real-world social exclusion that have led to violent aggression (Leary et al., 2003), people are seemingly excluded by others with whom they have no preexisting emotional attachments (Baumeister, Stillwell, & Heatherton, 1994). Moreover, they are often excluded for inherent characteristics rather than specific actions. Social exclusion under these circumstances may instigate a feeling of shame, rather than guilt. If the nature of the social exclusion fails to activate a feeling of guilt, it may not increase prosocial strivings aimed at staying in line with cultural standards of value. Indeed, a large literature has documented that a tendency to experience shame (an emotion related to self-esteem threat) leads to defensiveness and antisocial behaviors, whereas a tendency to experience guilt is associated with reparative actions, such as confessions, apologies, undoing the consequences of negative behaviors, and other-oriented empathy (see Tangney, Stuewig, & Mashek, 2007 for a review). Future research on social exclusion could therefore explore the possibility that whether people become more prosocial versus antisocial in response to social exclusion may depend on whether the situation of exclusion arouses feelings of guilt versus shame. If individuals suspect that they might be disliked or excluded because they have acted selfishly or failed to live up to group norms or standards, their tendency to experience guilt as a result might moderate their tendency to make reparations with members of the group.

Conclusions

A need for social cooperation led to more complex brains, which led to the existential dilemma: the realization that we are on the one hand out of nature but at the same time hopelessly trapped within it (Becker, 1973). However, human evolution produced a mind capable of seeing oneself as special and unique, and of tremendous freedom from fixed response patterns. But the fear that came along with this mental leap forward gave rise to the need to re-socialize back into human groups to calm the fear. So, we have had to give up some of the freedom afforded by our evolved intellectual proclivities so as to feel securely embedded into human groups. Thus, for modern humans, the basis for belonging goes beyond mere inclusion. Now we need to feel a part of groups because they give meaning and purpose to human life and provide a symbolic basis for achieving death transcendence. The human desires for inclusion and negative reactions to exclusion are most profitably viewed not as innate reflexive responses but as complex reactions resulting from the potent need to sustain a valued place within a symbolic reality, the primary buffer against the potential for terror engendered by the ever-present knowledge of one's own mortality.

At the outset of this chapter we mentioned that very little research or theoretical discussion has considered an existential function of belonging. However, some theorists who have considered the TMT perspective have dismissed it in favor of mechanistic evolutionary accounts of a basic need to belong on the basis of parsimony (Buss, 1997; Macdonald, 2006; Navarrete & Fessler, 2005). In other words, TMT should be dismissed because it involves unnecessary theoretical complexity (i.e., unconscious machinations and defenses) (Buss, 1997). But simplistic psychological theories lack the explanatory power to account for the complexity and diversity of human behavior; a simple theory without explanatory power is anything but parsimonious. From our view, the simple proposition that humans evolved mechanisms designed to detect exclusion and motivate inclusion is not theoretically complex enough to readily explain: (1) a large empirical literature showing that social exclusion causes people to think and act in ways that make them less desirable to any group or relationship partner, (2) the observation that human intellect evolved in the direction of less dependence on evolved mechanisms to govern behavior, and (3) a large TMT literature implicating thoughts of death in people's motivation to pursue meaning and self-worth through social connections of all kinds, and to distance from social connections that threaten meaning and self-worth. The TMT proposition, that social connections provide people with consensus for their cultural worldview and a personal sense of significance to alleviate death-related fear, is indeed more complex than the simple notion of an evolved need to belong. However, when simple theories are not complex enough to account for known data, more complex theoretical accounts like that offered by TMT should be considered. We therefore conclude by suggesting that the uniquely human fear of death and a corresponding need for self-esteem should be integrated and included (versus excluded) in further research and theorizing on the effects of social exclusion.

References

Arndt, J., Greenberg, J., Schimel, J., Pyszczynski, T., & Solomon, S. (2002). To belong or not to belong, that is the question: Terror management and identification with gender and ethnicity. *Journal of Personality and Social Psychology, 83*, 26–43.

Bassett, J. F. (2005). Does threatening valued components of cultural worldview alter explicit and implicit attitudes about death? *Individual Differences Research, 3*, 260–268.

Baumeister, R. F., & DeWall, C. N. (2005). The inner dimension of social exclusion: Intelligent thought and self-regulation among rejected persons. In K. D. Williams, J. P. Forgas, & W. von Hippel (Eds.), *The Social Outcast: Ostracism, Social Exclusion, Rejection, and Bullying* (pp. 53–73). New York: Psychology Press.

Baumeister, R. F., & Leary, M. R. (1995). The need to belong: Desire for interpersonal attachments as a fundamental human motivation. *Psychological Bulletin, 117*, 497–529.

Baumeister, R. F., Stillwell, A. M., & Heatherton, T. F. (1994). Guilt: An interpersonal approach. *Psychological Bulletin, 115*, 243–267.

Becker, E. (1962/1971). *The Birth and Death of Meaning: An Interdisciplinary Perspective on the Problem of Man*. New York: Free Press.

Becker, E. (1973). *The Denial of Death*. New York: Free Press.

Bowlby, J. (1969). *Attachment*. New York: Basic Books.

Brewer, M. B. (1991). The social self: On being the same and different at the same time. *Personality and Social Psychology Bulletin, 17*, 475–482.

Buss, D. M. (1997). Human social motivation in evolutionary perspective: Grounding terror management theory. *Psychological Inquiry, 8*, 22–26.

Carver, C. S., & Scheier, M. F. (1981). *Attention and Self-Regulation: A Control Theory Approach to Human Behavior*. New York: Springer.

Castano, E. (2004). In case of death, cling to the ingroup. *European Journal of Social Psychology, 34*, 375–384.

Castano, E., & Dechesne, M. (2005). On defeating death: Group reification and social identification as strategies for transcendence. In W. Stroebe, & M. Hewstone (Eds.), *European Review of Social Psychology*. Chichester, UK: Wiley, pp. 16, 221.

Castano, E. Yzerbyt, V., Paladino, M. P., & Sacchi, S. (2002). I belong, therefore I exist: Ingroup identification, ingroup entitativity, and ingroup bias. *Personality and Social Psychology Bulletin, 28*, 135–143

Cohen, S. (2004). Social relationships and health. *American Psychologist, 59*, 676–684.

Cox, C. R., & Arndt, J. (2012). *How Sweet It Is to Be Loved by You*: The Role of Perceived Regard in the Terror Management of Close Relationships. *Journal of Personality and Social Psychology, 102*, 616–632.

Cox, C. R., Arndt, J., Pyszczynski, T., Greenberg, J., Abdollahi, A., & Solomon, S. (2008). Terror management and adults' attachment to their parents: The safe haven remains. *Journal of Personality and Social Psychology, 94*, 696–717.

Dechesne, M., Greenberg, J., Arndt, J., & Schimel, J. (2000). Terror management and sports fan affiliation: The effects of mortality salience on fan identification and optimism. *European Journal of Social Psychology, 30*, 813–835.

Dechesne, M., Janssen, J., & van Knippenberg, A. (2000). Defense and distancing as terror management strategies: The moderating role of need for structure and permeability of group boundaries. *Journal of Personality and Social Psychology, 79*, 923–932.

Duval, S., & Wicklund, R. A. (1972). *A Theory of Objective Self-Awareness*. New York: Academic Press.

Eisenberger, N. I., & Lieberman, M. D. (2005). Why it hurts to be left out: the neurocognitive overlap between physical and social pain. In K. D. Williams, J. P. Forgas, & W. von Hippel (Eds.), *The Social Outcast: Ostracism, Social Exclusion, Rejection, and Bullying* (pp. 109–127). New York: Psychology Press.

Florian, V., Mikulincer, M., & Hirschberger, G. (2002). The anxiety-buffering function of close relationships: Evidence that relationship commitment acts as a terror management mechanism. *Journal of Personality and Social Psychology, 82*, 527–542.

Gonsalkorale, K., & Williams, K. D. (2006). The KKK won't let me play: Ostracism even by a despised outgroup hurts. *European Journal of Social Psychology, 37*, 1176–1186.

Greenberg, J., Koole, S. L., & Pyszczynski, T. (2004). *The Handbook of Experimental Existential Psychology*. New York: Guilford Press.

Greenberg, J., & Pyszczynski, T. (1985). Compensatory self-inflation: A response to the threat to self-regard of public failure. *Journal of Personality and Social Psychology, 49*, 273–280.

Greenberg, J., Pyszczynski, T., & Solomon, S. (1986). The causes and consequences of a need for self esteem: a terror management theory. In R. F. Baumeister (Ed.), *Public Self and Private Self* (pp. 189–212). New York: Springer-Verlag.

Greenberg, J., Pyszczynski, T., Solomon, S., Rosenblatt, A., Veeder, M., Kirkland, S., & Lyon, D. (1990). Evidence for terror management II: The effects of mortality salience on reactions to those who threaten or bolster the cultural worldview. *Journal of Personality and Social Psychology*, 58, 308–318.

Greenberg, J., Schimel, J., Martens, A., Solomon, S., & Pyszcznyski, T. (2001). Sympathy for the devil: Evidence that reminding Whites of their mortality promotes more favorable reactions to White racists. *Motivation and Emotion*, 25, 113–133.

Greenberg, J., Solomon, S., & Arndt, J. (2008). A basic but uniquely human motivation: Terror management. In J. Y. Shah, & W. L. Gardner (Eds.). *Handbook of Motivation Science* (pp. 114–134). New York: Guilford Press.

Hart, J., Shaver, P. R., & Goldenberg, J. L. (2005). Attachment, self-esteem, worldviews, and terror management: Evidence for a tripartite security system. *Journal of Personality and Social Psychology*, 88, 999–1013.

Hayes, J., Schimel, J., Arndt, J., & Faucher, E. H. (2010). A theoretical and empirical review of the death-thought accessibility concept in terror management research. *Psychological Bulletin*, 136, 699–739.

House, J. S, Landis, K. R., & Umberson, D. (1988). Social relationships and health. *Science*, 241, 540–545.

Jonas, E., Schimel, J., Greenberg, J., & Pyszczynski, P. (2002). The Scrooge effect: Evidence that mortality salience increases prosocial attitudes and behavior. *Personality and Social Psychology Bulletin*, 28, 1342–1353.

Karmiloff-Smith, A. (1992). *Beyond Modularity: A Developmental Perspective on Cognitive Science.* Cambridge, MA: MIT Press.

Kosloff, S., Greenberg, J., Sullivan, D., & Weise, D. (2010). Of trophies and pillars: Exploring the terror management functions of short-term and long-term relationship partners. *Personality and Social Psychology Bulletin*, 36, 1036–1051.

Leary, M. R., Kowalski, R. M., Smith, L., & Phillips, S. (2003). Teasing, rejection, and violence: Case studies of the school shootings. *Aggressive Behavior*, 29, 202–214.

de Leeuw, R. W. (1996). *The Letters of Vincent Van Gogh.* London: Penguin Books.

Lifton, R. J. (1979). *The Broken Connection: On Death and the Continuity of Life.* Washington, DC: American Psychiatric Press.

Lonetto, R. (1980). *Children's Conceptions of Death.* New York: Springer.

MacDonald, G. (2006). Self-esteem: A human elaboration of prehuman belongingness motivation. In C. Sedikides, & S. Spencer (Eds.), *The Self* (pp. 235–258). New York: Psychology Press.

Martens, A., Burke, B. L., Schimel, J., & Faucher, E. H. (2011). Same but different: Meta analytically examining the uniqueness of mortality salience effects. *European Journal of Social Psychology*, 41, 6–10.

McGregor, H., Lieberman, J. D., Solomon, S., Greenberg, J., Arndt, J., Simon, L., & Pyszczynski, T. (1998). Terror management and aggression: Evidence that mortality salience motivates aggression against worldview threatening others. *Journal of Personality and Social Psychology*, 74, 590–605.

Mikulincer, M., & Florian, V. (2000). Exploring individual differences in reactions to mortality salience: Does attachment style regulate terror management mechanisms? *Journal of Personality and Social Psychology*, 79, 260–273.

Mikulincer, M., Florian, V., Birnbaum, G., & Malishkevich, S. (2002). The death-anxiety buffering function of close relationships: Exploring the effects of separation reminders on death-thought accessibility. *Personality and Social Psychology Bulletin*, 28, 287–299.

Mikulincer, M., Florian, V., & Hirschberger, G. (2003). The existential function of close relationships: Introducing death into the science of love. *Personality and Social Psychology Review*, 7, 20–40.

Mikulincer, M., & Shaver, P. R. (2007). Boosting attachment security to promote mental health, prosocial values, and intergroup tolerance. *Psychological Inquiry*, 18, 139–156.

Mithen, S. (1996). *The Prehistory of the Mind.* London: Thames and Hudson.

Navarrete, D. C., & Fessler, D. M. T. (2005). Normative bias and adaptive challenges: A relational approach to coalitional psychology and a critique of terror management theory. *Evolutionary Psychology*, 3, 297–325.

Ochsmann, R., & Mathy, M. (1994). *Depreciation of and Distancing from Foreigners: Effects of Mortality Salience.* Unpublished manuscript. Universitat Mainz, Germany.

Rank, O. (1932/89). *Art and Artist.* New York: Norton.

Pyszczynski, T., Abdollahi, A., Solomon, S., Greenberg, J., Cohen, F., & Weise, D. (2006). Mortality salience, martyrdom, and military might: The Great Satan versus the Axis of Evil. *Personality and Social Psychology Bulletin*, 32, 525–537.

Pyszczynski, T., Greenberg, J., Solomon, S., Arndt, J., & Schimel, J. (2004). Why do people need self-esteem? A theoretical and empirical review. *Psychological Bulletin*, 130, 435–468.

Schimel, J., Hayes, J., Williams, T., & Jahrig, J. (2007). Is death really the worm at the core? Converging evidence that worldview threat increases death-thought accessibility. *Journal of Personality and Social Psychology*, 92, 789–803.

Simon, L., Greenberg, J., Arndt, J., Pyszczynski, T., Clement, R., & Solomon, S. (1997). Perceived consensus, uniqueness, and terror management: Compensatory responses to threats to inclusion and distinctiveness following mortality salience. *Personality and Social Psychology Bulletin*, 23, 1055–1065.

Speece, M. W., & Brent, S. B. (1996). The development of children's understanding of death. In C. A. Corr, & D. M. Corr (Eds.), *Handbook of Childhood Death and Bereavement* (pp. 29–49). New York: Springer.

Strachman, A., & Schimel, J. (2006). Terror management and close relationships: Evidence that mortality salience reduces commitment among partners with different worldviews. *Journal of Social and Personal Relationships*, 23, 965–978.

Tangney, J. P., Stuewig, J., & Mashek, D. J. (2007). Moral emotions and moral behavior. *Annual review of Psychology*, 58, 345–372.

Taubman-Ben-Ari, O., & Katz-Ben-Ami, L. (2008). Death awareness, maternal separation anxiety, and attachment style—A Terror Management perspective. *Death Studies*, 32, 737–756.

Twenge, J. M. (2006). The socially excluded self. In C. Sedikides, & S. Spencer (Eds.), *The Self* (pp. 311–324). New York: Psychology Press.

Twenge, J. M., Baumeister, R. F., DeWall, C. N., Ciarocco, N. J., & Bartels, J. M. (2007). Social exclusion decreases prosocial behavior. *Journal of Personality and Social Psychology*, 92, 56–66.

Walsh, P. E., & Smith, J. L. (2007). Opposing standards within the cultural worldview: Terror management and American women's desire for uniqueness versus inclusiveness. *Psychology of Women Quarterly, 31*(103), 113.

Webb, N. B. (2002). The child and death. In N. B. Webb (Ed.), *Helping Bereaved Children: A Handbook for Practitioners* (pp. 3–18). New York: Guilford Press.

Williams, K. D. (2001). *Ostracism: The Power of Silence.* New York: Guilford.

Williams, K. D. (2007). Ostracism. *Annual Review of Psychology, 58*, 425–452.

Williams, K. D., Cheung, C. K. T., & Choi, W. (2000). Cyberostracism: Effects of being ignored over the Internet. *Journal of Personality and Social Psychology, 79*, 748–762.

Williams, K. D., & Sommer, K. L. (1997). Social ostracism by one's coworkers: Does rejection lead to loafing or compensation? *Personality and Social Psychology Bulletin, 23*, 693–706.

Williams, K. D., & Zadro, L. (2005). Ostracism: The indiscriminate early detection system. In K. D. Williams, J. P. Forgas, & W. von Hippel (Eds.), *The Social Outcast: Ostracism, Social Exclusion, Rejection, and Bullying* (pp. 19–34). New York: Psychology Press.

Wisman, A., & Goldenberg, J. L. (2005). From the grave to the cradle: Evidence that mortality salience engenders a desire for offspring. *Journal of Personality and Social Psychology, 89*, 46–61.

Looking Back and Forward: Lessons Learned and Moving Ahead

C. Nathan DeWall

Abstract

Over the past 15 years, psychologists embraced the importance social connections more than ever before. The chapters that included in the Oxford Handbook of Social Exclusion offer the most comprehensive and cutting-edge research on the impact of social exclusion ever assembled. In this concluding chapter, I provide an overview of the six basic lessons we learned and suggest avenues for future research.

Key Words: social exclusion, social rejection, ostracism, need to belong, interpersonal relationships

Since its inception, the field of psychology emphasized the importance of social connections. Theorists differed regarding how and why they believed people form and maintain relationships, from repressing unwanted impulses to reaching self-actualization. But they agreed on the importance of having a few positive and lasting relationships—and on the seriousness of social exclusion. In many ways, the scientists featured in this volume showed remarkable similarity with these early theorists. They voiced some disagreement regarding how and why people experience social exclusion, but they shared an overarching premise that social exclusion represents a significant topic worthy of scientific study. This closing chapter looks back to what we learned from the research covered in this volume that can inform the next generation of social exclusion research.

A first lesson is that researchers ought to consider the role of social exclusion within an evolutionary context. Random social exclusion is rare. More often, people experience social exclusion because they compromised their group's ability to survive and reproduce (Leary & Cottrell, Chapter 2). This systematic social exclusion enables one's

group to thrive by promoting feelings of belonging, understanding, control, an enhanced self, and trust (North & Fiske, Chapter 4). Social exclusion not only strengthens groups by casting out "bad apples," but it can also benefit socially excluded people. By motivating them to become more useful, productive, and compassionate members of society, social isolation can help people repair broken bonds or form new ones (Cacioppo, Hawkley, & Correll, Chapter 17). Indeed, several lines of research suggest that social exclusion motivates people to change their behaviors to make them more desirable as potential friends (Lakin & Chartrand, Chapter 25; Molden & Maner, Chapter 12).

A second lesson is that social exclusion takes many different forms, which can produce diverse consequences. People may experience exclusion because of their physical appearance, (Madera & Hebl, Chapter 6; London & Rosenthal, Chapter 18), their partner no longer regards them positively (Cavallo & Holmes, Chapter 9), their spouse divorces them (Sbarra & Mason, Chapter 8), their poor work performance (Scott & Thau, Chapter 7), or because they have various psychological disorders (Mikami, Chapter 21; Van Orden & Joiner, Chapter 19). Experimental manipulations of social exclusion that exceed moderate levels of arousal inhibit pain reactions (Borsook & MacDonald, Chapter 16), whereas manipulations that hover below these arousal levels enhance pain reactions (Eisenberger, Chapter 15). Understanding the type of social exclusion people experience can aid in predicting whether they will aggress toward the source of exclusion, repair the relationship, or withdraw (Smart Richman, Chapter 5).

A third lesson is that researchers will do well by considering how different individuals respond to the same social exclusion experience. Instead of representing "noise" that muddies understanding of social exclusion experiences, researchers can gain useful insight into systematic differences between people. For example, women who are high (versus low) in gender-based rejection sensitivity show more self-doubt and less constructive responses to negative feedback (London & Rosenthal, Chapter 18). Likewise, elevated levels of anxious attachment (Shaver & Mikulincer, Chapter 22), narcissism (vanDellan, Allen, & Campbell, Chapter 20), and lower levels of self-esteem (vanDellan, Allen, & Campbell, Chapter 20) place people at risk for negative responses to social exclusion. In contrast, having high self-compassion relates to less negative responses to social exclusion (vanDellan, Allen, & Campbell, Chapter 20). Moving beyond traits to broader subtypes, some children generally respond to social exclusion with aggression, whereas others respond with withdrawal (Juvonen, Chapter 10). Thus, social exclusion is generally painful, but it is important also to consider how the chronic motivations, goals, and traits that people bring with them to the situation can help understand their responses.

A fourth lesson is that social exclusion poses such a serious threat that it influences a broad range of responses. Social exclusion increases salivary cortisol levels (Dickerson & Zoccola, Chapter 14) and blood flow to brain regions associated with physical pain (Eisenberger, Chapter 15). The threat of social exclusion also produces sweeping changes in attention, memory, meaningful existence, intelligent thought, self-regulation, and support for one's worldview (Knowles, Chapter 26; Schimel & Greenberg, Chapter 27; Shaver & Mikulincer, Chapter 22; Stillman & Baumeister, Chapter 13). At a behavioral level, social exclusion causes changes in aggression, mimicry, and prosocial behavior

(DeWall & Twenge, Chapter 11; Lakin & Chartrand, Chapter 25; Molden & Maner, Chapter 12). This dizzying array of responses to social exclusion supports the premise that it strikes at the core of well-being.

A fifth lesson is that researchers may consider the time course of responses to social exclusion. Whereas many studies offer a "snapshot" of the immediate aftermath of social exclusion, how people respond changes over time (Wesselmann & Williams, Chapter 3). To date, most research focuses on reflexive and reflective responses, which leaves a gaping hole in understanding the resignation stage. Wesselmann and Williams offer several innovative ideas for interventions that target people in the resignation stage.

A final lesson is that people use assorted ways to cope with social exclusion. Excluded people often attribute humanlike qualities to nonhuman objects, such as naming their cars, declaring that their computers are "happy," or feeling that God is a close relationship partner (Waytz, Chapter 23). Socially disconnected people also form one-sided attachments to media figures (e.g., television characters) to regain a sense of belonging (Knowles, Chapter 26). By giving nonhuman objects human qualities and forming so-called "parasocial attachments," excluded people substitute their lack of social bonds with readily accessible sources of acceptance. Interventions that train attention away from threatening images also reduce emotional responses related to social exclusion, such as anxiety (Baumeister & Tice, 1990; Schmidt, Chapter 24). Motivated by a desire for renewed affiliation, socially excluded people also put their best foot forward by mimicking and behaving generously toward potential new friends (Lakin & Chartrand, Chapter 25; Molden & Maner, Chapter 12).

Although not exhaustive, these lessons can help shape the next generation of social exclusion research. For example, future research may examine whether people who experience little discomfort from social exclusion have difficulty fulfilling functionally relevant goals (see Cacioppo et al., Chapter 17). If social exclusion alerts people to correct their behavior so as to repair their bonds or create new ones, then people who fail to experience a strong pain response may exhibit impairments in other domains. Some initial evidence supports this possibility. Adolescents with autism spectrum disorders, who have pervasive deficits in their ability to function socially, also show dampened brain activation in regions associated with peer exclusion (e.g., subgenual anterior cingulate cortex, anterior insula) compared with normally developing controls when they experience social exclusion (versus inclusion) (Masten et al., 2011). Future research may examine whether this reduced brain activation to peer exclusion relates to autistic adolescents' social deficits.

Other research may examine how different forms of social exclusion cause people to navigate through the reflexive, reflective, and resignation stages in distinct ways. People who experience stigma because of a long-lasting physical attribute (e.g., a facial deformity) may bypass the reflective stage and enter the resignation phase when they experience social exclusion related to their physical appearance. Convinced that no one would want them as social partners, they may withdraw from others or lash out. But the same people may seek out sources of connection when they experience social exclusion at work. Knowing that they can restore their thwarted need to belong by obtaining a new position, the same people who circumvent the reflective stage after one form of social exclusion may utilize effective coping responses during the reflective stage after another form of social exclusion.

Future research may also examine how pharmacological treatments and individual differences combine to shape responses to social exclusion. For example, recent research in the oxytocin literature suggests that intranasal administration of the drug increases behaviors that strengthen one's in-group (De Dreu et al., 2010). Oxytocin's effects often depend on contextual and individual difference factors (Bartz et al., 2011b). For example, intranasal oxytocin increases envy and gloating in competitive situations (Shamay-Tsoory, Fischer, Dvash, Harari, et al., 2009) and decreases cooperativeness among people who are highly rejection sensitive and prone to aggression (i.e., individuals with borderline personality disorder) (Bartz et al., 2011a). Therefore, oxytocin may modify responses to social exclusion, but this effect will likely depend on traits that people bring with them to the social exclusion experience.

Never has there been a more exciting time to study social exclusion. Although we now know more than ever before about social exclusion, we have only begun to scratch the surface. It is my hope that this volume stimulates further theory and research on this significant topic.

References

Bartz, J., Simeon, D., Hamilton, H., Kim, S. Crystal, S., Braun, A., Vincens, V., & Hollander, E. (2011a). Oxytocin can hinder trust and cooperation in borderline personality disorder. *Social Cognitive & Affective Neuroscience, 6*, 556–563.

Bartz, J. A., Zaki, J., Bolger, N. & Ochsner, K. N. (2011b). Social effects of oxytocin in humans: Context and person matter. *Trends in Cognitive Sciences, 15*, 301–309.

Baumeister, R. F., & Tice, D. M. (1990). Anxiety and social exclusion. *Journal of Social and Clinical Psychology, 9*, 165–195.

De Dreu, C. K. W., Greer, L. L., Handgraaf, M. J. J., Shalvi, S., Van Kleef, G. A., Baas, M., Ten Velden, F. S., Van Dijk, E., & Feith, S. W. W. (2010). The neuropeptide oxytocin regulates parochial altruism in intergroup conflict among humans. *Science, 328*, 1408–1411.

Masten, C. L., Colich, N. L., Rudie, J. D., Bookheimer, S. Y., Eisenberger, N. I., & Dapretto, M. (2011). An fMRI investigation of responses to peer rejection in adolescents with autism spectrum disorders. *Developmental Cognitive Neuroscience, 1*, 260–270.

Shamay-Tsoory, S.G., Fischer, M., Dvash, J., Harari, H., Perach-Bloom, N., Levkovitz, Y. (2009). Intranasal administration of oxytocin increases envy and schadenfreude (gloating). *Biological Psychiatry, 66*, 864–870.

INDEX

motivations for social exclusion, 37
overview, 297–98
parent–child relationship, 292
permeability, 293
role of others, 289–92
self-consciousness, 289
self-esteem, 286, 288–96
social exclusion, 294–96
socialization, 288, 289
validation, support, 289, 295–96
Terry, R., 105
Testosterone, 84
Thau, Stefan, 4
Thoennes , N., 84
Tjaden, P., 84
TMT. *see* terror management theory
(TMT)
Tooby , J., 12
Tout, K., 146
Trawalter, S., 198
Tropp, L. R., 203
Tucker, J. S., 82
Twenge, J. M., 4, 23, 25, 114, 116, 124,
136
Tylenol (acetaminophen), 26, 158–59, 167

V

Vaillancourt, T., 149
Van Dellen, M., 4
Van den Hout, M., 261
Van Dulmen, M. M. H., 146
Van Knippenberg, A., 293
Van Orden, K., 4
Vasey, M. W., 102, 262
Virginia Tech massacre, 113
Vohs, K. D., 21–22

Vonk, R., 224

W

Wall, S., 239
Wallace, A., 85
Walsh, P. E., 293
Warburton, W. A., 23
Watanabe Heritable Hyperlipidemic
rabbit, 186
Waters, E., 239
Waytz, A., 4–5
Weise, D., 291
Weiss, R., 179, 187, 189
Wesselmann, E. D., 4, 23, 24, 302
Wheeler, V. A., 47
White, B. J., 190
White, J., 260
White, R. W., 35
Williams, A., 58
Williams, K. D., 4, 13, 21–26, 46, 118,
119, 123, 133, 136, 144, 187, 198,
266, 267, 275, 277, 295, 302
Wilson, M. I., 85
Wirth, J. H., 21, 22
Wohl, R. R., 279, 280
Word, C. O., 60, 61
Work group exclusion
actual workplace exclusion, 68
aggression, 66, 67, 69, 71
behavioral responses to, 66–68, 71
belonging need, 65–66, 70–71
conformity, appeasement behaviors,
66, 67
depression, 69
dysfunctional organizational behavior,
66–70

exclusion finality, 66–69, 71
future research directions, 71
interpersonal discrimination, 60–61
model of, 65–66
motivations to exclude, 69–71
nonconformity to group norms, values,
69–70
overview, 65, 70–71
peer rejection, 69
performance, lowered, 66, 70
physical responses to, 68, 69
punishment norms, 69
reconnection, reinclusion, 66–71, 123
relationship repair perception, 66–67
risk-averse approach to, 70, 71
rumination, 67, 69
self-defeatism, 66
self-esteem, 66, 67, 69
self-regulation, 66, 67, 69
social burden-exclusion relationship, 70
supervisor exclusion, 67–69
survival threat, 67
Wound healing paradigm, 87n1

Y

Yale Interpersonal Stressor (YIPS), 146,
147
Yamada, M., 183
Young, S. G., 23

Z

Zadro, L., 13, 22, 24, 25
Zanna, M. P., 60, 61
Zhang , L., 23
Zhou, X., 21–22
Zoccola, P., 4